The GOLF OMNIBUS

P. G. WODEHOUSE

WINGS BOOKS
New York

This 1996 edition is published by Wings Books,
a division of Random House Value Publishing, Inc.,
201 East 50th Street, New York, New York 10022,
http://www.randomhouse.com/

Wings Books and colophon are trademarks
of Random House Value Publishing, Inc.

Random House
New York • Toronto • London • Sydney • Auckland
http://www.randomhouse.com/

Printed and bound in the United States of America

Library of Congress Cataloging-in-Publication Data
Wodehouse, P. G. (Pelham Grenville), 1881–1975.
  The golf omnibus/by P. G. Wodehouse
        p.   cm.
      ISBN 0-517-05794-8
      1. Golf stories, English. 1. Title.
      PR6045.053A6   1991
      823´.912—dc20   90-24778
                                                            CIP

15 14 13 12 11 10 9

CONTENTS

PREFACE

As I start to write this Preface, I am brooding a bit. My brow is furrowed, sort of, and I can't help sighing a good deal.

The trouble about reaching the age of ninety-two, which I did last October, is that regrets for a misspent life are bound to creep in, and whenever you see me with a furrowed brow you can be sure that what is on my mind is the thought that if only I had taken up golf earlier and devoted my whole time to it instead of fooling about writing stories and things, I might have got my handicap down to under eighteen. If only they had put a putter in my hands when I was four and taught me the use of the various clubs, who knows what heights I might not have reached. It is this reflection that has always made my writing so sombre, its whole aroma like that of muddy shoes in a Russian locker room.

And yet I may have managed to get a few rays of sunshine into the stories which follow. If so, this is due to the fact that while I was writing them I won my first and only trophy, a striped umbrella in a hotel tournament at Aiken, South Carolina, where, hitting them squarely on the meat for once, I went through a field of some of the fattest retired business men in America like a devouring flame.

I was never much of a golfer. Except for that glorious day at Aiken I was always one of the dregs, the sort of man whose tee shots, designed to go due north, invariably went nor-nor-east or in a westerly direction. But how I loved the game. I have sometimes wondered if we of the canaille don't get more pleasure out of it than the top-notchers. For an untouchable like myself two perfect drives in a round would wipe out all memory of sliced approach shots and foozled putts, whereas if Jack Nicklaus does a sixty-four he goes home and thinks morosely that if he had not just missed that eagle on the seventh, he would have had a sixty-three.

I have made no attempt to bring this book up to date, and many changes have taken place since I wrote "The Clicking of Cuthbert" in 1916. Time like an ever-rolling stream bears all its sons away, and with them have gone the names of most of the golf clubs so dear to me. I believe one still drives with a driver nowadays, though at any moment we may have to start calling it the Number One wood, but where is the mashie now, where the cleek, the spoon and the baffy?

All Scottish names, those, dating back to the days (1593 A.D.) when we are told that John Henrie and Pat Rogie were imprisoned for "playing of the Gowff on the links of Leith every Sabbath the time of the sermonses". It is very sad, the way the Scottish atmosphere has gone out of the game. In my youth, when the Badminton book was a comparatively new publication, one took it for granted that to be a good golfer you had to be Scottish, preferably with a name like Sandy McHoots or Jock Auchtermuchty. And how we reverenced them. "These," we said, "are the men whose drives fly far, like bullets from a rifle, who when they do a hole in par regard it as a trifle. Of such as these the bard has said, 'Hech thrawfu' raltie rorkie, wi' thecht ta' croonie clapperhead and fash wi' unco' pawkie'." And where are they now? How long is it since a native Scot won an Open? All Americans these days, except for an occasional Mexican.

No stopping Progress, of course, but I do think it a pity to cast away lovely names like mashie and baffy in favour of numbers. I like to think that when I got into a bunker (isn't it called a trap now?) I got out of it, if I ever did, with a niblick and not a wedge. I wonder what Tommy Morris, winner of the British Open four years in succession, would have had to say to all this number six iron, number twelve iron, number twenty-eight iron stuff. Probably he wouldn't have said anything, just made one of those strange Scottish noises at the back of his throat like someone gargling.

A FOOTNOTE. In one of these little opuses I allude to Stout Cortez staring at the Pacific. Shortly after the appearance of this narrative in the *Saturday Evening Post* I received a letter from a usually well-informed source which began

Dear Sir, *you big stiff.*

Where do you get that Cortez stuff? It was Balboa.

This, I believe, is historically accurate. On the other hand, if Cortez was good enough for Keats, he is good enough for me. Besides, even if it *was* Balboa, the Pacific was open for being stared at about that time, and I see no reason why Cortez should not have had a look at it as well.

P. G. WODEHOUSE

DEDICATION

TO THE
IMMORTAL MEMORY
OF
JOHN HENRIE AND PAT ROGIE
WHO
AT EDINBURGH IN THE YEAR 1593 A.D.
WERE IMPRISONED FOR
" PLAYING OF THE GOWFF ON THE LINKS OF
LEITH EVERY SABBATH THE TIME OF THE
SERMONSES",
ALSO OF
ROBERT ROBERTSON
WHO GOT IT IN THE NECK IN 1604 A.D.
FOR THE SAME REASON

ARCHIBALD'S BENEFIT

ARCHIBALD MEALING was one of those golfers in whom desire outruns performance. Nobody could have been more willing than Archibald. He tried, and tried hard. Every morning before he took his bath he would stand in front of his mirror and practise swings. Every night before he went to bed he would read the golden words of some master on the subject of putting, driving, or approaching. Yet on the links most of his time was spent in retrieving lost balls or replacing America. Whether it was that Archibald pressed too much or pressed too little, whether it was that his club deviated from the dotted line which joined the two points A and B in the illustrated plate of the man making the brassy shot in the *Hints on Golf* book, or whether it was that he was pursued by some malignant fate, I do not know. Archibald rather favoured the last theory.

The important point is that, in his thirty-first year, after six seasons of untiring effort, Archibald went in for a championship, and won it.

Archibald, mark you, whose golf was a kind of blend of hockey, Swedish drill, and buck-and-wing dancing.

I know the ordeal I must face when I make such a statement. I see clearly before me the solid phalanx of men from Missouri, some urging me to tell it to the King of Denmark, others insisting that I produce my Eskimoes. Nevertheless, I do not shrink. I state once more that in his thirty-first year Archibald Mealing went in for a golf championship, and won it.

Archibald belonged to a select little golf club, the members of which lived and worked in New York, but played in Jersey. Men of substance, financially as well as physically, they had combined their superflous cash and with it purchased a strip of land close to the sea. This land had been drained—to the huge discomfort of a colony of mosquitoes which had come to look on the place as their private property—and converted into links, which had become a sort of refuge for incompetent golfers. The members of the Cape Pleasant Club were easy-going refugees from other and more exacting clubs, men who pottered rather than raced round the links; men, in short, who had grown tired of having to stop their game and stand aside in order to allow perspiring experts to whiz past them. The Cape Pleasant golfers did not make themselves slaves to the game. Their language, when they foozled, was gently regretful rather than sulphurous. The moment in the day's play which they enjoyed most was when they were saying: "Well, here's luck!" in the club-house.

It will, therefore, be readily understood that Archibald's inability to do a hole in single figures did not handicap him at Cape Pleasant as it might have done at St. Andrews. His kindly clubmates took him to their bosoms to a man, and looked on him as a brother. Archibald's was one of those admirable natures which prompt their possessor frequently to remark: "These are on me!" and his fellow golfers were not slow to appreciate the fact. They all loved Archibald.

Archibald was on the floor of his bedroom one afternoon, picking up the fragments of his mirror—a friend had advised him to practise the Walter J. Travis lofting shot —when the telephone bell rang. He took up the receiver, and was hailed by the comfortable voice of McCay, the club secretary.

"Is that Mealing?" asked McCay. "Say, Archie, I'm putting your name down for our championship competition. That's right, isn't it?"

"Sure," said Archibald. "When does it start?"

"Next Saturday."

"That's me."

"Good for you. Oh, Archie."

"Hello?"

"A man I met to-day told me you were engaged. Is that a fact?"

"Sure," murmured Archibald, blushfully.

The wire hummed with McCay's congratulations.

"Thanks," said Archibald. "Thanks, old man. What? Oh, yes. Milsom's her name. By the way, her family have taken a cottage at Cape Pleasant for the summer. Some distance from the links. Yes, very convenient, isn't it? Good-bye."

He hung up the receiver and resumed his task of gathering up the fragments.

Now McCay happened to be of a romantic and sentimental nature. He was by profession a chartered accountant, and inclined to be stout; and all rather stout chartered accountants are sentimental. McCay was the sort of man who keeps old ball programmes and bundles of letters tied round with lilac ribbon. At country houses, where they lingered in the porch after dinner to watch the moonlight flooding the quiet garden, it was McCay and his colleague who lingered longest. McCay knew Ella Wheeler Wilcox by heart, and could take Browning without anaesthetics. It is not to be wondered at, therefore, that Archibald's remark about his fiancée coming to live at Cape Pleasant should give him food for thought. It appealed to him.

He reflected on it a good deal during the day, and, running across Sigsbee, a fellow Cape Pleasanter, after dinner that night at the Sybarites' Club, he spoke of the matter to him. It so happened that both had dined excellently, and were looking on the world with a sort of cosy benevolence. They were in the mood when men pat small boys on the head and ask them if they mean to be President when they grow up.

"I called up Archie Mealing to-day," said McCay. "Did you know he was engaged?"

"I did hear something about it. Girl of the name of Wilson, or——"

"Milsom. She's going to spend the summer at Cape Pleasant, Archie tells me."

"Then she'll have a chance of seeing him play in the championship competition."

McCay sucked his cigar in silence for a while, watching with dreamy eyes the blue smoke as it curled ceiling-ward. When he spoke his voice was singularly soft.

"Do you know, Sigsbee," he said, sipping his Maraschino with a gentle melancholy —"do you know, there is something wonderfully pathetic to me in this business. I see the whole things so clearly. There was a kind of quiver in the poor old chap's voice when he said: 'She is coming to Cape Pleasant,' which told me more than any words could have done. It is a tragedy in its way, Sigsbee. We may smile at it, think it trivial; but it is none the less a tragedy. That warm-hearted, enthusiastic girl, all eagerness to see the man she loves do well—Archie, poor old Archie, all on fire to prove to her that her trust in him is not misplaced, and the end—Disillusionment— Disappointment—Unhappiness."

"He ought to keep his eye on the ball," said the more practical Sigsbee.

"Quite possibly," continued McCay, "he has told her that he will win the championship."

"If Archie's mutt enough to have told her that," said Sigsbee decidedly, "he deserves all he gets. Waiter, two Scotch highballs."

McCay was in no mood to subscribe to this stony-hearted view.

"I tell you," he said, "I'm *sorry* for Archie. I'm *sorry* for the poor old chap. And I'm more than sorry for the girl."

"Well, I don't see what we can do," said Sigsbee. "We can hardly be expected to foozle on purpose, just to let Archie show off before his girl."

McCay paused in the act of lighting his cigar, as one smitten with a great thought.

"Why not?" he said. "Why not, Sigsbee? Sigsbee, you've hit it!"

"Eh?"

"You have! I tell you, Sigsbee, you've solved the whole thing. Archie's such a bully good fellow, why not give him a benefit? Why not let him win this championship? You aren't going to tell me that you care whether you win a tin medal or not?"

Sigsbee's benevolence was expanding under the influence of the Scotch highball and his cigar. Little acts of kindness on Archie's part, here a cigar, there a lunch, at another time seats for the theatre, began to rise to the surface of his memory like rainbow-coloured bubbles. He wavered.

"Yes, but what about the rest of the men?" he said. "There will be a dozen or more in for the medal."

"We can square them," said McCay confidently. "We will broach the matter to them at a series of dinners at which we will be joint hosts. They are all white men who will be charmed to do a little thing like this for a sport like Archie."

"How about Gossett?" asked Sigsbee.

McCay's face clouded. Gossett was an unpopular subject with members of the

Cape Pleasant Golf Club. He was the serpent in their Eden. Nobody seemed quite to know how he had got in, but there, unfortunately, he was. Gossett had introduced into Cape Pleasant golf a cheerless atmosphere of the rigour of the game. It was to enable them to avoid just such golfers as Gossett that the Cape Pleasanters had founded their club. Genial courtesy rather than strict attention to the rules had been the leading characteristics of their play till his arrival. Up to that time it had been looked on as rather bad form to exact a penalty. A cheery give-and-take system had prevailed. Then Gossett had come, full of strange rules, and created about the same stir in the community which a hawk would create in a gathering of middle-aged doves.

"You can't square Gossett," said Sigsbee.

McCay looked unhappy.

"I forgot him," he said. "Of course, nothing will stop him trying to win. I wish we could think of something. I would almost as soon see him lose as Archie win. But, after all, he does have off days sometimes."

"You need to have a very off day to be as bad as Archie."

They sat and smoked in silence.

"I've got it," said Sigsbee suddenly. "Gossett is a fine golfer, but nervous. If we upset his nerves enough, he will go right off his stroke. Couldn't we think of some way?"

McCay reached out for his glass.

"Yours is a noble nature, Sigsbee," he said.

"Oh, no," said the paragon modestly. "Have another cigar?"

In order that the reader may get that mental half-Nelson on the plot of this narrative which is so essential if a short story is to charm, elevate, and instruct, it is necessary now, for the nonce (but only for the nonce), to inspect Archibald's past life.

Archibald, as he stated to McCay, was engaged to a Miss Milsom—Miss Margaret Milsom. How few men, dear reader, are engaged to girls with svelte figures, brown hair, and large blue eyes, now sparkling and vivacious, now dreamy and soulful, but always large and blue! How few, I say. You are, dear reader, and so am I, but who else? Archibald was one of the few who happened to be.

He was happy. It is true that Margaret's mother was not, as it were, wrapped up in him. She exhibited none of that effervescent joy at his appearance which we like to see in our mothers-in-law elect. On the contrary, she generally cried bitterly whenever she saw him, and at the end of ten minutes was apt to retire sobbing to her room, where she remained in a state of semi-coma till an advanced hour. She was by way of being a confirmed invalid, and something about Archibald seemed to get right in among her nerve centres, reducing them for the time being to a complicated hash. She did not like Archibald. She said she liked big, manly men. Behind his back she not infrequently referred to him as a "gaby"; sometimes even as that "guffin."

She did not do this to Margaret, for Margaret, besides being blue-eyed, was also a shade quick-tempered. Whenever she discussed Archibald, it was with her son Stuyvesant. Stuyvesant Milsom, who thought Archibald a bit of an ass, was always ready to sit and listen to his mother on the subject, it being, however, an understood thing that at the conclusion of the séance she yielded one or two saffron-coloured bills towards his racing debts. For Stuyvesant, having developed a habit of backing horses which either did not start at all or else sat down and thought in the middle of the race, could always do with ten dollars or so. His prices for these interviews worked out, as a rule, at about three cents a word.

In these circumstances it was perhaps natural that Archibald and Margaret should prefer to meet, when they did meet, at some other spot than the Milsom home. It suited them both better that they should arrange a secret tryst on these occasions. Archibald preferred it because being in the same room with Mrs. Milsom always made him feel like a murderer with particularly large feet; and Margaret preferred it because, as she told Archibald, these secret meetings lent a touch of poetry to what might otherwise have been a commonplace engagement.

Archibald thought this charming; but at the same time he could not conceal from himself the fact that Margaret's passion for the poetic cut, so to speak, both ways. He admired and loved the loftiness of her soul, but, on the other hand, it was a tough job having to live up to it. For Archibald was a very ordinary young man. They had tried to inoculate him with a love of poetry at school, but it had not taken. Until he was thirty he had been satisfied to class all poetry (except that of Mr. George Cohan) under the general heading of punk. Then he met Margaret, and the trouble began. On the day he first met her, at a picnic, she had looked so soulful, so aloof from this world, that he had felt instinctively that here was a girl who expected more from a man than a mere statement that the weather was great. It so chanced that he knew just one quotation from the classics, to wit, Tennyson's critique of the Island-Valley of Avilion. He knew this because he had had the passage to write out one hundred and fifty times at school, on the occasion of his being caught smoking by one of the faculty who happened to be a passionate admirer of the "Idylls of the King."

A remark of Margaret's that it was a splendid day for a picnic and that the country looked nice gave him his opportunity.

"It reminds me," he said, "it reminds me strongly of the Island-Valley of Avilion, where falls not hail, or rain, or any snow, nor ever wind blows loudly; but it lies deep-meadow'd, happy, fair, with orchard lawns . . . ."

He broke off here to squash a hornet; but Margaret had heard enough.

"Are you fond of the poets, Mr. Mealing?" she said, with a far-off look.

"Me?" said Archibald fervently. "Me? Why, I eat 'em alive!"

And that was how all the trouble had started. It had meant unremitting toil for Archibald. He felt that he had set himself a standard from which he must not fall. He bought every new volume of poetry which was praised in the press, and learned the reviews by heart. Every evening he read painfully a portion of the classics. He plodded through the poetry sections of Bartlett's *Familiar Quotations*. Margaret's devotion to the various bards was so enthusiastic, and her reading so wide, that there were times when Archibald wondered if he could endure the strain. But he persevered heroically, and so far had not been found wanting. But the strain was fearful.

The early stages of the Cape Pleasant golf tournament need no detailed description. The rules of match play governed the contests, and Archibald disposed of his first three opponents before the twelfth hole. He had been diffident when he teed off with McCay in the first round, but, finding that he defeated the secretary with ease, he met one Butler in the second round with more confidence. Butler, too, he routed; with the result that, by the time he faced Sigsbee in round three, he was practically the conquering hero. Fortune seemed to be beaming upon him with almost insipid sweetness. When he was trapped in the bunker at the seventh hole, Sigsbee became trapped as well. When he sliced at the sixth tee, Sigsbee pulled. And Archibald, striking a brilliant vein, did the next three holes in eleven, nine, and twelve; and, romping home, qualified for the final.

Gossett, that serpent, meanwhile, had beaten each of his three opponents without much difficulty.

The final was fixed for the following Thursday morning. Gossett, who was a broker, had made some frivolous objection about the difficulty of absenting himself from Wall Street, but had been overruled. When Sigsbee pointed out that he could easily defeat Archibald and get to the city by lunch-time if he wished, and that in any case his partner would be looking after things, he allowed himself to be persuaded, though reluctantly. It was a well-known fact that Gossett was in the midst of some rather sizeable deals at that time.

Thursday morning suited Archibald admirably. It had occurred to him that he could bring off a double event. Margaret had arrived at Cape Pleasant on the previous evening, and he had arranged by telephone to meet her at the end of the board-walk, which was about a mile from the links, at one o'clock, supply her with lunch, and spend the afternoon with her on the water. If he started his match with Gossett at eleven-thirty, he would have plenty of time to have his game and be at the end of the board-walk at the appointed hour. He had no delusions about the respective merits of Gossett and himself as golfers. He knew that Gossett would win the necessary ten holes off the reel. It was saddening, but it was a scientific fact. There was no avoiding it. One simply had to face it.

Having laid these plans, he caught his train on the Thursday morning with the consoling feeling that, however sadly the morning might begin, it was bound to end well.

The day was fine, the sun warm, but tempered with a light breeze. One or two of the club had come to watch the match, among them Sigsbee.

Sigsbee drew Gossett aside.

"You must let me caddie for you, old man," he said. "I know your temperament so exactly. I know how little it takes to put you off your stroke. In an ordinary game you might take one of these boys, I know, but on an important occasion like this you must not risk it. A grubby boy, probably with a squint, would almost certainly get on your nerves. He might even make comments on the game, or whistle. But I understand you. You must let me carry your clubs."

"It's very good of you," said Gossett.

"Not at all," said Sigsbee.

Archibald was now preparing to drive off from the first tee. He did this with great care. Everyone who has seen Archibald Mealing play golf knows that his teeing off is one of the most impressive sights ever witnessed on the links. He tilted his cap over his eyes, waggled his club a little, shifted his feet, waggled his club some more, gazed keenly towards the horizon for a moment, waggled his club again, and finally, with the air of a Strong Man lifting a bar of iron, raised it slowly above his head. Then, bringing it down with a sweep, he drove the ball with a lofty slice some fifty yards. It was rarely that he failed either to slice or pull his ball. His progress from hole to hole was generally a majestic zigzag.

Gossett's drive took him well on the way to the green. He holed out in five. Archibald, mournful but not surprised made his way to the second tee.

The second hole was shorter. Gossett won it in three. The third he took in six, the fourth in four. Archibald began to feel that he might just as well not be there. He was practically a spectator.

At this point he reached in his pocket for his tobacco-pouch, to console himself with smoke. To his dismay he found that it was not there. He had had it in the train, but now it had vanished. This added to his gloom, for the pouch had been given to him by Margaret, and he had always thought it one more proof of the way her nature towered over the natures of other girls that she had not woven a monogram on it in forget-me-nots. This record pouch was missing, and Archibald mourned for the loss.

His sorrows were not alleviated by the fact that Gossett won the fifth and sixth holes.

It was a quarter-past twelve, and Archibald reflected with moody satisfaction that the massacre must soon be over, and that he would be able to forget it in the society of Margaret.

As Gossett was about to drive off from the seventh tee, a telegraph boy approached the little group.

"Mr. Gossett," he said.

Gossett lowered his driver, and wheeled round, but Sigsbee had snatched the envelope from the boy's hand.

"It's all right, old man," he said. "Go right ahead. I'll keep it safe for you."

"Give it to me," said Gossett anxiously. "It may be from the office. Something may have happened to the market. I may be needed."

"No, no," said Sigsbee, soothingly. "Don't you worry about it. Better not open it.

It might have something in it that would put you off your stroke. Wait till the end of the game."

"Give it to me. I want to see it."

Sigsbee was firm.

"No," he said, "I'm here to see you win this championship and I won't have you taking any risks. Besides, even if it was important, a few minutes won't make any difference."

"Well, at any rate, open it and read it."

"It is probably in cipher," said Sigsbee. "I wouldn't understand it. Play on, old man. You've only a few more holes to win."

Gossett turned and addressed his ball again. Then he swung. The club tipped the ball, and it rolled sluggishly for a couple of feet. Archibald approached the tee. Now there were moments when Archibald could drive quite decently. He always applied a considerable amount of muscular force to his efforts. It was in direction that, as a rule, he erred. On this occasion, whether inspired by his rival's failure or merely favoured by chance, he connected with his ball at precisely the right moment. It flew from the tee, straight, hard, and low, struck the ground near the green, bounded on and finally rocked to within a foot of the hole. No such long ball had been driven on the Cape Pleasant links since their foundation.

That it should have taken him three strokes to hole out from this promising position was unfortunate, but not fatal, for Gossett, who seemed suddenly to have fallen off his game, only reached the green in seven. A moment later a murmur of approval signified the fact that Archibald had won his first hole.

"Mr. Gossett," said a voice.

Those murmuring approval observed that the telegraph boy was once more in their midst. This time he bore two missives. Sigsbee dexterously impounded both.

"No," he said with decision, "I absolutely refuse to let you look at them till the game is over. I know your temperament."

Gossett gesticulated.

"But they must be important. They must come from my office. Where else would I get a stream of telegrams? Something has gone wrong. I am urgently needed."

Sigsbee nodded gravely.

"That is what I fear," he said. "That is why I cannot risk having you upset. Time enough, Gossett, for bad news after the game. Play on, man, and dismiss it from your mind. Besides, you couldn't get back to New York just yet, in any case. There are no trains. Dismiss the whole thing from your mind and just play your usual, and you're sure to win."

Archibald had driven off during this conversation, but without his previous success. This time he had pulled his ball into some long grass. Gossett's drive was, however, worse; and the subsequent movement of the pair to the hole resembled more than anything else the manoeuvres of two men rolling pea-nuts with toothpicks as the result of an election bet. Archibald finally took the hole in twelve after Gossett had played his fourteenth.

When Archibald won the next in eleven and the tenth in nine, hope began to flicker feebly in his bosom. But when he won two more holes, bringing the score to like-as-we-lie, it flamed up within him like a beacon.

The ordinary golfer, whose scores per hole seldom exceed those of Colonel Bogey, does not understand the whirl of mixed sensations which the really incompetent performer experiences on the rare occasions when he does strike a winning vein. As stroke follows stroke, and he continues to hold his opponent, a wild exhilaration surges through him, followed by a sort of awe, as if he was doing something wrong, even irreligious. Then all these yeasty emotions subside and are blended into one glorious sensation of grandeur and majesty, as of a giant among pigmies.

By the time that Archibald, putting with the care of one brushing flies off a sleeping Venus, had holed out and won the thirteenth, he was in the full grip of this feeling. And as he walked to the fifteenth tee, after winning the fourteenth, he felt that this was Life, that till now he had been a mere mollusc.

Just at that moment he happened to look at his watch, and the sight was like a douche of cold water. The hands stood at five minutes to one.

Let us pause and ponder on this point for a while. Let us not dismiss it as if it were some mere trivial, everyday difficulty. You, dear reader, play an accurate, scientific game and beat your opponent with ease every time you go to the links, and so do I; but Archibald was not like us. This was the first occasion on which he had ever felt that he was playing well enough to give him a chance of defeating a really good man. True, he had beaten McCay, Sigsbee and Butler in the earlier rounds; but they were ignoble rivals compared with Gossett. To defeat Gossett, however, meant the championship. On the other hand, he was passionately devoted to Margaret Milsom, whom he was due to meet at the end of the board-walk at one sharp. It was now five minutes to one, and the end of the board-walk still a mile away.

The mental struggle was brief but keen. A sharp pang, and his mind was made up. Cost what it might, he must stay on the links. If Margaret broke off the engagement —well, it might be that Time would heal the wound, and that after many years he would find some other girl for whom he might come to care in a wrecked, broken sort of way. But a chance like this could never come again. What is Love compared with holing out before your opponent?

The excitement now became so intense that a small boy, following with the crowd, swallowed his chewing-gum; for a slight improvement had become noticeable in Gossett's play, and a slight improvement in the play of almost anyone meant that it became vastly superior to Archibald's. At the next hole the improvement was not marked enough to have its full effect, and Archibald contrived to halve. This made him two up and three to play. What an average golfer would consider a commanding lead. But Archibald was no average golfer. A commanding lead for him would have been two up and one to play.

To give the public of his best, your golfer should have his mind cool and intent upon the game. Inasmuch as Gossett was worrying about the telegrams, while Archibald, strive as he might to dismiss it, was haunted by a vision of Margaret standing alone and deserted on the board-walk, play became, as it were, ragged. Fine putting enabled Gossett to do the sixteenth hole in twelve, and when, winning the seventeenth in nine, he brought his score level with Archibald's the match seemed over. But just then—

"Mr. Gossett!" said a familiar voice.

Once more was the much-enduring telegraph boy among those present.

"T'ree dis time!" he observed.

Gossett sprang, but again the watchful Sigsbee was too swift.

"Be brave, Gossett—be brave," he said. "This is a crisis in the game. Keep your nerve. Play just as if nothing existed outside the links. To look at these telegrams now would be fatal."

Eye-witnesses of that great encounter will tell the story of the last hole to their dying day. It was one of those Titanic struggles which Time cannot efface from the memory. Archibald was fortunate in getting a good start. He only missed twice before he struck his ball on the tee. Gossett had four strokes ere he achieved the feat. Nor did Archibald's luck desert him in the journey to the green. He was out of the bunker in eleven. Gossett emerged only after sixteen. Finally, when Archibald's twenty-first stroke sent the ball trickling into the hole, Gossett had played his thirtieth.

The ball had hardly rested on the bottom of the hole before Gossett had begun to tear the telegrams from their envelopes. As he read, his eyes bulged in their sockets.

"Not bad news, I hope," said a sympathetic bystander.

Sigsbee took the sheaf of telegrams.

The first ran: "Good luck. Hope you win. McCay." The second also ran: "Good luck, Hope you win. McCay." So, singularly enough, did the third, fourth, fifth, sixth, and seventh.

"Great Scott!" said Sigsbee. "He seems to have been pretty anxious not to run any risk of missing you, Gossett."

As he spoke, Archibald, close behind him, was looking at his watch. The hands stood at a quarter to two.

Margaret and her mother were seated in the parlour when Archibald arrived. Mrs. Milsom, who had elicited the fact that Archibald had not kept his appointment, had been saying "I told you so" for some time, and this had not improved Margaret's temper. When, therefore, Archibald, damp and dishevelled, was shown in, the chill in the air nearly gave him frost-bite. Mrs. Milsom did her celebrated imitation of the Gorgon, while Margaret, lightly humming an air, picked up a weekly paper and became absorbed in it.

"Margaret, let me explain," panted Archibald. Mrs. Milsom was understood to remark that she dared say. Margaret's attention was riveted by a fashion plate.

"Driving in a taximeter to the ferry this morning," resumed Archibald, "I had an accident."

This was the net result of some rather feverish brainwork on the way from the links to the cottage.

The periodical flapped to the floor.

"Oh, Archie, are you hurt?"

"A few scratches, nothing more; but it made me miss my train."

"What train did you catch?" asked Mrs. Milsom sepulchrally.

"The one o'clock. I came straight on here from the station."

"Why," said Margaret, "Stuyvesant was coming home on the one o'clock train. Did you see him?"

Archibald's jaw dropped slightly.

"Er—no," he said.

"How curious," said Margaret.

"Very curious," said Archibald.

"Most curious," said Mrs. Milsom.

They were still reflecting on the singularity of this fact when the door opened, and the son of the house entered in person.

"Thought I should find you here, Mealing," he said. "They gave me this at the station to give to you; you dropped it this morning when you got out of the train."

He handed Archibald the missing pouch.

"Thanks," said the latter huskily. "When you say this morning, of course you mean this afternoon, but thanks all the same—thanks—thanks."

"No, Archibald Mealing, he does *not* mean this afternoon," said Mrs. Milsom. "Stuyvesant, speak! From what train did that guf—did Mr. Mealing alight when he dropped the tobacco-pouch?"

"The ten o'clock, the fellow told me. Said he would have given it back to him then only he sprinted off in the deuce of a hurry."

Six eyes focused themselves upon Archibald.

"Margaret," he said, "I will not try to deceive you——"

"You may try," observed Mrs. Milsom, "but you will not succeed."

"Well, Archibald?"

Archibald fingered his collar.

"There was no taximeter accident."

"Ah!" said Mrs. Milsom.

"The fact is, I have been playing in a golf tournament."

Margaret uttered an exclamation of surprise.

"Playing golf!"

Archibald bowed his head with manly resignation.

"Why didn't you tell me? Why didn't you arrange for us to meet on the links? I should have loved it."

Archibald was amazed.

"You take an interest in golf, Margaret? You! I thought you scorned it, considered it an unintellectual game. I thought you considered all games unintellectual."

"Why, I play golf myself. Not very well."

"Margaret! Why didn't you tell me?"

"I thought you might not like it. You were so spiritual, so poetic. I feared you would despise me."

Archibald took a step forward. His voice was tense and trembling.

"Margaret," he said, "this is no time for misunderstandings. We must be open with one another. Our happiness is at stake. Tell me honestly, *do* you like poetry really?"

Margaret hesitated, then answered bravely:

"No, Archibald," she said, "it is as you suspect. I am not worthy of you. I do *not* like poetry. Ah, you shudder! You turn away! Your face grows hard and scornful!"

"I don't!" yelled Archibald. "It doesn't! It doesn't do anything of the sort! You've made me another man!"

She stared, wild-eyed, astonished.

"What! Do you mean that you, too——"

"I should just say I do. I tell you I hate the beastly stuff. I only pretended to like it because I thought you did. The hours I've spent learning it up! I wonder I've not got brain fever."

"Archie! Used you to read it up, too? Oh, if I'd only known!"

"And you forgive me—this morning, I mean?"

"Of course. You couldn't leave a golf tournament. By the way, how did you get on?"

Archibald coughed.

"Rather well," he said modestly. "Pretty decently. In fact, not badly. As a matter of fact, I won the championship."

"The championship!" whispered Margaret. "Of America?"

"Well, not *absolutely* of America," said Archibald. "But all the same a championship."

"My hero."

"You won't be wanting me for a while, I guess?" said Stuyvesant nonchalantly. "Think I'll smoke a cigarette on the porch."

And sobs from the stairs told that Mrs. Milsom was already on her way to her room.

2

THE CLICKING OF CUTHBERT

THE YOUNG MAN came into the smoking-room of the club-house, and flung his bag with a clatter on the floor. He sank moodily into an arm-chair and pressed the bell.

"Waiter!"

"Sir?"

The young man pointed at the bag with every evidence of distaste.

"You may have these clubs," he said. "Take them away. If you don't want them yourself, give them to one of the caddies."

Across the room the Oldest Member gazed at him with a grave sadness through the smoke of his pipe. His eye was deep and dreamy—the eye of a man who, as the poet says, has seen Golf steadily and seen it whole.

"You are giving up golf?" he said.

He was not altogether unprepared for such an attitude on the young man's part: for from his eyrie on the terrace above the ninth green he had observed him start out on the afternoon's round and had seen him lose a couple of balls in the lake at the second hole after taking seven strokes at the first.

"Yes!" cried the young man fiercely. "For ever, dammit! Footling game! Blanked infernal fat-headed silly ass of a game! Nothing but a waste of time."

The Sage winced.

"Don't say that, my boy."

"But I do say it. What earthly good is golf? Life is stern and life is earnest. We live in a practical age. All round us we see foreign competition making itself unpleasant. And we spend our time playing golf! What do we get out of it? Is golf any *use*? That's what I'm asking you. Can you name me a single case where devotion to this pestilential pastime has done a man any practical good?"

The Sage smiled gently.

"I could name a thousand."

"One will do."

"I will select," said the Sage, "from the innumerable memories that rush to my mind, the story of Cuthbert Banks."

"Never heard of him."

"Be of good cheer," said the Oldest Member. "You are going to hear of him now."

It was in the picturesque little settlement of Wood Hills (said the Oldest Member) that the incidents occurred which I am about to relate. Even if you have never been in Wood Hills, that suburban paradise is probably familiar to you by name. Situated at a convenient distance from the city, it combines in a notable manner the advantages of town life with the pleasant surroundings and healthful air of the country. Its inhabitants live in commodious houses, standing in their own grounds, and enjoy so many luxuries—such as gravel soil, main drainage, electric light, telephone, baths (h. and c.), and company's own water, that you might be pardoned for imagining life to be so ideal for them that no possible improvement could be added to their lot. Mrs. Willoughby Smethurst was under no such delusion. What Wood Hills needed to make it perfect, she realized, was Culture. Material comforts are all very well, but, if the *summum bonum* is to be achieved, the Soul also demands a look in, and it was Mrs. Smethurst's unfaltering resolve that never while she had her strength should the Soul be handed the loser's end. It was her intention to make Wood Hills a centre of all that was most cultivated and refined, and, golly! how she had succeeded. Under her presidency the Wood Hills Literary and Debating Society had tripled its membership.

But there is always a fly in the ointment, a caterpillar in the salad. The local golf club, an institution to which Mrs. Smethurst strongly objected, had also tripled its membership; and the division of the community into two rival camps, the Golfers and the Cultured, had become more marked than ever. This division, always acute, had attained now to the dimensions of a Schism. The rival sects treated one another with a cold hostility.

Unfortunate episodes came to widen the breach. Mrs. Smethurst's house adjoined the links, standing to the right of the fourth tee: and, as the Literary Society was in the habit of entertaining visiting lecturers, many a golfer had foozled his drive owing to sudden loud outbursts of applause coinciding with his down-swing. And not long before this story opens a sliced ball, whizzing in at the open window, had come within an ace of incapacitating Raymond Parslow Devine, the rising young novelist (who rose at that moment a clear foot and a half) from any further exercise of his art. Two inches, indeed, to the right and Raymond must inevitably have handed in his dinner-pail.

To make matters worse, a ring at the front-door bell followed almost immediately, and the maid ushered in a young man of pleasing appearance in a sweater and baggy knickerbockers who apologetically but firmly insisted on playing his ball where it lay, and, what with the shock of the lecturer's narrow escape and the spectacle of the intruder standing on the table and working away with a niblick, the afternoon's session had to be classed as a complete frost. Mr. Devine's determination, from which no argument could swerve him, to deliver the rest of his lecture in the coal-cellar gave the meeting a jolt from which it never recovered.

I have dwelt upon this incident, because it was the means of introducing Cuthbert Banks to Mrs. Smethurst's niece, Adeline. As Cuthbert, for it was he who had so nearly reduced the muster-roll of rising novelists by one, hopped down from the table after his stroke, he was suddenly aware that a beautiful girl was looking at him intently. As a matter of fact, everyone in the room was looking at him intently, none more so than Raymond Parsloe Devine, but none of the others were beautiful girls. Long as the members of Wood Hills Literary Society were on brain, they were short on looks, and, to Cuthbert's excited eye, Adeline Smethurst stood out like a jewel in a pile of coke.

He had never seen her before, for she had only arrived at her aunt's house on the previous day, but he was perfectly certain that life, even when lived in the midst of gravel soil, main drainage, and company's own water, was going to be a pretty poor affair if he did not see her again. Yes, Cuthbert was in love: and it is interesting to record, as showing the effect of the tender emotion on a man's game that twenty minutes after he had met Adeline he did the short eleventh in one, and as near as a toucher got a three on the four-hundred-yard twelfth.

I will skip lightly over the intermediate stages of Cuthbert's courtship and come to the moment when—at the annual ball in aid of the local Cottage Hospital, the only occasion during the year on which the lion, so to speak, lay down with the lamb, and the Golfers and the Cultured met on terms of easy comradeship, their differences temporarily laid aside—he proposed to Adeline and was badly stymied.

That fair, soulful girl could not see him with a spy-glass.

"Mr. Banks," she said, "I will speak frankly."

"Charge right ahead," assented Cuthbert.

"Deeply sensible as I am of——"

"I know. Of the honour and the compliment and all that. But, passing lightly over all that guff, what seems to be the trouble? I love you to distraction——"

"Love is not everything."

"You're wrong," said Cuthbert earnestly. "You're right off it. Love——" And he was about to dilate on the theme when she interrupted him.

"I am a girl of ambition."

"And very nice, too," said Cuthbert.

"I am a girl of ambition," repeated Adeline, "and I realize that the fulfilment of my ambitions must come through my husband. I am very ordinary myself——"

"What!" cried Cuthbert. "You ordinary? Why, you are a pearl among women, the queen of your sex. You can't have been looking in a glass lately. You stand alone. Simply alone. You make the rest look like battered repaints."

"Well," said Adeline, softening a trifle, "I believe I am fairly good-looking——"

"Anybody who was content to call you fairly good-looking would describe the Taj Mahal as a pretty nifty tomb."

"But that is not the point. What I mean is, if I marry a nonentity I shall be a nonentity myself for ever. And I would sooner die than be a nonentity."

"And, if I follow your reasoning, you think that that lets *me* out?"

"Well, really, Mr. Banks, *have* you done anything, or are you likely ever to do anything worth while?"

Cuthbert hesitated.

"It's true," he said, "I didn't finish in the first ten in the Open, and I was knocked out in the semi-final of the Amateur, but I won the French Open last year."

"The—what?"

"The French Open Championship. Golf, you know."

"Golf! You waste all your time playing golf. I admire a man who is more spiritual, more intellectual."

A pang of jealousy rent Cuthbert's bosom.

"Like What's-his-name Devine?" he said, sullenly.

"Mr. Devine," replied Adeline, blushing faintly, "is going to be a great man. Already he has achieved much. The critics say that he is more Russian than any other young English writer."

"And is that good?"

"Of course it's good."

"I should have thought the wheeze would be to be more English than any other young English writer."

"Nonsense! Who wants an English writer to be English? You've got to be Russian or Spanish or something to be a real success. The mantle of the great Russians has descended on Mr. Devine."

"From what I've heard of Russians, I should hate to have that happen to *me*."

"There is no danger of that," said Adeline scornfully.

"Oh! Well, let me tell you that there is a lot more in me than you think."

"That might easily be so."

"You think I'm not spiritual and intellectual," said Cuthbert, deeply moved. "Very well. Tomorrow I join the Literary Society."

Even as he spoke the words his leg was itching to kick himself for being such a chump, but the sudden expression of pleasure on Adeline's face soothed him; and he went home that night with the feeling that he had taken on something rather attractive. It was only in the cold grey light of the morning that he realized what he had let himself in for.

I do not know if you have had any experience of suburban literary societies, but the one that flourished under the eye of Mrs. Willoughby Smethurst at Wood Hills was rather more so than the average. With my feeble powers of narrative, I cannot hope to make clear to you all that Cuthbert Banks endured in the next few weeks. And, even if I could, I doubt if I should do so. It is all very well to excite pity and terror, as Aristotle recommends, but there are limits. In the ancient Greek tragedies it was an ironclad rule that all the real rough stuff should take place off-stage, and I shall follow this admirable principle. It will suffice if I say merely that J. Cuthbert Banks had a thin time. After attending eleven debates and fourteen lectures on *vers libre* Poetry, the Seventeenth-Century Essayists, the Neo-Scandinavian Movement in Portuguese Literature, and other subjects of a similar nature, he grew so enfeebled that, on the rare occasions when he had time for a visit to the links, he had to take a full iron for his mashie shots.

It was not simply the oppressive nature of the debates and lectures that sapped his vitality. What really got right in amongst him was the torture of seeing Adeline's adoration of Raymond Parsloe Devine. The man seemed to have made the deepest possible impression upon her plastic emotions. When he spoke, she leaned forward with parted lips and looked at him. When he was not speaking—which was seldom—she leaned back and looked at him. And when he happened to take the next seat to her, she leaned sideways and looked at him. One glance at Mr. Devine would have been more than enough for Cuthbert; but Adeline found him a spectacle that never palled. She could not have gazed at him with a more rapturous intensity if she had been a small child and he a saucer of ice-cream. All this Cuthbert had to witness while still endeavouring to retain the possession of his faculties sufficiently to enable him to duck and back away if somebody suddenly asked him what he thought of the sombre realism of Vladimir Brusiloff. It is little wonder that he tossed in bed, picking at the coverlet, through sleepless nights, and had to have all his waistcoats taken in three inches to keep them from sagging.

This Vladimir Brusiloff to whom I have referred was the famous Russian novelist, and, owing to the fact of his being in the country on a lecturing tour at the moment, there had been something of a boom in his works. The Wood Hills Literary Society had been studying them for weeks, and never since his first entrance into intellectual circles had Cuthbert Banks come nearer to throwing in the towel. Vladimir specialized in grey studies of hopeless misery, where nothing happened till page three hundred and eighty, when the moujik decided to commit suicide. It was tough going for a man whose deepest reading hitherto had been Vardon on the Push-Shot, and there can be no greater proof of the magic of love than the fact that Cuthbert stuck it without a cry. But the strain was terrible and I am inclined to think that he must have cracked, had it not been for the daily reports in the papers of the internecine strife which was proceeding so briskly in Russia. Cuthbert was an optimist at heart, and it seemed to him that, at the rate at which the inhabitants of that interesting country were murdering one another, the supply of Russian novelists must eventually give out.

One morning, as he tottered down the road for the short walk which was now almost the only exercise to which he was equal, Cuthbert met Adeline. A spasm of anguish flitted through all his nerve-centres as he saw that she was accompanied by Raymond Parsloe Devine.

"Good morning, Mr. Banks," said Adeline.

"Good morning," said Cuthbert hollowly.

"Such good news about Vladimir Brusiloff."

"Dead?" said Cuthbert, with a touch of hope.

"Dead? Of course not. Why should he be? No, Aunt Emily met his manager after his lecture at Queen's Hall yesterday, and he has promised that Mr. Brusiloff shall come to her next Wednesday reception.

"Oh, ah!" said Cuthbert, dully.

"I don't know how she managed it. I think she must have told him that Mr. Devine would be there to meet him."

"But you said he was coming," argued Cuthbert.

"I shall be very glad," said Raymond Devine, "of the opportunity of meeting Brusiloff."

"I'm sure," said Adeline, "he will be very glad of the opportunity of meeting you."

"Possibly," said Mr. Devine. "Possibly. Competent critics have said that my work closely resembles that of the great Russian Masters."

"Your psychology is so deep."

"Yes, yes."

"And your atmosphere."

"Quite."

Cuthbert in a perfect agony of spirit prepared to withdraw from this love-feast. The sun was shining brightly, but the world was black to him. Birds sang in the tree-tops, but he did not hear them. He might have been a moujik for all the pleasure he found in life.

"You will be there, Mr. Banks?" said Adeline, as he turned away.

"Oh, all right," said Cuthbert.

When Cuthbert had entered the drawing-room on the following Wednesday and had taken his usual place in a distant corner where, while able to feast his gaze on Adeline, he had a sporting chance of being overlooked or mistaken for a piece of furniture, he perceived the great Russian thinker seated in the midst of a circle of admiring females. Raymond Parsloe Devine had not yet arrived.

His first glance at the novelist surprised Cuthbert. Doubtless with the best motives, Vladimir Brusiloff had permitted his face to become almost entirely concealed behind a dense zareba of hair, but his eyes were visible through the undergrowth, and it seemed to Cuthbert that there was an expression in them not unlike that of a cat in a strange backyard surrounded by small boys. The man looked forlorn and hopeless, and Cuthbert wondered whether he had had bad news from home.

This was not the case. The latest news which Vladimir Brusiloff had had from Russia had been particularly cheering. Three of his principal creditors had perished in the last massacre of the *bourgeoisie,* and a man whom he owed for five years for a samovar and a pair of overshoes had fled the country, and had not been heard of since. It was not bad news from home that was depressing Vladimir. What was wrong with him was the fact that this was the eighty-second suburban literary reception he had been compelled to attend since he had landed in the country on his lecturing tour, and he was sick to death of it. When his agent had first suggested the trip, he had signed on the dotted line without an instant's hesitation. Worked out in roubles, the fees offered had seemed just about right. But now, as he peered through the brushwood at the faces round him, and realized that eight out of ten of those present had manuscripts of some sort concealed on their persons, and were only waiting for an opportunity to whip them out and start reading, he wished that he had stayed at his quiet home in Nijni-Novgorod, where the worst thing that could happen to a fellow was a brace of bombs coming in through the window and mixing themselves up with his breakfast egg.

At this point in his meditations he was aware that his hostess was looming up before him with a pale young man in horn-rimmed spectacles at her side. There was in Mrs. Smethurst's demeanour something of the unction of the master-of-ceremonies at the big fight who introduces the earnest gentleman who wishes to challenge the winner.

"Oh, Mr. Brusiloff," said Mrs. Smethurst, "I do so want you to meet Mr. Raymond Parsloe Devine, whose work I expect you know. He is one of our younger novelists."

The distinguished visitor peered in a wary and defensive manner through the shrubbery, but did not speak. Inwardly he was thinking how exactly like Mr. Devine was to the eighty-one other younger novelists to whom he had been introduced at various hamlets throughout the country. Raymond Parsloe Devine bowed courteously, while Cuthbert, wedged into his corner, glowered at him.

"The critics," said Mr. Devine, "have been kind enough to say that my poor efforts contain a good deal of the Russian spirit. I owe much to the great Russians. I have been greatly influenced by Sovietski."

Down in the forest something stirred. It was Vladimir Brusiloff's mouth opening, as he prepared to speak. He was not a man who prattled readily, especially in a foreign tongue. He gave the impression that each word was excavated from his interior by some up-to-date process of mining. He glared bleakly at Mr. Devine, and allowed three words to drop out of him.

"Sovietski no good!"

He paused for a moment, set the machinery working again, and delivered five more at the pithead.

"I spit me of Sovietski!"

There was a painful sensation. The lot of a popular idol is in many ways an enviable one, but it has the drawback of uncertainty. Here today and gone tomorrow. Until this moment Raymond Parsloe Devine's stock had stood at something considerably over par in Wood Hills intellectual circles, but now there was a rapid slump. Hitherto he had been greatly admired for being influenced by Sovietski, but it appeared now that this was not a good thing to be. It was evidently a rotten thing to be. The law could not touch you for being influenced by Sovietski, but there is an ethical as well as a legal code, and this it was obvious that Raymond Parsloe Devine had transgressed. Women drew away from him slightly, holding their skirts. Men looked at him censoriously. Adeline Smethurst started violently, and dropped a tea-cup. And Cuthbert Banks, doing his popular imitation of a sardine in his corner, felt for the first time that life held something of sunshine.

Raymond Parsloe Devine was plainly shaken, but he made an adroit attempt to recover his lost prestige.

"When I say I have been influenced by Sovietski, I mean, of course, that I was once under his spell. A young writer commits many follies. I have long since passed through that phase. The false glamour of Sovietski has ceased to dazzle me. I now belong whole-heartedly to the school of Nastikoff."

There was a reaction. People nodded at one another sympathetically. After all, we cannot expect old heads on young shoulders, and a lapse at the outset of one's career should not be held against one who has eventually seen the light.

"Nastikoff no good," said Vladimir Brusiloff, coldly. He paused, listening to the machinery.

"Nastikoff worse than Sovietski."

He paused again.

"I spit me of Nastikoff!" he said.

This time there was no doubt about it. The bottom had dropped out of the market, and Raymond Parsloe Devine Preferred were down in the cellar with no takers. It was clear to the entire assembled company that they had been all wrong about Raymond Parsloe Devine. They had allowed him to play on their innocence and sell them a pup. They had taken him at his own valuation, and had been cheated into admiring him as a man who amounted to something, and all the while he had belonged to the school of Nastikoff. You never can tell. Mrs. Smethurst's guests were well-bred, and there was consequently no violent demonstration, but you could see by their faces what they felt. Those nearest Raymond Parsloe jostled to get further away. Mrs. Smethurst eyed him stonily through a raised lorgnette. One or two low hisses were heard, and over at the other end of the room somebody opened the window in a marked manner.

Raymond Parsloe Devine hesitated for a moment, then, realizing his situation, turned and slunk to the door. There was an audible sigh of relief as it closed behind him.

Vladimir Brusiloff proceeded to sum up.

"No novelists any good except me. Sovietski—yah! Nastikoff—bah! I spit me of zem all. No novelists anywhere any good except me. P. G. Wodehouse and Tolstoi not bad. Not good, but not bad. No novelists any good except me."

And, having uttered this dictum, he removed a slab of cake from a near-by plate, steered it through the jungle, and began to champ.

It is too much to say that there was a dead silence. There could never be that in any room in which Vladimir Brusiloff was eating cake. But certainly what you might call the general chit-chat was pretty well down and out. Nobody liked to be the first to speak. The members of the Wood Hills Literary Society looked at one another timidly. Cuthbert, for his part, gazed at Adeline; and Adeline gazed into space. It was plain that the girl was deeply stirred. Her eyes were opened wide, a faint flush crimsoned her cheeks, and her breath was coming quickly.

Adeline's mind was in a whirl. She felt as if she had been walking gaily along a pleasant path and had stopped suddenly on the very brink of a precipice. It would be idle to deny that Raymond Parsloe Devine had attracted her extraordinarily. She had taken him at his own valuation as an extremely hot potato, and her hero-worship had gradually been turning into love. And now her hero had been shown to have feet of clay. It was hard, I consider, on Raymond Parsloe Devine, but that is how it goes in this world. You get a following as a celebrity, and then you run up against another bigger celebrity and your admirers desert you. One could moralize on this at considerable length, but better not, perhaps. Enough to say that the glamour of Raymond Devine ceased abruptly in that moment for Adeline, and her most coherent thought at this juncture was the resolve, as soon as she got up to her room, to burn the three signed photographs he had sent her and to give the autographed presentation set of his books to the grocer's boy.

Mrs. Smethurst, meanwhile, having rallied somewhat, was endeavouring to set the feast of reason and flow of soul going again.

"And how do you like England, Mr. Brusiloff?" she asked.

The celebrity paused in the act of lowering another segment of cake.

"Dam good," he replied, cordially.

"I suppose you have travelled all over the country by this time?"

"You said it," agreed the Thinker.

"Have you met many of our great public men?"

"Yais—Yais—Quite a few of the nibs—Lloyid Gorge, I meet him. But——" Beneath the matting a discontented expression came into his face, and his voice took on a peevish note. "But I not meet your *real* great men—your Arbmishel, your Arreevadon—I not meet them. That's what gives me the pipovitch. Have *you* ever met Arbmishel and Arreevadon?"

A strained, anguished look came into Mrs. Smethurst's face and was reflected in the faces of the other members of the circle. The eminent Russian had sprung two entirely new ones on them, and they felt that their ignorance was about to be exposed. What would Vladimir Brusiloff think of the Wood Hills Literary Society? The reputation of the Wood Hills Literary Society was at stake, trembling in the balance, and coming up for the third time. In dumb agony Mrs. Smethurst rolled her eyes about the room searching for someone capable of coming to the rescue. She drew blank.

And then, from a distant corner, there sounded a deprecating cough, and those nearest Cuthbert Banks saw that he had stopped twisting his right foot round his left ankle and his left foot round his right ankle and was sitting up with a light of almost human intelligence in his eyes.

"Er——" said Cuthbert, blushing as every eye in the room seemed to fix itself on him, "I think he means Abe Mitchell and Harry Vardon."

"Abe Mitchell and Harry Vardon?" repeated Mrs. Smethurst, blankly. "I never heard of——"

"Yais! Yais! Most! Very!" shouted Vladimir Brusiloff, enthusiastically.

"Arbmishel and Arreevadon. You know them, yes, what, no, perhaps?"

"I've played with Abe Mitchell often, and I was partnered with Harry Vardon in last year's Open."

The great Russian uttered a cry that shook the chandelier.

"You play in ze Open? Why," he demanded reproachfully of Mrs. Smethurst, "was I not been introduced to this young man who play in opens?"

"Well, really," faltered Mrs. Smethurst. "Well, the fact is, Mr. Brusiloff——"

She broke off. She was unequal to the task of explaining, without hurting anyone's feelings, that she had always regarded Cuthbert as a piece of cheese and a blot on the landscape.

"Introduct me!" thundered the Celebrity.

"Why, certainly, certainly, of course. This is Mr. ——." She looked appealingly at Cuthbert.

"Banks," prompted Cuthbert.

"Banks!" cried Vladimir Brusiloff. "Not Cootaboot Banks?"

"*Is* your name Cootaboot?" asked Mrs. Smethurst, faintly.

"Well, it's Cuthbert."

"Yais! Yais! Cootaboot!" There was a rush and swirl, as the effervescent Muscovite burst his way through the throng and rushed to where Cuthbert sat. He stood for a moment eyeing him excitedly, then, stooping swiftly, kissed him on both cheeks before Cuthbert could get his guard up. "My dear young man, I saw you win ze French Open. Great! Great! Grand! Superb! Hot stuff, and you can say I said so! Will you permit one who is but eighteen at Nijni-Novgorod to salute you once more?"

And he kissed Cuthbert again. Then, brushing aside one or two intellectuals who were in the way, he dragged up a chair and sat down.

"You are a great man!" he said.

"Oh, no," said Cuthbert modestly.

"Yais! Great. Most! Very! The way you lay your approach-putts dead from anywhere!"

"Oh, I don't know."

Mr. Brusiloff drew his chair closer.

"Let me tell you one vairy funny story about putting. It was one day I play at Nijni-Novgorod with the pro. against Lenin and Trotsky, and Trotsky had a two-inch putt for the hole. But, just as he addresses the ball, someone in the crowd he tries to assassinate Lenin with a rewolwer—you know that is our great national sport, trying to assassinate Lenin with rewolwers—and the bang puts Trotsky off his stroke and he goes five yards past the hole, and then Lenin, who is rather shaken, you understand, he misses again himself, and we win the hole and match and I clean up three hundred and ninety-six thousand roubles, or fifteen shillings in your money. Some gameovitch! And now let me tell you one other vairy funny story——"

Desultory conversation had begun in murmurs over the rest of the room, as the

Wood Hills intellectuals politely endeavoured to conceal the fact that they realized that they were about as much out of it at this re-union of twin souls as cats at a dog-show. From time to time they started as Vladimir Brusiloff's laugh boomed out. Perhaps it was a consolation to them to know that he was enjoying himself.

As for Adeline, how shall I describe her emotions? She was stunned. Before her very eyes the stone which the builders had rejected had become the main thing, the hundred-to-one shot had walked away with the race. A rush of tender admiration for Cuthbert Banks flooded her heart. She saw that she had been all wrong. Cuthbert, whom she had always treated with a patronizing superiority, was really a man to be looked up to and worshipped. A deep, dreamy sigh shook Adeline's fragile form.

Half an hour later Vladimir and Cuthbert Banks rose.

"Goot-a-bye, Mrs. Smet-thirst," said the Celebrity. "Zank you for a most charm-ing visit. My friend Cootaboot and me we go now to shoot a few holes. You will lend me clobs, friend Cootaboot?"

"Any you want."

"The niblicksky is what I use most. Goot-a-bye, Mrs. Smet-thirst."

They were moving to the door, when Cuthbert felt a light touch on his arm. Adeline was looking up at him tenderly.

"May I come, too, and walk round with you?"

Cuthbert's bosom heaved.

"Oh," he said, with a tremor in his voice, "that you would walk round with me for life!"

Her eyes met his.

"Perhaps," she whispered, softly, "it could be arranged."

"And so" (concluded the Oldest Member), "you see that golf can be of the greatest practical assistance to a man in Life's struggle. Raymond Parsloe Devine, who was no player, had to move out of the neighbourhood immediately, and is now, I believe, writing scenarios out in California for the Flicker Film Company. Adeline is married to Cuthbert, and it was only his earnest pleading which prevented her from having their eldest son christened Abe Mitchell Ribbed-Faced Mashie Banks, for she is now as keen a devotee of the great game as her husband. Those who know them say that theirs is a union so devoted, so——"

The Sage broke off abruptly, for the young man had rushed to the door and out into the passage. Through the open door he could hear him crying passionately to the waiter to bring back his clubs.

3
A WOMAN IS ONLY A WOMAN

ON A FINE DAY in the spring, summer, or early autumn, there are few spots more delightful than the terrace in front of our Golf Club. It is a vantage-point peculiarly fitted to the man of philosophic mind: for from it may be seen that varied, never-ending pageant, which men call Golf, in a number of its aspects. To your right, on the first tee, stand the cheery optimists who are about to make their opening drive, happily conscious that even a topped shot will trickle a measurable distance down the steep hill. Away in the valley, directly in front of you, is the lake hole, where these same optimists will be converted to pessimism by the wet splash of a new ball. At your side is the ninth green, with its sinuous undulations which have so often wrecked the returning traveller in sight of home. And at various points within your line of vision are the third tee, the sixth tee, and the sinister bunkers about the eighth green—none of them lacking in food for the reflective mind.

It is on this terrace that the Oldest Member sits, watching the younger generation knocking at the divot. His gaze wanders from Jimmy Fothergill's two-hundred-and-twenty-yard drive down the hill to the silver drops that flash up in the sun, as young Freddie Woosley's mashie-shot drops weakly into the waters of the lake. Returning, it rests upon Peter Willard, large and tall, and James Todd, small and slender, as they struggle up the fairway of the ninth.

Love (says the Oldest Member) is an emotion which your true golfer should always treat with suspicion. Do not misunderstand me. I am not saying that love is a bad thing, only that it is an unknown quantity. I have known cases where marriage improved a man's game, and other cases where it seemed to put him right off his stroke. There seems to be no fixed rule. But what I do say is that a golfer should be cautious. He should not be led away by the first pretty face. I will tell you a story that illustrates the point. It is the story of those two men who have just got on to the ninth green—Peter Willard and James Todd.

There is about great friendships between man and man (said the Oldest Member) a certain inevitability that can only be compared with the age-old association of ham and eggs. No one can say when it was that these two wholesome and palatable food-stuffs first came together, nor what was the mutual magnetism that brought their deathless partnership about. One simply feels that it is one of the things that must be so. Similarly with men. Who can trace to its first beginnings the love of Damon for Pythias, of David for Jonathan, of Swan for Edgar? Who can explain what it was about Crosse that first attracted Blackwell? We simply say, "These men are friends," and leave it at that.

In the case of Peter Willard and James Todd, one may hazard the guess that the first link in the chain that bound them together was the fact that they took up golf within a few days of each other, and contrived, as time went on, to develop such equal form at the game that the most expert critics are still baffled in their efforts to decide which is the worse player. I have heard the point argued a hundred times without any conclusion being reached. Supporters of Peter claim that his driving off the tee entitles him to an unchallenged pre-eminence among the world's most hopeless foozlers—only to be discomfited later when the advocates of James show, by means of diagrams, that no one has ever surpassed their man in absolute incompetence with the spoon. It is one of those problems where debate is futile.

Few things draw two men together more surely than a mutual inability to master golf, coupled with an intense and ever-increasing love for the game. At the end of the first few months, when a series of costly experiments had convinced both Peter and James that there was not a tottering grey-beard nor a toddling infant in the neighbourhood whose downfall they could encompass, the two became inseparable. It was pleasanter, they found, to play together, and go neck and neck round the eighteen holes, than to take on some lissom youngster who could spatter them all over the course with one old ball and a cut-down cleek stolen from his father; or some spavined elder who not only rubbed it into them, but was apt, between strokes, to bore them with personal reminiscences of the Crimean War. So they began to play together early and late. In the small hours before breakfast, long ere the first faint piping of the waking caddie made itself heard from the caddie-shed, they were half-way through their opening round. And at close of day, when bats wheeled against the steely sky and the "pro's" had stolen home to rest, you might see them in the deepening dusk, going through the concluding exercises of their final spasm. After dark, they visited each other's houses and read golf books.

If you have gathered from what I have said that Peter Willard and James Todd were fond of golf, I am satisfied. That is the impression I intended to convey. They were real golfers, for real golf is a thing of the spirit, not of mere mechanical excellence of stroke.

It must not be thought, however, that they devoted too much of their time and their thoughts to golf—assuming, indeed, that such a thing is possible. Each was connected with a business in the metropolis; and often, before he left for the links, Peter would go to the trouble and expense of ringing up the office to say he would not be coming in that day; while I myself have heard James—and this not once, but frequently— say while lunching in the club-house, that he had half a mind to get Gracechurch Street on the 'phone and ask how things were going. They were, in fact, the type of men of whom England is proudest—the backbone of a great country, toilers in the mart, untired businessmen, keen red-blooded men of affairs. If they played a little golf besides, who shall blame them?

So they went on, day by day, happy and contented. And then the Woman came into their lives, like the Serpent in the Links of Eden, and perhaps for the first time they realized that they were not one entity—not one single, indivisible Something that made for topped drives and short putts—but two individuals, in whose breasts Nature had implanted other desires than the simple ambition some day to do the dog-leg hole on the second nine in under double figures. My friends tell me that, when I am relating a story, my language is inclined at times a little to obscure my meaning; but, if you understand from what I have been saying that James Todd and Peter Willard both fell in love with the same woman—all right, let us carry on. That is precisely what I was driving at.

I have not the pleasure of an intimate acquaintance with Grace Forrester. I have seen her in the distance, watering the flowers in her garden, and on these occasions her stance struck me as graceful. And once, at a picnic, I observed her killing wasps with a teaspoon, and was impressed by the freedom of the wrist-action of her back-swing. Beyond this, I can say little. But she must have been attractive, for there can be no doubt of the earnestness with which both Peter and James fell in love with her. I doubt if either slept a wink the night of the dance at which it was their privilege first to meet her.

The next afternoon, happening to encounter Peter in the bunker near the eleventh green, James said:

"That was a nice girl, that Miss What's-her-name."

And Peter, pausing for a moment from his trench-digging, replied:

"Yes."

And then James, with a pang, knew that he had a rival, for he had not mentioned Miss Forrester's name, and yet Peter had divined that it was to her that he had referred.

Love is a fever which, so to speak, drives off without wasting time on the address. On the very next morning after the conversation which I have related, James Todd rang Peter Willard up on the 'phone and cancelled their golf engagements for the day, on the plea of a sprained wrist. Peter, acknowledging the cancellation, stated that he himself had been on the point of ringing James up to say that he would be unable to play owing to a slight headache. They met at tea-time at Miss Forrester's house. James asked how Peter's headache was, and Peter said it was a little better. Peter inquired after James's sprained wrist, and was told it seemed on the mend. Miss Forrester dispensed tea and conversation to both impartially.

They walked home together. After an awkward silence of twenty minutes, James said:

"There is something about the atmosphere—the aura, shall I say?—that emanates from a good woman that makes a man feel that life has a new, a different meaning."

Peter replied:

"Yes."

When they reached James's door, James said:

"I won't ask you in tonight, old man. You want to go home and rest and cure that headache."

"Yes," said Peter.

There was another silence. Peter was thinking that, only a couple of days before, James had told him that he had a copy of Sandy MacBean's "How to Become a Scratch Man Your First Season by Studying Photographs" coming by parcel-post from town, and they had arranged to read it aloud together. By now, thought Peter, it must be lying on his friend's table. The thought saddened him. And James, guessing what was in Peter's mind, was saddened too. But he did not waver. He was in no mood to read MacBean's masterpiece that night. In the twenty minutes of silence after leaving Miss Forrester he had realized that "Grace" rhymes with "face", and he wanted to sit alone in his study and write poetry. The two men parted with a distant nod. I beg your pardon? Yes, you are right. Two distant nods. It was always a failing of mine to count the score erroneously.

It is not my purpose to weary you by a minute recital of the happenings of each day that went by. On the surface, the lives of these two men seemed unchanged. They still played golf together, and during the round achieved towards each other a manner that, superficially, retained all its ancient cheeriness and affection. If—I should say—when, James topped his drive, Peter never failed to say "Hard luck!" And when—or, rather, if Peter managed not to top his, James invariably said "Great!" But things were not the same, and they knew it.

It so happened, as it sometimes will on these occasions, for Fate is a dramatist who gets his best effects with a small cast, that Peter Willard and James Todd were the only visible aspirants for the hand of Miss Forrester. Right at the beginning young Freddie Woosley had seemed attracted by the girl, and had called once or twice with flowers and chocolates, but Freddie's affections never centred themselves on one object for more than a few days, and he had dropped out after the first week. From that time on it became clear to all of us that, if Grace Forrester intended to marry anyone in the place, it would be either James or Peter; and a good deal of interest was taken in the matter by the local sportsmen. So little was known of the form of the two men, neither having figured as principal in a love-affair before, that even money was the best you could get, and the market was sluggish. I think my own flutter of twelve golf-balls, taken up by Percival Brown, was the most substantial of any of the wagers. I selected James as the winner. Why, I can hardly say, unless that he had an aunt who contributed occasional stories to the "Woman's Sphere". These things sometimes weigh with a girl. On the other hand, George Lucas, who had half-a-dozen of ginger-ale on Peter, based his calculations on the fact that James wore knickerbockers on the links, and that no girl could possibly love a man with calves like that. In short, you see, we really had nothing to go on.

Nor had James and Peter. The girl seemed to like them both equally. They never saw her except in each other's company. And it was not until one day when Grace

Forrester was knitting a sweater that there seemed a chance of getting a clue to her hidden feelings.

When the news began to spread through the place that Grace was knitting this sweater there was a big sensation. The thing seemed to us practically to amount to a declaration.

That was the view that James Todd and Peter Willard took of it, and they used to call on Grace, watch her knitting, and come away with their heads full of complicated calculations. The whole thing hung on one point—to wit, what size the sweater was going to be. If it was large, then it must be for Peter; if small, then James was the lucky man. Neither dared to make open inquiries, but it began to seem almost impossible to find out the truth without them. No masculine eye can reckon up purls and plains and estimate the size of chest which the garment is destined to cover. Moreover, with amateur knitters there must always be allowed a margin for involuntary error. There were many cases during the war where our girls sent sweaters to their sweethearts which would have induced strangulation in their young brothers. The amateur sweater of those days was, in fact, practically tantamount to German propaganda.

Peter and James were accordingly baffled. One evening the sweater would look small, and James would come away jubilant; the next it would have swollen over a vast area, and Peter would walk home singing. The suspense of the two men can readily be imagined. On the one hand, they wanted to know their fate; on the other, they fully realized that whoever the sweater was for would have to wear it. And, as it was a vivid pink and would probably not fit by a mile, their hearts quailed at the prospect.

In all affairs of human tension there must come a breaking point. It came one night as the two men were walking home.

"Peter," said James, stopping in mid-stride. He mopped his forehead. His manner had been feverish all the evening.

"Yes?" said Peter.

"I can't stand this any longer. I haven't had a good night's rest for weeks. We must find out definitely which of us is to have that sweater."

"Let's go back and ask her, ' said Peter.

So they turned back and rang the bell and went into the house and presented themselves before Miss Forrester.

"Lovely evening," said James, to break the ice.

"Superb," said Peter.

"Delightful," said Miss Forrester, looking a little surprised at finding the troupe playing a return date without having booked it in advance.

"To settle a bet," said James, "will you please tell us who—I should say, whom—you are knitting that sweater for?"

"It is not a sweater," replied Miss Forrester, with a womanly candour that well became her. "It is a sock. And it is for my cousin Juliet's youngest son, Willie."

"Good night," said James.

"Good night," said Peter.

"Good night," said Grace Forrester.

It was during the long hours of the night, when ideas so often come to wakeful men, that James was struck by an admirable solution of his and Peter's difficulty. It seemed to him that, were one or the other to leave Woodhaven, the survivor would find himself in a position to conduct his wooing as wooing should be conducted. Hitherto, as I have indicated, neither had allowed the other to be more than a few minutes alone with the girl. They watched each other like hawks. When James called, Peter called. When Peter dropped in, James invariably popped round. The thing had resolved itself into a stalemate.

The idea which now came to James was that he and Peter should settle their rivalry by an eighteen-hole match on the links. He thought very highly of the idea before he finally went to sleep, and in the morning the scheme looked just as good to him as it had done overnight.

James was breakfasting next morning, preparatory to going round to disclose his plan to Peter, when Peter walked in, looking happier than he had done for days.

" 'Morning," said James.

" 'Morning," said Peter.

Peter sat down and toyed absently with a slice of bacon.

"I've got an idea," he said.

"One isn't many," said James, bringing his knife down with a jerk-shot on a fried egg. "What is your idea?"

"Got it last night as I was lying awake. It struck me that, if either of us was to clear out of this place, the other would have a fair chance. You know what I mean— with Her. At present we've got each other stymied. Now, how would it be," said Peter, abstractedly spreading marmalade on his bacon, "if we were to play an eighteen-hole match, the loser to leg out of the neighbourhood and stay away long enough to give the winner the chance to find out exactly how things stood?"

James started so violently that he struck himself in the left eye with his fork.

"That's exactly the idea I got last night, too."

"Then it's a go?"

"It's the only thing to do."

There was silence for a moment. Both men were thinking. Remember, they were friends. For years they had shared each other's sorrows, joys, and golf-balls, and sliced into the same bunkers.

Presently Peter said:

"I shall miss you."

"What do you mean, miss me?"

"When you're gone, Woodhaven won't seem the same place. But of course you'll soon be able to come back. I sha'n't waste any time proposing."

"Leave me your address," said James, "and I'll send you a wire when you can return. You won't be offended if I don't ask you to be best man at the wedding? In the circumstances it might be painful to you."

Peter sighed dreamily.

"We'll have the sitting-room done in blue. Her eyes are blue."

"Remember," said James, "there will always be a knife and fork for you at our little nest. Grace is not the woman to want me to drop my bachelor friends."

"Touching this match," said Peter. "Strict Royal and Ancient rules, of course?"

"Certainly."

"I mean to say—no offence, old man—but no grounding niblicks in bunkers."

"Precisely. And, without hinting at anything personal, the ball shall be considered holed-out only when it is in the hole, not when it stops on the edge."

"Undoubtedly. And—you know I don't want to hurt your feelings—missing the ball counts as a stroke, not as a practice-swing."

"Exactly. And—you'll forgive me if I mention it—a player whose ball has fallen in the rough, may not pull up all the bushes within a radius of three feet."

"In fact, strict rules."

"Strict rules."

They shook hands without more words. And presently Peter walked out, and James, with a guilty look over his shoulder, took down Sandy MacBean's great work from the bookshelf and began to study the photograph of the short approach-shot showing Mr. MacBean swinging from Point A, through dotted line B–C, to Point D, his head the while remaining rigid at the spot marked with a cross. He felt a little guiltily that he had stolen a march on his friend, and that the contest was as good as over.

I cannot recall a lovelier summer day than that on which the great Todd-Willard eighteen-hole match took place. It had rained during the night, and now the sun shone down from a clear blue sky on to turf that glistened more greenly than the young grass of early spring. Butterflies flitted to and fro; birds sang merrily. In short, all Nature smiled. And it is to be doubted if nature ever had a better excuse for smiling—or even laughing outright; for matches like that between James Todd and Peter Willard do not occur every day.

Whether it was that love had keyed them up, or whether hours of study of Braid's "Advanced Golf" and the Badminton Book had produced a belated effect, I cannot say; but both started off quite reasonably well. Our first hole, as you can see, is a bogey four, and James was dead on the pin in seven, leaving Peter, who had twice hit the United Kingdom with his mashie in mistake for the ball, a difficult putt for the half. Only one thing could happen when you left Peter a difficult putt; and James advanced to the lake-hole one up, Peter, as he followed, trying to console himself with the thought that many of the best golfers prefer to lose the first hole and save themselves for a strong finish.

Peter and James had played over the lake-hole so often that they had become

accustomed to it, and had grown into the habit of sinking a ball or two as a preliminary formality with much the same stoicism displayed by those kings in ancient and
superstitious times who used to fling jewellery into the sea to propitiate it before
they took a voyage. But today, by one of those miracles without which golf would
not be golf, each of them got over with his first shot—and not only over, but dead
on the pin. Our "pro" himself could not have done better.

I think it was at this point that the two men began to go to pieces. They were in an
excited frame of mind, and this thing unmanned them. You will no doubt recall
Keats's poem about stout Cortez staring with eagle eyes at the Pacific while all his
men gazed at each other with a wild surmise, silent upon a peak in Darien. Precisely
so did Peter Willard and James Todd stare with eagle eyes at the second lake hole,
and gaze at each other with a wild surmise, silent upon a tee in Woodhaven. They
had dreamed of such a happening so often and woke to find the vision false, that at
first they could not believe that the thing had actually occurred.

"I got over!" whispered James, in an awed voice.

"So did I!" muttered Peter.

"In one!"

"With my very first!"

They walked in silence round the edge of the lake, and holed out. One putt was
enough for each, and they halved the hole with a two. Peter's previous record was
eight, and James had once done a seven. There are times when strong men lose their
self-control, and this was one of them. They reached the third tee in a daze, and it
was here that mortification began to set in.

The third hole is another bogey four, up the hill and past the tree that serves as a
direction-post, the hole itself being out of sight. On his day, James had often done
it in ten and Peter in nine; but now they were unnerved. James, who had the honour,
shook visibly as he addressed his ball. Three times he swung and only connected with
the ozone; the fourth time he topped badly. The discs had been set back a little way,
and James had the mournful distinction of breaking a record for the course by
playing his fifth shot from the tee. It was a low, raking brassey-shot, which carried
a heap of stones twenty feet to the right and finished in a furrow. Peter, meanwhile,
had popped up a lofty ball which came to rest behind a stone.

It was now that the rigid rules governing this contest began to take their toll. Had
they been playing an ordinary friendly round, each would have teed up on some
convenient hillock and probably been past the tree with their second, for James
would, in ordinary circumstances, have taken his drive back and regarded the strokes
he had made as a little preliminary practice to get him into mid-season form. But
today it was war to the niblick, and neither man asked nor expected quarter. Peter's
seventh shot dislodged the stone, leaving him a clear field, and James, with his
eleventh, extricated himself from the furrow. Fifty feet from the tree James was
eighteen, Peter twelve; but then the latter, as every golfer does at times, suddenly
went right off his game. He hit the tree four times, then hooked into the sand-bunkers

to the left of the hole. James, who had been playing a game that was steady without being brilliant, was on the green in twenty-six, Peter taking twenty-seven. Poor putting lost James the hole. Peter was down in thirty-three, but the pace was too hot for James. He missed a two-foot putt for the half, and they went to the fourth tee all square.

The fourth hole follows the curve of the road, on the other side of which are picturesque woods. It presents no difficulties to the expert, but it has pitfalls for the novice. The dashing player stands for a slice, while the more cautious are satisfied if they can clear the bunker that spans the fairway and lay their ball well out to the left, whence an iron shot will take them to the green. Peter and James combined the two policies. Peter aimed to the left and got a slice, and James, also aiming to the left, topped into the bunker. Peter, realizing from experience the futility of searching for his ball in the woods, drove a second, which also disappeared into the jungle, as did his third. By the time he had joined James in the bunker he had played his sixth.

It is the glorious uncertainty of golf that makes it the game it is. The fact that James and Peter, lying side by side in the same bunker, had played respectively one and six shots, might have induced an unthinking observer to fancy the chances of the former. And no doubt, had he not taken seven strokes to extricate himself from the pit, while his opponent, by some act of God, contrived to get out in two, James's chances might have been extremely rosy. As it was, the two men staggered out on to the fairway again with a score of eight apiece. Once past the bunker and round the bend of the road, the hole becomes simple. A judicious use of the cleek put Peter on the green in fourteen, while James, with a Braid iron, reached it in twelve. Peter was down in seventeen, and James contrived to halve. It was only as he was leaving the hole that the latter discovered that he had been putting with his niblick, which cannot have failed to exercise a prejudicial effect on his game. These little incidents are bound to happen when one is in a nervous and highly-strung condition.

The fifth and sixth holes produced no unusual features. Peter won the fifth in eleven, and James the sixth in ten. The short seventh they halved in nine. The eighth, always a tricky hole, they took no liberties with, James, sinking a long putt with his twenty-third, just managing to halve. A ding-dong race up the hill for the ninth found James first at the pin, and they finished the first nine with James one up.

As they left the green James looked a little furtively at his companion.

"You might be strolling on to the tenth," he said. "I want to get a few balls at the shop. And my mashie wants fixing up. I sha'n't be long."

"I'll come with you," said Peter.

"Don't bother," said James. "You go on and hold our place at the tee."

I regret to say that James was lying. His mashie was in excellent repair, and he still had a dozen balls in his bag, it being his prudent practice always to start out with eighteen. No! What he had said was mere subterfuge. He wanted to go to his locker and snatch a few minutes with Sandy MacBean's "How to Become a Scratch Man". He felt sure that one more glance at the photograph of Mr. MacBean driving would give him the mastery of the stroke and so enable him to win the match. In this I think he was a little sanguine. The difficulty about Sandy MacBean's method of tuition was that he laid great stress on the fact that the ball should be directly in a line with a point exactly in the centre of the back of the player's neck; and so far James's efforts to keep his eye on the ball and on the back of his neck simultaneously had produced no satisfactory results.

It seemed to James, when he joined Peter on the tenth tee, that the latter's manner was strange. He was pale. There was a curious look in his eye.

"James, old man," he said.

"Yes?" said James.

"While you were away I have been thinking. James, old man, do you really love this girl?"

James stared. A spasm of pain twisted Peter's face.

"Suppose," he said in a low voice, "she were not all you—we—think she is!"

"What do you mean?"

"Nothing, nothing."

"Miss Forrester is an angel."

"Yes, yes. Quite so."

"I know what it is," said James passionately. "You're trying to put me off my stroke. You know that the least thing makes me lose my form."

"No, no!"

"You hope that you can take my mind off the game and make me go to pieces, and then you'll win the match."

"On the contrary," said Peter. "I intend to forfeit the match."

James reeled.

"What!"

"I give up."

"But—but——" James shook with emotion. His voice quavered. "Ah!" he cried. "I see now: I understand! You are doing this for me because I am your pal. Peter, this is noble! This is the sort of thing you read about in books. I've seen it in the movies. But I can't accept the sacrifice."

"You must!"

"No, no!"

"I insist!"

"Do you mean this?"

"I give her up, James, old man. I—I hope you will be happy."

"But I don't know what to say. How can I thank you?"

"Don't thank me."

"But, Peter, do you fully realize what you are doing? True, I am one up, but there are nine holes to go, and I am not right on my game today. You might easily beat me. Have you forgotten that I once took forty-seven at the dog-leg hole? This may be one of my bad days. Do you understand that if you insist on giving up I shall go to Miss Forrester tonight and propose to her?"

"I understand."

"And yet you stick to it that you are through?"

"I do. And, by the way, there's no need for you to wait till tonight. I saw Miss Forrester just now outside the tennis court. She's alone."

James turned crimson.

"Then I think perhaps——"

"You'd better go to her at once."

"I will." James extended his hand. "Peter, old man, I shall never forget this."

"That's all right."

"What are you going to do?"

"Now, do you mean? Oh, I shall potter round the second nine. If you want me, you'll find me somewhere about."

"You'll come to the wedding, Peter?" said James, wistfully.

"Of course," said Peter. "Good luck."

He spoke cheerily, but, when the other had turned to go, he stood looking after him thoughtfully. Then he sighed a heavy sigh.

James approached Miss Forrester with a beating heart. She made a charming picture as she stood there in the sunlight, one hand on her hip, the other swaying a tennis racket.

"How do you do?" said James.

"How are you, Mr. Todd? Have you been playing golf?"

"Yes."

"With Mr. Willard?"

"Yes. We were having a match."

"Golf," said Grace Forrester, "seems to make men very rude. Mr. Willard left me without a word in the middle of our conversation."

James was astonished.

"Were you talking to Peter?"

"Yes. Just now. I can't understand what was the matter with him. He just turned on his heel and swung off."

"You oughtn't to turn on your heel when you swing." said James; "only on the ball of the foot."

"I beg your pardon?"

"Nothing, nothing. I wasn't thinking. The fact is, I've something on my mind. So has Peter. You mustn't think too hardly of him. We have been playing an important match, and it must have got on his nerves. You didn't happen by any chance to be watching us?"

"No."

"Ah! I wish you had seen me at the lake-hole. I did it one under par."

"Was your father playing?"

"You don't understand. I mean I did it in one better than even the finest player is supposed to do it. It's a mashie-shot, you know. You mustn't play too light, or you fall in the lake; and you mustn't play it too hard, or you go past the hole into the woods. It requires the nicest delicacy and judgment, such as I gave it. You might have to wait a year before seeing anyone do it in two again. I doubt if the 'pro' often does it in two. Now, directly we came to this hole today, I made up my mind that there was going to be no mistake. The great secret of any shot at golf is ease, elegance, and the ability to relax. The majority of men, you will find, think it important that their address should be good."

"How snobbish! What does it matter where a man lives?"

"You don't absolutely follow me. I refer to the waggle and the stance before you make the stroke. Most players seem to fix in their minds the appearance of the angles which are presented by the position of the arms, legs, and club shaft, and it is largely the desire to retain these angles which results in their moving their heads and stiffening their muscles so that there is no freedom in the swing. There is only one point which vitally affects the stroke, and the only reason why that should be kept constant is that you are enabled to see your ball clearly. That is the pivotal point marked at the base of the neck, and a line drawn from this point to the ball should be at right angles to the line of flight."

James paused for a moment for air, and as he paused Miss Forrester spoke.

"This is all gibberish to me," she said.

"Gibberish!" gasped James. "I am quoting verbatim from one of the best authorities on golf."

Miss Forrester swung her tennis racket irritably.

"Golf," she said, "bores me pallid. I think it is the silliest game ever invented!"

The trouble about telling a story is that words are so feeble a means of depicting the supreme moments of life. That is where the artist has the advantage over the historian. Were I an artist, I should show James at this point falling backwards with his feet together and his eyes shut, with a semi-circular dotted line marking the progress of his flight and a few stars above his head to indicate moral collapse. There are no words that can adequately describe the sheer, black horror that froze the blood in his veins as this frightful speech smote his ears.

He had never inquired into Miss Forrester's religious views before, but he had always assumed that they were sound. And now here she was polluting the golden summer air with the most hideous blasphemy. It would be incorrect to say that James's love was turned to hate. He did not hate Grace. The repulsion he felt was deeper than mere hate. What he felt was not altogether loathing and not wholly pity. It was a blend of the two.

There was a tense silence. The listening world stood still. Then, without a word, James Todd turned and tottered away.

Peter was working moodily in the twelfth bunker when his friend arrived. He looked up with a start. Then, seeing that the other was alone, he came forward hesitatingly.

"Am I to congratulate you?"

James breathed a deep breath.

"You are!" he said. "On an escape!"

"She refused you?"

"She didn't get the chance. Old man, have you ever sent one right up the edge of that bunker in front of the seventh and just not gone in?"

"Very rarely."

"I did once. It was my second shot, from a good lie, with the light iron, and I followed well through and thought I had gone just too far, and, when I walked up, there was my ball on the edge of the bunker, nicely teed up on a chunk of grass, so that I was able to lay it dead with my mashie-niblick, holing out in six. Well, what I mean to say is, I feel now as I felt then—as if some unseen power had withheld me in time from some frightful disaster."

"I know just how you feel," said Peter, gravely.

"Peter, old man, that girl said golf bored her pallid. She said she thought it was the silliest game ever invented." He paused to mark the effect of his words. Peter merely smiled a faint, wan smile. "You don't seem revolted," said James.

"I am revolted, but not surprised. You see, she said the same thing to me only a few minutes before."

"She did!"

"It amounted to the same thing. I had just been telling her how I did the lake-hole today in two, and she said that in her opinion golf was a game for children with water on the brain who weren't athletic enough to play Animal Grab."

The two men shivered in sympathy.

"There must be insanity in the family," said James at last.

"That," said Peter, "is the charitable explanation."

"We were fortunate to find it out in time."

"We were!"

"We mustn't run a risk like that again."

"Never again!"

"I think we had better take up golf really seriously. It will keep us out of mischief."

"You're quite right. We ought to do our four rounds a day regularly."

"In spring, summer, and autumn. And in winter it would be rash not to practise most of the day at one of those indoor schools."

"We ought to be safe that way."

"Peter, old man," said James, "I've been meaning to speak to you about it for some time. I've got Sandy MacBean's new book, and I think you ought to read it. It is full of helpful hints."

"James!"

"Peter!"

Silently the two men clasped hands. James Todd and Peter Willard were themselves again.

And so (said the Oldest Member) we come back to our original starting-point—to wit, that, while there is nothing to be said definitely against love, your golfer should be extremely careful how he indulges in it. It may improve his game or it may not. But, if he finds that there is any danger that it may not—if the object of his affections is not the kind of girl who will listen to him with cheerful sympathy through the long evenings, while he tells her, illustrating stance and grip and swing with the kitchen poker, each detail of the day's round—then, I say unhesitatingly, he had better leave it alone. Love has had a lot of press-agenting from the oldest times; but there are higher, nobler things than love. A woman is only a woman, but a hefty drive is a slosh.

4
A MIXED THREESOME

IT WAS the holiday season, and during the holidays the Greens Committees have decided that the payment of twenty guineas shall entitle fathers of families not only to infest the course themselves, but also to decant their nearest and dearest upon it in whatever quantity they please. All over the links, in consequence, happy, laughing groups of children had broken out like a rash. A wan-faced adult, who had been held up for ten minutes while a drove of issue quarrelled over whether little Claude had taken two hundred or two hundred and twenty approach shots to reach the ninth green sank into a seat beside the Oldest Member.

"What luck?" inquired the Sage.

"None to speak of," returned the other, moodily. "I thought I had bagged a small boy in a Lord Fauntleroy suit on the sixth, but he ducked. These children make me tired. They should be bowling their hoops in the road. Golf is a game for grown-ups. How can a fellow play, with a platoon of progeny blocking him at every hole?"

The Oldest Member shook his head. He could not subscribe to these sentiments.

No doubt (said the Oldest Member) the summer golf-child is, from the point of view of the player who likes to get round the course in a single afternoon, something of a trial; but, personally, I confess, it pleases me to see my fellow human beings—and into this category golf-children, though at the moment you may not be broad-minded enough to admit it, undoubtedly fall—taking to the noblest of games at an early age. Golf, like measles, should be caught young, for, if postponed to riper years, the results may be serious. Let me tell you the story of Mortimer Sturgis, which illustrates what I mean rather aptly.

Mortimer Sturgis, when I first knew him, was a care-free man of thirty-eight, of amiable character and independent means, which he increased from time to time by judicious ventures on the Stock Exchange. Although he had never played golf, his had not been altogether an ill-spent life. He swung a creditable racket at tennis, was always ready to contribute a baritone solo to charity concerts, and gave freely to the poor. He was what you might call a golden-mean man, good-hearted rather than magnetic, with no serious vices and no heroic virtues. For a hobby, he had taken up the collecting of porcelain vases, and he was engaged to Betty Weston, a charming girl of twenty-five, a lifelong friend of mine.

I like Mortimer. Everybody liked him. But, at the same time, I was a little surprised that a girl like Betty should have become engaged to him. As I said before, he was not magnetic; and magnetism, I thought, was the chief quality she would have demanded in a man. Betty was one of those ardent, vivid girls, with an intense capacity for hero-worship, and I would have supposed that something more in the nature of a plumed knight or a corsair of the deep would have been her ideal. But, of course, if there is a branch of modern industry where the demand is greater than the supply, it is the manufacture of knights and corsairs; and nowadays a girl, however flaming her aspirations, has to take the best she can get. I must admit that Betty seemed perfectly content with Mortimer.

Such, then, was the state of affairs when Eddie Denton arrived, and the trouble began.

I was escorting Betty home one evening after a tea-party at which we had been fellow-guests, when, walking down the road, we happened to espy Mortimer. He broke into a run when he saw us, and galloped up, waving a piece of paper in his hand. He was plainly excited, a thing which was unusual in this well-balanced man. His broad, good-humoured face was working violently.

"Good news!" he cried. "Good news! Dear old Eddie's back!"

"Oh, how nice for you, dear!" said Betty. "Eddie Denton is Mortimer's best friend," she explained to me. "He has told me so much about him. I have been looking forward to his coming home. Mortie thinks the world of him."

"So will you, when you know him," cried Mortimer. "Dear old Eddie! He's a wonder! The best fellow on earth! We were at schòol and the 'Varsity together. There's nobody like Eddie! He landed yesterday. Just home from Central Africa. He's an explorer, you know," he said to me. "Spends all his time in places where it's death for a white man to go."

"An explorer!" I heard Betty breathe, as if to herself. I was not so impressed, I fear, as she was. Explorers, as a matter of fact, leave me a trifle cold. It has always seemed to me that the difficulties of their life are greatly exaggerated—generally by themselves. In a large country like Africa, for instance, I should imagine that it was almost impossible for a man not to get somewhere if he goes on long enough. Give *me* the fellow who can plunge into the bowels of the earth at Piccadilly Circus and find the right Tube train with nothing but a lot of misleading signs to guide him. However, we are not all constituted alike in this world and it was apparent from the flush on her cheek and the light in her eyes that Betty admired explorers.

"I wired to him at once," went on Mortimer, "and insisted on his coming down here. It's two years since I saw him. You don't know how I have looked forward, dear, to you and Eddie meeting. He is just your sort. I know how romantic you are and keen on adventure and all that. Well, you should hear Eddie tell the story of how he brought down the bull *bongo* with his last cartridge after all the *pongos*, or native bearers, had fled into the *dongo*, or undergrowth."

"I should love to!" whispered Betty, her eyes glowing. I suppose to an impressionable girl these things really are of absorbing interest. For myself *bongos* intrigue me even less than *pongos*, while *dongos* frankly bore me. "When do you expect him?"

"He will get my wire tonight. I'm hoping we shall see the dear old fellow tomorrow afternoon some time. How surprised old Eddie will be to hear that I'm engaged. He's such a confirmed bachelor himself. He told me once that he considered the wisest thing ever said by human tongue was the Swahili proverb—'Whoso taketh a woman into his kraal depositeth himself straightway in the *wongo*.' *Wongo*, he tells me, is a sort of broth composed of herbs and meat-bones, corresponding to our soup. You must get Eddie to give it you in the original Swahili. It sounds even better."

I saw the girl's eyes flash, and there came into her face that peculiar set expression which married men know. It passed in an instant, but not before it had given me material for thought which lasted me all the way to my house and into the silent watches of the night. I was fond of Mortimer Sturgis, and I could see trouble ahead for him as plainly as though I had been a palmist reading his hand at two guineas a visit. There are other proverbs fully as wise as the one which Mortimer had translated from the Swahili, and one of the wisest is that quaint old East London saying, handed down from one generation of costermongers to another, and whispered at midnight in the wigwams of the whelk-seller! "Never introduce your donah to a pal." In those seven words is contained the wisdom of the ages.

I could read the future so plainly. What but one thing could happen after Mortimer had influenced Betty's imagination with his stories of his friend's romantic career, and added the finishing touch by advertising him as a woman-hater? He might just as well have asked for his ring back at once. My heart bled for Mortimer.

I happened to call at his house on the second evening of the explorer's visit, and already the mischief had been done.

Denton was one of those lean, hard-bitten men with smouldering eyes and a brick-red complexion. He looked what he was, the man of action and enterprise. He had the wiry frame and strong jaw without which no explorer is complete, and Mortimer, beside him, seemed but a poor, soft product of our hot-house civilization. Mortimer, I forgot to say, wore glasses; and, if there is one time more than another when a man should not wear glasses, it is while a strong-faced, keen-eyed wanderer in the wilds is telling a beautiful girl the story of his adventures.

For this was what Denton was doing. My arrival seemed to have interrupted him in the middle of his narrative. He shook my hand in a strong, silent sort of way, and resumed:

"Well, the natives seemed fairly friendly, so I decided to stay the night."

I made a mental note never to seem fairly friendly to an explorer. If you do, he always decides to stay the night.

"In the morning they took me down to the river. At this point it widens into a *kongo*, or pool, and it was here, they told me, that the crocodile mostly lived, subsisting on the native oxen—the short-horned *jongos*—which, swept away by the current while crossing the ford above, were carried down on the *longos*, or rapids.

It was not, however, till the second evening that I managed to catch sight of his ugly snout above the surface. I waited around, and on the third day I saw him suddenly come out of the water and heave his whole length on to a sandbank in midstream and go to sleep in the sun. He was certainly a monster—fully thirty—you have never been in Central Africa, have you, Miss Weston? No? You ought to go there!—fully fifty feet from tip to tail. There he lay, glistening. I shall never forget the sight."

He broke off to light a cigarette. I heard Betty draw in her breath sharply. Mortimer was beaming through his glasses with the air of the owner of a dog which is astonishing a drawing-room with its clever tricks.

"And what did you do then, Mr. Denton?" asked Betty, breathlessly.

"Yes, what did you do then, old chap?" said Mortimer.

Denton blew out the match and dropped it on the ash-tray.

"Eh? Oh," he said, carelessly, "I swam across and shot him."

"Swam across and shot him!"

"Yes. It seemed to me that the chance was too good to be missed. Of course, I might have had a pot at him from the bank, but the chances were I wouldn't have hit him in a vital place. So I swam across to the sandbank, put the muzzle of my gun in his mouth, and pulled the trigger. I have rarely seen a crocodile so taken aback."

"But how dreadfully dangerous!"

"Oh, danger!" Eddie Denton laughed lightly. "One drops into the habit of taking a few risks out there, you know. Talking of *danger*, the time when things really did look a little nasty was when the wounded *gongo* cornered me in a narrow *tongo* and I only had a pocket-knife with everything in it broken except the corkscrew and the thing for taking stones out of horses' hoofs. It was like this——"

I could bear no more. I am a tender-hearted man, and I made some excuse and got away. From the expression on the girl's face I could see that it was only a question of days before she gave her heart to this romantic newcomer.

As a matter of fact, it was on the following afternoon that she called on me and told me that the worst had happened. I had known her from a child, you understand, and she always confided her troubles to me.

"I want your advice," she began. "I'm so wretched!"

She burst into tears. I could see the poor girl was in a highly nervous condition, so I did my best to calm her by describing how I had once done the long hole in four. My friends tell me that there is no finer soporific, and it seemed as though they may be right, for presently, just as I had reached the point where I laid my approach-putt dead from a distance of fifteen feet, she became quieter. She dried her eyes, yawned once or twice, and looked at me bravely.

"I love Eddie Denton!" she said.

"I feared as much. When did you feel this coming on?"

"It crashed on me like a thunderbolt last night after dinner. We were walking in the garden, and he was just telling me how he had been bitten by a poisonous *zongo*, when I seemed to go all giddy. When I came to myself I was in Eddie's arms. His face was pressed against mine, and he was gargling."

"Gargling?"

"I thought so at first. But he reassured me. He was merely speaking in one of the lesser-known dialects of the Walla-Walla natives of Eastern Uganda, into which he always drops in moments of great emotion. He soon recovered sufficiently to give me a rough translation, and then I knew that he loved me. He kissed me. I kissed him. We kissed each other."

"And where was Mortimer all this while?"

"Indoors, cataloguing his collection of vases."

For a moment, I confess, I was inclined to abandon Mortimer's cause. A man, I felt, who could stay indoors cataloguing vases while his *fiancée* wandered in the moonlight with explorers deserved all that was coming to him. I overcame the feeling.

"Have you told him?"

"Of course not."

"You don't think it might be of interest to him?"

"How can I tell him? It would break his heart. I am awfully fond of Mortimer. So is Eddie. We would both die rather than do anything to hurt him. Eddie is the soul of honour. He agrees with me that Mortimer must never know."

"Then you aren't going to break off your engagement?"

"I couldn't. Eddie feels the same. He says that, unless something can be done, he will say good-bye to me and creep far, far away to some distant desert, and there, in the great stillness, broken only by the cry of the prowling *yongo,* try to forget."

"When you say 'unless something can be done,' what do you mean? What can be done?"

"I thought you might have something to suggest. Don't you think it possible that somehow Mortimer might take it into his head to break the engagement himself?"

"Absurd! He loves you devotedly."

"I'm afraid so. Only the other day I dropped one of his best vases, and he just smiled and said it didn't matter."

"I can give you even better proof than that. This morning Mortimer came to me and asked me to give him secret lessons in golf."

"Golf! But he despises golf."

"Exactly. But he is going to learn it for your sake."

"But why secret lessons?"

"Because he wants to keep it a surprise for your birthday. Now can you doubt his love?"

"I am not worthy of him!" she whispered.

The words gave me an idea.

"Suppose," I said, "we could convince Mortimer of that!"

"I don't understand."

"Suppose, for instance, he could be made to believe that you were, let us say, a dipsomaniac."

She shook her head. "He knows that already."

"What!"

"Yes; I told him I sometimes walked in my sleep."

"I mean a secret drinker."

"Nothing will induce me to pretend to be a secret drinker."

"Then a drug-fiend?" I suggested, hopefully.

"I hate medicine."

"I have it!" I said. "A kleptomaniac."

"What is that?"

"A person who steals things."

"Oh, that's horrid."

"Not at all. It's a perfectly ladylike thing to do. You don't know you do it."

"But, if I don't know I do it, how do I know I do it?"

"I beg your pardon?"

"I mean, how can I tell Mortimer I do it if I don't know?"

"You don't tell him. I will tell him. I will inform him tomorrow that you called on me this afternoon and stole my watch and"—I glanced about the room—"my silver matchbox."

"I'd rather have that little vinaigrette."

"You don't get either. I merely say you stole it. What will happen?"

"Mortimer will hit you with a cleek."

"Not at all. I am an old man. My white hairs protect me. What he will do is to insist on confronting me with you and asking you to deny the foul charge."

"And then?"

"Then you admit it and release him from his engagement."

She sat for a while in silence. I could see that my words had made an impression.

"I think it's a splendid idea. Thank you very much." She rose and moved to the door. "I knew you would suggest something wonderful." She hesitated. "You don't think it would make it sound more plausible if I really took the vinaigrette?" she added, a little wistfully.

"It would spoil everything," I replied, firmly, as I reached for the vinaigrette and locked it carefully in my desk.

She was silent for a moment, and her glance fell on the carpet. That, however, did not worry me. It was nailed down.

"Well, good-bye," she said.

"*Au revoir*," I replied. "I am meeting Mortimer at six-thirty tomorrow. You may expect us round at your house at about eight."

Mortimer was punctual at the tryst next morning. When I reached the tenth tee he was already there. We exchanged a brief greeting and I handed him a driver, outlined the essentials of grip and swing, and bade him go to it.

"It seems a simple game," he said, as he took his stance. "You're sure it's fair to have the ball sitting up on top of a young sand-hill like this?"

"Perfectly fair."

"I mean, I don't want to be coddled because I'm a beginner."

"The ball is always teed up for the drive," I assured him.

"Oh, well, if you say so. But it seems to me to take all the element of sport out of the game. Where do I hit it?"

"Oh, straight ahead."

"But isn't it dangerous? I mean, suppose I smash a window in that house over there?"

He indicated a charming bijou residence some five hundred yards down the fairway.

"In that case," I replied, "the owner comes out in his pyjamas and offers you the choice between some nuts and a cigar."

He seemed reassured, and began to address the ball. Then he paused again.

"Isn't there something you say before you start?" he asked. " 'Five', or something?"

"You may say 'Fore!' if it makes you feel any easier. But it isn't necessary."

"If I am going to learn this silly game," said Mortimer, firmly, "I am going to learn it *right*. Fore!"

I watched him curiously. I never put a club into the hand of a beginner without something of the feeling of the sculptor who surveys a mass of shapeless clay. I experience the emotions of a creator. Here, I say to myself, is a semi-sentient being into whose soulless carcass I am breathing life. A moment before, he was, though technically living, a mere clod. A moment hence he will be a golfer.

While I was still occupied with these meditations Mortimer swung at the ball. The club, whizzing down, brushed the surface of the rubber sphere, toppling it off the tee and propelling it six inches with a slight slice on it.

"Damnation!" said Mortimer, unravelling himself.

I nodded approvingly. His drive had not been anything to write to the golfing journals about, but he was picking up the technique of the game.

"What happened then?"

I told him in a word.

"Your stance was wrong, and your grip was wrong, and you moved your head, and swayed your body, and took your eye off the ball, and pressed, and forgot to use your wrists, and swung back too fast, and let the hands get ahead of the club, and lost your balance, and omitted to pivot on the ball of the left foot, and bent your right knee."

He was silent for a moment.

"There is more in this pastime," he said, "than the casual observer would suspect."

I have noticed, and I suppose other people have noticed, that in the golf education of every man there is a definite point at which he may be said to have crossed the dividing line—the Rubicon, as it were—that separates the golfer from the non-golfer. This moment comes immediately after his first good drive. In the ninety minutes in which I instructed Mortimer Sturgis that morning in the rudiments of the game, he made every variety of drive known to science; but it was not till we were about to leave that he made a good one.

A moment before he had surveyed his blistered hands with sombre disgust.

"It's no good," he said. "I shall never learn this beast of a game. And I don't want to either. It's only fit for lunatics. Where's the sense in it? Hitting a rotten little ball with a stick! If I want exercise, I'll take a stick and go and rattle it along the railings. There's something in that! Well, let's be getting along. No good wasting the whole morning out here."

"Try one more drive, and then we'll go."

"All right. If you like. No sense in it, though."

He teed up the ball, took a careless stance, and flicked moodily. There was a sharp crack, the ball shot off the tee, flew a hundred yards in a dead straight line never ten feet above the ground, soared another seventy yards in a graceful arc, struck the turf, rolled, and came to rest within easy mashie distance of the green.

"Splendid!" I cried.

The man seemed stunned.

"How did that happen?"

I told him very simply.

"Your stance was right, and your grip was right, and you kept your head still, and didn't sway your body, and never took your eye off the ball, and slowed back, and let the arms come well through, and rolled the wrists, and let the club-head lead, and kept your balance, and pivoted on the ball of the left foot, and didn't duck the right knee."

"I see," he said. "Yes, I thought that must be it."

"Now let's go home."

"Wait a minute. I just want to remember what I did while it's fresh in my mind. Let me see, this was the way I stood. Or was it more like this? No, like this." He turned to me, beaming. "What a great idea it was, my taking up golf! It's all nonsense what you read in the comic papers about people foozling all over the place and breaking clubs and all that. You've only to exercise a little reasonable care. And what a corking game it is! Nothing like it in the world! I wonder if Betty is up yet. I must go round and show her how I did that drive. A perfect swing, with every ounce of weight, wrist, and muscle behind it. I meant to keep it a secret from the dear girl till I had really learned, but of course I have learned now. Let's go round and rout her out."

He had given me my cue. I put my hand on his shoulder and spoke sorrowfully.

"Mortimer, my boy, I fear I have bad news for you."

"Slow back—keep the head—— What's that? Bad news?"

"About Betty."

"About Betty? What about her? Don't sway the body—keep the eye on the———"

"Prepare yourself for a shock, my boy. Yesterday afternoon Betty called to see me. When she had gone I found that she had stolen my silver matchbox."

"Stolen your matchbox?"

"Stolen my matchbox."

"Oh, well, I dare say there were faults on both sides," said Mortimer. "Tell me if I sway my body this time."

"You don't grasp what I have said! Do you realize that Betty, the girl you are going to marry, is a kleptomaniac?"

"A kleptomaniac!"

"That is the only possible explanation. Think what this means, my boy. Think how you will feel every time your wife says she is going out to do a little shopping! Think of yourself, left alone at home, watching the clock, saying to yourself, 'Now she is lifting a pair of silk stockings!' 'Now she is hiding gloves in her umbrella!' 'Just about this moment she is getting away with a pearl necklace!'"

"Would she do that?"

"She would! She could not help herself. Or, rather, she could not refrain from helping herself. How about it, my boy?"

"It only draws us closer together," he said.

I was touched, I own. My scheme had failed, but it had proved Mortimer Sturgis to be of pure gold. He stood gazing down the fairway, wrapped in thought.

"By the way," he said, meditatively, "I wonder if the dear girl ever goes to any of those sales—those auction-sales, you know, where you're allowed to inspect the things the day before? They often have some pretty decent vases."

He broke off and fell into a reverie.

From this point onward Mortimer Sturgis proved the truth of what I said to you about the perils of taking up golf at an advanced age. A lifetime of observing my fellow-creatures has convinced me that Nature intended us all to be golfers. In every human being the germ of golf is implanted at birth, and suppression causes it to grow and grow till—it may be at forty, fifty, sixty—it suddenly bursts its bonds and sweeps over the victim like a tidal wave. The wise man, who begins to play in childhood, is enabled to let the poison exude gradually from his system, with no harmful results. But a man like Mortimer Sturgis, with thirty-eight golfless years behind him, is swept off his feet. He is carried away. He loses all sense of proportion. He is like the fly that happens to be sitting on the wall of the dam just when the crack comes.

Mortimer Sturgis gave himself up without a struggle to an orgy of golf such as I have never witnessed in any man. Within two days of that first lesson he had accumulated a collection of clubs large enough to have enabled him to open a shop; and he went on buying them at the rate of two and three a day. On Sundays, when

it was impossible to buy clubs, he was like a lost spirit. True, he would do his regular
four rounds on the day of rest, but he never felt happy. The thought, as he sliced into
the rough, that the patent wooden-faced cleek which he intended to purchase next
morning might have made all the difference, completely spoiled his enjoyment.

I remember him calling me up on the telephone at three o'clock one morning to
tell me that he had solved the problem of putting. He intended in future, he said, to
use a croquet mallet, and he wondered that no one had ever thought of it before. The
sound of his broken groan when I informed him that croquet mallets were against
the rules haunted me for days.

His golf library kept pace with his collection of clubs. He bought all the standard
works, subscribed to all the golfing papers, and, when he came across a paragraph
in a magazine to the effect that Mr. Hutchings, an ex-amateur champion, did not
begin to play till he was past forty, and that his opponent in the final, Mr. S. H.
Fry, had never held a club till his thirty-fifth year, he had it engraved on vellum and
framed and hung up beside his shaving-mirror.

And Betty, meanwhile? She, poor child, stared down the years into a bleak future,
in which she saw herself parted for ever from the man she loved, and the golf-widow
of another for whom—even when he won a medal for lowest net at a weekly handicap
with a score of a hundred and three minus twenty-four—she could feel nothing
warmer than respect. Those were dreary days for Betty. We three—she and I and
Eddie Denton—often talked over Mortimer's strange obsession. Denton said that,
except that Mortimer had not come out in pink spots, his symptoms were almost
identical with those of the dreaded *mongo-mongo,* the scourge of the West African
hinterland. Poor Denton! He had already booked his passage for Africa, and spent
hours looking in the atlas for good deserts.

In every fever of human affairs there comes at last the crisis. We may emerge from
it healed or we may plunge into still deeper depths of soul-sickness; but always the
crisis comes. I was privileged to be present when it came in the affairs of Mortimer
Sturgis and Betty Weston.

I had gone into the club-house one afternoon at an hour when it is usually empty,
and the first thing I saw, as I entered the main room, which looks out on the ninth
green, was Mortimer. He was grovelling on the floor, and I confess that, when I
caught sight of him, my heart stood still. I feared that his reason, sapped by
dissipation, had given way. I knew that for weeks, day in and day out, the niblick
had hardly ever been out of his hand, and no constitution can stand that.

He looked up as he heard my footstep.

"Hallo," he said. "Can you see a ball anywhere?"

"A ball?" I backed away, reaching for the door-handle. "My dear boy," I said
soothingly, "you have made a mistake. Quite a natural mistake. One anybody would
have made. But, as a matter of fact, this is the club-house. The links are outside there.
Why not come away with me very quietly and let us see if we can't find some balls

on the links? If you will wait here a moment, I will call up Doctor Smithson. He was telling me only this morning that he wanted a good spell of ball-hunting to put him in shape. You don't mind if he joins us?"

"It was a Silver King with my initials on it," Mortimer went on, not heeding me. "I got on the ninth green in eleven with a nice mashie-niblick, but my approach-putt was a little too strong. It came in through that window."

I perceived for the first time that one of the windows facing the course was broken, and my relief was great. I went down on my knees and helped him in his search. We ran the ball to earth finally inside the piano.

"What's the local rule?" inquired Mortimer. "Must I play it where it lies, or may I tee up and lose a stroke? If I have to play it where it lies, I suppose a niblick would be the club?"

It was at this moment that Betty came in. One glance at her pale, set face told me that there was to be a scene, and I would have retired, but that she was between me and the door.

"Hallo, dear," said Mortimer, greeting her with a friendly waggle of his niblick. "I'm bunkered in the piano. My approach-putt was a little strong, and I over-ran the green."

"Mortimer," said the girl, tensely, "I want to ask you one question."

"Yes, dear? I wish, darling, you could have seen my drive at the eighth just now. It was a pip!"

Betty looked at him steadily.

"Are we engaged," she said, "or are we not?"

"Engaged? Oh, to be married? Why, of course. I tried the open stance for a change, and——"

"This morning you promised to take me for a ride. You never appeared. Where were you?"

"Just playing golf."

"Golf! I'm sick of the very name!"

A spasm shook Mortimer.

"You mustn't let people hear you saying things like that!" he said. "I somehow felt, the moment I began my up-swing, that everything was going to be all right. I——"

"I'll give you one more chance. Will you take me for a drive in your car this evening?"

"I can't."

"Why not? What are you doing?"

"Just playing golf!"

"I'm tired of being neglected like this!" cried Betty, stamping her foot. Poor girl, I saw her point of view. It was bad enough for her being engaged to the wrong man, without having him treat her as a mere acquaintance. Her conscience fighting with her love for Eddie Denton had kept her true to Mortimer, and Mortimer accepted the sacrifice with an absent-minded carelessness which would have been galling to any girl. "We might just as well not be engaged at all. You never take me anywhere."

"I asked you to come with me to watch the Open Championship."

"Why don't you ever take me to dances?"

"I can't dance."

"You could learn."

"But I'm not sure if dancing is a good thing for a fellow's game. You never hear of any first-class pro dancing. James Braid doesn't dance."

"Well, my mind's made up. Mortimer, you must choose between golf and me."

"But, darling, I went round in a hundred and one yesterday. You can't expect a fellow to give up golf when he's at the top of his game."

"Very well. I have nothing more to say. Our engagement is at an end."

"Don't throw me over, Betty," pleaded Mortimer, and there was that in his voice which cut me to the heart. "You'll make me so miserable. And, when I'm miserable, I always slice my approach shots."

Betty Weston drew herself up. Her face was hard.

"Here is your ring!" she said, and swept from the room.

For a moment after she had gone Mortimer remained very still, looking at the glistening circle in his hand. I stole across the room and patted his shoulder.

"Bear up, my boy, bear up!" I said.

He looked at me piteously.

"Stymied!" he muttered.

"Be brave!"

He went on, speaking as if to himself.

"I had pictured—ah, how often I had pictured!—our little home! Hers and mine. She sewing in her arm-chair, I practising putts on the hearth-rug——" He choked. "While in the corner, little Harry Vardon Sturgis played with little J. H. Taylor Sturgis. And round the room—reading, busy with their childish tasks—little George Duncan Sturgis, Abe Mitchell Sturgis, Harold Hilton Sturgis, Edward Ray Sturgis, Horace Hutchinson Sturgis, and little James Braid Sturgis."

"My boy! My boy!" I cried.

"What's the matter?"

"Weren't you giving yourself rather a large family?"

He shook his head moodily.

"Was I?" he said, dully. "I don't know. What's bogey?"

There was a silence.

"And yet——" he said, at last, in a low voice. He paused. An odd, bright look had come into his eyes. He seemed suddenly to be himself again, the old happy Mortimer Sturgis I had known so well. "And yet," he said, "who knows? Perhaps it is all for the best. They might all have turned out tennis-players!" He raised his niblick again, his face aglow. "Playing thirteen!" he said. "I think the game here would be to chip out through the door and work round the club-house to the green, don't you?"

Little remains to be told. Betty and Eddie have been happily married for years. Mortimer's handicap is now down to eighteen, and he is improving all the time. He was not present at the wedding, being unavoidably detained by a medal tournament; but, if you turn up the files and look at the list of presents, which were both numerous and costly, you will see—somewhere in the middle of the column, the words:
STURGIS, J. MORTIMER.
   Two dozen Silver King Golf-balls and one patent Sturgis Aluminium Self-Adjusting, Self-Compensating Putting-Cleek.

5
SUNDERED HEARTS

IN the smoking-room of the club-house a cheerful fire was burning, and the Oldest Member glanced from time to time out of the window into the gathering dusk. Snow was falling lightly on the links. From where he sat, the Oldest Member had a good view of the ninth green; and presently, out of the greyness of the December evening, there appeared over the brow of the hill a golf-ball. It trickled across the green and stopped within a yard of the hole. The Oldest Member nodded approvingly. A good approach-shot.

A young man in a tweed suit clambered on to the green, holed out with easy confidence, and, shouldering his bag, made his way to the club-house. A few moments later he entered the smoking-room, and uttered an exclamation of rapture at the sight of the fire.

"I'm frozen stiff!"

He rang for a waiter and ordered a hot drink. The Oldest Member gave a gracious assent to the suggestion that he should join him.

"I like playing in winter," said the young man. "You get the course to yourself, for the world is full of slackers who only turn out when the weather suits them. I cannot understand where they get the nerve to call themselves golfers."

"Not everyone is as keen as you are, my boy," said the Sage, dipping gratefully into his hot drink. "If they were, the world would be a better place, and we should hear less of all this modern unrest."

"I *am* pretty keen," admitted the young man.

"I have only encountered one man whom I could describe as keener. I allude to Mortimer Sturgis."

"The fellow who took up golf at thirty-eight and let the girl he was engaged to marry go off with someone else because he hadn't the time to combine golf with courtship? I remember. You were telling me about him the other day."

"There is a sequel to that story, if you would care to hear it," said the Oldest Member.

"You have the honour," said the young man. "Go ahead!"

Some people (began the Oldest Member) considered that Mortimer Sturgis was too wrapped up in golf, and blamed him for it. I could never see eye to eye with them. In the days of King Arthur nobody thought the worse of a young knight if he suspended all his social and business engagements in favour of a search for the Holy Grail. In the Middle Ages a man could devote his whole life to the Crusades, and the public fawned upon him. Why, then, blame the man of today for a zealous attention to the modern equivalent, the Quest of Scratch! Mortimer Sturgis never became a scratch player, but he did eventually get his handicap down to nine, and I honour him for it.

The story which I am about to tell begins in what might be called the middle period of Sturgis's career. He had reached the stage when his handicap was a wobbly twelve; and, as you are no doubt aware, it is then that a man really begins to golf in the true sense of the word. Mortimer's fondness for the game until then had been merely tepid compared with what it became now. He had played a little before, but now he really buckled to and got down to it. It was at this point, too, that he began once more to entertain thoughts of marriage. A profound statistician in this one department, he had discovered that practically all the finest exponents of the art are married men; and the thought that there might be something in the holy state which improved a man's game, and that he was missing a good thing, troubled him a great deal. Moreover, the paternal instinct had awakened in him. As he justly pointed out, whether marriage improved your game or not, it was to Old Tom Morris's marriage that the existence of young Tommy Morris, winner of the British Open Championship four times in succession, could be directly traced. In fact, at the age of forty-two, Mortimer Sturgis was in just the frame of mind to take some nice girl aside and ask her to become a step-mother to his eleven drivers, his baffy, his twenty-eight putters, and the rest of the ninety-four clubs which he had accumulated in the course of his golfing career. The sole stipulation, of course, which he made when dreaming his day-dreams was that the future Mrs. Sturgis must be a golfer. I can still recall the horror in his face when one girl, admirable in other respects, said that she had never heard of Harry Vardon, and didn't he mean Dolly Vardon? She has since proved an excellent wife and mother, but Mortimer Sturgis never spoke to her again.

With the coming of January, it was Mortimer's practice to leave England and go to the South of France, where there was sunshine and crisp dry turf. He pursued his usual custom this year. With his suit-case and his ninety-four clubs he went off to Saint Brüle, staying as he always did at the Hôtel Superbe, where they knew him, and treated with an amiable tolerance his habit of practising chip-shots in his bedroom. On the first evening, after breaking a statuette of the Infant Samuel in Prayer, he dressed and went down to dinner. And the first thing he saw was Her.

Mortimer Sturgis, as you know, had been engaged before, but Betty Weston had never inspired the tumultuous rush of emotion which the mere sight of this girl set loose in him. He told me later that just to watch her holing out her soup gave him a sort of feeling you get when your drive collides with a rock in the middle of a tangle of rough and kicks back into the middle of the fairway. If golf had come late in life to Mortimer Sturgis, love came later still, and just as the golf, attacking him in middle life, had been some golf, so was the love considerable love. Mortimer finished his dinner in a trance, which is the best way to do it at some hotels, and then scoured the place for someone who would introduce him. He found such a person eventually and the meeting took place.

She was a small and rather fragile-looking girl, with big blue eyes and a cloud of golden hair. She had a sweet expression, and her left wrist was in a sling. She looked up at Mortimer as if she had at last found something that amounted to something. I am inclined to thing it was a case of love at first sight on both sides.

"Fine weather we're having," said Mortimer, who was a capital conversationalist.

"Yes," said the girl.

"I like fine weather."

"So do I."

"There's something about fine weather!"

"Yes."

"It's—it's—well, fine weather's so much finer than weather that isn't fine," said Mortimer.

He looked at the girl a little anxiously, fearing he might be taking her out of her depth, but she seemed to have followed his train of thought perfectly.

"Yes, isn't it?" she said. "It's so—so fine."

"That's just what I meant," said Mortimer. "So fine. You've just hit it."

He was charmed. The combination of beauty with intelligence is so rare.

"I see you've hurt your wrist," he went on, pointing to the sling.

"Yes. I strained it a little playing in the championship."

"The championship?" Mortimer was interested. "It's awfully rude of me," he said, apologetically, "but I didn't catch your name just now."

"My name is Somerset."

Mortimer had been bending forward solicitously. He overbalanced and nearly fell off his chair. The shock had been stunning. Even before he had met and spoken to her, he had told himself that he loved this girl with the stored-up love of a lifetime. And she was Mary Somerset! The hotel lobby danced before Mortimer's eyes.

The name will, of course, be familiar to you. In the early rounds of the Ladies' Open Golf Championship of that year nobody had paid much attention to Mary Somerset. She had survived her first two matches, but her opponents had been nonentities like herself. And then, in the third round, she had met and defeated the champion. From that point on, her name was on everybody's lips. She became favourite. And she justified the public confidence by sailing into the final and winning easily. And here she was, talking to him like an ordinary person, and, if he could read the message in her eyes, not altogether indifferent to his charms, if you could call them that.

"Golly!" said Mortimer, awed.

Their friendship ripened rapidly, as friendships do in the South of France. In that favoured clime, you find the girl and Nature does the rest. On the second morning of their acquaintance Mortimer invited her to walk round the links with him and watch him play. He did it a little diffidently, for his golf was not of the calibre that would be likely to extort admiration from a champion. On the other hand, one should never let slip the opportunity of acquiring wrinkles on the game, and he thought that Miss Somerset, if she watched one or two of his shots, might tell him just what he ought to do. And sure enough, the opening arrived on the fourth hole, where Mortimer, after a drive which surprised even himself, found his ball in a nasty cuppy lie.

He turned to the girl.

"What ought I to do here?" he asked.

Miss Somerset looked at the ball. She seemed to be weighing the matter in her mind.

"Give it a good hard knock," she said.

Mortimer knew what she meant. She was advocating a full iron. The only trouble was that, when he tried anything more ambitious than a half-swing, except off the tee, he almost invariably topped. However, he could not fail this wonderful girl, so he swung well back and took a chance. His enterprise was rewarded. The ball flew out of the indentation in the turf as cleanly as though John Henry Taylor had been behind it, and rolled, looking neither to left nor to right, straight for the pin. A few moments later Mortimer Sturgis had holed out one under bogey, and it was only the fear that, having known him for so short a time, she might be startled and refuse him that kept him from proposing then and there. This exhibition of golfing generalship on her part had removed his last doubts. He know that, if he lived for ever, there could be no other girl in the world for him. With her at his side, what might he not do? He might get his handicap down to six—to three—to scratch—to plus something! Good heavens, why, even the Amateur Championship was not outside the range of possibility. Mortimer Sturgis shook his putter solemnly in the air, and vowed a silent vow that he would win this pearl among women.

Now, when a man feels like that, it is impossible to restrain him long. For a week Mortimer Sturgis's soul sizzled within him: then he could contain himself no longer. One night, at one of the informal dances at the hotel, he drew the girl out on to the moonlit terrace.

"Miss Somerset——" he began, stuttering with emotion like an imperfectly-corked bottle of ginger-beer. "Miss Somerset—may I call you Mary?"

The girl looked at him with eyes that shone softly in the dim light.

"Mary?" she repeated. "Why, of course, if you like——"

"If I like!" cried Mortimer. "Don't you know that it is my dearest wish? Don't you know that I would rather be permitted to call you Mary than do the first hole at Muirfield in two? Oh, Mary, how I have longed for this moment! I love you! I love you! Ever since I met you I have known that you were the one girl in this vast world whom I would die to win! Mary, will you be mine? Shall we go round together? Will you fix up a match with me on the links of life which shall end only when the Grim Reaper lays us both a stymie?"

She drooped towards him.

"Mortimer!" she murmured.

He held out his arms, then drew back. His face had grown suddenly tense, and there were lines of pain about his mouth.

"Wait!" he said, in a strained voice. "Mary, I love you dearly, and because I love you so dearly I cannot let you trust your sweet life to me blindly. I have a confession to make. I am not—I have not always been"—he paused—"a good man," he said, in a low voice.

She started indignantly.

"How can you say that? You are the best, the kindest, the bravest man I have ever met! Who but a good man would have risked his life to save me from drowning?"

"Drowning?" Mortimer's voice seemed perplexed. "You? What do you mean?"

"Have you forgotten the time when I fell in the sea last week, and you jumped in with all your clothes on——"

"Of course, yes," said Mortimer. "I remember now. It was the day I did the long seventh in five. I got off a good tee-shot straight down the fairway, took a baffy for my second, and—— But that is not the point. It is sweet and generous of you to think so highly of what was the merest commonplace act of ordinary politeness, but I must repeat, that judged by the standards of your snowy purity, I am not a good man. I do not come to you clean and spotless as a young girl should expect her husband to come to her. Once, playing in a foursome, my ball fell in some long grass. Nobody was near me. We had no caddies, and the others were on the fairway. God knows——" His voice shook. "God knows I struggled against the temptation. But I fell. I kicked the ball on to a little bare mound, from which it was an easy task with a nice half-mashie to reach the green for a snappy seven. Mary, there have been times when, going round by myself, I have allowed myself ten-foot putts on three holes in succession, simply in order to be able to say I had done the course in under a hundred. Ah! you shrink from me! You are disgusted!"

"I'm not disgusted! And I don't shrink! I only shivered because it is rather cold."

"Then you can love me in spite of my past?"

"Mortimer!"

She fell into his arms.

"My dearest," he said presently, "what a happy life ours will be. That is, if you do not find that you have made a mistake."

"A mistake!" she cried, scornfully.

"Well, my handicap is twelve, you know, and not so darned twelve at that. There are days when I play my second from the fairway of the next hole but one, days when I couldn't putt into a coal-hole with 'Welcome!' written over it. And you are a

Ladies' Open Champion. Still, if you think it's all right——. Oh, Mary, you little know how I have dreamed of some day marrying a really first-class golfer! Yes, that was my vision—of walking up the aisle with some sweet plus two girl on my arm. You shivered again. You are catching cold."

"It is a little cold," said the girl. She spoke in a small voice.

"Let me take you in, sweetheart," said Mortimer. "I'll just put you in a comfortable chair with a nice cup of coffee, and then I think I really must come out again and tramp about and think how perfectly splendid everything is."

They were married a few weeks later, very quietly, in the little village church of Saint Brûle. The secretary of the local golf-club acted as best man for Mortimer, and a girl from the hotel was the only bridesmaid. The whole business was rather a disappointment to Mortimer, who had planned out a somewhat florid ceremony at St. George's, Hanover Square, with the Vicar of Tooting (a scratch player excellent at short approach shots) officiating, and "The Voice That Breathed O'er St. Andrews" booming from the organ. He had even had the idea of copying the military wedding and escorting his bride out of the church under an arch of crossed cleeks. But she would have none of this pomp. She insisted on a quiet wedding, and for the honeymoon trip preferred a tour through Italy. Mortimer, who had wanted to go to Scotland to visit the birthplace of James Braid, yielded amiably, for he loved her dearly. But he did not think much of Italy. In Rome, the great monuments of the past left him cold. Of the Temples of Vespasian, all he thought was that it would be a devil of a place to be bunkered behind. The Colosseum aroused a faint spark of interest in him, as he speculated whether Abe Mitchell would use a full brassey to carry it. In Florence, the view over the Tuscan Hills from the Torre Rosa, Fiesole, over which his bride waxed enthusiastic, seemed to him merely a nasty bit of rough which would take a deal of getting out of.

And so, in the fullness of time, they came home to Mortimer's cosy little house adjoining the links.

Mortimer was so busy polishing his ninety-four clubs on the evening of their arrival that he failed to notice that his wife was preoccupied. A less busy man would have perceived at a glance that she was distinctly nervous. She started at sudden noises, and once, when he tried the newest of his mashie-niblicks and broke one of the drawing-room windows, she screamed sharply. In short her manner was strange, and, if Edgar Allan Poe had put her into "The Fall of the House of Usher", she would have fitted it like the paper on the wall. She had the air of one waiting tensely for the approach of some imminent doom. Mortimer, humming gaily to himself as he sand-papered the blade of his twenty-second putter, observed nothing of this. He was thinking of the morrow's play.

"Your wrist's quite well again now, darling, isn't it?" he said.

"Yes. Yes, quite well."

"Fine!" said Mortimer. "We'll breakfast early—say at half-past seven—and then we'll be able to get in a couple of rounds before lunch. A couple more in the afternoon will about see us through. One doesn't want to over-golf oneself the first day." He swung the putter joyfully. "How had we better play do you think? We might start with you giving me a half."

She did not speak. She was very pale. She clutched the arm of her chair tightly till the knuckles showed white under the skin.

To anybody but Mortimer her nervousness would have been even more obvious on the following morning, as they reached the first tee. Her eyes were dull and heavy, and she started when a grasshopper chirruped. But Mortimer was too occupied with thinking how jolly it was having the course to themselves to notice anything.

He scooped some sand out of the box, and took a ball out of her bag. His wedding present to her had been a brand-new golf-bag, six dozen balls, and a full set of the most expensive clubs, all born in Scotland.

"Do you like a high tee?" he asked.

"Oh, no," she replied, coming with a start out of her thoughts. "Doctors say it's indigestible."

Mortimer laughed merrily.

"Deuced good!" he chuckled. "Is that your own or did you read it in a comic paper? There you are!" He placed the ball on a little hill of sand, and got up. "Now let's see some of that championship form of yours!"

She burst into tears.

"My darling!"

Mortimer ran to her and put his arms round her. She tried weakly to push him away.

"My angel! What is it?"

She sobbed brokenly. Then, with an effort, she spoke.

"Mortimer, I have deceived you!"

"Deceived me?"

"I have never played golf in my life! I don't even know how to hold the caddie!"

Mortimer's heart stood still. This sounded like the gibberings of an unbalanced mind, and no man likes his wife to begin gibbering immediately after the honeymoon.

"My precious! You are not yourself!"

"I am! That's the whole trouble! I'm myself and not the girl you thought I was!"

Mortimer stared at her, puzzled. He was thinking that it was a little difficult and that, to work it out properly, he would need a pencil and a bit of paper.

"My name is not Mary!"

"But you said it was."

"I didn't. You asked if you could call me Mary, and I said you might, because I loved you too much to deny your smallest whim. I was going on to say that it wasn't my name, but you interrupted me."

"Not Mary!" The horrid truth was coming home to Mortimer. "You were not Mary Somerset?"

"Mary is my cousin. My name is Mabel."

"But you said you had sprained your wrist playing in the championship."

"So I had. The mallet slipped in my hand."

"The mallet!" Mortimer clutched at his forehead. "You didn't say 'the mallet'?"

"Yes, Mortimer! The mallet!"

A faint blush of shame mantled her cheek, and into her blue eyes there came a look of pain, but she faced him bravely.

"I am the Ladies' Open Croquet Champion!" she whispered.

Mortimer Sturgis cried aloud, a cry that was like the shriek of some wounded animal.

"Croquet!" He gulped, and stared at her with unseeing eyes. He was no prude, but he had those decent prejudices of which no self-respecting man can wholly rid himself, however broad-minded he may try to be. "Croquet!"

There was a long silence. The light breeze sang in the pines above them. The grasshoppers chirruped at their feet.

She began to speak again in a low, monotonous voice.

"I blame myself! I should have told you before, while there was yet time for you to withdraw. I should have confessed this to you that night on the terrace in the moonlight. But you swept me off my feet, and I was in your arms before I realized what you would think of me. It was only then that I understood what my supposed skill at golf meant to you, and then it was too late. I loved you too much to let you go! I could not bear the thought of you recoiling from me. Oh, I was mad—mad! I knew that I could not keep up the deception for ever, that you must find me out in time. But I had a wild hope that by then we should be so close to one another that you might find it in your heart to forgive. But I was wrong. I see it now. There are some things that no man can forgive. Some things," she repeated, dully, "which no man can forgive."

She turned away. Mortimer awoke from his trance.

"Stop!" he cried. "Don't go!"

"I must go."

"I want to talk this over."

She shook her head sadly and started to walk slowly across the sunlit grass. Mortimer watched her, his brain in a whirl of chaotic thoughts. She disappeared through the trees.

Mortimer sat down on the tee-box, and buried his face in his hands. For a time he could thing of nothing but the cruel blow he had received. This was the end of those rainbow visions of himself and her going through life side by side, she lovingly criticizing his stance and his back-swing, he learning wisdom from her. A croquet-player! He was married to a woman who hit coloured balls through hoops. Mortimer Sturgis writhed in torment. A strong man's agony.

The mood passed. How long it had lasted, he did not know. But suddenly, as he sat there, he became once more aware of the glow of the sunshine and the singing of the birds. It was as if a shadow had lifted. Hope and optimism crept into his heart.

He loved her. He loved her still. She was part of him, and nothing that she could do had power to alter that. She had deceived him, yes. But why had she deceived him? Because she loved him so much that she could not bear to lose him. Dash it all, it was a bit of a compliment.

And, after all, poor girl, was it her fault? Was it not rather the fault of her upbringing? Probably she had been taught to play croquet when a mere child, hardly able to distinguish right from wrong. No steps had been taken to eradicate the virus from her system, and the thing had become chronic. Could she be blamed? Was she not more to be pitied than censured?

Mortimer rose to his feet, his heart swelling with generous forgiveness. The black horror had passed from him. The future seemed once more bright. It was not too late. She was still young, many years younger than he himself had been when he took up golf, and surely, if she put herself into the hands of a good specialist and practised every day, she might still hope to become a fair player. He reached the house and ran in, calling her name.

No answer came. He sped from room to room, but all were empty.

She had gone. The house was there. The furniture was there. The canary sang in its cage, the cook in the kitchen. The pictures still hung on the walls. But she had gone. Everything was at home except his wife.

Finally, propped up against the cup he had once won in a handicap competition, he saw a letter. With a sinking heart he tore open the envelope.

It was a pathetic, a tragic letter, the letter of a woman endeavouring to express all the anguish of a torn heart with one of those fountain-pens which suspend the flow of ink about twice in every three words. The gist of it was that she felt she had wronged him; that, though he might forgive, he could never forget; and that she was going away, away out into the world alone.

Mortimer sank into a chair, and stared blankly before him. She had scratched the match.

I am not a married man myself, so have had no experience of how it feels to have one's wife whiz off silently into the unknown; but I should imagine that it must be something like taking a full swing with a brassey and missing the ball. Something, I take it, of the same sense of mingled shock, chagrin, and the feeling that nobody loves one, which attacks a man in such circumstances, must come to the bereaved husband. And one can readily understand how terribly the incident must have shaken Mortimer Sturgis. I was away at the time, but I am told by those who saw him that his game went all to pieces.

He had never shown much indication of becoming anything in the nature of a first-class golfer, but he had managed to acquire one or two decent shots. His work with the light iron was not at all bad, and he was a fairly steady putter. But now, under the shadow of this tragedy, he dropped right back to the form of his earliest period. It was a pitiful sight to see this gaunt, haggard man with the look of dumb anguish behind his spectacles taking as many as three shots sometimes to get past the ladies' tee. His slice, of which he had almost cured himself, returned with such virulence that in the list of ordinary hazards he had now to include the tee-box. And, when he was not slicing, he was pulling. I have heard that he was known, when driving at the sixth, to get bunkered in his own caddie, who had taken up his position directly behind him. As for the deep sand-trap in front of the seventh green, he spent so much of his time in it that there was some informal talk among the members of the committee of charging him a small weekly rent.

A man of comfortable independent means, he lived during these days on next to nothing. Golf-balls cost him a certain amount, but the bulk of his income he spent in efforts to discover his wife's whereabouts. He advertised in all the papers. He employed private detectives. He even, much as it revolted his finer instincts, took to travelling about the country, watching croquet matches. But she was never among the players. I am not sure that he did not find a melancholy comfort in this, for it seemed to show that, whatever his wife might be and whatever she might be doing, she had not gone right under.

Summer passed. Autumn came and went. Winter arrived. The days grew bleak and chill, and an early fall of snow, heavier than had been known at that time of the year for a long while, put an end to golf. Mortimer spent his days indoors, staring gloomily through the window at the white mantle that covered the earth.

It was Christmas Eve.

The young man shifted uneasily on his seat. His face was long and sombre.

"All this is very depressing," he said.

"These soul tragedies," agreed the Oldest Member, "are never very cheery."

"Look here," said the young man, firmly, "tell me one thing frankly, as man to man. Did Mortimer find her dead in the snow, covered except for her face, on which still lingered that faint, sweet smile which he remembered so well? Because, if he did, I'm going home."

"No, no," protested the Oldest Member. "Nothing of that kind."

"You're sure? You aren't going to spring it on me suddenly?"

"No, no!"

The young man breathed a relieved sigh.

"It was your saying that about the white mantle covering the earth that made me suspicious."

The Sage resumed.

It was Christmas Eve. All day the snow had been falling, and now it lay thick and deep over the countryside. Mortimer Sturgis, his frugal dinner concluded—what with losing his wife and not being able to get any golf, he had little appetite these days—was sitting in his drawing-room, moodily polishing the blade of his jigger. Soon wearying of this once congenial task, he laid down the club and went to the front door to see if there was any chance of a thaw. But no. It was freezing. The snow, as he tested it with his shoe, crackled crisply. The sky above was black and full of cold stars. It seemed to Mortimer that the sooner he packed up and went to the South of France, the better. He was just about to close the door, when suddenly he thought he heard his own name called.

"Mortimer!"

Had he been mistaken? The voice had sounded faint and far away.

"Mortimer!"

He thrilled from head to foot. This time there could be no mistake. It was the voice he knew so well, his wife's voice, and it had come from somewhere down near the garden-gate. It is difficult to judge distance where sounds are concerned, but Mortimer estimated that the voice had spoken about a short mashie-niblick and an easy putt from where he stood.

The next moment he was racing down the snow-covered path. And then his heart stood still. What was that dark something on the ground just inside the gate? He leaped towards it. He passed his hands over it. It was a human body. Quivering, he struck a match. It went out. He struck another. That went out, too. He struck a third, and it burnt with a steady flame; and, stooping, he saw that it was his wife who lay there, cold and stiff. Her eyes were closed, and on her face still lingered that faint, sweet smile which he remembered so well.

The young man rose with a set face. He reached for his golf-bag.

"I call that a dirty trick," he said, "after you promised—" The Sage waved him back to his seat.

"Have no fear! She had only fainted."

"You said she was cold."

"Wouldn't you be cold if you were lying in the snow?"

"And stiff."

"Mrs. Sturgis was stiff because the train-service was bad, it being the holiday-season, and she had had to walk all the way from the junction, a distance of eight miles. Sit down and allow me to proceed."

Tenderly, reverently, Mortimer Sturgis picked her up and began to bear her into the house. Half-way there, his foot slipped on a piece of ice and he fell heavily, barking his shin and shooting his lovely burden out on to the snow.

The fall brought her to. She opened her eyes.

"Mortimer, darling!" she said.

Mortimer had just been going to say something else, but he checked himself.

"Are you alive?" he asked.

"Yes," she replied.

"Thank God!" said Mortimer, scooping some of the snow out of the back of his collar.

Together they went into the house, and into the drawing-room. Wife gazed at husband, husband at wife. There was a silence.

"Rotten weather!" said Mortimer.

"Yes, isn't it!"

The spell was broken. They fell into each other's arms. And presently they were sitting side by side on the sofa, holding hands, just as if that awful parting had been but a dream.

It was Mortimer who made the first reference to it.

"I say, you know," he said, "you oughtn't to have nipped away like that!"

"I thought you hated me!"

"Hated *you*! I love you better than life itself! I would sooner have smashed my pet driver than have had you leave me!"

She thrilled at the words.

"Darling!"

Mortimer fondled her hand.

"I was just coming back to tell you that I loved you still. I was going to suggest that you took lessons from some good professional. And I found you gone!"

"I wasn't worthy of you, Mortimer!"

"My angel!" He pressed his lips to her hair, and spoke solemnly. "All this has taught me a lesson, dearest. I knew all along, and I know it more than ever now, that it is you—you that I want. Just you! I don't care if you don't play golf. I don't care——" He hesitated, then went on manfully. "I don't care even if you play croquet, so long as you are with me!"

For a moment her face showed rapture that made it almost angelic. She uttered a low moan of ecstasy. She kissed him. Then she rose.

"Mortimer, look!"

"What at?"

"Me. Just look!"

The jigger which he had been polishing lay on a chair close by. She took it up. From the bowl of golf-balls on the mantelpiece she selected a brand new one. She placed it on the carpet. She addressed it. Then, with a merry cry of "Fore!" she drove it hard and straight through the glass of the china-cupboard.

"Good God!" cried Mortimer, astounded. It had been a bird of a shot.

She turned to him, her whole face alight with that beautiful smile.

"When I left you, Mortie," she said, "I had but one aim in life, somehow to make myself worthy of you. I saw your advertisements in the papers, and I longed to answer them, but I was not ready. All this long, weary while I have been in the village of Auchtermuchtie, in Scotland, studying under Tamms McMickle."

"Not the Tamms McMickle who finished fourth in the Open Championship of

1911, and had the best ball in the foursome in 1912 with Jock McHaggis, Andy McHeather, and Sandy McHoots!"

"Yes, Mortimer, the very same. Oh, it was difficult at first. I missed my mallet, and longed to steady the ball with my foot and use the toe of the club. Wherever there was a direction post I aimed at it automatically. But I conquered my weakness. I practised steadily. And now Mr. McMickle says my handicap would be a good twenty-four on any links." She smiled apologetically. "Of course, that doesn't sound much to you! You were a twelve when I left you, and now I suppose you are down to eight or something."

Mortimer shook his head.

"Alas, no!" he replied, gravely. "My game went right off for some reason or other, and I'm twenty-four, too."

"For some reason or other!" She uttered a cry. "Oh, I know what the reason was! How can I ever forgive myself! I have ruined your game!"

The brightness came back to Mortimer's eyes. He embraced her fondly.

"Do not reproach yourself, dearest," he murmured. "It is the best thing that could have happened. From now on, we start level, two hearts that beat as one, two drivers that drive as one. I could not wish it otherwise. By George! It's just like that thing of Tennyson's."

He recited the lines softly:

> *My bride,*
> *My wife, my life. Oh, we will walk the links*
> *Yoked in all exercise of noble end,*
> *And so thro' those dark bunkers off the course*
> *That no man knows. Indeed, I love thee: come,*
> *Yield thyself up: our handicaps are one;*
> *Accomplish thou my manhood and thyself;*
> *Lay thy sweet hands in mine and trust to me.*

She laid her hands in his.

"And now, Mortie, darling," she said, "I want to tell you all about how I did the long twelfth at Auchtermuchtie in one under bogey."

6

THE SALVATION OF GEORGE MACKINTOSH

THE young man came into the club-house. There was a frown on his usually cheerful face, and he ordered a ginger-ale in the sort of voice which an ancient Greek would have used when asking the executioner to bring on the hemlock.

Sunk in the recesses of his favourite settee the Oldest Member had watched him with silent sympathy.

"How did you get on?" he inquired.

"He beat me."

The Oldest Member nodded his venerable head.

"You have had a trying time, if I am not mistaken. I feared as much when I saw you go out with Pobsley. How many a young man have I seen go out with Herbert Pobsley exulting in his youth, and crawl back at eventide looking like a toad under the harrow! He talked?"

"All the time, confound it! Put me right off my stroke."

The Oldest Member sighed.

"The talking golfer is undeniably the most pronounced pest of our complex modern civilization," he said, "and the most difficult to deal with. It is a melancholy thought that the noblest of games should have produced such a scourge. I have frequently marked Herbert Pobsley in action. As the crackling of thorns under a pot . . . He is almost as bad as poor George Mackintosh in his worst period. Did I ever tell you about George Mackintosh?"

"I don't think so."

"His," said the Sage, "is the only case of golfing garrulity I have ever known where a permanent cure was effected. If you would care to hear about it——?"

George Mackintosh (said the Oldest Member), when I first knew him, was one of the most admirable young fellows I have ever met. A handsome, well-set-up man, with no vices except a tendency to use the mashie for shots which should have been made with the light iron. And as for his positive virtues, they were too numerous to mention. He never swayed his body, moved his head, or pressed. He was always ready to utter a tactful grunt when his opponent foozled. And when he himself achieved a glaring fluke, his self-reproachful click of the tongue was music to his adversary's bruised soul. But of all his virtues the one that most endeared him to me and to all thinking men was the fact that, from the start of a round to the finish, he never spoke a word except when absolutely compelled to do so by the exigencies of the game. And it was this man who subsequently, for a black period which lives in the memory of all his contemporaries, was known as Gabby George and became a shade less popular than the germ of Spanish Influenza. Truly, *corruptio optimi pessima!*

One of the things that sadden a man as he grows older and reviews his life is the reflection that his most devastating deeds were generally the ones which he did with the best motives. The thought is disheartening. I can honestly say that, when George Mackintosh came to me and told me his troubles, my sole desire was to ameliorate his lot. That I might be starting on the downward path a man whom I liked and respected never once occurred to me.

One night after dinner when George Mackintosh came in, I could see at once that there was something on his mind, but what this could be I was at a loss to imagine, for I had been playing with him myself all the afternoon, and he had done an eighty-one and a seventy-nine. And, as I had not left the links till dusk was beginning to fall, it was practically impossible that he could have gone out again and done badly. The idea of financial trouble seemed equally out of the question. George had a good job with the old-established legal firm of Peabody, Peabody, Peabody, Peabody, Cootes, Toots, and Peabody. The third alternative, that he might be in love, I rejected at once. In all the time I had known him I had never seen a sign that George Mackintosh gave a thought to the opposite sex.

Yet this, bizarre as it seemed, was the true solution. Scarcely had he seated himself and lit a cigar when he blurted out his confession.

"What would you do in a case like this?" he said.

"Like what?"

"Well——" He choked, and a rich blush permeated his surface. "Well, it seems a silly thing to say and all that, but I'm in love with Miss Tennant, you know!"

"You are in love with Celia Tennant?"

"Of course I am. I've got eyes, haven't I? Who else is there that any sane man could possibly be in love with? That," he went on, moodily, "is the whole trouble. There's a field of about twenty-nine, and I should think my place in the betting is about thirty-three to one."

"I cannot agree with you there," I said. "You have every advantage, it appears to me. You are young, amiable, good-looking, comfortably off, scratch——"

"But I can't talk, confound it!" he burst out. "And how is a man to get anywhere at this sort of game without talking?"

"You are talking perfectly fluently now."

"Yes, to you. But put me in front of Celia Tennant, and I simply make a sort of gurgling noise like a sheep with the botts. It kills my chances stone dead. You know these other men. I can give Claude Mainwaring a third and beat him. I can give Eustace Brinkley a stroke or hole and simply trample on his corpse. But when it comes to talking to a girl, I'm not in their class."

"You must not be diffident."

"But I *am* diffident. What's the good of saying I mustn't be diffident when I'm the man who wrote the words and music, when Diffidence is my middle name and my telegraphic address? I can't help being diffident."

"Surely you could overcome it?"

"But how? It was in the hope that you might be able to suggest something that I came round tonight."

And this was where I did the fatal thing. It happened that, just before I took up "Braid on the Push-Shot," I had been dipping into the current number of a magazine, and one of the advertisements, I chanced to remember, might have been framed with a special eye to George's unfortunate case. It was that one, which I have no doubt you have seen, which treats of "How to Become a Convincing Talker". I picked up this magazine now and handed it to George.

He studied it for a few minutes in thoughtful silence. He looked at the picture of the Man who had taken the course being fawned upon by lovely women, while the man who had let this opportunity slip stood outside the group gazing with a wistful envy.

"They never do that to me," said George.

"Do what, my boy?"

"Cluster round, clinging cooingly."

"I gather from the letterpress that they will if you write for the booklet."

"You think there is really something in it?"

"I see no reason why eloquence should not be taught by mail. One seems to be able to acquire every other desirable quality in that manner nowadays."

"I might try it. After all, it's not expensive. There's no doubt about it," he murmured, returning to his perusal, "that fellow does look popular. Of course, the evening dress may have something to do with it."

"Not at all. The other man, you will notice, is also wearing evening dress, and yet he is merely among those on the outskirts. It is simply a question of writing for the booklet."

"Sent post free."

"Sent, as you say, post free."

"I've a good mind to try it."

"I see no reason why you should not."

"I will, by Duncan!" He tore the page out of the magazine and put it in his pocket. "I'll tell you what I'll do. I'll give this thing a trial for a week or two, and at the end of that time I'll go to the boss and see how he reacts when I ask for a rise of salary. If he crawls, it'll show there's something in this. If he flings me out, it will prove the thing's no good."

We left it at that, and I am bound to say—owing, no doubt, to my not having written for the booklet of the Memory Training Course advertised on the adjoining page of the magazine—the matter slipped from my mind. When, therefore, a few weeks later, I received a telegram from young Mackintosh which ran:

Worked like magic

I confess I was intensely puzzled. It was only a quarter of an hour before George himself arrived that I solved the problem of its meaning.

"So the boss crawled?" I said, as he came in.

He gave a light, confident laugh. I had not seen him, as I say, for some time, and I was struck by the alteration in his appearance. In what exactly this alteration consisted I could not at first have said; but gradually it began to impress itself on me that his eye was brighter, his jaw squarer, his carriage a trifle more upright than it had been. But it was his eye that struck me most forcibly. The George Mackintosh I had known had had a pleasing gaze, but, though frank and agreeable, it had never been more dynamic than a fried egg. This new George had an eye that was a combination of a gimlet and a searchlight. Coleridge's Ancient Mariner, I imagine, must have been somewhat similarly equipped. The Ancient Mariner stopped a wedding guest on his way to a wedding; George Mackintosh gave me the impression that he could have stopped the Cornish Riviera express on its way to Penzance. Self-confidence—aye, and more than self-confidence—a sort of sinful, overbearing swank seemed to exude from his very pores.

"Crawled?" he said. "Well, he didn't actually lick my boots, because I saw him coming and side-stepped; but he did everything short of that. I hadn't been talking an hour when——"

"An hour!" I gasped. "Did you talk for an hour?"

"Certainly. You wouldn't have had me be abrupt, would you? I went into his private office and found him alone. I think at first he would have been just as well pleased if I had retired. In fact, he said as much. But I soon adjusted that outlook. I took a seat and a cigarette, and then I started to sketch out for him the history of my connection with the firm. He began to wilt before the end of the first ten minutes. At the quarter of an hour mark he was looking at me like a lost dog that's just found its owner. By the half-hour he was making little bleating noises and massaging my coat-sleeve. And when, after perhaps an hour and a half, I came to my peroration and suggested a rise, he choked back a sob, gave me double what I had asked, and invited me to dine at his club next Tuesday. I'm a little sorry now I cut the thing so short. A few minutes more, and I fancy he would have given me his sock-suspenders and made over his life-insurance in my favour."

"Well," I said, as soon as I could speak, for I was finding my young friend a trifle overpowering, "this is most satisfactory."

"So-so," said George. "Not un-so-so. A man wants an addition to his income when he is going to get married."

"Ah!" I said. "That, of course, will be the real test."

"What do you mean?"

"Why, when you propose to Celia Tennant. You remember you were saying when we spoke of this before——"

"Oh, that!" said George, carelessly. "I've arranged all that."

"What!"

"Oh, yes. On my way up from the station. I looked in on Celia about an hour ago, and it's all settled."

"Amazing!"

"Well, I don't know. I just put the thing to her, and she seemed to see it."

"I congratulate you. So now, like Alexander, you have no more worlds to conquer."

"Well, I don't know so much about that," said George. "The way it looks to me is that I'm just starting. This eloquence is a thing that rather grows on one. You didn't hear about my after-dinner speech at the anniversary banquet of the firm, I suppose? My dear fellow, a riot! A positive stampede. Had 'em laughing and then crying and then laughing again and then crying once more till six of 'em had to be led out and the rest down with hiccoughs. Napkins waving . . . three tables broken . . . waiters in hysterics. I tell you, I played on them as on a stringed instrument . . ."

"Can you play on a stringed instrument?"

"As it happens, no. But as I would have played on a stringed instrument if I could play on a stringed instrument. Wonderful sense of power it gives you. I mean to go in pretty largely for that sort of thing in future."

"You must not let it interfere with your golf."

He gave a laugh which turned my blood cold.

"Golf!" he said. "After all, what is golf? Just pushing a small ball into a hole. A child could do it. Indeed, children have done it with great success. I see an infant of fourteen has just won some sort of championship. Could that stripling convulse a roomful of banqueters? I think not! To sway your fellow-men with a word, to hold them with a gesture . . . that is the real salt of life. I don't suppose I shall play much more golf now. I'm making arrangements for a lecturing-tour, and I'm booked up for fifteen lunches already."

Those were his words. A man who had once done the lake-hole in one. A man whom the committee were grooming for the amateur championship. I am no weakling, but I confess they sent a chill shiver down my spine.

George Mackintosh did not, I am glad to say, carry out his mad project to the letter. He did not altogether sever himself from golf. He was still to be seen occasionally on the links. But now—and I know of nothing more tragic that can befall a man—he found himself gradually shunned, he who in the days of his sanity had been besieged with more offers of games than he could manage to accept. Men simply would not stand his incessant flow of talk. One by one they dropped off, until the only person he could find to go round with him was old Major Moseby, whose hearing completely petered out as long ago as the year '98. And, of course, Celia

Tennant would play with him occasionally; but it seemed to me that even she, greatly
as no doubt she loved him, was beginning to crack under the strain.

So surely had I read the pallor of her face and the wild look of dumb agony in her
eyes that I was not surprised when, as I sat one morning in my garden reading Ray
on Taking Turf, my man announced her name. I had been half expecting her to
come to me for advice and consolation, for I had known her ever since she was a child.
It was I who had given her her first driver and taught her infant lips to lisp "Fore!"
It is not easy to lisp the word "Fore!" but I had taught her to do it, and this
constituted a bond between us which had been strengthened rather than weakened
by the passage of time.

She sat down on the grass beside my chair, and looked up at my face in silent pain.
We had known each other so long that I know that it was not my face that pained
her, but rather some unspoken *malaise* of the soul. I waited for her to speak, and
suddenly she burst out impetuously as though she could hold back her sorrow no
longer.

"Oh, I can't stand it! I can't stand it!"

"You mean . . .?" I said, though I knew only too well.

"This horrible obsession of poor George's," she cried passionately. "I don't think
he has stopped talking once since we have been engaged."

"He *is* chatty," I agreed. "Has he told you the story about the Irishman?"

"Half a dozen times. And the one about the Swede oftener than that. But I would
not mind an occasional anecdote. Women have to learn to bear anecdotes from the
men they love. It is the curse of Eve. It is his incessant easy flow of chatter on all
topics that is undermining even my devotion."

"But surely, when he proposed to you, he must have given you an inkling of the
truth. He only hinted at it when he spoke to me, but I gather that he was eloquent."

"When he proposed," said Celia dreamily, "he was wonderful. He spoke for
twenty minutes without stopping. He said I was the essence of his every hope, the
tree on which the fruit of his life grew; his Present, his Future, his Past . . . oh, and
all that sort of thing. If he would only confine his conversation now to remarks of a
similar nature, I could listen to him all day long. But he doesn't. He talks politics
and statistics and philosophy and . . . oh, and everything. He makes my head ache."

"And your heart also, I fear," I said gravely.

"I love him!" she replied simply. "In spite of everything, I love him dearly. But
what to do? What to do? I have an awful fear that when we are getting married
instead of answering 'I will,' he will go into the pulpit and deliver an address on
Marriage Ceremonies of All Ages. The world to him is a vast lecture-platform. He
looks on life as one long after-dinner, with himself as the principal speaker of the
evening. It is breaking my heart. I see him shunned by his former friends. Shunned!
They run a mile when they see him coming. The mere sound of his voice outside the
club-house is enough to send brave men diving for safety beneath the sofas. Can you

wonder that I am in despair? What have I to live for?"

"There is always golf."

"Yes, there is always golf," she whispered bravely.

"Come and have a round this afternoon."

"I had promised to go for a walk . . ." She shuddered, then pulled herself together, ". . . for a walk with George."

I hesitated for a moment.

"Bring him along," I said, and patted her hand. "It may be that together we shall find an opportunity of reasoning with him."

She shook her head.

"You can't reason with George. He never stops talking long enough to give you time."

"Nevertheless, there is no harm in trying. I have an idea that this malady of his is not permanent and incurable. The very violence with which the germ of loquacity has attacked him gives me hope. You must remember that before this seizure he was rather a noticeably silent man. Sometimes I think that it is just Nature's way of restoring the average, and that soon the fever may burn itself out. Or it may be that a sudden shock . . . At any rate, have courage."

"I will try to be brave."

"Capital! At half-past two on the first tee, then."

"You will have to give me a stroke on the third, ninth, twelfth, fifteenth, sixteenth and eighteenth," she said, with a quaver in her voice. "My golf has fallen off rather lately."

I patted her hand again.

"I understand," I said gently. "I understand."

The steady drone of a baritone voice as I alighted from my car and approached the first tee told me that George had not forgotten the tryst. He was sitting on the stone seat under the chestnut-tree, speaking a few well-chosen words on the Labour Movement

"To what conclusion, then, do we come?" he was saying. "We come to the foregone and inevitable conclusion that . . ."

"Good afternoon, George," I said.

He nodded briefly, but without verbal salutation. He seemed to regard my remark as he would have regarded the unmannerly heckling of someone at the back of the hall. He proceeded evenly with his speech, and was still talking when Celia addressed her ball and drove off. Her drive, coinciding with a sharp rhetorical question from George, wavered in mid-air, and the ball trickled off into the rough half-way down the hill. I can see the poor girl's tortured face even now. But she breathed no word of reproach. Such is the miracle of women's love.

"Where you went wrong there," said George, breaking off his remarks on Labour, "was that you have not studied the dynamics of golf sufficiently. You did not pivot properly. You allowed your left heel to point down the course when you were at the top of your swing. This makes for instability and loss of distance. The fundamental law of the dynamics of golf is that the left foot shall be solidly on the ground at the moment of impact. If you allow your heel to point down the course, it is almost impossible to bring it back in time to make the foot a solid fulcrum."

I drove, and managed to clear the rough and reach the fairway. But it was not one of my best drives. George Mackintosh, I confess, had unnerved me. The feeling he gave me resembled the self-conscious panic which I used to experience in my childhood when informed that there was One Awful Eye that watched my every movement and saw my every act. It was only the fact that poor Celia appeared even more affected by his espionage that enabled me to win the first hole in seven.

On the way to the second tee George discoursed on the beauties of Nature, pointing out at considerable length how exquisitely the silver glitter of the lake harmonized with the vivid emerald turf near the hole and the duller green of the rough beyond it. As Celia teed up her ball, he directed her attention to the golden glory of the sand-pit to the left of the flag. It was not the spirit in which to approach the lake-hole, and I was not surprised when the unfortunate girl's ball fell with a sickening plop half-way across the water.

"Where you went wrong there," said George, "was that you made the stroke a sudden heave instead of a smooth, snappy flick of the wrists. Pressing is always bad, but with the mashie——"

"I think I will give you this hole," said Celia to me, for my shot had cleared the water and was lying on the edge of the green. "I wish I hadn't used a new ball."

"The price of golf-balls," said George, as we started to round the lake, "is a matter to which economists should give some attention. I am credibly informed that rubber at the present time is exceptionally cheap. Yet we see no decrease in the price of golf-balls, which, as I need scarcely inform you, are rubber-cored. Why should this be so? You will say that the wages of skilled labour have gone up. True. But——"

"One moment, George, while I drive," I said. For we had now arrived at the third tee.

"A curious thing, concentration," said George, "and why certain phenomena should prevent us from focusing our attention—— This brings me to the vexed question of sleep. Why is it that we are able to sleep through some vast convulsion of Nature when a dripping tap is enough to keep us awake? I am told that there were people who slumbered peacefully through the San Francisco earthquake, merely stirring drowsily from time to time to tell an imaginary person to leave it on the mat. Yet these same people——"

Celia's drive bounded into the deep ravine which yawns some fifty yards from the tee. A low moan escaped her.

"Where you went wrong there——" said George.

"I know," said Celia. "I lifted my head."

I had never heard her speak so abruptly before. Her manner, in a girl less noticeably pretty, might almost have been called snappish. George, however, did not appear to have noticed anything amiss. He filled his pipe and followed her into the ravine.

"Remarkable," he said, "how fundamental a principle of golf is this keeping the head still. You will hear professionals tell their pupils to keep their eye on the ball. Keeping the eye on the ball is only a secondary matter. What they really mean is that the head should be kept rigid, as otherwise it is impossible to——"

His voice died away. I had sliced my drive into the woods on the right, and after playing another had gone off to try to find my ball, leaving Celia and George in the ravine behind me. My last glimpse of them showed me that her ball had fallen into a stone-studded cavity in the side of the hill, and she was drawing her niblick from her bag as I passed out of sight. George's voice, blurred by distance to a monotonous murmur, followed me until I was out of earshot.

I was just about to give up the hunt for my ball in despair, when I heard Celia's voice calling to me from the edge of the undergrowth. There was a sharp note in it which startled me.

I came out, trailing a portion of some unknown shrub which had twined itself about my ankle.

"Yes?" I said, picking twigs out of my hair.

"I want your advice," said Celia.

"Certainly. What is the trouble? By the way," I said, looking round, "where is your *fiancé*?"

"I have no *fiancé*," she said, in a dull, hard voice.

"You have broken off the engagement?"

"Not exactly. And yet—well, I suppose it amounts to that."

"I don't quite understand."

"Well, the fact is," said Celia, in a burst of girlish frankness, "I rather think I've killed George."

"Killed him, eh?"

It was a solution that had not occurred to me, but now that it was presented for my inspection I could see its merits. In these days of national effort, when we are all working together to try to make our beloved land fit for heroes to live in, it was astonishing that nobody before had thought of a simple, obvious thing like killing George Mackintosh. George Mackintosh was undoubtedly better dead, but it had taken a woman's intuition to see it.

"I killed him with my niblick," said Celia.

I nodded. If the thing was to be done at all, it was unquestionably a niblick shot.

"I had just made my eleventh attempt to get out of that ravine," the girl went on, "with George talking all the time about the recent excavations in Egypt, when suddenly—you know what it is when something seems to snap——"

"I had the experience with my shoe-lace only this morning."

"Yes, it was like that. Sharp—sudden—happening all in a moment. I suppose I must have said something, for George stopped talking about Egypt and said that he was reminded by a remark of the last speaker's of a certain Irishman———"

I pressed her hand.

"Don't go on if it hurts you," I said, gently.

"Well, there is very little more to tell. He bent his head to light his pipe, and well —the temptation was too much for me. That's all."

"You were quite right."

"You really think so?"

"I certainly do. A rather similar action, under far less provocation, once made Jael the wife of Heber the most popular woman in Israel."

"I wish I could think so too," she murmured. "At the moment, you know, I was conscious of nothing but an awful elation. But—but—oh, he was such a darling before he got this dreadful affliction. I can't help thinking of G-George as he used to be."

She burst into a torrent of sobs.

"Would you care for me to view the remains?" I said.

"Perhaps it would be as well."

She led me silently into the ravine. George Mackintosh was lying on his back where he had fallen.

"There!" said Celia.

And, as she spoke, George Mackintosh gave a kind of snorting groan and sat up. Celia uttered a sharp shriek and sank on her knees before him. George blinked once or twice and looked about him dazedly.

"Save the women and children!" he cried. "I can swim."

"Oh, George!" said Celia.

"Feeling a little better?" I asked.

"A little. How many people were hurt?"

"Hurt?"

"When the express ran into us." He cast another glance around him. "Why, how did I get here?"

"You were here all the time," I said.

"Do you mean after the roof fell in or before?"

Celia was crying quietly down the back of his neck.

"Oh, George!" she said, again.

He groped out feebly for her hand and patted it.

"Brave little woman!" he said. "Brave little woman! She stuck by me all through. Tell me—I am strong enough to bear it—what caused the explosion?"

It seemed to me a case where much unpleasant explanation might be avoided by the exercise of a little tact.

"Well, some say one thing and some another," I said. "Whether it was a spark from a cigarette———"

Celia interrupted me. The woman in her made her revolt against this well-intentioned subterfuge.

"I hit you, George!"

"Hit me?" he repeated, curiously. "What with? The Eiffel Tower?"

"With my niblick."

"You hit me with your niblick? But why?"

She hesitated. Then she faced him bravely.

"Because you wouldn't stop talking."

He gaped.

"Me!" he said. "*I* wouldn't stop talking! But I hardly talk at all. I'm noted for it."

Celia's eyes met mine in agonized inquiry. But I saw what had happened. The blow, the sudden shock, had operated on George's brain-cells in such a way as to effect a complete cure. I have not the technical knowledge to be able to explain it, but the facts were plain.

"Lately, my dear fellow," I assured him, "you have dropped into the habit of talking rather a good deal. Ever since we started out this afternoon you have kept up an incessant flow of conversation!"

"Me! On the links! It isn't possible."

"It is only too true, I fear. And that is why this brave girl hit you with her niblick. You started to tell her a funny story just as she was making her eleventh shot to get her ball out of this ravine, and she took what she considered the necessary steps."

"Can you ever forgive me, George?" cried Celia.

George Mackintosh stared at me. Then a crimson blush mantled his face.

"So I did! It's all beginning to come back to me. Oh, heavens!"

"*Can* you forgive me, George?" cried Celia again.

He took her hand in his.

"Forgive you?" he muttered. "Can *you* forgive *me*? Me—a tee-talker, a green-gabbler, a prattler on the links, the lowest form of life known to science! I am unclean, unclean!"

"It's only a little mud, dearest," said Celia, looking at the sleeve of his coat. "It will brush off when it's dry."

"How can you link your lot with a man who talks when people are making their shots?"

"You will never do it again."

"But I have done it. And you stuck to me all through! Oh, Celia!"

"I loved you, George!"

The man seemed to swell with a sudden emotion. His eye lit up, and he thrust one hand into the breast of his coat while he raised the other in a sweeping gesture. For an instant he appeared on the verge of a flood of eloquence. And then, as if he had been made sharply aware of what it was that he intended to do, he suddenly sagged. The gleam died out of his eyes. He lowered his hand.

"Well, I must say that was rather decent of you," he said.

A lame speech, but one that brought an infinite joy to both his hearers. For it showed that George Mackintosh was cured beyond possibility of relapse.

"Yes, I must say you are rather a corker," he added.

"George!" cried Celia.

I said nothing, but I clasped his hand; and then, taking my clubs, I retired. When I looked round she was still in his arms. I left them there alone, alone together in the great silence.

And so (concluded the Oldest Member) you see that a cure is possible, though it needs a woman's gentle hand to bring it about. And how few women are capable of doing what Celia Tennant did. Apart from the difficulty of summoning up the necessary resolution, an act like hers requires a straight eye and a pair of strong and supple wrists. It seems to me that for the ordinary talking golfer there is no hope. And the race seems to be getting more numerous every day. Yet the finest golfers are always the least loquacious. It is related of the illustrious Sandy McHoots that when, on the occasion of his winning the British Open Championship, he was interviewed by reporters from the leading daily papers as to his views on Tariff Reform, Bimetallism, the Trial by Jury System, and the Modern Craze for Dancing, all they could extract from him was the single word "Mphm!" Having uttered which, he shouldered his bag and went home to tea. A great man. I wish there were more like him.

7

ORDEAL BY GOLF

A PLEASANT breeze played among the trees on the terrace outside the Marvis Bay
Golf and Country Club. It ruffled the leaves and cooled the forehead of the Oldest
Member, who, as was his custom of a Saturday afternoon, sat in the shade on a
rocking-chair, observing the younger generation as it hooked and sliced in the valley
below. The eye of the Oldest Member was thoughtful and reflective. When it looked
into yours you saw in it that perfect peace, that peace beyond understanding, which
comes at its maximum only to the man who has given up golf.

The Oldest Member has not played golf since the rubber-cored ball superseded
the old dignified gutty. But as a spectator and philosopher he still finds pleasure in
the pastime. He is watching it now with keen interest. His gaze, passing from the
lemonade which he is sucking through a straw, rests upon the Saturday foursome
which is struggling raggedly up the hill to the ninth green. Like all Saturday foursomes, it is in difficulties. One of the patients is zigzagging about the fairway like a
liner pursued by submarines. Two others seem to be digging for buried treasure,
unless—it is too far off to be certain—they are killing snakes. The remaining cripple,
who has just foozled a mashie-shot, is blaming his caddie. His voice, as he upbraids
the innocent child for breathing during his up-swing, comes clearly up the hill.

The Oldest Member sighs. His lemonade gives a sympathetic gurgle. He puts it
down on the table.

How few men, says the Oldest Member, possess the proper golfing temperament!
How few indeed, judging by the sights I see here on Saturday afternoons, possess
any qualification at all for golf except a pair of baggy knickerbockers and enough
money to enable them to pay for the drinks at the end of the round. The ideal golfer
never loses his temper. When I played, I never lost my temper. Sometimes, it is true,
I may, after missing a shot, have broken my club across my knees; but I did it in a
calm and judicial spirit, because the club was obviously no good and I was going to
get another one anyway. To lose one's temper at golf is foolish. It gets you nothing,
not even relief. Imitate the spirit of Marcus Aurelius. "Whatever may befall thee,"
says that great man in his "Meditations", "it was preordained for thee from ever-
lasting. Nothing happens to anybody which he is not fitted by nature to bear." I like
to think that this noble thought came to him after he had sliced a couple of new balls
into the woods, and that he jotted it down on the back of his score-card. For there

can be no doubt that the man was a golfer, and a bad golfer at that. Nobody who had not had a short putt stop on the edge of the hole could possibly have written the words: "That which makes the man no worse than he was makes life no worse. It has no power to harm, without or within." Yes, Marcus Aurelius undoubtedly played golf, and all the evidence seems to indicate that he rarely went round in under a hundred and twenty. The niblick was his club.

Speaking of Marcus Aurelius and the golfing temperament recalls to my mind the case of young Mitchell Holmes. Mitchell, when I knew him first, was a promising young man with a future before him in the Paterson Dyeing and Refining Company, of which my old friend, Alexander Paterson, was the president. He had many engaging qualities—among them an unquestioned ability to imitate a bulldog quarrelling with a Pekingese in a way which had to be heard to be believed. It was a gift which made him much in demand at social gatherings in the neighbourhood, marking him off from other young men who could only almost play the mandolin or recite bits of Gunga Din; and no doubt it was this talent of his which first sowed the seeds of love in the heart of Millicent Boyd. Women are essentially hero-worshippers, and when a warm-hearted girl like Millicent has heard a personable young man imitating a bulldog and a Pekingese to the applause of a crowded drawing-room, and has been able to detect the exact point at which the Pekingese leaves off and the bulldog begins, she can never feel quite the same to other men. In short, Mitchell and Millicent were engaged, and were only waiting to be married till the former could bite the Dyeing and Refining Company's ear for a bit of extra salary.

Mitchell Holmes had only one fault. He lost his temper when playing golf. He seldom played a round without becoming piqued, peeved, or—in many cases—chagrined. The caddies on our links, it was said, could always worst other small boys in verbal argument by calling them some of the things they had heard Mitchell call his ball on discovering it in a cuppy lie. He had a great gift of language, and he used it unsparingly. I will admit that there was some excuse for the man. He had the makings of a brilliant golfer, but a combination of bad luck and inconsistent play invariably robbed him of the fruits of his skill. He was the sort of player who does the first two holes in one under bogey and then takes an eleven at the third. The least thing upsets him on the links. He missed short putts because of the uproar of the butterflies in the adjoining meadows.

It seemed hardly likely that this one kink in an otherwise admirable character would ever seriously affect his working or professional life, but it did. One evening, as I was sitting in my garden, Alexander Paterson was announced. A glance at his face told me that he had come to ask my advice. Rightly or wrongly, he regarded me as one capable of giving advice. It was I who had changed the whole current of his life by counselling him to leave the wood in his bag and take a driving-iron off the tee; and in one or two other matters, like the choice of a putter (so much more important than the choice of a wife), I had been of assistance to him.

Alexander sat down and fanned himself with his hat, for the evening was warm. Perplexity was written upon his fine face.

"I don't know what to do," he said.

"Keep the head still—slow back—don't press," I said, gravely. There is no better rule for a happy and successful life.

"It's nothing to do with golf this time," he said. " It's about the treasurership of my company. Old Smithers retires next week, and I've got to find a man to fill his place."

"That should be easy. You have simply to select the most deserving from among your other employees."

"But which is the most deserving? That's the point. There are two men who are capable of holding the job quite adequately. But then I realize how little I know of their real characters. It is the treasurership, you understand, which has to be filled. Now, a man who was quite good at another job might easily get wrong ideas into his head when he became a treasurer. He would have the handling of large sums of money. In other words, a man who in ordinary circumstances had never been conscious of any desire to visit the more distant portions of South America might feel the urge, so to speak, shortly after he became a treasurer. That is my difficulty. Of course, one always takes a sporting chance with any treasurer; but how am I to find out which of these two men would give me the more reasonable opportunity of keeping some of my money?"

I did not hesitate a moment. I held strong views on the subject of character-testing.

"The only way," I said to Alexander, "of really finding out a man's true character is to play golf with him. In no other walk of life does the cloven hoof so quickly display itself. I employed a lawyer for years, until one day I saw him kick his ball out of a heel-mark. I removed my business from his charge next morning. He has not yet run off with any trust funds, but there is a nasty gleam in his eye, and I am convinced that it is only a question of time. Golf, my dear fellow, is the infallible test. The man who can go into a patch of rough alone, with the knowledge that only God is watching him, and play his ball where it lies, is the man who will serve you faithfully and well. The man who can smile bravely when his putt is diverted by one of those beastly wormcasts is pure gold right through. But the man who is hasty, unbalanced, and violent on the links will display the same qualities in the wider field of everyday life. You don't want an unbalanced treasurer do you?"

"Not if his books are likely to catch the complaint."

"They are sure to. Statisticians estimate that the average of crime among good golfers is lower than in any class of the community except possibly bishops. Since Willie Park won the first championship at Prestwick in the year 1860 there has, I believe, been no instance of an Open Champion spending a day in prison. Whereas the bad golfers—and by bad I do not mean incompetent, but black-souled—the men who fail to count a stroke when they miss the globe; the men who never replace a divot; the men who talk while their opponent is driving; and the men who let their angry passions rise—these are in and out of Wormwood Scrubs all the time. They find it hardly worth while to get their hair cut in their brief intervals of liberty."

Alexander was visibly impressed.

"That sounds sensible, by George!" he said.

"It is sensible."

"I'll do it! Honestly, I can't see any other way of deciding between Holmes and Dixon."

I started.

"Holmes? Not Mitchell Holmes?"

"Yes. Of course you must know him? He lives here, I believe."

"And by Dixon do you mean Rupert Dixon?"

"That's the man. Another neighbour of yours."

I confess that my heart sank. It was as if my ball had fallen into the pit which my niblick had digged. I wished heartily that I had thought of waiting to ascertain the names of the two rivals before offering my scheme. I was extremely fond of Mitchell Holmes and of the girl to whom he was engaged to be married. Indeed, it was I who had sketched out a few rough notes for the lad to use when proposing; and results had shown that he had put my stuff across well. And I had listened many a time with a sympathetic ear to his hopes in the matter of securing a rise of salary which would enable him to get married. Somehow, when Alexander was talking, it had not occurred to me that young Holmes might be in the running for so important an office as the treasurership. I had ruined the boy's chances. Ordeal by golf was the one test which he could not possibly undergo with success. Only a miracle could keep him from losing his temper, and I had expressly warned Alexander against such a man.

When I thought of his rival my heart sank still more. Rupert Dixon was rather an unpleasant young man, but the worst of his enemies could not accuse him of not possessing the golfing temperament. From the drive off the tee to the holing of the final putt he was uniformly suave.

When Alexander had gone, I sat in thought for some time. I was faced with a problem. Strictly speaking, no doubt, I had no right to take sides; and, though secrecy had not been enjoined upon me in so many words, I was very well aware that Alexander was under the impression that I would keep the thing under my hat and not reveal to either party the test that awaited him. Each candidate was, of course, to remain ignorant that he was taking part in anything but a friendly game.

But when I thought of the young couple whose future depended on this ordeal, I hesitated no longer. I put on my hat and went round to Miss Boyd's house, where I knew that Mitchell was to be found at this hour.

The young couple were out in the porch, looking at the moon. They greeted me heartily, but their heartiness had rather a tinny sound, and I could see that on the whole they regarded me as one of those things which should not happen. But when I told my story their attitude changed. They began to look on me in the pleasanter light of a guardian, philosopher, and friend.

"Wherever did Mr. Paterson get such a silly idea?" said Miss Boyd, indignantly. I had—from the best motives—concealed the source of the scheme. "It's ridiculous!"

"Oh, I don't know," said Mitchell. "The old boy's crazy about golf. It's just the sort of scheme he would cook up. Well, it dishes *me*!"

"Oh, come!" I said.

"It's no good saying 'Oh, come!' You know perfectly well that I'm a frank, outspoken golfer. When my ball goes off nor'-nor'-east when I want it to go due west I can't help expressing an opinion about it. It is a curious phenomenon which calls for comment, and I give it. Similarly, when I top my drive, I have to go on record as saying that I did not do it intentionally. And it's just these trifles, as far as I can make out, that are going to decide the thing."

"Couldn't you learn to control yourself on the links, Mitchell, darling?" asked Millicent. "After all, golf is only a game!"

Mitchell's eyes met mine, and I have no doubt that mine showed just the same look of horror which I saw in his. Women say these things without thinking. It does not mean that there is any kink in their character. They simply don't realize what they are saying.

"Hush!" said Mitchell, huskily, patting her hand and overcoming his emotion with a strong effort. "Hush, dearest!"

Two or three days later I met Millicent coming from the post-office. There was a new light of happiness in her eyes, and her face was glowing.

"Such a splendid thing has happened," she said. "After Mitchell left that night I happened to be glancing through a magazine, and I came across a wonderful advertisement. It began by saying that all the great men in history owed their success to being able to control themselves, and that Napoleon wouldn't have amounted to anything if he had not curbed his fiery nature, and then it said that we can all be like Napoleon if we fill in the accompanying blank order-form for Professor Orlando Rollitt's wonderful book, 'Are You Your Own Master?' absolutely free for five days and then seven shillings, but you must write at once because the demand is enormous and pretty soon it may be too late. I wrote at once, and luckily I was in time, because Professor Rollitt did have a copy left, and it's just arrived. I've been looking through it, and it seems splendid."

She held out a small volume. I glanced at it. There was a frontispiece showing a signed photograph of Professor Orlando Rollitt controlling himself in spite of having long white whiskers, and then some reading matter, printed between wide margins. One look at the book told me the professor's methods. To be brief, he had simply swiped Marcus Aurelius's best stuff, the copyright having expired some two thousand years ago, and was retailing it as his own. I did not mention this to Millicent. It was no affair of mine. Presumably, however obscure the necessity, Professor Rollitt had to live.

"I'm going to start Mitchell on it today. Don't you think this is good? 'Thou seest how few be the things which if a man has at his command his life flows gently on and is divine.' I think it will be wonderful if Mitchell's life flows gently on and is divine for seven shillings, don't you?"

At the club-house that evening I encountered Rupert Dixon. He was emerging from a shower-bath, and looked as pleased with himself as usual.

"Just been going round with old Paterson," he said. "He was asking after you. He's gone back to town in his car."

I was thrilled. So the test had begun!

"How did you come out?" I asked.

Rupert Dixon smirked. A smirking man, wrapped in a bath towel, with a wisp of wet hair over one eye, is a repellent sight.

"Oh, pretty well. I won by six and five. In spite of having poisonous luck."

I felt a gleam of hope at these last words.

"Oh, you had bad luck?"

"The worst. I over-shot the green at the third with the best brassey-shot I've ever made in my life—and that's saying a lot—and lost my ball in the rough beyond it."

"And I suppose you let yourself go, eh?"

"Let myself go?"

"I take it that you made some sort of demonstration?"

"Oh, no. Losing your temper doesn't get you anywhere at golf. It only spoils your next shot."

I went away heavy-hearted. Dixon had plainly come through the ordeal as well as any man could have done. I expected to hear every day that the vacant treasurership had been filled, and that Mitchell had not even been called upon to play his test round. I suppose, however, that Alexander Paterson felt that it would be unfair to the other competitor not to give him his chance, for the next I heard of the matter was when Mitchell Holmes rang me up on the Friday and asked me if I would accompany him round the links next day in the match he was playing with Alexander, and give him my moral support.

"I shall need it," he said. "I don't mind telling you I'm pretty nervous. I wish I had had longer to get the stranglehold on that 'Are You Your Own Master?' stuff. I can see, of course, that it is the real tabasco from start to finish, and absolutely as mother makes it, but the trouble is I've only had a few days to soak it into my system. It's like trying to patch up a motor car with string. You never know when the thing will break down. Heaven knows what will happen if I sink a ball at the water-hole. And something seems to tell me I am going to do it."

There was a silence for a moment.

"Do you believe in dreams?" asked Mitchell.

"Believe in what?"

"Dreams."

"What about them?"

"I said, 'Do you believe in dreams?' Because last night I dreamed that I was playing in the final of the Open Championship, and I got into the rough, and there was a cow there, and the cow looked at me in a sad sort of way and said, 'Why don't you use the two-V grip instead of the interlocking?' At the time it seemed an odd sort of thing to happen, but I've been thinking it over and I wonder if there isn't something in it. These things must be sent to us for a purpose."

"You can't change your grip on the day of an important match."

"I suppose not. The fact is, I'm a bit jumpy, or I wouldn't have mentioned it. Oh, well! See you tomorrow at two."

The day was bright and sunny, but a tricky cross-wind was blowing when I reached the club-house. Alexander Paterson was there, practising swings on the first tee; and almost immediately Mitchell Holmes arrived, accompanied by Millicent.

"Perhaps," said Alexander, "we had better be getting under way. Shall I take the honour?"

"Certainly," said Mitchell.

Alexander teed up his ball.

Alexander Paterson has always been a careful rather than a dashing player. It is his custom, a sort of ritual, to take two measured practice-swings before addressing the ball, even on the putting-green. When he does address the ball he shuffles his feet for a moment or two, then pauses, and scans the horizon in a suspicious sort of way, as if he had been expecting it to play some sort of trick on him when he was not looking. A careful inspection seems to convince him of the horizon's *bona fides*, and he turns his attention to the ball again. He shuffles his feet once more, then raises his club. He waggles the club smartly over the ball three times, then lays it behind the globule. At this point he suddenly peers at the horizon again, in the apparent hope of catching it off its guard. This done, he raises his club very slowly, brings it back very slowly till it almost touches the ball, raises it again, brings it down again, raises it once more, and brings it down for the third time. He then stands motionless, wrapped in thought, like some Indian fakir contemplating the infinite. Then he raises his club again and replaces it behind the ball. Finally he quivers all over, swings very slowly back, and drives the ball for about a hundred and fifty yards in a dead straight line.

It is a method of procedure which proves sometimes a little exasperating to the highly strung, and I watched Mitchell's face anxiously to see how he was taking his first introduction to it. The unhappy lad had blenched visibly. He turned to me with the air of one in pain.

"Does he always do that?" he whispered.

"Always," I replied.

"Then I'm done for! No human being could play golf against a one-ring circus like that without blowing up!"

I said nothing. It was, I feared, only too true. Well-poised as I am, I had long since been compelled to give up playing with Alexander Paterson, much as I esteemed him. It was a choice between that and resigning from the Baptist Church.

At this moment Millicent spoke. There was an open book in her hand. I recognized it as the life-work of Professor Rollitt.

"Think on this doctrine," she said, in her soft, modulated voice, "that to be patient is a branch of justice, and that men sin without intending it."

Mitchell nodded briefly, and walked to the tee with a firm step.

"Before you drive, darling," said Millicent, "remember this. Let no act be done at haphazard, nor otherwise than according to the finished rules that govern its kind."

The next moment Mitchell's ball was shooting through the air, to come to rest two hundred yards down the course. It was a magnificent drive. He had followed the counsel of Marcus Aurelius to the letter.

An admirable iron-shot put him in reasonable proximity to the pin, and he holed out in one under bogey with one of the nicest putts I have ever beheld. And when at the next hole, the dangerous water-hole, his ball soared over the pond and lay safe, giving him bogey for the hole, I began for the first time to breathe freely. Every golfer has his day, and this was plainly Mitchell's. He was playing faultless golf. If he could continue in this vein, his unfortunate failing would have no chance to show itself.

The third hole is long and tricky. You drive over a ravine—or possibly into it. In the latter event you breathe a prayer and call for your niblick. But, once over the ravine, there is nothing to disturb the equanimity. Bogey is five, and a good drive, followed by a brassey-shot, will put you within easy mashie-distance of the green.

Mitchell cleared the ravine by a hundred and twenty yards. He strolled back to me, and watched Alexander go through his ritual with an indulgent smile. I knew just how he was feeling. Never does the world seem so sweet and fair and the foibles of our fellow human beings so little irritating as when we have just swatted the pill right on the spot.

"I can't see why he does it," said Mitchell, eyeing Alexander with a toleration that almost amounted to affection. "If I did all those Swedish exercises before I drove, I should forget what I had come out for and go home." Alexander concluded the movements, and landed a bare three yards on the other side of the ravine. "He's what you would call a steady performer, isn't he? Never varies!"

Mitchell won the hole comfortably. There was a jauntiness about his stance on the fourth tee which made me a little uneasy. Over-confidence at golf is almost as bad as timidity.

My apprehensions were justified. Mitchell topped his ball. It rolled twenty yards into the rough, and nestled under a dock-leaf. His mouth opened, then closed with a snap. He came over to where Millicent and I were standing.

"I didn't say it!" he said. "What on earth happened then?"

"Search men's governing principles," said Millicent, "and consider the wise, what they shun and what they cleave to."

"Exactly," I said. "You swayed your body."

"And now I've got to go and look for that infernal ball."

"Never mind, darling," said Millicent. "Nothing has such power to broaden the mind as the ability to investigate systematically and truly all that comes under thy observation in life."

"Besides," I said, "you're three up."

"I shan't be after this hole."

He was right. Alexander won it in five, one above bogey, and regained the honour.

Mitchell was a trifle shaken. His play no longer had its first careless vigour. He lost the next hole, halved the sixth, lost the short seventh, and then, rallying, halved the eighth.

The ninth hole, like so many on our links, can be a perfectly simple four, although the rolling nature of the green makes bogey always a somewhat doubtful feat; but, on the other hand, if you foozle your drive, you can easily achieve double figures. The tee is on the farther side of the pond, beyond the bridge, where the water narrows almost to the dimensions of a brook. You drive across this water and over a tangle of trees and undergrowth on the other bank. The distance to the fairway cannot be more than sixty yards, for the hazard is purely a mental one, and yet how many fair hopes have been wrecked there!

Alexander cleared the obstacles comfortably with his customary short, straight drive, and Mitchell advanced to the tee.

I think the loss of the honour had been preying on his mind. He seemed nervous. His up-swing was shaky, and he swayed back perceptibly. He made a lunge at the ball, sliced it, and it struck a tree on the other side of the water and fell in the long grass. We crossed the bridge to look for it; and it was here that the effect of Professor Rollitt began definitely to wane.

"Why on earth don't they mow this darned stuff?" demanded Mitchell, querulously, as he beat about the grass with his niblick.

"You have to have rough on a course," I ventured.

"Whatever happens at all," said Millicent, "happens as it should. Thou wilt find this true if thou shouldst watch narrowly."

"That's all very well," said Mitchell, watching narrowly in a clump of weeds but seeming unconvinced. "I believe the Greens Committee run this bally club purely in the interests of the caddies. I believe they encourage lost balls, and go halves with the little beasts when they find them and sell them!"

Millicent and I exchanged glances. There were tears in her eyes.

"Oh, Mitchell! Remember Napoleon!"

"Napoleon! What's Napoleon got to do with it? Napoleon never was expected to drive through a primeval forest. Besides, what did Napoleon ever do? Where did Napoleon get off, swanking round as if he amounted to something? Poor fish! All he ever did was to get hammered at Waterloo!"

Alexander rejoined us. He had walked on to where his ball lay.

"Can't find it, eh? Nasty bit of rough, this!"

"No, I can't find it. But tomorrow some miserable, chinless, half-witted reptile of a caddie with pop eyes and eight hundred and thirty-seven pimples will find it, and will sell it to someone for sixpence! No, it was a brand-new ball. He'll probably get a shilling for it. That'll be sixpence for himself and sixpence for the Greens Committee. No wonder they're buying cars quicker than the makers can supply them. No wonder you see their wives going about in mink coats and pearl necklaces. Oh, dash it! I'll drop another!"

"In that case," Alexander pointed out, "you will, of course, under the rules governing match-play, lose the hole."

"All right, then. I'll give up the hole."

"Then that, I think, makes me one up on the first nine," said Alexander. "Excellent! A very pleasant, even game."

"Pleasant! On second thoughts I don't believe the Greens Committee let the wretched caddies get any of the loot. They hang round behind trees till the deal's concluded, and then sneak out and choke it out of them!"

I saw Alexander raise his eyebrows. He walked up the hill to the next tee with me.

"Rather a quick-tempered young fellow, Holmes!" he said, thoughtfully. "I should never have suspected it. It just shows how little one can know of a man, only meeting him in business hours."

I tried to defend the poor lad.

"He has an excellent heart, Alexander. But the fact is—we are such old friends that I know you will forgive my mentioning it—your style of play gets, I fancy, a little on his nerves."

"My style of play? What's wrong with my style of play?"

"Nothing is actually wrong with it, but to a young and ardent spirit there is apt to be something a trifle upsetting in being compelled to watch a man play quite so slowly as you do. Come now, Alexander, as one friend to another, is it necessary to take two practice-swings before you putt?"

"Dear, dear!" said Alexander. "You really mean to say that that upsets him? Well, I'm afraid I am too old to change my methods now."

I had nothing more to say.

As we reached the tenth tee, I saw that we were in for a few minutes' wait. Suddenly I felt a hand on my arm. Millicent was standing beside me, dejection written on her face. Alexander and young Mitchell were some distance away from us.

"Mitchell doesn't want me to come round the rest of the way with him," she said, despondently. "He says I make him nervous."

I shook my head.

"That's bad! I was looking on you as a steadying influence."

"I thought I was, too. But Mitchell says no. He says my being there keeps him from concentrating."

"Then perhaps it would be better for you to remain in the club-house till we return. There is, I fear, dirty work ahead."

A choking sob escaped the unhappy girl.

"I'm afraid so. There is an apple tree near the thirteenth hole, and Mitchell's caddie is sure to start eating apples. I am thinking of what Mitchell will do when he hears the crunching when he is addressing his ball."

"That is true."

"Our only hope," she said, holding out Professor Rollitt's book, "is this. Will you please read him extracts when you see him getting nervous? We went through the book last night and marked all the passages in blue pencil which might prove helpful. You will see notes against them in the margin, showing when each is supposed to be used."

It was a small favour to ask. I took the book and gripped her hand silently. Then I joined Alexander and Mitchell on the tenth tee. Mitchell was still continuing his speculations regarding the Greens Committee.

"The hole after this one," he said, "used to be a short hole. There was no chance of losing a ball. Then, one day, the wife of one of the Greens Committee happened to mention that the baby needed new shoes, so now they've tacked on another hundred and fifty yards to it. You have to drive over the brow of a hill, and if you slice an eighth of an inch you get into a sort of No Man's Land, full of rocks and bushes and crevices and old pots and pans. The Greens Committee practically live there in the summer. You see them prowling round in groups, encouraging each other with merry cries as they fill their sacks. Well, I'm going to fool them today. I'm going to drive an old ball which is just hanging together by a thread. It'll come to pieces when they pick it up!"

Golf, however, is a curious game—a game of fluctuations. One might have supposed that Mitchell, in such a frame of mind, would have continued to come to grief. But at the beginning of the second nine he once more found his form. A perfect drive put him in position to reach the tenth green with an iron-shot, and, though the ball was several yards from the hole, he laid it dead with his approach-putt and holed his second for a bogey four. Alexander could only achieve a five, so that they were all square again.

The eleventh, the subject of Mitchell's recent criticism, is certainly a tricky hole, and it is true that a slice does land the player in grave difficulties. Today, however, both men kept their drives straight, and found no difficulty in securing fours.

"A little more of this," said Mitchell, beaming, "and the Greens Committee will have to give up piracy and go back to work."

The twelfth is a long, dog-leg hole, bogey five. Alexander plugged steadily round the bend, holing out in six, and Mitchell, whose second shot had landed him in some long grass, was obliged to use his niblick. He contrived, however, to halve the hole with a nicely-judged mashie-shot to the edge of the green.

Alexander won the thirteenth. It is a three hundred and sixty yard hole, free from bunkers. It took Alexander three strokes to reach the green, but his third laid the ball dead; while Mitchell, who was on in two, required three putts.

"That reminds me," said Alexander, chattily, "of a story I heard. Friend calls out to a beginner, 'How are you getting on, old man?' and the beginner says, 'Splendidly. I just made three perfect putts on the last green!'"

Mitchell did not appear amused. I watch his face anxiously. He had made no remark, but the missed putt which would have saved the hole had been very short, and I feared the worst. There was a brooding look in his eye as we walked to the fourteenth tee.

There are few more picturesque spots in the whole of the countryside than the neighbourhood of the fourteenth tee. It is a sight to charm the nature-lover's heart.

But, if golf has a defect, it is that it prevents a man being a whole-hearted lover of nature. Where the layman sees waving grass and romantic tangles of undergrowth, your golfer beholds nothing but a nasty patch of rough from which he must divert his ball. The cry of the birds, wheeling against the sky, is to the golfer merely something that may put him off his putt. As a spectator, I am fond of the ravine at the bottom of the slope. It pleases the eye. But, as a golfer, I have frequently found it the very devil.

The last hole had given Alexander the honour again. He drove even more deliberately than before. For quite half a minute he stood over his ball, pawing at it with his driving-iron like a cat investigating a tortoise. Finally he despatched it to one of the few safe spots on the hillside. The drive from this tee has to be carefully calculated, for, if it be too straight, it will catch the slope and roll down into the ravine.

Mitchell addressed his ball. He swung up, and then, from immediately behind him came a sudden sharp crunching sound. I looked quickly in the direction whence it came. Mitchell's caddie, with a glassy look in his eyes, was gnawing a large apple. And even as I breathed a silent prayer, down came the driver, and the ball, with a terrible slice on it, hit the side of the hill and bounded into the ravine.

There was a pause—a pause in which the world stood still. Mitchell dropped his club and turned. His face was working horribly.

"Mitchell!" I cried. "My boy! Reflect! Be calm!"

"Calm! What's the use of being calm when people are chewing apples in thousands all round you? What *is* this, anyway—a golf match or a pleasant day's outing for the children of the poor? Apples! Go on, my boy, take another bite. Take several. Enjoy yourself! Never mind if it seems to cause me a fleeting annoyance. Go on with your lunch! You probably had a light breakfast, eh, and are feeling a little peckish, yes? If you wait here, I will run to the clubhouse and get you a sandwich and a bottle of ginger-ale. Make yourself at home, you lovable little fellow! Sit down and have a good time!"

I turned the pages of Professor Rollitt's book feverishly. I could not find a passage that had been marked in blue pencil to meet this emergency. I selected one at random.

"Mitchell," I said, "one moment. How much time he gains who does not look to see what his neighbour says or does, but only at what he does himself, to make it just and holy."

"Well, look what I've done myself! I'm somewhere down at the bottom of that dashed ravine, and it'll take me a dozen strokes to get out. Do you call that just and holy? Here, give me that book for a moment!"

He snatched the little volume out of my hands. For an instant he looked at it with a curious expression of loathing, then he placed it gently on the ground and jumped on it a few times. Then he hit it with his driver. Finally, as if feeling that the time for half measures had passed, he took a little run and kicked it strongly into the long grass.

He turned to Alexander, who had been an impassive spectator of the scene.

"I'm through!" he said. "I concede the match. Good-bye. You'll find me in the bay!"

"Going swimming?"

"No. Drowning myself."

A gentle smile broke out over my old friend's usually grave face. He patted Mitchell's shoulder affectionately.

"Don't do that, my boy," he said. "I was hoping you would stick around the office awhile as treasurer of the company."

Mitchell tottered. He grasped my arm for support. Everything was very still. Nothing broke the stillness but the humming of the bees, the murmur of the distant wavelets, and the sound of Mitchell's caddie going on with his apple.

"What!" cried Mitchell.

"The position," said Alexander, "will be falling vacant very shortly, as no doubt you know. It is yours, if you care to accept it."

"You mean—you mean—you're going to give me the job?"

"You have interpreted me exactly."

Mitchell gulped. So did his caddie. One from a spiritual, the other from a physical cause.

"If you don't mind excusing me," said Mitchell huskily, "I think I'll be popping back to the club-house. Someone I want to see."

He disappeared through the trees, running strongly. I turned to Alexander.

"What does this mean?" I asked. "I am delighted, but what becomes of the test?"

My old friend smiled gently.

"The test," he replied, "has been eminently satisfactory. Circumstances, perhaps, have compelled me to modify the original idea of it, but nevertheless it has been a completely successful test. Since we started out, I have been doing a good deal of thinking, and I have come to the conclusion that what the Paterson Dyeing and Refining Company really needs is a treasurer whom I can beat at golf. And I have discovered the ideal man. Why," he went on, a look of holy enthusiasm on his fine old face, "do you realize that I can always lick the stuffing out of that boy, good player as he is, simply by taking a little trouble? I can make him get the wind up every time, simply by taking one or two extra practice-swings! That is the sort of man I need for a responsible post in my office."

"But what about Rupert Dixon?" I asked.

He gave a gesture of distaste.

"I wouldn't trust that man. Why, when I played with him, everything went wrong, and he just smiled and didn't say a word. A man who can do that is not the man to trust with the control of large sums of money. It wouldn't be safe. Why, the fellow isn't honest! He can't be." He paused for a moment. "Besides," he added thoughtfully, "he beat me by six and five. What's the good of a treasurer who beats the boss by six and five?"

8

THE LONG HOLE

THE YOUNG MAN, as he sat filling his pipe in the club-house smoking-room, was inclined to be bitter.

"If there's one thing that gives me a pain squarely in the centre of the gizzard," he burst out, breaking a silence that had lasted for some minutes, "it's a golf-lawyer. They oughtn't to be allowed on the links."

The Oldest Member, who had been meditatively putting himself outside a cup of tea and a slice of seed-cake, raised his white eyebrows.

"The Law," he said, "is an honourable profession. Why should its practitioners be restrained from indulgence in the game of games?"

"I don't mean actual lawyers," said the young man, his acerbity mellowing a trifle under the influence of tobacco. "I mean the blighters whose best club is the book of rules. You know the sort of excrescences. Every time you think you've won a hole, they dig out Rule eight hundred and fifty-three, section two, sub-section four, to prove that you've disqualified yourself by having an ingrowing toe-nail. Well, take my case." The young man's voice was high and plaintive. "I go out with that man Hemmingway to play an ordinary friendly round—nothing depending on it except a measly ball—and on the seventh he pulls me up and claims the hole simply because I happened to drop my niblick in the bunker. Oh, well, a tick's a tick, and there's nothing more to say, I suppose."

The Sage shook his head.

"Rules are rules, my boy, and must be kept. It is odd that you should have brought up this subject, for only a moment before you came in I was thinking of a somewhat curious match which ultimately turned upon a question of the rule-book. It is true that, as far as the actual prize was concerned, it made little difference. But perhaps I had better tell you the whole story from the beginning."

The young man shifted uneasily in his chair.

"Well, you know, I've had a pretty rotten time this afternoon already——"

"I will call my story," said the Sage, tranquilly, " 'The Long Hole', for it involved the playing of what I am inclined to think must be the longest hole in the history of golf. In its beginnings the story may remind you of one I once told you about Peter Willard and James Todd, but you will find that it develops in quite a different manner. Ralph Bingham . . ."

"I half promised to go and see a man——"

"But I will begin at the beginning," said the Sage. "I see that you are all impatience to hear the full details."

Ralph Bingham and Arthur Jukes (said the Oldest Member) had never been friends—their rivalry was too keen to admit of that—but it was not till Amanda Trivett came to stay here that a smouldering distaste for each other burst out into the flames of actual enmity. It is ever so. One of the poets, whose name I cannot recall, has a passage, which I am unable at the moment to remember, in one of his works, which for the time being has slipped my mind, which hits off admirably this age-old situation. The gist of his remarks is that lovely woman rarely fails to start something. In the weeks that followed her arrival, being the the same room with the two men was like dropping in on a reunion of Capulets and Montagues.

You see, Ralph and Arthur were so exactly equal in their skill on the links that life for them had for some time past resolved itself into a silent, bitter struggle in which first one, then the other, gained some slight advantage. If Ralph won the May medal by a stroke, Arthur would be one ahead in the June competition, only to be nosed out again in July. It was a state of affairs which, had they been men of a more generous stamp, would have bred a mutual respect, esteem, and even love. But I am sorry to say that, apart from their golf, which was in a class of its own as far as this neighbourhood was concerned, Ralph Bingham and Arthur Jukes were a sorry pair—and yet, mark you, far from lacking in mere superficial good looks. They were handsome fellows, both of them, and well aware of the fact; and when Amanda Trivett came to stay they simply straightened their ties, twirled their moustaches, and expected her to do the rest.

But there they were disappointed. Perfectly friendly though she was to both of them, the lovelight was conspicuously absent from her beautiful eyes. And it was not long before each had come independently to a solution of this mystery. It was plain to them that the whole trouble lay in the fact that each neutralized the other's attractions. Arthur felt that, if he could only have a clear field, all would be over except the sending out of the wedding invitations; and Ralph was of the opinion that, if he could just call on the girl one evening without finding the place all littered up with Arthur, his natural charms would swiftly bring home the bacon. And, indeed, it was true that they had no rivals except themselves. It happened at the moment that Woodhaven was very short of eligible bachelors. We marry young in this delightful spot, and all the likely men were already paired off. It seemed that, if Amanda Trivett intended to get married, she would have to select either Ralph Bingham or Arthur Jukes. A dreadful choice.

It had not occurred to me at the outset that my position in the affair would be anything closer than that of a detached and mildly interested spectator. Yet it was to me that Ralph came in his hour of need. When I returned home one evening, I found that my man had brought him in and laid him on the mat in my sitting-room.

I offered him a chair and a cigar, and he came to the point with commendable rapidity.

"Leigh," he said, directly he had lighted his cigar, "is too small for Arthur Jukes and myself."

"Ah, you have been talking it over and decided to move?" I said, delighted. "I think you are perfectly right. Leigh *is* overbuilt. Men like you and Jukes need a lot of space. Where do you think of going?"

"I'm not going."

"But I thought you said——"

"What I meant was that the time has come when one of us must leave."

"Oh, only one of you?" It was something, of course, but I confess I was disappointed, and I think my disappointment must have shown in my voice; for he looked at me, surprised.

"Surely you wouldn't mind Jukes going?" he said.

"Why, certainly not. He really is going, is he?"

A look of saturnine determination came into Ralph's face.

"He is. He thinks he isn't, but he is."

I failed to understand him, and said so. He looked cautiously about the room, as if to reassure himself that he could not be overheard.

"I suppose you've noticed," he said, "the disgusting way that man Jukes has been hanging round Miss Trivett, boring her to death?"

"I have seen them together sometimes."

"I love Amanda Trivett!" said Ralph.

"Poor girl!" I sighed.

"I beg your pardon?"

"Poor girl!" I said. "I mean, to have Arthur Jukes hanging round her."

"That's just what I think," said Ralph Bingham. "And that's why we're going to play this match."

"What match?"

"This match we've decided to play. I want you to act as one of the judges, to go along with Jukes and see that he doesn't play any of his tricks. You know what he is! And in a vital match like this——"

"How much are you playing for?"

"The whole world!"

"I beg your pardon?"

"The whole world. It amounts to that. The loser is to leave Leigh for good, and the winner stays on and marries Amanda Trivett. We have arranged all the details. Rupert Bailey will accompany me, acting as the other judge."

"And you want me to go round with Jukes?"

"Not round," said Ralph Bingham. "Along."

"What is the distinction?"

"We are not going to play a round. Only one hole."

"Sudden death, eh?"

"Not so very sudden. It's a longish hole. We start on the first tee here and hole out in the town in the doorway of the Majestic Hotel in Royal Square. A distance, I imagine, of about sixteen miles."

I was revolted. About that time a perfect epidemic of freak matches had broken out in the club, and I had strongly opposed them from the start. George Willis had begun it by playing a medal round with the pro., George's first nine against the pro.'s complete eighteen. After that came the contest between Herbert Widgeon and Montague Brown, the latter, a twenty-four handicap man, being entitled to shout "Boo!" three times during the round at moments selected by himself. There had been many more of these degrading travesties on the sacred game, and I had writhed to see them. Playing freak golf-matches is to my mind like ragging a great classical melody. But of the whole collection this one, considering the sentimental interest and the magnitude of the stakes, seemed to me the most terrible. My face, I imagine, betrayed my disgust, for Bingham attempted extenuation.

"It's the only way," he said. "You know how Jukes and I are on the links. We are as level as two men can be. This, of course, is due to his extraordinary luck. Everybody knows that he is the world's champion fluker. I, on the other hand, invariably have the worst luck. The consequence is that in an ordinary round it is always a toss-up which of us wins. The test we propose will eliminate luck. After sixteen miles of give-and-take play, I am certain—that is to say, the better man is certain to be ahead. That is what I meant when I said that Arthur Jukes would shortly be leaving Leigh. Well, may I take it that you will consent to act as one of the judges?"

I considered. After all, the match was likely to be historic, and one always feels tempted to hand one's name down to posterity.

"Very well," I said.

"Excellent. You will have to keep a sharp eye on Jukes, I need scarcely remind you. You will, of course, carry a book of rules in your pocket and refer to them when you wish to refresh your memory. We start at daybreak, for, if we put it off till later, the course at the other end might be somewhat congested when we reach it. We want to avoid publicity as far as possible. If I took a full iron and hit a policeman, it would excite a remark."

"It would. I can tell you the exact remark which it would excite."

"We will take bicycles with us, to minimize the fatigue of covering the distance. Well, I am glad that we have your co-operation. At daybreak tomorrow on the first tee, and don't forget to bring your rule-book.

The atmosphere brooding over the first tee when I reached it on the following morning, somewhat resembled that of a duelling-ground in the days when these affairs were settled with rapiers or pistols. Rupert Bailey, an old friend of mine, was the only cheerful member of the party. I am never at my best in the early morning, and the two rivals glared at each other with silent sneers. I had never supposed till that moment that men ever really sneered at one another outside the movies, but these two were indisputably doing so. They were in the mood when men say "Pshaw!"

They tossed for the honour, and Arthur Jukes, having won, drove off with a fine ball that landed well down the course. Ralph Bingham, having teed up, turned to Rupert Bailey.

"Go down on to the fairway of the seventeenth," he said. "I want you to mark my ball."

Rupert stared.

"The seventeenth!"

"I am going to take that direction," said Ralph, pointing over the trees.

"But that will land your second or third shot in the lake."

"I have provided for that. I have a flat-bottomed boat moored close by the sixteenth green. I shall use a mashie-niblick and chip my ball aboard, row across to the other side, chip it ashore, and carry on. I propose to go across country as far as Woodfield. I think it will save me a stroke or two."

I gasped. I had never before realized the man's devilish cunning. His tactics gave him a flying start. Arthur, who had driven straight down the course, had as his objective the high road, which adjoins the waste ground beyond the first green. Once there, he would play the orthodox game by driving his ball along till he reached the bridge. While Arthur was winding along the high road, Ralph would have cut off practically two sides of a triangle. And it was hopeless for Arthur to imitate his enemy's tactics now. From where his ball lay he would have to cross a wide tract of marsh in order to reach the seventeenth fairway—an impossible feat. And, even if it had been feasible, he had no boat to take him across the water.

He uttered a violent protest. He was an unpleasant young man, almost—it seems absurd to say so, but almost as unpleasant as Ralph Bingham; yet at the moment I am bound to say I sympathized with him.

"What are you doing?" he demanded. "You can't play fast and loose with the rules like that."

"To what rule do you refer?" said Ralph, coldly.

"Well, that bally boat of yours is a hazard, isn't it? And you can't row a hazard about all over the place."

"Why not?"

The simple question seemed to take Arthur Jukes aback.

"Why not?" he repeated. "Why not? Well, you can't. That's why."

"There is nothing in the rules," said Ralph Bingham, "against moving a hazard. If a hazard can be moved without disturbing the ball, you are at liberty, I gather, to move it wherever you please. Besides, what is all this about moving hazards? I have a perfect right to go for a morning row, haven't I? If I were to ask my doctor, he would probably actually recommend it. I am going to row my boat across the sound.

If it happens to have my ball on board, that is not my affair. I shall not disturb my ball, and I shall play it from where it lies. Am I right in saying that the rules enact that the ball shall be played from where it lies?"

We admitted that it was.

"Very well, then," said Ralph Bingham. "Don't let us waste any more time. We will wait for you at Woodfield."

He addressed his ball, and drove a beauty over the trees. It flashed out of sight in the direction of the seventeenth tee. Arthur and I made our way down the hill to play our second.

It is a curious trait of the human mind that, however little personal interest one may have in the result, it is impossible to prevent oneself taking sides in any event of a competitive nature. I had embarked on this affair in a purely neutral spirit, not caring which of the two won and only sorry that both could not lose. Yet, as the morning wore on, I found myself almost unconsciously becoming distinctly pro-Jukes. I did not like the man. I objected to his face, his manners, and the colour of his tie. Yet there was something in the dogged way in which he struggled against adversity which touched me and won my grudging support. Many men, I felt, having been so outmanœuvred at the start, would have given up the contest in despair; but Arthur Jukes, for all his defects, had the soul of a true golfer. He declined to give up. In grim silence he hacked his ball through the rough till he reached the high road; and then, having played twenty-seven, set himself resolutely to propel it on its long journey.

It was a lovely morning, and, as I bicycled along, keeping a fatherly eye on Arthur's activities, I realized for the first time in my life the full meaning of that exquisite phrase of Coleridge:

> " *Clothing the palpable and familiar*
> *With golden exhalations of the dawn,*"

for in the pellucid air everything seemed weirdly beautiful, even Arthur Juke's heather-mixture knickerbockers, of which hitherto I had never approved. The sun gleamed on their seat, as he bent to make his shots, in a cheerful and almost a poetic way. The birds were singing gaily in the hedgerows, and such was my uplifted state that I, too, burst into song, until Arthur petulantly desired me to refrain, on the plea that, though he yielded to no man in his enjoyment of farmyard imitations in their proper place, I put him off his stroke. And so we passed through Bayside in silence and started to cover that long stretch of road which ends in the railway bridge and the gentle descent into Woodfield.

Arthur was not doing badly. He was at least keeping them straight. And in the circumstances straightness was to be preferred to distance. Soon after leaving Little Hadley he had become ambitious and had used his brassey with disastrous results, slicing his fifty-third into the rough on the right of the road. It had taken him ten with the niblick to get back on to the car tracks, and this had taught him prudence.

He was now using his putter for every shot, and, except when he got trapped in the cross-lines at the top of the hill just before reaching Bayside, he had been in no serious difficulties. He was playing a nice easy game, getting the full face of the putter on to each shot.

At the top of the slope that drops down into Woodfield High Street he paused.

"I think I might try my brassie again here," he said. "I have a nice lie."

"Is it wise?" I said.

He looked down the hill.

"What I was thinking," he said, "was that with it I might wing that man Bingham. I see he is standing right out in the middle of the fairway."

I followed his gaze. It was perfectly true. Ralph Bingham was leaning on his bicycle in the roadway, smoking a cigarette. Even at this distance one could detect the man's disgustingly complacent expression. Rupert Bailey was sitting with his back against the door of the Woodfield Garage, looking rather used up. He was a man who liked to keep himself clean and tidy, and it was plain that the cross-country trip had done him no good. He seemed to be scraping mud off his face. I learned later that he had had the misfortune to fall into a ditch just beyond Bayside.

"No," said Arthur. "On second thoughts, the safe game is the one to play. I'll stick to the putter."

We dropped down the hill, and presently came up with the opposition. I had not been mistaken in thinking that Ralph Bingham looked complacent. The man was smirking.

"Playing three hundred and ninety-six," he said, as we drew near. "How are you?"

I consulted my score-card.

"We have played a snappy seven hundred and eleven," I said.

Ralph exulted openly. Rupert Bailey made no comment. He was too busy with the alluvial deposits on his person.

"Perhaps you would like to give up the match?" said Ralph to Arthur.

"Tchah!" said Arthur.

"Might just as well."

"Pah!" said Arthur.

"You can't win now."

"Pshaw!" said Arthur.

I am aware that Arthur's dialogue might have been brighter, but he had been through a trying time.

Rupert Bailey sidled up to me.

"I'm going home," he said.

"Nonsense!" I replied. "You are in an official capacity. You must stick to your post. Besides, what could be nicer than a pleasant morning ramble?"

"Pleasant morning ramble my number nine foot!" he replied, peevishly. "I want to get back to civilization and set an excavating party with pickaxes to work on me."

"You take too gloomy a view of the matter. You are a little dusty. Nothing more."

"And it's not only the being buried alive that I mind. I cannot stick Ralph Bingham much longer."

"You have found him trying?"

"Trying! Why, after I had fallen into that ditch and was coming up for the third time, all the man did was simply to call to me to admire an infernal iron shot he had just made. No sympathy, mind you! Wrapped up in himself. Why don't you make your man give up the match? He can't win.

"I refuse to admit it. Much may happen between here and Royal Square."

I have seldom known a prophecy more swiftly fulfilled. At this moment the doors of the Woodfield Garage opened and a small car rolled out with a grimy young man in a sweater at the wheel. He brought the machine out into the road, and alighted and went back into the garage, where we heard him shouting unintelligibly to someone in the rear premises. The car remained puffing and panting against the kerb.

Engaged in conversation with Rupert Bailey, I was paying little attention to this evidence of an awakening world, when suddenly I heard a hoarse, triumphant cry from Arthur Jukes, and, turned, I perceived his ball dropping neatly into the car's interior. Arthur himself, brandishing a niblick, was dancing about in the fairway.

"Now what about your moving hazards?" he cried.

At this moment the man in the sweater returned, carrying a spanner. Arthur Jukes sprang towards him.

"I'll give you five pounds to drive me to Royal Square," he said.

I do not know what the sweater-clad young man's engagements for the morning had been originally, but nothing could have been more obliging than the ready way in which he consented to revise them at a moment's notice. I dare say you have noticed that the sturdy peasantry of our beloved land respond to an offer of five pounds as to a bugle-call.

"You're on," said the youth.

"Good!" said Arthur Jukes.

"You think you're darned clever," said Ralph Bingham.

"I know it," said Arthur.

"Well, then," said Ralph, "perhaps you will tell us how you propose to get the ball out of the car when you reach Royal Square?"

"Certainly," replied Arthur. "You will observe on the side of the vehicle a convenient handle which, when turned, opens the door. The door thus opened, I shall chip my ball out!"

"I see," said Ralph. "Yes, I never thought of that."

There was something in the way the man spoke that I did not like. His mildness seemed to me suspicious. He had the air of a man who has something up his sleeve. I was still musing on this when Arthur called to me impatiently to get in. I did so, and we drove off. Arthur was in great spirits. He had ascertained from the young man at the wheel that there was no chance of the opposition being able to hire another car at the garage. This machine was his own property, and the only other one at present in the shop was suffering from complicated trouble of the oiling-system and would not be able to be moved for at least another day.

I, however, shook my head when he pointed out the advantages of his position. I was still wondering about Ralph.

"I don't like it," I said.

"Don't like what?"

"Ralph Bingham's manner."

"Of course not," said Arthur. "Nobody does. There have been complaints on all sides."

"I mean, when you told him how you intended to get the ball out of the car."

"What was the matter with him?"

"He was too—ha!"

"How do you mean he was too—ha?"

"I have it!"

"What?"

"I see the trap he was laying for you. It has just dawned on me. No wonder he didn't object to your opening the door and chipping the ball out. By doing so you would forfeit the match."

"Nonsense! Why?"

"Because," I said, "it is against the rules to tamper with a hazard. If you had got into a sand-bunker, would you smooth away the sand? If you had put your shot under a tree, could your caddie hold up the branches to give you a clear shot? Obviously you would disqualify yourself if you touched that door."

Arthur's jaw dropped.

"What! Then how the deuce am I to get it out?"

"That," I said, gravely, "is a question between you and your Maker."

It was here that Arthur Jukes forfeited the sympathy which I had begun to feel for him. A crafty, sinister look came into his eyes.

"Listen!" he said. "It'll take them an hour to catch up with us. Suppose, during that time, that door happened to open accidentally, as it were, and close again? You wouldn't think it necessary to mention the fact, eh? You would be a good fellow and keep your mouth shut, yes? You might even see your way to go so far as to back me up in a statement to the effect that I hooked it out with my——?"

I was revolted.

"I am a golfer," I said, coldly, "and I obey the rules."

"Yes, but——"

"Those rules were drawn up by——"—I bared by head reverently—"by the Committee of the Royal and Ancient at St. Andrews. I have always respected them, and I shall not deviate on this occasion from the policy of a lifetime."

Arthur Jukes relapsed into a moody silence. He broke it once, crossing the West

Street Bridge, to observe that he would like to know if I called myself a friend of his —a question which I was able to answer with a whole-hearted negative. After that he did not speak till the car drew up in front of the Majestic Hotel in Royal Square.

Early as the hour was, a certain bustle and animation already prevailed in that centre of the city, and the spectacle of a man in a golf-coat and plus-four knicker-bockers hacking with a niblick at the floor of a car was not long in collecting a crowd of some dimensions. Three messenger-boys, four typists, and a gentleman in full evening-dress, who obviously possessed or was friendly with someone who possessed a large cellar, formed the nucleus of it; and they were joined about the time when Arthur addressed the ball in order to play his nine hundred and fifteenth by six news-boys, eleven charladies, and perhaps a dozen assorted loafers, all speculating with the liveliest interest as to which particular asylum had had the honour of sheltering Arthur before he had contrived to elude the vigilance of his custodians.

Arthur had prepared for some such contingency. He suspended his activities with the niblick, and drew from his pocket a large poster, which he proceeded to hang over the side of the car. It read:

COME
TO
McCLURG AND MACDONALD,
18, WEST STREET,
FOR
ALL GOLFING SUPPLIES.

His knowledge of psychology had not misled him. Directly they gathered that he was advertising something, the crowd declined to look at it; they melted away, and Arthur returned to his work in solitude.

He was taking a well-earned rest after playing his eleven hundred and fifth, a nice niblick shot with lots of wrist behind it, when out of Bridle Street there trickled a weary-looking golf-ball, followed in the order named by Ralph Bingham, resolute but going a trifle at the knees, and Rupert Bailey on a bicycle. The latter, on whose face and limbs the mud had dried, made an arresting spectacle.

"What are you playing?" I inquired.

"Eleven hundred," said Rupert. "We got into a casual dog."

"A casual dog?"

"Yes, just before the bridge. We were coming along nicely, when a stray dog grabbed our nine hundred and ninety-eighth and took it nearly back to Woodfield, and we had to start all over again. How are you getting on?"

"We have just played our eleven hundred and fifth. A nice even game." I looked at Ralph's ball, which was lying close to the kerb. "You are farther from the hole, I think. Your shot, Bingham."

Rupert Bailey suggested breakfast. He was a man who was altogether too fond of creature comforts. He had not the true golfing spirit.

"Breakfast!" I exclaimed.

"Breakfast," said Rupert, firmly. "If you don't know what it is, I can teach you in half a minute. You play it with a pot of coffee, a knife and fork, and about a hundred-weight of scrambled eggs. Try it. It's a pastime that grows on you."

I was surprised when Ralph Bingham supported the suggestion. He was so near holing out that I should have supposed that nothing would have kept him from finishing the match. But he agreed heartily.

"Breakfast," he said, "is an excellent idea. You go along in. I'll follow in a moment. I want to buy a paper."

We went into the hotel, and a few minutes later he joined us. Now that we were actually at the table, I confess that the idea of breakfast was by no means repugnant to me. The keen air and the exercise had given me an appetite, and it was some little time before I was able to assure the waiter definitely that he could cease bringing orders of scrambled eggs. The others having finished also, I suggested a move. I was anxious to get the match over and be free to go home.

We filed out of the hotel, Arthur Jukes leading. When I had passed through the swing-doors, I found him gazing perplexedly up and down the street.

"What is the matter?" I asked.

"It's gone!"

"What has gone?"

"The car!"

"Oh, the car?" said Ralph Bingham. "That's all right. Didn't I tell you about that? I bought it just now and engaged the driver as my chauffeur. I've been meaning to buy a car for a long time. A man ought to have a car."

"Where is it?" said Arthur, blankly. The man seemed dazed.

"I couldn't tell you to a mile or two," replied Ralph. "I told the man to drive to Glasgow. Why? Had you any message for him?"

"But my ball was inside it!"

"Now that," said Ralph, "is really unfortunate! Do you mean to tell me you hadn't managed to get it out yet? Yes, that *is* a little awkward for you. I'm afraid it means that you lose the match."

"Lose the match?"

"Certainly. The rules are perfectly definite on that point. A period of five minutes is allowed for each stroke. The player who fails to make his stroke within that time loses the hole. Unfortunate, but there it is!"

Arthur Jukes sank down on the path and buried his face in his hands. He had the appearance of a broken man. Once more, I am bound to say, I felt a certain pity for him. He had certainly struggled gamely, and it was hard to be beaten like this on the post.

"Playing eleven hundred and one," said Ralph Bingham, in his odiously self-satisfied voice, he as addressed his ball. He laughed jovially. A messenger-boy had paused close by and was watching the proceedings gravely. Ralph Bingham patted him on the head.

"Well, sonny," he said, "what club would you use here?"

"I claim the match!" cried Arthur Jukes, springing up. Ralph Bingham regarded him coldly.

"I beg your pardon!"

"I claim the match!" repeated Arthur Jukes. "The rules say that a player who asks advice from any person other than his caddie shall lose the hole."

"This is absurd!" said Ralph, but I noticed that he had turned pale.

"I appeal to the judges."

"We sustain the appeal," I said, after a brief consultation with Rupert Bailey. "The rule is perfectly clear."

"But you had lost the match already by not playing within five minutes," said Ralph, vehemently.

"It was not my turn to play. You were farther from the pin."

"Well, play now. Go on! Let's see you make your shot."

"There is no necessity," said Arthur, frigidly. "Why should I play when you have already disqualified yourself?"

"I claim a draw!"

"I deny the claim."

"I appeal to the judges."

"Very well. We will leave it to the judges."

I consulted with Rupert Bailey. It seemed to me that Arthur Jukes was entitled to the verdict. Rupert, who, though an amiable and delightful companion, had always been one of Nature's fat-heads, could not see it. We had to go back to our principals and announce that we had been unable to agree.

"This is ridiculous," said Ralph Bingham. "We ought to have had a third judge."

At this moment, who should come out of the hotel but Amanda Trivett! A veritable goddess from the machine.

"It seems to me," I said, "that you would both be well advised to leave the decision to Miss Trivett. You could have no better referee."

"I'm game," said Arthur Jukes.

"Suits *me*," said Ralph Bingham.

"Why, whatever are you all doing here with your golf-clubs?" asked the girl, wonderingly.

"These two gentlemen," I explained, "have been playing a match, and a point has arisen on which the judges do not find themselves in agreement. We need an unbiased outside opinion, and we should like to put it up to you. The facts are as follows."

Amanda Trivett listened attentively, but, when I had finished, she shook her head.

"I'm afraid I don't know enough about the game to be able to decide a question like that," she said.

"Then we must consult St. Andrews," said Rupert Bailey.

"I'll tell you who might know," said Amanda Trivett, after a moment's thought.

"Who is that?" I asked.

"My *fiancé*. He has just come back from a golfing holiday. That's why I'm in town this morning. I've been to meet him. He is very good at golf. He won a medal at Little-Mudbury-in-the-Wold the day before he left."

There was a tense silence. I had the delicacy not to look at Ralph or Arthur. Then the silence was broken by a sharp crack. Ralph Bingham had broken his mashie-niblick across his knee. From the direction where Arthur Jukes was standing there came a muffled gulp.

"Shall I ask him?" said Amanda Trivett.

"Don't bother," said Ralph Bingham.

"It doesn't matter," said Arthur Jukes.

9

THE HEEL OF ACHILLES

ON the young man's face, as he sat sipping his ginger-ale in the club-house smoking-room, there was a look of disillusionment. "Never again!" he said.

The Oldest Member glanced up from his paper.

"You are proposing to give up golf once more?" he queried.

"Not golf. Betting on golf." The Young Man frowned. "I've just been let down badly. Wouldn't you have thought I had a good thing, laying seven to one on McTavish against Robinson?"

"Undoubtedly," said the Sage. "The odds, indeed, generous as they are, scarcely indicate the former's superiority. Do you mean to tell me that the thing came unstitched?"

"Robinson won in a walk, after being three down at the turn."

"Strange! What happened?"

"Why, they looked in at the bar to have a refresher before starting for the tenth," said the young man, his voice quivering, "and McTavish suddenly discovered that there was a hole in his trouser-pocket and sixpence had dropped out. He worried so frightfully about it that on the second nine he couldn't do a thing right. Went completely off his game and didn't win a hole."

The Sage shook his head gravely.

"If this is really going to be a lesson to you, my boy, never to bet on the result of a golf-match, it will be a blessing in disguise. There is no such thing as a certainty in golf. I wonder if I ever told you a rather curious episode in the career of Vincent Jopp?"

"*The* Vincent Jopp? The American multi-millionaire?"

"The same. You never knew he once came within an ace of winning the American Amateur Championship, did you?"

"I never heard of his playing golf."

"He played for one season. After that he gave it up and has not touched a club since. Ring the bell and get me a small lime-juice, and I will tell you all."

It was long before your time (said the Oldest Member) that the events which I am about to relate took place. I had just come down from Cambridge, and was feeling particularly pleased with myself because I had secured the job of private and confidential secretary to Vincent Jopp, then a man in the early thirties, busy in laying the foundations of his present remarkable fortune. He engaged me, and took me with him to Chicago.

Jopp was, I think, the most extraordinary personality I have encountered in a long and many-sided life. He was admirably equipped for success in finance, having the steely eye and square jaw without which it is hopeless for a man to enter that line of business. He possessed also an overwhelming confidence in himself, and the ability to switch a cigar from one corner of his mouth to the other without wiggling his ears, which, as you know, is the stamp of the true Monarch of the Money Market. He was the nearest approach to the financier on the films, the fellow who makes his jaw-muscles jump when he is telephoning, that I have ever seen.

Like all successful men, he was a man of method. He kept a pad on his desk on which he would scribble down his appointments, and it was my duty on entering the office each morning to take this pad and type its contents neatly in a loose-leaved ledger. Usually, of course, these entries referred to business appointments and deals which he was contemplating, but one day I was interested to note, against the date May 3rd, the entry:

> " *Propose to Amelia.*"

I was interested, as I say, but not surprised. Though a man of steel and iron, there was nothing of the celibate about Vincent Jopp. He was one of those men who marry early and often. On three separate occasions before I joined his service he had jumped off the dock, to scramble back to shore again later by means of the Divorce Court lifebelt. Scattered here and there about the country there were three ex-Mrs. Jopps, drawing their monthly envelope, and now, it seemed, he contemplated the addition of a fourth to the platoon.

I was not surprised, I say, at this resolve of his. What did seem a little remarkable to me was the thorough way in which he had thought the thing out. This iron-willed man recked nothing of possible obstacles. Under the date of June 1st was the entry:

> " *Marry Amelia* ";

while in March of the following year he had arranged to have his first-born christened Thomas Reginald. Later on, the short-coating of Thomas Reginald was arranged for, and there was a note about sending him to school. Many hard things have been said of Vincent Jopp, but nobody has ever accused him of not being a man who looked ahead.

On the morning of May 4th Jopp came into the office, looking, I fancied, a little thoughtful. He sat for some moments staring before him with his brow a trifle furrowed; then he seemed to come to himself. He rapped his desk.

"Hi! You!" he said. "It was thus that he habitually addressed me.

"Mr. Jopp?" I replied.

"What's golf?"

I had at that time just succeeded in getting my handicap down into single figures, and I welcomed the opportunity of dilating on the noblest of pastimes. But I had barely begun my eulogy when he stopped me.

"It's a game, is it?"

"I suppose you could call it that," I said, "but it is an off-hand way of describing the holiest——"

"How do you play it?"

"Pretty well," I said. "At the beginning of the season I didn't seem able to keep 'em straight at all, but lately I've been doing fine. Getting better every day. Whether it was that I was moving my head or gripping too tightly with the right hand——"

"Keep the reminiscences for your grandchildren during the long winter evenings," he interrupted, abruptly, as was his habit. "What I want to know is what a fellow does when he plays golf. Tell me in as few words as you can just what it's all about."

"You hit a ball with a stick till it falls into a hole."

"Easy!" he snapped. "Take dictation."

I produced my pad.

"May the fifth, take up golf. What's an Amateur Championship?"

"It is the annual competition to decide which is the best player among the amateurs. There is also a Professional Championship, and an Open Event."

"Oh, there are golf professionals, are there? What do they do?"

"They teach golf."

"Which is the best of them?"

"Sandy McHoots won both British and American Open events last year."

"Wire him to come here at once."

"But McHoots is in Inverlochty, in Scotland."

"Never mind. Get him; tell him to name his own terms. When is the Amateur Championship?"

"I think it is on September the twelfth this year."

"All right, take dictation. September twelfth win Amateur Championship."

I stared at him in amazement, but he was not looking at me.

"Got that?" he said. "September thir—— Oh, I was forgetting! Add September twelfth, corner wheat. September thirteenth, marry Amelia."

"Marry Amelia," I echoed, moistening my pencil.

"Where do you play this—what's-its-name—golf?"

"There are clubs all over the country. I belong to the Wissahicky Glen."

"That a good place?"

"Very good."

"Arrange today for my becoming a member."

Sandy McHoots arrived in due course, and was shown into the private office.

"Mr. McHoots?" said Vincent Jopp.

"Mphm!" said the Open Champion.

"I have sent for you, Mr. McHoots, because I hear that you are the greatest living exponent of this game of golf."

"Aye," said the champion, cordially. "I am that."

"I wish you to teach me the game. I am already somewhat behind schedule owing to the delay incident upon your long journey, so let us start at once. Name a few of the most important points in connection with the game. My secretary will make notes of them, and I will memorize them. In this way we shall save time. Now, what is the most important thing to remember when playing golf?"

"Keep your heid still."

"A simple task."

"Na sae simple as it soonds."

"Nonsense!" said Vincent Jopp, curtly. "If I decide to keep my head still, I shall keep it still. What next?"

"Keep yer ee on the ba'."

"It shall be attended to. And the next?"

"Dinna press."

"I won't. And to resume."

Mr. McHoots ran through a dozen of the basic rules, and I took them down in shorthand. Vincent Jopp studied the list.

"Very good. Easier than I had supposed. On the first tee at Wissahicky Glen at eleven sharp tomorrow, Mr. McHoots. Hi! You!"

"Sir?" I said.

"Go out and buy me a set of clubs, a red jacket, a cloth cap, a pair of spiked shoes, and a ball."

"One ball?"

"Certainly. What need is there of more?"

"It sometimes happens," I explained, "that a player who is learning the game fails to hit his ball straight, and then he often loses it in the rough at the side of the fairway."

"Absurd!" said Vincent Jopp. "If I set out to drive my ball straight, I shall drive it straight. Good morning, Mr. McHoots. You will excuse me now. I am busy cornering Woven Textiles."

Golf is in its essence a simple game. You laugh in a sharp, bitter, barking manner when I say this, but nevertheless it is true. Where the average man goes wrong is in making the game difficult for himself. Observe the non-player, the man who walks round with you for the sake of the fresh air. He will hole out with a single care-free flick of his umbrella the twenty-foot putt over which you would ponder and hesitate for a full minute before sending it right off the line. Put a driver in his hands and he pastes the ball into the next county without a thought. It is only when he takes to the game in earnest that he becomes self-conscious and anxious, and tops his shots even as you and I. A man who could retain through his golfing career the almost scornful confidence of the non-player would be unbeatable. Fortunately such an attitude of mind is beyond the scope of human nature.

It was not, however, beyond the scope of Vincent Jopp, the superman. Vincent Jopp, was, I am inclined to think, the only golfer who ever approached the game in a spirit of Pure Reason. I have read of men who, never having swum in their lives, studied a text-book on their way down to the swimming bath, mastered its contents, and dived in and won the big race. In just such a spirit did Vincent Jopp start to play golf. He committed McHoots's hints to memory, and then went out on the links and put them into practice. He came to the tee with a clear picture in his mind of what he had to do, and he did it. He was not intimidated, like the average novice, by the thought that if he pulled in his hands he would slice, or if he gripped too tightly with the right he would pull. Pulling in the hands was an error, so he did not pull in his hands. Gripping too tightly was a defect, so he did not grip too tightly. With that weird concentration which had served him so well in business he did precisely what he had set out to do—no less and no more. Golf with Vincent Jopp was an exact science.

The annals of the game are studded with the names of those who have made rapid progress in their first season. Colonel Quill, we read in our Vardon, took up golf at the age of fifty-six, and by devising an ingenious machine consisting of a fishing-line and a sawn-down bedpost was enabled to keep his head so still that he became a scratch player before the end of the year. But no one, I imagine, except Vincent Jopp, has ever achieved scratch on his first morning on the links.

The main difference, we are told, between the amateur and the professional golfer is the fact that the latter is always aiming at the pin, while the former has in his mind a vague picture of getting somewhere reasonably near it. Vincent Jopp invariably went for the pin. He tried to hole out from anywhere inside two hundred and twenty yards. The only occasion on which I ever heard him express any chagrin or disappointment was during the afternoon round on his first day out, when from the tee on the two hundred and eighty yard seventh he laid his ball within six inches of the hole.

"A marvellous shot!" I cried, genuinely stirred.

"Too much to the right," said Vincent Jopp, frowning.

He went on from triumph to triumph. He won the monthly medal in May, June, July, August, and September. Towards the end of May he was heard to complain that Wissahicky Glen was not a sporting course. The Greens Committee sat up night after night trying to adjust his handicap so as to give other members an outside chance against him. The golf experts of the daily papers wrote columns about his play. And it was pretty generally considered throughout the country that it would be a pure formality for anyone else to enter against him in the Amateur Championship—an opinion which was borne out when he got into the final without losing a hole. A safe man to have betted on, you would have said. But mark the sequel.

The American Amateur Championship was held that year in Detroit. I had accompanied my employer there; for, though engaged on this nerve-wearing contest, he refused to allow his business to be interfered with. As he had indicated in his schedule, he was busy at the time cornering wheat; and it was my task to combine the duties of caddie and secretary. Each day I accompanied him round the links with my note-book and his bag of clubs, and the progress of his various matches was somewhat complicated by the arrival of a stream of telegraph-boys bearing important messages. He would read these between the strokes and dictate replies to me, never, however, taking more than the five minutes allowed by the rules for an interval between strokes. I am inclined to think that it was this that put the finishing touch on his opponents' discomfiture. It is not soothing for a nervous man to have the game hung up on the green while his adversary dictates to his caddie a letter beginning "Yours of the 11th inst. received and contents noted. In reply would state——"

This sort of thing puts a man off his game.

I was resting in the lobby of our hotel after a strenuous day's work, when I found that I was being paged. I answered the summons, and was informed that a lady wished to see me. Her card bore the name "Miss Amelia Merridew." Amelia! The name seemed familiar. Then I remembered. Amelia was the name of the girl Vincent Jopp intended to marry, the fourth of the long line of Mrs. Jopps. I hurried to present myself, and found a tall, slim girl, who was plainly labouring under a considerable agitation.

"Miss Merridew?" I said.

"Yes," she murmured. "My name will be strange to you."

"Am I right," I queried, "in supposing that you are the lady to whom Mr. Jopp——"

"I am! I am!" she replied. "And, oh, what shall I do?"

"Kindly give me particulars," I said, taking out my pad from force of habit.

She hesitated a moment, as if afraid to speak.

"You are caddying for Mr. Jopp in the Final tomorrow?" she said at last.

"I am."

"Then could you—would you mind—would it be giving you too much trouble if I asked you to shout 'Boo!' at him when he is making his stroke, if he looks like winning?"

I was perplexed.

"I don't understand."

"I see that I must tell you all. I am sure you will treat what I say as absolutely confidential."

"Certainly."

"I am provisionally engaged to Mr. Jopp."

"Provisionally?"

She gulped.

"Let me tell you my story. Mr. Jopp asked me to marry him, and I would rather do anything on earth than marry him. But how could I say 'No!' with those awful eyes of his boring me through? I knew that if I said 'No', he would argue me out of it in two minutes. I had an idea. I gathered that he had never played golf, so I told him that I would marry him if he won the Amateur Championship this year. And now I find that he has been a golfer all along, and, what is more, a plus man! It isn't fair!"

"He was not a golfer when you made that condition," I said. "He took up the game on the following day."

"Impossible! How could he have become as good as he is in this short time?"

"Because he is Vincent Jopp! In his lexicon there is no such word as impossible." She shuddered.

"What a man! But I can't marry him," she cried. "I want to marry somebody else. Oh, won't you help me? Do shout 'Boo!' at him when he is starting his down-swing!"

I shook my head.

"It would take more than a single 'boo' to put Vincent Jopp off his stroke."

"But won't you try it?"

"I cannot. My duty is to my employer."

"Oh, do!"

"No, no. Duty is duty, and paramount with me. Besides, I have a bet on him to win."

The stricken girl uttered a faint moan, and tottered away.

I was in our suite shortly after dinner that night, going over some of the notes I had made that day, when the telephone rang. Jopp was out at the time, taking a short stroll with his after-dinner cigar. I unhooked the receiver, and a female voice spoke.

"Is that Mr. Jopp?"

"Mr. Jopp's secretary speaking. Mr. Jopp is out."

"Oh, it's nothing important. Will you say that Mrs. Luella Mainprice Jopp called up to wish him luck? I shall be on the course tomorrow to see him win the Final."

I returned to my notes. Soon afterwards the telephone rang again.

"Vincent, dear?"

"Mr. Jopp's secretary speaking."

"Oh, will you say that Mrs. Jane Jukes Jopp called up to wish him luck? I shall be there tomorrow to see him play."

I resumed my work. I had hardly started when the telephone rang for the third time.

"Mr. Jopp?"

"Mr. Jopp's secretary speaking."

"This is Mrs. Agnes Parsons Jopp. I just called up to wish him luck. I shall be looking on tomorrow."

I shifted my work nearer to the telephone-table so as to be ready for the next call. I had heard that Vincent Jopp had only been married three times, but you never knew.

Presently Jopp came in.

"Anybody called up?" he asked.

"Nobody on business. An assortment of your wives were on the wire wishing you luck. They asked me to say that they will be on the course tomorrow."

For a moment it seemed to me that the man's iron repose was shaken.

"Luella?" he asked.

"She was the first."

"Jane?"

"And Jane."

"And Agnes?"

"Agnes," I said, "is right."

"H'm!" said Vincent Jopp. And for the first time since I had known him I thought that he was ill at ease.

The day of the Final dawned bright and clear. At least, I was not awake at the time to see, but I suppose it did; for at nine o'clock, when I came down to breakfast, the sun was shining brightly. The first eighteen holes were to be played before lunch, starting at eleven. Until twenty minutes before the hour Vincent Jopp kept me busy taking dictation, partly on matters connected with his wheat deal and partly on a signed article dealing with the Final, entitled "How I Won." At eleven sharp we were out on the first tee.

Jopp's opponent was a nice-looking young man, but obviously nervous. He giggled in a distraught sort of way as he shook hands with my employer.

"Well, may the best man win," he said.

"I have arranged to do so," replied Jopp, curtly, and started to address his ball.

There was a large crowd at the tee, and, as Jopp started his down-swing, from somewhere on the outskirts of this crowd there came suddenly a musical "Boo!" It rang out in the clear morning air like a bugle.

I had been right in my estimate of Vincent Jopp. His forceful stroke never wavered. The head of his club struck the ball, despatching it a good two hundred yards down the middle of the fairway. As we left the tee I saw Amelia Merridew being led away with bowed head by two members of the Greens Committee. Poor girl! My heart bled for her. And yet, after all, Fate had been kind in removing her from the scene, even in custody, for she could hardly have borne to watch the proceedings. Vincent Jopp made rings round his antagonist. Hole after hole he won in his remorseless, machine-like way, until when lunch-time came at the end of the eighteenth he was ten up. All the other holes had been halved.

It was after lunch, as we made our way to the first tee, that the advance-guard of the Mrs. Jopps appeared in the person of Luella Mainprice Jopp, a kittenish little woman with blond hair and a Pekingese dog. I remember reading in the papers that she had divorced my employer for persistent and aggravated mental cruelty, calling witnesses to bear out her statement that he had said he did not like her in pink, and that on two separate occasions had insisted on her dog eating the leg of a chicken instead of the breast; but Time, the great healer, seemed to have removed all bitterness, and she greeted him affectionately.

"Wassums going to win great big championship against nasty rough strong man?" she said.

"Such," said Vincent Jopp, "is my intention. It was kind of you, Luella, to trouble to come and watch me. I wonder if you know Mrs. Agnes Parsons Jopp?" he said, courteously, indicating a kind-looking, motherly woman who had just come up. "How are you, Agnes?"

"If you had asked me that question this morning, Vincent," replied Mrs. Agnes Parsons Jopp, "I should have been obliged to say that I felt far from well. I had an odd throbbing feeling in the left elbow, and I am sure my temperature was above the normal. But this afternoon I am a little better. How are you, Vincent?"

Although she had, as I recalled from the reports of the case, been compelled some years earlier to request the Court to sever her marital relations with Vincent Jopp on the ground of calculated and inhuman brutality, in that he had callously refused, in spite of her pleadings, to take old Dr. Bennett's Tonic Swamp-Juice three times a day, her voice, as she spoke, was kind and even anxious. Badly as this man had treated her—and I remember hearing that several of the jury had been unable to restrain their tears when she was in the witness-box giving her evidence—there still seemed to linger some remnants of the old affection.

"I am quite well, thank you, Agnes," said Vincent Jopp.

"Are you wearing your liver-pad?"

A frown flitted across my employer's strong face.

"I am not wearing my liver-pad," he replied, brusquely.

"Oh, Vincent, how rash of you!"

He was about to speak, when a sudden exclamation from his rear checked him. A genial-looking woman in a sports coat was standing there, eyeing him with a sort of humorous horror.

"Well, Jane," he said.

I gathered that this was Mrs. Jane Jukes Jopp, the wife who had divorced him for systematic and ingrowing fiendishness on the ground that he had repeatedly outraged her feelings by wearing a white waistcoat with a dinner-jacket. She continued to look at him dumbly, and then uttered a sort of strangled, hysterical laugh.

"Those legs!" she cried. "Those legs!"

Vincent Jopp flushed darkly. Even the strongest and most silent of us have our weaknesses, and my employer's was the rooted idea that he looked well in knicker-bockers. It was not my place to try to dissuade him, but there was no doubt that they did not suit him. Nature, in bestowing upon him a massive head and a jutting chin, had forgotten to finish him off at the other end. Vincent Jopp's legs were skinny.

"You poor dear man!" went on Mrs. Jane Jukes Jopp. "What practical joker ever lured you into appearing in public in knickerbockers?"

"I don't object to the knickerbockers," said Mrs. Agnes Parsons Jopp, "but when he foolishly comes out in quite a strong east wind without his liver-pad——"

"Little Tinky-Ting don't need no liver-pad, he don't," said Mrs. Luella Mainprice Jopp, addressing the animal in her arms, "because he was his muzzer's pet, he was."

I was standing quite near to Vincent Jopp, and at this moment I saw a bead of perspiration spring out on his forehead, and into his steely eyes there came a positively hunted look. I could understand and sympathize. Napoleon himself would have wilted if he had found himself in the midst of a trio of females, one talking baby-talk, another fussing about his health, and the third making derogatory observations on his lower limbs. Vincent Jopp was becoming unstrung.

"May as well be starting, shall we?"

It was Jopp's opponent who spoke. There was a strange, set look on his face—the look of a man whose back is against the wall. Ten down on the morning's round, he had drawn on his reserves of courage and was determined to meet the inevitable bravely.

Vincent Jopp nodded absently, then turned to me.

"Keep those women away from me," he whispered tensely. "They'll put me off my stroke!"

"Put *you* off your stroke!" I exclaimed, incredulously.

"Yes, me! How the deuce can I concentrate, with people babbling about liver-pads, and—and knickerbockers all round me? Keep them away!"

He started to address his ball, and there was a weak uncertainty in the way he did it that prepared me for what was to come. His club rose, wavered, fell; and the ball, badly topped, trickled two feet and sank into a cuppy lie.

"Is that good or bad?" inquired Mrs. Luella Mainprice Jopp.

A sort of desperate hope gleamed in the eye of the other competitor in the Final. He swung with renewed vigour. His ball sang through the air, and lay within chip-shot distance of the green.

"At the very least," said Mrs. Agnes Parsons Jopp, "I hope, Vincent, that you are wearing flannel next your skin."

I heard Jopp give a stifled groan as he took his spoon from the bag. He made a gallant effort to retrieve the lost ground, but the ball struck a stone and bounded away into the long grass to the side of the green. His opponent won the hole.

We moved to the second tee.

"Now, *that* young man," said Mrs. Jane Jukes Jopp, indicating her late husband's blushing antagonist, "is quite right to wear knickerbockers. He can carry them off. But a glance in the mirror must have shown you that you——"

"I'm sure you're feverish, Vincent," said Mrs. Agnes Parsons Jopp, solicitously. "You are quite flushed. There is a wild gleam in your eyes."

"Muzzer's pet got little buttons of eyes, that don't never have no wild gleam in zem because he's muzzer's own darling, he was!" said Mrs. Luella Mainprice Jopp.

A hollow groan escaped Vincent Jopp's ashen lips.

I need not recount the play hole by hole, I think. There are some subjects that are too painful. It was pitiful to watch Vincent Jopp in his downfall. By the end of the first nine his lead had been reduced to one, and his antagonist, rendered a new man by success, was playing magnificent golf. On the next hole he drew level. Then with a superhuman effort Jopp contrived to halve the eleventh, twelfth, and thirteenth. It seemed as though his iron will might still assert itself, but on the fourteenth the end came.

He had driven a superb ball, outdistancing his opponent by a full fifty yards. The latter played a good second to within a few feet of the green. And then, as Vincent Jopp was shaping for his stroke, Luella Mainprice gave tongue.

"Vincent!"

"Well?"

"Vincent, that other man—bad man—not playing fair. When your back was turned just now, he gave his ball a great bang. *I* was watching him."

"At any rate," said Mrs. Agnes Parsons Jopp, "I do hope, when the game is over, Vincent, that you will remember to cool slowly."

"Flesho!" cried Mrs. Jane Jukes Jopp triumphantly. "I've been trying to remember the name all the afternoon. I saw about it in one of the papers. The advertisements speak most highly of it. You take it before breakfast and again before retiring, and they guarantee it to produce firm, healthy flesh on the most sparsely-covered limbs in next to no time. Now, *will* you remember to get a bottle tonight? It comes in two sizes, the five-shilling (or large size) and the smaller at half-a-crown. G. K. Chesterton writes that he used it regularly for years."

Vincent Jopp uttered a quavering moan, and his hand, as he took the mashie from his bag, was trembling like an aspen.

Ten minutes later, he was on his way back to the club-house, a beaten man.

And so (concluded the Oldest Member) you see that in golf there is no such thing as a soft snap. You can never be certain of the finest player. Anything may happen to the greatest expert at any stage of the game. In a recent competition George Duncan took eleven shots over a hole which eighteen-handicap men generally do in five. No! Back horses or go down to Throgmorton Street and try to take it away from the Rothschilds, and I will applaud you as a shrewd and cautious financier. But to bet at golf is pure gambling.

10

THE ROUGH STUFF

INTO the basking warmth of the day there had crept, with the approach of evening, that heartening crispness which heralds the advent of autumn. Already, in the valley by the ninth tee, some of the trees had begun to try on strange colours, in tentative experiment against the coming of nature's annual fancy dress ball, when the soberest tree casts off its workaday suit of green and plunges into a riot of reds and yellows. On the terrace in front of the club-house an occasional withered leaf fluttered down on the table where the Oldest Member sat, sipping a thoughtful seltzer and lemon and listening with courteous gravity to a young man in a sweater and golf breeches who occupied the neighbouring chair.

"She is a dear girl," said the young man a little moodily, "a dear girl in every respect. But somehow—I don't know—when I see her playing golf I can't help thinking that woman's place is in the home."

The Oldest Member inclined his frosted head.

"You think," he said, "that lovely woman loses in queenly dignity when she fails to slam the ball squarely on the meat?"

"I don't mind her missing the pill," said the young man. "But I think her attitude toward the game is too light-hearted."

"Perhaps it cloaks a deeper feeling. One of the noblest women I ever knew used to laugh merrily when she foozled a short putt. It was only later, when I learned that in the privacy of her home she would weep bitterly and bite holes in the sofa cushions, that I realized that she did but wear the mask. Continue to encourage your *fiancée* to play the game, my boy. Much happiness will reward you. I could tell you a story——"

A young woman of singular beauty and rather statuesque appearance came out of the club-house carrying a baby swaddled in flannel. As she drew near the table she said to the baby:

"Chicketty wicketty wicketty wipsey pop!"

In other respects her intelligence appeared to be above the ordinary.

"Isn't he a darling!" she said, addressing the Oldest Member.

The Sage cast a meditative eye upon the infant. Except to the eye of love, it looked like a skinned poached egg.

"Unquestionably so," he replied.

"Don't you think he looks more like his father every day?"

For a brief instant the Oldest Member seemed to hesitate.

"Assuredly!" he said. "Is your husband out on the links today?"

"Not today. He had to see Wilberforce off on the train to Scotland."

"Your brother is going to Scotland?"

"Yes. Ramsden has such a high opinion of the schools up there. I did say that Scotland was a long way off, and he said yes, that had occurred to him, but that we must make sacrifices for Willie's good. He was very brave and cheerful about it. Well, I mustn't stay. There's quite a nip in the air, and Rammikins will get a nasty cold in his precious little button of a nose if I don't walk him about. Say 'Bye-bye' to the gentleman, Rammy!"

The Oldest Member watched her go thoughtfully.

"There is a nip in the air," he said, "and, unlike our late acquaintance in the flannel, I am not in my first youth. Come with me, I want to show you something."

He led the way into the club-house, and paused before the wall of the smoking-room. This was decorated from top to bottom with bold caricatures of members of the club.

"These," he said, "are the work of a young newspaper artist who belongs here. A clever fellow. He has caught the expressions of these men wonderfully. His only failure, indeed, is that picture of myself." He regarded it with distaste, and a touch of asperity crept into his manner. "I don't know why the committee lets it stay there," he said, irritably. "It isn't a bit like." He recovered himself. "But all the others are excellent, excellent, though I believe many of the subjects are under the erroneous impression that they bear no resemblance to the originals. Here is the picture I wished to show you. That is Ramsden Waters, the husband of the lady who has just left us."

The portrait which he indicated was that of a man in the early thirties. Pale saffron hair surmounted a receding forehead. Pale blue eyes looked out over a mouth which wore a pale, weak smile, from the centre of which protruded two teeth of a rabbit-like character.

"Golly! What a map!" exclaimed the young man at his side.

"Precisely!" said the Oldest Member. "You now understand my momentary hesitation in agreeing with Mrs. Waters that the baby was like its father. I was torn by conflicting emotions. On the one hand, politeness demanded that I confirm any statement made by a lady. Common humanity, on the other hand, made it repugnant to me to knock an innocent child. Yes, that is Ramsden Waters. Sit down and take the weight off your feet, and I will tell you about him. The story illustrates a favourite theory of mine, that it is an excellent thing that women should be encouraged to take up golf. There are, I admit, certain drawbacks attendant on their presence on the links. I shall not readily forget the occasion on which a low, raking drive of mine at the eleventh struck the ladies' tee box squarely and came back and stunned my caddie, causing me to lose stroke and distance. Nevertheless, I hold that the advantages outnumber the drawbacks. Golf humanizes women, humbles their haughty natures, tends, in short, to knock out of their systems a certain modicum of that superciliousness, that swank, which makes wooing a tough proposition for the diffident male. You may have found this yourself?"

"Well, as a matter of fact," admitted the young man, "now I come to think of it I have noticed that Genevieve has shown me a bit more respect since she took up the game. When I drive 230 yards after she had taken six sloshes to cover fifty, I sometimes think that a new light comes into her eyes."

"Exactly," said the Sage.

From earliest youth (said the Oldest Member) Ramsden Waters had always been of a shrinking nature. He seemed permanently scared. Possibly his nurse had frightened him with tales of horror in his babyhood. If so, she must have been the Edgar Allan Poe of her sex, for, by the time he reached man's estate, Ramsden Waters had about as much ferocity and self-assertion as a blancmange. Even with other men he was noticeably timid, and with women he comported himself in a manner that roused their immediate scorn and antagonism. He was one of those men who fall over their feet and start apologizing for themselves the moment they see a woman. His idea of conversing with a girl was to perspire and tie himself into knots, making the while a strange gurgling sound like the language of some primitive tribe. If ever a remark of any coherence emerged from his tangled vocal cords it dealt with the weather and he immediately apologized and qualified it. To such a man women are merciless, and it speedily became an article of faith with the feminine population of this locality that Ramsden Waters was an unfortunate incident and did not belong. Finally, after struggling for a time to keep up a connection in social circles, he gave it up and became a sort of hermit.

I think that caricature I just showed you weighed rather heavily on the poor fellow. Just as he was nerving himself to make another attempt to enter society, he would catch sight of it and say to himself, "What hope is there for a man with a face like that?" These caricaturists are too ready to wound people simply in order to raise a laugh. Personally I am broad-minded enough to smile at that portrait of myself. It has given me great enjoyment, though why the committee permits it to— But then, of course, it isn't a bit like, whereas that of Ramsden Waters not only gave the man's exact appearance, very little exaggerated, but laid bare his very soul. That portrait is the portrait of a chump, and such Ramsden Waters undeniably was.

By the end of the first year in the neighbourhood, Ramsden, as I say, had become practically a hermit. He lived all by himself in a house near the fifteenth green, seeing nobody, going nowhere. His only solace was golf. His late father had given him an excellent education, and, even as early as his seventeenth year, I believe, he was going round difficult courses in par. Yet even this admirable gift, which might have done him social service, was rendered negligible by the fact that he was too shy and shrinking to play often with other men. As a rule, he confined himself to golfing by himself in the mornings and late evenings when the links were more or less deserted. Yes, in his twenty-ninth year, Ramsden Waters had sunk to the depth of becoming a secret golfer.

One lovely morning in summer, a scented morning of green and blue and gold, when the birds sang in the trees and the air had that limpid clearness which makes the first hole look about 100 yards long instead of 345, Ramsden Waters, alone as ever, stood on the first tee addressing his ball. For a space he waggled masterfully, then, drawing his club back with a crisp swish, brought it down. And, as he did so, a voice behind him cried:

"Bing!"

Ramsden's driver wabbled at the last moment. The ball flopped weakly among the trees on the right of the course. Ramsden turned to perceive, standing close beside him, a small fat boy in a sailor suit. There was a pause.

"Rotten!" said the boy austerely.

Ramsden gulped. And then suddenly he saw that the boy was not alone. About a medium approach-putt distance, moving gracefully and languidly towards him, was a girl of such pronounced beauty that Ramsden Waters's heart looped the loop twice in rapid succession. It was the first time that he had seen Eunice Bray, and, like most men who saw her for the first time, he experienced the sensations of one in an express lift at the tenth floor going down who has left the majority of his internal organs up on the twenty-second. He felt a dazed emptiness. The world swam before his eyes.

You yourself saw Eunice just now: and, though you are in a sense immune, being engaged to a charming girl of your own, I noticed that you unconsciously braced yourself up and tried to look twice as handsome as nature ever intended you to. You smirked and, if you had a moustache, you would have twiddled it. You can imagine, then, the effect which this vision of loveliness had on lonely, diffident Ramsden Waters. It got right in amongst him.

"I'm afraid my little brother spoiled your stroke," said Eunice. She did not speak at all apologetically, but rather as a goddess might have spoken to a swineherd.

Ramsden yammered noiselessly. As always in the presence of the opposite sex, and more than ever now, his vocal cords appeared to have tied themselves in a knot which would have baffled a sailor and might have perplexed Houdini. He could not even gargle.

"He is very fond of watching golf," said the girl.

She took the boy by the hand, and was about to lead him off, when Ramsden miraculously recovered speech.

"Would he like to come round with me?" he croaked. How he had managed to acquire the nerve to make the suggestion he could never understand. I suppose that in certain supreme moments a sort of desperate recklessness descends on nervous men.

"How very kind of you!" said the girl indifferently. "But I'm afraid——"

"I want to go!" shrilled the boy. "I want to go!"

Fond as Eunice Bray was of her little brother, I imagine that the prospect of having him taken off her hands on a fine summer morning, when all nature urged her to sit in the shade on the terrace and read a book, was not unwelcome.

"It would be very kind of you if you would let him," said Eunice. "He wasn't able to go to the circus last week, and it was a great disappointment; this will do instead."

She turned toward the terrace, and Ramsden, his head buzzing, tottered into the jungle to find his ball, followed by the boy.

I have never been able to extract full particulars of that morning's round from Ramsden. If you speak of it to him, he will wince and change the subject. Yet he seems to have had the presence of mind to pump Wilberforce as to the details of his home life, and by the end of the round he had learned that Eunice and her brother had just come to visit an aunt who lived in the neighbourhood. Their house was not far from the links; Eunice was not engaged to be married; and the aunt made a hobby of collecting dry seaweed, which she pressed and pasted in an album. One sometimes thinks that aunts live entirely for pleasure.

At the end of the round Ramsden staggered on to the terrace, tripping over his feet, and handed Wilberforce back in good condition. Eunice, who had just reached the chapter where the hero decides to give up all for love, thanked him perfunctorily without looking up from her book; and so ended the first spasm of Ramsden Waters's life romance.

There are few things more tragic than the desire of the moth for the star; and it is a curious fact that the spectacle of a star almost invariably fills the most sensible moth with thoughts above his station. No doubt, if Ramsden Waters had stuck around and waited long enough there might have come his way in the fullness of time some nice, homely girl with a squint and a good disposition who would have been about his form. In his modest day dreams he had aspired to nothing higher. But the sight of Eunice Bray seemed to have knocked all the sense out of the man. He must have known that he stood no chance of becoming anything to her other than a handy means of getting rid of little Wilberforce now and again. Why, the very instant that Eunice appeared in the place, every eligible bachelor for miles around her tossed his head with a loud, snorting sound, and galloped madly in her direction. Dashing young devils they were, handsome, well-knit fellows with the figures of Greek gods and the faces of movie heroes. Any one of them could have named his own price from the advertisers of collars. They were the sort of young men you see standing grandly beside the full-page picture of the seven-seater Magnifico car in the magazines. And it was against this field that Ramsden Waters, the man with the unshuffled face, dared to pit his feeble personality. One weeps.

Something of the magnitude of the task he had undertaken must have come home to Ramsden at a very early point in the proceedings. At Eunice's home, at the hour when women receive callers, he was from the start a mere unconsidered unit in the mob scene. While his rivals clustered thickly about the girl, he was invariably somewhere on the outskirts listening limply to the aunt. I imagine that seldom has any young man had such golden opportunities of learning all about dried seaweed. Indeed, by the end of the month Ramsden Waters could not have known more about seaweed if he had been a deep sea fish. And yet he was not happy. He was in a position, if he had been at a dinner party and things had got a bit slow, to have held the table spellbound with the first hand information about dried seaweed, straight from the stable; yet nevertheless he chafed. His soul writhed and sickened within him. He lost weight and went right off his approach shots. I confess that my heart bled for the man.

His only consolation was that nobody else, not even the fellows who worked their way right through the jam and got seats in the front row where they could glare into her eyes and hang on her lips and all that sort of thing, seemed to be making any better progress.

And so matters went on till one day Eunice decided to take up golf. Her motive for doing this was, I believe, simply because Kitty Manders, who had won a small silver cup at a monthly handicap, receiving thirty-six, was always dragging the conversation round to this trophy, and if there was one firm article in Eunice Bray's simple creed it was that she would be hanged if she let Kitty, who was by way of being a rival on a small scale, put anything over on her. I do not defend Eunice, but women are women, and I doubt if any of them really take up golf in that holy, quest-of-the-grail spirit which animates men. I have known girls to become golfers as an excuse for wearing pink jumpers, and one at least who did it because she had read in the beauty hints in the evening paper that it made you lissom. Girls will be girls.

Her first lessons Eunice received from the professional, but after that she saved money by distributing herself among her hordes of admirers, who were only too willing to give up good matches to devote themselves to her tuition. By degrees she acquired a fair skill and a confidence in her game which was not altogether borne out by results. From Ramsden Waters she did not demand a lesson. For one thing it never occurred to her that so poor-spirited a man could be of any use at the game, and for another Ramsden was always busy tooling round with little Wilberforce.

Yet it was with Ramsden that she was paired in the first competition for which she entered, the annual mixed foursomes. And it was on the same evening that the list of the draw went up on the notice board that Ramsden proposed.

The mind of a man in love works in strange ways. To you and to me there would seem to be no reason why the fact that Eunice's name and his own had been drawn out of a hat together should so impress Ramsden, but he looked on it as an act of God. It seemed to him to draw them close together, to set up a sort of spiritual affinity. In a word, it acted on the poor fellow like a tonic, and that very night he went round to her house, and having, after a long and extremely interesting conversation with her aunt, contrived to get her alone, coughed eleven times in a strangled sort of way, and suggested that the wedding bells should ring out.

Eunice was more startled than angry.

"Of course, I'm tremendously complimented, Mr.——" She had to pause to recall the name. "Mr.——"

"Waters," said Ramsden, humbly.

"Of course, yes. Mr. Waters. As I say, it's a great compliment——"

"Not at all!"

"A great compliment——"

"No, no!" murmured Ramsden obsequiously.

"I wish you wouldn't interrupt!" snapped Eunice with irritation. No girl likes to have to keep going back and trying over her speeches. "It's a great compliment, but it is quite impossible."

"Just as you say, of course," agreed Ramsden.

"What," demanded Eunice, "have you to offer me? I don't mean money. I mean something more spiritual. What is there in you, Mr. Walter——"

"Waters."

"Mr. Waters. What is there in you that would repay a girl for giving up the priceless boon of freedom?"

"I know a lot about dried seaweed," suggested Ramsden hopefully.

Eunice shook her head.

"No," she said, "it is quite impossible. You have paid me the greatest compliment a man can pay a woman, Mr. Waterson——"

"Waters," said Ramsden. "I'll write it down for you."

"Please don't trouble. I am afraid we shall never meet again——"

'But we are partners in the mixed foursomes tomorrow."

"Oh, yes, so we are!" said Eunice. Well, mind you play up. I want to win a cup more than anything on earth."

"Ah!" said Ramsden, "if only I could win what I want to win more than anything else on earth! You, I mean," he added, to make his meaning clear. "If I could win you——" His tongue tied itself in a bow knot round his uvula, and he could say no more. He moved slowly to the door, paused with his fingers on the handle for one last look over his shoulder, and walked silently into the cupboard where Eunice's aunt kept her collection of dried seaweed.

His second start was favoured with greater luck, and he found himself out in the hall, and presently in the cool air of the night, with the stars shining down on him. Had those silent stars ever shone down on a more broken-hearted man? Had the cool air of the night ever fanned a more fevered brow? Ah, yes! Or, rather, ah no!

There was not a very large entry for the mixed foursomes competition. In my experience there seldom is. Men are as a rule idealists, and wish to keep their illusions regarding women intact, and it is difficult for the most broad-minded man to preserve a chivalrous veneration for the sex after a woman has repeatedly sliced into the rough and left him a difficult recovery. Women, too—I am not speaking of the occasional champions, but of the average woman, the one with the handicap of 33, who plays in high-heeled shoes—are apt to giggle when they foozle out of a perfect lie, and this makes for misogyny. Only eight couples assembled on the tenth tee (where our foursomes matches start) on the morning after Ramsden Waters had proposed to Eunice. Six of these were negligible, consisting of males of average skill and young women who played golf because it kept them out in the fresh air. Looking over the field, Ramsden felt that the only serious rivalry was to be feared from Marcella Bingley and her colleague, a 16-handicap youth named George Perkins, with whom they were paired for the opening round. George was a pretty indifferent performer, but Marcella, a weather-beaten female with bobbed hair and the wrists of a welter-weight pugilist, had once appeared in the women's open championship and swung a nasty iron.

Ramsden watched her drive a nice, clean shot down the middle of the fairway, and spoke earnestly to Eunice. His heart was in this competition, for, though the first prize in the mixed foursomes does not perhaps entitle the winners to a place in the hall of fame, Ramsden had the soul of the true golfer. And the true golfer wants to win whenever he starts, whether he is playing in a friendly round or in the open championship.

"What we've got to do is to play steadily," he said. "Don't try any fancy shots. Go for safety. Miss Bingley is a tough proposition, but George Perkins is sure to foozle a few, and if we play safe we've got 'em cold. The others don't count."

You notice something odd about this speech. Something in it strikes you as curious. Precisely. It affected Eunice Bray in the same fashion. In the first place, it contains forty-four words, some of them of two syllables, others of even greater length. In the second place, it was spoken crisply, almost commandingly, without any of that hesitation and stammering which usually characterized Ramsden Waters's utterances. Eunice was puzzled. She was also faintly resentful. True, there was not a word in what he had said that was calculated to bring the blush of shame to the cheek of modesty; nevertheless, she felt vaguely that Ramsden Waters had exceeded the limits. She had been prepared for a gurgling Ramsden Waters, a Ramsden Waters who fell over his large feet and perspired; but here was a Ramsden Waters who addressed her not merely as an equal, but with more than a touch of superiority. She eyed him coldly, but he had turned to speak to little Wilberforce, who was to accompany them on the round.

"And you, my lad," said Ramsden curtly, "you kindly remember that this is a competition, and keep your merry flow of conversation as much as possible to yourself. You've got a bad habit of breaking into small talk when a man's addressing the ball."

"If you think that my brother will be in the way——" began Eunice coldly.

"Oh, I don't mind him coming round," said Ramsden, "if he keeps quiet."

Eunice gasped. She had not played enough golf to understand how that noblest of games changes a man's whole nature when on the links. She was thinking of something crushing to say to him, when he advanced to the tee to drive off.

He drove a perfect ball, hard and low with a lot of roll. Even Eunice was impressed.

"Good shot, partner!" she said.

Ramsden was apparently unaware that she had spoken. He was gazing down the fairway with his club over his left shoulder in an attitude almost identical with that of Sandy MacBean in the plate labelled "The Drive—Correct Finish", to face page twenty-four of his monumental work, "How to Become a Scratch Player Your First Season by Studying Photographs". Eunice bit her lip. She was piqued. She felt as if she had patted the head of a pet lamb, and the lamb had turned and bitten her in the finger.

"I said, 'Good shot, partner!' " she repeated coldly.

"Yes," said Ramsden, "but don't talk. It prevents one cencentrating." He turned to Wilberforce. "And don't let me have to tell you that again!" he said.

"Wilberforce has been like a mouse!"

"That is what I complain of," said Ramsden. "Mice make a beastly scratching sound, and that's what he was doing when I drove that ball."

"He was only playing with the sand in the tee box."

"Well, if he does it again, I shall be reluctantly compelled to take steps."

They walked in silence to where the ball had stopped. It was nicely perched up on the grass, and to have plunked it on to the green with an iron should have been for any reasonable golfer the work of a moment. Eunice, however, only succeeded in slicing it feebly into the rough.

Ramsden reached for his niblick and plunged into the bushes. And, presently, as if it had been shot up by some convulsion of nature, the ball, accompanied on the early stages of its journey by about a pound of mixed mud, grass, and pebbles, soared through the air and fell on the green. But the mischief had been done. Miss Bingley, putting forcefully, put the opposition ball down for a four and won the hole.

Eunice now began to play better, and, as Ramsden was on the top of his game, a ding-dong race ensued for the remainder of the first nine holes. The Bingley-Perkins combination, owing to some inspired work by the female of the species, managed to keep their lead up to the tricky ravine hole, but there George Perkins, as might have been expected of him, deposited the ball right in among the rocks, and Ramsden and Eunice drew level. The next four holes were halved and they reached the club-house with no advantage to either side. Here there was a pause while Miss Bingley went to the professional's shop to have a tack put into the leather of her mashie, which had worked loose. George Perkins and little Wilberforce, who believed in keeping up their strength, melted silently away in the direction of the refreshment bar, and Ramsden and Eunice were alone.

The pique which Eunice had felt at the beginning of the game had vanished by now. She was feeling extremely pleased with her performance on the last few holes, and would have been glad to go into the matter fully. Also, she was conscious of a feeling not perhaps of respect so much as condescending tolerance towards Ramsden.

He might be a pretty minus quantity in a drawing-room or at a dance, but in a bunker or out in the open with a cleek, Eunice felt, you'd be surprised. She was just about to address him in a spirit of kindliness, when he spoke.

"Better keep your brassie in the bag on the next nine," he said. "Stick to the iron. The great thing is to keep 'em straight!"

Eunice gasped. Indeed, had she been of a less remarkable beauty one would have said that she snorted. The sky turned black, and all her amiability was swept away in a flood of fury. The blood left her face and surged back in a rush of crimson. You are engaged to be married and I take it that there exists between you and your *fiancée* the utmost love and trust and understanding; but would you have the nerve, could you summon up the cold, callous gall to tell your Genevieve that she wasn't capable of using her wooden clubs? I think not. Yet this was what Ramsden Waters had told Eunice, and the delicately nurtured girl staggered before the coarse insult. Her refined, sensitive nature was all churned up.

Ever since she had made her first drive at golf, she had prided herself on her use of the wood. Her brother and her brassie were the only things she loved. And here was this man deliberately . . . Eunice choked.

"Mr. Waters!"

Before they could have further speech George Perkins and little Wilberforce ambled in a bloated way out of the club-house.

"I've had three ginger ales," observed the boy. "Where do we go from here?"

"Our honour," said Ramsden. "Shoot!"

Eunice took out her driver without a word. Her little figure was tense with emotion. She swung vigorously, and pulled the ball far out on to the fairway of the ninth hole.

"Even off the tee," said Ramsden, "you had better use an iron. You must keep 'em straight."

Their eyes met. Hers were glittering with the fury of a woman scorned. His were cold and hard. And, suddenly, as she looked at his awful, pale, set golf face, something seemed to snap in Eunice. A strange sensation of weakness and humility swept over her. So might the cave woman have felt when, with her back against a cliff and unable to dodge, she watched her suitor take his club in the interlocking grip, and, after a preliminary waggle, start his back swing.

The fact was that, all her life, Eunice had been accustomed to the homage of men. From the time she had put her hair up every man she had met had grovelled before her, and she had acquired a mental attitude toward the other sex which was a blend of indifference and contempt. For the cringing specimens who curled up and died all over the hearthrug if she spoke a cold word to them she had nothing but scorn. She dreamed wistfully of those brusque cavemen of whom she read in the novels which she took out of the village circulating library. The female novelist who was at that time her favourite always supplied with each chunk of wholesome and invigorating fiction one beetle-browed hero with a grouch and a scowl, who rode wild horses over the countryside till they foamed at the mouth, and treated women like dirt. That,

Eunice had thought yearningly, as she talked to youths whose spines turned to gelatine at one glance from her bright eyes, was the sort of man she wanted to meet and never seemed to come across.

Of all the men whose acquaintance she had made recently she had despised Ramsden Waters most. Where others had grovelled he had tied himself into knots. Where others had gazed at her like sheep he had goggled at her like a kicked spaniel. She had only permitted him to hang round because he seemed so fond of little Wilberforce. And here he was, ordering her about and piercing her with gimlet eyes, for all the world as if he were Claude Delamere, in the thirty-second chapter of "The Man of Chilled Steel", the one where Claude drags Lady Matilda around the smoking-room by her hair because she gave the rose from her bouquet to the Italian count.

She was half-cowed, half-resentful.

"Mr. Winklethorpe told me I was very good with the wooden clubs," she said defiantly.

"He's a great kidder," said Ramsden.

He went down the hill to where his ball lay. Eunice proceeded direct for the green. Much as she told herself that she hated this man, she never questioned his ability to get there with his next shot.

George Perkins, who had long since forfeited any confidence which his partner might have reposed in him, had topped his drive, leaving Miss Bingley a difficult second out of a sandy ditch. The hole was halved.

The match went on. Ramsden won the short hole, laying his ball dead with a perfect iron shot, but at the next, the long dog-leg hole, Miss Bingley regained the honour. They came to the last all square.

As the match had started on the tenth tee, the last hole to be negotiated was, of course, what in the ordinary run of human affairs is the ninth, possibly the trickiest on the course. As you know, it is necessary to carry with one's initial wallop that combination of stream and lake into which so many well-meant drives have flopped. This done, the player proceeds up the face of a steep slope, to find himself ultimately on a green which looks like the sea in the storm scene of a melodrama. It heaves and undulates, and is altogether a nasty thing to have happen to one at the end of a gruelling match. But it is the first shot, the drive, which is the real test, for the water and the trees form a mental hazard of unquestionable toughness.

George Perkins, as he addressed his ball for the vital stroke, manifestly wabbled. He was scared to the depths of his craven soul. He tried to pray, but all he could remember was the hymn for those in peril on the deep, into which category, he feared, his ball would shortly fall. Breathing a few bars of this he swung. There was a musical click, and the ball, singing over the water like a bird, breasted the hill like a homing aeroplane and fell in the centre of the fairway within easy distance of the plateau green.

"Nice work, partner," said Miss Bingley, speaking for the first and last time in the course of the proceedings.

George unravelled himself with a modest simper. He felt like a gambler who has placed his all on a number at roulette and sees the white ball tumble into the correct compartment.

Eunice moved to the tee. In the course of the last eight holes the girl's haughty soul had been rudely harrowed. She had foozled two drives and three approach shots and had missed a short putt on the last green but three. She had that consciousness of sin which afflicts the golfer off his game, that curious self-loathing which humbles the proudest. Her knees felt weak and all nature seemed to bellow at her that this was where she was going to blow up with a loud report.

Even as her driver rose above her shoulder she was acutely aware that she was making eighteen out of the twenty-three errors which complicate the drive at golf. She knew that her head had swayed like some beautiful flower in a stiff breeze. The heel of her left foot was pointing down the course. Her grip had shifted, and her wrists felt like sticks of boiled asparagus. As the club began to descend she perceived that she had under-estimated the total of her errors. And when the ball, badly topped, bounded down the slope and entered the muddy water like a timid diver on a cold morning she realized that she had a full hand. There are twenty-three things which it is possible to do wrong in the drive, and she had done them all.

Silently Ramsden Waters made a tee and placed thereon a new ball. He was a golfer who rarely despaired, but he was playing three, and his opponents' ball would undoubtedly be on the green, possibly even dead in two. Nevertheless, perhaps, by a supreme drive, and one or two miracles later on, the game might be saved. He concentrated his whole soul on the ball.

I need scarcely tell you that Ramsden Waters pressed . . .

Swish came the driver. The ball, fanned by the wind, rocked a little on the tee, then settled down in its original position. Ramsden Waters, usually the most careful of players, had missed the globe.

For a moment there was a silence—a silence which Ramsden had to strive with an effort almost physically painful not to break. Rich oaths surged to his lips, and blistering maledictions crashed against the back of his clenched teeth.

The silence was broken by little Wilberforce.

One can only gather that there lurks in the supposedly innocuous amber of ginger ale an elevating something which the temperance reformers have overlooked. Wilberforce Bray had, if you remember, tucked away no fewer than three in the spot where they would do most good. One presumes that the child, with all that stuff surging about inside him, had become thoroughly above himself. He uttered a merry laugh.

"Never hit it!" said little Wilberforce.

He was kneeling beside the tee box as he spoke, and now, as one who has seen all that there is to be seen and turns, sated, to other amusements, he moved round and began to play with the sand. The spectacle of his alluring trouser seat was one which a stronger man would have found it hard to resist. To Ramsden Waters, it had the aspect of a formal invitation. For one moment his number 11 golf shoe, as supplied to all the leading professionals, wavered in mid-air, then crashed home.

Eunice screamed.

"How dare you kick my brother!"

Ramsden faced her, stern and pale.

"Madam," he said, "in similar circumstances I would have kicked the Archangel Gabriel!"

Then, stooping to his ball, he picked it up.

"The match is yours," he said to Miss Bingley, who, having paid no attention at all to the drama which had just concluded, was practising short chip shots with her mashie-niblick.

He bowed coldly to Eunice, cast one look of sombre satisfaction at little Wilberforce, who was painfully extricating himself from a bed of nettles into which he had rolled, and strode off. He crossed the bridge over the water and stalked up the hill.

Eunice watched him go, spellbound. Her momentary spurt of wrath at the kicking of her brother had died away, and she wished she had thought of doing it herself.

How splendid he looked, she felt, as she watched Ramsden striding up to the clubhouse—just like Carruthers Mordyke after he had flung Ermyntrude Vanstone from him in chapter forty-one of "Grey Eyes That Gleam". Her whole soul went out to him. This was the sort of man she wanted as a partner in life. How grandly he would teach her to play golf. It had sickened her when her former instructors, prefacing their criticism with glutinous praise, had mildly suggested that some people found it a good thing to keep the head still when driving and that though her methods were splendid it might be worth trying. They had spoken of her keeping her eye on the ball as if she were doing the ball a favour. What she wanted was a great, strong, rough brute of a fellow who would tell her not to move her damned head; a rugged Viking of a chap who, if she did not keep her eye on the ball, would black it for her. And Ramsden Waters was such a one. He might not look like a Viking, but after all it is the soul that counts and, as this afternoon's experience had taught her, Ramsden Waters had a soul that seemed to combine in equal proportions the outstanding characteristics of Nero, a wildcat, and the second mate of a tramp steamer.

That night Ramsden Waters sat in his study, a prey to the gloomiest emotions. The gold had died out of him by now, and he was reproaching himself bitterly for having ruined for ever his chance of winning the only girl he had ever loved. How could she forgive him for his brutality? How could she overlook treatment which would have caused comment in the stokehold of a cattle ship? He groaned and tried to forget his sorrows by forcing himself to read.

But the choicest thought of the greatest writers had no power to grip him. He tried Vardon "On the Swing", and the words swam before his eyes. He turned to Taylor "On the Chip Shot", and the master's pure style seemed laboured and involved. He found solace neither in Braid "On the Pivot" nor in Duncan "On the Divot".

He was just about to give it up and go to bed though it was only nine o'clock, when the telephone bell rang.

"Hello!"

"Is that you, Mr. Waters? This is Eunice Bray." The receiver shook in Ramsden's hand. "I've just remembered. Weren't we talking about something last night? Didn't you ask me to marry you or something? I know it was something."

Ramsden gulped three times.

"I did," he replied hollowly.

"We didn't settle anything, did we?"

"Eh?"

"I say, we sort of left it kind of open."

"Yuk!"

"Well, would it bore you awfully," said Eunice's soft voice, "to come round now and go on talking it over?"

Ramsden tottered.

"We shall be quite alone," said Eunice. "Little Wilberforce has gone to bed with a headache."

Ramsden paused a moment to disentangle his tongue from the back of his neck.

"I'll be right over!" he said huskily.

11

THE COMING OF GOWF

AFTER we had sent in our card and waited for a few hours in the marbled ante-room, a bell rang and the major-domo, parting the priceless curtains, ushered us in to where the editor sat writing at his desk. We advanced on all fours, knocking our head reverently on the Aubusson carpet.

"Well?" he said at length, laying down his jewelled pen.

"We just looked in," we said humbly, "to ask if it would be all right if we sent you an historical story."

"The public does not want historical stories," he said, frowning coldly.

"Ah, but the public hasn't seen one of ours!" we replied.

The editor placed a cigarette in a holder presented to him by a reigning monarch, and lit it with a match from a golden box, the gift of the millionaire president of the Amalgamated League of Working Plumbers.

"What this magazine requires," he said, "is red-blooded, one-hundred-per-cent dynamic stuff, palpitating with warm human interest and containing a strong, poignant love-motive."

"That," we replied, "is us all over, Mabel."

"What I need at the moment, however, is a golf story."

"By a singular coincidence, ours is a golf story."

"Ha! say you so?" said the editor, a flicker of interest passing over his finely-chiselled features. "Then you may let me see it."

He kicked us in the face, and we withdrew.

THE STORY

On the broad terrace outside his palace, overlooking the fair expanse of the Royal gardens, King Merolchazzar of Oom stood leaning on the low parapet, his chin in his hand and a frown on his noble face. The day was fine, and a light breeze bore up to him from the garden below a fragrant scent of flowers. But, for all the pleasure it seemed to give him, it might have been bone-fertilizer.

The fact is, King Merolchazzar was in love, and his suit was not prospering. Enough to upset any man.

Royal love affairs in those days were conducted on the correspondence system. A monarch, hearing good reports of a neighbouring princess, would despatch messengers with gifts to her Court, beseeching an interview. The Princess would name a date, and a formal meeting would take place; after which everything usually buzzed along pretty smoothly. But in the case of King Merolchazzar's courtship of the Princess of the Outer Isles there had been a regrettable hitch. She had acknowledged the gifts, saying that they were just what she had wanted and how had he guessed, and had added that, as regarded a meeting, she would let him know later. Since that day no word had come from her, and a gloomy spirit prevailed in the capital. At the Courtiers' Club, the meeting-place of the aristocracy of Oom, five to one in *pazazas* was freely offered against Merolchazzar's chances, but found no takers; while in the taverns of the common people, where less conservative odds were always to be had, you could get a snappy hundred to eight. "For in good sooth," writes a chronicler of the time on a half-brick and a couple of paving-stones which have survived to this day, "it did indeed begin to appear as though our beloved monarch, the son of the sun and the nephew of the moon, had been handed the bitter fruit of the citron."

The quaint old idiom is almost untranslatable, but one sees what he means.

As the King stood sombrely surveying the garden, his attention was attracted by a small bearded man with bushy eyebrows and a face like a walnut, who stood not far away on a gravelled path flanked by rose bushes. For some minutes he eyed this man in silence, then he called to the Grand Vizier, who was standing in the little group of courtiers and officials at the other end of the terrace. The bearded man, apparently unconscious of the Royal scrutiny, had placed a rounded stone on the gravel, and was standing beside it making curious passes over it with his hoe. It was this singular behaviour that had attracted the King's attention. Superficially it seemed silly, and yet Merolchazzar had a curious feeling that there was a deep, even a holy, meaning behind the action.

"Who," he inquired, "is that?"

"He is one of your Majesty's gardeners," replied the Vizier.

"I don't remember seeing him before. Who is he?"

The Vizier was a kind-hearted man, and he hesitated for a moment.

"It seems a hard thing to say of anyone, your Majesty," he replied, "but he is a Scotsman. One of your Majesty's invincible admirals recently made a raid on the inhospitable coast of that country at a spot known to the natives as S'nandrews and brought away this man."

"What does he think he's doing?" asked the King, as the bearded one slowly raised the hoe above his right shoulder, slightly bending the left knee as he did so.

"It is some species of savage religious ceremony, your Majesty. According to the admiral, the dunes by the seashore where he landed were covered with a multitude of men behaving just as this man is doing. They had sticks in their hands and they struck with these at small round objects. And every now and again———"

"Fo-o-ore!" called a gruff voice from below.

"And every now and again," went on the Vizier, "they would utter the strange melancholy cry which you have just heard. It is a species of chant."

The Vizier broke off. The hoe had descended on the stone, and the stone, rising in a graceful arc, had sailed through the air and fallen within a foot of where the King stood.

"Hi!" exclaimed the Vizier.

The man looked up.

"You mustn't do that! You nearly hit his serene graciousness the King!"

"Mphm!" said the bearded man nonchalantly, and began to wave his hoe mystically over another stone.

Into the King's careworn face there had crept a look of interest, almost of excitement.

"What god does he hope to propitiate by these rites?" he asked.

"The deity, I learn from your Majesty's admiral is called Gowf."

"Gowf? Gowf?" King Merolchazzar ran over in his mind the muster-roll of the gods of Oom. There were sixty-seven of them, but Gowf was not of their number. "It is a strange religion," he murmured. "A strange religion, indeed. But, by Belus, distinctly attractive. I have an idea that Oom could do with a religion like that. It has a zip to it. A sort of fascination, if you know what I mean. It looks to me extraordinarily like what the Court physician ordered. I will talk to this fellow and learn more of these holy ceremonies."

And, followed by the Vizier, the King made his way into the garden. The Vizier was now in a state of some apprehension. He was exercised in his mind as to the effect which the embracing of a new religion by the King might have on the formidable Church party. It would be certain to cause displeasure among the priesthood; and in those days it was a ticklish business to offend the priesthood, even for a monarch. And, if Merolchazzar had a fault, it was a tendency to be a little tactless in his dealings with that powerful body. Only a few mornings back the High Priest of Hec had taken the Vizier aside to complain about the quality of the meat which the King had been using lately for his sacrifices. He might be a child in worldly matters, said the High Priest, but if the King supposed that he did not know the difference between home-grown domestic and frozen imported foreign, it was time his Majesty was disabused of the idea. If, on top of this little unpleasantness, King Merolchazzar were to become an adherent of this new Gowf, the Vizier did not know what might not happen.

The King stood beside the bearded foreigner, watching him closely. The second stone soared neatly on to the terrace. Merolchazzar uttered an excited cry. His eyes were glowing, and he breathed quickly.

"It doesn't look difficult," he muttered.

"Hoo's!" said the bearded man.

"I believe I could do it," went on the King, feverishly. "By the eight green gods of the mountain, I believe I could! By the holy fire that burns night and day before the altar of Belus, I'm *sure* I could! By Hec, I'm going to do it now! Gimme that hoe!"

"Toots!" said the bearded man.

It seemed to the King that the fellow spoke derisively, and his blood boiled angrily. He seized the hoe and raised it above his shoulder, bracing himself solidly on widely-parted feet. His pose was an exact reproduction of the one in which the Court sculptor had depicted him when working on the life-size statue ("Our Athletic King") which stood in the principal square of the city; but it did not impress the stranger. He uttered a discordant laugh.

"Ye puir gonuph!" he cried, "whitkin' o' a staunce is that?"

The King was hurt. Hitherto the attitude had been generally admired.

"It's the way I always stand when killing lions," he said. " 'In killing lions,' " he added, quoting from the well-known treatise of Nimrod, the recognized text-book on the sport, " 'the weight at the top of the swing should be evenly balanced on both feet.' "

"Ah, weel, ye're no killing lions the noo. Ye're gowfing."

A sudden humility descended upon the King. He felt, as so many men were to feel in similar circumstances in ages to come, as though he were a child looking eagerly for guidance to an all-wise master—a child, moreover, handicapped by water on the brain, feet three sizes too large for him, and hands consisting mainly of thumbs.

"O thou of noble ancestors and agreeable disposition!" he said, humbly. "Teach me the true way."

"Use the interlocking grup and keep the staunce a wee bit open and slow back, and dinna press or sway the heid and keep yer e'e on the ba'."

"My which on the what?" said the King, bewildered.

"I fancy, your Majesty," hazarded the Vizier, "that he is respectfully suggesting that your serene graciousness should deign to keep your eye on the ball."

"Oh, ah!" said the King.

The first golf lesson ever seen in the kingdom of Oom had begun.

Up on the terrace, meanwhile, in the little group of courtiers and officials, a whispered consultation was in progress. Officially, the King's unfortunate love affair was supposed to be a strict secret. But you know how it is. These things get about. The Grand Vizier tells the Lord High Chamberlain; the Lord High Chamberlain whispers it in confidence to the Supreme Hereditary Custodian of the Royal Pet Dog; the Supreme Hereditary Custodian hands it on to the Exalted Overseer of the King's Wardrobe on the understanding that it is to go no farther; and, before you know where you are, the varlets and scurvy knaves are gossiping about it in the kitchens and the Society journalists have started to carve it out on bricks for the next issue of *Palace Prattlings*.

"The long and short of it is," said the Exalted Overseer of the King's Wardrobe, "we must cheer him up."

There was a murmur of approval. In those days of easy executions it was no light matter that a monarch should be a prey to gloom.

"But how?" queried the Lord High Chamberlain.

"I know," said the Supreme Hereditary Custodian of the Royal Pet Dog. "Try him with the minstrels."

"Here! Why us?" protested the leader of the minstrels.

"Don't be silly!" said the Lord High Chamberlain. "It's for your good just as much as ours. He was asking only last night why he never got any music nowadays. He told me to find out whether you supposed he paid you simply to eat and sleep, because if so he knew what to do about it."

"Oh, in that case!" The leader of the minstrels started nervously. Collecting his assistants and tip-toeing down the garden, he took up his stand a few feet in Merolchazzar's rear, just as that much-enduring monarch, after twenty-five futile attempts, was once more addressing his stone.

Lyric writers in those days had not reached the supreme pitch of excellence which has been produced by modern musical comedy. The art was in its infancy then, and the best the minstrels could do was this—and they did it just as Merolchazzar, raising the hoe with painful care, reached the top of his swing and started down:

> *"Oh, tune the string and let us sing*
> *Our godlike, great, and glorious King!*
> *He's a bear! He's a bear! He's a bear!"*

There were sixteen more verses, touching on their ruler's prowess in the realms of sport and war, but they were not destined to be sung on that circuit. King Merolchazzar jumped like a stung bullock, lifted his head, and missed the globe for the twenty-sixth time. He spun round on the minstrels, who were working pluckily through their song of praise:

> *"Oh, may his triumphs never cease!*
> *He has the strength of ten!*
> *First in war, first in peace,*
> *First in the hearts of his countrymen."*

"Get out!" roared the King.

"Your Majesty?" quavered the leader of the minstrels.

"Make a noise like an egg and beat it!" (Again one finds the chronicler's idiom impossible to reproduce in modern speech, and must be content with a literal translation.) "By the bones of my ancestors, it's a little hard! By the beard of the sacred goat, it's tough! What in the name of Belus and Hec do you mean, you yowling misfits, by starting that sort of stuff when a man's swinging? I was just shaping to hit it right that time when you butted in, you——"

The minstrels melted away. The bearded man patted the fermenting monarch paternally on the shoulder.

"Ma mannie," he said, "ye may no' be a gowfer yet, but hoots! ye're learning the language fine!"

King Merolchazzar's fury died away. He simpered modestly at these words of commendation, the first his bearded preceptor had uttered. With exemplary patience he turned to address the stone for the twenty-seventh time.

That night it was all over the city that the King had gone crazy over a new religion, and the orthodox shook their heads.

We of the present day, living in the midst of a million marvels of a complex civilization, have learned to adjust ourselves to conditions and to take for granted phenomena which in an earlier and less advanced age would have caused the profoundest excitement and even alarm. We accept without comment the telephone, the automobile, and the wireless telegraph, and we are unmoved by the spectacle of our fellow human beings in the grip of the first stages of golf fever. Far otherwise was it with the courtiers and officials about the Palace of Oon. The obsession of the King was the sole topic of conversation.

Every day now, starting forth at dawn and returning only with the falling of darkness, Merolchazzar was out on the Linx, as the outdoor temple of the new god was called. In a luxurious house adjoining this expanse the bearded Scotsman had been installed, and there he could be found at almost any hour of the day fashioning out of holy wood the weird implements indispensable to the new religion. As a recognition of his services, the King had bestowed upon him a large pension, innumerable *kaddiz* or slaves, and the title of Promoter of the King's Happiness, which for the sake of convenience was generally shortened to The Pro.

At present, Oom being a conservative country, the worship of the new god had not attracted the public in great numbers. In fact, except for the Grand Vizier, who, always a faithful follower of his sovereign's fortunes, had taken to Gowf from the start, the courtiers held aloof to a man. But the Vizier had thrown himself into the new worship with such vigour and earnestness that it was not long before he won from the King the title of Supreme Splendiferous Maintainer of the Twenty-Four Handicap Except on Windy Days when It Goes Up to Thirty—a title which in ordinary conversation was usually abbreviated to The Dub.

All these new titles, it should be said, were, so far as the courtiers were concerned, a fruitful source of discontent. There were black looks and mutinous whispers. The laws of precedence were being disturbed, and the courtiers did not like it. It jars a man who for years has had his social position all cut and dried—a man, to take an instance at random, who, as Second Deputy Shiner of the Royal Hunting Boots, knows that his place is just below the Keeper of the Eel-Hounds and just above the Second Tenor of the Corps of Minstrels—it jars him, we say, to find suddenly that he has got to go down a step in favour of the Hereditary Bearer of the King's Baffy.

But it was from the priesthood that the real, serious opposition was to be expected. And the priests of the sixty-seven gods of Oom were up in arms. As the white-bearded High Priest of Hec, who by virtue of his office was generally regarded as leader of the guild, remarked in a glowing speech at an extraordinary meeting of the Priests' Equity Association, he had always set his face against the principle of the Closed Shop hitherto, but there were moments when every thinking man had to admit that enough was sufficient, and it was his opinion that such a moment had now arrived. The cheers which greeted the words showed how correctly he had voiced popular sentiment.

Of all those who had listened to the High Priest's speech, none had listened more intently than the King's half-brother, Ascobaruch. A sinister, disappointed man, this Ascobaruch, with mean eyes and a crafty smile. All his life he had been consumed with ambition, and until now it had looked as though he must go to his grave with this ambition unfulfilled. All his life he had wanted to be King of Oom, and now he began to see daylight. He was sufficiently versed in Court intrigues to be aware that the priests were the party that really counted, the source from which all successful revolutions sprang. And of all the priests the one that mattered most was the venerable High Priest of Hec.

It was to this prelate, therefore, that Ascobaruch made his way at the close of the proceedings. The meeting had dispersed after passing a unanimous vote of censure on King Merolchazzar, and the High Priest was refreshing himself in the vestry— for the meeting had taken place in the Temple of Hec—with a small milk and honey.

"Some speech!" began Ascobaruch in his unpleasant, crafty way. None knew better than he the art of appealing to human vanity.

The High Priest was plainly gratified.

"Oh, I don't know," he said, modestly.

"Yessir!" said Ascobaruch. "Considerable oration! What I can never understand is how you think up all these things to say. I couldn't do it if you paid me. The other night I had to propose the Visitors at the Old Alumni dinner of Oom University, and my mind seemed to go all blank. But you just stand up and the words come fluttering out of you like bees out of a barn. I simply cannot understand it. The thing gets past me."

"Oh, it's just a knack."

"A divine gift, I should call it."

"Perhaps you're right," said the High Priest, finishing his milk and honey. He was wondering why he had never realized before what a capital fellow Ascobaruch was.

"Of course," went on Ascobaruch, "you had an excellent subject. I mean to say, inspiring and all that. Why, by Hec, even I—though, of course, I couldn't have approached your level—even I could have done something with a subject like that. I mean, going off and worshipping a new god no one has ever heard of. I tell you, my blood fairly boiled. Nobody has a greater respect and esteem for Merolchazzar than I have, but I mean to say, what! Not right, I mean, going off worshipping gods no one has ever heard of! I'm a peaceable man, and I've made it a rule never to mix in politics, but if you happened to say to me as we were sitting here, just as one reasonable man to another—if you happened to say, 'Ascobaruch, I think it's time that definite steps were taken,' I should reply frankly, 'My dear old High Priest, I absolutely agree with you, and I'm with you all the way.' You might even go so far as to suggest that the only way out of the muddle was to assassinate Merolchazzar and start with a clean slate."

The High Priest stroked his beard thoughtfully.

"I am bound to say I never thought of going quite so far as that."

"Merely a suggestion, of course," said Ascobaruch. "Take it or leave it. I shan't be offended. If you know a superior excavation, go to it. But as a sensible man—and I've always maintained that you are the most sensible man in the country—you must see that it would be a solution. Merolchazzar has been a pretty good king, of course. No one denies that. A fair general, no doubt, and a plus-man at lion-hunting. But, after all—look at it fairly—is life all battles and lion-hunting? Isn't there a deeper side? Wouldn't it be better for the country to have some good orthodox fellow who has worshipped Hec all his life, and could be relied on to maintain the old beliefs— wouldn't the fact that a man like that was on the throne be likely to lead to more general prosperity? There are dozens of men of that kind simply waiting to be asked. Let us say, purely for purposes of argument, that you approached *me*. I should reply, 'Unworthy though I know myself to be of such an honour, I can tell you this. If you put me on the throne, you can bet your bottom *pazaza* that there's one thing that won't suffer, and that is the worship of Hec!' That's the way I feel about it."

The High Priest pondered.

"O thou of unshuffled features but amiable disposition!" he said, "thy discourse soundeth good to me. Could it be done?"

"Could it!" Ascobaruch uttered a hideous laugh. "Could it! Arouse me in the night-watches and ask me! Question me on the matter, having stopped me for that purpose on the public highway! What I would suggest—I'm not dictating, mind you; merely trying to help you out—what I would suggest is that you took that long, sharp knife of yours, the one you use for the sacrifices, and toddled out to the Linx— you're sure to find the King there; and just when he's raising that sacrilegious stick of his over his shoulder——"

"O man of infinite wisdom," cried the High Priest, warmly, "verily hast thou spoken a fullness of the mouth!"

"Is it a wager?" said Ascobaruch.

"It is a wager!" said the High Priest.

"That's that, then," said Ascobaruch. "Now, I don't want to be mixed up in any unpleasantness, so what I think I'll do while what you might call the preliminaries are being arranged is to go and take a little trip abroad somewhere. The Middle Lakes are pleasant at this time of year. When I come back, it's possible that all the formalities have been completed, yes?"

"Rely on me, by Hec!" said the High Priest grimly, as he fingered his weapon.

The High Priest was as good as his word. Early on the morrow he made his way to the Linx, and found the King holing-out on the second green. Merolchazzar was in high good humour.

"Greetings, O venerable one!" he cried, jovially. "Hadst thou come a moment sooner, thou wouldst have seen me lay my ball dead—aye, dead as mutton, with the sweetest little half-mashie-niblick chip-shot ever seen outside the sacred domain of S'nandrew, on whom"—he bared his head reverently—"be peace! In one under bogey did I do the hole—yea, and that despite the fact that, slicing my drive, I became ensnared in yonder undergrowth."

The High Priest had not the advantage of understanding one word of what the King was talking about, but he gathered with satisfaction that Merolchazzar was pleased and wholly without suspicion. He clasped an unseen hand more firmly about the handle of his knife, and accompanied the monarch to the next altar. Merolchazzar stooped, and placed a small round white object on a little mound of sand. In spite of his austere views, the High Priest, always a keen student of ritual, became interested.

"Why does your Majesty do that?"

"I tee it up that it may fly the fairer. If I did not, then would it be apt to run along the ground like a beetle instead of soaring like a bird, and mayhap, for thou seest how rough and tangled is the grass before us, I should have to use a niblick for my second."

The High Priest groped for his meaning.

"It is a ceremony to propitiate the god and bring good luck?"

"You might call it that."

The High Priest shook his head.

"I may be old-fashioned," he said, "but I should have thought that, to propitiate a god, it would have been better to have sacrificed one of these *kaddiz* on his altar."

"I confess," replied the King, thoughtfully, "that I have often felt that it would be a relief to one's feelings to sacrifice one or two *kaddiz*, but The Pro for some reason or other has set his face against it." He swung at the ball, and sent it forcefully down the fairway. "By Abe, the son of Mitchell," he cried, shading his eyes, "a bird of a drive! How truly is it written in the book of the prophet Vadun, 'The left hand applieth the force, the right doth but guide. Grip not, therefore, too closely with the right hand!' Yesterday I was pulling all the time."

The High Priest frowned.

"It is written in the sacred book of Hec, your Majesty, 'Thou shalt not follow after strange gods'."

"Take thou this stick, O venerable one," said the King, paying no attention to the remark, "and have a shot thyself. True, thou art well stricken in years, but many a man has so wrought that he was able to give his grandchildren a stroke a hole. It is never too late to begin."

The High Priest shrank back, horrified. The King frowned.

"It is our Royal wish," he said, coldly.

The High Priest was forced to comply. Had they been alone, it is possible that he might have risked all on one swift stroke with his knife, but by this time a group of *kaddiz* had drifted up, and were watching the proceedings with that supercilious detachment so characteristic of them. He took the stick and arranged his limbs as the King directed.

"Now," said Merolchazzar, "slow back and keep your e'e on the ba'!"

A month later, Ascobaruch returned from his trip. He had received no word from the High Priest announcing the success of the revolution, but there might be many reasons for that. It was with unruffled contentment that he bade his charioteer drive him to the palace. He was glad to get back, for after all a holiday is hardly a holiday if you have left your business affairs unsettled.

As he drove, the chariot passed a fair open space, on the outskirts of the city. A sudden chill froze the serenity of Ascobaruch's mood. He prodded the charioteer sharply in the small of the back.

"What is that?" he demanded, catching his breath.

All over the green expanse could be seen men in strange robes, moving to and fro in couples and bearing in their hands mystic wands. Some searched restlessly in the bushes, others were walking briskly in the direction of small red flags. A sickening foreboding of disaster fell upon Ascobaruch.

The charioteer seemed surprised at the question.

"Yon's the muneecipal linx," he replied.

"The what?"

"The muneecipal linx."

"Tell me, fellow, why do you talk that way?"

"Whitway?"

"Why, like that. The way you're talking."

"Hoots, mon!" said the charioteer. "His Majesty King Merolchazzar—may his handicap decrease!—hae passit a law that a' his soobjects shall do it. Aiblins, 'tis the language spoken by The Pro, on whom be peace! Mphm!"

Ascobaruch sat back limply, his head swimming. The chariot drove on, till now it took the road adjoining the royal Linx. A wall lined a portion of this road, and suddenly, from behind this wall, there rent the air a great shout of laughter.

"Pull up!" cried Ascobaruch to the charioteer.

He had recognized that laugh. It was the laugh of Merolchazzar.

Ascobaruch crept to the wall and cautiously poked his head over it. The sight he saw drove the blood from his face and left him white and haggard.

The King and the Grand Vizier were playing a foursome against the Pro and the High Priest of Hec, and the Vizier had just laid the High Priest a dead stymie.

Ascobaruch tottered to the chariot.

"Take me back," he muttered, pallidly. "I've forgotten something!"

And so golf came to Oom, and with it prosperity uneaqualled in the whole history of the land. Everybody was happy. There was no more unemployment. Crime ceased. The chronicler repeatedly refers to it in his memoirs as the Golden Age. And yet there remained one man on whom complete felicity had not descended. It was all right while he was actually on the Linx, but there were blank, dreary stretches of the night when King Merolchazzar lay sleepless on his couch and mourned that he had nobody to love him.

Of course, his subjects loved him in a way. A new statue had been erected in the palace square, showing him in the act of getting out of casual water. The minstrels had composed a whole cycle of up-to-date songs, commemorating his prowess with the mashie. His handicap was down to twelve. But these things are not all. A golfer needs a loving wife, to whom he can describe the day's play through the long evenings. And this was just were Merolchazzar's life was empty. No word had come from the Princess of the Outer Isles, and, as he refused to be put off with just-as-good substitutes, he remained a lonely man.

But one morning, in the early hours of a summer day, as he lay sleeping after a disturbed night, Merolchazzar was awakened by the eager hand of the Lord High Chamberlain, shaking his shoulder.

"Now what?" said the King.

"Hoots, your Majesty! Glorious news! The Princess of the Outer Isles waits without—I mean wi'oot!"

The King sprang from his couch.

"A messenger from the Princess at last!"

"Nay, sire, the Princess herself—that is to say," said the Lord Chamberlain, who was an old man and had found it hard to accustom himself to the new tongue at his age, "her ain sel'! And believe me, or rather, mind ah'm telling ye," went on the honest man, joyfully, for he had been deeply exercised by his monarch's troubles, "her Highness is the easiest thing to look at these eyes hae ever seen. And you can say I said it!"

"She is beautiful?"

"Your Majesty, she is, in the best and deepest sense of the word, a pippin!"

King Merolchazzar was groping wildly for his robes.

"Tell her to wait!" he cried. "Go and amuse her. Ask her riddles! Tell her anecdotes! Don't let her go. Say I'll be down in a moment. Where in the name of

Zoroaster is our imperial mesh-knit underwear?"

A fair and pleasing sight was the Princess of the Outer Isles as she stood on the terrace in the clear sunshine of the summer morning, looking over the King's gardens. With her delicate littles nose she sniffed the fragrance of the flowers. Her blue eyes roamed over the rose bushes, and the breeze ruffled the golden curls about her temples. Presently a sound behind her caused her to turn, and she perceived a godlike man hurrying across the terrace pulling up a sock. And at the sight of him the Princess's heart sang within her like the birds in the garden.

"Hope I haven't kept you waiting," said Merolchazzar, apologetically. He, too, was conscious of a strange, wild exhilaration. Truly was this maiden, as his Chamberlain had said, noticeably easy on the eyes. Her beauty was as water in the desert, as fire on a frosty night, as diamonds, rubies, pearls, sapphires, and amethysts.

"Oh, no!" said the princess, "I've been enjoying myself. How passing beautiful are thy gardens, O King!"

"My gardens may be passing beautiful," said Merolchazzar, earnestly, "but they aren't half so passing beautiful as thy eyes. I have dreamed of thee by night and by day, and I will tell the world I was nowhere near it! My sluggish fancy came not within a hundred and fifty-seven miles of the reality. Now let the sun dim his face and the moon hide herself abashed. Now let the flowers bend their heads and the gazelle of the mountains confess itself a cripple. Princess, your slave!"

And King Merolchazzar, with that easy grace so characteristic of Royalty, took her hand in his and kissed it.

As he did so, he gave a start of surprise.

"By Hec!" he exclaimed. "What hast thou been doing to thyself? Thy hand is all over little rough places inside. Has some malignant wizard laid a spell upon thee, or what is it?"

The Princess blushed.

"If I make that clear to thee," she said, "I shall also make clear why it was that I sent thee no message all this long while. My time was so occupied, verily I did not seem to have a moment. The fact is, these sorenesses are due to a strange, new religion to which I and my subjects have but recently become converted. And O that I might make thee also of the true faith! 'Tis a wondrous tale, my lord. Some two moons back there was brought to my Court by wandering pirates a captive of an uncouth race who dwell in the north. And this man has taught us——"

King Merolchazzar uttered a loud cry.

"By Tom, the son of Morris! Can this truly be so? What is thy handicap?"

The Princess stared at him, wide-eyed.

"Truly this is a miracle! Art thou also a worshipper of the great Gowf?"

"Am I!" cried the King. "Am I!" He broke off. "Listen!"

From the minstrels' room high up in the palace there came the sound of singing. The minstrels were practising a new pæan of praise—words by the Grand Vizier, music by the High Priest of Hec—which they were to render at the next full moon at the banquet of the worshippers of Gowf. The words came clear and distinct through the still air:

> *"Oh, praises let us utter*
> *To our most glorious King!*
> *It fairly makes you stutter*
> *To see him start his swing!*
> *Success attend his putter!*
> *And luck be with his drive!*
> *And may he do each hole in two,*
> *Although the bogey's five!"*

The voices died away. There was a silence.

"If I hadn't missed a two-foot putt, I'd have done the long fifteenth in four yesterday," said the King.

"I won the Ladies' Open Championship of the Outer Isles last week," said the Princess.

They looked into each other's eyes for a long moment. And then, hand in hand, they walked slowly into the palace.

EPILOGUE

"Well?" we said, anxiously.

"I like it," said the editor.

"Good egg!" we murmured.

The editor pressed a bell, a single ruby set in a fold of the tapestry upon the wall. The major-domo appeared.

"Give this man a purse of gold," said the editor, "and throw him out."

12

THE HEART OF A GOOF

IT WAS a morning when all nature shouted "Fore!" The breeze, as it blew gently up from the valley, seemed to bring a message of hope and cheer, whispering of chip-shots holed and brassies landing squarely on the meat. The fairway, as yet unscarred by the irons of a hundred dubs, smiled greenly up at the azure sky; and the sun, peeping above the trees, looked like a giant golf-ball perfectly lofted by the mashie of some unseen god and about to drop dead by the pin of the eighteenth. It was the day of the opening of the course after the long winter, and a crowd of considerable dimensions had collected at the first tee. Plus fours gleamed in the sunshine, and the air was charged with happy anticipation.

In all that gay throng there was but one sad face. It belonged to the man who was waggling his driver over the new ball perched on its little hill of sand. This man seemed careworn, hopeless. He gazed down the fairway, shifted his feet, waggled, gazed down the fairway again, shifted the dogs once more, and waggled afresh. He waggled as Hamlet might have waggled, moodily, irresolutely. Then, at last, he swung, and, taking from his caddie the niblick which the intelligent lad had been holding in readiness from the moment when he had walked on to the tee, trudged wearily off to play his second.

The Oldest Member, who had been observing the scene with a benevolent eye from his favourite chair on the terrace, sighed.

"Poor Jenkinson," he said, "does not improve."

"No," agreed his companion, a young man with open features and a handicap of six. "And yet I happen to know that he has been taking lessons all the winter at one of those indoor places."

"Futile, quite futile," said the Sage with a shake of his snowy head. "There is no wizard living who could make that man go round in an average of sevens. I keep advising him to give up the game."

"You!" cried the young man, raising a shocked and startled face from the driver with which he was toying. "*You* told him to give up golf! Why I thought——"

"I understand and approve of your horror," said the Oldest Member, gently. "But you must bear in mind that Jenkinson's is not an ordinary case. You know and I know scores of men who have never broken a hundred and twenty in their lives, and yet contrive to be happy, useful members of society. However badly they may play, they are able to forget. But with Jenkinson it is different. He is not one of those who can take it or leave it alone. His only chance of happiness lies in complete abstinence. Jenkinson is a goof."

"A what?"

"A goof," repeated the Sage. "One of those unfortunate beings who have allowed this noblest of sports to get too great a grip upon them, who have permitted it to eat into their souls, like some malignant growth. The goof, you must understand, is not like you and me. He broods. He becomes morbid. His goofery unfits him for the battles of life. Jenkinson, for example, was once a man with a glowing future in the hay, corn, and feed business, but a constant stream of hooks, tops, and slices gradually made him so diffident and mistrustful of himself, that he let opportunity after opportunity slip, with the result that other, sterner, hay, corn, and feed merchants passed him in the race. Every time he had the chance to carry through some big deal in hay, or to execute some flashing *coup* in corn and feed, the fatal diffidence generated by a hundred rotten rounds would undo him. I understand his bankruptcy may be expected at any moment."

"My golly!" said the young man, deeply impressed. "I hope I never become a goof. Do you mean to say there is really no cure except giving up the game?"

The Oldest Member was silent for a while.

"It is curious that you should have asked that question," he said at last, "for only this morning I was thinking of the one case in my experience where a goof was enabled to overcome his deplorable malady. It was owing to a girl, of course. The longer I live, the more I come to see that most things are. But you will, no doubt, wish to hear the story from the beginning."

The young man rose with the startled haste of some wild creature, which, wandering through the undergrowth, perceives the trap in his path.

"I should love to," he mumbled, "only I shall be losing my place at the tee."

"The goof in question," said the Sage, attaching himself with quiet firmness to the youth's coat-button, "was a man of about your age, by name Ferdinand Dibble. I knew him well. In fact, it was to me——"

"Some other time, eh?"

"It was to me," proceeded the Sage, placidly, "that he came for sympathy in the great crisis of his life, and I am not ashamed to say that when he had finished laying bare his soul to me there were tears in my eyes. My heart bled for the boy."

"I bet it did. But——"

The Oldest Member pushed him gently back into his seat.

"Golf," he said, "is the Great Mystery. Like some capricious goddess——"

The young man, who had been exhibiting symptoms of feverishness, appeared to become resigned. He sighed softly.

"Did you ever read 'The Ancient Mariner'?" he said.

"Many years ago," said the Oldest Member. "Why do you ask?"

"Oh, I don't know," said the young man. "It just occurred to me."

Golf (resumed the Oldest Member) is the Great Mystery. Like some capricious goddess, it bestows its favours with what would appear an almost fat-headed lack of method and discrimination. On every side we see big two-fisted he-men floundering round in three figures, stopping every few minutes to let through little shrimps with knock-knees and hollow cheeks, who are tearing off snappy seventy-fours. Giants of finance have to accept a stroke per from their junior clerks. Men capable of governing empires fail to control a small, white ball, which presents no difficulties whatever to others with one ounce more brain than a cuckoo-clock. Mysterious, but there it is. There was no apparent reason why Ferdinand Dibble should not have been a competent golfer. He had strong wrists and a good eye. Nevertheless, the fact remains that he was a dub. And on a certain evening in June I realized that he was also a goof. I found it out quite suddenly as the result of a conversation which we had on this very terrace.

I was sitting here that evening thinking of this and that, when by the corner of the club-house I observed young Dibble in conversation with a girl in white. I could not see who she was, for her back was turned. Presently they parted and Ferdinand came slowly across to where I sat. His air was dejected. He had had the boots licked off him earlier in the afternoon by Jimmy Fothergill, and it was to this that I attributed his gloom. I was to find out in a few moments that I was partly but not entirely correct in this surmise. He took the next chair to mine, and for several minutes sat staring moodily down into the valley.

"I've just been talking to Barbara Medway," he said, suddenly breaking the silence.

"Indeed?" I said. "A delightful girl."

"She's going away for the summer to Marvis Bay."

"She will take the sunshine with her."

"You bet she will!" said Ferdinand Dibble, with extraordinary warmth, and there was another long silence.

Presently Ferdinand uttered a hollow groan. "I love her, dammit!" he muttered brokenly. "Oh golly, how I love her!"

I was not surprised at his making me the recipient of his confidences like this. Most of the young folk in the place brought their troubles to me sooner or later.

"And does she return your love?"

"I don't know. I haven't asked her."

"Why not? I should have thought the point not without its interest for you."

Ferdinand gnawed the handle of his putter distractedly.

"I haven't the nerve," he burst out at length. "I simply can't summon up the cold gall to ask a girl, least of all an angel like her, to marry me. You see, it's like this. Every time I work myself up to the point of having a dash at it, I go out and get trimmed by someone giving me a stroke a hole. Every time I feel I've mustered up enough pep to propose, I take on a bogey three. Every time I'm in good mid-season form for putting my fate to the test, to win or lose it all, something goes all blooey with my swing, and I slice into the rough at every tee. And then my self-confidence leaves me. I become nervous, tongue-tied, diffident. I wish to goodness I knew the man who invented this infernal game. I'd strangle him. But I suppose he's been dead for ages. Still, I could go and jump on his grave."

It was at this point that I understood all, and the heart within me sank like lead. The truth was out. Ferdinand Dibble was a goof.

"Come, come, my boy," I said, though feeling the uselessness of any words. "Master this weakness."

"I can't."

"Try!"

"I have tried."

He gnawed his putter again.

"She was asking me just now if I couldn't manage to come to Marvis Bay, too," he said.

"That surely is encouraging? It suggests that she is not entirely indifferent to your society."

"Yes, but what's the use? Do you know," a gleam coming into his eyes for a moment, "I have a feeling that if I could ever beat some really fairly good player— just once—I could bring the thing off." The gleam faded. "But what chance is there of that?"

It was a question which I did not care to answer. I merely patted his shoulder sympathetically, and after a little while he left me and walked away. I was still sitting there, thinking over his hard case, when Barbara Medway came out of the club-house.

She, too, seemed grave and preoccupied, as if there was something on her mind. She took the chair which Ferdinand had vacated, and sighed wearily.

"Have you ever felt," she asked, "that you would like to bang a man on the head with something hard and heavy? With knobs on?"

I said I had sometimes experienced such a desire, and asked if she had any particular man in mind. She seemed to hesitate for a moment before replying, then, apparently, made up her mind to confide in me. My advanced years carry with them certain pleasant compensations, one of which is that nice girls often confide in me. I frequently find myself enrolled as a father-confessor on the most intimate matters by beautiful creatures from whom many a younger man would give his eye-teeth to get a friendly word. Besides, I had known Barbara since she was a child. Frequently—though not recently—I had given her her evening bath. These things form a bond.

"Why are men such chumps?" she exclaimed.

"You still have not told me who it is that has caused these harsh words. Do I know him?"

"Of course you do. You've just been talking to him."

"Ferdinand Dibble? But why should you wish to bang Ferdinand Dibble on the head with something hard and heavy with knobs on?"

"Because he's such a goop."

"You mean a goof?" I queried, wondering how she could have penetrated the unhappy man's secret.

"No, a goop. A goop is a man who's in love with a girl and won't tell her so. I am as certain as I am of anything that Ferdinand is fond of me."

"Your instinct is unerring. He has just been confiding in me on that very point."

"Well, why doesn't he confide in *me*, the poor fish?" cried the high-spirited girl, petulantly flicking a pebble at a passing grasshopper. "I can't be expected to fling myself into his arms unless he gives some sort of a hint that he's ready to catch me."

"Would it help if I were to repeat to him the substance of this conversation of ours?"

"If you breathe a word of it, I'll never speak to you again," she cried. "I'd rather die an awful death than have any man think I wanted him so badly that I had to send relays of messengers begging him to marry me."

I saw her point.

"Then I fear," I said, gravely, "that there is nothing to be done. One can only wait and hope. It may be that in the years to come Ferdinand Dibble will acquire a nice lissom, wristy swing, with the head kept rigid and the right leg firmly braced and——"

"What are you talking about?"

"I was toying with the hope that some sunny day Ferdinand Dibble would cease to be a goof."

"You mean a goop?"

"No, a goof. A goof is a man who——" And I went on to explain the peculiar psychological difficulties which lay in the way of any declaration of affection on Ferdinand's part.

"But I have never heard of anything so ridiculous in my life," she ejaculated. "Do you mean to say that he is waiting till he is good at golf before he asks me to marry him?"

"It is not quite so simple as that," I said sadly. "Many bad golfers marry, feeling that a wife's loving solicitude may improve their game. But they are rugged, thick-skinned men, not sensitive and introspective, like Ferdinand. Ferdinand has allowed himself to become morbid. It is one of the chief merits of golf that non-success at the game induces a certain amount of decent humility, which keeps a man from pluming himself too much on any petty triumphs he may achieve in other walks of life; but in all things there is a happy mean, and with Ferdinand this humility has gone too far. It has taken all the spirit out of him. He feels crushed and worthless. He is grateful to caddies when they accept a tip instead of drawing themselves up to their full height and flinging the money in his face."

"Then do you mean that things have got to go on like this for ever?"

I thought for a moment.

"It is a pity," I said, "that you could not have induced Ferdinand to go to Marvis Bay for a month or two."

"Why?"

"Because it seems to me, thinking the thing over, that it is just possible that Marvis Bay might cure him. At the hotel there he would find collected a mob of golfers—I used the term in its broadest sense, to embrace the paralytics and the men who play left-handed—whom even he would be able to beat. When I was last at Marvis Bay, the hotel links were a sort of Sargasso Sea into which had drifted all the pitiful flotsam and jetsam of golf. I have seen things done on that course at which I shuddered and averted my eyes—and I am not a weak man. If Ferdinand can polish up his game so as to go round in a fairly steady hundred and five, I fancy there is hope. But I understand he is not going to Marvis Bay."

"Oh yes he is," said the girl.

"Indeed! He did not tell me that when we were talking just now."

"He didn't know it then. He will when I have had a few words with him."

And she walked with firm steps back into the club-house.

It has been well said that there are many kinds of golf, beginning at the top with the golf of professionals and the best amateurs and working down through the golf of ossified men to that of Scotch University professors. Until recently this last was looked upon as the lowest possible depth; but nowadays, with the growing popularity of summer hotels, we are able to add a brand still lower, the golf you find at places like Marvis Bay.

To Ferdinand Dibble, coming from a club where the standard of play was rather unusually high, Marvis Bay was a revelation, and for some days after his arrival there he went about dazed, like a man who cannot believe it is really true. To go out on the links at this summer resort was like entering a new world. The hotel was full of stout, middle-aged men, who, after a misspent youth devoted to making money, had taken to a game at which real proficiency can only be acquired by those who start playing in their cradles and keep their weight down. Out on the course each morning you could see representatives of every nightmare style that was ever invented. There was the man who seemed to be attempting to deceive his ball and lull it into a false security by looking away from it and then making a lightning slash in the apparent hope of catching it off its guard. There was the man who wielded his mid-iron like one killing snakes. There was the man who addressed his ball as if he were stroking a cat, the man who drove as if he were cracking a whip, the man who brooded over each shot like one whose heart is bowed down by bad news from home, and the man who scooped with his mashie as if he were ladling soup. By the end of the first week Ferdinand Dibble was the acknowledged champion of the place. He had gone through the entire menagerie like a bullet through a cream puff.

First, scarcely daring to consider the possibility of success, he had taken on the man who tried to catch his ball off its guard and had beaten him five up and four to play. Then, with gradually growing confidence, he tackled in turn the Cat-Stroker, the Whip-Cracker, the Heart Bowed Down, and the Soup-Scooper, and walked all over their faces with spiked shoes. And as these were the leading local amateurs, whose prowess the octogenarians and the men who went round in bath-chairs vainly strove to emulate, Ferdinand Dibble was faced on the eighth morning of his visit by the startling fact that he had no more worlds to conquer. He was monarch of all he surveyed, and, what is more, had won his first trophy, the prize in the great medal-play handicap tournament, in which he had nosed in ahead of the field by two strokes, edging out his nearest rival, a venerable old gentleman, by means of a brilliant and unexpected four on the last hole. The prize was a handsome pewter mug, about the size of the old oaken bucket, and Ferdinand used to go to his room immediately after dinner to croon over it like a mother over her child.

You are wondering, no doubt, why, in these circumstances, he did not take advantage of the new spirit of exhilarated pride which had replaced his old humility and instantly propose to Barbara Medway. I will tell you. He did not propose to Barbara because Barbara was not there. At the last moment she had been detained at home to nurse a sick parent and had been compelled to postpone her visit for a couple of weeks. He could, no doubt, have proposed in one of the daily letters which he wrote to her, but somehow, once he started writing, he found that he used up so much space describing his best shots on the links that day that it was difficult to squeeze in a declaration of undying passion. After all, you can hardly cram that sort of thing into a postscript.

He decided, therefore, to wait till she arrived, and meanwhile pursued his con-quering course. The longer he waited, the better, in one way, for every morning and afternoon that passed was adding new layers to his self-esteem. Day by day in every way he grew chestier and chestier.

Meanwhile, however, dark clouds were gathering. Sullen mutterings were to be heard in corners of the hotel lounge, and the spirit of revolt was abroad. For Fer-dinand's chestiness had not escaped the notice of his defeated rivals. There is nobody so chesty as a normally unchesty man who suddenly becomes chesty, and I am sorry to say that the chestiness which had come to Ferdinand was the aggressive type of chestiness which breeds enemies. He had developed a habit of holding the game up in order to give his opponent advice. The Whip-Cracker had not forgiven, and never would forgive, his well-meant but galling criticism of his back-swing. The Scooper, who had always scooped since the day when, at the age of sixty-four, he subscribed to the Correspondence Course which was to teach him golf in twelve lessons by mail, resented being told by a snip of a boy that the mashie-stroke should be a smooth, unhurried swing. The Snake-Killer—— But I need not weary you with a detailed recital of these men's grievances; it is enough to say that they all had it in for Ferdinand, and one night, after dinner, they met in the lounge to decide what was to be done about it.

A nasty spirit was displayed by all.

"A mere lad telling me how to use my mashie!" growled the Scooper. "Smooth and unhurried my left eyeball! I get it up, don't I? Well, what more do you want?"

"I keep telling him that mine is the old, full St. Andrew's swing," muttered the Whip-Cracker, between set teeth, "but he won't listen to me."

"He ought to be taken down a peg or two," hissed the Snake-Killer. It is not easy to hiss a sentence without a single "s" in it, and the fact that he succeeded in doing so shows to what a pitch of emotion the man had been goaded by Ferdinand's maddening air of superiority.

"Yes, but what can we do?" queried an octogenarian, when this last remark had been passed on to him down his ear-trumpet.

"That's the trouble," sighed the Scooper. "What can we do?" And there was a sorrowful shaking of heads.

"I know!" exclaimed the Cat-Stroker, who had not hitherto spoken. He was a lawyer, and a man of subtle and sinister mind. "I have it! There's a boy in my office—young Parsloe—who could beat this man Dibble hollow. I'll wire him to come down here and we'll spring him on this fellow and knock some of the conceit out of him."

There was a chorus of approval.

"But are you sure he can beat him?" asked the Snake-Killer, anxiously. "It would never do to make a mistake."

"Of course I'm sure," said the Cat-Stroker. "George Parsloe once went round in ninety-four."

"Many changes there have been since ninety-four," said the octogenarian, nodding sagely. "Ah, many, many changes. None of these motor-cars then, tearing about and killing——"

Kindly hands led him off to have an egg-and-milk, and the remaining conspirators returned to the point at issue with bent brows.

"Ninety-four?" said the Scooper, incredulously. "Do you mean counting every stroke?"

"Counting every stroke."

"Not conceding himself any putts?"

"Not one."

"Wire him to come at once," said the meeting with one voice.

That night the Cat-Stroker approached Ferdinand, smooth, subtle, lawyer-like.

"Oh, Dibble," he said, "just the man I wanted to see. Dibble, there's a young friend of mine coming down here who goes in for golf a little. George Parsloe is his name. I was wondering if you could spare time to give him a game. He is just a novice, you know."

"I shall be delighted to play a round with him," said Ferdinand kindly.

"He might pick up a pointer or two from watching you," said the Cat-Stroker.

"True, true," said Ferdinand.

"Then I'll introduce you when he shows up."

"Delighted," said Ferdinand.

He was in excellent humour that night, for he had had a letter from Barbara saying that she was arriving on the next day but one.

It was Ferdinand's healthy custom of a morning to get up in good time and take a dip in the sea before breakfast. On the morning of the day of Barbara's arrival, he arose, as usual, donned his flannels, took a good look at the cup, and started out. It was a fine, fresh morning, and he glowed both externally and internally. As he crossed the links, for the nearest route to the water was through the fairway of the seventh, he was whistling happily and rehearsing in his mind the opening sentences of his proposal. For it was his firm resolve that night after dinner to ask Barbara to marry him. He was proceeding over the smooth turf without a care in the world, when there was a sudden cry of "Fore!" and the next moment a golf-ball, missing him by inches, sailed up the fairway and came to a rest fifty yards from where he stood. He looked up and observed a figure coming towards him from the tee.

The distance from the tee was fully a hundred and thirty yards. Add fifty to that, and you have a hundred and eighty yards. No such drive had been made on the Marvis Bay links since their foundation, and such is the generous spirit of the true golfer that Ferdinand's first emotion, after the not inexcusable spasm of panic caused by the hum of the ball past his ear, was one of cordial admiration. By some kindly miracle, he supposed, one of his hotel acquaintances had been permitted for once in his life to time a drive right. It was only when the other man came up that there began to steal over him a sickening apprehension. The faces of all those who hewed divots on the hotel course were familiar to him, and the fact that this fellow was a stranger seemed to point with dreadful certainty to his being the man he had agreed to play.

"Sorry," said the man. He was a tall, strikingly handsome youth, with brown eyes and a dark moustache.

"Oh, that's all right," said Ferdinand. "Er—do you always drive like that?"

"Well, I generally get a bit longer ball, but I'm off my drive this morning. It's lucky I came out and got this practice. I'm playing a match tomorrow with a fellow named Dibble, who's a local champion, or something."

"Me," said Ferdinand, humbly.

"Eh? Oh, you?" Mr. Parsloe eyed him appraisingly. "Well, may the best man win."

As this was precisely what Ferdinand was afraid was going to happen, he nodded in a sickly manner and tottered off to his bathe. The magic had gone out of the morning. The sun still shone, but in a silly, feeble way; and a cold and depressing wind had sprung up. For Ferdinand's inferiority complex, which had seemed cured for ever, was back again, doing business at the old stand.

How sad it is in this life that the moment to which we have looked forward with the most glowing anticipation so often turns out on arrival, flat, cold, and disappointing. For ten days Barbara Medway had been living for that meeting with Ferdinand, when, getting out of the train, she would see him popping about on the horizon with the lovelight sparkling in his eyes and words of devotion trembling on his lips. The poor girl never doubted for an instant that he would unleash his pent-up emotions inside the first five minutes, and her only worry was lest he should give an embarrassing publicity to the sacred scene by falling on his knees on the station platform.

"Well, here I am at last," she cried gaily.

"Hullo!" said Ferdinand, with a twisted smile.

The girl looked at him, chilled. How could she know that his peculiar manner was due entirely to the severe attack of cold feet resultant upon his meeting with George Parsloe that morning? The interpretation which she placed upon it was that he was not glad to see her. If he had behaved like this before, she would, of course, have put it down to ingrowing goofery, but now she had his written statements to prove that for the last ten days his golf had been one long series of triumphs.

"I got your letters," she said, persevering bravely.

"I thought you would," said Ferdinand, absently.

"You seem to have been doing wonders."

"Yes."

There was a silence.

"Have a nice journey?" said Ferdinand.

"Very," said Barbara.

She spoke coldly, for she was madder than a wet hen. She saw it all now. In the ten days since they had parted, his love, she realized, had waned. Some other girl, met in the romantic surroundings of this picturesque resort, had supplanted her in his affections. She knew how quickly Cupid gets off the mark at a summer hotel, and for an instant she blamed herself for ever having been so ivory-skulled as to let him come to this place alone. Then regret was swallowed up in wrath, and she became so glacial that Ferdinand, who had been on the point of telling her the secret of his gloom, retired into his shell and conversation during the drive to the hotel never soared above a certain level. Ferdinand said the sunshine was nice and Barbara said yes, it was nice, and Ferdinand said it looked pretty on the water, and Barbara said yes, it did look pretty on the water, and Ferdinand said he hoped it was not going to rain, and Barbara said yes, it would be a pity if it rained. And then there was another lengthy silence.

"How is my uncle?" asked Barbara at last.

I omitted to mention that the individual to whom I have referred as the Cat-Stroker was Barbara's mother's brother, and her host at Marvis Bay.

"Your uncle?"

"His name is Tuttle. Have you met him?"

"Oh yes. I've seen a good deal of him. He has got a friend staying with him," said

Ferdinand, his mind returning to the matter nearest his heart. "A fellow named Parsloe."

"Oh, is George Parsloe here? How jolly!"

"Do you know him?" barked Ferdinand, hollowly. He would not have supposed that anything could have added to his existing depression, but he was conscious now of having slipped a few rungs farther down the ladder of gloom. There had been a horribly joyful ring in her voice. Ah, well, he reflected morosely, how like life it all was! We never know what the morrow may bring forth. We strike a good patch and are beginning to think pretty well of ourselves, and along comes a George Parsloe.

"Of course I do," said Barbara. "Why, there he is."

The cab had drawn up at the door of the hotel, and on the porch George Parsloe was airing his graceful person. To Ferdinand's fevered eye he looked like a Greek god, and his inferiority complex began to exhibit symptoms of elephantiasis. How could he compete at love or golf with a fellow who looked as if he had stepped out of the movies and considered himself off his drive when he did a hundred and eighty yards?

"Geor-gee!" cried Barbara blithely. "Hullo, George!"

"Why, hullo, Barbara!"

They fell into pleasant conversation, while Ferdinand hung miserably about in the offing. And presently, feeling that his society was not essential to their happiness, he slunk away.

George Parsloe dined at the Cat-Stroker's table that night, and it was with George Parsloe that Barbara roamed in the moonlight after dinner. Ferdinand, after a profitless hour at the billiard-table, went early to his room. But not even the rays of the moon, glinting on his cup, could soothe the fever in his soul. He practised putting sombrely into his tooth-glass for a while; then, going to bed, fell at last into a troubled sleep.

Barbara slept late the next morning and breakfasted in her room. Coming down towards noon, she found a strange emptiness in the hotel. It was her experience of summer hotels that a really fine day like this one was the cue for half the inhabitants to collect in the lounge, shut all the windows, and talk about conditions in the jute industry. To her surprise, though the sun was streaming down from a cloudless sky, the only occupant of the lounge was the octogenarian with the ear-trumpet. She observed that he was chuckling to himself in a senile manner.

"Good morning," she said, politely, for she had made his acquaintance on the previous evening.

"Hey?" said the octogenarian, suspending his chuckling and getting his trumpet into position.

"I said 'Good morning!'" roared Barbara into the receiver.

"Hey?"

"Good morning!"

"Ah! Yes, it's a very fine morning, a very fine morning. If it wasn't for missing my bun and glass of milk at twelve sharp," said the octogenarian, "I'd be down on the links. That's where I'd be, down on the links. If it wasn't for missing my bun and glass of milk."

This refreshment arriving at this moment, he dismantled the radio outfit and began to restore his tissues.

"Watching the match," he explained, pausing for a moment in his bun-mangling. "What match?"

The octogenarian sipped his milk.

"What match?" repeated Barbara.

"Hey?"

"What match?"

The octogenarian began to chuckle again and nearly swallowed a crumb the wrong way.

"Take some of the conceit out of him," he gurgled.

"Out of who?" asked Barbara, knowing perfectly well that she should have said "whom".

"Yes," said the octogenarian.

"Who is conceited?"

"Ah! This young fellow, Dibble. Very conceited. I saw it in his eye from the first, but nobody would listen to me. Mark my words, I said, that boy needs taking down a peg or two. Well, he's going to be this morning. Your uncle wired to young Parsloe to come down, and he's arranged a match between them. Dibble——" Here the octogenarian choked again and had to rinse himself out with milk, "Dibble doesn't know that Parsloe once went round in ninety-four!"

"What?"

Everything seemed to go black to Barbara. Through a murky mist she appeared to be looking at a negro octogenarian, sipping ink. Then her eyes cleared, and she found herself clutching for support at the back of a chair. She understood now. She realized why Ferdinand had been so distrait, and her whole heart went out to him in a spasm of maternal pity. How she had wronged him!

"Take some of the conceit out of him," the octogenarian was mumbling, and Barbara felt a sudden sharp loathing for the old man. For two pins she could have dropped a beetle in his milk. Then the need for action roused her. What action? She did not know. All she knew was that she must act.

"Oh!" she cried.

"Hey?" said the octogenarian, bringing his trumpet to the ready.

But Barbara had gone.

It was not far to the links, and Barbara covered the distance on flying feet. She reached the club-house, but the course was empty except for the Scooper, who was preparing to drive off the first tee. In spite of the fact that something seemed to tell her subconsciously that this was one of the sights she ought not to miss, the girl did not wait to watch. Assuming that the match had started soon after breakfast, it must by now have reached one of the holes on the second nine. She ran down the hill, looking to left and right, and was presently aware of a group of spectators clustered about a green in the distance. As she hurried towards them they moved away, and now she could see Ferdinand advancing to the next tee. With a thrill that shook her whole body she realized that he had the honour. So he must have won one hole, at any rate. Then she saw her uncle.

"How are they?" she gasped.

Mr. Tuttle seemed moody. It was apparent that things were not going altogether to his liking.

"All square at the fifteenth," he replied, gloomily.

"All square!"

"Yes. Young Parsloe," said Mr. Tuttle with a sour look in the direction of that lissom athlete, "doesn't seem to be able to do a thing right on the greens. He has been putting like a sheep with the botts."

From the foregoing remark of Mr. Tuttle you will, no doubt, have gleaned at least a clue to the mystery of how Ferdinand Dibble had managed to hold his long-driving adversary up to the fifteenth green, but for all that you will probably consider that some further explanation of this amazing state of affairs is required. Mere bad putting on the part of George Parsloe is not, you feel, sufficient to cover the matter entirely. You are right. There was another very important factor in the situation—to wit, that by some extraordinary chance Ferdinand Dibble had started right off from the first tee, playing the game of a lifetime. Never had he made such drives, never chipped his chips so shrewdly.

About Ferdinand's driving there was as a general thing a fatal stiffness and over-caution which prevented success. And with his chip-shots he rarely achieved accuracy owing to his habit of rearing his head like the lion of the jungle just before the club struck the ball. But today he had been swinging with a careless freedom, and his chips had been true and clean. The thing had puzzled him all the way round. It had not elated him, for, owing to Barbara's aloofness and the way in which she had gambolled about George Parsloe, like a young lamb in the springtime, he was in too deep a state of dejection to be elated by anything. And now, suddenly, in a flash of clear vision, he perceived the reason why he had been playing so well today. It was just because he was not elated. It was simply because he was so profoundly miserable.

That was what Ferdinand told himself as he stepped off the sixteenth, after hitting a screamer down the centre of the fairway, and I am convinced that he was right. Like so many indifferent golfers, Ferdinand Dibble had always made the game hard for himself by thinking too much. He was a deep student of the works of the masters, and whenever he prepared to play a stroke he had a complete mental list of all the mistakes which it was possible to make. He would remember how Taylor had warned against dipping the right shoulder, how Vardon had inveighed against any movement of the head; he would recall how Ray had mentioned the tendency to snatch back the club, how Braid had spoken sadly of those who sin against their better selves by stiffening the muscles and heaving.

The consequence was that when, after waggling in a frozen manner till mere shame urged him to take some definite course of action, he eventually swung, he invariably proceeded to dip his right shoulder, stiffen his muscles, heave, and snatch back the club, at the same time raising his head sharply as in the illustrated plate ("Some Frequent Faults of Beginners—No. 3—Lifting the Bean") facing page thirty-four of James Braid's *Golf Without Tears*. Today, he had been so preoccupied with his broken heart that he had made his shots absently, almost carelessly, with the result that at least one in every three had been a lallapaloosa.

Meanwhile, George Parsloe had driven off and the match was progressing. George was feeling a little flustered by now. He had been given to understand that this bird Dibble was a hundred-at-his-best man, and all the way round the fellow had been reeling off fives in great profusion, and had once actually got a four. True, there had been an occasional six, and even a seven, but that did not alter the main fact that the man was making the dickens of a game of it. With the haughty spirit of one who had once done a ninety-four, George Parsloe had anticipated being at least three up at the turn. Instead of which he had been two down, and had had to fight strenuously to draw level.

Nevertheless, he drove steadily and well, and would certainly have won the hole had it not been for his weak and sinful putting. The same defect caused him to halve the seventeenth, after being on in two, with Ferdinand wandering in the desert and only reaching the green with his fourth. Then, however, Ferdinand holed out from a distance of seven yards, getting a five; which George's three putts just enabled him to equal.

Barbara had watched the proceedings with a beating heart. At first she had looked on from afar; but now, drawn as by a magnet, she approached the tee. Ferdinand was driving off. She held her breath. Ferdinand held his breath. And all around one could see their respective breaths being held by George Parsloe, Mr. Tuttle, and the enthralled crowd of spectators. It was a moment of the acutest tension, and it was broken by the crack of Ferdinand's driver as it met the ball and sent it hopping along the ground for a mere thirty yards. At this supreme crisis in the match Ferdinand Dibble had topped.

George Parsloe teed up his ball. There was a smile of quiet satisfaction on his face. He snuggled the driver in his hands, and gave it a preliminary swish. This, felt George Parsloe, was where the happy ending came. He could drive as he had never driven before. He would so drive that it would take his opponent at least three shots to catch up with him. He drew back his club with infinite caution, poised it at the top of the swing——

"I always wonder——" said a clear, girlish voice, ripping the silence like the explosion of a bomb.

George Parsloe started. His club wobbled. It descended. The ball trickled into the long grass in front of the tee. There was a grim pause.

"You were saying, Miss Medway——" said George Parsloe, in a small, flat voice.

"Oh, I'm so sorry," said Barbara. "I'm afraid I put you off."

"A little, perhaps. Possibly the merest trifle. But you were saying you wondered about something. Can I be of any assistance?"

"I was only saying," said Barbara, "that I always wonder why tees are called tees."

George Parsloe swallowed once or twice. He also blinked a little feverishly. His eyes had a dazed, staring expression.

"I am afraid I cannot tell you off-hand," he said, "but I will make a point of consulting some good encyclopædia at the earliest opportunity."

"Thank you so much."

"Not at all. It will be a pleasure. In case you were thinking of inquiring at the moment when I am putting why greens are called greens, may I venture the suggestion now that it is because they are green?"

And, so saying, George Parsloe stalked to his ball and found it nestling in the heart of some shrub of which, not being a botanist, I cannot give you the name. It was a close-knit, adhesive shrub, and it twined its tentacles so lovingly around George Parsloe's niblick that he missed his first shot altogether. His second made the ball rock, and his third dislodged it. Playing a full swing with his brassie and being by now a mere cauldron of seething emotions he missed his fourth. His fifth came to within a few inches of Ferdinand's drive, and he picked it up and hurled it from him into the rough as if it had been something venomous.

"Your hole and match," said George Parsloe, thinly.

Ferdinand Dibble sat beside the glittering ocean. He had hurried off the course with swift strides the moment George Parsloe had spoken those bitter words. He wanted to be alone with his thoughts.

They were mixed thoughts. For a moment joy at the reflection that he had won a tough match came irresistibly to the surface, only to sink again as he remembered that life, whatever its triumphs, could hold nothing for him now that Barbara Medway loved another.

"Mr. Dibble!"

He looked up. She was standing at his side. He gulped and rose to his feet.

"Yes?"

There was a silence.

"Doesn't the sun look pretty on the water?" said Barbara.

Ferdinand groaned. This was too much.

"Leave me," he said, hollowly. "Go back to your Parsloe, the man with whom you walked in the moonlight beside this same water."

"Well, why shouldn't I walk with Mr. Parsloe in the moonlight beside this same water?" demanded Barbara, with spirit.

"I never said," replied Ferdinand, for he was a fair man at heart, "that you shouldn't walk with Mr. Parsloe beside this same water. I simply said you did walk with Mr. Parsloe beside this same water."

"I've a perfect right to walk with Mr. Parsloe beside this same water," persisted Barbara. "He and I are old friends."

Ferdinand groaned again.

"Exactly! There you are! As I suspected. Old friends. Played together as children, and what not, I shouldn't wonder."

"No, we didn't. I've only known him five years. But he is engaged to be married to my greatest chum, so that draws us together."

Ferdinand uttered a strangled cry.

"Parsloe engaged to be married!"

"Yes. The wedding takes place next month."

"But look here." Ferdinand's forehead was wrinkled. He was thinking tensely. "Look here," said Ferdinand, a close reasoner. "If Parsloe's engaged to your greatest chum, he can't be in love with *you*."

"No."

"And you aren't in love with him?"

"No."

"Then, by gad," said Ferdinand, "how about it?"

"What do you mean?"

"Will you marry me?" bellowed Ferdinand.

"Yes."

"You will?"

"Of course I will."

"Darling!" cried Ferdinand.

"There is only one thing that bothers me a bit," said Ferdinand, thoughtfully, as they strolled together over the scented meadows, while in the trees above them a thousand birds trilled Mendelssohn's Wedding March.

"What is that?"

"Well, I'll tell you," said Ferdinand. "The fact is, I've just discovered the great secret of golf. You can't play a really hot game unless you're so miserable that you don't worry over your shots. Take the case of a chip-shot, for instance. If you're really wretched, you don't care where the ball is going and so you don't raise your head to see. Grief automatically prevents pressing and over-swinging. Look at the top-notchers. Have you ever seen a happy pro?"

"No. I don't think I have."

"Well, then!"

"But pros are all Scotchmen," argued Barbara.

"It doesn't matter. I'm sure I'm right. And the darned thing is that I'm going to be so infernally happy all the rest of my life that I suppose my handicap will go up to thirty or something."

Barbara squeezed his hand lovingly.

"Don't worry, precious," she said, soothingly. "It will be all right. I am a woman, and, once we are married, I shall be able to think of at least a hundred ways of snootering you to such an extent that you'll be fit to win the Amateur Championship."

"You will?" said Ferdinand, anxiously. "You're sure?"

"Quite, quite sure, dearest," said Barbara.

"My angel!" said Ferdinand.

He folded her in his arms, using the interlocking grip.

13

HIGH STAKES

THE summer day was drawing to a close. Over the terrace outside the club-house the chestnut trees threw long shadows, and such bees as still lingered in the flower-beds had the air of tired business men who are about ready to shut up the office and go off to dinner and a musical comedy. The Oldest Member, stirring in his favourite chair, glanced at his watch and yawned.

As he did so, from the neighbourhood of the eighteenth green, hidden from his view by the slope of the ground, there came suddenly a medley of shrill animal cries, and he deduced that some belated match must just have reached a finish. His surmise was correct. The babble of voices drew nearer, and over the brow of the hill came a little group of men. Two, who appeared to be the ringleaders in the affair, were short and stout. One was cheerful and the other dejected. The rest of the company consisted of friends and adherents; and one of these, a young man who seemed to be amused, strolled to where the Oldest Member sat.

"What," inquired the Sage, "was all the shouting for?"

The young man sank into a chair and lighted a cigarette.

"Perkins and Broster," he said, "were all square at the seventeenth, and they raised the stakes to fifty pounds. They were both on the green in seven, and Perkins had a two-foot putt to halve the match. He missed it by six inches. They play pretty high, those two."

"It is a curious thing," said the Oldest Member, "that men whose golf is of a kind that makes hardened caddies wince always do. The more competent a player, the smaller the stake that contents him. It is only when you get down into the submerged tenth of the golfing world that you find the big gambling. However, I would not call fifty pounds anything sensational in the case of two men like Perkins and Broster. They are both well provided with the world's goods. If you would care to hear the story——"

The young man's jaw fell a couple of notches.

"I had no idea it was so late," he bleated. "I ought to be——"

"——of a man who played for really high stakes——"

"I promised to——"

"——I will tell it to you," said the Sage.

"Look here," said the young man, sullenly, "it isn't one of those stories about two men who fall in love with the same girl and play a match to decide which is to marry her, is it? Because if so——"

"The stake to which I allude," said the Oldest Member, "was something far higher and bigger than a woman's love. Shall I proceed?"

"All right," said the young man, resignedly. "Snap into it."

It has been well said—I think by the man who wrote the sub-titles for "Cage-Birds of Society" (began the Oldest Member)—that wealth does not always bring happiness. It was so with Bradbury Fisher, the hero of the story which I am about to relate. One of America's most prominent tainted millionaires, he had two sorrows in life—his handicap refused to stir from twenty-four and his wife disapproved of his collection of famous golf relics. Once, finding him crooning over the trousers in which Ouimet had won his historic replay against Vardon and Ray in the American Open, she had asked him why he did not collect something worth while, like Old Masters or first editions.

Worth while! Bradbury had forgiven, for he loved the woman, but he could not forget.

For Bradbury Fisher, like so many men who have taken to the game in middle age, after a youth misspent in the pursuits of commerce, was no half-hearted enthusiast. Although he still occasionally descended on Wall Street in order to prise the small investor loose from another couple of million, what he really lived for now was golf and his collection. He had begun the collection in his first year as a golfer, and he prized it dearly. And when he reflected that his wife had stopped him purchasing J. H. Taylor's shirt-stud, which he could have had for a few hundred pounds, the iron seemed to enter into his soul.

The distressing episode had occurred in London, and he was now on his way back to New York, having left his wife to continue her holiday in England. All through the voyage he remained moody and distrait; and at the ship's concert, at which he was forced to take the chair, he was heard to observe to the purser that if the alleged soprano who had just sung "My Little Grey Home in the West" had the immortal gall to take a second encore he hoped that she would trip over a high note and dislocate her neck.

Such was Bradbury Fisher's mood throughout the ocean journey, and it remained constant until he arrived at his palatial home at Goldenville, Long Island, where, as he sat smoking a moody after-dinner cigar in the Versailles drawing room, Blizzard, his English butler, informed him that Mr. Gladstone Bott desired to speak to him on the telephone.

"Tell him to go and boil himself," said Bradbury.

"Very good, sir."

"No, I'll tell him myself," said Bradbury. He strode to the telephone. "Hullo!" he said, curtly.

He was not fond of this Bott. There are certain men who seem fated to go through life as rivals. It was so with Bradbury Fisher and J. Gladstone Bott. Born in the same town within a few days of one another, they had come to New York in the same week, and from that moment their careers had run side by side. Fisher had made his first million two days before Bott, but Bott's first divorce had got half a column and two sticks more publicity than Fisher's.

At Sing-Sing, where each had spent several happy years of early manhood, they had run neck and neck for the prizes which that institution has to offer. Fisher secured the position of catcher on the baseball nine in preference to Bott, but Bott just nosed Fisher out when it came to the choice of a tenor for the glee club. Bott was selected for the debating contest against Auburn, but Fisher got the last place on the cross-word puzzle team, with Bott merely first reserve.

They had taken up golf simultaneously, and their handicaps had remained level ever since. Between such men it is not surprising that there was little love lost.

"Hullo!" said Gladstone Bott. "So you're back? Say, listen, Fisher. I think I've got something that'll interest you. Something you'll be glad to have in your golf collection."

Bradbury Fisher's mood softened. He disliked Bott, but that was no reason for not doing business with him. And though he had little faith in the man's judgment it might be that he had stumbled upon some valuable antique. There crossed his mind the comforting thought that his wife was three thousand miles away and that he was no longer under her penetrating eye—that eye which, so to speak, was always "about his bath and about his bed and spying out all his ways".

"I've just returned from a trip down South," proceeded Bott, "and I have secured the authentic baffy used by Bobby Jones in his first important contest—the Infants' All-In Championship of Atlanta, Georgia, open to those of both sexes not yet having finished teething."

Bradbury gasped. He had heard rumours that this treasure was in existence, but he had never credited them.

"You're sure?" he cried. "You're positive it's genuine?"

"I have a written guarantee from Mr. Jones, Mrs. Jones, and the nurse."

"How much, Bott, old man?" stammered Bradbury. "How much do you want for it, Gladstone, old top? I'll give you a hundred thousand dollars."

"Ha!"

"Five hundred thousand."

"Ha, ha!"

"A million."

"Ha, ha, ha!"

"Two million."

"Ha, ha, ha, ha!"

Bradbury Fisher's strong face twisted like that of a tortured fiend. He registered in quick succession rage, despair, hate, fury, anguish, pique, and resentment. But when he spoke again his voice was soft and gentle.

"Gladdy, old socks," he said, "we have been friends for years."

"No, we haven't," said Gladstone Bott.

"Yes, we have."

"No, we haven't."

"Well, anyway, what about two million five hundred?"

"Nothing doing. Say, listen. Do you really want that baffy?"

"I do, Botty, old egg, I do indeed."

"Then listen. I'll exchange it for Blizzard."

"For Blizzard?" quavered Fisher.

"For Blizzard."

It occurs to me that, when describing the closeness of the rivalry between these two men, I may have conveyed the impression that in no department of life could either claim a definite advantage over the other. If that is so, I erred. It is true that in a general way, whatever one had, the other had something equally good to counterbalance it; but in just one matter Bradbury Fisher had triumphed completely over Gladstone Bott. Bradbury Fisher had the finest English butler on Long Island.

Blizzard stood alone. There is a regrettable tendency on the part of English butlers today to deviate more and more from the type which made their species famous. The modern butler has a nasty knack of being a lissom young man in perfect condition who looks like the son of the house. But Blizzard was of the fine old school. Before coming to the Fisher home he had been for fifteen years in the service of an earl, and his appearance suggested that throughout those fifteen years he had not let a day pass without its pint of port. He radiated port and popeyed dignity. He had splay feet and three chins, and when he walked his curving waistcoat preceded him like the advance guard of some royal procession.

From the first, Bradbury had been perfectly aware that Bott coveted Blizzard, and the knowledge had sweetened his life. But this was the first time he had come out into the open and admitted it.

"Blizzard?" whispered Fisher.

"Blizzard," said Bott firmly. "It's my wife's birthday next week, and I've been wondering what to give her."

Bradbury Fisher shuddered from head to foot, and his legs wobbled like asparagus stalks. Beads of perspiration stood out on his forehead. The serpent was tempting him—tempting him grievously.

"You're sure you won't take three million—or four—or something like that?"

"No; I want Blizzard."

Bradbury Fisher passed his handkerchief over his streaming brow.

"So be it," he said in a low voice.

The Jones baffy arrived that night, and for some hours Bradbury Fisher gloated over it with the unmixed joy of a collector who has secured the prize of a lifetime. Then, stealing gradually over him, came the realization of what he had done.

He was thinking of his wife and what she would say when she heard of this. Blizzard was Mrs. Fisher's pride and joy. She had never, like the poet, rear'd a young gazelle, but, had she done so, her attitude towards it would have been identical with her attitude towards Blizzard. Although so far away, it was plain that her thoughts still lingered with the pleasure she had left at home, for on his arrival Bradbury had found three cables awaiting him.

The first ran:
"How is Blizzard? Reply."

The second:
"How is Blizzard's sciatica? Reply."

The third:
"Blizzard's hiccups. How are they? Suggest Doctor Murphy's Tonic Swamp-Juice. Highly spoken of. Three times a day after meals. Try for week and cable result."

It did not require a clairvoyant to tell Bradbury that, if on her return she found that he had disposed of Blizzard in exchange for a child's cut-down baffy, she would certainly sue for for divorce. And there was not a jury in America that would not give their verdict in her favour without a dissentient voice. His first wife, he recalled, had divorced him on far flimsier grounds. So had his second, third, and fourth. And Bradbury loved his wife. There had been a time in his life when, if he lost a wife, he had felt philosophically that there would be another along in a minute; but, as a man grows older, he tends to become set in his habits, and he could not contemplate existence without the company of the present incumbent.

What, therefore, to do? What, when you came right down to it, to do?

There seemed no way out of the dilemma. If he kept the Jones baffy, no other price would satisfy Bott's jealous greed. And to part with the baffy, now that it was actually in his possession, was unthinkable.

And then, in the small hours of the morning, as he tossed sleeplessly on his Louis Quinze bed, his giant brain conceived a plan.

.   .   .   .   .

On the following afternoon he made his way to the club-house, and was informed that Bott was out playing around with another millionaire of his acquaintance. Bradbury waited, and presently his rival appeared.

"Hey!" said Gladstone Bott, in his abrupt uncouth way. "When are you going to deliver that butler?"

"I will make the shipment at the earliest date," said Bradbury.

"I was expecting him last night."

"You shall have him shortly."

"What do you feed him on?" asked Gladstone Bott.

"Oh, anything you have yourselves. Put sulphur in his port in the hot weather. Tell me, how did your match go?"

"He beat me. I had rotten luck."

Bradbury Fisher's eyes gleamed. His moment had come.

"Luck?" he said. "What do you mean, luck? Luck has nothing to do with it. You're always beefing about your luck. The trouble with you is that you play rottenly."

"What!"

"It is no use trying to play golf unless you learn the first principles and do it properly. Look at the way you drive."

"What's wrong with my driving?"

"Nothing, except that you don't do anything right. In driving, as the club comes back in the swing, the weight should be shifted by degrees, quietly and gradually, until, when the club has reached its topmost point, the whole weight of the body is supported by the right leg, the left foot being turned at the time and the left knee bent in towards the right leg. But, regardless of how much you perfect your style, you cannot develop any method which will not require you to keep your head still so that you can see your ball clearly."

"Hey!"

"It is obvious that it is impossible to introduce a jerk or a sudden violent effort into any part of the swing without disturbing the balance or moving the head. I want to drive home the fact that it is absolutely essential to——"

"Hey!" cried Gladstone Bott.

The man was shaken to the core. From the local pro., and from scratch men of his acquaintance, he would gladly have listened to this sort of thing by the hour, but to hear these words from Bradbury Fisher, whose handicap was the same as his own, and out of whom it was his imperishable conviction that he could hammer the tar any time he got him out on the links, was too much.

"Where do you get off," he demanded, heatedly, "trying to teach me golf?"

Bradbury Fisher chuckled to himself. Everything was working out as his subtle mind had foreseen.

"My dear fellow," he said, "I was only speaking for your good."

"I like your nerve! I can lick you any time we start."

"It's easy enough to talk."

"I trimmed you twice the week before you sailed to England."

"Naturally," said Bradbury Fisher, "in a friendly round, with only a few thousand dollars on the match, a man does not extend himself. You wouldn't dare to play me for anything that really mattered."

"I'll play you when you like for anything you like."

"Very well. I'll play you for Blizzard."

"Against what?"

"Oh, anything you please. How about a couple of railroads?"

"Make it three."

"Very well."

"Next Friday suit you?"

"Sure," said Bradbury Fisher.

It seemed to him that his troubles were over. Like all twenty-four-handicap men, he had the most perfect confidence in his ability to beat all other twenty-four-handicap men. As for Gladstone Bott, he knew that he could disembowel him at any time he was able to lure him out of the club-house.

Nevertheless, as he breakfasted on the morning of the fateful match, Bradbury Fisher was conscious of an unwonted nervousness. He was no weakling. In Wall Street his phlegm in moments of stress was a byword. On the famous occasion when the B. and G. crowd had attacked C. and D., and in order to keep control of L. and M. he had been compelled to buy so largely of S. and T., he had not turned a hair. And yet this morning, in endeavouring to prong up segments of bacon, he twice missed the plate altogther and on a third occasion speared himself in the cheek with his fork. The spectacle of Blizzard, so calm, so competent, so supremely the perfect butler, unnerved him.

"I am jumpy today, Blizzard," he said, forcing a laugh.

"Yes, sir. You do, indeed, appear to have the willies."

"Yes. I am playing a very important golf-match this morning."

"Indeed, sir?"

"I must pull myself together, Blizzard."

"Yes, sir. And, if I may respectfully make the suggestion, you should endeavour, when in action, to keep the head down and the eye rigidly upon the ball."

"I will, Blizzard, I will," said Bradbury Fisher, his keen eyes clouding under a sudden mist of tears. "Thank you, Blizzard, for the advice."

"Not at all, sir."

"How is your sciatica, Blizzard?"

"A trifle improved, I thank you, sir."

"And your hiccups?"

"I am conscious of a slight though possibly only a temporary relief, sir."

"Good," said Bradbury Fisher.

He left the room with a firm step and, proceeding to his library, read for a while portions of that grand chapter in James Braid's *Advanced Golf* which deals with driving into the wind. It was a fair and cloudless morning, but it was as well to be prepared for emergencies. Then, feeling that he had done all that could be done, he ordered the car and was taken to the links.

Gladstone Bott was awaiting him on the first tee, in company with two caddies. A curt greeting, a spin of the coin, and Gladstone Bott, securing the honour, stepped out to begin the contest.

Although there are, of course, endless sub-species in their ranks, not all of which have yet been classified by science, twenty-four-handicap golfers may be stated broadly to fall into two classes, the dashing and the cautious—those, that is to say, who endeavour to do every hole in a brilliant one and those who are content to win with a steady nine. Gladstone Bott was one of the cautious brigade. He fussed about for a few moments like a hen scratching gravel, then with a stiff quarter-swing sent his ball straight down the fairway for a matter of seventy yards, and it was Bradbury Fisher's turn to drive.

Now, normally, Bradbury Fisher was essentially a dasher. It was his habit, as a rule, to raise his left foot some six inches from the ground and, having swayed forcefully back on to his right leg, to sway sharply forward again and lash out with sickening violence in the general direction of the ball. It was a method which at times produced excellent results, though it had the flaw that it was somewhat uncertain. Bradbury Fisher was the only member of the club, with the exception of the club champion, who had ever carried the second green with his drive; but, on the other hand, he was also the only member who had ever laid his drive on the eleventh dead to the pin of the sixteenth.

But today the magnitude of the issues at stake had wrought a change in him. Planted firmly on both feet, he fiddled at the ball in the manner of one playing spillikens. When he swung, it was with a swing resembling that of Gladstone Bott; and, like Bott, he achieved a nice, steady, rainbow-shaped drive of some seventy yards straight down the middle. Bott replied with an eighty-yard brassie shot. Bradbury held him with another. And so, working their way cautiously across the prairie, they came to the green, where Bradbury, laying his third putt dead, halved the hole.

The second was a repetition of the first, the third and fourth repetitions of the second. But on the fifth green the fortunes of the match began to change. Here Gladstone Bott, faced with a fifteen-foot putt to win, smote his ball firmly off the line, as had been his practice at each of the preceding holes, and the ball, hitting a worm-cast and bounding off to the left, ran on a couple of yards, hit another worm-cast, bounded to the right, and finally, bumping into a twig, leaped to the left again and clattered into the tin.

"One up," said Gladstone Bott. "Tricky, some of these greens are. You have to gauge the angles to a nicety."

At the sixth a donkey in an adjoining field uttered a raucous bray just as Bott was addressing his ball with a mashie-niblick on the edge of the green. He started violently and, jerking his club with a spasmodic reflex action of the forearm, holed out.

"Nice work," said Gladstone Bott.

The seventh was a short hole, guarded by two large bunkers between which ran a narrow footpath of turf. Gladstone Bott's mashie-shot, falling short, ran over the rough, peered for a moment into the depths to the left, then, winding up the path, trickled on to the green, struck a fortunate slope, acquired momentum, ran on, and dropped into the hole.

"Nearly missed it," said Gladstone Bott, drawing a deep breath.

Bradbury Fisher looked out upon a world that swam and danced before his eyes. He had not been prepared for this sort of thing. The way things were shaping, he felt that it would hardly surprise him now if the cups were to start jumping up and snapping at Bott's ball like starving dogs.

"Three up," said Gladstone Bott.

With a strong effort Bradbury Fisher mastered his feelings. His mouth set grimly. Matters, he perceived, had reached a crisis. He saw now that he had made a mistake in allowing himself to be intimidated by the importance of the occasion into being scientific. Nature had never intended him for a scientific golfer, and up till now he had been behaving like an animated illustration out of a book by Vardon. He had taken his club back along and near the turf, allowing it to trend around the legs as far as was permitted by the movement of the arms. He had kept his right elbow close to the side, this action coming into operation before the club was allowed to describe a section of a circle in an upward direction, whence it was carried by means of a slow, steady, swinging movement. He had pivoted, he had pronated the wrists, and he had been careful about the lateral hip-shift.

And it had been all wrong. That sort of stuff might suit some people, but not him. He was a biffer, a swatter, and a slosher; and it flashed upon him now that only by biffing, swatting, and sloshing as he had never biffed, swatted, and sloshed before could he hope to recover the ground he had lost.

Gladstone Bott was not one of those players who grow careless with success. His drive at the eighth was just as steady and short as ever. But this time Bradbury Fisher made no attempt to imitate him. For seven holes he had been checking his natural instincts, and now he drove with all the banked-up fury that comes with release from long suppression.

For an instant he remained poised on one leg like a stork; then there was a whistle and a crack, and the ball, smitten squarely in the midriff, flew down the course and, soaring over the bunkers, hit the turf and gambolled to within twenty yards of the green.

He straightened out the kinks in his spine with a grim smile. Allowing himself the regulation three putts, he would be down in five, and only a miracle could give Gladstone Bott anything better than a seven.

"Two down," he said some minutes later, and Gladstone Bott nodded sullenly.

It was not often that Bradbury Fisher kept on the fairway with two consecutive drives, but strange things were happening today. Not only was his drive at the ninth a full two hundred and forty yards, but it was also perfectly straight.

"One down," said Bradbury Fisher, and Bott nodded even more sullenly than before.

There are few things more demoralizing than to be consistently outdriven; and when he is outdriven by a hundred and seventy yards at two consecutive holes the bravest man is apt to be shaken. Gladstone Bott was only human. It was with a sinking heart that he watched his opponent heave and sway on the tenth tee; and when the ball once more flew straight and far down the course a strange weakness seemed to come over him. For the first time he lost his morale and topped. The ball trickled into the long grass, and after three fruitless stabs at it with a niblick he picked up, and the match was squared.

At the eleventh Bradbury Fisher also topped, and his tee-shot, though nice and straight, travelled only a couple of feet. He had to scramble to halve in eight.

The twelfth was another short hole; and Bradbury, unable to curb the fine, careless rapture which had crept into his game, had the misfortune to overshoot the green by some sixty yards, thus enabling his opponent to take the lead once more.

The thirteenth and fourteenth were halved, but Bradbury, driving another long ball, won the fifteenth, squaring the match.

It seemed to Bradbury Fisher, as he took his stand on the sixteenth tee, that he now had the situation well in hand. At the thirteenth and fourteenth his drive had flickered, but on the fifteenth it had come back in all its glorious vigour and there appeared to be no reason to suppose that it had not come to stay. He recollected exactly how he had done that last colossal slosh, and he now prepared to reproduce the movements precisely as before. The great thing to remember was to hold the breath on the back-swing and not to release it before the moment of impact. Also, the eyes should not be closed until late in the down-swing. All great golfers have their little secrets, and that was Bradbury's.

With these aids to success firmly fixed in his mind, Bradbury Fisher prepared to give the ball the nastiest bang that a golf-ball had ever had since Edward Blackwell was in his prime. He drew in his breath and, with lungs expanded to their fullest capacity, heaved back on to his large, flat right foot. Then, clenching his teeth, he lashed out.

When he opened his eyes, they fell upon a horrid spectacle. Either he had closed those eyes too soon or else he had breathed too precipitately—whatever the cause, the ball, which should have gone due south, was travelling with great speed sou'-sou'-east. And, even as he gazed, it curved to earth and fell into as uninviting a bit of rough as he had ever penetrated. And he was a man who had spent much time in many roughs.

Leaving Gladstone Bott to continue his imitation of a spavined octogenarian rolling peanuts with a toothpick, Bradbury Fisher, followed by his caddie, set out on the long trail into the jungle.

Hope did not altogether desert him as he walked. In spite of its erratic direction, the ball had been so shrewdly smitten that it was not far from the green. Provided luck was with him and the lie not too desperate, a mashie would put him on the carpet. It was only when he reached the rough and saw what had happened that his heart sank. There the ball lay, half hidden in the grass, while above it waved the straggling tentacle of some tough-looking shrub. Behind it was a stone, and behind the stone, at just the elevation required to catch the back-swing of the club, was a tree. And, by an ironical stroke of fate which drew from Bradbury a hollow, bitter laugh, only a few feet to the right was a beautiful smooth piece of turf from which it would have been a pleasure to play one's second.

Dully, Bradbury looked to see how Bott was getting on. And then suddenly, as he found that Bott was completely invisible behind the belt of bushes through which he had just passed, a voice seemed to whisper to him, "Why not?"

Bradbury Fisher, remember, had spent thirty years in Wall Street.

It was at this moment that he realized that he was not alone. His caddie was standing at his side.

Bradbury Fisher gazed upon the caddie, whom until now he had not had any occasion to observe with any closeness.

The caddie was not a boy. He was a man, apparently in the middle forties, with bushy eyebrows and a walrus moustache; and there was something about his appearance which suggested to Bradbury that here was a kindred spirit. He reminded Bradbury a little of Spike Huggins, the safe-blower, who had been a fresher with him at Sing-Sing. It seemed to him that this caddie could be trusted in a delicate matter involving secrecy and silence. Had he been some babbling urchin, the risk might have been too great.

"Caddie," said Bradbury.

"Sir?" said the caddie.

"Yours is an ill-paid job," said Bradbury.

"It is, indeed, sir," said the caddie.

"Would you like to earn fifty dollars?"

"I would prefer to earn a hundred."

"I meant a hundred," said Bradbury.

He produced a roll of bills from his pocket, and peeled off one of that value. Then, stooping, he picked up his ball and placed it on the little oasis of turf. The caddie bowed intelligently.

"You mean to say," cried Gladstone Bott, a few moments later, "that you were out with your second? With your second!"

"I had a stroke of luck."

"You're sure it wasn't about six strokes of luck?"

"My ball was right out in the open in an excellent lie."

"Oh!" said Gladstone Bott, shortly.

"I have four for it, I think."

"One down," said Gladstone Bott.

"And two to play," trilled Bradbury.

It was with a light heart that Bradbury Fisher teed up on the seventeenth. The match, he felt, was as good as over. The whole essence of golf is to discover a way of getting out of the rough without losing strokes; and with this sensible, broad-minded man of the world caddying for him he seemed to have discovered the ideal way. It cost him scarcely a pang when he saw his drive slice away into a tangle of long grass, but for the sake of appearances he affected a little chagrin.

"Tut, tut!" he said.

"I shouldn't worry," said Gladstone Bott. "You will probably find it sitting upon an india-rubber tee which someone has dropped there."

He spoke sardonically, and Bradbury did not like his manner. But then he never had liked Gladstone Bott's manner, so what of that? He made his way to where the ball had fallen. It was lying under a bush.

"Caddie," said Bradbury.

"Sir?" said the caddie.

"A hundred?"

"And fifty."

"And fifty," said Bradbury Fisher.

Gladstone Bott was still toiling along the fairway when Bradbury reached the green.

"How many?" he asked, eventually winning to the goal.

"On in two," said Bradbury. "And you?"

"Playing seven."

"Then let me see. If you take two putts, which is most unlikely, I shall have six for the hole and match."

A minute later Bradbury had picked up his ball out of the cup. He stood there, basking in the sunshine, his heart glowing with quiet happiness. It seemed to him that he had never seen the countryside looking so beautiful. The birds appeared to be singing as they had never sung before. The trees and the rolling turf had taken on a charm beyond anything he had ever encountered. Even Gladstone Bott looked almost bearable.

"A very pleasant match," he said, cordially, "conducted throughout in the most sporting spirit. At one time I thought you were going to pull it off, old man, but there—class will tell."

"I will now make my report," said the caddie with the walrus moustache.

"Do so," said Gladstone Bott, briefly.

Bradbury Fisher stared at the man with blanched cheeks. The sun had ceased to shine, the birds had stopped singing. The trees and the rolling turf looked pretty rotten, and Gladstone Bott perfectly foul. His heart was leaden with a hideous dread.

"Your report? Your—your report? What do you mean?"

"You don't suppose," said Gladstone Bott, "that I would play you an important match unless I had detectives watching you, do you? This gentleman is from the

Quick Results Agency. What have you to report?" he said, turning to the caddie.

The caddie removed his bushy eyebrows, and with a quick gesture swept off his moustache.

"On the twelfth inst.," he began in a monotonous, sing-song voice, "acting upon instructions received, I made my way to the Goldenville Golf Links in order to observe the movements of the man Fisher. I had adopted for the occasion the Number Three disguise and——"

"All right, all right," said Gladstone Bott, impatiently. "You can skip all that. Come down to what happened at the sixteenth."

The caddie looked wounded, but bowed deferentially.

"At the sixteenth hole the man Fisher moved his ball into what—from his actions and furtive manner—I deduced to be a more favourable position."

"Ah!" said Gladstone Bott.

"On the seventeenth the man Fisher picked up his ball and threw it with a movement of the wrist on to the green."

"It's a lie. A foul and contemptible lie, shouted Bradbury Fisher.

"Realizing that the man Fisher might adopt this attitude, sir," said the caddie, "I took the precaution of snapshotting him in the act with my miniature wrist-watch camera, the detective's best friend."

Bradbury Fisher covered his face with his hands and uttered a hollow groan.

"My match," said Gladstone Bott, with vindictive triumph. "I'll trouble you to deliver that butler to me f.o.b. at my residence not later than noon tomorrow. Oh yes, and I was forgetting. You owe me three railroads."

Blizzard, dignified but kindly, met Bradbury in the Byzantine hall on his return home.

"I trust your golf-match terminated satisfactorily, sir?" said the butler.

A pang, almost too poignant to be borne, shot through Bradbury.

"No, Blizzard," he said. "No. Thank you for your kind inquiry, but I was not in luck."

"Too bad, sir," said Blizzard, sympathetically. "I trust the prize at stake was not excessive?"

"Well—er—well, it was rather big. I should like to speak to you about that a little later, Blizzard."

"At any time that is suitable to you, sir. If you will ring for one of the assistant-under-footmen when you desire to see me, sir, he will find me in my pantry. Meanwhile, sir, this cable arrived for you a short while back."

Bradbury took the envelope listlessly. He had been expecting a communication from his London agents announcing that they had bought Kent and Sussex, for which he had instructed them to make a firm offer just before he left England. No doubt this was their cable.

He opened the envelope, and started as if it had contained a scorpion. It was from his wife.

> "*Returning immediately 'Aquitania'*," (*it ran*). "*Docking Friday night. Meet without fail.*"

Bradbury stared at the words, frozen to the marrow. Although he had been in a sort of trance ever since that dreadful moment on the seventeenth green, his great brain had not altogether ceased to function; and, while driving home in the car, he had sketched out roughly a plan of action which, he felt, might meet the crisis. Assuming that Mrs. Fisher was to remain abroad for another month, he had practically decided to buy a daily paper, insert in it a front-page story announcing the death of Blizzard, forward the clipping to his wife, and then sell his house, and move to another neighbourhood. In this way it might be that she would never learn of what had occurred.

But if she was due back next Friday, the scheme fell through and exposure was inevitable.

He wondered dully what had caused her change of plans, and came to the conclusion that some feminine sixth sense must have warned her of peril threatening Blizzard. With a good deal of peevishness he wished that Providence had never endowed women with this sixth sense. A woman with merely five took quite enough handling.

"Sweet suffering soup-spoons!" groaned Bradbury.

"Sir?" said Blizzard.

"Nothing," said Bradbury.

"Very good, sir," said Blizzard.

For a man with anything on his mind, any little trouble calculated to affect the *joie de vivre,* there are few spots less cheering that the Customs sheds of New York. Draughts whistle dismally there—now to, now fro. Strange noises are heard. Customs officials chew gum and lurk grimly in the shadows, like tigers awaiting the luncheon-gong. It is not surprising that Bradbury's spirits, low when he reached the place, should have sunk to zero long before the gangplank was lowered and the passengers began to stream down it.

His wife was among the first to land. How beautiful she looked, thought Bradbury, as he watched her. And, alas, how intimidating. His tastes had always lain in the direction of spirited women. His first wife had been spirited. So had his second, third, and fourth. And the one at the moment of holding office was perhaps the most spirited of the whole platoon. For one long instant, as he went to meet her, Bradbury Fisher was conscious of a regret that he had not married one of those meek, mild girls who suffer uncomplainingly at their husband's hands in the more hectic type of feminine novel. What he felt he could have done with at the moment was the sort of wife who thinks herself dashed lucky if the other half of the sketch does not drag her round the billiard-room by her hair, kicking her the while with spiked shoes.

Three conversational openings presented themselves to him as he approached her.

"Darling, there is something I want to tell you——"

"Dearest, I have a small confession to make——"

"Sweetheart, I don't know if by any chance you remember Blizzard, our butler. Well, it's like this——"

But, in the event, it was she who spoke first.

"Oh, Bradbury," she cried, rushing into his arms, "I've done the most awful thing, and you must try to forgive me!"

Bradbury blinked. He had never seen her in this strange mood before. As she clung to him, she seemed timid, fluttering, and—although a woman who weighed a full hundred and fifty-seven pounds—almost fragile.

"What is it?" he inquired, tenderly. "Has somebody stolen your jewels?"

"No, no."

"Have you been losing money at bridge?"

"No, no. Worse than that."

Bradbury started.

"You didn't sing 'My Little Grey Home in the West' at the ship's concert?" he demanded, eyeing her closely.

"No, no! Ah, how can I tell you? Bradbury, look! You see that man over there?"

Bradbury followed her pointing finger. Standing in an attitude of negligent dignity beside a pile of trunks under the letter V was a tall, stout, ambassadorial man, at the very sight of whom, even at this distance, Bradbury Fisher felt an odd sense of inferiority. His pendulous cheeks, his curving waistcoat, his protruding eyes, and the sequence of rolling chins combined to produce in Bradbury that instinctive feeling of being in the presence of a superior which we experience when meeting scratch golfers, head-waiters of fashionable restaurants, and traffic-policemen. A sudden pang of suspicion pierced him.

"Well?" he said, hoarsely. "What of him?"

"Bradbury, you must not judge me too harshly. We were thrown together and I was tempted——"

"Woman," thundered Bradbury Fisher, "who is this man?"

"His name is Vosper."

"And what is there between you and him, and when did it start, and why and how and where?"

Mrs. Fisher dabbed at her eyes with her handkerchief.

"It was at the Duke of Bootle's, Bradbury. I was invited there for the week-end."

"And this man was there?"

"Yes."

"Ha! Proceed!"

"The moment I set eyes on him, something seemed to go all over me."

"Indeed!"

"At first it was his mere appearance. I felt that I had dreamed of such a man all my life, and that for all these wasted years I had been putting up with the second-best."

"Oh, you did, eh? Really? Is that so? You did, did you?" snorted Bradbury Fisher.

"I couldn't help it, Bradbury. I know I have always seemed so devoted to Blizzard, and so I was. But, honestly, there is no comparison between them—really there isn't. You should see the way Vosper stood behind the Duke's chair. Like a high priest presiding over some mystic religious ceremony. And his voice when he asks you if you will have sherry or hock! Like the music of some wonderful organ. I couldn't resist him. I approached him delicately, and found that he was willing to come to America. He had been eighteen years with the Duke, and he told me he couldn't stand the sight of the back of his head any longer. So——"

Bradbury Fisher reeled.

"This man—this Vosper. Who is he?"

"Why, I'm telling you, honey. He was the Duke's butler, and now he's ours. Oh, you know how impulsive I am. Honestly, it wasn't till we were half-way across the Atlantic that I suddenly said to myself, 'What about Blizzard?' What am I to do, Bradbury? I simply haven't the nerve to fire Blizzard. And yet what will happen when he walks into his pantry and finds Vosper there? Oh, think, Bradbury, think!"

Bradbury Fisher was thinking—and for the first time in a week without agony.

"Evangeline," he said, gravely, "this is awkward."

"I know."

'Extremely awkward."

"I know, I know. But surely you can think of some way out of the muddle?"

"I may, I cannot promise, but I may." He pondered deeply. "Ha! I have it! It is just possible I may be able to induce Gladstone Bott to take on Blizzard."

"Do you really think he would?"

"He may—if I play my cards carefully. At any rate, I will try to persuade him. For the moment you and Vosper had better remain in New York, while I go home and put the negotiations in train. If I am successful, I will let you know."

"Do try your very hardest."

"I think I shall be able to manage it. Gladstone and I are old friends, and he would stretch a point to oblige me. But let this be a lesson to you, Evangeline."

"Oh, I will."

"By the way," said Bradbury Fisher, "I am cabling my London agents today to instruct them to buy J. H. Taylor's shirt-stud for my collection."

"Quite right, Bradbury, darling. And anything else you want in that way you will get, won't you?"

"I will," said Bradbury Fisher.

14

KEEPING IN WITH VOSPER

THE YOUNG man in the heather-mixture plus fours, who for some time had been pacing the terrace above the ninth green like an imprisoned jaguar, flung himself into a chair and uttered a snort of anguish.

"Women," said the young man, "are the limit."

The Oldest Member, ever ready to sympathize with youth in affliction, turned a courteous ear.

"What," he inquired, "has the sex been pulling on you now?"

"My wife is the best little woman in the world."

"I can readily believe it."

"But," continued the young man, "I would like to bean her with a brick, and bean her good. I told her, when she wanted to play a round with me this afternoon, that we must start early, as the days are drawing in. What did she do? Having got into her things, she decided that she didn't like the look of them and made a complete change. She then powdered her nose for ten minutes. And when finally I got her on to the first tee, an hour late, she went back into the clubhouse to phone to her dressmaker. It will be dark before we've played six holes. If I had my way, golf-clubs would make a rigid rule that no wife be allowed to play with her husband."

The Oldest Member nodded gravely.

"Until this is done," he agreed, "the millennium cannot but be set back indefinitely. Although we are told nothing about it, there can be little doubt that one of Job's chief trials was that his wife insisted on playing golf with him. And, as we are on this topic, it may interest you to hear a story."

"I have no time to listen to stories now."

"If your wife is telephoning to her dressmaker, you have ample time," replied the Sage. "The story which I am about to relate deals with a man named Bradbury Fisher——"

"You told me that one."

"I think not."

"Yes, you did. Bradbury Fisher was a Wall Street millionaire who had an English butler named Blizzard, who had been fifteen years with an earl. Another millionaire coveted Blizzard, and they played a match for him, and Fisher lost. But, just as he was wondering how he could square himself with his wife, who valued Blizzard very highly, Mrs. Fisher turned up from England with a still finer butler named Vosper, who had been eighteen years with a duke. So all ended happily."

"Yes," said the Sage. "You appear to have the facts correctly. The tale which I am about to relate is a sequel to that story, and runs as follows:

You say (began the Oldest Member) that all ended happily. That was Bradbury Fisher's opinion, too. It seemed to Bradbury in the days that followed Vosper's taking of office as though Providence, recognizing his sterling merits, had gone out of its way to smooth the path of life for him. The weather was fine; his handicap, after remaining stationary for many years, had begun to decrease; and his old friend Rupert Worple had just come out of Sing-Sing, where he had been taking a post-graduate course, and was paying him a pleasant visit at his house in Goldenville, Long Island.

The only thing, in fact, that militated against Bradbury's complete tranquillity was the information he had just received from his wife that her mother, Mrs. Lora Smith Maplebury, was about to infest the home for an indeterminate stay.

Bradbury had never liked his wives' mothers. His first wife, he recalled, had had a particularly objectionable mother. So had his second, third, and fourth. And the present holder of the title appeared to him to be scratch. She had a habit of sniffing in a significant way whenever she looked at him, and this can never make for a spirit of easy comradeship between man and woman. Given a free hand, he would have tied a brick to her neck and dropped her in the water-hazard at the second; but, realizing that this was but a Utopian dream, he sensibly decided to make the best of things and to content himself with jumping out of the window whenever she came into a room in which he happened to be sitting.

His mood, therefore, as he sat in his Louis Quinze library on the evening on which this story opens, was perfectly contented. And when there was a knock at the door and Vosper entered, no foreboding came to warn him that the quiet peace of his life was about to be shattered.

"Might I have a word, sir?" said the butler.

"Certainly, Vosper. What is it?"

Bradbury Fisher beamed upon the man. For the hundredth time, as he eyed him, he reflected how immeasurably superior he was to the departed Blizzard. Blizzard had been fifteen years with an earl, and no one disputes that earls are all very well in their way. But they are not dukes. About a butler who has served in a ducal household there is something which cannot be duplicated by one who has passed the formative years of his butlerhood in humbler surroundings.

"It has to do with Mr. Worple, sir."

"What about him?"

"Mr. Worple," said the butler, gravely, "must go. I do not like his laugh, sir."

"Eh?"

"It is too hearty, sir. It would not have done for the Duke."

Bradbury Fisher was an easy-going man, but he belonged to a free race. For freedom his fathers had fought, and if he had heard the story correctly, bled. His eyes flashed.

"Oh!" he cried. "Oh, indeed!"

"Yes, sir."

"Is zat so?"

"Yes, sir."

"Well, let me tell you something, Bill——"

"My name is Hildebrand, sir."

"Well, let me tell you, whatever your scarlet name is, that no butler is going to boss me in my own home. You can darned well go yourself."

"Very good, sir."

Vosper withdrew like an ambassador who has received his papers; and presently there was a noise without like hens going through a hedge, and Mrs. Fisher plunged in.

"Bradbury," she cried, "are you mad? Of course, Mr. Worple must go if Vosper says so. Don't you realize that Vosper will leave us if we don't humour him?"

"I should worry about him leaving!"

A strange, set look came into Mrs. Fisher's face.

"Bradbury," she said, "if Vosper leaves us, I shall die. And, what is more, just before dying I shall get a divorce. Yes, I will."

"But, darling," gasped Bradbury, "Rupert Worple! Old Rupie Worple! We've been friends all our lives."

"I don't care."

"We were freshers at Sing-Sing together."

"I don't care."

"We were initiated into the same Frat, the dear old Cracka-Bitta-Rock, on the same day."

"I don't care. Heaven has sent me the perfect butler, and I'm not going to lose him."

There was a tense silence.

"Ah, well!" said Bradbury Fisher with a deep sigh.

That night he broke the news to Rupert Worple.

"I never thought," said Rupert Worple sadly, "when we sang together on the glee-club at the old Alma Mater, that it would ever come to this."

"Nor I," said Bradbury Fisher. "But so it must be. You wouldn't have done for the Duke, Rupie, you wouldn't have done for the Duke."

"Good-bye, Number 8,097,564," said Rupert Worple in a low voice.

"Good-bye, Number 8,097,565," whispered Bradbury Fisher.

And with a silent hand-clasp the two friends parted.

With the going of Rupert Worple a grey cloud seemed to settle upon the glowing radiance of Bradbury Fisher's life. Mrs. Lora Smith Maplebury duly arrived; and, having given a series of penetrating sniffs as he greeted her in the entrance-hall, dug herself in and settled down to what looked like the visit of a life-time. And then, just as Bradbury's cup seemed to be full to over-flowing, Mrs. Fisher drew him aside one evening.

"Bradbury," said Mrs. Fisher. "I have some good news for you."

"Is your mother leaving?" asked Bradbury eagerly.

"Of course not. I said good news. I am taking up golf again."

Bradbury Fisher clutched at the arms of his chair, and an ashen pallor spread itself over his clean-cut face.

"What did you say?" he muttered.

"I'm taking up golf again. Won't it be nice? We'll be able to play together every day."

Bradbury Fisher shuddered strongly. It was many years since he had played with his wife, but, like an old wound, the memory of it still troubled him occasionally.

"It was Vosper's idea."

"Vosper!"

A sudden seething fury gripped Bradbury. This pestilent butler was an absolute home-wrecker. He toyed with the idea of poisoning Vosper's port. Surely, if he were to do so, a capable lawyer could smooth things over and get him off with, at the worst, a nominal fine.

"Vosper says I need exercise. He says he does not like my wheezing."

"Your what?"

"My wheezing. I do wheeze, you know."

"Well, so does he."

"Yes, but a good butler is expected to wheeze. A wheezing woman is quite a different thing. My wheezing would never have done for the Duke, Vosper says."

Bradbury Fisher breathed tensely.

"Ha!" he said.

"I think it's so nice of him, Bradbury. It shows he has our interests at heart, just like a faithful old retainer. He says wheezing is an indication of heightened blood-pressure and can be remedied by gentle exercise. So we'll have our first round tomorrow morning, shall we?"

"Just as you say," said Bradbury dully. "I had a sort of date to make one of a foursome with three men at the club, but——"

"Oh, you don't want to play with those silly men any more. It will be much nicer, just you and I playing together."

It has always seemed to me a strange and unaccountable thing that nowadays, when gloom is at such a premium in the world's literature and all around us stern young pessimists are bringing home the bacon with their studies in the greyly grim, no writer has thought of turning his pen to a realistic portrayal of the golfing wife. No subject could be more poignant, and yet it has been completely neglected. One can only suppose that even modern novelists feel that the line should be drawn somewhere.

Bradbury Fisher's emotions, as he stood by the first tee watching his wife prepare to drive off, were far beyond my poor power to describe. Compared with him at that moment, the hero of a novel of the Middle West would have seemed almost offensively chirpy. This was the woman he loved, and she was behaving in a manner that made the iron sink deep into his soul.

Most women golfers are elaborate wagglers, but none that Bradbury had ever seen had made quite such a set of Swedish exercises out of the simple act of laying the clubhead behind the ball and raising it over the right shoulder. For fully a minute, it seemed to him, Mrs. Fisher fiddled and pawed at the ball; while Bradbury, realizing that there are eighteen tees on a course and that this Russian Ballet stuff was consequently going to happen at least seventeen times more, quivered in agony and clenched his hands till the knuckles stood out white under the strain. Then she drove, and the ball trickled down the hill into a patch of rough some five yards distant.

"Tee-hee!" said Mrs. Fisher.

Bradbury uttered a sharp cry. He was married to a golfing giggler.

"What did I do then?"

"God help you, woman," said Bradbury, "you jerked your head up till I wonder it didn't come off at the neck."

It was at the fourth hole that further evidence was afforded the wretched man of how utterly a good, pure woman may change her nature when once she gets out on the links. Mrs. Fisher had played her eleventh, and, having walked the intervening three yards, was about to play her twelfth when behind them, grouped upon the tee, Bradbury perceived two of his fellow-members of the club. Remorse and shame pierced him.

"One minute, honey," he said, as his life's partner took a stranglehold on her mashie and was about to begin the movements. "We'd better let these men through."

"What men?"

"We're holding up a couple of fellows. I'll wave to them."

"You will do nothing of the sort," cried Mrs. Fisher. "The idea!"

"But, darling——"

"Why should they go through us? We started before them."

"But, pettie——"

"They shall not pass!" said Mrs. Fisher. And, raising her mashie, she dug a grim divot out of the shrinking turf. With bowed head, Bradbury followed her on the long, long trail.

The sun was sinking as they came at last to journey's end.

"How right Vosper is!" said Mrs. Fisher, nestling into the cushions of the automobile. "I feel ever so much better already."

"Do you?" said Bradbury wanly. "Do you?"

"We'll play again tomorrow afternoon," said his wife.

Bradbury Fisher was a man of steel. He endured for a week. But on the last day of the week Mrs. Fisher insisted on taking as a companion on the round Alfred, her pet Airedale. In vain Bradbury spoke of the Greens Committee and their prejudice against dogs on the links. Mrs. Fisher—and Bradbury, as he heard the ghastly words, glanced involuntarily up at the summer sky, as if preparing to dodge the lightning-bolt which could scarcely fail to punish such blasphemy—said that the Greens Committee were a lot of silly, fussy old men, and she had no patience with them.

So Alfred came along—barking at Bradbury as he endeavoured to concentrate on the smooth pronation of the wrists, pounding ahead to frolic round distant players who were shaping for delicate chip-shots, and getting a deep toe-hold on the turf of each successive green. Hell, felt Bradbury, must be something like this; and he wished that he had led a better life.

But that retribution which waits on all, both small and great, who defy Greens Committees had marked Alfred down. Taking up a position just behind Mrs. Fisher as she began her down swing on the seventh, he received so shrewd a blow on his right foreleg that with a sharp yelp he broke into a gallop, raced through a foursome on the sixth green, and, charging across country, dived headlong into the water-hazard on the second; where he remained until Bradbury, who had been sent in pursuit, waded in and fished him out.

Mrs. Fisher came panting up, full of concern.

"What shall we do? The poor little fellow is quite lame. I know, you can carry him, Bradbury."

Bradbury Fisher uttered a low, bleating sound. The water had had the worst effect on the animal. Even when dry, Alfred was always a dog of powerful scent. Wet, he had become definitely one of the six best-smellers. His aroma had what the advertisement-writers call "strong memory value".

"Carry him? To the car, do you mean?"

"Of course not. Round the links. I don't want to miss a day's golf. You can put him down when you play your shots."

For a long instant Bradbury hesitated. The words "Is zat so?" trembled on his lips.

"Very well," he said, swallowing twice.

That night, in his du Barri bedroom, Bradbury Fisher lay sleepless far into the dawn. A crisis, he realized, had come in his domestic affairs. Things, he saw clearly, could not go on like this. It was not merely the awful spiritual agony of playing these daily rounds of golf with his wife that was so hard to endure. The real trouble was that the spectacle of her on the links was destroying his ideals, sapping away that love and respect which should have been as imperishable as steel.

To a good man his wife should be a goddess, a being far above him to whom he can offer worship and reverence, a beacon-star guiding him over the tossing seas of life. She should be ever on a pedestal and in a shrine. And when she waggles for a minute and a half and then jerks her head and tops the ball, she ceases to be so. And Mrs. Fisher was not merely a head-lifter and a super-waggler; she was a scoffer at Golf's most sacred things. She held up scratchmen. She omitted to replace divots. She spoke lightly of Green Committees.

The sun was gilding Goldenville in its morning glory when Bradbury made up his mind. He would play with her no more. To do so would be fair neither to himself nor to her. At any moment, he felt, she might come out on the links in high heels or stop to powder her nose on the green while frenzied foursomes waited to play their approach-shots. And then love would turn to hate, and he and she would go through life estranged. Better to end it now, while he still retained some broken remains of the old esteem.

He had got everything neatly arranged. He would plead business in the City and sneak off each day to play on another course five miles away.

"Darling," he said at breakfast, "I'm afraid we shan't be able to have our game for a week or so. I shall have to be at the office early and late."

"Oh, what a shame!" said Mrs. Fisher.

"You will, no doubt, be able to get a game with the pro. or somebody. You know how bitterly this disappoints me. I had come to look on our daily round as the bright spot of the day. But business is business."

"I thought you had retired from business," said Mrs. Lora Smith Maplebury, with a sniff that cracked a coffee-cup.

Bradbury Fisher looked at her coldly. She was a lean, pale-eyed woman with high cheek-bones, and for the hundredth time since she had come into his life he felt how intensely she needed a punch on the nose.

"Not altogether," he said. "I still retain large interests in this and that, and I am at the moment occupied with affairs which I cannot mention without revealing secrets which might—which would—which are—— Well, anyway, I've got to go to the office."

"Oh, quite," said Mrs. Maplebury.

"What do you mean, quite?" demanded Bradbury.

"I mean just what I say. Quite!"

"Why quite?"

"Why not quite? I suppose I can say 'Quite!' can't I?"

"Oh, quite," said Bradbury.

He kissed his wife and left the room. He felt a little uneasy. There had been something in the woman's manner which had caused him a vague foreboding.

Had he been able to hear the conversation that followed his departure, he would have been still more uneasy.

"Suspicious!" said Mrs. Maplebury.

"What is?" asked Mrs. Fisher.

"That man's behaviour."

"What do you mean?"

"Did you observe him closely while he was speaking?"

"No."

"The tip of his nose wiggled. Always distrust a man who wiggles the tip of his nose."

"I am sure Bradbury would not deceive you."

"So am I. But he might try to."

"I don't understand, mother. Do you mean you think Bradbury is not going to the office?"

"I am sure he is not."

"You think——?"

"I do."

"You are suggesting——?"

"I am."

"You would imply——?"

"I would."

A moan escaped Mrs. Fisher.

"Oh, mother, mother!" she cried. "If I thought Bradbury was untrue to me, what I wouldn't do to that poor clam!"

"I certainly think that the least you can do, as a good womanly woman, is to have a capable lawyer watching your interests."

"But we can easily find out if he is at the office. We can ring them up on the phone and ask."

"And be told that he is in conference. He will not have neglected to arrange for that."

"Then what shall I do?"

"Wait," said Mrs. Maplebury. "Wait and be watchful."

The shades of night were falling when Bradbury returned to his home. He was fatigued but jubilant. He had played forty-five holes in the society of his own sex. He had kept his head down and his eye on the ball. He had sung negro spirituals in the locker-room.

"I trust, Bradbury," said Mrs. Maplebury, "that you are not tired after your long day?"

"A little," said Bradbury. "Nothing to signify." He turned radiantly to his wife.

"Honey," he said, "you remember the trouble I was having with my iron? Well, today——"

He stopped aghast. Like every good husband it had always been his practice hitherto to bring his golfing troubles to his wife, and in many a cosy after-dinner chat he had confided to her the difficulty he was having in keeping his iron-shots straight. And he had only just stopped himself now from telling her that today he had been hitting 'em sweetly on the meat right down the middle.

"Your iron?"

"Er—ah—yes. I have large interests in Iron—as also in Steel, Jute, Woollen Fabrics, and Consolidated Peanuts. A gang has been trying to hammer down my stock. Today I fixed them."

"You did, did you?" said Mrs. Maplebury.

"I said I did," retorted Bradbury defiantly.

"So did I. I said you did, did you?"

"What do you mean, did you?"

"Well, you did, didn't you?"

"Yes, I did."

"Exactly what I said. You did. Didn't you?"

"Yes, I did."

"Yes, you did!" said Mrs. Maplebury.

Once again Bradbury felt vaguely uneasy. There was nothing in the actual dialogue which had just taken place to cause him alarm—indeed, considered purely as dialogue, it was bright and snappy and well calculated to make things gay about the home. But once more there had been a subtle something in his mother-in-law's manner which had jarred upon him. He mumbled and went off to dress for dinner.

"Ha!" said Mrs. Maplebury, as the door closed.

Such, then, was the position of affairs in the Fisher home. And now that I have arrived thus far in my story and have shown you this man systematically deceiving the woman he had vowed—at one of the most exclusive altars in New York—to love and cherish, you—if you are the sort of husband I hope you are—must be saying to yourself: "But what of Bradbury Fisher's conscience?" Remorse, you feel, must long since have begun to gnaw at his vitals; and the thought suggests itself to you that surely by this time the pangs of self-reproach must have interfered seriously with his short game, even if not as yet sufficiently severe to affect his driving off the tee.

You are overlooking the fact that Bradbury Fisher's was the trained and educated conscience of a man who had passed a large portion of his life in Wall Street; and years of practice had enabled him to reduce the control of it to a science. Many a time in the past, when an active operator on the Street, he had done things to the Small Investor which would have caused raised eyebrows in the fo'c'sle of a pirate sloop—and done them without a blush. He was not the man, therefore, to suffer torment merely because he was slipping one over on the Little Woman.

Occasionally he would wince a trifle at the thought of what would happen if she ever found out; but apart from that, I am doing no more than state the plain truth when I say that Bradbury Fisher did not care a whoop.

Besides, at this point his golf suddenly underwent a remarkable improvement. He had always been a long driver, and quite abruptly he found that he was judging them nicely with the putter. Two weeks after he had started on his campaign of deception he amazed himself and all who witnessed the performance by cracking a hundred for the first time in his career. And every golfer knows that in the soul of the man who does that there is no room for remorse. Conscience may sting the player who is going round in a hundred and ten, but when it tries to make itself unpleasant to the man who is doing ninety-sevens and ninety-eights, it is simply wasting its time.

I will do Bradbury Fisher justice. He did regret that he was not in a position to tell his wife all about that first ninety-nine of his. He would have liked to take her into a corner and show her with the aid of a poker and a lump of coal just how he had chipped up to the pin on the last hole and left himself a simple two-foot putt. And the forlorn feeling of being unable to confide his triumphs to a sympathetic ear deepened a week later when, miraculously achieving ninety-six in the medal round, he qualified for the sixth sixteen in the annual invitation tournament of the club to which he had attached himself.

"Shall I?" he mused, eyeing her wistfully across the Queen Anne table in the Crystal Boudoir, to which they had retired to drink their after-dinner coffee. "Better not, better not," whispered Prudence in his ear.

"Bradbury," said Mrs. Fisher.

"Yes, darling?"

"Have you been hard at work today?"

"Yes, precious. Very, very hard at work."

"Ho!" said Mrs. Maplebury.

"What did you say?" said Bradbury.

"I said ho!"

"What do you mean, ho?"

"Just ho. There is no harm, I imagine, in my saying ho, if I wish to."

"Oh no," said Bradbury. "By no means. Not at all. Pray do so."

"Thank you," said Mrs. Maplebury. "Ho!"

"You do have to slave at the office, don't you?" said Mrs. Fisher.

"I do, indeed."

"It must be a great strain."

"A terrible strain. Yes, yes, a terrible strain."

"Then you won't object to giving it up, will you?"

Bradbury started.

"Giving it up?"

"Giving up going to the office. The fact is, dear," said Mrs. Fisher, "Vosper has complained."

"What about?"

"About you going to the office. He says he has never been in the employment of anyone engaged in commerce, and he doesn't like it. The Duke looked down on commerce very much. So I'm afraid, darling, you will have to give it up."

Bradbury Fisher stared before him, a strange singing in his ears. The blow had been so sudden that he was stunned.

His fingers picked feverishly at the arm of his chair. He had paled to the very lips. If the office was barred to him, on what pretext could he sneak away from home? And sneak he must for tomorrow and the day after the various qualifying sixteens were to play the match-rounds for the cups; and it was monstrous and impossible that he should not be there. He must be there. He had done a ninety-six, and the next best medal score in his sixteen was a hundred and one. For the first time in his life he had before him the prospect of winning a cup; and, highly though the poets have spoken of love, that emotion is not to be compared with the frenzy which grips a twenty-four-handicap man who sees himself within reach of a cup.

Blindly he tottered from the room and sought his study. He wanted to be alone. He had to think, think.

The evening paper was lying on the table. Automatically he picked it up and ran his eye over the front page. And, as he did so, he uttered a sharp exclamation.

He leaped from his chair and returned to the boudoir, carrying the paper.

"Well, what do you know about this?" said Bradbury Fisher, in a hearty voice.

"We know a great deal about a good many things," said Mrs. Maplebury.

"What is it, Bradbury?" said Mrs. Fisher.

"I'm afraid I shall have to leave you for a couple of days. Great nuisance, but there it is. But, of course, I must be there."

"Where?"

"Ah, where?" said Mrs. Maplebury.

"At Sing-Sing. I see in the paper that tomorrow and the day after they are inaugurating the new Osborne Stadium. All the men of my class will be attending, and I must go, too."

"Must you really?"

"I certainly must. Not to do so would be to show a lack of college spirit. The boys are playing Yale, and there is to be a big dinner afterwards. I shouldn't wonder if I had to make a speech. But don't worry, honey," he said, kissing his wife affectionately. "I shall be back before you know I've gone." He turned sharply to Mrs. Maplebury. "I beg your pardon?" he said stiffly.

"I did not speak."

"I thought you did."

"I merely inhaled. I simply drew in air through my nostrils. If I am not at liberty to draw in air through my nostrils in your house, pray inform me."

"I would prefer that you didn't," said Bradbury, between set teeth.

"Then I would suffocate."

"Yes," said Bradbury Fisher.

Of all the tainted millionaires who, after years of plundering the widow and the orphan, have devoted the evening of their life to the game of golf, few can ever have been so boisterously exhilarated as was Bradbury Fisher when, two nights later, he returned to his home. His dreams had all come true. He had won his way to the foot of the rainbow. In other words, he was the possessor of a small pewter cup, value three dollars, which he had won by beating a feeble old gentleman with one eye in the final match of the competition for the sixth sixteen at the Squashy Hollow Golf Club Invitation Tournament.

He entered the house, radiant.

"Tra-la!" sang Bradbury Fisher. "Tra-la!"

"I beg your pardon, sir?" said Vosper, who had encountered him in the hall.

"Eh? Oh, nothing. Just tra-la."

"Very good, sir."

Bradbury Fisher looked at Vosper. For the first time it seemed to sweep over him like a wave that Vosper was an uncommonly good fellow. The past was forgotten, and he beamed upon Vosper like the rising sun.

"Vosper," he said, "what wages are you getting?"

"I regret to say, sir," replied the butler, "that, at the moment, the precise amount of the salary of which I am in receipt has slipped my mind. I could refresh my memory by consulting my books, if you so desire it, sir."

"Never mind. Whatever it is, it's doubled."

"I am obliged, sir. You will, no doubt, send me a written memo to that effect?"

"Twenty, if you like."

"One will be ample, sir."

Bradbury curvetted past him through the baronial hall and into the Crystal Boudoir. His wife was there alone.

"Mother has gone to bed," she said. "She has a bad headache."

"You don't say!" said Bradbury. It was as if everything was conspiring to make this a day of days. "Well, it's great to be back in the old home."

"Did you have a good time?"

"Capital."

"You saw all your old friends?"

"Every one of them."

"Did you make a speech at the dinner?"

"Did I! They rolled out of their seats and the waiters swept them up with dusters."

"A very big dinner, I suppose?"

"Enormous."

"How was the football game?"

"Best I've ever seen. We won. Number 432,986 made a hundred-and-ten-yard run for a touchdown in the last five minutes."

"Really?"

"And that takes a bit of doing, with a ball and chain round your ankle, believe me!"

"Bradbury," said Mrs. Fisher, "where have you been these last two days?"

Bradbury's heart missed a beat. His wife was looking exactly like her mother. It was the first time he had ever been able to believe that she could be Mrs. Maplebury's daughter.

"Been? Why, I'm telling you."

"Bradbury," said Mrs. Fisher, "just one word. Have you seen the paper this morning?"

"Why, no. What with all the excitement of meeting the boys and this and that——"

"Then you have not seen that the inauguration of the new Stadium at Sing-Sing was postponed on account of an outbreak of mumps in the prison?"

Bradbury gulped.

"There was no dinner, no football game, no gathering of Old Grads—nothing! So—where have you been, Bradbury?"

Bradbury gulped again.

"You're sure you haven't got this wrong?" he said at length.

"Quite."

"I mean, sure it wasn't some other place?"

"Quite."

"Sing-Sing? You got the name correctly?"

"Quite. Where, Bradbury, have you been these last two days?"

"Well—er——"

Mrs. Fisher coughed dryly.

"I merely ask out of curiosity. The facts will, of course, come out in court."

"In court!"

"Naturally I propose to place this affair in the hands of my lawyer immediately."

Bradbury started convulsively.

"You mustn't!"

"I certainly shall."

A shudder shook Bradbury from head to foot. He felt worse that he had done when his opponent in the final had laid him a stymie on the last green, thereby squaring the match and taking it to the nineteenth hole.

"I will tell you all," he muttered.

"Well?"

"Well—it was like this."

"Yes?"

"Er—like this. In fact, this way."

"Proceed."

Bradbury clenched his hands; and, as far as that could be managed, avoided her eye.

"I've been playing golf," he said in a low, toneless voice.

"Playing golf?"

"Yes." Bradbury hesitated. "I don't mean it in an offensive spirit, and no doubt most men would have enjoyed themselves thoroughly, but I—well, I am curiously constituted, angel, and the fact is I simply couldn't stand playing with you any longer. The fault, I am sure, was mine, but—well, there it is. If I had played another round with you, my darling, I think that I should have begun running about in circles, biting my best friends. So I thought it all over, and, not wanting to hurt your feelings by telling you the truth, I stooped to what I might call a ruse. I said I was going to the office; and, instead of going to the office, I went off to Squashy Hollow and played there."

Mrs. Fisher uttered a cry.

"You were there today and yesterday?"

In spite of his trying situation, the yeasty exhilaration which had been upon him when he entered the room returned to Bradbury.

"Was I!" he cried. "You bet your Russian boots I was! Only winning a cup, that's all!"

"You won a cup?"

"You bet your diamond tiara I won a cup. Say, listen," said Bradbury, diving for a priceless Boule table and wrenching a leg off it. "Do you know what happened in the semi-final?" He clasped his fingers over the table-leg in the overlapping grip. "I'm here, see, about fifteen feet off the green. The other fellow lying dead, and I'm playing the like. Best I could hope for was a half, you'll say, eh? Well, listen. I just walked up to that little white ball, and I gave it a little flick, and, believe me or believe me not, that little white ball never stopped running till in plunked into the hole."

He stopped. He perceived that he had been introducing into the debate extraneous and irrelevant matter.

"Honey," he said, fervently, "you mustn't get mad about this. Maybe, if we try again, it will be all right. Give me another chance. Let me come out and play a round tomorrow. I think perhaps your style of play is a thing that wants getting used to. After all, I didn't like olives the first time I tried them. Or whisky. Or caviare, for that matter. Probably if——"

Mrs. Fisher shook her head.

"I shall never play again."

"Oh, but, listen——"

She looked at him fondly, her eyes dim with happy tears.

"I should have known you better, Bradbury. I suspected you. How foolish I was."

"There, there," said Bradbury.

"It was mother's fault. She put ideas into my head."

There was much that Bradbury would have liked to say about her mother, but he felt that this was not the time.

"And you really forgive me for sneaking off, and playing at Squashy Hollow?"

"Of course."

"Then why not a little round tomorrow?"

"No, Bradbury, I shall never play again. Vosper says I mustn't."

"What!"

"He saw me one morning on the links, and he came to me and told me—quite nicely and respectfully—that it must not occur again. He said with the utmost deference that I was making a spectacle of myself and that this nuisance must now cease. So I gave it up. But it's all right. Vosper thinks that gentle massage will cure my wheezing, so I'm having it every day, and really I do think there's an improvement already."

"Where is Vosper?" said Bradbury hoarsely.

"You aren't going to be rude to him, Bradbury? He is so sensitive."

But Bradbury Fisher had left the room.

"You rang, sir?" said Vosper, entering the Byzantine smoking-room some few minutes later.

"Yes," said Bradbury. "Vosper, I am a plain, rugged man and I do not know all that there is to be known about these things. So do not be offended if I ask you a question."

"Not at all, sir."

"Tell me, Vosper, did the Duke ever shake hands with you?"

"Once only, sir—mistaking me in a dimly-lit hall for a visiting archbishop."

"Would it be all right for me to shake hands with you now?"

"If you wish it, sir, certainly."

"I want to thank you, Vosper. Mrs. Fisher tells me that you have stopped her playing golf. I thing that you have saved my reason, Vosper."

"That is extremely gratifying, sir."

"Your salary is trebled."

"Thank you very much, sir. And, while we are talking, sir, if I might—— There is one other little matter I wished to speak of, sir."

"Shoot, Vosper."

"It concerns Mrs. Maplebury, sir."

"What about her?"

"If I might say so, sir, she would scarcely have done for the Duke."

A sudden wild thrill shot through Bradbury.

"You mean——?" he stammered.

"I mean, sir, that Mrs. Maplebury must go. I make no criticism of Mrs. Maplebury, you understand, sir. I merely say that she would decidedly not have done for the Duke."

Bradbury drew in his breath sharply.

"Vosper," he said, "the more I hear of that Duke of yours, the more I seem to like him. You really think he would have drawn the line at Mrs. Maplebury?"

"Very firmly, sir."

"Splendid fellow! Splendid fellow! She shall go tomorrow, Vosper."

"Thank you very much, sir."

"And, Vosper."

"Sir?"

"Your salary. It is quadrupled."

"I am greatly obliged, sir."

"Tra-la, Vosper!"

"Tra-la, sir. Will that be all?"

"That will be all. Tra-la!"

"Tra-la, sir," said the butler.

15

CHESTER FORGETS HIMSELF

THE afternoon was warm and heavy. Butterflies loafed languidly in the sunshine, birds panted in the shady recesses of the trees.

The Oldest Member, snug in his favourite chair, had long since succumbed to the drowsy influence of the weather. His eyes were closed, his chin sunk upon his breast. The pipe which he had been smoking lay beside him on the turf, and ever and anon there proceeded from him a muffled snore.

Suddenly the stillness was broken. There was a sharp, cracking sound as of splitting wood. The Oldest Member sat up, blinking. As soon as his eyes had become accustomed to the glare, he perceived that a foursome had holed out on the ninth and was disintegrating. Two of the players were moving with quick, purposeful steps in the direction of the side door which gave entrance to the bar; a third was making for the road that led to the village, bearing himself as one in profound dejection; the fourth came on to the terrace.

"Finished?" said the Oldest Member.

The other stopped, wiping a heated brow. He lowered himself into the adjoining chair and stretched his legs out.

"Yes. We started at the tenth. Golly, I'm tired. No joke playing in this weather."

"How did you come out?"

"We won on the last green. Jimmy Fothergill and I were playing the vicar and Rupert Blake."

"What was that sharp, cracking sound I heard?" asked the Oldest Member.

"That was the vicar smashing his putter. Poor old chap, he had rotten luck all the way round, and it didn't seem to make it any better for him that he wasn't able to relieve his feelings in the ordinary way."

"I suspected some such thing," said the Oldest Member, "from the look of his back as he was leaving the green. His walk was the walk of an overwrought soul."

His companion did not reply. He was breathing deeply and regularly.

"It is a moot question," proceeded the Oldest Member, thoughtfully, "whether the clergy, considering their peculiar position, should not be more liberally handicapped at golf than the laymen with whom they compete. I have made a close study of the game since the days of the feather ball, and I am firmly convinced that to refrain entirely from oaths during a round is almost equivalent to giving away three bisques. There are certain occasions when an oath seems to be so imperatively demanded that the strain of keeping it in must inevitably affect the ganglions or nerve-centres in such a manner as to diminish the steadiness of the swing."

The man beside him slipped lower down in his chair. His mouth had opened slightly.

"I am reminded in this connection," said the Oldest Member, "of the story of young Chester Meredith, a friend of mine whom you have not, I think, met. He moved from this neighbourhood shortly before you came. There was a case where a man's whole happiness was very nearly wrecked purely because he tried to curb his instincts and thwart nature in this very respect. Perhaps you would care to hear the story?"

A snore proceeded from the next chair.

"Very well, then," said the Oldest Member, "I will relate it."

Chester Meredith (said the Oldest Member) was one of the nicest young fellows of my acquaintance. We had been friends ever since he had come to live here as a small boy, and I had watched him with a fatherly eye through all the more important crises of a young man's life. It was I who taught him to drive, and when he had all that trouble in his twenty-first year with shanking his short approaches, it was to me that he came for sympathy and advice. It was an odd coincidence, therefore, that I should have been present when he fell in love.

I was smoking my evening cigar out here and watching the last couples finishing their rounds, when Chester came out of the club-house and sat by me. I could see that the boy was perturbed about something, and wondered why, for I knew that he had won his match.

"What," I inquired, "is on your mind?"

"Oh, nothing," said Chester. "I was only thinking that there are some human misfits who ought not to be allowed on any decent links."

"You mean——?"

"The Wrecking Crew," said Chester, bitterly. "They held us up all the way round, confound them. Wouldn't let us through. What can you do with people who don't know enough of the etiquette of the game to understand that a single has right of way over a four-ball foursome? We had to loaf about for hours on end while they scratched at the turf like a lot of crimson hens. Eventually all four of them lost their balls simultaneously at the eleventh and we managed to get by. I hope they choke."

I was not altogether surprised at his warmth. The Wrecking Crew consisted of four retired business men who had taken up the noble game late in life because their doctors had ordered them air and exercise. Every club, I suppose, has a cross of this kind to bear, and it was not often that our members rebelled; but there was un-doubtedly something particularly irritating in the methods of the Wrecking Crew. They tried so hard that it seemed almost inconceivable that they should be so slow.

"They are all respectable men," I said, "and were, I believe, highly thought of in their respective businesses. But on the links I admit that they are a trial."

"They are the direct lineal descendants of the Gadarene swine," said Chester firmly. "Every time they come out I expect to see them rush down the hill from the first tee and hurl themselves into the lake at the second. Of all the——"

"Hush!" I said.

Out of the corner of my eye I had seen a girl approaching, and I was afraid lest Chester in his annoyance might use strong language. For he was one of those golfers who are apt to express themselves in moments of emotion with a good deal of generous warmth.

"Eh?" said Chester.

I jerked my head, and he looked round. And, as he did so, there came into his face an expression which I had seen there only once before, on the occasion when he won the President's Cup on the last green by holing a thirty-yard chip with his mashie. It was a look of ecstasy and awe. His mouth was open, his eyebrows raised, and he was breathing heavily through his nose.

"Golly!" I heard him mutter.

The girl passed by. I could not blame Chester for staring at her. She was a beautiful young thing, with a lissom figure and a perfect face. Her hair was a deep chestnut, her eyes blue, her nose small and laid back with about as much loft as a light iron. She disappeared, and Chester, after nearly dislocating his neck trying to see her round the corner of the club-house, emitted a deep, explosive sigh.

"Who is she?" he whispered.

I could tell him that. In one way and another I get to know most things around this locality.

"She is a Miss Blakeney. Felicia Blakeney. She has come to stay for a month with the Waterfields. I understand she was at school with Jane Waterfield. She is twenty-three, has a dog named Joseph, dances well, and dislikes parsnips. Her father is a distinguished writer on sociological subjects; her mother is Wilmot Royce, the well-known novelist, whose last work, *Sewers of the Soul,* was, you may recall, jerked before a tribunal by the Purity League. She has a brother, Crispin Blakeney, an eminent young reviewer and essayist, who is now in India studying local conditions with a view to a series of lectures. She only arrived here yesterday, so this is all I have been able to find out about her as yet."

Chester's mouth was still open when I began speaking. By the time I had finished it was open still wider. The ecstatic look in his eyes had changed to one of dull despair.

"My God!" he muttered. "If her family is like that, what chance is there for a rough-neck like me?"

"You admire her?"

"She is the alligator's Adam's apple," said Chester, simply.

I patted his shoulder.

"Have courage, my boy," I said. "Always remember that the love of a good man to whom the pro. can give only a couple of strokes in eighteen holes is not to be despised."

"Yes, that's all very well. But this girl is probably one solid mass of brain. She will look on me as an uneducated warthog."

"Well, I will introduce you, and we will see. She looked a nice girl."

"You're a great describer, aren't you?" said Chester. "A wonderful flow of language you've got, I don't think! Nice girl! Why, she's the only girl in the world. She's a pearl among women. She's the most marvellous, astounding, beautiful, heavenly thing that ever drew perfumed breath." He paused, as if his train of thought had been interrupted by an idea. "Did you say that her brother's name was Crispin?"

"I did. Why?"

Chester gave vent to a few manly oaths.

"Doesn't that just show you how things go in this rotten world?"

"What do you mean?"

"I was at school with him."

"Surely that should form a solid basis for friendship?"

"Should it? Should it, by gad? Well, let me tell you that I probably kicked that blighted worm Crispin Blakeney a matter of seven hundred and forty-six times in the few years I knew him. He was the world's worst. He could have walked straight into the Wrecking Crew and no questions asked. Wouldn't it jar you? I have the luck to know her brother, and it turns out that we couldn't stand the sight of each other."

"Well, there is no need to tell her that."

"Do you mean——?" He gazed at me wildly. "Do you mean I might pretend we were pals?"

"Why not? Seeing that he is in India, he can hardly contradict you."

"My gosh!" He mused for a moment. I could see that the idea was beginning to sink in. It was always thus with Chester. You had to give him time. "By Jove, it mightn't be a bad scheme at that. I mean, it would start me off with a rush, like being one up on bogey in the first two. And there's nothing like a good start. By gad, I'll do it."

"I should."

"Reminiscences of the dear old days when we were lads together and all that sort of thing."

"Precisely."

"It isn't going to be easy, mind you," said Chester, meditatively. "I'll do it because I love her, but nothing else in this world would make me say a civil word about the blister. Well, then, that's settled. Get on with the introduction stuff, will you? I'm in a hurry."

One of the privileges of age is that it enables a man to thrust his society on a beautiful girl without causing her to draw herself up and say "Sir!" It was not difficult for me to make the acquaintance of Miss Blakeney, and, this done, my first act was to unleash Chester on her.

"Chester," I said, summoning him as he loafed with an over-done carelessness on the horizon, one leg almost inextricably entwined about the other, "I want you to meet Miss Blakeney. Miss Blakeney, this is my young friend Chester Meredith. He was at school with your brother Crispin. You were great friends, were you not?"

"Bosom," said Chester, after a pause.

"Oh, really?" said the girl. There was a pause. "He is in India now."

"Yes," said Chester.

There was another pause.

"Great chap," said Chester, gruffly.

"Crispin is very popular," said the girl, "with some people."

"Always been my best pal," said Chester.

"Yes?"

I was not altogether satisfied with the way matters were developing. The girl seemed cold and unfriendly, and I was afraid that this was due to Chester's repellent manner. Shyness, especially when complicated by love at first sight, is apt to have strange effects on a man, and the way it had taken Chester was to make him abnormally stiff and dignified. One of the most charming things about him, as a rule, was his delightful boyish smile. Shyness had caused him to iron this out of his countenance till no trace of it remained. Not only did he not smile, he looked like a man who never had smiled and never would. His mouth was a thin, rigid line. His back was stiff with what appeared to be contemptuous aversion. He looked down his nose at Miss Blakeney as if she were less than the dust beneath his chariot-wheels.

I thought the best thing to do was to leave them alone together to get acquainted. Perhaps, I thought, it was my presence that was cramping Chester's style. I excused myself and receded.

It was some days before I saw Chester again. He came round to my cottage one night after dinner and sank into a chair, where he remained silent for several minutes.

"Well?" I said at last.

"Eh?" said Chester, starting violently.

"Have you been seeing anything of Miss Blakeney lately?"

"You bet I have."

"And how do you feel about her on further acquaintance?"

"Eh?" said Chester, absently.

"Do you still love her?"

Chester came out of his trance.

"Love her?" he cried, his voice vibrating with emotion. "Of course I love her. Who wouldn't love her? I'd be a silly chump not loving her. Do you know," the boy went on, a look in his eyes like that of some young knight seeing the Holy Grail in a vision, "do you know, she is the only woman I ever met who didn't overswing. Just a nice, crisp, snappy half-slosh, with a good full follow-through. And another thing. You'll hardly believe me, but she waggles almost as little as George Duncan. You know how women waggle as a rule, fiddling about for a minute and a half like kittens playing with a ball of wool. Well, she just makes one firm pass with the club and then *bing!* There is none like her, none."

"Then you have been playing golf with her?"

"Nearly every day."

"How is your game?"

"Rather spotty. I seem to be mistiming them."

I was concerned.

"I do hope, my dear boy," I said, earnestly, "that you are taking care to control your feelings when out on the links with Miss Blakeney. You know what you are like. I trust you have not been using the sort of language you generally employ on occasions when you are not timing them right?"

"Me?" said Chester, horrified. "Who, me? You don't imagine for a moment that I would dream of saying a thing that would bring a blush to her dear cheek, do you? Why, a bishop could have gone round with me and learned nothing new."

I was relieved.

"How do you find you manage the dialogue these days?" I asked. "When I introduced you, you behaved—you will forgive an old friend for criticizing—you behaved a little like a stuffed frog with laryngitis. Have things got easier in that respect?"

"Oh yes. I'm quite the prattler now. I talk about her brother mostly. I put in the greater part of my time boosting the tick. It seems to be coming easier. Will-power, I suppose. And then, of course, I talk a good deal about her mother's novels."

"Have you read them?"

"Every damned one of them—for her sake. And if there's a greater proof of love than that, show me! My gosh, what muck that woman writes! That reminds me, I've got to send to the bookshop for her latest—out yesterday. It's called *The Stench of Life*. A sequel, I understand, to *Grey Mildew*."

"Brave lad," I said, pressing his hand. "Brave, devoted lad!"

"Oh, I'd do more than that for her." He smoked for a while in silence. "By the way, I'm going to propose to her tomorrow."

"Already?"

"Can't put it off a minute longer. It's been as much as I could manage, bottling it up till now. Where do you think would be the best place? I mean, it's not the sort of thing you can do while you're walking down the street or having a cup of tea. I thought of asking her to have a round with me and taking a stab at it on the links."

"You could not do better. The links—Nature's cathedral."

"Right-o, then! I'll let you know how I come out."

"I wish you luck, my boy," I said.

And what of Felicia, meanwhile? She was, alas, far from returning the devotion which scorched Chester's vital organs. He seemed to her precisely the sort of man she most disliked. From childhood up Felicia Blakeney had lived in an atmosphere of highbrowism, and the type of husband she had always seen in her daydreams was the man who was simple and straightforward and earthy and did not know whether Artbashiekeff was a suburb of Moscow or a new kind of Russian drink. A man like Chester, who on his own statement would rather read one of her mother's novels than eat, revolted her. And his warm affection for her brother Crispin set the seal on her distaste.

Felicia was a dutiful child, and she loved her parents. It took a bit of doing, but she did it. But at her brother Crispin she drew the line. He wouldn't do, and his friends were worse than he was. They were high-voiced, supercilious, pince-nezed young men who talked patronizingly of Life and Art, and Chester's unblushing confession that he was one of them had put him ten down and nine to play right away.

You may wonder why the boy's undeniable skill on the links had no power to soften the girl. The unfortunate fact was that all the good effects of his prowess were neutralized by his behaviour while playing. All her life she had treated golf with a proper reverence and awe, and in Chester's attitude towards the game she seemed to detect a horrible shallowness. The fact is, Chester, in his efforts to keep himself from using strong language, had found a sort of relief in a girlish giggle, and it made her shudder every time she heard it.

His deportment, therefore, in the space of time leading up to the proposal could not have been more injurious to his cause. They started out quite happily, Chester doing a nice two-hundred-yarder off the first tee, which for a moment awoke the girl's respect. But at the fourth, after a lovely brassie-shot, he found his ball deeply embedded in the print of a woman's high heel. It was just one of those rubs of the green which normally would have caused him to ease his bosom with a flood of sturdy protest, but now he was on his guard.

"Tee-hee!" simpered Chester, reaching for his niblick. "Too bad, too bad!" and the girl shuddered to the depths of her soul.

Having holed out, he proceeded to enliven the walk to the next tee with a few remarks on her mother's literary style, and it was while they were walking after their drives that he proposed.

His proposal, considering the circumstances, could hardly have been less happily worded. Little knowing that he was rushing upon his doom, Chester stressed the Crispin note. He gave Felicia the impression that he was suggesting this marriage more for Crispin's sake than anything else. He conveyed the idea that he thought how nice it would be for brother Crispin to have his old chum in the family. He drew a picture of their little home, with Crispin for ever popping in and out like a rabbit. It is not to be wondered at that, when at length he had finished and she had time to speak, the horrified girl turned him down with a thud.

It is at moments such as these that a man reaps the reward of a good upbringing.

In similar circumstances those who have not had the benefit of a sound training in golf are too apt to go wrong. Goaded by the sudden anguish, they take to drink, plunge into dissipation, and write *vers libre*. Chester was mercifully saved from this.

I saw him the day after he had been handed the mitten, and was struck by the look of grim determination in his face. Deeply wounded though he was, I could see that he was the master of his fate and the captain of his soul.

"I am sorry, my boy," I said, sympathetically, when he had told me the painful news.

"It can't be helped," he replied, bravely.

"Her decision was final?"

"Quite."

"You do not contemplate having another pop at her?"

"No good. I know when I'm licked."

I patted him on the shoulder and said the only thing it seemed possible to say.

"After all, there is always golf."

He nodded.

"Yes. My game needs a lot of tuning up. Now is the time to do it. From now on I go at this pastime seriously. I make it my life-work. Who knows?" he murmured, with a sudden gleam in his eyes. "The Amateur Championship——"

"The Open!" I cried, falling gladly into his mood.

"The American Amateur," said Chester, flushing.

"The American Open," I chorused.

"No one has ever copped all four."

"No one."

"Watch me!" said Chester Meredith, simply.

It was about two weeks after this that I happened to look in on Chester at his house one morning. I found him about to start for the links. As he had foreshadowed in the conversation which I have just related, he now spent most of the daylight hours on the course. In these two weeks he had gone about his task of achieving perfection with a furious energy which made him the talk of the club. Always one of the best players in the place, he had developed an astounding brilliance. Men who had played him level were now obliged to receive two and even three strokes. The pro. himself, conceding one, had only succeeded in halving their match. The struggle for the President's Cup came round once more, and Chester won it for the second time with ridiculous ease.

When I arrived, he was practising chip-shots in his sitting-room. I noticed that he seemed to be labouring under some strong emotion, and his first words gave me the clue.

"She's going away tomorrow," he said, abruptly, lofting a ball over the whatnot on to the Chesterfield.

I was not sure whether I was sorry or relieved. Her absence would leave a terrible blank, of course, but it might be that it would help him to get over his infatuation.

"Ah!" I said, non-committally.

Chester addressed his ball with a well-assumed phlegm, but I could see by the way his ears wiggled that he was feeling deeply. I was not surprised when he topped his shot into the coal-scuttle.

"She has promised to play a last round with me this morning," he said.

Again I was doubtful what view to take. It was a pretty, poetic idea, not unlike Browning's "Last Ride Together", but I was not sure if it was altogether wise. However, it was none of my business, so I merely patted him on the shoulder and he gathered up his clubs and went off.

Owing to motives of delicacy I had not offered to accompany him on his round, and it was not till later that I learned the actual details of what occurred. At the start, it seems, the spiritual anguish which he was suffering had a depressing effect on his game. He hooked his drive off the first tee and was only enabled to get a five by means of a strong niblick shot out of the rough. At the second, the lake hole, he lost a ball in the water and got another five. It was only at the third that he began to pull himself together.

The test of a great golfer is his ability to recover from a bad start. Chester had this quality to a pre-eminent degree. A lesser man, conscious of being three over bogey for the first two holes, might have looked on his round as ruined. To Chester it simply meant that he had to get a couple of "birdies" right speedily, and he set about it at once. Always a long driver, he excelled himself at the third. It is, as you know, an uphill hole all the way, but his drive could not have come far short of two hundred and fifty yards. A brassie-shot of equal strength and unerring direction put him on the edge of the green, and he holed out with a long putt two under bogey. He had hoped for a "birdie" and he had achieved an "eagle".

I think that this splendid feat must have softened Felicia's heart, had it not been for the fact that misery had by this time entirely robbed Chester of the ability to smile. Instead, therefore, of behaving in the wholesome, natural way of men who get threes at bogey-five holes, he preserved a drawn, impassive countenance; and as she watched him tee up her ball, stiff, correct, polite, but to all outward appearance absolutely inhuman, the girl found herself stifling that thrill of what for a moment had been almost adoration. It was, she felt, exactly how her brother Crispin would have comported himself if he had done a hole in two under bogey.

And yet she could not altogether check a wistful sigh when, after a couple of fours at the next two holes, he picked up another stroke on the sixth and with an inspired spoon-shot brought his medal-score down to one better than bogey by getting a two at the hundred-and-seventy-yard seventh. But the brief spasm of tenderness passed, and when he finished the first nine with two more fours she refrained from anything warmer than a mere word of stereotyped congratulation.

"One under bogey for the first nine," she said. "Splendid!"

"One under bogey!" said Chester, woodenly.

"Out in thirty-four. What is the record for the course?"

Chester started. So great had been his preoccupation that he had not given a thought to the course record. He suddenly realized now that the pro., who had done the lowest medal-score to date—the other course record was held by Peter Willard with a hundred and sixty-one, achieved in his first season—had gone out in only one better than his own figures that day.

"Sixty-eight," he said.

"What a pity you lost those strokes at the beginning!"

"Yes," said Chester.

He spoke absently—and, as it seemed to her, primly and without enthusiasm—for the flaming idea of having a go at the course record had only just occurred to him. Once before he had done the first nine in thirty-four, but on that occasion he had not felt that curious feeling of irresistible force which comes to a golfer at the very top of his form. Then he had been aware all the time that he had been putting chancily. They had gone in, yes, but he had uttered a prayer per putt. Today he was superior to any weak doubtings. When he tapped the ball on the green, he knew it was going to sink. The course record? Why not? What a last offering to lay at her feet? She would go away, out of his life for ever; she would marry some other bird; but the memory of that supreme round would remain with her as long as she breathed. When he won the Open and Amateur for the second—the third—the fourth time, she would say to herself, "I was with him when he dented the record for his home course!" And he had only to pick up a couple of strokes on the last nine, to do threes at holes where he was wont to be satisfied with fours. Yes, by Vardon, he would take a whirl at it.

You, who are acquainted with these links, will no doubt say that the task which Chester Meredith had sketched out for himself—cutting two strokes off thirty-five for the second nine—was one at which Humanity might well shudder. The pro. himself, who had finished sixth in the last Open Championship, had never done better than a thirty-five, playing perfect golf and being one under par. But such was Chester's mood that, as he teed up on the tenth, he did not even consider the possibility of failure. Every muscle in his body was working in perfect co-ordination with its fellows, his wrists felt as if they were made of tempered steel, and his eyes had just that hawk-like quality which enables a man to judge his short approaches to the inch. He swung forcefully, and the ball sailed so close to the direction-post that for a moment it seemed as if it had hit it.

"Oo!" cried Felicia.

Chester did not speak. He was following the flight of the ball. It sailed over the brow of the hill, and with his knowledge of the course he could tell almost the exact patch of turf on which it must have come to rest. An iron would do the business from there, and a single putt would give him the first of the "birdies" he required. Two minutes later he had holed out a six-foot putt for a three.

"Oo!" said Felicia again.

Chester walked to the eleventh tee in silence.

"No, never mind," she said, as he stooped to put her ball on the sand. "I don't think I'll play any more. I'd much rather just watch you."

"Oh, that you could watch me through life!" said Chester, but he said it to himself. His actual words were "Very well!" and he spoke them with a stiff coldness which chilled the girl.

The eleventh is one of the trickiest holes on the course, as no doubt you have found out for yourself. It looks absurdly simple, but that little patch of wood on the right that seems so harmless is placed just in the deadliest position to catch even the most slightly sliced drive. Chester's lacked the austere precision of his last. A hundred yards from the tee it swerved almost imperceptibly, and, striking a branch, fell in the tangled undergrowth. It took him two strokes to hack it out and put it on the green, and then his long putt, after quivering on the edge of the hole, stayed there. For a swift instant red-hot words rose to his lips, but he caught them just as they were coming out and crushed them back. He looked at his ball and looked at the hole.

"Tut!" said Chester.

Felicia uttered a deep sigh. The niblick-shot out of the rough had impressed her profoundly. If only, she felt, this superb golfer had been more human! If only she were able to be constantly in this man's society, to see exactly what it was that he did with his left wrist that gave that terrific snap to his drives, she might acquire the knack herself one of these days. For she was a clear-thinking, honest girl, and thoroughly realized that she did not get the distance she ought to with her wood. With a husband like Chester beside her to stimulate and advise, of what might she not be capable? If she got wrong in her stance, he could put her right with a word. If she had a bout of slicing, how quickly he would tell her what caused it. And she knew that she had only to speak the word to wipe out the effects of her refusal, to bring him to her side for ever.

But could a girl pay such a price? When he had got that "eagle" on the third, he had looked bored. When he had missed this last putt, he had not seemed to care. "Tut!" What a word to use at such a moment! No, she felt sadly, it could not be done. To marry Chester Meredith, she told herself, would be like marrying a composite of Soames Forsyte, Sir Willoughby Patterne, and all her brother Crispin's friends. She sighed and was silent.

Chester, standing on the twelfth tee, reviewed the situation swiftly, like a general before a battle. There were seven holes to play, and he had to do these in two better than bogey. The one that faced him now offered few opportunities. It was a long, slogging, dog-leg hole, and even Ray and Taylor, when they had played their exhibition game on the course, had taken fives. No opening there.

The thirteenth—up a steep hill with a long iron-shot for one's second and a blind green fringed with bunkers? Scarcely practicable to hope for better than a four. The fourteenth—into the valley with the ground sloping sharply down to the ravine? He had once done it in three, but it had been a fluke. No; on these three holes he must be content to play for a steady par and trust to picking up a stroke on the fifteenth.

The fifteenth, straightforward up to the plateau green with its circle of bunkers, presents few difficulties to the finished golfer who is on his game. A bunker meant nothing to Chester in his present conquering vein. His mashie-shot second soared almost contemptuously over the chasm and rolled to within a foot of the pin. He came to the sixteenth with the clear-cut problem before him of snipping two strokes off par on the last three holes.

To the unthinking man, not acquainted with the lay-out of our links, this would no doubt appear a tremendous feat. But the fact is, the Green Committee, with perhaps an unduly sentimental bias towards the happy ending, have arranged a comparatively easy finish to the course. The sixteenth is a perfectly plain hole with broad fairway and a down-hill run; the seventeenth, a one-shot affair with no difficulties for the man who keeps them straight; and the eighteenth, though its up-hill run makes it deceptive to the stranger and leads the unwary to take a mashie instead of a light iron for his second, has no real venom in it. Even Peter Willard has occasionally come home in a canter with a six, five, and seven, conceding himself only two eight-foot putts. It is, I think, this mild conclusion to a tough course that makes the refreshment-room of our club so noticeable for its sea of happy faces. The bar every day is crowded with rejoicing men who, forgetting the agonies of the first fifteen, are babbling of what they did on the last three. The seventeenth, with its possibilities of holing out a topped second, is particularly soothing.

.   .   .   .   .

Chester Meredith was not the man to top his second on any hole, so this supreme bliss did not come his way; but he laid a beautiful mashie-shot dead and got a three; and when with his iron he put his first well on the green at the seventeenth and holed out for two, life, for all his broken heart, seemed pretty tolerable. He now had the situation well in hand. He had only to play his usual game to get a four on the last and lower the course record by one stroke.

It was at this supreme moment of his life that he ran into the Wrecking Crew.

You doubtless find it difficult to understand how it came about that if the Wrecking Crew were on the course at all he had not run into them long before. The explanation is that, with a regard for the etiquette of the game unusual in these miserable men, they had for once obeyed the law that enacts that foursomes shall start at the tenth. They had begun their dark work on the second nine, accordingly, at almost the exact moment when Chester Meredith was driving off at the first, and this had enabled them to keep ahead until now. When Chester came to the eighteenth tee, they were just leaving it, moving up the fairway with their caddies in mass formation and looking to his exasperated eye like one of those great race-migrations of the Middle Ages. Wherever Chester looked he seemed to see human, so to speak, figures. One was doddering about in the long grass fifty yards from the tee, others debouched to the left and right. The course was crawling with them.

Chester sat down on the bench with a weary sigh. He knew these men. Self-centred, remorseless, deaf to all the promptings of their better nature, they never let anyone through. There was nothing to do but wait.

The Wrecking Crew scratched on. The man near the tee rolled his ball ten yards, then twenty, then thirty—he was improving. Ere long he would be out of range. Chester rose and swished his driver.

But the end was not yet. The individual operating in the rough on the left had been advancing in slow stages, and now, finding his ball teed up on a tuft of grass, he opened his shoulders and let himself go. There was a loud report, and the ball, hitting a tree squarely, bounded back almost to the tee, and all the weary work was to do again. By the time Chester was able to drive, he was reduced by impatience, and the necessity of refraining from commenting on the state of affairs as he would have wished to comment, to a frame of mind in which no man could have kept himself from pressing. He pressed, and topped. The ball skidded over the turf for a meagre hundred yards.

"D-d-d-dear me!" said Chester.

The next moment he uttered a bitter laugh. Too late a miracle had happened. One of the foul figures in front was waving its club. Other ghastly creatures were withdrawing to the side of the fairway. Now, when the harm had been done, these outcasts were signalling to him to go through. The hollow mockery of the thing swept over Chester like a wave. What was the use of going through now? He was a good three hundred yards from the green, and he needed a bogey at this hole to break the record. Almost absently he drew his brassie from his bag; then, as the full sense of his wrongs bit into his soul, he swung viciously.

Golf is a strange game. Chester had pressed on the tee and foozled. He pressed now, and achieved the most perfect shot of his life. The ball shot from its place as if a charge of powerful explosive were behind it. Never deviating from a straight line, never more than six feet from the ground, it sailed up the hill, crossed the bunker, eluded the mounds beyond, struck the turf, rolled, and stopped fifty feet from the hole. It was a brassie-shot of a lifetime, and shrill senile yippings of excitement and congratulations floated down from the Wrecking Crew. For, degraded though they were, these men were not wholly devoid of human instincts.

Chester drew a deep breath. His ordeal was over. That third shot, which would lay the ball right up to the pin, was precisely the sort of thing he did best. Almost from boyhood he had been a wizard at the short approach. He could hole out in two now on his left ear. He strode up the hill to his ball. It could not have been lying better. Two inches away there was a nasty cup in the turf; but it had avoided this and was sitting nicely perched up, smiling an invitation to the mashie-niblick. Chester shuffled his feet and eyed the flag keenly. Then he stooped to play, and Felicia watched him breathlessly. Her whole body seemed to be concentrated on him. She had forgotten everything save that she was seeing a course record get broken.

She could not have been more wrapped up in his success if she had had large sums of money on it.

. . . . .

The Wrecking Crew, meanwhile, had come to life again. They had stopped twittering about Chester's brassie-shot and were thinking of resuming their own game. Even in foursomes where fifty yards is reckoned a good shot somebody must be away, and the man whose turn it was to play was the one who had acquired from his brother-members of the club the nickname of the First Grave-Digger.

A word about this human wen. He was—if there can be said to be grades in such a sub-species—the star performer of the Wrecking Crew. The lunches of fifty-seven years had caused his chest to slip down into the mezzanine floor, but he was still a powerful man, and had in his youth been a hammer-thrower of some repute. He differed from his colleagues—the Man With the Hoe, Old Father Time, and Consul, the Almost Human—in that, while they were content to peck cautiously at the ball, he never spared himself in his efforts to do it a violent injury. Frequently he had cut a blue dot almost in half with his niblick. He was completely muscle-bound, so that he seldom achieved anything beyond a series of chasms in the turf, but he was always trying, and it was his secret belief that, given two or three miracles happening simultaneously, he would one of these days bring off a snifter. Years of disappointment had, however, reduced the flood of hope to a mere trickle, and when he took his brassie now and addressed the ball he had no immediate plans beyond a vague intention of rolling the thing a few yards farther up the hill.

The fact that he had no business to play at all till Chester had holed out did not occur to him; and even if it had occurred he would have dismissed the objection as finicking. Chester, bending over his ball, was nearly two hundred yards away—or the distance of three full brassie-shots. The First Grave-Digger did not hesitate. He whirled up his club as in distant days he had been wont to swing the hammer, and with the grunt which this performance always wrung from him, brought it down.

Golfers—and I stretch this term to include the Wrecking Crew—are a highly imitative race. The spectacle of a flubber flubbing ahead of us on the fairway inclines to make us flub as well; and, conversely, it is immediately after we have seen a magnificent shot that we are apt to eclipse ourselves. Consciously the Grave-Digger had no notion how Chester had made that superb brassie-biff of his, but all the while I suppose his subconscious self had been taking notes. At any rate, on this occasion he, too, did the shot of a lifetime. As he opened his eyes, which he always shut tightly at the moment of impact, and started to unravel himself from the complicated tangle in which his follow-through had left him, he perceived the ball breasting the hill like some untamed jack-rabbit of the Californian prairie.

For a moment his only emotion was one of dreamlike amazement. He stood looking at the ball with a wholly impersonal wonder, like a man suddenly confronted with some terrific work of Nature. Then, as a sleep-walker awakens, he came to himself with a start. Directly in front of the flying ball was a man bending to make an approach-shot.

Chester, always a concentrated golfer when there was man's work to do, had scarcely heard the crack of the brassie behind him. Certainly he had paid no attention to it. His whole mind was fixed on his stroke. He measured with his eye the distance to the pin, noted the down-slope of the green, and shifted his stance a little to allow for it. Then, with a final swift waggle, he laid his club-head behind the ball and slowly raised it. It was just coming down when the world became full of shouts of "Fore!" and something hard smote him violently on the seat of his plus fours.

The supreme tragedies of life leave us momentarily stunned. For an instant which seemed an age Chester could not understand what had happened. True, he realized that there had been an earthquake, a cloud-burst, and a railway accident, and that a high building had fallen on him at the exact moment when somebody had shot him with a gun, but these happenings would account for only a small part of his sensations. He blinked several times, and rolled his eyes wildly. And it was while rolling them that he caught sight of the gesticulating Wrecking Crew on the lower slopes and found enlightenment. Simultaneously, he observed his ball only a yard and a half from where it had been when he addressed it.

Chester Meredith gave one look at his ball, one look at the flag, one look at the Wrecking Crew, one look at the sky. His lips writhed, his forehead turned vermilion. Beads of perspiration started out on his forehead. And then, with his whole soul seething like a cistern struck by a thunderbolt, he spoke.

"! ! ! ! ! ! ! ! ! ! ! ! ! ! !" cried Chester.

Dimly he was aware of a wordless exclamation from the girl beside him, but he was too distraught to think of her now. It was as if all the oaths pent up within his bosom for so many weary days were struggling and jostling to see which could get out first. They cannoned into each other, they linked hands and formed parties, they got themselves all mixed up in weird vowel-sounds, the second syllable of some red-hot verb forming a temporary union with the first syllable of some blistering noun.

"——! ——!! ——!!! ——!!!! ——!!!!!" cried Chester.

Felicia stood starring at him. In her eyes was the look of one who sees visions.

"***!!! ***!!! ***!!! ***!!!" roared Chester, in part.

A great wave of emotion flooded over the girl. How she had misjudged this silver-tongued man! She shivered as she thought that, had this not happened, in another five minutes they would have parted for ever, sundered by seas of misunderstanding, she cold and scornful, he with all his music still within him.

"Oh, Mr. Meredith!" she cried, faintly.

With a sickening abruptness Chester came to himself. It was as if somebody had poured a pint of ice-cold water down his back. He blushed vividly. He realized with horror and shame how grossly he had offended against all the canons of decency and good taste. He felt like the man in one of those "What Is Wrong With This

Picture?" things in the advertisements of the etiquette books.

"I beg—I beg your pardon!" he mumbled, humbly. "Please please, forgive me. I should not have spoken like that."

"You should! You should!" cried the girl, passionately. "You should have said all that and a lot more. That awful man ruining your record round like that! Oh, why am I a poor weak woman with practically no vocabulary that's any use for anything!"

Quite suddenly, without knowing that she had moved, she found herself at his side, holding his hand.

"Oh, to think how I misjudged you!" she wailed. "I thought you cold, stiff, formal, precise. I hated the way you sniggered when you foozled a shot. I see it all now! You were keeping it in for my sake. Can you ever forgive me?

Chester, as I have said, was not a very quick-minded young man, but it would have taken a duller youth than he to fail to read the message in the girl's eyes, to miss the meaning of the pressure of her hand on his.

"My gosh!" he exclaimed wildly. "Do you mean——? Do you think——? Do you really——? Honestly, has this made a difference? Is there any chance for a fellow, I mean?"

Her eyes helped him on. He felt suddenly confident and masterful.

"Look here—no kidding—will you marry me?" he said.

"I will! I will!"

"Darling!" cried Chester.

He would have said more, but at this point he was interrupted by the arrival of the Wrecking Crew who panted up full of apologies; and Chester, as he eyed them, thought that he had never seen a nicer, cheerier, pleasanter lot of fellows in his life. His heart warmed to them. He made a mental resolve to hunt them up some time and have a good long talk. He waved the Grave-Digger's remorse airily aside.

"Don't mention it," he said. "Not at all. Faults on both sides. By the way, my fiancée, Miss Blakeney."

The Wrecking Crew puffed acknowledgment.

"But, my dear fellow," said the Grave-Digger, "it was—really it was—unforgivable. Spoiling your shot. Never dreamed I would send the ball that distance. Lucky you weren't playing an important match."

"But he was," moaned Felicia. "He was trying for the course-record, and now he can't break it."

The Wrecking Crew paled behind their whiskers, aghast at this tragedy, but Chester, glowing with the yeasty intoxication of love, laughed lightly.

"What do you mean, can't break it?" he cried, cheerily. "I've one more shot."

And, carelessly addressing the ball, he holed out with a light flick of his mashie-niblick.

"Chester, darling!" said Felicia.

They were walking slowly through a secluded glade in the quiet evenfall.

"Yes, precious?"

Felicia hesitated. What she was going to say would hurt him, she knew, and her love was so great that to hurt him was agony.

"Do you think——" she began. "I wonder whether—— It's about Crispin."

"Good old Crispin!"

Felicia sighed, but the matter was too vital to be shirked. Cost what it might, she must speak her mind.

"Chester, darling, when we are married, would you mind very, *very* much if we didn't have Crispin with us *all* the time?"

Chester started.

"Good Lord!" he exclaimed. "Don't you like him?"

"Not very much," confessed Felicia. "I don't think I'm clever enough for him. I've rather disliked him ever since we were children. But I know what a friend he is of yours——"

Chester uttered a joyous laugh.

"Friend of mine! Why, I can't stand the blighter! I loathe the worm! I abominate the excrescence! I only pretended we were friends because I thought it would put me in solid with you. The man is a pest and should have been strangled at birth. At school I used to kick him every time I saw him. If your brother Crispin tries so much as to set foot across the threshold of our little home, I'll set the dog on him."

"Darling!" whispered Felicia. "We shall be very, very happy." She drew her arm through his. "Tell me, dearest," she murmured, "all about how you used to kick Crispin at school."

And together they wandered off into the sunset.

16

THE MAGIC PLUS FOURS

"AFTER ALL," said the young man, "golf is only a game."

He spoke bitterly and with the air of one who has been following a train of thought. He had come into the smoking-room of the club-house in low spirits at the dusky close of a November evening, and for some minutes had been sitting, silent and moody, staring at the log fire.

"Merely a pastime," said the young man.

The Oldest Member, nodding in his arm-chair, stiffened with horror, and glanced quickly over his shoulder to make sure that none of the waiters had heard these terrible words.

"Can this be George William Pennefather speaking!" he said, reproachfully. "My boy, you are not yourself."

The young man flushed a little beneath his tan: for he had had a good upbringing and was not bad at heart.

"Perhaps I ought not to have gone quite so far as that," he admitted. "I was only thinking that a fellow's got no right, just because he happens to have come on a bit in his form lately, to treat a fellow as if a fellow was a leper or something."

The Oldest Member's face cleared, and he breathed a relieved sigh.

"Ah! I see," he said. "You spoke hastily and in a sudden fit of pique because something upset you out on the links today. Tell me all. Let me see, you were playing with Nathaniel Frisby this afternoon, were you not? I gather that he beat you."

"Yes, he did. Giving me a third. But it isn't being beaten that I mind. What I object to is having the blighter behave as if he were a sort of champion condescending to a mere mortal. Dash it, it seemed to bore him playing with me! Every time I sliced off the tee he looked at me as if I were a painful ordeal. Twice when I was having a bit of trouble in the bushes I caught him yawning. And after we had finished he started talking about what a good game croquet was, and he wondered more people didn't take it up. And it's only a month or so ago that I could play the man level!"

The Oldest Member shook his snowy head sadly.

"There is nothing to be done about it," he said. "We can only hope that the poison will in time work its way out of the man's system. Sudden success at golf is like the sudden acquisition of wealth. It is apt to unsettle and deteriorate the character. And,

as it comes almost miraculously, so only a miracle can effect a cure. The best advice
I can give you is to refrain from playing with Nathaniel Frisby till you can keep
your tee-shots straight."

"Oh, but don't run away with the idea that I wasn't pretty good off the tee this
afternoon!" said the young man. "I should like to describe to you the shot I did on
the——"

"Meanwhile," proceeded the Oldest Member, "I will relate to you a little story
which bears on what I have been saying."

"From the very moment I addressed the ball——"

"It is the story of two loving hearts temporarily estranged owing to the sudden
and unforeseen proficiency of one of the couple——"

"I waggled quickly and strongly, like Duncan. Then, swinging smoothly back,
rather in the Vardon manner——"

"But as I see," said the Oldest Member, "that you are all impatience for me to
begin, I will do so without further preamble."

To the philosophical student of golf like myself (said the Oldest Member) perhaps
the most outstanding virtue of this noble pursuit is the fact that it is a medicine for
the soul. Its great service to humanity is that it teaches human beings that, whatever
petty triumphs they may have achieved in other walks of life, they are after all
merely human. It acts as a corrective against sinful pride. I attribute the insane
arrogance of the later Roman emperors almost entirely to the fact that, never having
played golf, they never knew that strange chastening humility which is engendered
by a topped chip-shot. If Cleopatra had been outed in the first round of the Ladies'
Singles, we should have heard a lot less of her proud imperiousness. And, coming
down to modern times, it was undoubtedly his rotten golf that kept Wallace Chesney
the nice unspoiled fellow he was. For in every other respect he had everything in the
world calculated to make a man conceited and arrogant. He was the best-looking
man for miles around; his health was perfect; and, in addition to this, he was rich;
danced, rode, played bridge and polo with equal skill; and was engaged to be
married to Charlotte Dix. And when you saw Charlotte Dix you realized that being
engaged to her would by itself have been quite enough luck for any one man.

But Wallace, as I say, despite all his advantages, was a thoroughly nice, modest
young fellow. And I attribute this to the fact that, while one of the keenest golfers
in the club, he was also one of the worst players. Indeed, Charlotte Dix used to say
to me in his presence that she could not understand why people paid money to go
to the circus when by merely walking over the brow of a hill they could watch
Wallace Chesney trying to get out of the bunker by the eleventh green. And Wallace
took the gibe with perfect good humour, for there was a delightful camaraderie
between them which robbed it of any sting. Often at lunch in the club-house I used
to hear him and Charlotte planning the handicapping details of a proposed match
between Wallace and a non-existent cripple whom Charlotte claimed to have

discovered in the village—it being agreed finally that he should accept seven bisques from the cripple, but that, if the latter ever recovered the use of his arms, Wallace should get a stroke a hole.

In short, a thoroughly happy and united young couple. Two hearts, if I may coin an expression, that beat as one.

I would not have you misjudge Wallace Chesney. I may have given you the impression that his attitude towards golf was light and frivolous, but such was not the case. As I have said, he was one of the keenest members of the club. Love made him receive the joshing of his *fiancée* in the kindly spirit in which it was meant, but at heart he was as earnest as you could wish. He practised early and late; he bought golf books; and the mere sight of a patent club of any description acted on him like catnip on a cat. I remember remonstrating with him on the occasion of his purchasing a wooden-faced driving-mashie which weighed about two pounds, and was, taking it for all in all, as foul an instrument as ever came out of the workshop of a clubmaker who had been dropped on the head by his nurse when a baby.

"I know, I know," he said, when I had finished indicating some of the weapon's more obvious defects. "But the point is, I believe in it. It gives me confidence. I don't believe you could slice with a thing like that if you tried."

Confidence! That was what Wallace Chesney lacked, and that, as he saw it, was the prime grand secret of golf. Like an alchemist on the track of the Philosopher's Stone, he was for ever seeking for something which would really give him confidence. I recollect that he even tried repeating to himself fifty times every morning the words, "Every day in every way I grow better and better." This, however, proved such a black lie that he gave it up. The fact is, the man was a visionary, and it is to auto-hypnosis of some kind that I attribute the extraordinary change that came over him at the beginning of his third season.

You may have noticed in your perambulations about the City a shop bearing above its door and upon its windows the legend:

COHEN BROS.
SECOND-HAND CLOTHIERS

a statement which is borne out by endless vistas seen through the door of every variety of what is technically known as Gents' Wear. But the Brothers Cohen, though their main stock-in-trade is garments which have been rejected by their owners for one reason or another, do not confine their dealings to Gents' Wear. The place is a museum of derelict goods of every description. You can get a second-hand revolver there, or a second-hand sword, or a second-hand umbrella. You can do a cheap deal in field-glasses, trunks, dog collars, canes, photograph frames, attaché cases, and bowls for goldfish. And on the bright spring morning when Wallace Chesney happened to pass by there was exhibited in the window a putter of such pre-eminently lunatic design that he stopped dead as if he had run into an invisible wall, and then, panting like an overwrought fish, charged in through the door.

The shop was full of the Cohen family, sombre-eyed, smileless men with purposeful expressions; and two of these, instantly descending upon Wallace Chesney like leopards, began in swift silence to thrust him into a suit of yellow tweed. Having worked the coat over his shoulders with a shoe-horn, they stood back to watch the effect.

"A beautiful fit," announced Isidore Cohen.

"A little snug under the arms," said his brother Irving. "But that'll give."

"The warmth of the body will make it give," said Isidore.

"Or maybe you'll lose weight in the summer," said Irving.

Wallace, when he had struggled out of the coat and was able to breathe, said that he had come into buy a putter. Isidore therefore sold him the putter, a dog collar, and a set of studs, and Irving sold him a fireman's helmet: and he was about to leave when their elder brother Lou, who had just finished fitting out another customer, who had come in to buy a cap, with two pairs of trousers and a miniature aquarium for keeping newts in, saw that business was in progress and strolled up. His fathomless eye rested on Wallace, who was toying feebly with the putter.

"You play golf?" asked Lou. "Then looka here!"

He dived into an alleyway of dead clothing, dug for a moment, and emerged with something at the sight of which Wallace Chesney, hardened golfer that he was, blenched and threw up an arm defensively.

"No, no!" he cried.

The object which Lou Cohen was waving insinuatingly before his eyes was a pair of those golfing breeches which are technically known as Plus Fours. A player of two years' standing, Wallace Chesney was not unfamiliar with Plus Fours—all the club cracks wore them—but he had never seen Plus Fours like these. What might be termed the main *motif* of the fabric was a curious vivid pink, and with this to work on the architect had let his imagination run free, and had produced so much variety in the way of chessboard squares of white, yellow, violet, and green that the eye swam as it looked upon them.

"These were made to measure for Sandy McHoots, the Open Champion," said Lou, stroking the left leg lovingly. "But he sent 'em back for some reason or other."

"Perhaps they frightened the children," said Wallace, recollecting having heard that Mr. McHoots was a married man.

"They'll fit you nice," said Lou.

"Sure they'll fit him nice," said Isidore, warmly.

"Why, just take a look at yourself in the glass," said Irving, "and see if they don't fit you nice."

And, as one who wakes from a trance, Wallace discovered that his lower limbs were now encased in the prismatic garment. At what point in the proceedings the brethren had slipped them on him, he could not have said. But he was undeniably in.

Wallace looked in the glass. For a moment, as he eyed his reflection, sheer horror gripped him. Then suddenly, as he gazed, he became aware that his first feelings were changing. The initial shock over, he was becoming calmer. He waggled his right leg with a certain sang-froid.

There is a certain passage in the works of the poet Pope with which you may be familiar. It runs as follows:

> *"Vice is a monster of so frightful mien*
> *As to be hated needs but to be seen;*
> *Yet seen too oft, familiar with her face,*
> *We first endure, then pity, then embrace."*

Even so was it with Wallace Chesney and these Plus Fours. At first he had recoiled from them as any decent-minded man would have done. Then, after a while, almost abruptly he found himself in the grip of a new emotion. After an unsuccessful attempt to analyse this, he suddenly got it. Amazing as it may seem, it was pleasure that he felt. He caught his eye in the mirror, and it was smirking. Now that the things were actually on, by Hutchinson, they didn't look half bad. By Braid, they didn't. There was a sort of something about them. Take away that expanse of bare leg with its unsightly sock-suspender and substitute a woolly stocking, and you would have the lower section of a golfer. For the first time in his life, he thought, he looked like a man who could play golf.

There came to him an odd sensation of masterfulness. He was still holding the putter, and now he swung it up above his shoulder. A fine swing, all lissomness and supple grace, quite different from any swing he had ever done before.

Wallace Chesney gasped. He knew that at last he had discovered that prime grand secret of golf for which he had searched so long. It was the costume that did it. All you had to do was wear Plus Fours. He had always hitherto played in grey flannel trousers. Naturally he had not been able to do himself justice. Golf required an easy dash, and how could you be easily dashing in concertina-shaped trousers with a patch on the knee? He saw now—what he had never seen before—that it was not because they were crack players that crack players wore Plus Fours: it was because they wore Plus Fours that they were crack players. And these Plus Fours had been the property of an Open Champion. Wallace Chesney's bosom swelled, and he was filled, as by some strange gas, with joy—with excitement—with confidence. Yes, for the first time in his golfing life, he felt really confident.

True, the things might have been a shade less gaudy: they might perhaps have hit the eye with a slightly less violent punch: but what of that? True, again, he could scarcely hope to avoid the censure of his club-mates when he appeared like this on the links: but what of *that?* His club-mates must set their teeth and learn to bear these Plus Fours like men. That was what Wallace Chesney thought about it. If they did not like his Plus Fours, let them go and play golf somewhere else.

"How much?" he muttered, thickly. And the Brothers Cohen clustered grimly round with notebooks and pencils.

In predicting a stormy reception for his new apparel, Wallace Chesney had not been unduly pessimistic. The moment he entered the club-house Disaffection reared its ugly head. Friends of years' standing called loudly for the committee, and there was a small and vehement party of the left wing, headed by Raymond Gandle, who was an artist by profession, and consequently had a sensitive eye, which advocated the tearing off and public burial of the obnoxious garment. But, prepared as he had been for some such demonstration on the part of the coarser-minded, Wallace had hoped for better things when he should meet Charlotte Dix, the girl who loved him. Charlotte, he had supposed, would understand and sympathize.

Instead of which, she uttered a piercing cry and staggered to a bench, whence a moment later she delivered her ultimatum.

"Quick!" she said. "Before I have to look again."

"What do you mean?"

"Pop straight back into the changing-room while I've got my eyes shut, and remove the fancy-dress."

"What's wrong with them?"

"Darling," said Charlotte, "I think it's sweet and patriotic of you to be proud of your cycling-club colours or whatever they are, but you mustn't wear them on the links. It will unsettle the caddies."

"They *are* a trifle on the bright side,'" admitted Wallace. "But it helps my game, wearing them. I was trying a few practice-shots just now, and I couldn't go wrong. Slammed the ball on the meat every time. They inspire me, if you know what I mean. Come on, let's be starting."

Charlotte opened her eyes incredulously.

"You can't seriously mean that you're really going to *play* in—those? It's against the rules. There must be a rule somewhere in the book against coming out looking like a sunset. Won't you go and burn them for my sake?"

"But I tell you they give me confidence. I sort of squint down at them when I'm addressing the ball, and I feel like a pro."

"Then the only thing to do is for me to play you for them. Come on, Wally, be a sportsman. I'll give you a half and play you for the whole outfit—the breeches, the red jacket, the little cap, and the belt with the snake's-head buckle. I'm sure all those things must have gone with the breeches. Is it a bargain?"

Strolling on the club-house terrace some two hours later, Raymond Gandle encountered Charlotte and Wallace coming up from the eighteenth green.

"Just the girl I wanted to see," said Raymond. "Miss Dix, I represent a select committee of my fellow-members, and I have come to ask you on their behalf to use the influence of a good woman to induce Wally to destroy those Plus Fours of his, which we all consider nothing short of Bolshevik propaganda and a menace to the public weal. May I rely on you?"

"You may not," retorted Charlotte. "They are the poor boy's mascot. You've no idea how they have improved his game. He has just beaten me hollow. I am going to try to learn to bear them, so you must. Really, you've no notion how he has come on. My cripple won't be able to give him more than a couple of bisques if he keeps up this form."

"It's something about the things," said Wallace. "They give me confidence."

"They give *me* a pain in the neck," said Raymond Gandle.

To the thinking man nothing is more remarkable in this life than the way in which Humanity adjusts itself to conditions which at their outset might well have appeared intolerable. Some great cataclysm occurs, some storm or earthquake, shaking the community to its foundations; and after the first pardonable consternation one finds the sufferers resuming their ordinary pursuits as if nothing had happened. There have been few more striking examples of this adaptability than the behaviour of the members of our golf-club under the impact of Wallace Chesney's Plus Fours. For the first few days it is not too much to say that they were stunned. Nervous players sent their caddies on in front of them at blind holes, so that they might be warned in time of Wallace's presence ahead and not have him happening to them all of a sudden. And even the pro. was not unaffected. Brought up in Scotland in an atmosphere of tartan kilts, he nevertheless winced, and a startled "Hoots!" was forced from his lips when Wallace Chesney suddenly appeared in the valley as he was about to drive from the fifth tee.

But in about a week conditions were back to normal. Within ten days the Plus Fours became a familiar feature of the landscape, and were accepted as such without comment. They were pointed out to strangers together with the waterfall, the Lovers' Leap, and the view from the eighth green as things you ought not to miss when visiting the course; but apart from that one might almost say they were ignored. And meanwhile Wallace Chesney continued day by day to make the most extraordinary progress in his play.

As I have said before, and I think you will agree with me when I have told you what happened subsequently, it was probably a case of auto-hypnosis. There is no other sphere in which a belief in oneself has such immediate effects as it has in golf. And Wallace, having acquired self-confidence, went on from strength to strength. In under a week he had ploughed his way through the Unfortunate Incidents—of which class Peter Willard was the best example—and was challenging the fellows who kept three shots in five somewhere on the fairway. A month later he was holding his own with ten-handicap men. And by the middle of the summer he was so far advanced that his name occasionally cropped up in speculative talks on the subject of the July medal. One might have been excused for supposing that, as far as Wallace Chesney was concerned, all was for the best in the best of all possible worlds.

And yet——

The first inkling I received that anything was wrong came through a chance meeting with Raymond Gandle who happened to pass my gate on his way back from the links just as I drove up in my taxi; for I had been away from home for many weeks on a protracted business tour. I welcomed Gandle's advent and invited him in to smoke a pipe and put me abreast of local gossip. He came readily enough—and seemed, indeed to have something on his mind and to be glad of the opportunity of revealing it to a sympathetic auditor.

"And how," I asked him, when we were comfortably settled, "did your game this afternoon come out?"

"Oh, he beat me," said Gandle, and it seemed to me that there was a note of bitterness in his voice.

"Then He, whoever he was, must have been an extremely competent performer," I replied, courteously, for Gandle was one of the finest players in the club. "Unless, of course, you were giving him some impossible handicap."

"No; we played level."

"Indeed! Who was your opponent?"

"Chesney."

"Wallace Chesney! And he beat you playing level! This is the most amazing thing I have ever heard."

"He's improved out of all knowledge."

"He must have done. Do you think he would ever beat you again?"

"No. Because he won't have the chance."

"You surely do not mean that you will not play him because you are afraid of being beaten?"

"It isn't being beaten I mind——"

And if I omit to report the remainder of his speech it is not merely because it contained expresssions with which I am reluctant to sully my lips, but because, omitting these expletives, what he said was almost word for word what you were saying to me just now about Nathaniel Frisby. It was, it seemed, Wallace Chesney's manner, his arrogance, his attitude of belonging to some superior order of being that had so wounded Raymond Gandle. Wallace Chesney had, it appeared, criticized Gandle's mashie-play in no friendly spirit; had hung up the game on the fourteenth tee in order to show him how to place his feet; and on the way back to the club-house had said that the beauty of golf was that the best player could enjoy a round even with a dud, because, though there might be no interest in the match, he could always amuse himself by playing for his medal score.

I was profoundly shaken.

"Wallace Chesney!" I exclaimed. "Was it really Wallace Chesney who behaved in the manner you describe?"

"Unless he's got a twin brother of the same name, it was."

"Wallace Chesney a victim to swelled head! I can hardly credit it."

"Well, you needn't take my word for it unless you want to. Ask anybody. It isn't often he can get anyone to play with him now."

"You horrify me!"

Raymond Gandle smoked a while in brooding silence.

"You've heard about his engagement?" he said at length.

"I have heard nothing, nothing. What about his engagement?"

"Charlotte Dix has broken it off."

"No!"

"Yes. Couldn't stand him any longer."

I got rid of Gandle as soon as I could. I made my way as quickly as possible to the house where Charlotte lived with her aunt. I was determined to sift this matter to the bottom and to do all that lay in my power to heal the breach between two young people for whom I had a great affection.

"I have just heard the news," I said, when the aunt had retired to some secret lair, as aunts do, and Charlotte and I were alone.

"What news?" said Charlotte, dully. I thought she looked pale and ill, and she had certainly grown thinner.

"This dreadful news about your engagement to Wallace Chesney. Tell me, why did you do this thing? Is there no hope of a reconciliation?"

"Not unless Wally becomes his old self again."

"But I had always regarded you two as ideally suited to one another."

"Wally has completely changed in the last few weeks. Haven't you heard?"

"Only sketchily, from Raymond Gandle."

"I refuse," said Charlotte, proudly, all the woman in her leaping to her eyes, "to marry a man who treats me as if I were a kronen at the present rate of exchange, merely because I slice an occasional tee-shot. The afternoon I broke off the engagement"—her voice shook, and I could see that her indifference was but a mask—"the afternoon I broke off the en-gug-gug-gagement, he t-told me I ought to use an iron off the tee instead of a dud-dud-driver."

And the stricken girl burst into an uncontrollable fit of sobbing. And realizing that, if matters had gone as far as that, there was little I could do, I pressed her hand silently and left her.

But though it seemed hopeless I decided to persevere. I turned my steps towards Wallace Chesney's bungalow, resolved to make one appeal to the man's better feelings. He was in his sitting-room when I arrived, polishing a putter; and it seemed significant to me, even in that tense moment, that the putter was quite an ordinary one, such as any capable player might use. In the brave old happy days of his dudhood, the only putters you ever found in the society of Wallace Chesney were patent self-adjusting things that looked like croquet mallets that had taken the wrong turning in childhood.

"Well, Wallace, my boy," I said.

"Hallo!" said Wallace Chesney. "So you're back?"

We fell into conversation, and I had not been in the room two minutes before I realized that what I had been told about the change in him was nothing more than the truth. The man's bearing and his every remark were insufferably bumptious. He spoke of his prospects in the July medal competition as if the issue were already settled. He scoffed at his rivals.

I had some little difficulty in bringing the talk round to the matter which I had come to discuss.

"My boy," I said at length, "I have just heard the sad news."

"What sad news?"

"I have been talking to Charlotte——"

"Oh, that!" said Wallace Chesney.

"She was telling me——"

"Perhaps it's all for the best."

"All for the best? What do you mean?"

"Well," said Wallace, "one doesn't wish, of course, to say anything ungallant, but, after all, poor Charlotte's handicap *is* fourteen and wouldn't appear to have much chance of getting any lower. I mean, there's such a thing as a fellow throwing himself away."

Was I revolted at these callous words? For a moment, yes. Then it struck me that, though he had uttered them with a light laugh, that laugh had had in it more than a touch of bravado. I looked at him keenly. There was a bored, discontented expression in his eyes, a line of pain about his mouth.

"My boy," I said, gravely, "you are not happy."

For an instant I think he would have denied the imputation. But my visit had coincided with one of those twilight moods in which a man requires, above all else, sympathy. He uttered a weary sigh.

"I'm fed up," he admitted. "It's a funny thing. When I was a dud, I used to think how perfect it must be to be scratch. I used to watch the cracks buzzing round the course and envy them. It's all a fraud. The only time when you enjoy golf is when an occasional decent shot is enough to make you happy for the day. I'm plus two, and I'm bored to death. I'm too good. And what's the result? Everybody's jealous of me. Everybody's got it in for me. Nobody loves me."

His voice rose in a note of anguish, and at the sound his terrier, which had been sleeping on the rug, crept forward and licked his hand.

"The dog loves you," I said, gently, for I was touched.

"Yes, but I don't love the dog," said Wallace Chesney.

"Now come, Wallace," I said. "Be reasonable, my boy. It is only your unfortunate manner on the links which has made you perhaps a little unpopular at the moment. Why not pull yourself up? Why ruin your whole life with this arrogance? All that you need is a little tact, a little forbearance. Charlotte, I am sure, is just as fond of you as ever, but you have wounded her pride. Why must you be unkind about her tee-shots?"

Wallace Chesney shook his head despondently.

"I can't help it," he said. "It exasperates me to see anyone foozling, and I have to say so."

"Then there is nothing to be done," I said, sadly.

All the medal competitions at our club are, as you know, important events; but, as you are also aware, none of them is looked forward to so keenly or contested so hotly as the one in July. At the beginning of the year of which I am speaking, Raymond Gandle had been considered the probable winner of the fixture; but as the season progressed and Wallace Chesney's skill developed to such a remarkable extent most of us were reluctantly inclined to put our money on the latter. Reluctantly, because Wallace's unpopularity was now so general that the thought of his winning was distasteful to all. It grieved me to see how cold his fellow-members were towards him. He drove off from the first tee without a solitary hand-clap; and, though the drive was of admirable quality and nearly carried the green, there was not a single cheer. I noticed Charlotte Dix among the spectators. The poor girl was looking sad and wan.

In the draw for partners Wallace had had Peter Willard allotted to him; and he muttered to me in a quite audible voice that it was as bad as handicapping him half a dozen strokes to make him play with such a hopeless performer. I do not think Peter heard, but it would not have made much difference to him if he had, for I doubt if anything could have had much effect for the worse on his game. Peter Willard always entered for the medal competition, because he said that competition-play was good for the nerves.

On this occasion he topped his ball badly, and Wallace lit his pipe with the exaggeratedly patient air of an irritated man. When Peter topped his second also, Wallace was moved to speech.

"For goodness' sake," he snapped, "what's the good of playing at all if you insist on lifting your head? Keep it down, man, keep it down. You don't need to watch to see where the ball is going. It isn't likely to go as far as all that. Make up your mind to count three before you look up."

"Thanks," said Peter, meekly. There was no pride in Peter to be wounded. He knew the sort of player he was.

The couples were now moving off with smooth rapidity, and the course was dotted with the figures of players and their accompanying spectators. A fair proportion of these latter had decided to follow the fortunes of Raymond Gandle, but by far the larger number were sticking to Wallace, who right from the start showed that Gandle or anyone else would have to return a very fine card to beat him. He was out in thirty-seven, two above bogey, and with the assistance of a superb second, which landed the ball within a foot of the pin, got a three on the tenth, where a four is considered good. I mention this to show that by the time he arrived at the short lake-hole Wallace Chesney was at the top of his form. Not even the fact that he had been obliged to let the next couple through owing to Peter Willard losing his ball had been enough to upset him.

The course has been rearranged since, but at that time the lake-hole, which is now the second, was the eleventh, and was generally looked on as the crucial hole in a medal round. Wallace no doubt realized this, but the knowledge did not seem to affect him. He lit his pipe with the utmost coolness: and, having replaced the match-box in his hip-pocket, stood smoking nonchalantly as he waited for the couple in front to get off the green.

They holed out eventually, and Wallace walked to the tee. As he did so, he was startled to receive a resounding smack.

"Sorry," said Peter Willard, apologetically. "Hope I didn't hurt you. A wasp."

And he pointed to the corpse, which was lying in a used-up attitude on the ground.

"Afraid it would sting you," said Peter.

"Oh, thanks," said Wallace.

He spoke a little stiffly, for Peter Willard had a large, hard, flat hand, the impact of which had shaken him up considerably. Also, there had been laughter in the crowd. He was fuming as he bent to address the ball, and his annoyance became acute when, just as he reached the top of his swing, Peter Willard suddenly spoke.

"Just a second, old man," said Peter. Wallace spun round, outraged.

"What *is* it? I do wish you would wait till I've made my shot."

"Just as you like," said Peter, humbly.

"There is no greater crime that a man can commit on the links than to speak to a fellow when he's making his stroke."

"Of course, of course," acquiesced Peter, crushed.

Wallace turned to his ball once more. He was vaguely conscious of a discomfort to which he could not at the moment give a name. At first he thought that he was having a spasm of lumbago, and this surprised him, for he had never in his life been subject to even a suspicion of that malady. A moment later he realized that this diagnosis had been wrong.

"Good heavens!" he cried, leaping nimbly some two feet into the air. "I'm on fire!"

"Yes," said Peter, delighted at his ready grasp of the situation. "That's what I wanted to mention just now."

Wallace slapped vigorously at the seat of his Plus Fours.

"It must have been when I killed that wasp," said Peter, beginning to see clearly into the matter. "You had a match-box in your pocket."

Wallace was in no mood to stop and discuss first causes. He was springing up and down on his pyre, beating at the flames.

"Do you know what I should do if I were you?" said Peter Willard. "I should jump into the lake."

One of the cardinal rules of golf is that a player shall accept no advice from anyone but his own caddie; but the warmth about his lower limbs had now become so generous that Wallace was prepared to stretch a point. He took three rapid strides and entered the water with a splash.

The lake, though muddy, is not deep, and presently Wallace was to be observed standing up to his waist some few feet from the shore.

"That ought to have put it out," said Peter Willard. "It was a bit of luck that it happened at this hole." He stretched out a hand to the bather. "Catch hold, old man, and I'll pull you out."

"No!" said Wallace Chesney.

"Why not?"

"Never mind!" said Wallace, austerely. He bent as near to Peter as he was able.

"Send a caddie up to the club-house to fetch my grey flannel trousers from my locker," he whispered, tensely.

"Oh, ah!" said Peter.

It was some little time before Wallace, encircled by a group of male spectators, was enabled to change his costume; and during the interval he continued to stand waist-deep in the water, to the chagrin of various couples who came to the tee in the course of their round and complained with not a little bitterness that his presence there added a mental hazard to an already difficult hole. Eventually, however, he found himself back ashore, his ball before him, his mashie in his hand.

"Carry on," said Peter Willard, as the couple in front left the green. "All clear now."

Wallace Chesney addressed his ball. And, even as he did so, he was suddenly aware that an odd psychological change had taken place in himself. He was aware of a strange weakness. The charred remains of the Plus Fours were lying under an adjacent bush; and, clad in the old grey flannels of his early golfing days, Wallace felt diffident, feeble, uncertain of himself. It was as though virtue had gone out of him, as if some indispensable adjunct to good play had been removed. His corrugated trouser-leg caught his eye as he waggled, and all at once he became acutely alive to the fact that many eyes were watching him. The audience seemed to press on him like a blanket. He felt as he had been wont to feel in the old days when he had had to drive off the first tee in front of a terrace-full of scoffing critics.

The next moment his ball had bounded weakly over the intervening patch of turf and was in the water.

"Hard luck!" said Peter Willard, ever a generous foe. And the words seemed to touch some almost atrophied chord in Wallace's breast. A sudden love for his species flooded over him. Dashed decent of Peter, he thought, to sympathize. Peter was a good chap. So were the spectators good chaps. So was everybody, even his caddie.

Peter Willard, as if resolved to make his sympathy practical, also rolled his ball into the lake.

"Hard luck!" said Wallace Chesney, and started as he said it; for many weeks had passed since he had commiserated with an opponent. He felt a changed man. A better, sweeter, kindlier man. It was as if a curse had fallen from him.

He teed up another ball, and swung.

"Hard luck!" said Peter.

"Hard luck!" said Wallace, a moment later.

"Hard luck!" said Peter, a moment after that.

Wallace Chesney stood on the tee watching the spot in the water where his third ball had fallen. The crowd was now openly amused, and, as he listened to their happy laughter, it was borne in upon Wallace that he, too, was amused and happy. A weird, almost effervescent exhilaration filled him. He turned and beamed upon the spectators. He waved his mashie cheerily at them. This, he felt, was something like golf. This was golf as it should be—not the dull, mechanical thing which had bored him during all these past weeks of his perfection, but a gay, rollicking adventure. That was the soul of golf, the thing that made it the wonderful pursuit it was—that speculativeness, that not knowing where the dickens your ball was going when you hit it, that eternal hoping for the best, that never-failing chanciness. It is better to travel hopefully than to arrive, and at last this great truth had come home to Wallace Chesney. He realized now why pro's. were all grave, silent men who seemed to struggle manfully against some secret sorrow. It was because they were too darned good. Golf had no surprises for them, no gallant spirit of adventure.

"I'm going to get a ball over if I stay here all night," cried Wallace Chesney, gaily, and the crowd echoed his mirth. On the face of Charlotte Dix was the look of a mother whose prodigal son had rolled into the old home once more. She caught Wallace's eye and gesticulated to him blithely.

"The cripple says he'll give you a stroke a hole, Wally!" she shouted.

"I'm ready for him!" bellowed Wallace.

"Hard *luck*!" said Peter Willard.

Under their bush the Plus Fours, charred and dripping, lurked unnoticed. But Wallace Chesney saw them. They caught his eye as he sliced his eleventh into the marshes on the right. It seemed to him that they looked sullen. Disappointed. Baffled.

Wallace Chesney was himself again.

17

THE AWAKENING OF ROLLO PODMARSH

Down on the new bowling-green behind the club-house some sort of competition was in progress. The seats about the smooth strip of turf were crowded, and the weak-minded yapping of the patients made itself plainly audible to the Oldest Member as he sat in his favourite chair in the smoking-room. He shifted restlessly, and a frown marred the placidity of his venerable brow. To the Oldest Member a golf-club was a golf-club, and he resented the introduction of any alien element. He had opposed the institution of tennis-courts; and the suggestion of a bowling-green had stirred him to his depths.

A young man in spectacles came into the smoking-room. His high forehead was aglow, and he lapped up a ginger-ale with the air of one who considers that he has earned it.

"Capital exercise!" he said, beaming upon the Oldest Member.

The Oldest Member laid down his *Vardon On Casual Water,* and peered suspiciously at his companion.

"What did you go round in?" he asked.

"Oh, I wasn't playing golf," said the young man. "Bowls."

"A nauseous pursuit!" said the Oldest Member, coldly, and resumed his reading.

The young man seemed nettled.

"I don't know why you should say that," he retorted. "It's a splendid game."

"I rank it," said the Oldest Member, "with the juvenile pastime of marbles."

The young man pondered for some moments.

"Well, anyway," he said at length, "it was good enough for Drake."

"As I have not the pleasure of the acquaintance of your friend Drake, I am unable to estimate the value of his endorsement."

"*The* Drake. The Spanish Armada Drake. He was playing bowls on Plymouth Hoe when they told him that the Armada was in sight. 'There is time to finish the game,' he replied. That's what Drake thought of bowls."

"If he had been a golfer he would have ignored the Armada altogether."

"It's easy enough to say that," said the young man, with spirit, "but can the history of golf show a parallel case?"

"A million, I should imagine."

"But you've forgotten them, eh?" said the young man, satirically.

"On the contrary," said the Oldest Member. "As a typical instance, neither more

nor less remarkable than a hundred others, I will select the story of Rollo Podmarsh."
He settled himself comfortably in his chair, and placed the tips of his fingers
together. "This Rollo Podmarsh——"

"No, I say!" protested the young man, looking at his watch.

"This Rollo Podmarsh——"

"Yes, but——"

This Rollo Podmarsh (said the Oldest Member) was the only son of his mother,
and she was a widow; and like other young men in that position he had rather allowed
a mother's tender care to take the edge off what you might call his rugged manliness.
Not to put too fine a point on it, he had permitted his parent to coddle him ever since
he had been in the nursery; and now, in his twenty-eighth year, he invariably wore
flannel next his skin, changed his shoes the moment they got wet, and—from
September to May, inclusive—never went to bed without partaking of a bowl of hot
arrowroot. Not, you would say, the stuff of which heroes are made. But you would
be wrong. Rollo Podmarsh was a golfer, and consequently pure gold at heart; and
in his hour of crisis all the good in him came to the surface.

In giving you this character-sketch of Rollo, I have been at pains to make it crisp,
for I observe that you are wriggling in a restless manner and you persist in pulling
out that watch of yours and gazing at it. Let me tell you that, if a mere skeleton
outline of the man has this effect upon you, I am glad for your sake that you never
met his mother. Mrs. Podmarsh could talk with enjoyment for hours on end about her
son's character and habits. And, on the September evening on which I introduce
her to you, though she had, as a fact, been speaking only for some ten minutes, it had
seemed like hours to the girl, Mary Kent, who was the party of the second part to
the conversation.

Mary Kent was the daughter of an old school-friend of Mrs. Podmarsh, and she
had come to spend the autumn and winter with her while her parents were abroad.
The scheme had never looked particularly good to Mary, and after ten minutes of
her hostess on the subject of Rollo she was beginning to weave dreams of knotted
sheets and a swift getaway through the bedroom window in the dark of the night.

"He is a strict teetotaller," said Mrs. Podmarsh.

"Really?"

"And has never smoked in his life."

"Fancy that!"

"But here is the dear boy now," said Mrs. Podmarsh, fondly.

Down the road towards them was coming a tall, well-knit figure in a Norfolk coat
and grey flannel trousers. Over his broad shoulders was suspended a bag of golf-clubs.

"Is *that* Mr. Podmarsh?" exclaimed Mary.

She was surprised. After all she had been listening to about the arrowroot and the
flannel next the skin and the rest of it, she had pictured the son of the house as a far
weedier specimen. She had been expecting to meet a small, slender young man with

an eyebrow moustache, and pince-nez; and this person approaching might have stepped straight out of Jack Dempsey's training-camp.

"Does he play golf?" asked Mary, herself an enthusiast.

"Oh yes," said Mrs. Podmarsh. "He makes a point of going out on the links once a day. He says the fresh air gives him such an appetite."

Mary, who had taken a violent dislike to Rollo on the evidence of his mother's description of his habits, had softened towards him on discovering that he was a golfer. She now reverted to her previous opinion. A man who could play the noble game from such ignoble motives was beyond the pale.

"Rollo is exceedingly good at golf," proceeded Mrs. Podmarsh. "He scores more than a hundred and twenty every time, while Mr. Burns, who is supposed to be one of the best players in the club, seldom manages to reach eighty. But Rollo is very modest—modesty is one of his best qualities—and you would never guess he was so skilful unless you were told."

"Well, Rollo darling, did you have a nice game? You didn't get your feet wet, I hope? This is Mary Kent, dear."

Rollo Podmarsh shook hands with Mary. And at her touch the strange dizzy feeling which had come over him at the sight of her suddenly became increased a thousand-fold. As I see that you are consulting your watch once more, I will not describe his emotions as exhaustively as I might. I will merely say that he had never felt anything resembling this sensation of dazed ecstasy since the occasion when a twenty-foot putt of his, which had been going well off the line, as his putts generally did, had hit a worm-cast sou'-sou'-east of the hole and popped in, giving him a snappy six. Rollo Podmarsh, as you will have divined, was in love at first sight. Which makes it all the sadder to think Mary at the moment was regarding him as an outcast and a blister.

Mrs. Podmarsh, having enfolded her son in a vehement embrace, drew back with a startled exclamation, sniffing.

"Rollo!" she cried. "You smell of tobacco-smoke."

Rollo looked embarrassed.

"Well, the fact is, mother——"

A hard protuberance in his coat-pocket attracted Mrs. Podmarsh's notice. She swooped and drew out a big-bowled pipe.

"Rollo!" she exclaimed, aghast.

"Well, the fact is, mother——"

"Don't you know," cried Mrs. Podmarsh, "that smoking is poisonous, and injurious to the health?"

"Yes. But the fact is, mother——"

"It causes nervous dyspepsia, sleeplessness, gnawing of the stomach, headache, weak eyes, red spots on the skin, throat irritation, asthma, bronchitis, heart failure, lung trouble, catarrh, melancholy, neurasthenia, loss of memory, impaired will-power, rheumatism, lumbago, sciatica, neuritis, heartburn, torpid liver, loss of appetite, enervation, lassitude, lack of ambition, and falling out of hair."

"Yes, I know, mother. But the fact is, Ted Ray smokes all the time he's playing, and I thought it might improve my game."

And it was at these splendid words that Mary Kent felt for the first time that something might be made of Rollo Podmarsh. That she experienced one-millionth of the fervour which was gnawing at his vitals I will not say. A woman does not fall in love in a flash like a man. But at least she no longer regarded him with loathing. On the contrary, she found herself liking him. There was, she considered, the right stuff in Rollo. And if, as seemed probable from his mother's conversation, it would take a bit of digging to bring it up, well—she liked rescue-work and had plenty of time.

Mr. Arnold Bennett, in a recent essay, advises young bachelors to proceed with a certain caution in matters of the heart. They should, he asserts, first decide whether or not they are ready for love; then, whether it is better to marry earlier or later; thirdly, whether their ambitions are such that a wife will prove a hindrance to their career. These romantic preliminaries concluded, they may grab a girl and go to it. Rollo Podmarsh would have made a tough audience for these precepts. Since the days of Antony and Cleopatra probably no one had ever got more swiftly off the mark. One may say that he was in love before he had come within two yards of the girl. And each day that passed found him more nearly up to his eyebrows in the tender emotion.

He thought of Mary when he was changing his wet shoes; he dreamed of her while putting flannel next his skin; he yearned for her over the evening arrowroot. Why, the man was such a slave to his devotion that he actually went to the length of purloining small articles belonging to her. Two days after Mary's arrival Rollo Podmarsh was driving off the first tee with one of her handkerchiefs, a powder-puff, and a dozen hairpins secreted in his left breast-pocket. When dressing for dinner he used to take them out and look at them, and at night he slept with them under his pillow. Heavens, how he loved that girl!

One evening when they had gone out into the garden together to look at the new moon—Rollo, by his mother's advice, wearing a woollen scarf to protect his throat—he endeavoured to bring the conversation round to the important subject. Mary's last remark had been about earwigs. Considered as a cue, it lacked a subtle something; but Rollo was not the man to be discouraged by that.

"Talking of earwigs, Miss Kent," he said, in a low musical voice, "have you ever been in love?"

Mary was silent for a moment before replying.

"Yes, once. When I was eleven. With a conjurer who came to perform at my birthday-party. He took a rabbit and two eggs out of my hair, and life seemed one grand sweet song."

"Never since then?"

"Never."

"Suppose—just for the sake of argument—suppose you ever did love anyone—er —what sort of man would it be?"

"A hero," said Mary, promptly.

"A hero?" said Rollo, somewhat taken aback. "What sort of hero?"

"Any sort. I could only love a really brave man—a man who had done some wonderful heroic action."

"Shall we go in?" said Rollo, hoarsely. "The air is a little chilly."

We have now, therefore, arrived at a period in Rollo Podmarsh's career which might have inspired those lines of Henley's about "the night that covers me, black as the Pit from pole to pole". What with one thing and another, he was in an almost Job-like condition of despondency. I say "one thing and another", for it was not only hopeless love that weighed him down. In addition to being hopelessly in love, he was greatly depressed about his golf.

On Rollo in his capacity of golfer I have so far not dwelt. You have probably allowed yourself, in spite of the significant episode of the pipe, to dismiss him as one of those placid, contented—shall I say dilettante?—golfers who are so frequent in these degenerate days. Such was not the case. Outwardly placid, Rollo was consumed inwardly by an ever-burning fever of ambition. His aims were not extravagant. He did not want to become amateur champion, nor even to win a monthly medal; but he did, with his whole soul, desire one of these days to go round the course in under a hundred. This feat accomplished, it was his intention to set the seal on his golfing career by playing a real money-match; and already he had selected his opponent, a certain Colonel Bodger, a tottery performer of advanced years who for the last decade had been a martyr to lumbago.

But it began to look as if even the modest goal he had marked out for himself were beyond his powers. Day after day he would step on to the first tee, glowing with zeal and hope, only to crawl home in the quiet evenfall with another hundred and twenty on his card. Little wonder, then, that he began to lose his appetite and would moan feebly at the sight of a poached egg.

With Mrs. Podmarsh sedulously watching over her son's health, you might have supposed that this inability on his part to teach the foodstuffs to take a joke would have caused consternation in the home. But it so happened that Rollo's mother had recently been reading a medical treatise in which an eminent physician stated that we all eat too much nowadays, and that the secret of a happy life is to lay off the carbohydrates to some extent. She was, therefore, delighted to observe the young man's moderation in the matter of food, and frequently held him up as an example to be noted and followed by little Lettice Willoughby, her grand-daughter, who was a good and consistent trencherwoman, particularly rough on the puddings. Little Lettice, I should mention, was the daughter of Rollo's sister Enid, who lived in the neighbourhood. Mrs. Willoughby had been compelled to go away on a visit a few days before and had left her child with Mrs. Podmarsh during her absence.

You can fool some of the people all the time, but Lettice Willoughby was not of the type that is easily deceived. A nice, old-fashioned child would no doubt have accepted without questioning her grandmother's dictum that roly-poly pudding could not fail to hand a devastating wallop to the blood-pressure, and that to take two helpings of it was practically equivalent to walking right into the family vault. A child with less decided opinions of her own would have been impressed by the spectacle of her uncle refusing sustenance, and would have received without demur the statement that he did it because he felt that abstinence was good for his health. Lettice was a modern child and knew better. She had had experience of this loss of appetite and its significance. The first symptom which had preceded the demise of poor old Ponto, who had recently handed in his portfolio after holding office for ten years as the Willoughby family dog, had been this same disinclination to absorb nourishment. Besides, she was an observant child, and had not failed to note the haggard misery in her uncle's eyes. She tackled him squarely on the subject one morning after breakfast. Rollo had retired into the more distant parts of the garden, and was leaning forward, when she found him, with his head buried in his hands.

"Hallo, uncle," said Lettice.

Rollo looked up wanly.

"Ah, child!" he said. He was fond of his niece.

"Aren't you feeling well, uncle?"

"Far, far from well."

"It's old age, I expect," said Lettice.

"I feel old," admitted Rollo. "Old and battered. Ah, Lettice, laugh and be gay while you can."

"All right, uncle."

"Make the most of your happy, careless, smiling halcyon childhood."

"Right-o, uncle."

"When you get to my age, dear, you will realize that it is a sad, hopeless world. A world where, if you keep your head down, you forget to let the club-head lead: where even if you do happen by a miracle to keep 'em straight with your brassie, you blow up on the green and foozle a six-inch putt."

Lettice could not quite understand what Uncle Rollo was talking about, but she gathered broadly that she had been correct in supposing him to be in a bad state, and her warm, childish heart was filled with pity for him. She walked thoughtfully away, and Rollo resumed his reverie.

Into each life, as the poet says, some rain must fall. So much had recently been falling into Rollo's that, when Fortune at last sent along a belated sunbeam, it exercised a cheering effect out of all proportion to its size. By this I mean that when, some four days after his conversation with Lettice, Mary Kent asked him to play golf with her, he read into the invitation a significance which only a lover could have seen in it. I will not go so far as to say that Rollo Podmarsh looked on Mary Kent's suggestion that they should have a round together as actually tantamount to a revelation of undying love; but he certainly regarded it as a most encouraging sign. It seemed to him that things were beginning to move, that Rollo Preferred were on a rising market. Gone was the gloom of the past days. He forgot those sad, solitary wanderings of his in the bushes at the bottom of the garden; he forgot that his mother had bought him a new set of winter woollies which felt like horsehair; he forgot that for the last few evenings his arrowroot had tasted rummy. His whole mind was occupied with the astounding fact that she had voluntarily offered to play golf with him, and he walked out on to the first tee filled with a yeasty exhilaration which nearly caused him to burst into song.

"How shall we play?" asked Mary. "I am a twelve. What is your handicap?"

Rollo was under the disadvantage of not actually possessing a handicap. He had a sort of private system of book-keeping of his own by which he took strokes over if they did not seem to him to be up to sample, and allowed himself five-foot putts at discretion. So he had never actually handed in the three cards necessary for handicapping purposes.

"I don't exactly know," he said. "It's my ambition to get round in under a hundred, but I've never managed it yet."

"Never?"

"Never! It's strange, but something always seems to go wrong."

"Perhaps you'll manage it today," said Mary, encouragingly, so encouragingly that it was all that Rollo could do to refrain from flinging himself at her feet and barking like a dog. "Well, I'll start you two holes up, and we'll see how we get on. Shall I take the honour?"

She drove off one of those fair-to-medium balls which go with a twelve handicap. Not a great length, but nice and straight.

"Splendid!" cried Rollo, devoutly.

"Oh, I don't know," said Mary. "I wouldn't call it anything special."

Titanic emotions were surging in Rollo's bosom as he addressed his ball. He had never felt like this before, especially on the first tee—where as a rule he found himself overcome with a nervous humility.

"Oh, Mary! Mary!" he breathed to himself as he swung.

You who squander your golden youth fooling about on a bowling-green will not understand the magic of those three words. But if you were a golfer, you would realize that in selecting just that invocation to breathe to himself Rollo Podmarsh had hit, by sheer accident, on the ideal method of achieving a fine drive. Let me explain. The first two words, tensely breathed, are just sufficient to take a man with the proper slowness to the top of his swing; the first syllable of the second "Mary" exactly coincides with the striking of the ball; and the final "ry!" takes care of the follow-through. The consequence was that Rollo's ball, instead of hopping down the hill like an embarrassed duck, as was its usual practice, sang off the tee with a scream like a shell, nodded in passing Mary's ball, where it lay some hundred and fifty yards down the course, and, carrying on from there, came to rest within easy distance of the green. For the first time in his golfing life Rollo Podmarsh had hit a nifty.

Mary followed the ball's flight with astonished eyes.

"But this will never do!" she exclaimed. "I can't possibly start you two up if you're going to do this sort of thing."

Rollo blushed.

"I shouldn't think it would happen again," he said. "I've never done a drive like that before."

"But it must happen again," said Mary, firmly. "This is evidently your day. If you don't get round in under a hundred today, I shall never forgive you."

Rollo shut his eyes, and his lips moved feverishly. He was registering a vow that, come what might, he would not fail her. A minute later he was holing out in three, one under bogey.

The second hole is the short lake-hole. Bogey is three, and Rollo generally did it in four; for it was his custom not to count any balls he might sink in the water, but to start afresh with one which happened to get over, and then take three putts. But today something seemed to tell him that he would not require the aid of this ingenious system. As he took his mashie from the bag, he *knew* that his first shot would soar successfully on to the green.

"Ah, Mary!" he breathed as he swung.

These subtleties are wasted on a worm, if you will pardon the expression, like yourself, who, possibly owing to a defective education, is content to spend life's springtime rolling wooden balls across a lawn; but I will explain that in altering and shortening his soliloquy at this juncture Rollo had done the very thing any good pro. would have recommended. If he had murmured, "Oh, Mary! Mary!" as before he would have over-swung. "Ah, Mary!" was exactly right for a half-swing with the mashie. His ball shot up in a beautiful arc, and trickled to within six inches of the hole.

Mary was delighted. There was something about this big, diffident man which had appealed from the first to everything in her that was motherly.

"Marvellous!" she said. "You'll get a two. Five for the first two holes! Why, you simply must get round in under a hundred now." She swung, but too lightly; and her ball fell in the water. "I'll give you this," she said, without the slightest chagrin, for this girl had a beautiful nature. "Let's go on to the third. Four up! Why, you're wonderful!"

And not to weary you with too much detail, I will simply remark that, stimulated by her gentle encouragement, Rollo Podmarsh actually came off the ninth green with a medal score of forty-six for the half-round. A ten on the seventh had spoiled his card to some extent, and a nine on the eighth had not helped, but nevertheless here he was in forty-six, with the easier half of the course before him. He tingled all over —partly because he was wearing the new winter woollies to which I have alluded previously, but principally owing to triumph, elation, and love. He gazed at Mary as Dante might have gazed at Beatrice on one of his particularly sentimental mornings.

Mary uttered an exclamation.

"Oh, I've just remembered," she exclaimed. "I promised to write last night to Jane Simpson and give her that new formula for knitting jumpers. I think I'll phone her now from the club-house and then it'll be off my mind. You go on to the tenth, and I'll join you there."

Rollo proceeded over the brow of the hill to the tenth tee, and was filling in the time with practice-swings when he heard his name spoken.

"Good gracious, Rollo! I couldn't believe it was you at first."

He turned to see his sister, Mrs. Willoughby, the mother of the child Lettice.

"Hallo!" he said. "When did you get back?"

"Late last night. Why, it's extraordinary!"

"Hope you had a good time. What's extraordinary? Listen, Enid. Do you know what I've done? Forty-six for the first nine! Forty-six! And holing out every putt."

"Oh, then that accounts for it."

"Accounts for what?"

"Why, your looking so pleased with life. I got an idea from Letty, when she wrote to me, that you were at death's door. Your gloom seems to have made a deep impression on the child. Her letter was full of it."

Rollo was moved.

"Dear little Letty! She is wonderfully sympathetic."

"Well, I must be off now," said Enid Willoughby. "I'm late. Oh, talking of Letty. Don't children say the funniest things! She wrote in her letter that you were very old and wretched and that she was going to put you out of your misery."

"Ha ha ha!" laughed Rollo.

"We had to poison poor old Ponto the other day, you know, and poor little Letty was inconsolable till we explained to her that it was really the kindest thing to do, because he was so old and ill. But just imagine her thinking of wanting to end *your* sufferings!"

"Ha ha!" laughed Rollo. "Ha ha h——!"

His voice trailed off into a broken gurgle. Quite suddenly a sinister thought had come to him.

The arrowroot had tasted rummy!

"Why, what on earth is the matter?" asked Mrs. Willoughby, regarding his ashen face.

Rollo could find no words. He yammered speechlessly. Yes, for several nights the arrowroot had tasted very rummy. Rummy! There was no other adjective. Even as he plied the spoon he had said to himself: "This arrowroot tastes rummy!" And—he uttered a sharp yelp as he remembered—it had been little Lettice who had brought it to him. He recollected being touched at the time by the kindly act.

"What *is* the matter, Rollo?" demanded Mrs. Willoughby, sharply. "Don't stand there looking like a dying duck."

"I am a dying duck," responded Rollo, hoarsely. "A dying man, I mean. Enid, that infernal child has poisoned me!"

"Don't be ridiculous! And kindly don't speak of her like that!"

"I'm sorry. I shouldn't blame her, I suppose. No doubt her motives were good. But the fact remains."

"Rollo, you're too absurd."

"But the arrowroot tasted rummy."

"I never knew you could be such an idiot," said his exasperated sister with sisterly outspokenness. "I thought you would think it quaint. I thought you would roar with laughter."

"I did—till I remembered about the rumminess of the arrowroot."

Mrs. Willoughby uttered an impatient exclamation and walked away.

Rollo Podmarsh stood on the tenth tee, a volcano of mixed emotions. Mechanically he pulled out his pipe and lit it. But he found that he could not smoke. In this supreme crisis of his life tobacco seemed to have lost its magic. He put the pipe back in his pocket and gave himself up to his thoughts. Now terror gripped him; anon a sort of gentle melancholy. It was so hard that he should be compelled to leave the world just as he had begun to hit 'em right.

And then in the welter of his thoughts there came one of practical value. To wit, that by hurrying to the doctor's without delay he might yet be saved. There might be antidotes.

He turned to go and there was Mary Kent standing beside him with her bright, encouraging smile.

"I'm sorry I kept you so long," she said. "It's your honour. Fire away, and remember that you've got to do this nine in fifty-three at the outside."

Rollo's thought flitted wistfully to the snug surgery where Dr. Brown was probably sitting at this moment surrounded by the finest antidotes.

"Do you know, I think I ought to——"

"Of course you ought to," said Mary. "If you did the first nine in forty-six, you can't possibly take fifty-three coming in."

For one long moment Rollo continued to hesitate—a moment during which the instinct of self-preservation seemed as if it must win the day. All his life he had been brought up to be nervous about his health, and panic gripped him. But there is a deeper, nobler instinct than that of self-preservation—the instinctive desire of a golfer who is at the top of his form to go on and beat his medal-score record. And little by little this grand impulse began to dominate Rollo. If, he felt, he went off now to take antidotes, the doctor might possibly save his life; but reason told him that never again would he be likely to do the first nine in forty-six. He would have to start all over afresh.

Rollo Podmarsh hesitated no longer. With a pale, set face he teed up his ball and drove.

If I were telling this story to a golfer instead of to an excrescence—I use the word in the kindliest spirit—who spends his time messing about on a bowling-green, nothing would please me better than to describe shot by shot Rollo's progress over the remaining nine holes. Epics have been written with less material. But these details would, I am aware, be wasted on you. Let it suffice that by the time his last approach trickled on to the eighteenth green he had taken exactly fifty shots.

"Three for it!" said Mary Kent. "Steady now! Take it quite easy and be sure to lay your second dead."

It was prudent counsel, but Rollo was now thoroughly above himself. He had got his feet wet in a puddle on the sixteenth, but he did not care. His winter woollies seemed to be lined with ants, but he ignored them. All he knew was that he was on the last green in ninety-six, and he meant to finish in style. No tame three putts for him! His ball was five yards away, but he aimed for the back of the hole and brought his putter down with a whack. Straight and true the ball sped, hit the tin, jumped high in the air, and fell into the hole with a rattle.

"Oo!" cried Mary.

Rollo Podmarsh wiped his forehead and leaned dizzily on his putter. For a moment, so intense is the fervour induced by the game of games, all he could think of was that he had gone round in ninety-seven. Then, as one waking from a trance, he began to appreciate his position. The fever passed, and a clammy dismay took possession of him. He had achieved his life's ambition; but what now? Already he was conscious of a curious discomfort within him. He felt as he supposed Italians of the Middle Ages must have felt after dropping in to take pot-luck with the Borgias. It was hard. He had gone round in ninety-seven, but he could never take the next step in the career which he had mapped out in his dreams—the money-match with the lumbago-stricken Colonel Bodger.

Mary Kent was fluttering round him, bubbling congratulations, but Rollo sighed.

"Thanks," he said. "Thanks very much. But the trouble is, I'm afraid I'm going to die almost immediately. I've been poisoned!"

"Poisoned!"

"Yes. Nobody is to blame. Everything was done with the best intentions. But there it is."

"But I don't understand."

Rollo explained. Mary listened pallidly.

"Are you sure?" she gasped.

"Quite sure," said Rollo, gravely. "The arrowroot tasted rummy."

"But arrowroot always does."

Rollo shook his head.

"No," he said. "It tastes like warm blotting-paper, but not rummy."

Mary was sniffing.

"Don't cry," urged Rollo tenderly. "Don't cry."

"But I must. And I've come out without a handkerchief."

"Permit me," said Rollo, producing one of her best from his left breast-pocket.

"I wish I had a powder-puff," said Mary.

"Allow me," said Rollo. "And your hair has become a little disordered. If I may
——" And from the same reservoir he drew a handful of hairpins.

Mary gazed at these exhibits with astonishment.

"But these are mine," she said.

"Yes. I sneaked them from time to time."

"But why?"

"Because I loved you," said Rollo. And in a few moving sentences which I will not
trouble you with he went on to elaborate this theme.

Mary listened with her heart full of surging emotions, which I cannot possibly go
into if you persist in looking at that damned watch of yours. The scales had fallen
from her eyes. She had thought slightingly of this man because he had been a little
over-careful of his health, and all the time he had had within him the potentiality
of heroism. Something seemed to snap inside her.

"Rollo!" she cried, and flung herself into his arms.

"Mary!" muttered Rollo, gathering her up.

"I told you it was all nonsense," said Mrs. Willoughby, coming up at this tense
moment and going on with the conversation where she had left off. "I've just seen
Letty, and she said she meant to put you out of your misery but the chemist wouldn't
sell her any poison, so she let it go."

Rollo disentangled himself from Mary.

"What?" he cried.

Mrs. Willoughby repeated her remarks.

"You're sure?" he said.

"Of course I'm sure."

"Then why did the arrowroot taste rummy?"

"I made inquiries about that. It seems that mother was worried about your taking
to smoking, and she found an advertisement in one of the magazines about the
Tobacco Habit Cured in Three Days by a secret method without the victim's
knowledge. It was a gentle, safe, agreeable method of eliminating the nicotine poison
from the system, strengthening the weakened membranes, and overcoming the
craving; so she put some in your arrowroot every night."

There was a long silence. To Rollo Podmarsh it seemed as though the sun had
suddenly begun to shine, the birds to sing, and the grasshoppers to toot. All Nature
was one vast substantial smile. Down in the valley by the second hole he caught sight
of Wallace Chesney's Plus Fours gleaming as their owner stooped to play his shot,
and it seemed to him that he had never in his life seen anything so lovely.

"Mary," he said, in a low, vibrant voice, "will you wait here for me? I want to go into the club-house for a moment."

"To change your wet shoes?"

"No!" thundered Rollo. "I'm never going to change my wet shoes again in my life." He felt in his pocket, and hurled a box of patent pills far into the undergrowth. "But I *am* going to change my winter woollies. And when I've put those dashed barbed-wire entanglements into the club-house furnace, I'm going to phone to old Colonel Bodger. I hear his lumbago's worse than ever. I'm going to fix up a match with him for a shilling a hole. And if I don't lick the boots off him you can break the engagement!"

"My hero!" murmured Mary.

Rollo kissed her, and with long, resolute steps strode to the club-house.

18

RODNEY FAILS TO QUALIFY

THERE was a sound of revelry by night, for the first Saturday in June had arrived and the Golf Club was holding its monthly dance. Fairy lanterns festooned the branches of the chestnut trees on the terrace above the ninth green, and from the big dining-room, cleared now of its tables and chairs, came a muffled slithering of feet and the plaintive sound of saxophones moaning softly like a man who has just missed a short putt. In a basket-chair in the shadows, the Oldest Member puffed a cigar and listened, well content. His was the peace of the man who has reached the age when he is no longer expected to dance.

A door opened, and a young man came out of the club-house. He stood on the steps with folded arms, gazing to left and right. The Oldest Member, watching him from the darkness, noted that he wore an air of gloom. His brow was furrowed and he had the indefinable look of one who has been smitten in the spiritual solar plexus.

Yes, where all around him was joy, jollity, and song, this young man brooded.

The sound of a high tenor voice, talking rapidly and entertainingly on the subject of modern Russian thought, now intruded itself on the peace of the night. From the farther end of the terrace a girl came into the light of the lantern, her arm in that of a second young man. She was small and pretty, he tall and intellectual. The light shone on his high forehead and glittered on his tortoiseshell-rimmed spectacles. The girl was gazing up at him with reverence and adoration, and at the sight of these twain the youth on the steps appeared to undergo some sort of spasm. His face became contorted and he wobbled. Then, with a gesture of sublime despair, he tripped over the mat and stumbled back into the club-house. The couple passed on and disappeared, and the Oldest Member had the night to himself, until the door opened once more and the club's courteous and efficient secretary trotted down the steps. The scent of the cigar drew him to where the Oldest Member sat, and he dropped into the chair beside him.

"Seen young Ramage tonight?" asked the secretary.

"He was standing on those steps only a moment ago," replied the Oldest Member. "Why do you ask?"

"I thought perhaps you might have had a talk with him and found out what's the matter. Can't think what's come to him tonight. Nice, civil boy as a rule, but just now, when I was trying to tell him about my short approach on the fifth this afternoon, he was positively abrupt. Gave a sort of hollow gasp and dashed away in the middle of a sentence."

The Oldest Member sighed.

"You must overlook his brusqueness," he said. "The poor lad is passing through a trying time. A short while back I was the spectator of a little drama that explains everything. Mabel Patmore is flirting disgracefully with that young fellow Purvis."

"Purvis? Oh, you mean the man who won the club Bowls Championship last week?"

"I can quite believe that he may have disgraced himself in the manner you describe," said the Sage, coldly. "I know he plays that noxious game. And it is for that reason that I hate to see a nice girl like Mabel Patmore, who only needs a little more steadiness off the tee to become a very fair golfer, wasting her time on him. I suppose his attraction lies in the fact that he has a great flow of conversation, while poor Ramage is, one must admit, more or less of a dumb Isaac. Girls are too often snared by a glib tongue. Still, it is a pity, a great pity. The whole affair recalls irresistibly to my mind the story——"

The secretary rose with a whirr like a rocketing pheasant.

"——the story," continued the Sage, "of Jane Packard, William Bates and Rodney Spelvin—which, as you have never heard it, I will now proceed to relate."

"Can't stop now, much as I should like——"

"It is a theory of mine," proceeded the Oldest Member, attaching himself to the other's coat-tails, and pulling him gently back into his seat, "that nothing but misery can come of the union between a golfer and an outcast whose soul has not been purified by the noblest of games. This is well exemplified by the story of Jane Packard, William Bates, and Rodney Spelvin."

"All sorts of things to look after——"

"That is why I am hoping so sincerely that there is nothing more serious than a temporary flirtation in this business of Mabel Patmore and bowls-playing Purvis. A girl in whose life golf has become a factor, would be mad to trust her happiness to a blister whose idea of enjoyment is trundling wooden balls across a lawn. Sooner or later he is certain to fail her in some crisis. Lucky for her if this failure occurs before the marriage knot has been inextricably tied and so opens her eyes to his inadequacy—as was the case in the matter of Jane Packard, William Bates, and Rodney Spelvin. I will now," said the Oldest Member, "tell you all about Jane Packard, William Bates, and Rodney Spelvin."

The secretary uttered a choking groan.

"I shall miss the next dance," he pleaded.

"A bit of luck for some nice girl," said the Sage, equably.

He tightened his grip on the other's arm.

Jane Packard and William Bates (said the Oldest Member) were not, you must understand, officially engaged. They had grown up together from childhood, and there existed between them a sort of understanding—the understanding being that, if ever William could speed himself up enough to propose, Jane would accept him, and they would settle down and live stodgily and happily ever after. For William was not one of your rapid wooers. In his affair of the heart he moved somewhat slowly and ponderously, like a motor-lorry, an object which both in physique and temperament he greatly resembled. He was an extraordinarily large, powerful, ox-like young man, who required plenty of time to make up his mind about any given problem. I have seen him in the club dining-room musing with a thoughtful frown for fifteen minutes on end while endeavouring to weigh the rival merits of a chump chop and a sirloin steak as a luncheon dish. A placid, leisurely man, I might almost call him lymphatic. I *will* call him lymphatic. He was lymphatic.

The first glimmering of an idea that Jane might possibly be a suitable wife for him had come to William some three years before this story opens. Having brooded on the matter tensely for six months, he then sent her a bunch of roses. In the October of the following year, nothing having occurred to alter his growing conviction that she was an attractive girl, he presented her with a two-pound box of assorted chocolates. And from then on his progress, though not rapid, was continuous, and there seemed little reason to doubt that, should nothing come about to weaken Jane's regard for him, another five years or so would see the matter settled.

And it did not appear likely that anything would weaken Jane's regard. They had much in common, for she was a calm, slow-moving person, too. They had a mutual devotion to golf, and played together every day; and the fact that their handicaps were practically level formed a strong bond. Most divorces, as you know, spring from the fact that the husband is too markedly superior to his wife at golf; this leading him, when she starts criticizing his relations, to say bitter and unforgivable things about her mashie-shots. Nothing of this kind could happen with William and Jane. They would build their life on a solid foundation of sympathy and understanding. The years would find them consoling and encouraging each other, happy married lovers. If, that is to say, William ever got round to proposing.

It was not until the fourth year of this romance that I detected the first sign of any alteration in the schedule. I had happened to call on the Packards one afternoon and found them all out except Jane. She gave me tea and conversed for a while, but she seemed distrait. I had known her since she wore rompers, so felt entitled to ask if there was anything wrong.

"Not exactly wrong," said Jane, and she heaved a sigh.

"Tell me," I said.

She heaved another sigh.

"Have you ever read *The Love that Scorches,* by Luella Periton Phipps?" she asked.

I said I had not.

"I got it out of the library yesterday," said Jane, dreamily, "and finished it at three this morning in bed. It is a very, very beautiful book. It is all about the desert and people riding on camels and a wonderful Arab chief with stern, yet tender, eyes, and a girl called Angela, and oases and dates and mirages, and all like that. There is a chapter where the Arab chief seizes the girl and clasps her in his arms and she feels his hot breath searing her face and he flings her on his horse and they ride off and all around was sand and night, and the mysterious stars. And somehow—oh, I don't know——"

She gazed yearningly at the chandelier.

"I wish mother would take me to Algiers next winter," she murmured, absently. "It would do her rheumatism so much good."

I went away frankly uneasy. These novelists, I felt, ought to be more careful. They put ideas into girls' heads and made them dissatisfied. I determined to look William up and give him a kindly word of advice. It was no business of mine, you may say, but they were so ideally suited to one another that it seemed a tragedy that anything should come between them. And Jane was in a strange mood. At any moment, I felt, she might take a good, square look at William and wonder what she could ever have seen in him. I hurried to the boy's cottage.

"William," I said, "as one who dandled you on his knee when you were a baby, I wish to ask you a personal question. Answer me this, and make it snappy. Do you love Jane Packard?"

A look of surprise came into his face, followed by one of intense thought. He was silent for a space.

"Who, me?" he said at length.

"Yes, you."

"Jane Packard?"

"Yes, Jane Packard."

"Do I love Jane Packard?" said William, assembling the material and arranging it neatly in his mind.

He pondered for perhaps five minutes.

"Why, of course I do," he said.

"Splendid!"

"Devotedly, dash it!"

"Capital!"

"You might say madly."

I tapped him on his barrel-like chest.

"Then my advice to you, William Bates, is to tell her so."

"Now that's rather a brainy scheme," said William, looking at me admiringly, "I see exactly what you're driving at. You mean it would kind of settle things, and all that?"

"Precisely."

"Well, I've got to go away for a couple of days tomorrow—it's the Invitation Tournament at Squashy Hollow—but I'll be back on Wednesday. Suppose I take her out on the links on Wednesday and propose?"

"A very good idea."

"At the sixth hole, say?"

"At the sixth hole would do excellently."

"Or the seventh?"

"The sixth would be better. The ground slopes from the tee, and you would be hidden from view by the dog-leg turn."

"Something in that."

"My own suggestion would be that you somehow contrive to lead her into that large bunker to the left of the sixth fairway."

"Why?"

"I have reason to believe that Jane would respond more readily to your wooing were it conducted in some vast sandy waste. And there is another thing," I proceeded, earnestly, "which I must impress upon you. See that there is nothing tame or tepid about your behaviour when you propose. You must show zip and romance. In fact, I strongly recommend you, before you even say a word to her, to seize her and clasp her in your arms and let your hot breath sear her face."

"Who, me?" said William.

"Believe me, it is what will appeal to her most."

"But, I say! Hot breath, I mean! Dash it all, you know, what?"

"I assure you it is indispensable."

"Seize her?" said William blankly.

"Precisely."

"Clasp her in my arms?"

"Just so."

William plunged into silent thought once more.

"Well, you *know*, I suppose," he said at length. "You've had experience, I take it. Still—— Oh, all right, I'll have a stab at it."

"There spoke the true William Bates!" I said. "Go to it, lad, and Heaven speed your wooing!"

In all human schemes—and it is this that so often brings failure to the subtlest strategists—there is always the chance of the Unknown Factor popping up, that unforeseen X for which we have made no allowance and which throws our whole plan of campaign out of gear. I had not anticipated anything of the kind coming along to mar the arrangements on the present occasion; but when I reached the first tee on the Wednesday afternoon to give William Bates that last word of encouragement, which means so much, I saw that I had been too sanguine. William had not yet arrived, but Jane was there, and with her a tall, slim, dark-haired, sickeningly romantic-looking youth in faultlessly fitting serge. A stranger to me. He was talking to her in a musical undertone, and she seemed to be hanging on his words. Her beautiful eyes were fixed on his face, and her lips slightly parted. So absorbed was she that it was not until I spoke that she became aware of my presence.

"William not arrived yet?"

She turned with a start.

"William? Hasn't he? Oh! No, not yet. I don't suppose he will be long. I want to introduce you to Mr. Spelvin. He has come to stay with the Wyndhams for a few weeks. He is going to walk round with us."

Naturally this information came as a shock to me, but I masked my feelings and greeted the young man with a well-assumed cordiality.

"Mr. George Spelvin, the actor?" I asked, shaking hands.

"My cousin," he said. "My name is Rodney Spelvin. I do not share George's histrionic ambitions. If I have any claim to—may I say renown?—it is as a maker of harmonies."

"A composer, eh?"

"Verbal harmonies," explained Mr. Spelvin. "I am, in my humble fashion, a poet."

"He writes the most beautiful poetry," said Jane, warmly. "He has just been reciting some of it to me."

"Oh, that little thing?" said Mr. Spelvin, deprecatingly. "A mere *morceau*. One of my juvenilia."

"It was too beautiful for words," persisted Jane.

"Ah, you," said Mr. Spelvin, "have the soul to appreciate it. I could wish that there were more like you, Miss Packard. We singers have much to put up with in a crass and materialistic world. Only last week, a man, a coarse editor, asked me what my sonnet, 'Wine of Desire', *meant*." He laughed indulgently. "I gave him answer, 'twas a sonnet, not a mining prospectus."

"It would have served him right," said Jane, heatedly, "if you had pasted him one on the nose!"

At this point a low whistle behind me attracted my attention, and I turned to perceive William Bates towering against the skyline.

"Hoy!" said William.

I walked to where he stood, leaving Jane and Mr. Spelvin in earnest conversation with their heads close together.

"I say," said William, in a rumbling undertone, "who's the bird with Jane?"

"A man named Spelvin. He is visiting the Wyndhams. I suppose Mrs. Wyndham made them acquainted."

"Looks a bit of a Gawd-help-us," said William critically.

"He is going to walk round with you."

It was impossible for a man of William Bates's temperament to start, but his face took on a look of faint concern.

"Walk round with us?"

"So Jane said."

"But look here," said William. "I can't possibly seize her and clasp her in my arms and do all that hot-breath stuff with this pie-faced exhibit hanging round on the outskirts."

"No, I fear not."

"Postpone it, then, what?" said William, with unmistakable relief. "Well, as a matter of fact, it's probably a good thing. There was a most extraordinarily fine steak-and-kidney pudding at lunch, and, between ourselves, I'm not feeling what you might call keyed up to anything in the nature of a romantic scene. Some other time, eh?"

I looked at Jane and the Spelvin youth, and a nameless apprehension swept over me. There was something in their attitude which I found alarming. I was just about to whisper a warning to William not to treat this new arrival too lightly, when Jane caught sight of him and called him over and a moment later they set out on their round.

I walked away pensively. This Spelvin's advent, coming immediately on top of that book of desert love, was undeniably sinister. My heart sank for William, and I waited at the club-house to have a word with him, after his match. He came in two hours later, flushed and jubilant.

"Played the game of my life!" he said. "We didn't hole out all the putts, but, making allowances for everything, you can chalk me up an eighty-three. Not so bad, eh? You know the eighth hole? Well, I was a bit short with my drive, and found my ball lying badly for the brassie, so I took my driving-iron and with a nice easy swing let the pill have it so squarely on the seat of the pants that it flew——"

"Where is Jane?" I interrupted.

"Jane? Oh, the bloke Spelvin has taken her home."

"Beware of him, William!" I whispered, tensely. "Have a care, young Bates! If you don't look out, you'll have him stealing Jane from you. Don't laugh. Remember that I saw them together before you arrived. She was gazing into his eyes as a desert maiden might gaze into the eyes of a sheik. You don't seem to realize, wretched William Bates, that Jane is an extremely romantic girl. A fascinating stranger like this, coming suddenly into her life, may well snatch her away from you before you know where you are."

"That's all right," said William, lightly. "I don't mind admitting that the same idea occurred to me. But I made judicious inquiries on the way round, and found out that the fellow's a poet. You don't seriously expect me to believe that there's any chance of Jane falling in love with a poet?"

He spoke incredulously, for there were three things in the world that he held in the smallest esteem—slugs, poets, and caddies with hiccups.

"I think it extremely possible, if not probable," I replied.

"Nonsense!" said William. "And, besides, the man doesn't play golf. Never had a club in his hand, and says he never wants to. That's the sort of fellow he is."

At this, I confess, I did experience a distinct feeling of relief. I could imagine Jane Packard, stimulated by exotic literature, committing many follies, but I was compelled to own that I could not conceive of her giving her heart to one who not only did not play golf but had no desire to play it. Such a man, to a girl of her fine nature and correct upbringing, would be beyond the pale. I walked home with William in a calm and happy frame of mind.

I was to learn but one short week later that Woman is the unfathomable, incalculable mystery, the problem we men can never hope to solve.

The week that followed was one of much festivity in our village. There were dances, picnics, bathing-parties, and all the other adjuncts of high summer. In these William Bates played but a minor part. Dancing was not one of his gifts. He swung, if called upon, an amiable shoe, but the disposition in the neighbourhood was to refrain from calling upon him; for he had an incurable habit of coming down with his full weight upon his partner's toes, and many a fair girl had had to lie up for a couple of days after collaborating with him in a foxtrot.

Picnics, again, bored him, and he always preferred a round on the links to the merriest bathing-party. The consequence was that he kept practically aloof from the revels, and all through the week Jane Packard was squired by Rodney Spelvin. With Spelvin she swayed over the waxed floor; with Spelvin she dived and swam; and it was Spelvin who, with zealous hand, brushed ants off her mayonnaise and squashed wasps with a chivalrous teaspoon. The end was inevitable. Apart from anything else, the moon was at its full and many of these picnics were held at night. And you know what that means. It was about ten days later that William Bates came to me in my little garden with an expression on his face like a man who didn't know it was loaded.

"I say," said William, "you busy?"

I emptied the remainder of the water-can on the lobelias, and was at his disposal.

"I say," said William, "rather a rotten thing has happened. You know Jane?"

I said I knew Jane.

"You know Spelvin?"

I said I knew Spelvin.

"Well, Jane's gone and got engaged to him," said William, aggrieved.

"What?"

"It's a fact."

"Already?"

"Absolutely. She told me this morning. And what I want to know," said the stricken boy, sitting down thoroughly unnerved on a basket of strawberries, "is, where do I get off?"

My heart bled for him, but I could not help reminding him that I had anticipated this.

"You should not have left them so much alone together," I said. "You must have known that there is nothing more conducive to love than the moon in June. Why, songs have been written about it. In fact, I cannot at the moment recall a song that has not been written about it."

"Yes, but how was I to guess that anything like this would happen?" cried William, rising and scraping strawberries off his person. "Who would ever have supposed Jane Packard would leap off the dock with a fellow who doesn't play golf?"

"Certainly, as you say, it seems almost incredible. You are sure you heard her correctly? When she told you about the engagement, I mean. There was no chance that you could have misunderstood?"

"Not a bit of it. As a matter of fact, what led up to the thing, if you know what I mean, was me proposing to her myself. I'd been thinking a lot during the last ten days over what you said to me about that, and the more I thought of it the more of a sound egg the notion seemed. So I got her alone up at the club-house and said, 'I say, old girl, what about it?' and she said, 'What about what?' and I said, 'What about marrying me? Don't if you don't want to, of course,' I said, 'but I'm bound to say it looks pretty good to me.' And then she said she loved another—this bloke Spelvin, to wit. A nasty jar, I can tell you, it was. I was just starting off on a round, and it made me hook my putts on every green."

"But did she say specifically that she was engaged to Spelvin?"

"She said she loved him."

"There may be hope. If she is not irrevocably engaged the fancy may pass. I think I will go and see Jane and make tactful inquiries."

"I wish you would," said William. "And, I say, you haven't any stuff that'll take strawberry-juice off a fellow's trousers, have you?"

My interview with Jane that evening served only to confirm the bad news. Yes, she was definitely engaged to the man Spelvin. In a burst of girlish confidence she told me some of the details of the affair.

"The moon was shining and a soft breeze played in the trees," she said. "And suddenly he took me in his arms, gazed deep into my eyes, and cried, 'I love you! I worship you! I adore you! You are the tree on which the fruit of my life hangs; my mate; my woman; predestined to me since the first star shone up in yonder sky!'"

"Nothing," I agreed, "could be fairer than that. And then?" I said, thinking how different it all must have been from William Bates's miserable, limping proposal.

"Then we fixed it up that we would get married in September."

"You are sure you are doing wisely?" I ventured.

Her eyes opened.

"Why do you say that?"

"Well, you know, whatever his other merits—and no doubt they are numerous—Rodney Spelvin does *not* play golf."

"No, but he's very broad-minded about it."

I shuddered. Women say these things so lightly.

"Broad-minded?"

"Yes. He has no objection to my going on playing. He says he likes my pretty enthusiasms."

There seemed nothing more to say on that subject.

"Well," I said, "I am sure I wish you every happiness. I had hoped, of course—

but never mind that."

"What?"

"I had hoped, as you insist on my saying it, that you and William Bates——"

A shadow passed over her face. Her eyes grew sad.

"Poor William! I'm awfully sorry about that. He's a dear."

"A splendid fellow," I agreed.

"He has been so wonderful about the whole thing. So many men would have gone off and shot grizzly bears or something. But William just said 'Right-o!' in a quiet voice, and he's going to caddie for me at Mossy Heath next week."

"There is good stuff in the boy."

"Yes." She sighed. "If it wasn't for Rodney—— Oh, well!"

I thought it would be tactful to change the subject.

"So you have decided to go to Mossy Heath again?"

"Yes. And I'm really going to qualify this year."

The annual Invitation Tournament at Mossy Heath was one of the most important fixtures of our local female golfing year. As is usual with these affairs, it began with a medal-play qualifying round, the thirty-two players with the lowest net scores then proceeding to fight it out during the remainder of the week by match-play. It gratified me to hear Jane speak so confidently of her chances, for this was the fourth year she had entered, and each time, though she had started out with the brightest prospects, she had failed to survive the qualifying round. Like so many golfers, she was fifty per cent. better at match-play than at medal-play. Mossy Heath, being a championship course, is full of nasty pitfalls, and on each of the three occasions on which she had tackled it one very bad hole had undone all her steady work on the other seventeen and ruined her card. I was delighted to find her so undismayed by failure.

"I am sure you will," I said. "Just play your usual careful game."

"It doesn't matter what sort of a game I play this time," said Jane, jubilantly. "I've just heard that there are only thirty-two entries this year, so that everybody who finishes is bound to qualify. I have simply got to get round somehow, and there I am."

"It would seem somewhat superfluous in these circumstances to play a qualifying round at all."

"Oh, but they must. You see, there are prizes for the best three scores, so they have to play it. But isn't it a relief to know that, even if I come to grief on that beastly seventh, as I did last year, I shall still be all right?"

"It is, indeed. I have a feeling that once it becomes a matter of match-play you will be irresistible."

"I do hope so. It would be lovely to win with Rodney looking on."

"Will he be looking on?"

"Yes. He's going to walk round with me. Isn't it sweet of him?"

Her *fiancé's* name having slid into the conversation again, she seemed inclined to become eloquent about him. I left her, however, before she could begin. To one so strongly pro-William as myself, eulogistic prattle about Rodney Spelvin was repugnant. I disapproved entirely of this infatuation of hers. I am not a narrow-minded man; I quite appreciate the fact that non-golfers are entitled to marry; but I could not countenance their marrying potential winners of the Ladies' Invitation Tournament at Mossy Heath.

The Greens Committee, as greens committees are so apt to do in order to justify their existence, have altered the Mossy Heath course considerably since the time of which I am speaking, but they have left the three most poisonous holes untouched. I refer to the fourth, the seventh, and the fifteenth. Even a soulless Greens Committee seems to have realized that golfers, long-suffering though they are, can be pushed too far, and that the addition of even a single extra bunker to any of these dreadful places would probably lead to armed riots in the club-house.

Jane Packard had done well on the first three holes, but as she stood on the fourth tee she was conscious, despite the fact that this seemed to be one of her good days, of a certain nervousness; and oddly enough, great as was her love for Rodney Spelvin, it was not his presence that gave her courage, but the sight of William Bates's large, friendly face and the sound of his pleasant voice urging her to keep her bean down and refrain from pressing.

As a matter of fact, to be perfectly truthful, there was beginning already to germinate within her by this time a faint but definite regret that Rodney Spelvin had decided to accompany her on this qualifying round. It was sweet of him to bother to come, no doubt, but still there was something about Rodney that did not seem to blend with the holy atmosphere of a championship course. He was the one romance of her life and their souls were bound together for all eternity, but the fact remained that he did not appear to be able to keep still while she was making her shots, and his light humming, musical though it was, militated against accuracy on the green. He was humming now as she addressed her ball, and for an instant a spasm of irritation shot through her. She fought it down bravely and concentrated on her drive, and when the ball soared over the cross-bunker she forgot her annoyance. There is nothing so mellowing, so conducive to sweet and genial thoughts, as a real juicy one straight down the middle, and this was a pipterino.

"Nice work," said William Bates, approvingly.

Jane gave him a grateful smile and turned to Rodney. It was his appreciation that she wanted. He was not a golfer, but even he must be able to see that her drive had been something out of the common.

Rodney Spelvin was standing with his back turned, gazing out over the rolling prospect, one hand shading his eyes.

"That vista there," said Rodney. "That calm, wooded hollow, bathed in the golden sunshine. It reminds me of the island-valley of Avilion——"

"Did you see my drive, Rodney?"

"——where falls not hail, or rain, or any snow, Nor ever wind blows loudly. Eh? Your drive? No, I didn't."

Again Jane Packard was aware of that faint, wistful regret. But this was swept away a few moments later in the ecstasy of a perfect iron-shot which plunked her ball nicely on to the green. The last time she had played this hole she had taken seven, for all round the plateau green are sinister sand-bunkers, each beckoning the ball into its hideous depths; and now she was on in two and life was very sweet. Putting was her strong point, so that there was no reason why she should not get a snappy four on one of the nastiest holes on the course. She glowed with a strange emotion as she took her putter, and as she bent over her ball the air seemed filled with soft music.

It was only when she started to concentrate on the line of her putt that this soft music began to bother her. Then, listening, she became aware that it proceeded from Rodney Spelvin. He was standing immediately behind her, humming an old French love-song. It was the sort of old French love-song to which she could have listened for hours in some scented garden under the young May moon, but on the green of the fourth at Mossy Heath it got right in amongst her nerve-centres.

"Rodney, *please*!"

"Eh?"

Jane found herself wishing that Rodney Spelvin would not say "Eh?" whenever she spoke to him.

"Do you mind not humming?" said Jane. "I want to putt."

"Putt on, child, putt on," said Rodney Spelvin, indulgently. "I don't know what you mean, but, if it makes you happy to putt, putt to your heart's content."

Jane bent over her ball again. She had got the line now. She brought back her putter with infinite care.

"My God!" exclaimed Rodney Spelvin, going off like a bomb.

Jane's ball, sharply jabbed, shot past the hole and rolled on about three yards. She spun round in anguish. Rodney Spelvin was pointing at the horizon.

"*What* a bit of colour!" he cried. "Did you ever see such a bit of colour?"

"Oh, Rodney!" moaned Jane.

"Eh?"

Jane gulped and walked to her ball. Her fourth putt trickled into the hole.

"Did you win?" said Rodney Spelvin, amiably.

Jane walked to the fifth tee in silence.

The fifth and sixth holes at Mossy Heath are long, but they offer little trouble to those who are able to keep straight. It is as if the architect of the course had relaxed over these two in order to ensure that his malignant mind should be at its freshest and keenest when he came to design the pestilential seventh. This seventh, as you may remember, is the hole at which Sandy McHoots, then Open Champion, took an eleven on an important occasion. It is a short hole, and a full mashie will take you nicely on to the green, provided you can carry the river that frolics just beyond the tee and seems to plead with you to throw it a ball to play with. Once on the green, however, the problem is to stay there. The green itself is about the size of a drawing-room carpet, and in the summer, when the ground is hard, a ball that has not the maximum of back-spin is apt to touch lightly and bound off into the river beyond; for this is an island green, where the stream bends like a serpent. I refresh your memory with these facts in order that you may appreciate to the full what Jane Packard was up against.

The woman with whom Jane was partnered had the honour, and drove a nice high ball which fell into one of the bunkers to the left. She was a silent, patient-looking woman, and she seemed to regard this as perfectly satisfactory. She withdrew from the tee and made way for Jane.

"Nice work!" said William Bates, a moment later. For Jane's ball, soaring in a perfect arc, was dropping, it seemed on the very pin.

"Oh, Rodney, look!" cried Jane.

"Eh?" said Rodney Spelvin.

His remark was drowned in a passionate squeal of agony from his betrothed. The most poignant of all tragedies had occurred. The ball, touching the green, leaped like a young lamb, scuttled past the pin, and took a running dive over the cliff.

There was a silence. Jane's partner, who was seated on the bench by the sand-box reading a pocket edition in limp leather of Vardon's *What Every Young Golfer Should Know,* with which she had been refreshing herself at odd moments all through the round, had not observed the incident. William Bates, with the tact of a true golfer, refrained from comment. Jane was herself swallowing painfully. It was left to Rodney Spelvin to break the silence.

"Good!" he said.

Jane Packard turned like a stepped-on worm.

"What do you mean, good?"

"You hit your ball farther than she did."

"I sent it into the river," said Jane, in a low, toneless voice.

"Capital!" said Rodney Spelvin, delicately masking a yawn with two fingers of his shapely right hand. "Capital! Capital!"

Her face contorted with pain, Jane put down another ball.

"Playing three," she said.

The student of Vardon marked the place in her book with her thumb, looked up, nodded, and resumed her reading.

"Nice w——" began William Bates, as the ball soared off the tee, and checked himself abruptly. Already he could see that the unfortunate girl had put too little beef into it. The ball was falling, falling. It fell. A crystal fountain flashed up towards the sun. The ball lay floating on the bosom of the stream, only some few feet short of the island. But, as has been well pointed out, that little less and how far away!

"Playing five!" said Jane, between her teeth.

"What," inquired Rodney Spelvin, chattily, lighting a cigarette, "is the record break?"

"Playing *five*," said Jane, with a dreadful calm, and gripped her mashie.

"Half a second," said William Bates, suddenly. "I say, I believe you could play that last one from where it floats. A good crisp slosh with a niblick would put you on, and you'd be there in four, with a chance for a five. Worth trying, what? I mean, no sense in dropping strokes unless you have to."

Jane's eyes were gleaming. She threw William a look of infinite gratitude.

"Why, I believe I could!"

"Worth having a dash."

"There's a boat down there!"

"I could row," said William.

"I could stand in the middle and slosh," cried Jane.

"And what's-his-name—*that*," said William, jerking his head in the direction of Rodney Spelvin, who was strolling up and down behind the tee, humming a gay Venetian barcarolle, "could steer."

"William," said Jane, fervently, "you're a darling."

"Oh, I don't know," said William, modestly.

"There's no one like you in the world. Rodney!"

"Eh?" said Rodney Spelvin.

"We're going out in that boat. I want you to steer."

Rodney Spelvin's face showed appreciation of the change of programme. Golf bored him, but what could be nicer than a gentle row in a boat.

"Capital!" he said. "Capital! Capital!"

There was a dreamy look in Rodney Spelvin's eyes as he leaned back with the tiller-ropes in his hands. This was just his idea of the proper way of passing a summer afternoon. Drifting lazily over the silver surface of the stream. His eyes closed. He began to murmur softly:

> " All today the slow sleek ripples hardly bear up shoreward,
> Charged with sighs more light than laughter, faint and fair,
> Like a woodland lake's weak wavelets lightly lingering forward,
> Soft and listless as the—— Here! Hi!"

For at this moment the silver surface of the stream was violently split by a vigorously-wielded niblick, the boat lurched drunkenly, and over his Panama-hatted head and down his grey-flannelled torso there descended a cascade of water.

"Here! Hi!" cried Rodney Spelvin.

He cleared his eyes and gazed reproachfully. Jane and William Bates were peering into the depths.

"I missed it," said Jane.

"There she spouts!" said William pointing. "Ready?"

Jane raised her niblick.

"Here! Hi!" bleated Rodney Spelvin, as a second cascade poured damply over him.

He shook the drops off his face, and perceived that Jane was regarding him with hostility.

"I do wish you wouldn't talk just as I am swinging," she said, pettishly. "Now you've made me miss it again! If you can't keep quiet, I wish you wouldn't insist on coming round with one. Can you see it, William?"

"There she blows," said William Bates.

"Here! You aren't going to do it *again,* are you?" cried Rodney Spelvin.

Jane bared her teeth.

"I'm going to get that ball on to the green if I have to stay here all night," she said.

Rodney Spelvin looked at her and shuddered. Was this the quiet, dreamy girl he had loved? This Mænad? Her hair was lying in damp wisps about her face, her eyes were shining with an unearthly light.

"No, but really——" he faltered.

Jane stamped her foot.

"What *are* you making all this fuss about, Rodney?" she snapped. "Where is it, William?"

"There she dips," said William. "Playing six."

"Playing six."

"Let her go," said William.

"Let her go it is!" said Jane.

A perfect understanding seemed to prevail between these two.

Splash!

The woman on the bank looked up from her Vardon as Rodney Spelvin's agonized scream rent the air. She saw a boat upon the water, a man rowing the boat, another man, hatless, gesticulating in the stern, a girl beating the water with a niblick. She nodded placidly and understandingly. A niblick was the club she would have used herself in such circumstances. Everything appeared to her entirely regular and orthodox. She resumed her book.

Splash!

"Playing fifteen," said Jane.

"Fifteen is right," said William Bates.

Splash! Splash! Splash!

"Playing forty-four."

"Forty-four is correct."

Splash! Splash! Splash! Splash!

"Eighty-three?" said Jane, brushing the hair out of her eyes.

"No. Only eighty-two," said William Bates.

"Where is it?"

"There she drifts."

A dripping figure rose violently in the stern of the boat, spouting water like a public fountain. For what seemed to him like an eternity Rodney Spelvin had ducked and spluttered and writhed, and now it came to him abruptly that he was through. He bounded from his seat, and at the same time Jane swung with all the force of her supple body. There was a splash beside which all the other splashes had been as nothing. The boat overturned and went drifting away. Three bodies plunged into the stream. Three heads emerged from the water.

The woman on the bank looked absently in their direction. Then she resumed her book.

"It's all right," said William Bates, contentedly. "We're in our depth."

"My bag!" cried Jane. "My bag of clubs!"

"Must have sunk," said William.

"Rodney," said Jane, "my bag of clubs is at the bottom somewhere. Dive under and swim about and try to find it."

"It's bound to be around somewhere," said William Bates encouragingly.

Rodney Spelvin drew himself up to his full height. It was not an easy thing to do, for it was muddy where he stood, but he did it.

"Damn your bag of clubs!" he bellowed, lost to all shame. "I'm going home!"

With painful steps, tripping from time to time and vanishing beneath the surface, he sloshed to the shore. For a moment he paused on the bank, silhouetted against the summer sky, then he was gone.

Jane Packard and William Bates watched him go with amazed eyes.

"I never would have dreamed," said Jane, dazedly, "that he was that sort of man."

"A bad lot," said William Bates.

"The sort of man to be upset by the merest trifle!"

"Must have a naturally bad disposition," said William Bates.

"Why, if a little thing like this could make him so rude and brutal and horrid, it wouldn't be *safe* to marry him!"

"Taking a big chance," agreed William Bates. "Sort of fellow who would water the cat's milk and kick the baby in the face." He took a deep breath and disappeared. "Here are your clubs, old girl," he said, coming to the surface again. "Only wanted a bit of looking for."

"Oh, William," said Jane, "you are the most wonderful man on earth!"

"Would you go as far as that?" said William.

"I was mad, mad, ever to get engaged to that brute!"

"Now there," said William Bates, removing an eel from his left breast-pocket, "I'm absolutely with you. Thought so all along, but didn't like to say so. What I mean is, a girl like you—keen on golf and all that sort of thing—ought to marry a chap like me—keen on golf and everything of that description."

"William," cried Jane, passionately, detaching a newt from her right ear, "I will!"

"Silly nonsense, when you come right down to it, your marrying a fellow who doesn't play golf. Nothing in it."

"I'll break off the engagement the moment I get home."

"You couldn't make a sounder move, old girl."

"William!"

"Jane!"

The woman on the bank, glancing up as she turned a page, saw a man and a girl embracing, up to their waists in water. It seemed to have nothing to do with her. She resumed her book.

Jane looked lovingly into William's eyes.

"William," she said, "I think I have loved you all my life."

"Jane," said William, "I'm dashed sure I've loved *you* all *my* life. Meant to tell you so a dozen times, but something always seemed to come up."

"William," said Jane, "you're an angel and a darling. Where's the ball?"

"There she pops."

"Playing eighty-four?"

"Eighty-four it is," said William. "Slow back, keep your eye on the ball, and don't press."

The woman on the bank began Chapter Twenty-five.

19

JANE GETS OFF THE FAIRWAY

THE side-door leading into the smoking-room opened, and the golf-club's popular and energetic secretary came trotting down the steps on to the terrace above the ninth green. As he reached the gravel, a wandering puff of wind blew the door to with a sharp report, and the Oldest Member, who had been dozing in a chair over his *Wodehouse on the Niblick*, unclosed his eyes, blinking in the strong light. He perceived the secretary skimming to and fro like a questing dog.

"You have lost something?" he inquired, courteously.

"Yes, a book. I wish," said the secretary, annoyed, "that people would leave things alone. You haven't seen a novel called *The Man with the Missing Eyeball* anywhere about, have you? I'll swear I left it on one of these seats when I went in to lunch."

"You are better without it," said the Sage, with a touch of asperity. "I do not approve of these trashy works of fiction. How much more profitably would your time be spent in mastering the contents of such a volume as I hold in my hand. This is the real literature."

The secretary drew nearer, peering discontentedly about him; and as he approached the Oldest Member sniffed inquiringly.

"What," he said, "is that odour of——? Ah, I see that you are wearing them in your buttonhole. White violets," he murmured. "White violets. Dear me!"

The secretary smirked.

"A girl gave them to me," he said, coyly. "Nice, aren't they?" He squinted down complacently at the flowers, thus missing a sudden sinister gleam in the Oldest Member's eye—a gleam which, had he been on his guard, would have sent him scudding over the horizon, for it was the gleam which told that the Sage had been reminded of a story.

"White violets," said the Oldest Member, in a meditative voice. "A curious coincidence that you should be wearing white violets and looking for a work of fiction. The combination brings irresistibly to my mind——"

Realizing his peril too late, the secretary started violently. A gentle hand urged him into the adjoining chair.

"——the story," proceeded the Oldest Member, "of William Bates, Jane Packard, and Rodney Spelvin."

The secretary drew a deep breath of relief and the careworn look left his face.

"It's all right," he said, briskly. "You told me that one only the other day. I remember every word of it. Jane Packard got engaged to Rodney Spelvin, the poet, but her better feelings prevailed in time, and she broke it off and married Bates, who was a golfer. I recall the whole thing distinctly. This man Bates was an unromantic sort of chap, but he loved Jane Packard devotedly. Bless my soul, how it all comes back to me! No need to tell it me at all."

"What I am about to relate now," said the Sage, tightening his grip on the other's coat-sleeve, "is another story about William Bates, Jane Packard, and Rodney Spelvin."

Inasmuch (said the Oldest Member) as you have not forgotten the events leading up to the marriage of William Bates and Jane Packard, I will not repeat them. All I need say is that that curious spasm of romantic sentiment which had caused Jane to fall temporarily under the spell of a man who was not only a poet but actually a non-golfer appeared to have passed completely away, leaving no trace behind. From the day she broke off her engagement to Spelvin and plighted her troth to young Bates, nothing could have been more eminently sane and satisfactory than her behaviour. She seemed entirely her old self once more. Two hours after William had led her down the aisle, she and he were out on the links, playing off the final of the Mixed Foursomes, which—and we all thought it the best of omens for their married happiness—they won hands down. A deputation of all that was best and fairest in the village then escorted them to the station to see them off on their honeymoon, which was to be spent in a series of visits to well-known courses throughout the country.

Before the train left, I took young William aside for a moment. I had known both him and Jane since childhood, and the success of their union was very near my heart.

"William," I said, "a word with you."

"Make it snappy," said William.

"You have learned by this time," I said, "that there is a strong romantic streak in Jane. It may not appear on the surface, but it is there. And this romantic streak will cause her, like so many wives, to attach an exaggerated importance to what may seem to you trivial things. She will expect from her husband not only love and a constant tender solicitude——"

"Speed it up," urged William.

"What I am trying to say is that, after the habit of wives, she will expect you to remember each year the anniversary of your wedding day, and will be madder than a wet hen if you forget it."

"That's all right. I thought of that myself."

"It is not all right," I insisted. "Unless you take the most earnest precautions, you are absolutely certain to forget. A year from now you will come down to breakfast, and Jane will say to you, 'Do you know what day it is today?' and you will answer 'Tuesday' and reach for the ham and eggs, thus inflicting on her gentle heart a wound from which it will not readily recover."

"Nothing like it," said William, with extraordinary confidence. "I've got a system calculated to beat the game every time. You know how fond Jane is of white violets?"

"Is she?"

"She loves 'em. The bloke Spelvin used to give her a bunch every day. That's how I got the idea. Nothing like learning the shots from your opponent. I've arranged with a florist that a bunch of white violets is to be shipped to Jane every year on this day. I paid five years in advance. I am, therefore, speaking in the most conservative spirit, on velvet. Even if I forget the day, the violets will be there to remind me. I've looked at it from every angle, and I don't see how it can fail. Tell me frankly, is the scheme a wam or is it not?"

"A most excellent plan," I said, relieved. And the next moment the train came in. I left the station with my mind at rest. It seemed to me that the only possible obstacle to the complete felicity of the young couple had been removed.

Jane and William returned in due season from their honeymoon, and settled down to the normal life of a healthy young couple. Each day they did their round in the morning and their two rounds in the afternoon, and after dinner they would sit hand in hand in the peaceful dusk, reminding one another of the best shots they had brought off at the various holes. Jane would describe to William how she got out of the bunker on the fifth, and William would describe to Jane the low raking wind-cheater he did on the seventh, and then for a moment they would fall into that blissful silence which only true lovers know, until William, illustrating his remarks with a walking-stick, would show Jane how he did that pin-splitter with the mashie on the sixteenth. An ideally happy union, one would have said.

But all the while a little cloud was gathering. As the anniversary of their wedding day approached, a fear began to creep into Jane's heart that William was going to forget it. The perfect husband does not wait till the dawning of the actual day to introduce the anniversary *motif* into his conversation. As long as a week in advance he is apt to say, dreamily, "About this time a year ago I was getting the old silk hat polished up for the wedding," or "Just about now, a year ago, they sent home the sponge-bag trousers, as worn, and I tried them on in front of the looking-glass." But William said none of these things. Not even on the night before the all-important date did he make any allusion to it, and it was with a dull feeling of foreboding that Jane came down to breakfast next morning.

She was first at the table, and was pouring out the coffee when William entered. He opened the morning paper and started to peruse its contents in silence. Not a yip did he let out of him to the effect that this was the maddest, merriest day of all the glad new year.

"William," said Jane.

"Hullo?"

"William," said Jane, and her voice trembled a little, "what day is it today?"

William looked at her over the paper, surprised.

"Wednesday, old girl," he replied. "Don't you remember that yesterday was Tuesday? Shocking memory you've got."

He then reached out for the sausages and bacon and resumed his reading.

"Jane," he said, suddenly. "Jane, old girl, there's something I want to tell you."

"Yes?" said Jane, her heart beginning to flutter.

"Something important."

"Yes?"

"It's about these sausages. They are the very best," said William, earnestly, "that I have ever bitten. Where did you get them?"

"From Brownlow."

"Stick to him," said William.

Jane rose from the table and wandered out into the garden. The sun shone gaily, but for her the day was bleak and cold. That William loved her she did not doubt. But that streak of romance in her demanded something more than mere placid love. And when she realized that the poor mutt with whom she had linked her lot had forgotten the anniversary of their wedding day first crack out of the box, her woman's heart was so wounded that for two pins she could have beaned him with a brick.

It was while she was still brooding in this hostile fashion that she perceived the postman coming up the garden. She went to meet him, and was handed a couple of circulars and a mysterious parcel. She broke the string, and behold! a cardboard box containing white violets.

Jane was surprised. Who could be sending her white violets? No message accompanied them. There was no clue whatever to their origin. Even the name of the florist had been omitted.

"Now, who——?" mused Jane, and suddenly started as if she had received a blow. Rodney Spelvin! Yes, it must be he. How many a bunch of white violets had he given her in the brief course of their engagement! This was his poetic way of showing her that he had not forgotten. All was over between them, she had handed him his hat and given him the air, but he still remembered.

Jane was a good and dutiful wife. She loved her William, and no others need apply. Nevertheless, she was a woman. She looked about her cautiously. There was nobody in sight. She streaked up to her room and put the violets in water. And that night, before she went to bed, she gazed at them for several minutes with eyes that were a little moist. Poor Rodney! He could be nothing to her now, of course, but a dear lost friend; but he had been a good old scout in his day.

.   .   .   .   .

It is not my purpose to weary you with repetitious detail in this narrative. I will, therefore, merely state that the next year and the next year and the year after that precisely the same thing took place in the Bateses' home. Punctually every September the seventh William placidly forgot, and punctually every September the seventh the sender of the violets remembered. It was about a month after the fifth anniversary, when William had got his handicap down to nine and little Braid Vardon Bates, their only child, had celebrated his fourth birthday, that Rodney Spelvin, who had hitherto confined himself to poetry, broke out in a new place and inflicted upon the citizenry a novel entitled *The Purple Fan*.

I saw the announcement of the publication in the papers; but beyond a passing resolve that nothing would induce me to read the thing I thought no more of the matter. It is always thus with life's really significant happenings. Fate sneaks its deadliest wallops in on us with such seeming nonchalance. How could I guess what that book was to do to the married happiness of Jane and William Bates?

In deciding not to read *The Purple Fan* I had, I was to discover, over-estimated my powers of resistance. Rodney Spelvin's novel turned out to be one of those things which it is impossible not to read. Within a week of its appearance it had begun to go through the country like Spanish influenza; and, much as I desired to avoid it, a perusal was forced on me by sheer weight of mass-thinking. Every paper that I picked up contained reviews of the book, references to it, letters from the clergy denouncing it; and when I read that three hundred and sixteen mothers had signed a petition to the authorities to have it suppressed, I was reluctantly compelled to spring the necessary cash and purchase a copy.

I had not expected to enjoy it, and I did not. Written in the neodecadent style, which is so popular nowadays, its preciosity offended me; and I particularly objected to its heroine, a young woman of a type which, if met in real life, only ingrained chivalry could have prevented a normal man from kicking extremely hard. Having skimmed through it, I gave my copy to the man who came to inspect the drains. If I had any feeling about the thing, it was a reflection that, if Rodney Spelvin had had to get a novel out of his system, this was just the sort of novel he was bound to write. I remember experiencing a thankfulness that he had gone so entirely out of Jane's life. How little I knew!

Jane, like every other woman in the village, had bought her copy of *The Purple Fan*. She read it surreptitiously, keeping it concealed, when not in use, beneath a cushion on the Chesterfield. It was not its general tone that caused her to do this, but rather the subconscious feeling that she, a good wife, ought not to be deriving quite so much enjoyment from the work of a man who had occupied for a time such a romantic place in her life.

For Jane, unlike myself, adored the book. Eulalie French, its heroine, whose appeal I had so missed, seemed to her the most fascinating creature she had ever encountered.

She had read the thing through six times when, going up to town one day to do some shopping, she ran into Rodney Spelvin. They found themselves standing side by side on the pavement, waiting for the traffic to pass.

"Rodney!" gasped Jane.

It was a difficult moment for Rodney Spelvin. Five years had passed since he had last seen Jane, and in those five years so many delightful creatures had made a fuss of him that the memory of the girl to whom he had once been engaged for a few weeks had become a little blurred. In fact, not to put too fine a point on it, he had forgotten Jane altogether. The fact that she had addressed him by his first name seemed to argue that they must have met at some time somewhere; but, though he strained his brain, absolutely nothing stirred.

The situation was one that might have embarrassed another man, but Rodney Spelvin was a quick thinker. He saw at a glance that Jane was an extremely pretty girl, and it was his guiding rule in life never to let anything like that get past him. So he clasped her hand warmly, allowed an expression of amazed delight to sweep over his face, and gazed tensely into her eyes.

"You!" he murmured, playing it safe. "You, little one!"

Jane stood five feet seven in her stockings and had a forearm like the village blacksmith's, but she liked being called "little one".

"How strange that we should meet like this!" she said, blushing brightly.

"After all these years," said Rodney Spelvin, taking a chance. It would be a nuisance if it turned out that they had met at a studio-party the day before yesterday, but something seemed to tell him that she dated back a goodish way. Besides, even if they had met the day before yesterday, he could get out of it by saying that the hours had seemed like years. For you cannot stymie these modern poets. The boys are there.

"More than five," murmured Jane.

"Now where the deuce was I five years ago?" Rodney Spelvin asked himself.

Jane looked down at the pavement and shuffled her left shoe nervously.

"I got the violets, Rodney," she said.

Rodney Spelvin was considerably fogged, but he came back strongly.

"That's good!" he said. "You got the violets? That's capital. I was wondering if you would get the violets."

"It was like you to send them."

Rodney blinked, but recovered himself immediately. He waved his hand with a careless gesture, indicative of restrained nobility.

"Oh, as to that——!"

"Especially as I'm afraid I treated you rather badly. But it really was for the happiness of both of us that I broke off the engagement. You do understand that, don't you?"

A light broke upon Rodney Spelvin. He had been confident that it would if he only stalled along for a while. Now he placed this girl. She was Jane something, the girl he had been engaged to. By Jove, yes. He knew where he was now.

"Do not let us speak of it," he said, registering pain. It was quite easy for him to do this. All there was to it was tightening the lips and drawing up the left eyebrow. He had practised it in front of his mirror, for a fellow never knew when it might not come in useful.

"So you didn't forget me, Rodney?"

"Forget you!"

There was a short pause.

"I read your novel," said Jane. "I loved it."

She blushed again, and the colour in her cheeks made her look so remarkably pretty that Rodney began to feel some of the emotions which had stirred him five years ago. He decided that this was a good thing and wanted pushing along.

"I hoped that you might," he said in a low voice, massaging her hand. He broke off and directed into her eyes a look of such squashy sentimentality that Jane reeled where she stood. "I wrote it for you," he added, simply.

Jane gasped.

"For me?"

"I supposed you would have guessed," said Rodney. "Surely you saw the dedication?"

The Purple Fan had been dedicated, after Rodney Spelvin's eminently prudent fashion, to "One Who Will Understand". He had frequently been grateful for the happy inspiration.

"The dedication?"

" 'To One Who Will Understand'," said Rodney, softly. "Who would that be but you?"

"Oh, Rodney!"

"And didn't you recognize Eulalie, Jane? Surely you cannot have failed to recognize Eulalie?"

"Recognize her?"

"I drew her from you," said Rodney Spelvin.

Jane's mind was in a whirl as she went home in the train. To have met Rodney Spelvin again was enough in itself to stimulate into activity that hidden pulse of romance in her. To discover that she had been in his thoughts so continuously all these years and that she still held such sway over his faithful heart that he had drawn the heroine of his novel from her was simply devastating. Mechanically she got out at the right station and mechanically made her way to the cottage. She was relieved to find that William was still out on the links. She loved William devotedly, of course, but just at that moment he would have been in the way; for she wanted a quiet hour with *The Purple Fan*. It was necessary for her to re-read in the light of this new knowledge the more important of the scenes in which Eulalie French figured. She knew them practically by heart already, but nevertheless she wished to read them again. When William returned, warm and jubilant, she was so absorbed that she only just had time to slide the book under the sofa cushion before the door opened.

Some guardian angel ought to have warned William Bates that he was selecting a bad moment for his re-entry into the home, or at least to have hinted that a preliminary wash and brush-up would be no bad thing. There had been rain in the night, causing the links to become a trifle soggy in spots, and William was one of those energetic golfers who do not spare themselves. The result was that his pleasant features were a good deal obscured by mud. An explosion-shot out of the bunker on the fourteenth had filled his hair with damp sand, and his shoes were a disgrace to any refined home. No, take him for all in all, William did not look his best. He was fine if the sort of man you admired was the brawny athlete straight from the dust of the arena; but on a woman who was picturing herself the heroine of *The Purple Fan* he was bound to jar. Most of the scenes in which Eulalie French played anything like a fat part took place either on moonlit terraces or in beautifully furnished studios beneath the light of Oriental lamps with pink silk shades, and all the men who came in contact with her—except her husband, a clodhopping brute who spent most of his time in riding-kit—were perfectly dressed and had dark, clean-cut, sensitive faces.

William, accordingly, induced in Jane something closely approximating to the heeby-jeebies.

"Hullo, old girl!" said William, affectionately. "You back? What have you been doing with yourself?"

"Oh, shopping," said Jane, listlessly.

"See anyone you know?"

For a moment Jane hesitated.

"Yes," she said. "I met Rodney Spelvin."

Jealousy and suspicion had been left entirely out of William Bates's make-up. He did not start and frown; he did not clutch the arm of his chair; he merely threw back his head and laughed like a hyæna. And that laugh wounded Jane more than the most violent exhibition of mistrust could have done.

"Good Lord!" gurgled William, jovially. "You don't mean to say that bird is still going around loose? I should have thought he would have been lynched years ago. Looks like negligence somewhere."

There comes a moment in married life when every wife gazes squarely at her husband and the scales seem to fall from her eyes and she sees him as he is—one of Nature's Class A fatheads. Fortunately for married men, these times of clear vision do not last long, or there would be few homes left unbroken. It was so that Jane gazed at William now, but unhappily her conviction that he was an out-size in rough-neck chumps did not pass. Indeed, all through that evening it deepened. That night she went to bed feeling for the first time that, when the clergyman had said, "Wilt thou, Jane?" and she had replied in the affirmative, a mean trick had been played on an inexperienced girl.

And so began that black period in the married life of Jane and William Bates, the mere recollection of which in after years was sufficient to put them right off their short game and even to affect their driving from the tee. To William, having no clue to the cause of the mysterious change in his wife, her behaviour was inexplicable. Had not her perfect robustness made such a theory absurd, he would have supposed that she was sickening for something. She golfed now intermittently and often with positive reluctance. She was frequently listless and distrait. And there were other things about her of which he disapproved.

"I say, old girl," he said one evening, "I know you won't mind my mentioning it, and I don't suppose you're aware of it yourself, but recently you've developed a sort of silvery laugh. A nasty thing to have about the home. Try to switch it off, old bird, would you mind?"

Jane said nothing. The man was not worth answering. All through the pages of *The Purple Fan*, Eulalie French's silvery laugh had been highly spoken of and greatly appreciated by one and all. It was the thing about her that the dark, clean-cut, sensitive-faced men most admired. And the view Jane took of the matter was that if William did not like it the poor fish could do the other thing.

But this brutal attack decided her to come out into the open with the grievance which had been vexing her soul for weeks past.

"William," she said, "I want to say something. William, I am feeling stifled."

"I'll open the window."

"Stifled in this beastly little village, I mean," said Jane, impatiently. "Nobody ever does anything here except play golf and bridge, and you never meet an artist-soul from one year's end to the other. How can I express myself? How can I be myself? How can I fulfil myself?"

"Do you want to?" asked William, somewhat out of his depth.

"Of course I want to. And I shan't be happy unless we leave this ghastly place and go to live in a studio in town."

William sucked thoughtfully at his pipe. It was a tense moment for a man who hated metropolitan life as much as he did. Nevertheless, if the solution of Jane's recent weirdness was simply that she had got tired of the country and wanted to live in town, to the town they must go. After a first involuntary recoil, he nerved himself to the martyrdom like the fine fellow he was.

"We'll pop off as soon as I can sell the house," he said.

"I can't wait as long as that. I want to go now."

"All right," said William, amiably. "We'll go next week."

William's forebodings were quickly fulfilled. Before he had been in the Metropolis ten days he realized that he was up against it as he had never been up against it before. He and Jane and little Braid Vardon had established themselves in what the house-agent described as an attractive bijou studio-apartment in the heart of the artistic quarter. There was a nice bedroom for Jane, a delightful cupboard for Braid Vardon, and a cosy corner behind a Japanese screen for William. Most compact. The rest of the place consisted of a room with a large skylight, handsomely furnished with cushions and samovars, where Jane gave parties to the intelligentsia.

It was these parties that afflicted William as much as anything else. He had not realized that Jane intended to run a *salon*. His idea of a pleasant social evening was to have a couple of old friends in for a rubber of bridge, and the almost nightly incursion of a horde of extraordinary birds in floppy ties stunned him. He was unequal to the situation from the first. While Jane sat enthroned on her cushion, exchanging gay badinage with rising young poets and laughing that silvery laugh of hers, William would have to stand squashed in a corner, trying to hold off some bobbed-haired female who wanted his opinion of Augustus John.

The strain was frightful, and, apart from the sheer discomfort of it, he found to his consternation that it was beginning to affect his golf. Whenever he struggled out from the artistic zone now to one of the suburban courses, his jangled nerves unfitted him for decent play. Bit by bit his game left him. First he found that he could not express himself with the putter. Then he began to fail to be himself with the mashie-niblick. And when at length he discovered that he was only fulfilling himself about every fifth shot off the tee he felt that this thing must stop.

The conscientious historian will always distinguish carefully between the events leading up to a war and the actual occurrence resulting in the outbreak of hostilities. The latter may be, and generally is, some almost trivial matter, whose only importance is that it fulfils the function of the last straw. In the case of Jane and William what caused the definite rift was Jane's refusal to tie a can to Rodney Spelvin.

The author of *The Purple Fan* had been from the first a leading figure in Jane's *salon*. Most of those who attended these functions were friends of his, introduced by him, and he had assumed almost from the beginning the demeanour of a master of the revels. William, squashed into his corner, had long gazed at the man with sullen dislike, yearning to gather him up by the slack of his trousers and heave him into outer darkness; but it is improbable that he would have overcome his native amiability sufficiently to make any active move, had it not been for the black mood caused by his rotten golf. But one evening, when, coming home after doing the Mossy Heath course in five strokes over the hundred, he found the studio congested with Rodney Spelvin and his friends, many of them playing ukeleles, he decided that flesh and blood could bear the strain no longer.

As soon as the last guest had gone he delivered his ultimatum.

"Listen, Jane," he said. "Touching on this Spelvin bloke."

"Well?" said Jane, coldly. She scented battle from afar.

"He gives me a pain in the neck."

"Really?" said Jane, and laughed a silvery laugh.

"Don't do it, old girl," pleaded William, wincing.

"I wish you wouldn't call me 'old girl'."

"Why not?"

"Because I don't like it."

"You used to like it."

"Well, I don't now."

"Oh!" said William, and ruminated a while. "Well, be that as it may," he went on, "I want to tell you just one thing. Either you throw the bloke Spelvin out on his left ear and send for the police if he tries to get in again, or I push off. I mean it! I absolutely push off."

There was a tense silence.

"Indeed?" said Jane at last.

"Positively push off," repeated William, firmly. "I can stand a lot, but pie-faced Spelvin tries human endurance too high."

"He is not pie-faced," said Jane, warmly.

"He *is* pie-faced," insisted William. "Come round to the Vienna Bon-Ton Bakery tomorrow and I will show you an individual custard-pie that might be his brother."

"Well, I am certainly not going to be bullied into giving up an old friend just because——"

William stared.

"You mean you won't hand him the mitten?"

"I will not."

"Think what you are saying, Jane. You positively decline to give this false-alarm the quick exit?"

"I do."

"Then," said William, "all is over. I pop off."

Jane stalked without a word into her bedroom. With a mist before his eyes William began to pack. After a few moments he tapped at her door.

"Jane."

"Well?"

"I'm packing."

"Indeed?"

"But I can't find my spare mashie."

"I don't care."

William returned to his packing. When it was finished, he stole to her door again. Already a faint stab of remorse was becoming blended with his just indignation.

"Jane."

"Well?"

"I've packed."

"Really?"

"And now I'm popping."

There was silence behind the door.

"I'm popping, Jane," said William. And in his voice, though he tried to make it cold and crisp, there was a note of wistfulness.

Through the door there came a sound. It was the sound of a silvery laugh. And as he heard it William's face hardened. Without another word he picked up his suit-case and golf-bag, and with set jaw strode out into the night.

One of the things that tend to keep the home together in these days of modern unrest is the fact that exalted moods of indignation do not last. William, released from the uncongenial atmosphere of the studio, proceeded at once to plunge into an orgy of golf that for a while precluded regret. Each day he indulged his starved soul with fifty-four holes, and each night he sat smoking in bed, pleasantly fatigued, reviewing the events of the past twelve hours with complete satisfaction. It seemed to him that he had done the good and sensible thing.

And then, slowly at first, but day by day more rapidly, his mood began to change. That delightful feeling of jolly freedom ebbed away.

It was on the morning of the tenth day that he first became definitely aware that all was not well. He had strolled out on the links after breakfast with a brassie and a dozen balls for a bit of practice, and, putting every ounce of weight and muscle into the stroke, brought off a snifter with his very first shot. Straight and true the ball sped for the distant green, and William, forgetting everything in the ecstasy of the moment, uttered a gladsome cry.

"How about that one, old girl?" he exclaimed.

And then, with a sudden sinking of the heart, he realized that he was alone.

An acute spasm of regret shot through William's massive bosom. In that instant of clear thinking he understood that golf is not all. What shall it profit a man that he do the long hole in four, if there is no loving wife at his elbow to squeak congratulations? A dull sensation of forlorn emptiness afflicted William Bates. It passed, but it had been. And he knew it would come again.

It did. It came that same afternoon. It came next morning. Gradually it settled like a cloud on his happiness. He did his best to fight it down. He increased his day's output to sixty-three holes, but found no relief. When he reflected that he had had the stupendous luck to be married to a girl like Jane and had chucked the thing up, he could have kicked himself round the house. He was in exactly the position of the hero of the movie when the sub-title is flashed on the screen: "Came a Day When Remorse Bit Like An Adder Into Roland Spenlow's Soul." Of all the chumps who had ever tripped over themselves and lost a good thing, from Adam downwards, he, he told himself, was the woollen-headedest.

On the fifteenth morning it began to rain.

Now, William Bates was not one of your fair-weather golfers. It took more than a shower to discourage him. But this was real rain, with which not even the stoutest enthusiast could cope. It poured down all day in a solid sheet and set the seal on his melancholy. He pottered about the house, sinking deeper and deeper into the slough of despond, and was trying to derive a little faint distraction from practising putts into a tooth-glass when the afternoon post arrived.

There was only one letter. He opened it listlessly. It was from Jukes, Enderby, and Miller, florists, and what the firm wished to ascertain was whether, his deposit on white violets to be dispatched to Mrs. William Bates being now exhausted, he desired to renew his esteemed order. If so, on receipt of the money they would spring to the task of sending same.

William stared at the letter dully. His first impression was that Jukes, Enderby, and Miller were talking through their collective hats. White violets? What was all this drivel about white violets? Jukes was an ass. He knew nothing about white violets. Enderby was a fool. What had he got to do with white violets? Miller was a pin-head. He had never deposited any money to have white violets dispatched.

William gasped. Yes, by George, he had, though, he remembered with a sudden start. So he had, by golly! Good gosh! it all came back to him. He recalled the whole thing, by Jove! Crikey, yes!

The letter swam before William's eyes. A wave of tenderness engulfed him. All that had passed recently between Jane and himself was forgotten—her weirdness, her wish to live in the Metropolis, her silvery laugh—everything. With one long, loving gulp, William Bates dashed a not unmanly tear from his eye and, grabbing a hat and raincoat, rushed out of the house and sprinted for the station.

At about the hour when William flung himself into the train, Jane was sitting in her studio-apartment, pensively watching little Braid Vardon as he sported on the floor. An odd melancholy had gripped her. At first she had supposed that this was due to the rain, but now she was beginning to realize that the thing went much deeper than that. Reluctant though she was to confess it, she had to admit that what she was suffering from was a genuine soul-sadness, due entirely to the fact that she wanted William.

It was strange what a difference his going had made. William was the sort of fellow you shoved into a corner and forgot about, but when he was not there the whole scheme of things seemed to go blooey. Little by little, since his departure, she had found the fascination of her surroundings tending to wane, and the glamour of her new friends had dwindled noticeably. Unless you were in the right vein for them, Jane felt, they could be an irritating crowd. They smoked too many cigarettes and talked too much. And not far from being the worst of them, she decided, was Rodney Spelvin. It was with a sudden feeling of despair that she remembered that she had invited him to tea this afternoon and had got in a special seed-cake for the occasion. The last thing in the world that she wanted to do was to watch Rodney Spelvin eating cake.

It is a curious thing about men of the Spelvin type, how seldom they really last. They get off to a flashy start and for a while convince impressionable girls that the search for a soul-mate may be considered formally over; but in a very short while reaction always sets in. There had been a time when Jane could have sat and listened to Rodney Spelvin for hours on end. Then she began to feel that from fifteen to twenty minutes was about sufficient. And now the mere thought of having to listen to him at all was crushing her like a heavy burden.

She had got thus far in her meditations when her attention was attracted to little Braid Vardon, who was playing energetically in a corner with some object which Jane could not distinguish in the dim light.

"What have you got there, dear?" she asked.

"Wah," said little Braid, a child of few words, proceeding with his activities.

Jane rose and walked across the room. A sudden feeling had come to her, the remorseful feeling that for some time now she had been neglecting the child. How seldom nowadays did she trouble to join in his pastimes!

"Let mother play too," she said gently. "What are you playing? Trains?"

"Golf."

Jane uttered a sharp exclamation. With a keen pang she saw that what the child had got hold of was William's spare mashie. So he had left it behind after all! Since the night of his departure it must have been lying unnoticed behind some chair or sofa.

For a moment the only sensation Jane felt was an accentuation of that desolate feeling which had been with her all day. How many a time had she stood by William and watched him foozle with this club! Inextricably associated with him it was, and her eyes filled with sudden tears. And then she was abruptly conscious of a new, a more violent emotion, something akin to panic fear. She blinked, hoping against hope that she had been mistaken. But no. When she opened her eyes and looked again she saw what she had seen before.

The child was holding the mashie all wrong.

"Braid!" gasped Jane in an agony.

All the mother-love in her was shrieking at her, reproaching her. She realized now how paltry, how greedily self-centred she had been. Thinking only of her own pleasures, how sorely she had neglected her duty as a mother! Long ere this, had she been worthy of that sacred relation, she would have been brooding over her child, teaching him at her knee the correct Vardon grip, shielding him from bad habits, seeing to it that he did not get his hands in front of the ball, putting him on the right path as regarded the slow back-swing. But, absorbed in herself, she had sacrificed him to her shallow ambitions. And now there he was, grasping the club as if it had been a spade and scooping with it like one of those twenty-four-handicap men whom the hot weather brings out on seaside links.

She shuddered to the very depths of her soul. Before her eyes there rose a vision of her son, grown to manhood, reproaching her. "If you had but taught me the facts of life when I was a child, Mother," she seemed to hear him say, "I would not now be going round in a hundred and twenty, rising to a hundred and forty in anything like a high wind."

She snatched the club from his hands with a passionate cry. And at this precise moment in came Rodney Spelvin, all ready for tea.

"Ah, little one!" said Rodney Spelvin, gaily.

Something in her appearance must have startled him, for he stopped and looked at her with concern.

"Are you ill?" he asked.

Jane pulled herself together with an effort.

"No, quite well. Ha, ha!" she replied, hysterically.

She stared at him wildly, as she might have stared at a caterpillar in her salad. If it had not been for this man, she felt, she would have been with William in their snug little cottage, a happy wife. If it had not been for this man, her only child would have been laying the foundations of a correct swing under the eyes of a conscientious pro. If it had not been for this man—— She waved him distractedly to the door.

"Good-bye," she said." Thank you so much for calling."

Rodney Spelvin gaped. This had been the quickest and most tealess tea-party he had ever assisted at.

"You want me to go?" he said, incredulously.

"Yes, go! go!"

Rodney Spelvin cast a wistful glance at the gate-leg table. He had had a light lunch, and the sight of the seed-cake affected him deeply. But there seemed nothing to be done. He moved reluctantly to the door.

"Well, good-bye," he said. "Thanks for a very pleasant afternoon."

"So glad to have seen you," said Jane, mechanically.

The door closed. Jane returned to her thoughts. But she was not alone for long. A few minutes later there entered the female cubist painter from downstairs, a manly young woman with whom she had become fairly intimate.

"Oh, Bates, old chap!" said the cubist painter.

Jane looked up.

"Yes, Osbaldistone?"

"Just came in to borrow a cigarette. Used up all mine."

"So have I, I'm afraid."

"Too bad. Oh, well," said Miss Osbaldistone, resignedly, "I suppose I'll have to go out and get wet. I wish I had had the sense to stop Rodney Spelvin and send him. I met him on the stairs."

"Yes, he was in here just now," said Jane.

Miss Osbaldistone laughed in her hearty manly way.

"Good boy, Rodney," she said, "but too smooth for my taste. A little too ready with the salve."

"Yes?" said Jane, absently.

"Has he pulled that one on you yet about your being the original of the heroine of *The Purple Fan?*"

"Why, yes," said Jane, surprised. "He did tell me that he had drawn Eulalie from me."

Her visitor emitted another laugh that shook the samovars.

"He tells every girl he meets the same thing."

"What!"

"Oh yes. It's his first move. He actually had the nerve to try to spring it on me. Mind you, I'm not saying it's a bad stunt. Most girls like it. You're sure you've no cigarettes? No? Well, how about a shot of cocaine? Out of that too? Oh, well, I'll be going, then. Pip-pip, Bates."

"Toodle-oo, Osbaldistone," said Jane, dizzily. Her brain was reeling. She groped her way to the table, and in a sort of trance cut herself a slice of cake.

"Wah!" said little Braid Vardon. He toddled forward, anxious to count himself in on the share-out.

Jane gave him some cake. Having ruined his life, it was, she felt, the least she could do. In a spasm of belated maternal love she also slipped him a jam-sandwich. But how trivial and useless these things seemed now.

"Braid!" she cried, suddenly.

"What?"

"Come here."

"Why?"

"Let Mother show you how to hold that mashie."

"What's a mashie?"

A new gash opened in Jane's heart. Four years old, and he didn't know what a mashie was. And at only a slightly advanced age Bobby Jones had been playing in the American Open Championship.

"This is a mashie," she said, controlling her voice with difficulty.

"Why?"

"It is called a mashie."

"What is?"

"This club."

"Why?"

The conversation was becoming too metaphysical for Jane. She took the club from him and closed her hand over it.

"Now, look, dear," she said, tenderly. "Watch how mother does it. She puts the fingers——"

A voice spoke, a voice that had been absent all too long from Jane's life.

"You'll pardon me, old girl, but you've got the right hand much too far over. You'll hook for a certainty."

In the doorway, large and dripping, stood William. Jane stared at him dumbly.

"William!" she gasped at length.

"Hullo, Jane!" said William. "Hullo, Braid! Thought I'd look in."

There was a long silence.

"Beastly weather," said William.

"Yes," said Jane.

"Wet and all that," said William.

"Yes," said Jane.

There was another silence.

"Oh, by the way, Jane," said William. "Knew there was something I wanted to say. You know those violets?"

"Violets?"

"White violets. You remember those white violets I've been sending you every year on our wedding anniversary? Well, what I mean to say, our lives are parted and all that sort of thing, but you won't mind if I go on sending them—what? Won't hurt you, what I'm driving at, and'll please me, see what I mean? So, well, to put the thing in a nutshell, if you haven't any objection, that's that."

Jane reeled against the gate-leg table.

"William! Was it you who sent those violets?"

"Absolutely. Who did you think it was?"

"William!" cried Jane, and flung herself into his arms.

William scooped her up gratefully. This was the sort of thing he had been wanting for weeks past. He could do with a lot of this. He wouldn't have suggested it himself, but, seeing that she felt that way, he was all for it.

"William," said Jane, "can you ever forgive me?"

"Oh, rather," said William. "Like a shot. Though, I mean to say, nothing to forgive, and all that sort of thing."

"We'll go back right away to our dear little cottage."

"Fine!"

"We'll never leave it again."

"Topping!"

"I love you." said Jane, "more than life itself."

"Good egg!" said William.

Jane turned with shining eyes to little Braid Vardon.

"Braid, we're going home with Daddy!"

"Where?"

"Home. To our little cottage."

"What's a cottage?"

"The house where we used to be before we came here."

"What's here?"

"This is."

"Which?"

"Where we are now."

"Why?"

"I'll tell you what, old girl," said William. "Just shove a green-baize cloth over that kid, and then start in and brew me about five pints of tea as strong and hot as you can jolly well make it. Otherwise I'm going to get the cold of a lifetime."

20

THE PURIFICATION OF RODNEY SPELVIN

It was an afternoon on which one would have said that all Nature smiled. The air was soft and balmy; the links, fresh from the rains of spring, glistened in the pleasant sunshine; and down on the second tee young Clifford Wimple, in a new suit of plus fours, had just sunk two balls in the lake, and was about to sink a third. No element, in short, was lacking that might be supposed to make for quiet happiness.

And yet on the forehead of the Oldest Member, as he sat beneath the chestnut tree on the terrace overlooking the ninth green, there was a peevish frown; and his eye, gazing down at the rolling expanse of turf, lacked its customary genial benevolence. His favourite chair, consecrated to his private and personal use by unwritten law, had been occupied by another. That is the worst of a free country—liberty so often degenerates into licence.

The Oldest Member coughed.

"I trust," he said, "you find that chair comfortable?"

The intruder, who was the club's hitherto spotless secretary, glanced up in a goofy manner.

"Eh?"

"That chair—you find it fits snugly to the figure?"

"Chair? Figure? Oh, you mean this chair? Oh yes."

"I am gratified and relieved," said the Oldest Member.

There was a silence.

"Look here," said the secretary, "what would you do in a case like this? You know I'm engaged?"

"I do. And no doubt your *fiancée* is missing you. Why not go in search of her?"

"She's the sweetest girl on earth."

"I should lose no time."

"But jealous. And just now I was in my office, and that Mrs. Pettigrew came in to ask if there was any news of the purse which she lost a couple of days ago. It had just been brought to my office, so I produced it; whereupon the infernal woman, in a most unsuitably girlish manner, flung her arms round my neck and kissed me on my bald spot. And at that moment Adela came in. Death," said the secretary, "where is thy sting?"

The Oldest Member's pique melted. He had a feeling heart.

"Most unfortunate. What did you say?"

"I hadn't time to say anything. She shot out too quick."

The Oldest Member clicked his tongue sympathetically.

"These misunderstandings between young and ardent hearts are very frequent," he said. "I could tell you at least fifty cases of the same kind. The one which I will select is the story of Jane Parkard, William Bates, and Rodney Spelvin."

"You told me that the other day. Jane Packard got engaged to Rodney Spelvin, the poet, but the madness passed and she married William Bates, who was a golfer."

"This is another story of the trio."

"You told me that one, too. After Jane Packard married William Bates she fell once more under the spell of Spelvin, but repented in time."

"This is still another story. Making three in all."

The secretary buried his face in his hands.

"Oh, well," he said, "go ahead. What does anything matter now?"

"First," said the Oldest Member, "let us make ourselves comfortable. Take this chair. It is easier than the one in which you are sitting."

"No, thanks."

"I insist."

"Oh, all right."

"Woof!" said the Oldest Member, settling himself luxuriously.

With an eye now full of kindly good-will, he watched young Clifford Wimple play his fourth. Then, as the silver drops flashed up into the sun, he nodded approvingly and began.

The story which I am about to relate (said the Oldest Member) begins at a time when Jane and William had been married some seven years. Jane's handicap was eleven, William's twelve, and their little son, Braid Vardon, had just celebrated his sixth birthday.

Ever since that dreadful time, two years before, when, lured by the glamour of Rodney Spelvin, she had taken a studio in the artistic quarter, dropped her golf, and practically learned to play the ukelele, Jane had been unremitting in her efforts to be a good mother and to bring up her son on the strictest principles. And, in order that his growing mind might have every chance, she had invited William's younger sister, Anastatia, to spend a week or two with them and put the child right on the true functions of the mashie. For Anastatia had reached the semi-finals of the last Ladies' Open Championship and, unlike many excellent players, had the knack of teaching.

On the evening on which this story opens the two women were sitting in the drawing-room, chatting. They had finished tea; and Anastatia, with the aid of a lump of sugar, a spoon, and some crumpled cake, was illustrating the method by which she had got out of the rough on the fifth at Squashy Hollow.

"You're wonderful!" said Jane, admiringly. "And such a good influence for Braid! You'll give him his lesson tomorrow afternoon as usual?"

"I shall have to make it the morning," said Anastatia. "I've promised to meet a man in town in the afternoon."

As she spoke there came into her face a look so soft and dreamy that it roused Jane as if a bradawl had been driven into her leg. As her history has already shown, there was a strong streak of romance in Jane Bates.

"Who is he?" she asked, excitedly.

"A man I met last summer," said Anastatia.

And she sighed with such abandon that Jane could no longer hold in check her womanly nosiness.

"Do you love him?" she cried.

"Like bricks," whispered Anastatia.

"Does he love you?"

"Sometimes I think so."

"What's his name?"

"Rodney Spelvin."

"What!"

"Oh, I know he writes the most awful bilge," said Anastatia, defensively, misinterpreting the yowl of horror which had proceeded from Jane. "All the same, he's a darling."

Jane could not speak. She stared at her sister-in-law aghast. Although she knew that if you put a driver in her hands she could paste the ball into the next county, there always seemed to her something fragile and helpless about Anastatia. William's sister was one of those small, rose-leaf girls with big blue eyes to whom good men instinctively want to give a stroke a hole and on whom bad men automatically prey. And when Jane reflected that Rodney Spelvin had to all intents and purposes preyed upon herself, who stood five foot seven in her shoes and, but for an innate love of animals, could have felled an ox with a blow, she shuddered at the thought of how he would prey on this innocent half-portion.

"You really love him?" she quavered.

"If he beckoned to me in the middle of a medal round, I would come to him," said Anastatia.

Jane realized that further words were useless. A sickening sense of helplessness obsessed her. Something ought to be done about this terrible thing, but what could she do? She was so ashamed of her past madness that not even to warn this girl could she reveal that she had once been engaged to Rodney Spelvin herself; that he had recited poetry on the green while she was putting; and that, later, he had hypnotized her into taking William and little Braid to live in a studio full of samovars. These revelations would no doubt open Anastatia's eyes, but she could not make them.

And then, suddenly, Fate pointed out a way.

It was Jane's practice to go twice a week to the cinema palace in the village; and two nights later she set forth as usual and took her place just as the entertainment was about to begin.

At first she was only mildly interested. The title of the picture, "Tried in the

Furnace", had suggested nothing to her. Being a regular patron of the silver screen, she knew that it might quite easily turn out to be an educational film on the subject of clinker-coal. But as the action began to develop she found herself leaning forward in her seat, blindly crushing a caramel between her fingers. For scarcely had the operator started to turn the crank when inspiration came to her.

Of the main plot of "Tried in the Furnace" she retained, when finally she reeled out into the open air, only a confused recollection. It had something to do with money not bringing happiness or happiness not bringing money, she could not remember which. But the part which remained graven upon her mind was the bit where Gloria Gooch goes by night to the apartments of the libertine, to beg him to spare her sister, whom he has entangled in his toils.

Jane saw her duty clearly. She must go to Rodney Spelvin and conjure him by the memory of their ancient love to spare Anastatia.

It was not the easiest of tasks to put this scheme into operation. Gloria Gooch, being married to a scholarly man who spent nearly all his time in a library a hundred yards long, had been fortunately situated in the matter of paying visits to libertines; but for Jane the job was more difficult. William expected her to play a couple of rounds with him in the morning and another in the afternoon, which rather cut into her time. However, Fate was still on her side, for one morning at breakfast William announced that business called him to town.

"Why don't you come too?" he said.

Jane started.

"No. No, I don't think I will, thanks."

"Give you lunch somewhere."

"No. I want to stay here and do some practice-putting."

"All right. I'll try to get back in time for a round in the evening."

Remorse gnawed at Jane's vitals. She had never deceived William before. She kissed him with even more than her usual fondness when he left to catch the ten-forty-five. She waved to him till he was out of sight; then, bounding back into the house, leaped at the telephone and, after a series of conversations with the Marks-Morris Glue Factory, the Poor Pussy Home for Indigent Cats, and Messrs. Oakes, Oakes, and Parbury, dealers in fancy goods, at last found herself in communication with Rodney Spelvin.

"Rodney?" she said, and held her breath, fearful at this breaking of a two years' silence and yet loath to hear another strange voice say "Wadnumjerwant?" "Is that you, Rodney?"

"Yes. Who is that?"

"Mrs. Bates. Rodney, can you give me lunch at the Alcazar today at one?"

"Can I!" Not even the fact that some unknown basso had got on the wire and was asking if that was Mr. Bootle could blur the enthusiasm in his voice. "I should say so!"

"One o'clock, then," said Jane. His enthusiastic response had relieved her. If by merely speaking she could stir him so, to bend to her will when they met face to face would be pie.

"One o'clock," said Rodney.

Jane hung up the receiver and went to her room to try on hats.

The impression çame to Jane, when she entered the lobby of the restaurant and saw him waiting, that Rodney Spelvin looked somehow different from the Rodney she remembered. His handsome face had a deeper and more thoughtful expression, as if he had been through some ennobling experience.

"Well, here I am," she said, going to him and affecting a jauntiness which she did not feel.

He looked at her, and there was in his eyes that unmistakable goggle which comes to men suddenly addressed in a public spot by women whom, to the best of their recollection, they do not know from Eve.

"How are you?" he said. He seemed to pull himself together. "You're looking splendid."

"You're looking fine," said Jane.

"You're looking awfully well," said Rodney.

"You're looking awfully well," said Jane.

"You're looking fine," said Rodney.

There was a pause.

"You'll excuse me glancing at my watch," said Rodney. "I have an appointment to lunch with—er—somebody here, and it's past the time."

"But you're lunching with me," said Jane, puzzled.

"With you?"

"Yes. I rang you up this morning."

Rodney gaped.

"Was it you who phoned? I thought you said 'Miss Bates'."

"No, Mrs. Bates."

"Mrs. Bates?"

"Mrs. Bates."

"Of course. You're Mrs. Bates."

"Had you forgotten me?" said Jane, in spite of herself a little piqued.

"Forgotten you, dear lady! As if I could!" said Rodney, with a return of his old manner. "Well, shall we go in and have lunch?"

"All right," said Jane.

She felt embarrassed and ill at ease. The fact that Rodney had obviously succeeded in remembering her only after the effort of a lifetime seemed to her to fling a spanner into the machinery of her plans at the very outset. It was going to be difficult, she realized, to conjure him by the memory of their ancient love to spare Anastatia; for the whole essence of the idea of conjuring anyone by the memory of their ancient love is that the party of the second part should be aware that there ever was such a thing.

At the luncheon-table conversation proceeded fitfully. Rodney said that this morning he could have sworn it was going to rain, and Jane said she had thought so, too, and Rodney said that now it looked as if the weather might hold up, and Jane said Yes, didn't it? and Rodney said he hoped the weather would hold up because rain was such a nuisance, and Jane said Yes, wasn't it? Rodney said yesterday had been a nice day, and Jane said Yes, and Rodney said that it seemed to be getting a little warmer, and Jane said Yes, and Rodney said that summer would be here any moment now, and Jane said Yes, wouldn't it? and Rodney said he hoped it would not be too hot this summer, but that, as a matter of fact, when you came right down to it, what one minded was not so much the heat as the humidity, and Jane said Yes, didn't one?

In short, by the time they rose and left the restaurant, not a word had been spoken that could have provoked the censure of the sternest critic. Yet William Bates, catching sight of them as they passed down the aisle, started as if he had been struck by lightning. He had happened to find himself near the Alcazar at lunch-time and had dropped in for a chop; and, peering round the pillar which had hidden his table from theirs, he stared after them with saucer-like eyes.

"Oh, dash it!" said William.

This William Bates, as I have indicated in my previous references to him, was not an abnormally emotional or temperamental man. Built physically on the lines of a motor-lorry, he had much of that vehicle's placid and even phlegmatic outlook on life. Few things had the power to ruffle William, but, unfortunately, it so happened that one of these things was Rodney Spelvin. He had never been able entirely to overcome his jealousy of this man. It had been Rodney who had come within an ace of scooping Jane from him in the days when she had been Miss Packard. It had been Rodney who had temporarily broken up his home some years later by persuading Jane to become a member of the artistic set. And now, unless his eyes jolly well deceived him, this human gumboil was once more busy on his dastardly work. Too dashed thick, was William's view of the matter; and he gnashed his teeth in such a spasm of resentful fury that a man lunching at the next table told the waiter to switch off the electric fan, as it had begun to creak unendurably.

Jane was reading in the drawing-room when William reached home that night.

"Had a nice day?" asked William.

"Quite nice," said Jane.

"Play golf?" asked William.

"Just practised," said Jane.

"Lunch at the club?"

"Yes."

"I thought I saw that bloke Spelvin in town," said William.

Jane wrinkled her forehead.

"Spelvin? Oh, you mean Rodney Spelvin? Did you? I see he's got a new book coming out."

"You never run into him these days, do you?"

"Oh no. It must be two years since I saw him."

"Oh?" said William. "Well, I'll be going upstairs and dressing."

It seemed to Jane, as the door closed, that she heard a curious clicking noise, and she wondered for a moment if little Braid had got out of bed and was playing with the Mah-Jongg counters. But it was only William gnashing his teeth.

There is nothing sadder in this life than the spectacle of a husband and wife with practically identical handicaps drifting apart; and to dwell unnecessarily on such a spectacle is, to my mind, ghoulish. It is not my purpose, therefore, to weary you with a detailed description of the hourly widening of the breach between this once ideally united pair. Suffice it to say that within a few days of the conversation just related the entire atmosphere of this happy home had completely altered. On the Tuesday, William excused himself from the morning round on the plea that he had promised Peter Willard a match, and Jane said What a pity! On Tuesday afternoon William said that his head ached, and Jane said Isn't that too bad? On Wednesday morning William said he had lumbago, and Jane, her sensitive feelings now deeply wounded, said Oh, had he? After that, it came to be agreed between them by silent compact that they should play together no more.

Also, they began to avoid one another in the house. Jane would sit in the drawing-room, while William retired down the passage to his den. In short, if you had added a couple of ikons and a photograph of Trotsky, you would have had a *mise en scène* which would have fitted a Russian novel like the paper on the wall.

One evening, about a week after the beginning of this tragic state of affairs, Jane was sitting in the drawing-room, trying to read *Braid on Taking Turf*. But the print seemed blurred and the philosophy too metaphysical to be grasped. She laid the book down and stared sadly before her.

Every moment of these black days had affected Jane like a stymie on the last green. She could not understand how it was that William should have come to suspect, but that he did suspect was plain; and she writhed on the horns of a dilemma. All she had to do to win him back again was to go to him and tell him of Anastatia's fatal entanglement. But what would happen then? Undoubtedly he would feel it his duty as a brother to warn the girl against Rodney Spelvin; and Jane instinctively knew that William warning anyone against Rodney Spelvin would sound like a private of the line giving his candid opinion of the sergeant-major.

Inevitably, in this case, Anastatia, a spirited girl and deeply in love, would take offence at his words and leave the house. And if she left the house, what would be the effect on little Braid's mashie-play? Already, in less than a fortnight, the gifted girl had taught him more about the chip-shot from ten to fifteen yards off the green than the local pro. had been able to do in two years. Her departure would be absolutely disastrous.

What it amounted to was that she must sacrifice her husband's happiness or her child's future; and the problem of which was to get the loser's end was becoming daily more insoluble.

She was still brooding on it when the postman arrived with the evening mail, and the maid brought the letters into the drawing-room.

Jane sorted them out. There were three for William, which she gave to the maid to take to him in his den. There were two for herself, both bills. And there was one for Anastatia, in the well-remembered handwriting of Rodney Spelvin.

Jane placed this letter on the mantelpiece, and stood looking at it like a cat at a canary. Anastatia was away for the day, visiting friends who lived a few stations down the line; and every womanly instinct in Jane urged her to get hold of a kettle and steam the gum off the envelope. She had almost made up her mind to disembowel the thing and write "Opened in error" on it, when the telephone suddenly went off like a bomb and nearly startled her into a decline. Coming at that moment it sounded like the Voice of Conscience.

"Hullo?" said Jane.

"Hullo!" replied a voice.

Jane clucked like a hen with uncontrollable emotion. It was Rodney.

"It that you?" asked Rodney.

"Yes," said Jane.

And so it was, she told herself.

"Your voice is like music," said Rodney.

This may or may not have been the case, but at any rate it was exactly like every other female voice when heard on the telephone. Rodney prattled on without a suspicion.

"Have you got my letter yet?"

"No," said Jane. She hesitated. "What was in it?" she asked, tremulously.

"It was to ask you to come to my house tomorrow at four."

"To your house!" faltered Jane.

"Yes. Everything is ready. I will send the servants out, so that we shall be quite alone. You will come, won't you?"

The room was shimmering before Jane's eyes, but she regained command of herself with a strong effort.

"Yes," she said. "I will be there."

She spoke softly, but there was a note of menace in her voice. Yes, she would indeed be there. From the very moment when this man had made his monstrous proposal, she had been asking herself what Gloria Gooch would have done in a crisis like this. And the answer was plain. Gloria Gooch, if her sister-in-law was intending to visit the apartments of a libertine, would have gone there herself to save the poor child from the consequences of her infatuated folly.

"Yes," said Jane, "I will be there."

"You have made me the happiest man in the world," said Rodney. "I will meet you at the corner of the street at four, then." He paused. "What is that curious clicking noise?" he asked.

"I don't know," said Jane. "I noticed it myself. Something wrong with the wire, I suppose."

"I thought it was somebody playing the castanets. Until tomorrow, then, good-bye."

"Good-bye."

Jane replaced the receiver. And William, who had been listening to every word of the conversation on the extension in his den, replaced his receiver, too.

Anastatia came back from her visit late that night. She took her letter, and read it without comment. At breakfast next morning she said that she would be compelled to go into town that day.

"I want to see my dressmaker," she said.

"I'll come, too," said Jane. "I want to see my dentist."

"So will I," said William. "I want to see my lawyer."

"That will be nice," and Anastatia, after a pause.

"Very nice," said Jane, after another pause.

"We might all lunch together," said Anastatia. "My appointment is not till four."

"I should love it," said Jane. "My appointment is at four, too."

"So is mine," said William.

"What a coincidence!" said Jane, trying to speak brightly.

"Yes," said William. He may have been trying to speak brightly, too; but, if so, he failed. Jane was too young to have seen Salvini in *Othello,* but, had she witnessed that great tragedian's performance, she could not have failed to be struck by the resemblance between his manner in the pillow scene and William's now.

"Then shall we all lunch together?" said Anastatia.

"I shall lunch at my club," said William curtly.

"William seems to have a grouch," said Anastatia.

"Ha!" said William.

He raised his fork and drove it with sickening violence at his sausage.

So Jane had a quiet little woman's lunch at a confectioner's alone with Anastatia. Jane ordered a tongue-and-lettuce sandwich, two macaroons, marsh-mallows, ginger-ale and cocoa; and Anastatia ordered pineapple chunks with whipped cream, tomatoes stuffed with beetroot, three dill pickles, a raspberry nut sundae, and hot chocolate. And, while getting outside this garbage, they talked merrily, as women will, of every subject but the one that really occupied their minds. When Anastatia got up and said good-bye with a final reference to her dressmaker, Jane shuddered at the depths of deceit to which the modern girl can sink.

It was now about a quarter to three, so Jane had an hour to kill before going to the rendezvous. She wandered about the streets, and never had time appeared to her to pass so slowly, never had a city been so congested with hard-eyed and suspicious citizens. Every second person she met seemed to glare at her as if he or she had guessed her secret.

The very elements joined in the general disapproval. The sky had turned a sullen grey, and far-away thunder muttered faintly, like an impatient golfer held up on the tee by a slow foursome. It was a relief when at length she found herself at the back of Rodney Spelvin's house, standing before the scullery window, which it was her intention to force with the pocket-knife won in happier days as second prize in a competition at a summer hotel for those with handicaps above eighteen.

But the relief did not last long. Despite the fact that she was about to enter this evil house with the best motives, a sense of almost intolerable guilt oppressed her. If William should ever get to know of this! Wow! felt Jane.

How long she would have hesitated before the window, one cannot say. But at this moment, glancing guiltily round, she happened to catch the eye of a cat which was sitting on a near-by wall, and she read in this cat's eye such cynical derision that the urge came upon her to get out of its range as quickly as possible. It was a cat that had manifestly seen a lot of life, and it was plainly putting an entirely wrong construction on her behaviour. Jane shivered, and, with a quick jerk prised the window open and climbed in.

It was two years since she had entered this house, but once she had reached the hall she remembered its topography perfectly. She mounted the stairs to the large studio sitting-room on the first floor, the scene of so many Bohemian parties in that dark period of her artistic life. It was here, she knew, that Rodney would bring his victim.

The studio was one of those dim, over-ornamented rooms which appeal to men like Rodney Spelvin. Heavy curtains hung in front of the windows. One corner was cut off by a high-backed Chesterfield. At the far end was an alcove, curtained like the windows. Once Jane had admired this studio, but now it made her shiver. It seemed to her one of those nests in which, as the sub-title of *Tried in the Furnace* had said, only eggs of evil are hatched. She paced the thick carpet restlessly, and suddenly there came to her the sound of footsteps on the stairs.

Jane stopped, every muscle tense. The moment had arrived. She faced the door, tight-lipped. It comforted her a little in this crisis to reflect that Rodney was not one of those massive Ethel M. Dell libertines who might make things unpleasant for an intruder. He was only a welter-weight egg of evil; and, if he tried to start anything, a girl of her physique would have little or no difficulty in knocking the stuffing out of him.

The footsteps reached the door. The handle turned. The door opened. And in strode William Bates, followed by two men in bowler hats.

"Ha!" said William.

Jane's lips parted, but no sound came from them. She staggered back a pace or two. William, advancing into the centre of the room, folded his arms and gazed at her with burning eyes.

"So," said William, and the words seemed forced like drops of vitriol from between his clenched teeth, "I find you here, dash it!"

Jane choked convulsively. Years ago, when an innocent child, she had seen a conjuror produce a rabbit out of a top-hat which an instant before had been conclusively proved to be empty. The sudden apparition of William affected her with much the same sensations as she had experienced then.

"How-ow-ow——?" she said.

"I beg your pardon?" said William, coldly.

"How-ow-ow——?"

"Explain yourself," said William.

"How-ow-ow did you get here? And who-oo-oo are these men?"

William seemed to become aware for the first time of the presence of his two companions. He moved a hand in a hasty gesture of introduction.

"Mr. Reginald Brown and Mr. Cyril Delancey—my wife," he said, curtly.

The two men bowed slightly and raised their bowler hats.

"Pleased to meet you," said one.

"Most awfully charmed," said the other.

"They are detectives," said William.

"Detectives!"

"From the Quick Results Agency," said William. "When I became aware of your clandestine intrigue, I went to the agency and they gave me their two best men."

"Oh, well," said Mr. Brown, blushing a little.

"Most frightfully decent of you to put it that way," said Mr. Delancey.

William regarded Jane sternly.

"I knew you were going to be here at four o'clock," he said. "I overheard you making the assignation on the telephone."

"Oh, William!"

"Woman," said William, "where is your paramour?"

"Really, really," said Mr. Delancey, deprecatingly.

"Keep it clean," urged Mr. Brown.

"Your partner in sin, where is he? I am going to take him and tear him into little bits and stuff him down his throat and make him swallow himself."

"Fair enough," said Mr. Brown.

"Perfectly in order," said Mr. Delancey.

Jane uttered a stricken cry.

"William," she screamed, "I can explain all."

"All?" said Mr. Delancey.

"All?" said Mr. Brown.

"All," said Jane.

"All?" said William.

"All," said Jane.

William sneered bitterly.

"I'll bet you can't," he said.

"I'll bet I can," said Jane.

"Well?"

"I came here to save Anastatia."

"Anastatia?"

"Anastatia."

"My sister?"

"Your sister."

"His sister Anastatia," explained Mr. Brown to Mr. Delancey in an undertone.

"What from?" asked William.

"From Rodney Spelvin. Oh, William, can't you understand?"

"No, I'm dashed if I can."

"I, too," said Mr. Delancey, "must confess myself a little fogged. And you, Reggie?"

"Completely, Cyril," said Mr. Brown, removing his bowler hat with a puzzled frown, examining the maker's name, and putting it on again.

"The poor child is infatuated with this man."

"With the bloke Spelvin?"

"Yes. She is coming here with him at four o'clock."

"Important," said Mr. Brown, producing a notebook and making an entry.

"Important, if true," agreed Mr. Delancey.

"But I heard you making the appointment with the bloke Spelvin over the phone," said William.

"He thought I was Anastatia. And I came here to save her."

William was silent and thoughtful for a few moments.

"It all sounds very nice and plausible," he said, "but there's just one thing wrong. I'm not a very clever sort of bird, but I can see where your story slips up. If what you say is true, where is Anastatia?"

"Just coming in now," whispered Jane. "Hist!"

"Hist, Reggie!" whispered Mr. Delancey.

They listened. Yes, the front door had banged, and feet were ascending the staircase.

"Hide!" said Jane, urgently.

"Why?" said William.

"So that you can overhear what they say and jump out and confront them."

"Sound," said Mr. Delancey.

"Very sound," said Mr. Brown.

The two detectives concealed themselves in the alcove. William retired behind the curtains in front of the window. Jane dived behind the Chesterfield. A moment later the door opened.

Crouching in her corner, Jane could see nothing, but every word that was spoken came to her ears; and with every syllable her horror deepened.

"Give me your things," she heard Rodney say, "and then we will go upstairs."

Jane shivered. The curtains by the window shook. From the direction of the alcove there came a soft scratching sound, as the two detectives made an entry in their notebooks.

For a moment after this there was silence. Then Anastatia uttered a sharp, protesting cry.

"Ah, no, no! Please, please!"

"But why not?" came Rodney's voice.

"It is wrong—wrong."

"I can't see why."

"It is, it is! You must not do that. Oh, please, please don't hold so tight."

There was a swishing sound, and through the curtains before the window a large form burst. Jane raised her head above the Chesterfield.

William was standing there, a menacing figure. The two detectives had left the alcove and were moistening their pencils. And in the middle of the room stood Rodney Spelvin, stooping slightly and grasping Anastatia's parasol in his hands.

"I don't get it," he said. "Why is it wrong to hold the dam' thing tight?" He looked up and perceived his visitors. "Ah, Bates," he said, absently. He turned to Anastatia again. "I should have thought that the tighter you held it, the more force you would get into the shot."

"But don't you see, you poor zimp," replied Anastatia, "that you've got to keep the ball straight. If you grip the shaft as if you were a drowning man clutching at a straw and keep your fingers under like that, you'll pull like the dickens and probably land out of bounds or in the rough. What's the good of getting force into the shot if the ball goes in the wrong direction, you cloth-headed goof?"

"I see now," said Rodney, humbly. "How right you always are!"

"Look here," interrupted William, folding his arms. "What is the meaning of this?"

"You want to grip firmly but lightly," said Anastatia.

"Firmly but lightly," echoed Rodney.

"What is the meaning of this?"

"And with the fingers. Not with the palms."

"What is the meaning of this?" thundered William. "Anastatia, what are you doing in this man's rooms?"

"Giving him a golf lesson, of course. And I wish you wouldn't interrupt."

"Yes, yes," said Rodney, a little testily. "Don't interrupt, Bates, there's a good fellow. Surely you have things to occupy you elsewhere?"

"We'll go upstairs," said Anastatia, "where we can be alone."

"You will not go upstairs," barked William.

"We shall get on much better there," explained Anastatia. "Rodney has fitted up the top-floor back as an indoor practising room."

Jane darted forward with a maternal cry.

"My poor child, has the scoundrel dared to delude you by pretending to be a golfer? Darling, he is nothing of the kind."

Mr. Reginald Brown coughed. For some moments he had been twitching restlessly.

"Talking of golf," he said, "it might interest you to hear of a little experience I had the other day at Marshy Moor. I had got a nice drive off the tee, nothing record-breaking, you understand, but straight and sweet. And what was my astonishment on walking up to play my second to find——"

"A rather similar thing happened to me at Windy Waste last Tuesday," interrupted Mr. Delancey. "I had hooked my drive the merest trifle, and my caddie said to me, 'You're out of bounds.' 'I am not out of bounds,' I replied, perhaps a little tersely, for the lad had annoyed me by a persistent habit of sniffing. 'Yes, you are out of bounds,' he said. 'No, I am not out of bounds,' I retorted. Well, believe me or believe me not, when I got up to my ball——"

"Shut up!" said William.

"Just as you say, sir," replied Mr. Delancey, courteously.

Rodney Spelvin drew himself up, and in spite of her loathing for his villainy Jane could not help feeling what a noble and romantic figure he made. His face was pale, but his voice did not falter.

"You are right," he said. "I am not a golfer. But with the help of this splendid girl here, I hope humbly to be one some day. Ah, I know what you are going to say," he went on, raising a hand. "You are about to ask how a man who has wasted his life as I have done can dare to entertain the mad dream of ever acquiring a decent handicap. But never forget," proceeded Rodney, in a low, quivering voice, "that Walter J. Travis was nearly forty before he touched a club, and a few years later he won the British Amateur."

"True," murmured William.

"True, true," said Mr. Delancey and Mr. Brown. They lifted their bowler hats reverently.

"I am thirty-three years old," continued Rodney, "and for fourteen of these thirty-three years I have been writing poetry—aye, and novels with a poignant sex-appeal, and if ever I gave a thought to this divine game it was but to sneer at it. But last summer I saw the light."

"Glory! Glory!" cried Mr. Brown.

"One afternoon I was persuaded to try a drive. I took the club with a mocking, contemptuous laugh." He paused, and a wild light came into his eyes. "I brought off a perfect pip," he said, emotionally. "Two hundred yards and as straight as a whistle. And, as I stood there gazing after the ball, something seemed to run up my spine and bite me in the neck. It was the golf-germ."

"Always the way," said Mr. Brown. "I remember the first drive I ever made. I took a nice easy stance——"

"The first drive I made," said Mr. Delancey, "you won't believe this, but it's a fact, was a full——"

"From that moment," continued Rodney Spelvin, "I have had but one ambition— to somehow or other, cost what it might, get down into single figures." He laughed bitterly. "You see," he said, "I cannot even speak of this thing without splitting my infinitives. And even as I split my infinitives, so did I split my drivers. After that first heavenly slosh I didn't seem able to do anything right."

He broke off, his face working. William cleared his throat awkwardly.

"Yes, but dash it," he said, "all this doesn't explain why I find you alone with my sister in what I might call your lair."

"The explanation is simple," said Rodney Spelvin. "This sweet girl is the only person in the world who seems able to simply and intelligently and in a few easily understood words make clear the knack of the thing. There is none like her, none. I have been to pro. after pro. but not one has been any good to me. I am a tempera- mental man, and there is a lack of sympathy and human understanding about these professionals which jars on my artist soul. They look at you as if you were a half- witted child. They click their tongues. They make odd Scotch noises. I could not endure the strain. And then this wonderful girl, to whom in a burst of emotion I had confided my unhappy case, offered to give me private lessons. So I went with her to some of those indoor practising places. But here, too, my sensibilities were racked by the fact that unsympathetic eyes observed me. So I fixed up a room here where we could be alone."

"And instead of going there," said Anastatia, "we are wasting half the afternoon talking."

William brooded for a while. He was not a quick thinker.

"Well, look here," he said at length, "this is the point. This is the nub of the thing. This is where I want you to follow me very closely. Have you asked Anastatia to marry you?"

"Marry me?" Rodney gazed at him, shocked. "Have I asked her to marry me? I, who am not worthy to polish the blade of her niblick! I, who have not even a thirty handicap, ask a girl to marry me who was in the semi-final of last year's Ladies' Open! No, no, Bates, I may be a *vers-libre* poet, but I have some sense of what is fitting. I love her, yes. I love her with a fervour which causes me to frequently and for hours at a time lie tossing sleeplessly upon my pillow. But I would not dare to ask her to marry me."

Anastatia burst into a peal of girlish laughter.

"You poor chump!" she cried. "Is that what has been the matter all this time? I couldn't make out what the trouble was. Why, I'm crazy about you. I'll marry you any time you give the word."

Rodney reeled.

"What!"

"Of course I will."

"Anastatia!"

"Rodney!"

He folded her in his arms.

"Well, I'm dashed," said William. "It looks to me as if I had been making rather a lot of silly fuss about nothing. Jane, I wronged you."

"It was my fault."

"No, no!"

"Yes, yes!"

"Jane!"

"William!"

He folded her in his arms. The two detectives, having entered the circumstances in their notebooks, looked at one another with moist eyes.

"Cyril!" said Mr. Brown.

"Reggie!" said Mr. Delancey.

Their hands met in a brotherly clasp.

"And so," concluded the Oldest Member, "all ended happily. The storm-tossed lives of William Bates, Jane Packard, and Rodney Spelvin came safely at long last into harbour. At the subsequent wedding William and Jane's present of a complete golfing outfit, including eight dozen new balls, a cloth cap, and a pair of spiked shoes, was generally admired by all who inspected the gifts during the reception.

"From that time forward the four of them have been inseparable. Rodney and Anastatia took a cottage close to that of William and Jane, and rarely does a day pass without a close foursome between the two couples. William and Jane being steady tens and Anastatia scratch and Rodney a persevering eighteen, it makes an ideal match."

"What does?" asked the secretary, waking from his reverie.

"This one."

"Which?"

"I see," said the Oldest Member, sympathetically, "that your troubles, weighing on your mind, have caused you to follow my little narrative less closely than you might have done. Never mind, I will tell it again.

"The story" (said the Oldest Member) "which I am about to relate begins at a time when——"

21

THOSE IN PERIL ON THE TEE

I THINK the two young men in the chess-board knickerbockers were a little surprised when they looked up and perceived Mr. Mulliner brooding over their table like an affable Slave of the Lamp. Absorbed in their conversation, they had not noticed his approach. It was their first visit to the Anglers' Rest, and their first meeting with the Sage of its bar-parlour: and they were not yet aware that to Mr. Mulliner any assemblage of his fellow-men over and above the number of one constitutes an audience.

"Good evening, gentlemen," said Mr. Mulliner. "You have been playing golf, I see."

They said they had.

"You enjoy the game?"

They said they did.

"Perhaps you will allow me to request Miss Postlethwaite, princess of barmaids, to re-fill your glasses?"

They said they would.

"Golf," said Mr. Mulliner, drawing up a chair and sinking smoothly into it, "is a game which I myself have not played for some years. I was always an indifferent performer, and I gradually gave it up for the simpler and more straightforward pastime of fishing. It is a curious fact that, gifted though the Mulliners have been in virtually every branch of life and sport, few of us have ever taken kindly to golf. Indeed, the only member of the family I can think of who attained to any real proficiency with the clubs was the daughter of a distant cousin of mine—one of the Devonshire Mulliners who married a man named Flack. Agnes was the girl's name. Perhaps you have run across her? She is always playing in tournaments and competitions, I believe."

The young men said No, they didn't seem to know the name.

"Ah?" said Mr. Mulliner. "A pity. It would have made the story more interesting to you."

The two young men exchanged glances.

"Story?" said the one in the slightly more prismatic knickerbockers, speaking in a voice that betrayed agitation.

"Story?" said his companion, blenching a little.

"The story," said Mr. Mulliner, "of John Gooch, Frederick Pilcher, Sidney

McMurdo and Agnes Flack."

The first young man said he didn't know it was so late. The second young man said it was extraordinary how time went. They began to talk confusedly about trains.

"The story," repeated Mr. Mulliner, holding them with the effortless ease which makes this sort of thing such child's play to him, "of Agnes Flack, Sidney McMurdo, Frederick Pilcher and John Gooch."

It is an odd thing (said Mr. Mulliner) how often one finds that those who practise the Arts are quiet, timid little men, shy in company and unable to express themselves except through the medium of the pencil or the pen. I have noticed it again and again. John Gooch was like that. So was Frederick Pilcher. Gooch was a writer and Pilcher was an artist, and they used to meet a good deal at Agnes Flack's house, where they were constant callers. And every time they met John Gooch would say to himself as he watched Pilcher balancing a cup of tea and smiling his weak, propitia- tory smile, "I am fond of Frederick, but his best friend could not deny that he is a pretty dumb brick." And Pilcher, as he saw Gooch sitting on the edge of his chair and fingering his tie, would reflect, "Nice fellow as John is, he is certainly a total loss in mixed society."

Mark you, if ever men had an excuse for being ill at ease in the presence of the opposite sex, these two had. They were both eighteen-handicap men, and Agnes was exuberantly and dynamically scratch. Her physique was an asset to her, especially at the long game. She stood about five feet ten in her stockings, and had shoulders and forearms which would have excited the envious admiration of one of those muscular women on the music-halls, who good-naturedly allow six brothers, three sisters, and a cousin by marriage to pile themselves on her collar-bone while the orchestra plays a long-drawn chord and the audience hurries out to the bar. Her eye resembled the eye of one of the more imperious queens of history: and when she laughed, strong men clutched at their temples to keep the tops of their heads from breaking loose.

Even Sidney McMurdo was as a piece of damp blotting-paper in her presence. And he was a man who weighed two hundred and eleven pounds and had once been a semi-finalist in the Amateur Championship. He loved Agnes Flack with an ox-like devotion. And yet—and this will show you what life is—when she laughed, it was nearly always at him. I am told by those in a position to know that, on the occasion when he first proposed to her—on the sixth green—distant rumblings of her mirth were plainly heard in the club-house locker-room, causing two men who were afraid of thunderstorms to scratch their match.

Such, then, was Agnes Flack. Such, also, was Sidney McMurdo. And such were Frederick Pilcher and John Gooch.

Now John Gooch, though, of course, they had exchanged a word from time to time, was in no sense an intimate of Sidney McMurdo. It was consequently a surprise to him when one night, as he sat polishing up the rough draft of a detective story—for his was the talent that found expression largely in blood, shots in the night, and millionaires who are found murdered in locked rooms with no possible means of access except a window forty feet above the ground—the vast bulk of McMurdo lumbered across his threshold and deposited itself in a chair.

The chair creaked. Gooch stared. McMurdo groaned.

"Are you ill?" said John Gooch.

"Ha!" said Sidney McMurdo.

He had been sitting with his face buried in his hands, but now he looked up; and there was a red glare in his eyes which sent a thrill of horror through John Gooch. The visitor reminded him of the Human Gorilla in his novel, *The Mystery of the Severed Ear.*

"For two pins," said Sidney McMurdo, displaying a more mercenary spirit than the Human Gorilla, who had required no cash payment for his crimes, "I would tear you into shreds."

"Me?" said John Gooch, blankly.

"Yes, you. And that fellow Pilcher, too." He rose; and, striding to the mantelpiece, broke off a corner of it and crumbled it in his fingers. "You have stolen her from me."

"Stolen? Whom?"

"My Agnes."

John Gooch stared at him, thoroughly bewildered. The idea of stealing Agnes Flack was rather like the notion of sneaking off with the Albert Hall. He could make nothing of it.

"She is going to marry you."

"What!" cried John Gooch, aghast.

"Either you or Pilcher." McMurdo paused. "Shall I tear you into little strips and tread you into the carpet?" he murmured, meditatively.

"No," said John Gooch. His mind was blurred, but he was clear on that point.

"Why did you come butting in?" groaned Sidney McMurdo, absently taking up the poker and tying it into a lover's knot. "I was getting along splendidly until you two pimples broke out. Slowly but surely I was teaching her to love me, and now it can never be. I have a message for you. From her. I proposed to her for the eleventh time to-night; and when she had finished laughing she told me that she could never marry a mere mass of brawn. She said she wanted brain. And she told me to tell you and the pest Pilcher that she had watched you closely and realized that you both loved her, but were too shy to speak, and that she understood and would marry one of you."

There was a long silence.

"Pilcher is a splendid fellow," said John Gooch. "She must marry Pilcher."

"She will, if he wins the match."

"What match?"

"The golf match. She read a story in a magazine the other day where two men played a match at golf to decide which was to win the heroine; and about a week later she read another story in another magazine where two men played a match at golf to decide which was to win the heroine. And a couple of days ago she read three more stories in three more magazines where exactly the same thing happened; and she has decided to accept it as an omen. So you and the hound Pilcher are to play eighteen holes, and the winner marries Agnes."

"The winner?"

"Certainly."

"I should have thought—I forget what I was going to say."

McMurdo eyed him keenly.

"Gooch," he said, "You are not one of those thoughtless butterflies, I hope, who go about breaking girls' hearts?"

"No, no," said John Gooch, learning for the first time that this was what butterflies did.

"You are not one of those men who win a good girl's love and then ride away with a light laugh?"

John Gooch said he certainly was not. He would not dream of laughing, even lightly, at any girl. Besides, he added, he could not ride. He had once had three lessons in the Park, but had not seemed to be able to get the knack.

"So much the better for you," said Sidney McMurdo heavily. "Because, if I thought that, I should know what steps to take. Even now. . . ." He paused, and looked at the poker in a rather yearning sort of way. "No, no," he said, with a sigh, "better not, better not." He flung the thing down with a gesture of resignation. "Better, perhaps, on the whole not." He rose, frowning. "Well, good night, weed," he said. "The match will be played on Friday morning. And may the better—or, rather, the less impossibly foul—man win."

He banged the door, and John Gooch was alone.

But not for long. Scarcely half an hour had passed when the door opened once more to admit Frederick Pilcher. The artist's face was pale, and he was breathing heavily. He sat down, and after a brief interval contrived to summon up a smile. He rose and patted John Gooch on the shoulder.

"John," he said, "I am a man who as a general rule hides his feelings. I mask my affections. But I want to say, straight out, here and now, that I like you, John."

"Yes?" said John Gooch.

Frederick Pilcher patted his other shoulder.

"I like you so much, John, old man, that I can read your thoughts, strive to conceal them though you may. I have been watching you closely of late, John, and I know your secret. You love Agnes Flack."

"I don't!"

"Yes, you do. Ah, John, John," said Frederick Pilcher, with a gentle smile, "why try to deceive an old friend? You love her, John. You love that girl. And I have good news for you, John—tidings of great joy. I happen to know that she will look favourably on your suit. Go in and win, my boy, go in and win. Take my advice and dash round and propose without a moment's delay."

John Gooch shook his head. He, too smiled a gentle smile.

"Frederick," he said, "this is like you. Noble. That's what I call it. Noble. It's the sort of thing the hero does in act two. But it must not be, Frederick. It must not, shall not be. I also can read a friend's heart, and I know that you, too, love Agnes Flack. And I yield my claim. I am excessively fond of you Frederick, and I give her up to you. God bless you, old fellow. God, in fact, bless both of you."

"Look here," said Frederick Pilcher, "have you been having a visit from Sidney McMurdo?"

"He did drop in for a minute."

There was a tense pause.

"What I can't understand," said Frederick Pilcher, at length, peevishly, "is why, if you don't love this infernal girl, you kept calling at her house practically every night and sitting goggling at her with obvious devotion."

"It wasn't devotion."

"It looked like it."

"Well, it wasn't. And, if it comes to that, why did you call on her practically every night and goggle just as much as I did?"

"I had a very good reason," said Frederick Pilcher. "I was studying her face. I am planning a series of humorous drawings on the lines of Felix the Cat, and I wanted her as a model. To goggle at a girl in the interests of one's Art, as I did, is a very different thing from goggling wantonly at her, like you."

"Is that so?" said John Gooch. "Well, let me tell you that I wasn't goggling wantonly. I was studying her psychology for a series of stories which I am preparing, entitled *Madeline Monk, Murderess*."

Frederick Pilcher held out his hand.

"I wronged you, John," he said. "However, be that as it may, the point is that we both appear to be up against it very hard. An extraordinarily well-developed man, that fellow McMurdo."

"A mass of muscle."

"And of a violent disposition."

"Dangerously so."

Frederick Pilcher drew out his handkerchief and dabbed at his forehead.

"You don't think, John, that you might ultimately come to love Agnes Flack?"

"I do not."

"Love frequently comes after marriage, I believe."

"So does suicide."

"Then it looks to me," said Frederick Pilcher, "as if one of us was for it. I see no way out of playing that match."

"Nor I."

"The growing tendency on the part of the modern girl to read trashy magazine stories," said Frederick Pilcher severely, "is one that I deplore. I view it with alarm. And I wish to goodness that you authors wouldn't write tales about men who play golf matches for the hand of a woman."

"Authors must live," said John Gooch. "How is your game these days, Frederick?"

"Improved, unfortunately. I am putting better."

"I am steadier off the tee." John Gooch laughed bitterly. "When I think of the hours of practice I have put in, little knowing that a thing of this sort was in store for me, I appreciate the irony of life. If I had not bought Sandy McHoots' book last spring I might now be in a position to be beaten five and four."

"Instead of which, you will probably win the match on the twelfth."

John Gooch started.

"You can't be as bad as that!"

"I shall be on Friday."

"You mean to say you aren't going to try?"

"I do."

"You have sunk to such depths that you would deliberately play below your proper form?"

"I have."

"Pilcher," said John Gooch, coldly, "you are a hound, and I never liked you from the start."

You would have thought that, after the conversation which I have just related, no depth of low cunning on the part of Frederick Pilcher would have had the power to surprise John Gooch. And yet, as he saw the other come out of the club-house to join him on the first tee on the Friday morning, I am not exaggerating when I say that he was stunned.

John Gooch had arrived at the links early, wishing to get in a little practice. One of his outstanding defects as a golfer was a pronounced slice; and it seemed to him that, if he drove off a few balls before the match began, he might be able to analyse this slice and see just what was the best stance to take up in order that it might have full scope. He was teeing his third ball when Frederick Pilcher appeared.

"What—what—what——!" gasped John Gooch.

For Frederick Pilcher, discarding the baggy mustard-coloured plus-fours in which it was his usual custom to infest the links, was dressed in a perfectly fitting morning-coat, yellow waistcoat, striped trousers, spats, and patent-leather shoes. He wore a high stiff collar, and on his head was the glossiest top-hat ever seen off the Stock Exchange. He looked intensely uncomfortable; and yet there was on his face a smirk which he made no attempt to conceal.

"What's the matter?" he asked.

"Why are you dressed like that?" John Gooch uttered an exclamation. "I see it all. You think it will put you off your game."

"Some idea of the kind did occur to me," replied Frederick Pilcher, airily.

"You fiend!"

"Tut, tut, John. These are hard words to use to a friend."

"You are no friend of mine."

"A pity," said Frederick Pilcher, "for I was hoping that you would ask me to be your best man at the wedding." He took a club from his bag and swung it. "Amazing what a difference clothes make. You would hardly believe how this coat cramps the shoulders. I feel as if I were a sardine trying to wriggle in its tin."

The world seemed to swim before John Gooch's eyes. Then the mist cleared, and he fixed Frederick Pilcher with a hypnotic gaze.

"You are going to play well," he said, speaking very slowly and distinctly. "You are going to play well. You are going to play well. You——"

"Stop it!" cried Frederick Pilcher.

"You are going to play well. You are going——"

A heavy hand descended on his shoulder. Sidney McMurdo was regarding him with a black scowl.

"We don't want any of your confounded chivalry," said Sidney McMurdo. "This match is going to be played in the strictest spirit of—— What the devil are you dressed like that for?" he demanded, wheeling on Frederick Pilcher.

"I—I have to go into the City immediately after the match," said Pilcher. "I sha'n't have time to change."

"H'm. Well, it's your own affair. Come along," said Sidney McMurdo, gritting his teeth. "I've been told to referee this match, and I don't want to stay here all day. Toss for the honour, worms."

John Gooch spun a coin. Frederick Pilcher called tails. The coin fell heads up.

"Drive off, reptile," said Sidney McMurdo.

As John Gooch addressed his ball, he was aware of a strange sensation which he could not immediately analyse. It was only when, after waggling two or three times, he started to draw his club back that it flashed upon him that this strange sensation was confidence. For the first time in his life he seemed to have no doubt that the ball, well and truly struck, would travel sweetly down the middle of the fairway. And then the hideous truth dawned on him. His subconscious self had totally misunderstood the purport of his recent remarks and had got the whole thing nicely muddled up.

Much has been written of the subconscious self, and all that has been written goes to show that of all the thick-headed, blundering chumps who take everything they hear literally, it is the worst. Anybody of any intelligence would have realized that when John Gooch said, "You are going to play well," he was speaking to Frederick Pilcher; but his subconscious self had missed the point completely. It had heard John Gooch say, "You are going to play well," and it was seeing that he did so.

The unfortunate man did what he could. Realizing what had happened, he tried with a despairing jerk to throw his swing out of gear just as the club came above his shoulder. It was a fatal move. You may recall that when Arnaud Massy won the

British Open Championship one of the features of his play was a sort of wiggly twiggle at the top of the swing, which seemed to have the effect of adding yards to his drive. This wiggly twiggle John Gooch, in his effort to wreck his shot, achieved to a nicety. The ball soared over the bunker in which he had hoped to waste at least three strokes; and fell so near the green that it was plain that only a miracle could save him from getting a four.

There was a sardonic smile on Frederick Pilcher's face as he stepped on to the tee. In a few moments he would be one down, and it would not be his fault if he failed to maintain the advantage. He drew back the head of his club. His coat, cut by a fashionable tailor who, like all fashionable tailors, resented it if the clothes he made permitted his customers to breathe, was so tight that he could not get the club-head more than half-way up. He brought it to this point, then brought it down in a lifeless semi-circle.

"Nice!" said Sidney McMurdo, involuntarily. He despised and disliked Frederick Pilcher, but he was a golfer. And a golfer cannot refrain from giving a good shot its meed of praise.

For the ball, instead of trickling down the hill as Frederick Pilcher had expected, was singing through the air like a shell. It fell near John Gooch's ball and, bounding past it, ran on to the green.

The explanation was, of course, simple. Frederick Pilcher was a man who, in his normal golfing costume, habitually over-swung. This fault the tightness of his coat had now rendered impossible. And his other pet failing, the raising of the head, had been checked by the fact that he was wearing a top-hat. It had been Pilcher's intention to jerk his head till his spine cracked; but the unseen influence of genera-tions of ancestors who had devoted the whole of their intellect to the balancing of top-hats on windy days was too much for him.

A minute later the two men had halved the hole in four.

The next hole, the water-hole, they halved in three. The third, long and over the hill, they halved in five.

And it was as they moved to the fourth tee that a sort of madness came upon both Frederick Pilcher and John Gooch simultaneously.

These two, you must remember, were eighteen-handicap men. That is to say, they thought well of themselves if they could get sixes on the first, sevens on the third, and anything from fours to elevens on the second—according to the number of balls they sank in the water. And they had done these three holes in twelve. John Gooch looked at Frederick Pilcher and Frederick Pilcher looked at John Gooch. Their eyes were gleaming, and they breathed a little stertorously through their noses.

"Pretty work," said John Gooch.

"Nice stuff," said Frederick Pilcher.

"Get a move on, blisters," growled Sidney McMurdo.

It was at this point that the madness came upon these two men.

Picture to yourself their position. Each felt that by continuing to play in this form he was running a deadly risk of having to marry Agnes Flack. Each felt that his opponent could not possibly keep up so hot a pace much longer, and the prudent course, therefore, was for himself to ease off a bit before the crash came. And each, though fully aware of all this, felt that he was dashed if he wasn't going to have a stab at doing the round of his life. It might well be that, having started off at such a clip, he would find himself finishing somewhere in the eighties. And that, surely, would compensate for everything.

After all, felt John Gooch, suppose he did marry Agnes Flack, what of it? He had faith in his star, and it seemed to him that she might quite easily get run over by a truck or fall off a cliff during the honeymoon. Besides, with all the facilities for divorce which modern civilization so beneficently provides, what was there to be afraid of in marriage, even with an Agnes Flack?

Frederick Pilcher's thoughts were equally optimistic. Agnes Flack, he reflected, was undeniably a pot of poison; but so much the better. Just the wife to keep an artist up to the mark. Hitherto he had had a tendency to be a little lazy. He had avoided his studio and loafed about the house. Married to Agnes Flack, his studio would see a lot more of him. He would spend all day in it—probably have a truckle bed put in and never leave it at all. A sensible man, felt Frederick Pilcher, can always make a success of marriage if he goes about it in the right spirit.

John Gooch's eyes gleamed. Frederick Pilcher's jaw protruded. And neck and neck, fighting grimly for their sixes and sometimes even achieving fives, they came to the ninth green, halved the hole, and were all square at the turn.

It was at this point that they perceived Agnes Flack standing on the club-house terrace.

"Yoo-hoo!" cried Agnes in a voice of thunder.

And John Gooch and Frederick Pilcher stopped dead in their tracks, blinking like abruptly-awakened somnambulists.

She made a singularly impressive picture, standing there with her tweed-clad form outlined against the white of the club-house wall. She had the appearance of one who is about to play Boadicea in a pageant; and John Gooch, as he gazed at her, was conscious of a chill that ran right down his back and oozed out at the soles of his feet.

"How's the match coming along?" she yelled, cheerily.

"All square," replied Sidney McMurdo, with a sullen scowl. "Wait where you are for a minute, germs," he said "I wish to have a word with Miss Flack."

He drew Agnes aside and began to speak to her in a low rumbling voice. And presently it was made apparent to all within a radius of half a mile that he had been proposing to her once again, for suddenly she threw her head back and there went reverberating over the countryside that old familiar laugh.

"Ha, ha, ha, ha, ha, ha, HA!" laughed Agnes Flack.

John Gooch shot a glance at his opponent. The artist, pale to the lips, was removing his coat and hat and handing them to his caddie. And, even as John Gooch looked, he unfastened his braces and tied them round his waist. It was plain that from now on Frederick Pilcher intended to run no risk of not overswinging.

John Gooch could appreciate his feelings. The thought of how that laugh would sound across the bacon and eggs on a rainy Monday morning turned the marrow in his spine to ice and curdled every red corpuscle in his veins. Gone was the exhilarating ferment which had caused him to skip like a young ram when a long putt had given him a forty-six for the first nine. How bitterly he regretted now those raking drives, those crisp flicks of the mashie-niblick of which he had been so proud ten minutes ago. If only he had not played such an infernally good game going out, he reflected, he might at this moment be eight or nine down and without a care in the world.

A shadow fell between him and the sun; and he turned to see Sidney McMurdo standing by his side, glaring with a singular intensity.

"Bah!" said Sidney McMurdo, having regarded him in silence for some moments. He turned on his heel and made for the club-house.

"Where are you going, Sidney?" asked Agnes Flack.

"I am going home," replied Sidney McMurdo, "before I murder these two miserable harvest-bugs. I am only flesh and blood, and the temptation to grind them into powder and scatter them to the four winds will shortly become too strong. Good morning."

Agnes emitted another laugh like a steam-riveter at work.

"Isn't he funny?" she said, addressing John Gooch, who had clutched at his scalp and was holding it down as the vibrations died away. "Well, I suppose I shall have to referee the rest of the match myself. Whose honour? Yours? Then drive off and let's get at it."

The demoralizing effects of his form on the first nine holes had not completely left John Gooch. He drove long and straight, and stepped back appalled. Only a similar blunder on the part of his opponent could undo the damage.

But Frederick Pilcher had his wits well about him. He overswung as he had never overswung before. His ball shot off into the long grass on the right of the course, and he uttered a pleased cry.

"Lost ball, I fancy," he said. "Too bad!"

"I marked it," said John Gooch, grimly. "I will come and help you find it."

"Don't trouble."

"It is no trouble."

"But it's your hole, anyway. It will take me three or four to get out of there."

"It will take me four or five to get a yard from where I am."

"Gooch," said Frederick Pilcher, in a cautious whisper, "you are a cad."

"Pilcher," said John Gooch, in tones equally hushed, "you are a low bounder.

And if I find you kicking that ball under a bush, there will be blood shed—and in large quantities."

"Ha, ha!"

"Ha, ha to you!" said John Gooch.

The ball was lying in a leathery tuft, and, as Pilcher had predicted, it took three strokes to move it back to the fairway. By the time Frederick Pilcher had reached the spot where John Gooch's drive had finished, he had played seven.

But there was good stuff in John Gooch. It is often in times of great peril that the artistic temperament shows up best. Missing the ball altogether with his next three swings, he topped it with his fourth, topped it again with his fifth, and, playing the like, sent a low, skimming shot well over the green into the bunker beyond. Frederick Pilcher, aiming for the same bunker, sliced and landed on the green. The six strokes which it took John Gooch to get out of the sand decided the issue. Frederick Pilcher was one up at the tenth.

But John Gooch's advantage was short-lived. On the right, as you approach the eleventh green there is a deep chasm, spanned by a wooden bridge. Frederick Pilcher, playing twelve, just failed to put his ball into this, and it rolled on to within a few feet of the hole. It seemed to John Gooch that the day was his. An easy mashie-shot would take him well into the chasm, from which no eighteen-handicap player had ever emerged within the memory of man. This would put him two down—a winning lead. He swung jubilantly, and brought off a nicely-lofted shot which seemed to be making for the very centre of the pit.

And so, indeed, it was; and it was this fact that undid John Gooch's schemes. The ball, with all the rest of the chasm to choose from, capriciously decided to strike the one spot on the left-hand rail of the wooden bridge which would deflect it towards the flag. It bounded high in the air, fell on the green, and the next moment, while John Gooch stood watching with fallen jaw and starting eyes, it had trickled into the hole.

There was a throbbing silence. Then Agnes Flack spoke.

"Important, if true," she said. "All square again. I will say one thing for you two— you make this game very interesting."

And once more she sent the birds shooting out of the tree-tops with that hearty laugh of hers. John Gooch, coming slowly to after the shattering impact of it, found that he was clutching Frederick Pilcher's arm. He flung it from him as if it had been a loathsome snake.

A grimmer struggle than that which took place over the next six holes has probably never been seen on any links. First one, then the other seemed to be about to lose the hole, but always a well-judged slice or a timely top enabled his opponent to rally. At the eighteenth tee the game was still square; and John Gooch, taking advantage of the fact that Agnes had stopped to tie her shoe-lace endeavoured to appeal to his one-time friend's better nature.

"Frederick," he said, "this is not like you."

"What isn't like me?"

"Playing this low-down game. It is not like the old Frederick Pilcher."

"Well, what sort of a game do you think you are playing?"

"A little below my usual, it is true," admitted John Gooch. "But that is due to nervousness. You are deliberately trying to foozle, which is not only painting the lily but very dishonest. And I can't see what motive you have, either."

"You can't, can't you?"

John Gooch laid a hand persuasively on the other's shoulder.

"Agnes Flack is a most delightful girl."

"Who is?"

"Agnes Flack."

"A delightful girl?"

"Most delightful."

"Agnes Flack is a delightful girl?"

"Yes."

"Oh?"

"She would make you very happy."

"Who would?"

"Agnes Flack."

"Make me happy?"

"Very happy."

"Agnes Flack would make me happy?"

"Yes."

"Oh?"

John Gooch was conscious of a slight discouragement. He did not seem to be making headway.

"Well, then, look here," he said, "what we had better do is to have a gentleman's agreement."

"Who are the gentlemen?"

"You and I."

"Oh?"

John Gooch did not like the other's manner, nor did he like the tone of voice in which he had spoken. But then there were so many things about Frederick Pilcher that he did not like that it seemed useless to try to do anything about it. Moreover, Agnes Flack had finished tying her shoe-lace, and was making for them across the turf like a mastodon striding over some prehistoric plain. It was no time for wasting words.

"A gentleman's agreement to halve the match," he said hurriedly.

"What's the good of that? She would only make us play extra holes."

"We would halve those too."

"Then we should have to play it off another day."

"But before that we could leave the neighbourhood."

"Sidney McMurdo would follow us to the ends of the earth."

"Ah, but suppose we didn't go there? Suppose we simply lay low in the city and grew beards?"

"There's something in it," said Frederick Pilcher, reflectively.

"You agree?"

"Very well."

"Splendid!"

"What's splendid?" asked Agnes Flack, thudding up.

"Oh—er—the match," said John Gooch. "I was saying to Pilcher that this was a splendid match."

Agnes Flack sniffed. She seemed quieter than she had been at the outset, as though something were on her mind.

"I'm glad you think so," she said. "Do you two always play like this?"

"Oh, yes. Yes. This is about our usual form."

"H'm! Well, push on."

It was with a light heart that John Gooch addressed his ball for the last drive of the match. A great weight had been lifted from his mind, and he told himself that now there was no objection to bringing off a real sweet one. He swung lustily; and the ball, struck on its extreme left side, shot off at right angles, hit the ladies' tee-box, and, whizzing back at a high rate of speed, would have mown Agnes Flack's ankles from under her, had she not at the psychological moment skipped in a manner extraordinarily reminiscent of the high hills mentioned in Sacred Writ.

"Sorry, old man," said John Gooch, hastily, flushing as he encountered Frederick Pilcher's cold look of suspicion. "Frightfully sorry, Frederick, old man. Absolutely unintentional."

"What are you apologizing to *him* for?" demanded Agnes Flack with a good deal of heat. It had been a near thing, and the girl was ruffled.

Frederick Pilcher's suspicions had plainly not been allayed by John Gooch's words. He drove a cautious thirty yards, and waited with the air of one suspending judgment for his opponent to play his second. It was with a feeling of relief that John Gooch, smiting vigorously with his brassie, was enabled to establish his *bona fides* with a shot that rolled to within mashie-niblick distance of the green.

Frederick Pilcher seemed satisfied that all was well. He played his second to the edge of the green. John Gooch ran his third up into the neighbourhood of the pin.

Frederick Pilcher stooped and picked his ball up.

"Here!" cried Agnes Flack.

"Hey!" ejaculated John Gooch.

"What on earth do you think you're doing?" said Agnes Flack.

Frederick Pilcher looked at them with mild surprise.

"What's the matter?" he said. "There's a blob of mud on my ball. I just wanted to brush it off."

"Oh, my heavens!" thundered Agnes Flack. "Haven't you ever read the rules? You're disqualified."

"Disqualified?"

"Dis-jolly-well-qualified," said Agnes Flack, her eyes flashing scorn. "This cripple here wins the match."

Frederick Pilcher heaved a sigh.

"So be it," he said. "So be it."

"What do you mean, so be it? Of course it is."

"Exactly. Exactly. I quite understand. I have lost the match. So be it."

And, with drooping shoulders, Frederick Pilcher shuffled off in the direction of the bar.

John Gooch watched him go with a seething fury which for the moment robbed him of speech. He might, he told himself, have expected something like this. Frederick Pilcher, lost to every sense of good feeling and fair play, had double-crossed him. He shuddered as he realized how inky must be the hue of Frederick Pilcher's soul; and he wished in a frenzy of regret that he had thought of picking his own ball up. Too late! Too late!

For an instant the world had been blotted out for John Gooch by a sort of red mist. This mist clearing, he now saw Agnes Flack standing looking at him in a speculative sort of way, an odd expression in her eyes. And beyond her, leaning darkly against the club-house wall, his bulging muscles swelling beneath his coat and his powerful fingers tearing to pieces what appeared to be a section of lead piping, stood Sidney McMurdo.

John Gooch did not hesitate. Although McMurdo was some distance away, he could see him quite clearly; and with equal clearness he could remember every detail of that recent interview with him. He drew a step nearer to Agnes Flack, and having gulped once or twice, began to speak.

"Agnes," he said huskily, "there is something I want to say to you. Oh, Agnes, have you not guessed——"

"One moment," said Agnes Flack. If you're trying to propose to me, sign off. There is nothing doing. The idea is all wet."

"All wet?"

"All absolutely wet. I admit that there was a time when I toyed with the idea of marrying a man with brains, but there are limits. I wouldn't marry a man who played golf as badly as you do if he were the last man in the world. Sid-nee!" she roared, turning and cupping her mouth with her hands; and a nervous golfer down by the lake-hole leaped three feet and got his mashie entangled between his legs.

"Hullo?"

"I'm going to marry you, after all."

"Me?"

"Yes, you."

"Three rousing cheers!" bellowed McMurdo.

Agnes Flack turned to John Gooch. There was something like commiseration in her eyes, for she was a woman. Rather on the large side, but still a woman.

"I'm sorry," she said.

"Don't mention it," said John Gooch.

"I hope this won't ruin your life."

"No, no."

"You still have your Art."

"Yes, I still have my Art."

"Are you working on anything just now?" asked Agnes Flack.

"I'm starting a new story to-night," said John Gooch. "It will be called *Saved From The Scaffold.*"

22

THE LETTER OF THE LAW

"Fo—o—o—re!"

The cry, in certain of its essentials not unlike the wail of a soul in torment, rolled out over the valley, and the young man on the seventh tee, from whose lips it had proceeded, observing that the little troupe of spavined octogenarians doddering along the fairway paid no attention whatever, gave his driver a twitch as if he was about to substitute action for words. Then he lowered the club and joined his companion on the bench.

"Better not, I suppose," he said, moodily.

The Oldest Member, who often infested the seventh tee on a fine afternoon, nodded.

"I think you are wise," he agreed. "Driving into people is a thing one always regrets. I have driven into people in my golfing days, and I was always sorry later. There is something about the reproachful eye of the victim as you meet it subsequently in the bar of the club-house which cannot fail to jar the man of sensibility. Like a wounded oyster. Wait till they are out of distance, says the good book. The only man I ever knew who derived solid profit from driving into somebody who was not out of distance was young Wilmot Byng. . . ."

The two young men started.

"Are you going to tell us a story?"

"I am."

"But——"

"I knew you would be pleased," said the Oldest Member.

Wilmot Byng at the time of which I speak (the sage proceeded) was an engaging young fellow with a clear-cut face and a drive almost as long as the Pro's. Strangers, watching him at his best, would express surprise that he had never taken a couple of days off and won the Open Championship, and you could have knocked them down with a putter when you informed them that his handicap was six. For Wilmot's game had a fatal defect. He was impatient. If held up during a round, he tended to press. Except for that, however, he had a sterling nature and frank blue eyes which won all hearts.

It was the fact that for some days past I had observed in these eyes a sort of cloud that led me to think that the lad had something on his mind. And when we were lunching together in the club-house one afternoon and he listlessly refused a most admirable steak and kidney pudding I shot at him a glance so significant that, blushing profusely, he told me all.

He loved, it seemed, and the partner he had selected for life's medal round was a charming girl named Gwendoline Poskitt.

I knew the girl well. Her father was one of my best friends. We had been at the University together. As an undergraduate, he had made a name as a hammer thrower. More recently, he had taken up golf, and being somewhat short-sighted and completely muscle-bound, had speedily won for himself in our little community the affectionate sobriquet of the First Grave Digger.

"Indeed?" I said. "So you love Gwendoline Poskitt, do you? Very sensible. Were I a younger man, I would do it myself. But she scorns your suit?"

"She doesn't scorn any such dashed thing," rejoined Wilmot with some heat. "She is all for my suit."

"You mean she returns your love?"

"She does."

"Then why refuse steak and kidney pudding?"

"Because her father will never consent to her becoming my wife. And it's no good saying Why not elope? because I suggested that and she would have none of it. She loves me dearly, she says—as a matter of fact, she admitted in so many words that I was the tree on which the fruit of her life hung—but she can't bring herself to forgo the big church wedding, with full choral effects and the Bishop doing his stuff and photographs in the illustrated weekly papers. As she quite rightly pointed out, were we to sneak off and get married at the registrar's, bim would go the Bishop and phut the photographs. I can't shake her."

"You ought not to want to shake her."

"Move her, I mean. Alter her resolution. So I've got to get her father's consent. And how can I, when he has it in for me the way he has?"

He gave a groan and began to crumble my bread. I took another piece and put it on the opposite side of my plate.

"Has it in for you?"

"Yes. It's like this. You know the Wrecking Crew?"

He was alluding to the quartet of golfing cripples of which Joseph Poskitt was a regular member. The others were Old Father Time, The Man With The Hoe, and Consul, the Almost Human.

"You know the way they dodder along and won't let anyone through. There have been ugly mutterings about it in the Club for months, and it came even harder on me than on most of the crowd, for, as you know, I like to play quick. Well, the other day I cracked under the strain. I could endure it no longer. I——"

"Drove into them?"

"Drove into them. Using my brassie for the shot. I took a nice easy stance, came back slow, keeping my head well down, and let fly—firing into the brown, as it were, and just trusting to luck which of them I hit. The man who drew the short straw was old Poskitt. I got him on the right leg. Did you tell me he got his blue at Oxford for throwing the hammer?"

"Throwing the hammer, yes."

"Not the high jump?"

"No."

"Odd. I should have said——"

I was deeply concerned. To drive into the father of the girl you love, no matter what the provocation, seemed to me an act of the most criminal folly and so I told him.

He quivered and broke a tumbler.

"Now there," he said, "you have touched on another cause for complaint. At the time, I had no notion that he was the father of the girl I loved. As a matter of fact, he wasn't, because I had not met Gwendoline then. She blew in later, having been on one of those round-the-world cruises. I must say I think that old buffers who hold people up and won't let them through ought to wear some sort of label indicating that they have pretty daughters who will be arriving shortly. Then one would know where one was and act accordingly. Still, there it is. I gave old Poskitt this juicy one, as described, and from what he said to me later in the changing room I am convinced that any suggestions on my part that I become his son-in-law will not be cordially received."

I ate cheese gravely. I could see that the situation was a difficult one.

"Well, the only thing I can advise," I said, "is that you cultivate him assiduously. Waylay him and give him cigars. Ask after his slice. Tell him it's a fine day. He has a dog named Edward. Seek Edward out and pat him. Many a young man has won over the father of the girl he loves by such tactics, so why not you?"

He agreed to do so, and in the days which followed Poskitt could not show his face in the club-house without having Wilmot spring out at him with perfectos. The dog Edward began to lose hair off his ribs through incessant patting. And gradually, as I had hoped, the breach healed. Came a morning when Wilmot, inquiring after my old friend's slice, was answered not with the usual malevolent grunt but with a reasonably cordial statement that it now showed signs of becoming a hook.

"Ah?" said Wilmot. "A cigar?"

"Thanks," said Poskitt.

"Nice doggie," said Wilmot, pursuing his advantage by administering a hearty buffet to Edward's aching torso before the shrinking animal could side-step.

"Ah," said Poskitt.

That afternoon, for the first time for weeks, Wilmot Byng took twice of steak and kidney pudding at lunch and followed it up with treacle tart and a spot of Stilton.

And so matters stood when the day arrived for the annual contest for the President's Cup.

The President's Cup, for all its high-sounding name, was one of the lowliest and most humble trophies offered for competition to the members of our club, ranking in the eyes of good judges somewhere between the Grandmothers' Umbrella and the Children's All-Day Sucker (open to boys and girls not yet having celebrated their seventh birthday). It has been instituted by a kindly committee for the benefit of the canaille of our little golfing world, those retired military, naval and business men who withdraw to the country and take up golf in their fifties. The contest was decided by medal play, if you could call it that, and no exponent with a handicap of under twenty-four was allowed to compete.

Nevertheless, there was no event on the fixture list which aroused among those involved a tenser enthusiasm. Centenarians sprang from their bathchairs to try their skill, and I have seen men with waist lines of sixty doing bending and stretching exercises for weeks in advance in order to limber themselves up for the big day. Form was eagerly discussed in the smoking room, and this year public opinion wavered between two men: Joseph Poskitt, the First Grave Digger, and Wadsworth Hemmingway, better known in sporting circles as Palsied Percy.

The betting, as I say, hovered uncertainly between these two, but there was no question as to which was the people's choice. Everybody was fond of Poskitt. You might wince as you saw his iron plough through the turf, but you could not help liking him, whereas Hemmingway was definitely unpopular. He was a retired solicitor, one of those dark, subtle, sinister men who carry the book of rules in their bag, and make it their best club. He was a confirmed hole-claimer, and such are never greatly esteemed by the more easy-going. He had, moreover, a way of suddenly clearing his throat on the greens which alone would have been sufficient to ensure dislike.

The President's Cup was an event which I always made a point of watching, if I could, considering it a spectacle that purged the soul with pity and terror: but on this occasion business in London unfortunately claimed me and I was compelled to deprive myself of my annual treat. I had a few words with Wilmot before leaving to catch my train. I was pleased with the lad.

"You've done splendidly, my boy," I said. "I notice distinct signs of softening on our friend's part."

"Me too," agreed Wilmot jubilantly. "He thanks me now when I give him a cigar."

"So I observed. Well, continue to spare no effort. Did you wish him success for this afternoon?"

"Yes. He seemed pleased."

"It might be a good idea if you were to offer to caddie for him. He would appreciate your skilled advice."

"I thought of that, but I'm playing myself."

"Today?"

I was surprised, for President's Cup day is usually looked on as a sort of Walpurgis

Night, when fearful things are abroad and the prudent golfer stays at home.

"I promised a fellow a game, and I can't get out of it."

"You will be held up a good deal, I am afraid."

"I suppose so."

"Well, don't go forgetting yourself and driving into Poskitt."

"I should say not, ha, ha! Not likely, ho, ho! One doesn't do that sort of thing twice, does one? But excuse me now, if you don't mind. I have an appointment to wander in the woods with Gwendoline."

It was late in the evening when I returned home. I was about to ring up Poskitt to ask how the contest had come out, when the telephone rang and I was surprised to hear Hemmingway's voice.

"Hullo," said Hemmingway. "Are you doing anything tomorrow morning?"

"Nothing," I replied. "How did things come out this afternoon?"

"That is what I rang up about. Poskitt and I tied for a low score at a hundred and fifteen. I put the matter up to the Committee and they decided that there must be a play off—match play."

"You mean stroke play?"

"No, match play. It was my suggestion. I pointed out to Poskitt that by this method he would only have to play the first ten holes, thus saving wear and tear on his niblick."

"I see. But why was it necessary to refer the thing to the Committee?"

"Oh, there was some sort of foolish dispute. It turned on a question of rubs of the green. Well, if you aren't doing anything tomorrow, will you referee the play off?"

"Delighted."

"Thanks. I want somebody who knows the rules. Poskitt does not seem to realize that there are any."

"Why do you say that?"

"Well, he appears to think that when you're playing in a medal competition you can pick and choose which strokes you are going to count and which you aren't. Somebody drove into him when he was addressing his ball at the eleventh and he claims that that is what made him send it at right angles into a bush. As I told him, and the Committee supported me . . ."

A nameless fear caused the receiver to shake in my hand.

"Who drove into him?"

"I forget his name. Tall, good-looking young fellow with red hair——"

I had heard enough. Five minutes later, I was at Wilmot's door, beating upon it. As he opened it, I noticed that his face was flushed, his eye wild.

"Wilmot!" I cried.

"Yes, I know," he said impatiently, leading the way to the sitting-room. "I suppose you've been talking to Poskitt."

"To Hemmingway. He told me——"

"I know, I know. You were surprised?"

"I was shocked. Shocked to the core. I thought there was better stuff in you, young Byng. Why, when the desire to drive into people grips you, do you not fight against it and conquer it like a man? Have you no will power? Cannot you shake off this frightful craving?"

"It wasn't that at all."

"What wasn't what at all?"

"All that stuff about having no will power. I was in full possession of my faculties when I tickled up old Poskitt this afternoon. I acted by the light of pure reason. Seeing that I had nothing to lose——"

"Nothing to lose?"

"Not a thing. Gwendoline broke off the engagement this morning."

"What?"

"Yes. As you are aware, we went to wander in the woods. Well, you know how you feel when you are wandering in the woods with a girl you adore. The sunlight streamed through the overhanging branches, forming a golden pattern on the green below: the air was heavy with fragrant scents and murmurous with the drone of fleeting insects, and what with one thing and another I was led to remark that I loved her as no one had ever loved before. Upon which, she said that I did not love her as much as she loved me. I said yes, I did, because my love stood alone. She said no, it didn't, because hers did. I said it couldn't because mine did.

"Hot words ensued, and a few moments later she was saying that she never wanted to see or speak to me again, because I was an obstinate, fatheaded son of an Army mule. She then handed back my letters, which she was carrying in a bundle tied round with lilac ribbon somewhere in the interior of her costume, and left me. Naturally, then, when Poskitt and his accomplice held us up for five minutes on the eleventh, I saw no reason to hesitate. My life's happiness was wrecked, and I found a sort of melancholy consolation in letting him have it on the seat of the pants with a wristy spoon shot."

In the face of the profounder human tragedies there is little that one can say. I was pondering in gloomy silence on this ruin of two young lives, when the door bell rang. Wilmot went to answer it and came back carrying a letter in his hand. There was a look upon his face which I had not seen since the occasion when he missed the short putt on the eighteenth which would have given him the Spring medal.

"Listen," said Wilmot. "Cyanide. Do you happen to have any cyanide on you?"

"Cyanide?"

"Or arsenic would do. Read this. On second thoughts, I'll give you the gist. There is some rather fruity stuff in Para. One which I feel was intended for my eye alone. The nub is that Gwendoline says she's sorry and it's all on again."

The drama of the situation hit me like a stuffed eelskin.

"She loves you as of yore?"

"Rather more than of yore, if anything, I gather."

"And you——"

"And I——"

"Have driven——"

"Have driven——"

"Into——"

"Into old Poskitt, catching him bending——"

"Causing him to lose a stroke and thereby tie for the President's Cup instead of winning it."

I had not thought that the young fellow's jaw could drop any farther, but at these words it fell another inch.

"You don't mean that?"

"Hemmingway rang me up just now to tell me that he and Poskitt turned in the same score and are playing it off tomorrow."

"Gosh!"

"Quite."

"What shall I do?"

I laid my hand upon his shoulder.

"Pray, my boy, that Poskitt will win tomorrow."

"But even then——"

"No. You have not studied the psychology of the long-handicap golfer as I have. It would not be possible for a twenty-four handicap man who had just won his first cup to continue to harbour resentment against his bitterest foe. In the hour of triumph Poskitt must inevitably melt. So pray, my boy."

A quick gleam lit up Wilmot Byng's blue eyes.

"You bet I'll pray," he said. "The way I'll pray will be nobody's business. Push off, and I'll start now."

At eleven o'clock the following morning I joined Poskitt and Hemmingway on the first tee, and a few minutes later the play off for the President's Cup had begun. From the very outset it was evident that this was to be a battle of styles. Two men of more sharply contrasted methods can seldom have come together on a golf course.

Poskitt, the d'Artagnan of the links, was a man who brought to the tee the tactics which in his youth had won him such fame as a hammer thrower. His plan was to clench his teeth, shut his eyes, whirl the club round his head and bring it down with sickening violence in the general direction of the sphere. Usually, the only result would be a ball topped along the ground or—as had been known to happen when he used his niblick—cut in half. But there would come times when by some mysterious dispensation of Providence he managed to connect, in which event the gallery would be stunned by the spectacle of a three-hundred-yarder down the middle. The whole thing, as he himself recognized, was a clean, sporting venture. He just let go and hoped for the best.

In direct antithesis to these methods were those of Wadsworth Hemmingway. It was his practice before playing a shot to stand over the ball for an appreciable time, shaking gently in every limb and eyeing it closely as if it were some difficult point of law. When eventually he began his back swing, it was with a slowness which reminded those who had travelled in Switzerland of moving glaciers. A cautious pause at the top, and the clubhead would descend to strike the ball squarely and dispatch it fifty yards down the course in a perfectly straight line.

The contest, in short, between a man who—on, say, the long fifteenth—oscillated between a three and a forty-two and one who on the same hole always got his twelve —never more, never less. The Salt of Golf, as you might say.

And yet, as I took my stand beside the first tee, I had no feeling of pleasurable anticipation. To ensure the enjoyment of the spectator of a golf match, one thing is essential. He must feel that the mimic warfare is being conducted in the gallant spirit of a medieval tourney, not in the mood of a Corsican vendetta. And today it was only too plain from the start that bitterness and hostility were rampant.

The dullest mind would have been convinced of this by the manner in which, when Hemmingway had spun a half-crown and won the honour, Poskitt picked up the coin and examined it on both sides with a hard stare. Reluctantly convinced by his inspection that there was no funny business afoot, he drew back and allowed his opponent to drive. And presently Hemmingway had completed his customary fifty-yarder, and it was Poskitt's turn to play.

A curious thing I have noticed about golf is that a festering grievance sometimes does wonders for a man's drive. It is as if pent-up emotion added zip to his swing. It was so on the present occasion. Assailing his ball with hideous violence, Poskitt sent it to within ten yards of the green, and a few moments later, despite the fact that Hemmingway cleared his throat both before and during the first, second and third putts, he was one up.

But this pent-up emotion is a thing that cuts both ways. It had helped Poskitt on the first. On the second, the short lake hole, it undid him. With all this generous wrath surging about inside him, he never looked like accomplishing the restrained mashie shot which would have left him by the pin. Outdriving the green by some hundred and seventy yards, he reached the woods that lay beyond it, and before he could extricate himself Hemmingway was on the green and he was obliged to concede. They went to the third all square.

Here Poskitt did one of his celebrated right-angle drives, and took seven to get out of the rough. Hemmingway, reaching the green with a steady eight, had six for it and won without difficulty.

The fourth is a dog-leg. Hemmingway drove short of the bunker. Poskitt followed with a stroke which I have never seen executed on the links before or since, a combination hook and slice. The ball, starting off as if impelled by dynamite, sailed well out to the left, then, after travelling one hundred and fifty yards, seemed to catch sight of the hole round the bend, paused in mid-air and, turning sharply to the right, soared on to the green.

All square once more, a ding-dong struggle brought them to the seventh, which

Poskitt won. Hemmingway, recovering, secured the eighth.

The ninth brings you back to the water again, though to a narrower part of it, and when Poskitt, with another of his colossal drives, finished within fifty yards of the pin, it seemed as if the hole must be his. Allowing him four approach shots and three putts, he would be down in eight, a feat far beyond the scope of his opponent. He watched Hemmingway's drive just clear the water, and with a grunt of satisfaction started to leave the tee.

"One moment," said Hemmingway.

"Eh?"

"Are you not going to drive?"

"Don't you call that a drive?"

"I do not. A nice practice shot, but not a drive. You took the honour when it was not yours. I, if you recollect, won the last hole. I am afraid I must ask you to play again."

"What?"

"The rules are quite definite on this point," said Hemmingway, producing a well-thumbed volume.

There was an embarrassing silence.

"And what do the rules say about clearing your throat on the green when your opponent is putting?"

"There is no rule against that."

"Oh, no?"

"It is recognized that a tendency to bronchial catarrh is a misfortune for which the sufferer should be sympathized with rather than penalized."

"Oh yes?"

"Quite." Hemmingway glanced at his watch. "I notice that three minutes have elapsed since I made my drive. I must point out to you that if you delay more than five minutes, you automatically lose the hole."

Poskitt returned to the tee and put down another ball. There was a splash.

"Playing three," said Hemmingway.

Poskitt drove again.

"Playing five," said Hemmingway.

"Must you recite?" said Poskitt.

"There is no rule against calling the score."

"I concede the hole," said Poskitt.

Wadsworth Hemmingway was one up at the turn.

There is nothing (said the Oldest Member) which, as a rule, I enjoy more than recounting stroke by stroke the course of a golf match. Indeed I have been told that I am sometimes almost too meticulous in my attention to detail. But there is one match which I have never been able to bring myself to report in this manner, and that is the play off for the President's Cup between Wadsworth Hemmingway and Joseph

Poskitt.

The memory is too painful. As I said earlier, really bad golf is a thing which purges the soul, and a man becomes a better and broader man from watching it. But this contest, from the tenth hole—where Poskitt became all square—onwards, was so poisoned by the mental attitude of the principals that to recall it even today makes me shudder. It resolved itself into a struggle between a great-souled slosher, playing far above his form, and a subtle Machiavellian schemer who, outdriven on every hole, held his own by constant reference to the book of rules.

I need merely say that Poskitt, after a two hundred and sixty yard drive at the eleventh, lost the hole through dropping his club in a bunker, that, having accomplished an equally stupendous stroke at the twelfth, he became two down owing to a careless inquiry as to whether I did not think he could get on from there with a mashie ("seeking advice of one who was not his caddie") and that, when he had won the thirteenth, he became two down once more at the short fourteenth when a piece of well-timed throat-clearing on the part of his opponent caused him to miss the putt which should have given him a half.

But there was good stuff in Joseph Poskitt. He stuck to it manfully. The long fifteenth I had expected him to win, and he did, but I had not been prepared for his clever seven on the sixteenth. And when he obtained a half on the seventeenth by holing out from a bunker a hundred and fifty yards short of the green, I felt that all might yet be well. I could see that Hemmingway, confident that he would be dormy one, was a good deal shaken at coming to the eighteenth all square.

The eighteenth was one of those objectionable freak holes, which, in my opinion, deface a golf course. Ten yards from the tee the hill rose almost sheer to the table-land where the green had been constructed. I suppose that from tee to pin was a distance of not more than fifty yards. A certain three if you were on, anything if you were not.

It was essentially a hole unsuited to Poskitt's particular style. What Poskitt required, if he was to give of his best, was a great wide level prairie stretching out before him into the purple distance. Conditions like those of the eighteenth hole put him very much in the position of a house-painter who is suddenly called upon to execute a miniature. I could see that he was ill at ease as he teed his ball up, and I was saddened, but not surprised, when he topped it into the long grass at the foot of the hill.

But the unnerving experience of seeing his opponent hole out from bunkers had taken its toll of Hemmingway. He, too, was plainly not himself. He swung with his usual care, but must have swerved from the policy of a lifetime and lifted his head. He finished his stroke with a nice, workmanlike follow through, but this did him no good, for he had omitted to hit the ball. When he had disentangled himself, there it was, still standing up on its little mountain of sand.

"You missed it," said Poskitt.

"I am aware of the fact," said Hemmingway.

"What made you do that? Silly. You can't expect to get anywhere if you don't hit the ball."

"If you will kindly refrain from talking, I will play my second."

"Well, don't miss this one."

"Please."

"You'll never win at golf if you do things in this slipshod way. The very first thing is to hit the ball. If you don't you cannot make real progress. I should have thought you would have realized that."

Hemmingway appealed to me.

"Umpire, I should be glad if you would instruct my opponent to be quiet. Otherwise, I shall claim the hole and match."

"There is nothing in the rules," I said, "against the opponent offering genial sympathy and advice."

"Exactly," said Poskitt. "You don't want to miss it again, do you? Very well. All I'm doing is telling you not to."

I pursed my lips. I was apprehensive. I knew Hemmingway. Another man in his position might have been distracted by these cracks, but I could see that they had but solidified his determination to put his second up to the pin. I had seen wrath and resentment work a magic improvement in Poskitt's game, and I felt sure that they were about to do so in Wadsworth Hemmingway.

Nor was I mistaken. Concentration was written in every line of the man's face as he swung back. The next moment, the ball was soaring through the air, to fall three feet from the hole. And there was Poskitt faced with the task of playing two from the interior of a sort of jungle. Long grass twined itself about his ball, wild flowers draped it, a beetle was sitting on it. His caddie handed him a niblick, but I could not but feel that what was really required was a steam shovel. It was not a golf shot at all. The whole contract should have been handed to some capable excavation company.

But I had not realized to what lengths an ex-hammer-thrower can go, when armed with a niblick and really up against it. Just as film stars are happiest among their books, so was Joseph Poskitt happiest among the flowering shrubs with his niblick. His was a game into which the niblick had always entered very largely. It was the one club with which he really felt confident of expressing his personality. It removed all finicky science from the proceedings and put the issue squarely up to the bulging biceps and the will to win.

Even though the sight of his starting eyes and the knotted veins on his forehead had prepared me for an effort on the major scale, I gave an involuntary leap as the club came down. It was as if a shell had burst in my immediate neighbourhood. Nor were the effects so very dissimilar to those which a shell would have produced. A gaping chasm opened in the hillside. The air became full of a sort of macedoine of grass, dirt, flowers and beetles. And dimly, in the centre of this moving hash, one perceived the ball, travelling well. Accompanied by about a pound of mixed solids, it cleared the brow and vanished from our sight.

But when we had climbed the steep ascent and reached the green, my heart bled for Poskitt. He had made a gallant effort as ever man made and had reduced the lower slopes to what amounted to a devastated area, but he was lying a full ten feet from the hole and Hemmingway, an unerring putter over the short distance, was safe for three. Unless he could sink this ten-footer and secure a half, it seemed to me inevitable that my old friend must lose the match.

He did not sink it. He tried superbly, but when the ball stopped rolling three inches separated it from the hole.

One could see from Hemmingway's bearing as he poised his club that he had no doubts or qualms. A sinister smile curved his thin lips.

"This for it," he said, with sickening complacency.

He drew back the clubhead, paused for an instant, and brought it down.

And, as he did so, Poskitt coughed.

I have heard much coughing in my time. I am a regular theatre-goer, and I was once at a luncheon where an operatic basso got a crumb in his windpipe. But never have I heard a cough so stupendous as that which Joseph Poskitt emitted at this juncture. It was as if he had put a strong man's whole soul into the thing.

The effect on Wadsworth Hemmingway was disintegrating. Not even his cold self-control could stand up against it. A convulsive start passed through his whole frame. His club jerked forward, and the ball, leaping past the hole, skimmed across the green, took the edge in its stride and shot into the far bunker.

"Sorry," said Poskitt. "Swallowed a fly or something."

There was a moment when all Nature seemed to pause, breathless.

"Umpire," said Hemmingway.

"It's no good appealing to the umpire," said Poskitt. "I know the rules. They covered your bronchial catarrh, and they cover my fly or something. You had better concede the hole and match."

"I will not concede the hole and match."

"Well, then, hurry up and shoot," said Poskitt, looking at his watch, "because my wife's got a big luncheon party today, and I shall get hell if I'm late."

"Ah!" said Hemmingway.

"Well, snap into it," said Poskitt.

"I beg your pardon?"

"I said, 'Snap into it'."

"Why?"

"Because I want to go home."

Hemmingway pulled up the knees of his trousers and sat down.

"Your domestic arrangements have nothing to do with me," he said. "The rules allow me five minutes between strokes. I propose to take them."

I could see that Poskitt was shaken. He looked at his watch again.

"All right," he said. "I can manage another five minutes."

"You will have to manage a little more than that," said Hemmingway. "With my next stroke I shall miss the ball. I shall then rest for another five minutes. I shall then miss the ball again . . . ."

"But we can't go on all day."

"Why not?"

"I must be at that lunch."

"Then what I would suggest is that you pick up and concede the hole and match."

"Caddie," said Poskitt.

"Sir?" said the caddie.

"Go to the club and get my house on the phone and tell my wife that I am unavoidably detained and shall not be able to attend that luncheon party."

He turned to me.

"Is this five minutes business really right?"

"Would you care to look at my book of the rules?" said Hemmingway. "I have it here in my bag."

"Five minutes," mused Poskitt.

"And as four and a half have now elapsed," said Hemmingway, "I will now go and play my third."

He disappeared.

"Missed it," he said, returning and sitting down again. The caddie came back.

"Well?"

"The lady said 'Oh, yeah?' "

"She said what?"

" 'Oh, yeah?' I tell her what you tell me to tell her and she said 'Oh, yeah?' "

I saw Poskitt's face pale. Nor was I surprised. Any husband would pale if his wife, in response to his telephone message that he proposed to absent himself from her important luncheon party, replied "Oh, yeah?" And of all such husbands, Joseph Poskitt was the one who might be expected to pale most. Like so many of these big, muscle-bound men, he was a mere serf in the home. His wife ruled him with an unremitting firmness from the day they had stepped across the threshold of St. Peter's, Eaton Square.

He chewed his lower lip thoughtfully.

"You're sure it wasn't 'Oh, *yes*'—like that—without the mark of interrogation— as much as to say that she quite understood and that it would be perfectly all right?"

"She said, 'Oh, yeah?' "

"H'm," said Poskitt.

I walked away. I could not bear the spectacle of this old friend of mine in travail. What wives do to their husbands who at the eleventh hour edge out of important luncheon parties I am not able, as a bachelor, to say, but a mere glance was enough to tell me that in the Poskitt home, at least, it was something special. And yet to pick up and lose the first cup he had ever had a chance of winning. . . . No wonder Joseph Poskitt clutched his hair and rolled his eyes.

And so, as I say, I strolled off, and my wandering footsteps took me in the direction of the practice tee. Wilmot Byng was there, with an iron and a dozen balls.

He looked up, as I approached, with a pitiful eagerness.

"Is it over?"

Not yet."

"They haven't holed out?"

"Not yet."

"But they must have done," said Wilmot, amazed. "I saw them both land on the green."

"Poskitt has played three and is lying dead."

"Well, where's Hemmingway?"

I peered round the bush which hides the eighteenth green from the practice tee.

"Just about to play five from the far bunker."

"And Poskitt is dead in three?"

"Yes."

"Well, then . . ."

I explained the circumstances. Wilmot was aghast.

"But what's going to happen?"

I shook my head sadly.

"I fear that Poskitt has no alternative but to pick up. His wife, informed over the telephone that he would not be back to lunch, said 'Oh, yeah?'"

For a space Wilmot Byng stood brooding.

"You'd better be getting along," he advised. "From what you tell me, this seems to be one of those matches where an umpire on the spot is rather required."

I did so, for I could see that there was much in what he said. I found Poskitt pacing the green. Hemmingway climbed out of the bunker a moment later to announce that he had once more been unsuccessful in striking the ball.

He seemed disposed to conversation.

"A lot of wasps there are about this summer," he said. "One sang right past my ear just then."

"I wish it had bitten you," said Poskitt.

"Wasps," replied Hemmingway, who dabbled in Natural History, "do not bite. They sting. You are thinking of snakes."

"Your society would make anyone think of snakes."

"Gentlemen," I said. "Gentlemen!"

Saddened, I strolled away again. Golf to me is a sacred thing, and it pained me to see it played in this spirit. Moreover, I was beginning to want my lunch. It was partly the desire to converse with a rational human being and partly the reflection that he could pop into the clubhouse and bring me out a couple of ham sandwiches that led me to seek Wilmot Byng again. I made my way to the practice tee, and as I came in sight of it I stopped dead.

Wilmot Byng, facing the bunker, was addressing a ball with his iron. And standing in the bunker, his club languidly raised for his sixth, or it may have been his seventh, was Wadsworth Hemmingway.

The next moment Wilmot had swung, and almost simultaneously a piercing cry of agony rang out over the countryside. A magnificent low, raking shot, with every ounce of wrist and weight behind it, had taken Hemmingway on the left leg.

Wilmot turned to me, and in his eyes there was the light which comes into the eyes of those who have set themselves a task and accomplished it.

"You'll have to disqualify that bird," he said. "He has dropped his club in a bunker."

Little (said the Oldest Member) remains to be told. When, accompanied by Wilmot, I returned to the green, I formally awarded the match and cup to Poskitt, at the same time condoling with his opponent on having had the bad luck to be in the line of flight of somebody's random practice drive. These things, I pointed out, were all in the game and must be accepted as rubs of the green. I added that Wilmot was prepared to apologize, and Wilmot said, Yes, fully prepared. Hemmingway was, however, none too well pleased, I fear, and shortly afterwards he left us, his last words being that he proposed to bring an action against Wilmot in the civil courts.

The young fellow appeared not to have heard the threat. He was gazing at Poskitt, pale but resolute.

"Mr. Poskitt," he said. "May I have a word with you?"

"A thousand," replied Poskitt, beaming on his benefactor, for whom it was plain that he had now taken a fancy amounting to adoration. "But later on, if you don't mind. I have to run like a . . ."

"Mr. Poskitt, I love your daughter."

"So do I," said Poskitt. "Very nice girl."

"I want to marry her."

"Well, why don't you?"

"You will give your consent?"

A kindly smile flickered over my old friend's face. He looked at his watch again, then patted Wilmot affectionately on the shoulder.

"I will do better than that, my boy," he said. "I will formally refuse my consent. I will forbid the match *in toto* and oppose it root and branch. That will fix everything nicely. When you have been married as long as I have, you will know that what these things require is tact and the proper handling."

And so it proved. Two minutes after Poskitt had announced that young Wilmot Byng wished to marry their daughter Gwendoline and that he, Poskitt, was resolved that this should be done only over his, Poskitt's, dead body, Mrs. Poskitt was sketching out the preliminary arrangements for the sacred ceremony. It took place a few weeks later at a fashionable church with full choral effects, and all were agreed that the Bishop had seldom been in finer voice. The bride, as one was able to see from the photographs in the illustrated weekly papers, looked charming.

23

FAREWELL TO LEGS

SQUEALS of feminine merriment woke the Oldest Member from the doze into which he had fallen. The door of the cardroom, in which it was his custom to take refuge when there was Saturday-night revelry at the club-house, had opened to admit a gloomy young man.

"Not butting in, am I?" said the gloomy young man. "I can't stand it out there any longer."

The Sage motioned him to a chair. He sank into it and for a while sat glowering darkly.

"Tricks with string!" he muttered at length.

"I beg your pardon?"

"Josh Hook is doing tricks with bits of string, and the girls are fawning on him as if he were Clark Gable. Makes me sick."

The Oldest Member began to understand.

"Is your *fiancée* among them?"

"Yes, she is. She keeps saying, 'Oh, Mr. *Hook*!' with a sort of rising inflection and giving him pats on the arm. Loving pats, or so it seemed to me."

The Sage smiled sympathetically. In his hot youth he had been through this sort of thing himself. "Cheer up," he said. "I know just how you feel, but rest assured that all will be well. Josh Hook's string tricks may be sweeping the girl off her feet for the moment, but his glamour will pass. She will wake tomorrow morning her true self again, thankful that she has the love of a good man who seldom shoots worse than eighty-three."

His companion brightened. His face lost its drawn look.

"You think so?"

"I am convinced of it. I have seen so many of these party hounds. They dazzle for a while, but they never last. I have observed this Hook. His laughter is as the crackling of thorns under the pot and his handicap is twenty-four. Just another Legs Mortimer?"

"Who was Legs Mortimer?"

"That was precisely what Angus McTavish wanted to know when he saw him blowing kisses at Evangeline Brackett from the club-house veranda."

Angus McTavish (said the Oldest Member), as one might infer from his name, was a man who all his life had taken golf with a proper seriousness, and in Evangeline Brackett he seemed to have found his female counterpart. She was not one of those girls who titter "tee-hee" when they top a drive. It was, indeed, her habit of biting her lips and rolling her eyes on such occasions which had first drawn Angus to her. On her side, respect for a man who, though slight of build and weighing ten stone two, could paste the ball two hundred yards from the tee, had speedily ripened into passion, and at the time of which I speak they had just become engaged; and the only cloud on Angus's happiness, until the series of events began which I am about to describe, was the fact that his great love occasionally caused him to fluff a chip shot. He would be swinging and he would suddenly think of Evangeline and jerk his head towards the sky, as if asking Heaven to make him worthy of her, thus shanking. He told me he had lost several holes that way.

However, the iron self-control of the McTavishes was rendering these lapses less frequent, and, as I say, there was virtually no flaw in his happiness until the spring morning when, coming up from the eighteenth green with the girl of his dreams, to whom he had been giving a third, he was shocked to observe that there was a young man on the club-house veranda, leaning over the rail and blowing kisses at her.

Now, no recently betrothed lover likes this sort of thing, and it jars him all the more sharply when, as in the present case, the blower is a man of extraordinary physical attractions, with large brown eyes and a natural wave in his hair. There was a certain coldness in Angus's voice as he spoke.

"Who," he asked, "is that bird?"

"Eh?" said Evangeline. She was polishing her ball with a sponge and her head was bent.

"Fellow on the veranda. Seems to know you."

Evangeline looked up. She stared for a moment, then uttered a delightful yowl.

"Why, it's Legs! Yoo-hoo!"

"Yoo-hoo!"

"Yoo-hoo!"

"Yoo-hoo!"

As, at the beginning of the episode, they had not been more than four Yoo-hoos' length from the veranda, they were now standing beside the handsome stranger.

"Why, Legs Mortimer!" said Evangeline. "Whatever are you doing here?"

The young man explained—in a manner which may have been merely brotherly, but which seemed to Angus McTavish rather fresher than an April breeze—that he had come to settle in the neighbourhood and that while his bungalow was being made ready he was temporarily established at the clubhouse. In making this statement, he addressed Evangeline once as "sweetness", twice as "kid", and three times as "darling".

"Splendid!" said Evangeline. "You'll wake the place up."

"Trust me, beautiful. Trust old Legs, kid. There will be many a jocund party thrown in yonder club-house."

"Well, mind you invite me. By the way, this is my *fiancé*, Angus McTavish."

"Angus McTavish," cried Legs Mortimer. "Hoots, mon! Scots wha hae! Hoo's a' wi' ye the morn's morn?"

And Angus, hearing these words and watching their speaker break into what appeared to be a Highland fling, became aware with a sinking heart that here, as he had already begun to suspect, was a life-and-soul-of-the-party man, a perfect scream, and an absolutely priceless fellow who simply makes you die with the things he says.

He was thoughtful as he accompanied Evangeline to her home.

"This Mortimer," he said dubiously.

"What about him?"

"Well, what about him? Who is he? Where did you meet him? What is his handicap?"

"I met him when I was over in Switzerland last winter. He was staying at the hotel. I believe he has a lot of money of his own. He doesn't play golf."

"Doesn't play golf?" said Angus incredulously.

"No. But he's wonderful at ski-ing."

"Faugh!"

"What?"

"I said 'Faugh!' Ski-ing, indeed! What on earth does the fellow want to ski for? Isn't there enough sadness in life without going out of your way to fasten long planks to your feet and jump off mountains? And don't forget this—from ski-ing to yodelling is but a short step. Do we want a world full of people going about the place singing, 'Ti-ra-ra-la-i-te,' or something amounting to very much the same thing? I'll bet this Mortimer man of yours is a confirmed yodeller."

"He did yodel a good deal," admitted Evangeline. "He yodelled to the waiters."

"Why to the waiters?"

"They were Swiss, you see. So he yodelled to them. He made us all scream. And he was always playing jokes on people."

"Jokes?"

"Like giving them trick cigars, you know. There was a Bishop staying at the hotel, and Legs gave him a cigar and the Bishop went off with a bang. We all expired with mirth."

Angus drew his breath in sharply.

"So," he said, "the man is not only a dangerous incendiary, but utterly lacking in respect for the Cloth. Faugh!"

"I wish you wouldn't say 'Faugh!'"

"Enough to make one say 'Faugh!'" said Angus sombrely.

The joy had gone out of his world. A dark fog seemed to be spreading over the sunlit uplands of his bliss, and there was a marked shortage of blue birds.

He viewed the future with concern. And he had good reason to do so. Little by little, as the days went by, the conviction was forced upon him that Evangeline Brackett was becoming infatuated with this yodelling, trick-cigar merchant. That very first morning he had thought them a great deal too matey. A week later, he was compelled to recognize that matiness was a feeble and inadequate word. It was Legs this and Legs that and Oh, Legs, and Yoo-hoo, Legs, till he began to feel like a super standing in the wings watching Romeo and Juliet play their balcony scene. A great bitterness of spirit began to descend on Angus McTavish, and he twice took sixes at holes at which in happier days he had often got threes.

There is no question (said the Oldest Member) that these party lizards like Legs Mortimer are a terrible menace when they sneak out into the rural districts. In a great city their noxious influence is less marked. The rushing life of a metropolis seems to fortify girls against their meretricious spell. But in a peaceful hamlet like that in which Angus McTavish and Evangeline Brackett resided there are so few counter-attractions that the poison may be said to work without anything in the nature of an antidote.

Except, of course, golf. The one consolation which Angus had during this dark period was the fact that Evangeline had not yet faltered in her devotion to golf. She was practising diligently for the Ladies' Spring Medal.

And yet, though, as I say, this consoled Angus, it did so only faintly. If Evangeline could still turn out with her bag of clubs and practise for the Spring Medal, it showed, of course, that her better self was not entirely dead. But of what avail was it to practise, he asked himself, if Legs Mortimer gave almost nightly parties and she persisted in attending them? Until the other's arrival, Evangeline had been accustomed to go to bed at eleven after spending the evening with some good book such as Braid on Taking Turf. Now, it seemed a perpetual race between her and the milkman as to which should reach her door first, with the milkman winning three times out of four.

He tried to reason with her one morning when a sudden yawn had caused her to top a mashie niblick shot which a month before she would have laid dead to the pin.

"What can you expect," he said, "if you stop up half the night at parties?"

She was plainly impressed.

"You don't really think it's hurting my game, do you?"

"It is ruining your game."

"But everybody goes to parties."

"Not when they have an important match in prospect."

"And Legs's parties are such fun. He makes them go so."

"Oh yes?" said Angus coldly.

"He's a perfect scream. You should have seen him last night. He told Jack Prescott he wanted him to help him with a trick, and he got him to lay his hands on the table, palms downward. Then he put a full glass of water on each hand . . ."

"And then——?" said Angus, with deepening gloom, for his whole soul was revolted at the thought of Jack Prescott, a four handicap man, lending himself to such childishness.

"Why, then he just walked away and left him, and Jack couldn't get his hands free without drenching himself with water. We simply howled."

"Well," said Angus, when he had ceased shuddering, "if you will take my advice, you will cut out these orgies from now on."

"I must go to the one next week."

"Why?"

"I promised I would. It's Legs's birthday."

"Then," said Angus, "I shall come, too."

"But you'll only go to sleep. You ought to see Legs's imitation of you going to sleep at a party. It's a scream."

"Possibly," said Angus stiffly, "I may doze off for a while. But I shall wake up in time to take you home at a reasonable hour."

"But I don't want to go home at a reasonable hour."

"You would prefer to finish about sixteenth in the Spring Medal?"

The girl paled.

"Don't say that."

"I do say that."

"Sixteenth?"

"Or seventeenth."

She drew in her breath sharply.

"All right, then. You shall take me home before midnight."

"Good," said Angus.

Being of Scottish descent, he never smiled, but he came within an ace of smiling as he heard those words. For the first time in weeks he was conscious of something that might roughly be called a gleam of light on the darkness of his horizon.

Nothing but love and his determination to save the girl he worshipped from crawling into bed at four in the morning could have forced Angus McTavish, when the appointed night arrived, to fish out the old stiff shirt and put on dress clothes and present himself at the club-house. The day had been unusually warm for the time of year and he had played three rounds and was feeling that desire for repose and solitude which comes to men who have done their fifty-four holes under a hot sun. But tomorrow was the day of the Ladies' Spring Medal, and at whatever cost to himself it was imperative that Evangeline be withdrawn from the revels at an hour which would enable her to get a good night's sleep. So he fought down the desire to put on pyjamas, and presently was mingling with Legs Mortimer's guests, trying to stifle the yawns which nearly tore him asunder.

Equally hard to stifle was the austre disgust which swept over him as he surveyed his surroundings. Legs Mortimer was a man who prided himself on doing these things well, and the club-house had broken out into an eruption of roses, smilax, Chinese lanterns, gold-toothed saxophonists, giggling girls and light refreshments. An inhabitant of ancient Babylon would have beamed approvingly on the spectacle, but it made Angus McTavish sick. His idea of a club-house was a sort of cathedral filled with serious-minded men telling one another in quiet undertones how they got a four on the long fifteenth.

His rising nausea was in no way allayed by the sight of Evangeline treading the measure in the arms of his host. Angus had never learned to dance, fearing that it might spoil his game, and so knew nothing of the technicalities of the modern fox-trot. He was unable to say, accordingly, whether Legs Mortimer should or should not have been holding Evangeline like that. It might be all right. On the other hand, it might not be all right. All Angus knew was that he had seen melodramas on the stage in which heroines had told villains to unhand them on far less provocation.

Finally, he could endure the thing no longer. There was a sort of annexe, soothingly dark, at the end of the room, and into this he withdrew. He sank into a chair, and almost immediately fell into a restful slumber.

How long he slept, he could not have said. It seemed to him but a moment, but no doubt it was in reality a good deal longer. He was aroused by someone shaking his shoulder and, blinking up, perceived Legs Mortimer at his side. Legs Mortimer's face was contorted with alarm, and he was shouting something which, after a brief interval of dazed misapprehension, Angus discovered was the word "Fire!"

The last mists of sleep rolled away from Angus McTavish. He was his keen, alert self once more. He had grasped the situation and realized what must be done.

His first thought was of Evangeline. He must start by saving her. Then he must save the trophies in the glass case on the smoking-room mantelpiece, including the ball used by Henry Cotton when breaking the course record. After that he must attend to the female guests, and after that rescue the man who mixed the club's special cocktails, and finally, if there was still time, he must save himself.

It was a comprehensive programme, calling for prompt action and an early start, and he embarked upon it immediately. With a cry of "Evangeline!" he sprang to his feet, and the next moment had shot into the ball-room with incredible velocity and was skidding along the polished floor on one ear.

Only then did he observe that during his slumbers some hidden hand had fastened roller-skates to his feet with stout straps. Simultaneously with this discovery came the sound of musical mirth on every side, and looking up he found himself the centre of a ring of merry, laughing faces. The merriest of these faces, and the one that laughed most, was that of Evangeline Brackett.

It was a grim, moody Angus McTavish who, some five minutes later, after taking three more tosses in a manner which he distinctly heard Evangeline compare to the delivery of coals in sacks, withdrew on all fours to the kitchen, where a kindly waiter cut the straps with a knife. It was a stern, soured Angus McTavish who, having tipped his preserver, strode off through the night to his cottage. He had a nasty bruise on his right thigh, but it was in his soul that he suffered most.

His love, he told himself, was dead. He felt that he had been deceived in Evangeline. A girl capable of laughing like a hyena at her betrothed in the circumstances in which Evangeline Brackett had laughed like a hyena at him was not, he reasoned, worthy of a good man's devotion. If this was the sort of girl she was, let her link her lot with that of Legs Mortimer. If her spiritual mate was a fellow who could outrage all the sacred laws of hospitality by fastening roller-skates to his guests' feet and then shouting "Fire!" in their ears, let her have him.

He rubbed himself with liniment and went to bed.

When he woke on the morrow, however, his mood, as so often happens, had become softer and gentler. He still chafed at the thought that Evangeline could have lowered herself to behave like a hyena, and a mentally arrested hyena at that, but now he was charitably inclined to put her conduct down to cerebral excitement induced by the insidious atmosphere of Chinese lanterns and smilax. Briefly, what he felt was that the girl had been temporarily led astray, and that it must be his task to win her back to the straight and narrow fairway. When, therefore, the telephone rang and he heard her voice, he greeted her amiably.

"How's the boy?" asked Evangeline. "All right?"

"Splendid," said Angus.

"No ill effects after last night?"

"None."

"You're caddying for me in the Ladies' Medal today, aren't you?"

"Of course."

"That's good. I was afraid you might want to be off somewhere, roller-skating. Ha, ha, ha," said Evangeline, laughing a silvery laugh. "He, he, he," she added, laughing another.

Now, against silvery laughs *qua* silvery laughs there is, of course, nothing to be said. But there are moments in a man's life when he is ill-attuned to them, and it must be confessed that this particular couple, proceeding whence they did, stirred Angus McTavish up to no little extent. A good deal of the softness and gentleness was missing from his composition when he presented himself on the first tee. In fact, not to put too fine a point upon it, he was as sore as a gumboil. And as this showed plainly in his demeanour, and as Evangeline was noticeably off her game during the opening holes, they came to the ninth green with a certain constraint between them. Angus was still thinking of those silvery laughs and feeling that they had been, all things considered, in the most dubious taste, while Evangeline, on her side, was asking herself petulantly how on earth a girl could be expected to shoot to form in the society of a caddie who looked like a V-shaped depression off the coast of Ireland.

And at this crucial point in the affairs of the young couple, when it needed but a spark to precipitate an explosion, whom should they see leaning over the club-house veranda but Legs Mortimer.

"Greetings, fair gentles," said Legs Mortimer. "And how is our bright and beautiful Evangeline this bright and beautiful morning?"

"Oh, Legs, you're a scream," said Evangeline. "Did you," she inquired of her betrothed, "speak?"

"I did not," said Angus, who had snorted.

"And the McTavish of McTavish," proceeded Legs Mortimer. "How is the

McTavish of McTavish? Listen," he said, "I think it's all right. I've been in communication with the management of an important circus this morning, and they tell me if that roller-skating act of yours is as good as I say it is they will book you solid."

"Oh, yes?" said Angus.

He was well aware that it was not much of a retort, but then no mere verbal thrust would have satisfied him. What he would have liked to do was to take Legs Mortimer's neck in his two hands, twist it, and continue twisting till it came unstuck. But he was slender of physique, and the other, like so many ski-iers and yodellers, was massive and well-proportioned, so he was compelled to confine himself to saying "Oh yes?" and adding, "Is that so?" His deportment, while making these observations, was that of an offended cobra.

"Well, boys and girls," said Legs Mortimer, "I will now withdraw to the bar and take a short, quick one. I have a slight headache, and meseems a hair of the dog that bit me is indicated."

Beaming in the insufferable manner that is so frequent with these party lizards, he walked away, and Evangeline, turning imperiously on Angus, said: "Oh, for goodness' sake." And when Angus said What did she mean by saying "Oh for goodness' sake," she said that he knew very well what she meant by saying "Oh, for goodness' sake."

"Behaving like that to poor Legs!"

"Like what?"

"Like a sulky schoolboy."

"Faugh!"

"I was ashamed of you."

"Faugh!"

"Don't say 'Faugh!'"

"Pshaw!"

"And don't say 'Pshaw,' either."

"Can't I speak?"

"Not if you're only going to say 'Faugh!' and 'Pshaw!'"

Angus was half inclined to remark that he had also been going to say "Tchah!" and "Pah!" but he restrained himself and kicked moodily at the woodwork.

"I simply can't understand you."

"You can't, can't you?"

"Any man with a grain of humour would have laughed himself sick at what happened last night."

"He would, would he?"

"Yes, he would. When Legs played that trick on the Prince of Schlossing-Lossing, the prince was fearfully amused."

"He was, was he?"

"Yes, he was. He laughed heartily, looking bronzed and fit."

"He did, did he?"

"Yes, he did."

"Well, I'm not a prince."

"I'll say you're not."

"What do you mean by that?"

"You're a—well, I don't know what you are."

"Is that so?"

"Yes, that is so."

"Indeed?"

"Yes, indeed."

The hot blood of the McTavishes boiled over.

"Well, I'll tell you," said Angus, "what you are."

"What?"

"You want to know?"

"I do."

"All right, then. You're the girl who's going to finish twenty-seventh in the Ladies' Medal."

"Don't talk nonsense."

"I'm not talking nonsense."

"Then it's the first time."

"I'm talking cold sense. You know as well as I do that all this party stuff has turned you from a fine, resolute, upstanding beater of the ball to a wretched, wobbling foozler who ought never to have entered her name for so important a contest as the Ladies' Medal. You have your little mirror with you, I presume? Gaze into it, Evangeline Brackett, and read its message. Your eye is dull and fishy, woman. Your hand trembles. You waggle your putter as if it were a cocktail shaker. And as for the way you have been playing—if I may employ the word 'playing'— with your wooden clubs . . ."

Evangeline's face was very cold and hard.

"Yes?" she said, "Proceed."

"No," replied Angus. "The subject is too painful. But I will say this: If I were you, I'd keep my wood in the bag from now on."

It was the unforgivable insult. A sock on the jaw Evangeline Brackett might have condoned, a kick in the eye she might have overlooked, but this was too much. Now that Angus McTavish had forfeited her affection by his uncouth and sullen behaviour, there were two things only that she loved—her mother and her steel-shafted driver.

"Good morning, Mr. McTavish," she said. "If you will kindly hand me that bag of clubs, I will not trouble you to come round with me any longer."

A swift revulsion of feeling swept over Angus McTavish. He perceived that he had gone too far. He loved this girl, and he had hurt her.

"Evangeline!" he cried.

"My name," said the girl, "is Brackett. A 'Miss' goes with it."

"But listen," pleaded Angus. "This is absurd. You know I worship the very tee you walk on. Are we to part like this just because that Mortimer excrescence has come into our lives? Shall our dream Paradise be shattered by a snake in the bosom—or is it grass—who is not worth a thought from either of us? If you will but reflect, you will see how right I am in regarding him as a worm and a pustule. Consider. The man yodels. He does not play golf. He . . ."

"My bag of clubs, if you please," said Evangeline haughtily, "and look slippy with it, if you will be so good. I do not wish to remain here all day. Ah, here comes Legs. Dear old Legs! Legs, darling, will you carry for me?"

"Carry what, sweetest of your sex?"

"My clubs."

"Oh, the jolly old hockey-knockers? Certainly, certainly, certainly."

"Hockey-knockers!" hissed Angus in her ear. "You heard what he said! One of the finest steel-shafted, rubber-grip, self-compensating sets of clubs ever made by the Pro, and he called them hockey-knockers. I warn you, girl, have a care. Do not trust that man. Somehow, somewhere, in some manner, at some time and place, he will let you down, and with a bump. Beware!"

"Come on, Legs darling," said Evangeline, laughing a silvery laugh. "My partner's waiting."

Standing there on the veranda with folded arms, Angus McTavish watched them depart. Evangeline, her face like stone, did not vouchsafe him so much as a glance over her shoulder. Cold and aloof, she made her way to the tenth tee, and Legs Mortimer, having tilted his hat to one side, put on a false moustache which he produced from an inner pocket, and danced a few steps, said "Hot dog," shouldered the bag and followed her.

Now, it may well be (said the Oldest Member) that, listening to what I have been telling you and particularly taking into consideration the remarks of Angus McTavish during the scene which I have just described, you will have formed the impression that after her performance going out it was scarcely worth Evangeline Brackett's while to bother to play the second nine. Having made a start like that, you probably feel, she might just as well, for all the chance she had of winning the Ladies' Medal, have torn up her card and gone home.

But you must make allowances for the exaggeration—shall I say the imagery?—of a jealous lover still smarting from the fact of having had roller-skates put on him by his rival in the presence of the adored object, and then having been laughed at by her, first in a hyena-like and then in a silvery manner. These things distort the judgment and lend acid to the tongue. When Angus had referred so bitingly to Evangeline's inefficiency with the wood, he had had in mind merely the circumstance of her having topped a couple of spoon shots. His remark about the putter and the cocktail shaker was based on a slight disposition on her part to fail to lay approach shots dead. The truth was that Evangeline, though perhaps five strokes in excess of what a pure-minded girl with her handicap might have expected to take on nine holes, was still well in the running. And the resentment with which she was seething as the result of her ex-*fiancé's* uncouth behaviour resulted now, as resentment so often does on the golf course, in her striking a patch of positive brilliance.

The thought of Angus McTavish and those low cracks of his lent her an almost superhuman vigour. Every time she drove off the tee she did it with a sort of controlled fury, as if she were imagining that she had seen Angus McTavish standing in the middle of the fairway and that a well-directed shot would catch him on the spot where it would do him most good. When she chipped, it was as if she were chipping Angus. And whenever she made a recovery from a bunker with her niblick, she hit the ball as though it were Angus McTavish's shin.

By these means, she was enabled to get fours on the tenth, eleventh and twelfth, a five on the thirteenth, and on the short fourteenth one of those lucky twos which, as James Braid once said to J. H. Taylor, seem like a dome of many-coloured glass to stain the white radiance of Eternity. In short, to condense the thing into cold figures, by the time she had holed out at the seventeenth, she had played a net seventy-three. And when she learned from a bystander that her only two possible rivals had each turned in net seventy-nine, she not unnaturally considered that the contest was as good as over. The eighteenth had always been a favourite hole of hers, and she was supremely confident of securing a four on it. Not even in the stress of a medal round had she the slightest apprehension of failing to be on near the pin with, at the worst, her third.

In these circumstances, it is not to be wondered at that she gazed at Legs Mortimer with an affection bordering on something even warmer. As was his practice when wearing a false moustache, he was waggling the ends of it, and she thought she had never seen anything so droll. How vast an improvement, she felt, not only in the capacity of a caddie but in that of a mate for life, was this sunny, light-hearted merry-maker on such a human pain in the tonsils as Angus McTavish. Going round with Angus McTavish carrying your bag, she mused, was equivalent to about four bisques to the opposition. Angus McTavish was the sort of man who, just by going about looking like a frozen asset, takes all the edge and zip out of a girl's game. She felt that she had had a merciful escape from Angus McTavish.

"What I love about you, Legs," she said, as they walked to the eighteenth tee, "is your wonderful sense of humour. Don't you hate people with no sense of humour? Scotchmen, I mean, and people like that. I mean people who get stuffy if somebody plays a harmless good-natured practical joke on them. Like—well, Scotchmen, I mean."

"Quite," said Legs Mortimer, putting on a false nose.

"I'm sure I should be the first to laugh if anything of that sort ever happened to me. But then, thank goodness, I have always had a sense of humour."

"Great gift," said Legs.

"Well, it's just the way one happens to be born, I suppose," said Evangeline modestly. "You either have it or you haven't. I think I'll have a new ball here, Legs, darling. I don't want to make any mistake over this hole."

The confidence which Evangeline Brackett had felt on holing out at the seventeenth had lost none of its force at this supreme moment. It seemed to inflate her as with some invisible gas as she surveyed the glistening white globe perched up on its wooden tee. Every golfer knows that sensation of power and mastery which comes when he has just played a series of holes in perfect style and is conscious that his stance is right and his wrists are right and all things working together for good. Evangeline had it now. Here was she and there was the ball, and in another moment she was going to slap it squarely in the tummy and send it a mile and a quarter. Her only fear was lest she might overdrive the green, which was a mere three hundred and eighty yards distant.

She waggled for an instant. Then, raising her club with an effortless swing, she brought it down.

And what of Angus, meanwhile? For some little time after Evangeline had left him, he stood rooted to the spot. For some little time after that, he had paced the terrace with knitted brow, reminding not a few of the members who watched him through the windows of Napoleon at St. Helena. Eventually, finding conditions rather cramped and feeling that he needed more space in which to express himself, he had gone for a walk round the links, and by one of those odd coincidences was approaching the eighteenth tee from the rear at the exact moment when Evangeline made her drive. And as he drew near his reverie was suddenly shattered by a hideous, cackling shout of laughter from the other side of the bushes which hid the tee from his view.

He stopped, frowning. Laughter on the links was a thing which always offended his sense of the reverent, and the current burst of merriment he had recognized immediately as emanating from Legs Mortimer. Nobody else's mirth had just that quacking sound.

"Faugh!" said Angus, and was about to repeat the word, when it died on his lips, and he stood gaping. There was a sort of thudding sound as of feet spurning the turf, and then round the corner of the bushes came Legs Mortimer, cutting out an excellent pace, and after him, her face flushed, her eyes staring, Evangeline Brackett, brandishing in her hand a steel-shafted driver. She seemed to be endeavouring to brain the other, if it is possible to brain a man like Legs Mortimer.

There was very little vulgar curiosity in the composition of Angus McTavish, but what there was was sufficient to make him follow the pair at his best speed. He came up with the hunt just as Legs, apparently despairing of shaking off the girl's challenge, dodged behind a leafy tree and, with an adroitness born, no doubt, of his Swiss mountaineering, shinned up it like a squirrel and remained there.

It was at this moment that Evangeline saw Angus.

"Oh, Angus!" she cried, and the next moment she was in his arms.

Scotch blood, it has always been my experience, makes for solid worth rather than nimbleness of wit, for a certain rugged stability of character rather than quick intuition, but even a man as Scotch as Angus McTavish was able to perceive—and that without delay—that here was a good thing which should be pushed along. He would have been the first to admit that he did not quite follow the run of the scenario, but he divined that for some reason which would doubtless be made clear at a later date the past was forgotten and Evangeline's heart his once more. Reaching out, accordingly, he clasped her to his bosom, and for a space he remained there, hiccoughing.

"Oh, Angus!" she sobbed at length. "How right you were!"

"When?" asked Angus McTavish.

"When you warned me against that man. 'Do not trust him,' you said. 'Somehow, somewhere, in some manner, at some time of place, he will let you down, and with a bump.' "

"And did he?"

"Did he not!" replied Evangeline Brackett. "I needed a five on the eighteenth to win the medal, and I asked him to get me out a new ball and do you know what he did?"

"What?"

"I'll tell you what. He put down a s-s-s-s-s."

Anguish robbed Evangeline of speech. There was something scarcely human in her expression, and in endeavouring to frame the last word she had sunk to the level of a soda-siphon.

Angus groped for her meaning.

"He put down what?"

"A s-s-s-s-s."

"Sand?"

She shook her head violently.

"No, no! Not s-s-s-s-s. A s-s-s-s-s."

"S-s-s-s-s?"

"S-s-s-s-s."

"S-s-s-s-s?"

"A soap-ball," said Evangeline, suddenly becoming articulate.

If he had not been holding on to the girl, Angus McTavish would have reeled—Scotch-reeled, as no doubt Legs Mortimer would have described it. If his reverent nature revolted at smilax in the club-house and laughter on the links it revolted with a far greater sensation of outraged nausea at the sight of those cakes of soap which manufacturers, dead to every decent instinct and making a mockery out of sacred things, turn out in the shape of regulation golf-balls. Many a time, going into a chemist's shop to purchase a tube of toothpaste, he had recoiled with a hoarse cry on seeing them on the counter, to take his custom elsewhere. And until now he had always supposed that the ultimate depth possible for Humanity to reach had been reached by the perpetrators of these loathsome travesties.

And now a new low level had been hit. A man—or, rather, a creature bearing the outward semblance of a man—had teed up one of the dreadful things for a girl, a fragile, sensitive girl, to drive—not, which would have been bad enough, in some casual morning round, but at the very crisis of the Ladies' Spring Medal Competition.

"I came down on it like a thousand of bricks," proceeded Evangeline, quivering at the memory, "with every ounce of weight and muscle behind the shot. I thought for a moment I had broken in half. And talking," she went on, a more cheerful note creeping into her voice, "of breaking things in half, if you wouldn't mind, darling, just climbing that tree and handing me down its contents, I will see what can be done with this driver."

But Angus McTavish, who had been scanning the tree closely, shook his head. It was as if he deprecated the violence at which she hinted. Gently he led her from the spot, and it was not until they were the distance of a good iron shot away that he released her and replied to the protestations which she had been uttering.

"It is quite all right, dear," he said. "Everything is in order."

"Everything in order?" she faced him passionately. "What do you mean?"

Angus patted her hand.

"You were a little too overwrought to observe it, no doubt," he said, "but there was a hornets' nest two inches above his head. I think we cannot be accused of being unduly sanguine if we assume that when he starts to . . . Ah!" said Angus, "Hark!"

Unmusical cries were ruining the peace of the spring evening.

"And look," added Angus.

As he spoke, a form came sliding hastily down out of the tree. At a rapid pace it moved across the turf to the water beyond the eighteenth tee. It dived in and, having done so, seemed anxious to remain below the surface, for each time a head emerged from those smelly depths it went under again.

"Nature's remedy," said Angus.

For a long minute Evangeline Brackett stood gazing silently, with parted lips. Then she threw her head back and from those parted lips there proceeded a silvery laugh so piercing in its timbre that an old gentleman practising approach shots at the seventeenth jerked his mashie sharply and holed out from eighty yards.

Angus McTavish patted her hand fondly. He was broad-minded, and felt that there were moments when laughter on the links was permissible.

24

THERE'S ALWAYS GOLF

IT WAS the day of the annual contest for the Mixed Foursomes Cup, and the Oldest Member, accompanied by the friend who was visiting him for the week-end, had strolled to the edge of the terrace to watch the first of the competitors drive off. As they came in sight of the tee the friend uttered an exclamation of astonishment, almost of awe.

"What an extraordinarily handsome woman," he whispered.

He was alluding to the girl who had just teed up her ball and was now inspecting, with a sort of queenly dignity, the bag of clubs offered to her by her caddie—who, one felt, had he any sense of the fitness of things, not that caddies ever have, would have dropped on one knee like a medieval page in the presence of royalty.

The Oldest Member nodded.

"Yes," he agreed. "Mrs. Plinlimmon is much admired in our little circle."

"Her face seems oddly familiar. I have seen it before somewhere."

"No doubt in the newspapers. As Clarice Fitch she was a good deal in the public eye."

"Clarice Fitch? The girl who used to fly oceans and things and cross Africa on foot and what not?"

"Precisely. She is now Mrs. Ernest Plinlimmon."

The Oldest Member's friend eyed her thoughtfully as she took a driver from the bag.

"So that is Clarice Fitch. It must require a good deal of nerve to marry a girl like that. She reminds me of Cleopatra. What sort of fellow is her husband?"

"You see him now, going up to speak to her. The smallish man with the spectacles."

"What! The little chap who looks like the second vice-president of something?"

"Darling," said the small man in the spectacles.

"Yes, darling?"

"Not the driver, darling."

"Oh, darling!"

"No, darling, You know how shaky you are with the wood, darling. Take your iron, darling."

"Must I, darling?"

"Yes, darling."

"Very well. You know best, darling."

On the face of the Oldest Member's friend, as the Sage led him back to their table, there was a look of profound amazement.

"Well," he said, "if I hadn't heard it with my own ears, I would never have believed it. If you had told me that a girl like that would merely coo meekly when informed that she was incapable of using her wooden clubs, I should have laughed derisively. If ever a wife had all the earmarks of being the dominant member of the firm——"

"Quite," assented the Oldest Member. "I admit that that is the impression she conveys. But I can assure you that ever since they were united it is Ernest Plinlimmon who, kindly but with quiet decision, has ruled the home."

"What is he? A lion tamer?"

"No. He is, and has been for many years, an average-adjuster."

"Good at his job, I'll bet."

"Very. I am told by those in a position to know that he adjusts a beautiful average. He is also a devout and quite skilful golfer, playing nowadays to a handicap of four. The inside story of his wooing is a curious one, and affords a striking illustration of a truth in which I have always been a firm believer—that there is a Providence which watches over all pious golfers. In the events which led up to the union of Ernest Plinlimmon and Clarice Fitch one sees the hand of this Providence clearly in operation."

When Clarice Fitch, some two years ago, came to spend the summer with an aunt who resides in this neighbourhood, the effect of her advent upon the unattached males of the place was, as you can readily imagine (said the Oldest Member), stupendous. There was a sort of universal gasp, and men who had been playing for years in baggy flannel trousers with mud stains on them rushed off in a body to their tailors, bidding them work night and day on form-fitting suits of plus-fours. Moustaches were curled, ties straightened, and shoes cleaned that had not been cleaned for months.

And of all those stunned by the impact of her personality, none was more powerfully affected than Ernest Faraday Plinlimmon. Within half an hour of their first meeting, he had shaved twice, put on three clean collars, given all his hats to the odd-job man, and started reading Portuguese Love Sonnets. I met him later in the day at the chemist's. He was buying Stick-o, a preparation for smoothing the hair and imparting to it a brilliant gloss, and inquiring of the man behind the counter if he knew of anything that would be good for freckles.

But, like all the others, he made no progress in his wooing, and eventually, as nearly everybody does around these parts sooner or later, he came to consult me.

"It is killing me, this great love of mine," he said. "I cannot eat, cannot sleep. It has begun to affect my work. Sometimes in my office, as I start to adjust an average, her face rises between me and it, so that I adjust it all crooked and have to start over again. What can I do to melt that proud, cold heart? There must be some method, if one only knew."

One of the compensations of age is that it enables a man to stand aside from the seething cauldron of sex and note in a calm and dispassionate spirit what is going on inside the pot. In my capacity of oldest inhabitant of this hamlet I have often been privileged to see more than can the hot-blooded young principals involved. I had very clear ideas as to what Clarice Fitch found wrong with the attentions to which she had been subjected since her arrival, and these I imparted now to Ernest Plinlimmon.

"What none of you young fellows appear to realize," I said, "is that Clarice Fitch is essentially a romantic girl. The fact that she crosses Africa on foot, when it would be both quicker and cheaper to take a train, proves this. And, being romantic, she demands a romantic lover. You, like all the rest, cringe before her. Naturally, she compares you to your disadvantage with such a man as 'Mgoopi 'Mgwumpi."

Ernest Plinlimmon's eyes widened and his mouth fell open, causing him to look exactly like a fish I once caught off Brighton pier.

"Such a man as—what was that name again?"

" 'Mgoopi 'Mgwumpi. He was the chief, if I remember rightly, of the Lesser 'Mgowpi. I gather that his personality made a deep impression upon Miss Fitch, and that, but for the fact that he was as black as the ace of spades and already had twenty-seven wives and a hundred spares, something might have come of it. At any rate, she as good as told me the other day that what she was looking for was someone who, while possessing the engaging spiritual qualities of this chief, was rather blonder and a bachelor."

"H'm," said Ernest Plinlimmon.

"I can give you another pointer," I proceeded. "She was speaking to me yesterday in terms of admiration of the hero of a novel by a female writer, whose custom it was to wear riding-boots and to kick the girl of his heart with them."

Ernest paled.

"You don't really think she wants a man like that?"

"I do."

"You don't feel that if a fellow had a nice singing voice and was gentle and devoted——"

"I do not."

"But this kicking business . . . I mean, to start with, I haven't any riding-boots . . ."

"Sir Jasper Medallion-Carteret would also on occasion drag the girl round the room by her hair."

"He would?"

"He would."

And Miss Fitch appeared to approve?"

"She did."

"I see," said Ernest Plinlimmon. "I see. Yes. Yes, I see. Well, good night."

He withdrew with bent head, and I watched him go with a pang of pity. It all seemed so hopeless, and I knew it would be futile to try to console him with any idle talk about time effecting a cure. Ernest Plinlimmon was not one of your butterflies who flit from flower to flower. He was an average-adjuster, and average-adjusters are like chartered accountants. When they love, they give their hearts for ever.

Nor did it seem likely that any words of mine to Clarice would bring about an improvement in the general conditions. Still, I supposed I had better try what I could do. My advanced years had enabled me to form an easy friendship with the girl, so it was not difficult for me to bring the conversation round to her intimate affairs. What in a younger man would be impertinence becomes, when the hair has whitened, mere kindly interest.

Taking advantage, accordingly, of a statement on her part to the effect that she was bored, that life seemed to stretch before her, arid and monotonous, like the Gobi Desert, I ventured to suggest that she ought to get married.

She raised her shapely eyebrows.

"To one of these local stiffs, do you mean?"

I sighed. I could not feel that this was promising.

"You are not attracted by the young bloods of our little community?"

A laugh like the screech of a parakeet in the jungles of Peru broke from her lips.

"Young what? Of all the human rabbits I ever encountered, of all the corpses that had plainly been some little time in the water . . ." She paused for an instant, and seemed to muse. "Listen," she went on, her voice soft with a kind of wistfulness, "do you think that novelists draw their characters from real people?"

I sighed again.

"I was reading Chapter Twenty-six of that book last night. There's a meet, and Lady Pamela rides over hounds, and Sir Jasper catches her a juicy one with his hunting crop just on the spot where it would make her think a bit. What a man!"

I sighed for the third time. It seemed so useless to try to give my unhappy young friend a build-up. When a woman is to all intents and purposes wailing for a demon lover, it requires super-salesmanship to induce her to accept on the this-is-just-as-good principle an Ernest Plinlimmon.

However, I made the attempt.

"I know a man living in this vicinity who loves you fondly."

"I know fifty, the poor jellyfish. To which of the prawns in aspic do you refer?"

"Ernest Plinlimmon."

She laughed again, jovially this time.

"Oh, golly! The 'Trees' bird."

"I beg your pardon?"

"He was round at our house last night, and my aunt dragged him to the piano, and he sang 'Only God Can Make A Tree'."

My heart sank. I was stunned that Ernest Plinlimmon could have been guilty of such a piece of mad folly. I could have warned him, had I known that he was a man who had it in his system, that there is something about that particular song which seems to take all the virility out of the singer and leave him spiritually filleted.

Genghis Khan or Attila the Hun, singing that passage about "A nest of robins in her hair," or whatever it is, would have seemed mild and spineless.

"You have mentioned," said Clarice Fitch, sneering visibly, "the one man on this earth whom I wouldn't marry to please a dying grandfather."

"He has a handicap of seven," I urged.

"What at?"

"I refer to the game of golf."

"Well, I don't play golf, so that's wasted on me. All I know is that he's the worst yesser in a neighbourhood congested with yes-men and looks like a shrimp with dyspepsia. Weedy little brute. Wears spectacles. Sort of fellow who couldn't say Bo to a cassowary. What do you imagine this Plinlimmon pimple would do if he had to face a leaping lion?"

"I have no doubt that he would conduct himself like a perfect gentleman," I said, a little coldly, for the girl's hard arrogance had annoyed me.

"Well, you can tell him from me," said Clarice Fitch, "that if he was the last man in the world, I wouldn't give him a second look. Nothing could be fairer than that."

I broke the news to Ernest that evening. It seemed to me kinder to acquaint him with the true position of affairs than to allow him to go on eating his heart out in empty hope. I found him practising chip shots near the seventh green and put the thing to him squarely.

I could see that he was sorely shaken. He topped a shot into the bunker.

"Weedy little brute, did she say?"

"That's right. Weedy little brute."

"And she wouldn't marry me to please a dying uncle?"

"Grandfather."

"Well, I'll tell you," said Ernest Plinlimmon. "The way it looks to me is that I haven't much chance."

"Not a great deal. Of course, if you could bring yourself to hit her over the head with your number three iron——"

He frowned petulantly.

"I won't," he said sharply. "Once and for all, I will not hit her over the head with my number three iron. No, I shall try to forget."

"It seems the only thing to do."

"I shall thrust her image from my mind. Immerse myself in my work. Stay longer at the office. Adjust more averages. And," he said, forcing a brave smile, "there is always golf."

"Well spoken, Ernest Plinlimmon!" I cried. "Yes, there is always golf. And from the way you're hitting them these days it seems to me that, receiving seven, you might quite easily win the summer medal."

A gleam that I liked to see shone through the young fellow's spectacles.

"You think so?"

"Quite easily, if you practise hard."

"You bet I'll practise hard. It has always been the dream of my life to win a medal competition. The only trouble is, I've always felt that half the fun would be telling one's grandchildren about it. And now, apparently, there aren't going to be any grandchildren."

"There will be other people's grandchildren."

"That's right too. Very well, then. From now on, I stifle my love and buckle down to it."

I must confess, however, that, though speaking in airy fashion about winning summer medals, I had done so rather with the idea of giving the unfortunate young man an interest in life than because I actually fancied his chances. It was true that, receiving seven strokes, he might come quite near the top of the list, but there were at least three men in the club who were capable of giving him ten and beating him. Alfred Jukes, for one. Wilberforce Bream, for another. And, for a third, George Peabody.

Still, when I watched him practising, I felt that I had been justified in falsifying the facts. There is something about practice at golf, about the steady self-discipline of playing shot after shot with the same club at the same objective, that gives strength to the soul, and it seemed to me that, as the days went by, Ernest Plinlimmon was becoming a stronger, finer man. And an incident that occurred the day before the competition gave proof of this. I was enjoying a quiet smoke on the terrace, when Clarice Fitch came out of the club-house. It was plain that something had upset her, for there was a frown on her lovely forehead and she was breathing through the nose with a low, whistling sound, like an escape of steam.

"Little worm!" she said.

"I beg your pardon?"

"Miserable undersized microbe!"

"You allude to——?"

"That bacillus in the goggles. The germ with the headlights. The tree crooner. Ernest Plinlimmon, in short. The nerve of the little glass-eyed insect!"

"What has Ernest Plinlimmon been doing to incur your displeasure?"

"Why, I told him to take my aunt to a matinée tomorrow, and he had the crust to say he couldn't."

"But, my dear child, tomorrow is the day of the summer medal competition."

"What in the name of the eight bearded gods of the Isisi is a summer medal competition?"

I explained.

"What!" cried Clarice Fitch. "You mean that he refused to do what I asked him simply because he wanted to stay here and fool about with golf balls? Well, I'm——! Of all the——! Can you beat it! I never heard of such a thing."

She strode off, fuming like an Oriental queen who has been having trouble with the domestic staff, and I resumed my cigar with an uplifted heart. I was proud of Ernest Plinlimmon. This incident showed that he had at last remembered that he was

a golfer and a man. I felt that all he needed now was to do well in this medal competition, and the thrall in which Clarice Fitch held him would be broken for ever. I have
seen it happen so many times. Golfers go off their drive or their approaches or, it
may be, their putting, and while in the enfeebled state induced by this loss of form
fall in love. Then one day they try a new stance and get back on their game and do
not give the girl another thought. My knowledge of human nature told me that,
should Ernest Plinlimmon by some miracle win the summer medal competition, he
would have no time for mooning about and pining for Clarice Fitch. His whole being
would be absorbed by the effort to bring himself down to scratch.

I was delighted, therefore, when I woke next morning, to see that the weather was
fine and the breeze mild, for this meant that play would take place under conditions
most favourable to Ernest's game. He was one of those golfers whom rain or a high
wind upset. It looked as if this might be the young fellow's day.

And so it proved. Confidence gleamed from his spectacles as he strode on to his
first tee, and his opening drive sent the ball sweetly down the middle of the course.
He holed out in a nice four.

It was an auspicious start, and had I been younger and more lissom I would have
liked to follow him round. Nowadays, however, I find that I enjoy these contests more
from a chair on the terrace, relying for my information on those who drop in from
time to time from the Front. It was thus that I learned that Ernest's most dangerous
rivals were decidedly off their game. Their tee shots at the third had been weak, and
at the lake hole Wilberforce Bream had put two into the water. And an hour or so
later there came another bulletin. Wilberforce Bream had torn up his card, George
Peabody had got into a casual sardine tin in the rough on the eleventh and had taken
ten, and Alfred Jukes would be lucky if he did a ninety.

"Right off it, all three of them," said Alexander Bassett, who was my informant.
"Strange."

"Not so very. I happen to know," said Alexander Bassett, who knows everything,
"that that Fitch girl turned them down, one after the other, at intervals during
yesterday evening. This has naturally affected them—off the tee mostly. You know
how it is. If you have a broken heart, it's bound to give you a twinge every now and
then, and if this happens when you are starting your down swing you neglect to let
the clubhead lead."

Well, I was sorry, of course, in a way, for one does not like to think of tragedy
entering the lives of scratch men, but my commiseration waned as I reflected what
this would mean to Ernest Plinlimmon. There is always, in these medal competitions,
the danger of a long-handicap man striking his big day and turning in a net sixty-
eight, but apart from such a contingency it seemed to me that, if he had kept his early
form, he ought now to win. And Alexander's next words encouraged this hope.

"Plinlimmon's playing a nice game," he said. "Nice and steady. Now that the
tigers are off the map, I'm backing him. Though there is one of the submerged tenth,

they tell me—twenty-four handicap man named Perkins—who seems in the money."

Alexander Bassett left me, to resume his inspection of the contest, and I think that shortly afterwards I must have fallen into a doze, for when I opened my eyes, which I had closed for a moment in order to meditate, I found that the sun was perceptibly lower. The cool of the evening was in the air, and I realized that by this time the competition must be drawing to a close. I was about to rise and cross the green to see if there was anything of interest happening on the eighteenth fairway, when Clarice Fitch came over the brow of the hill.

I gave you a description of her aspect on the occasion when she had been telling me how Ernest Plinlimmon, with splendid firmness, had refused to take her aunt to the matinée. She was looking very much like that now. There was the same frown, the same outraged glitter in her imperious eyes, the same escape-of-steam effects through the delicately chiselled nostrils. In addition, she appeared to be walking with some difficulty.

"Has something happened?" I asked, concerned. "You are limping."

She uttered a sharp, staccato howl, not unlike the battle-cry of the West African wild cat.

"So would you be limping, if a human boll-weevil had just hit you with a hard ball."

"What!"

"Yes. I was strolling along and I had stooped to tie my shoe-lace, when suddenly something came whizzing along like a bullet and struck me."

"Good heavens! Where?"

"Never mind," said Clarice Fitch austerely.

"I mean," I hastened to explain, "where did this happen?"

"Down in that field there."

"You mean the eighteenth fairway?"

"I don't know what you call it."

"Was the man driving off the tee?"

"He was standing on a sort of grass platform thing, if that is what you mean."

"What did he say when he came up to you?"

"He hasn't come up to me yet. Wait till he does! Yes, by the sacred crocodile of the Zambesi, just give me two minutes to rub in arnica and another to powder my nose, and I'll be ready for him. Ready and waiting! I'll startle his weak intellect, the miserable little undersized microbe!"

I started at the familiar phrase.

"Was it Ernest Plinlimmon who did this?"

"It was. Well, wait till I meet him."

She limped into the clubhouse, and I hurried down to the eighteenth fairway. I felt that Ernest Plinlimmon should be warned that there lurked against his coming an infuriated female explorer whose bite might well be fatal.

The course has been altered recently, but at the time of which I am speaking the eighteenth hole was the one which terminated below the terrace. It was a nice two-shotter—uphill, but with nothing to trouble the man who was steady off the tee. A good drive left you with a mashie-niblick chip for your second: after a drive that was merely moderate a full mashie or even an iron was required. As I came over the hill, I saw Ernest Plinlimmon and his partner, in whom I recognized a prominent local dub, emerging from the rough on the right. Apparently, the latter had sliced from the tee, and Ernest had been helping him find his ball. Ernest's own blue dot was lying well up the slope, some eighty yards short of the green. I eyed it with respect. Clarice Fitch's evidence had shown that it had been travelling with considerable speed when it encountered her person. But for that unfortunate incident, therefore, it would, presumably, have been good for at least another fifty yards. A superb drive.

The dub played a weak and sinful spoon shot out to the right, and I met Ernest where his ball lay. He blinked at me inquiringly as he came up, and I saw with surprise that his face was totally bare of glass.

"Oh, it's you," he said. "I didn't recognize you at first. I broke my spectacles at the fifteenth, and can't see a thing unless it's within a dozen yards or so."

I clicked my tongue sympathetically.

"Then you are out of the running, I suppose?"

"Out of the running?" cried Ernest Plinlimmon jubilantly. "I should say not. I've been playing like a book. Not being able to see seems to help me to concentrate. Knowing that I can't follow the ball, I don't lift my head. I've got this medal competition in the bag."

"You have?"

"Definitely in the good old sack. I've just been talking to Bassett, and he tells me that Perkins, leading the field by a matter of three strokes, has finished in a net seventy-five. There's nobody behind me, so that when I finish the returns will be all in. I have just played a net seventy-one. I shall be on with a net seventy-two. Then lay it dead with my approach putt and stuff it in with my second, and there I shall be—net seventy-four. It's a walk-over. The thing that makes me a little sore, though, is that, if it hadn't been for the sheep, I might have chipped to the pin and needed only one putt. The animal must have lost me a full fifty yards."

"Ernest," I began.

"My drive—an absolute pippin—was stopped by a sheep. It was standing in the middle of the fairway when I teed up just now. I should have waited, I suppose, but I hate waiting on the tee. So I took a chance, and, apparently, plugged it. Infernal nuisance. It was one of those low, skimming shots and would have run a mile but for that. Still, it doesn't really matter. I can get down in three more on my head."

I reconsidered my intention of warning the young man of what awaited him at journey's end. Obviously, if the state of the score was as he had said, nothing would deter him from holing out. It might be, I felt, that he would be able to make a quick getaway after sinking the winning putt. After all, Clarice Fitch, though she had talked lightly of taking two minutes for the rubbing of arnica on her wounds, would probably not emerge once more into public life for much nearer ten. I said nothing, accordingly, and watched him play a nice mashie shot.

"Where did it go?" he asked.

"On," I replied, "but a little wide of the pin."

"How wide?"

"Possibly fifteen feet."

"Easy," said Ernest Plinlimmon. "I've been laying fifteen footers dead all the way round."

I preserved a tactful silence, but I was disturbed in my mind. I had not liked the airy way in which he had spoken of being on with a net seventy-two, and I did not like the airy way in which he now spoke of laying fifteen-foot putts dead. Confidence, of course, is an admirable asset to a golfer, but it should be an unspoken confidence. It is perilous to put it into speech. The gods of golf lie in wait to chasten the presumptuous.

Ernest Plinlimmon did not lay his approach putt dead. The green was one of those tricky ones. It undulated. Sometimes at the close of a tight match I have fancied that I have seen it heave, like a stage sea. Ernest putted well, but not well enough. A hummock for which he had not allowed caught the ball and deflected it, leaving him a yard and a half from the hole, that fatal distance which has caused championships to change hands.

He shaped for the shot, however, with undiminished confidence.

"And now," Ernest Plinlimmon, "to stuff it in."

His partner, who had picked up and joined us, caught my eye. He had pursed his lips gravely. He was thinking, I knew, as I was, that no good could come of this loose talk.

Ernest Plinlimmon addressed his ball. The line was quite straight and clear, and all that was needed was the right strength. But, alas, nothing is more difficult at the end of a tense round than to estimate strength. As the ball left the clubhead, it looked to me destined for the happy ending. It trickled straight for the hole, and I was just expecting the joyful rattle which would signify that all was well, when it seemed to falter. Two feet . . . one foot . . . six inches . . . it was still moving. Three inches . . . two inches . . . I held my breath.

Would it? Could it?

No! Barely an inch from the cup it wavered, hesitated and stopped. He tapped it in, but it was too late. Ernest Plinlimmon had merely tied for the summer medal, and would have to undergo all the spiritual agonies of a play-off.

It was a moment when unthinking men would have said "Tough luck!" or some such banality. But Ernest's partner and I were seasoned golfers and knew that on these occasions silence is best. We exchanged a mute glance of pity and terror, and then our attention was diverted to the noticeable behaviour of the young man himself.

I had always known Ernest Plinlimmon as a mild, reserved man, and the sight of his contorted face gave me, I must confess, a rather painful shock. His eyes were wild, and the veins stood out on his forehead. I waited with something like apprehension for his first words, but when he spoke it was to utter a simple query.

"Where," inquired Ernest Plinlimmon, "is that sheep?"

"What sheep?" said his partner.

"*The* sheep. The sheep I drove into." His eyes rolled. "The best drive I ever made in my life, a drive that would have put me within easy chip shot of the pin, ruined by a blasted sheep. I now wish to be led into the presence of that sheep, so that I may strangle it with my bare hands."

"It didn't look like a sheep to me," said his partner. "More like Miss Fitch, if you follow what I mean."

"Miss Fitch?"

I gave a violent start. The excitement of watching those final putts had driven everything from my mind. I now remembered that the lad stood in imminent peril, and must be warned to fly while there was yet time. At any moment Clarice Fitch would be coming out of the clubhouse, breathing fire.

"Ernest," I said rapidly, "our friend here is quite correct. Miss Fitch was on the fairway, tying her shoelace . . ."

"What!"

"Tying her shoelace."

"What!"

"Tying her . . ."

My voice died away. Clarice Fitch was standing on the edge of the green, her arms folded, her eyes shooting out little sparks.

"Let us get this straight," said Ernest Plinlimmon, in a strange, quiet voice. "You say that this infernal girl stopped in the middle of the eighteenth fairway, in the middle of a medal competition, in the middle of a man's drive who only needed a four to win, in order to tie her shoelace . . . her blasted shoelace . . . her damned blanked . . ."

A dark flood swept over the young man's face. His teeth came together with a click. For an instant, his mouth opened and his nose twitched and he seemed to be struggling for utterance: then, as if realizing the futility of trying to find words that would do justice to his feelings, he raised his putter and hurled it violently from him. And Clarice Fitch, who had unfolded her arms and was advancing with a slow sinister stride, like the snow leopard of the Himalayas, got it squarely on the shinbone.

It was a moment which I shall not readily forget. I have always ranked it, indeed, among the high spots of my life. Looking back, I find each smallest detail of the scene rising before my eyes as if it had happened yesterday. I see the setting sun crimsoning the western sky. I see the long shadows creeping over the terrace. I see Clarice Fitch hopping about on one leg, while Ernest Plinlimmon, his wrath turned off as if with a tap, stands gaping at the sight of what he has done. And over all, after that first sharp, shrill, piercing cry of agony, there broods a strange, eerie silence.

How long this silence lasted I am not able to say, for at these supreme moments one cannot measure time. But presently Clarice Fitch ceased to hop and, coming to a halt with a hand pressed to her shin, began to speak.

One of the advantages enjoyed by a girl who gets about a bit is that in the crises of life she is not confined to the poor resources of her native tongue. I doubt if Clarice Fitch would have been able to say a tithe of the things she wished to say, had she been compelled to say them in English. The fact that as the result of her travels she had at her command a round dozen or so of African dialects enabled her now to express herself with a rich breadth which could not but awe even one who, like myself, did not understand a single word. There was no need to understand words. Given the situation, one got the general sense, and as the address gathered speed and volume I found myself edging away from Ernest Plinlimmon, fearful lest the lightning playing about his head might include me in its activities. So might the children of Israel have edged away from one of their number who had been so unfortunate as to fall out with the prophet Jeremiah.

And Ernest, as I say, stood gaping. One can dimly picture the young man's feelings. There before him was the shin he loved to touch, and he had sloshed it with a putter. In a similar situation, no doubt, Sir Jasper Medallion-Carteret would merely have sneered. Or he might even have followed up the putter with the number four iron. But Ernest was no Sir Jasper. He had the air of one who is out on his feet.

Over the quiet green the stream of words flowed on without a break. There seemed to be no reason why it should not go on for ever. And then, suddenly, in the very midst of what appeared to be a particularly powerful passage, Clarice Fitch broke down. Bursting into tears, she buried her face in her hands and began hopping again.

I cannot explain this. An instant before, one would have said that she was incapable of such a feminine weakness. The only theory I can advance is that, having reached this point in her remarks, she had suddenly become aware once more of the agony which oratory had for the time enabled her to forget. At any rate, be that as it may, she now burst into tears and buried her face in her hands.

The effect on Ernest Plinlimmon was as if some magic spell had been removed, bringing life again to his congealed frame. He had been standing transfixed, incapable of movement. He now gave a convulsive start, like a somnambulist rudely awakened, and bounded forward—unless I am mistaken in my conjecture—with the idea of grovelling at her feet and beating his head upon the ground. His eyes were glaring. His lips were twisted. He waved his arms in frantic appeal. And just as he reached the girl she raised her head, and his fist, shooting out in a passionate gesture of remorse, caught her on the right eye.

The result was extraordinary. If he had been practising for weeks with a punching bag he could not have brought off a sweeter left jab. It travelled about eight inches with all his weight behind it, and it sent Clarice Fitch over the side of the green as if she had been shot from a gun. One moment, she was among those present; the next, she had disappeared and a fountain of sand showed that she had found the pot bunker which stands at the base of the slope to catch a hooked second.

Ernest Plinlimmon congealed once more, and again time stood still.

As before, one could, in a dim way, picture his feelings. Plainly, he was running over in his mind the recent series of events. He loved this girl and yearned for her to be his. And, in addition to singing "Only God Can Make A Tree" in her presence, he had—in the course of some fifteen minutes—biffed her with a golf ball, cracked her over the shin with a putter and pasted her in the right eye with his fist. Not so good, he was evidently thinking. I saw him put up a hand to straighten his spectacles, only to lower it again on finding no spectacles there. The action was that of a man in a trance.

And he was still standing there, when there was a scrabbling sound and Clarice's head appeared over the edge of the green. And at the sight of it I uttered an involuntary cry of joy, for in her left eye—the other was closed and already assuming a blackish tint—I saw the light of love.

A moment ago, I said that I had been able to read Ernest Plinlimmon's mind. Now, even more clearly, I could read that of Clarice Fitch. It did not need words to tell me that she had been thinking things over in the bunker and had arrived at an arresting conclusion.

That drive that had struck her amidships she had attributed to carelessness. That hurled putter had seemed to her a putter hurled at random. But this punch in the eye had put an entirely different complexion on the matter. That, she knew, had been deliberate and calculated, the violent attempt at self-expression of a man who, though mild of aspect and intensely spectacled, possessed the soul of an infuriated rhinoceros and did not intend to allow girls to abuse him in Swahili without lodging a protest. And if that blow had been deliberate, so must the assault with the driver and putter have been deliberate. In other words, this man, crazed with love, had been wooing her just as she had hoped some day some man would come and woo her. Even the chief of the Lesser 'Mgowpi had not been so rough as this, and, as for Sir Jasper Medallion-Carteret, he became, in comparison with Ernest Plinlimmon, mere small-town stuff.

For an instant, she stood there, rubbing her shin and her eye alternately. Then with oustretched hands she advanced towards young Plinlimmon.

"My man!" she said.

Ernest Plinlimmon did not appear to get it.

"Eh?" he said, blinking. "Your what?"

"My great, strong, wonderful man!"

Once more, he blinked.

"Who, me?"

She flung her arms about his neck in an ecstasy of devotion, so that even Ernest Plinlimmon was able, though still somewhat fogged, to get the general idea. He was bewildered, yes, but he retained sufficient intelligence to do his bit. I saw him stand on tiptoe, for she was considerably the taller, and kiss her. Then with a little sigh of happiness, he adjusted himself to her embrace as if he had been an average, and I turned to his partner who, during the recent events, had been practising short putts.

"Come," I said. "Let us leave them together."

25

UP FROM THE DEPTHS

As THE Oldest Member stood chatting with his week-end guest on the terrace over-looking the ninth green, there came out of the club-house a girl of radiant beauty who, greeting the Sage cordially drew his attention to the bracelet on her shapely arm.

"Isn't it lovely!" she said. "Ambrose gave it me for my birthday."

She passed on, and the guest heaved a moody sigh.

"Once again!" he said. "I've never known it to fail. What on earth is the good of Nature turning out girls like that, seeing that before an honest man can put in his bid they have always gone and got an Ambrose attached to them? Or if not an Ambrose, a Jim or a Tim, or a Fred or a Ned or a Mike or a Spike or a Percival. Sometimes I think I shall go into a monastery and get away from it all."

"You admired my little friend?"

"She is what the doctor ordered."

"It is odd that you should say that, for she is what the doctor got. She is the wife of our local medicine man, Ambrose Gussett."

"I'll bet he isn't worthy of her."

"On the contrary. You might say that he married beneath him. He is a scratch, she a mere painstaking eighteen. But then we must remember that until shortly before her marriage she had never touched a golf club. She was a tennis player," said the Oldest Member, wincing. A devout golfer from the days of the gutty ball, his attitude towards exponents of the rival game had always resembled that of the early Christians towards the Ebionites.

"Well, anyway," said the guest. "I'm glad he remembers her birthday."

"He will always do so. That is one date which is graven on his memory in letters of brass. The time may come when in an absent-minded moment Ambrose Gussett will forgot to pronate the wrists and let the clubhead lead, but he will never forget his wife's birthday. And I'll tell you why," said the Oldest Member, securing his companion's attention by digging him in the lower ribs with the handle of a putter.

Ambrose Gussett (the Sage proceeded) had been a member of our little community for some months before Evangeline Tewkesbury came into his life. We all liked Ambrose and wished him well. He was a pleasant clean-cut young fellow with frank blue eyes and an easy swing, and several of our Society matrons with daughters on their hands were heard to express a regret that he should remain a bachelor.

Attempts to remedy this, however, had come to nothing. Like so many young doctors with agreeable manners and frank blue eyes, Ambrose Gussett continued to be an iodoform-scented butterfly flitting from flower to flower but never resting on any individual bloom long enough to run the risk of having to sign on the dotted line.

And then Evangeline Tewkesbury arrived on a visit to her aunt, Miss Martha Tewkesbury, and he fell for her with a thud which you could have heard in the next county.

It generally happens around these parts that young men who fall in love look me up in my favourite chair on this terrace in order to obtain sympathy and advice as to how to act for the best. Ambrose Gussett was no exception. Waking from a light doze one evening, I perceived him standing before me, scratching his chin coyly with a number three iron.

"I love her, I love her, I love her, I love her," said Ambrose Gussett, getting down to it without preamble. "When in her presence I note a marked cachexia. My temperature goes up, and a curious burning is accompanied by a well-marked yearning. There are floating spots before my eyes, and I am conscious of an over-powering urge to clasp her in my arms and cry 'My mate!'"

"You are speaking of——?"

"Didn't I mention that? Evangeline Tewkesbury."

"Good God!"

"What do you mean?"

I felt it best to be frank.

"My dear Ambrose, I am sorry to give you pain, but Miss Tewkesbury is a tennis player. I have seen her with my own eyes leaping about the court shouting 'Forty love,' 'Thirty all' and similar obscenities."

He astounded me by receiving my words with a careless nod.

"Yes, she told me she played tennis."

"And you still love her?"

"Of course I still love her."

"But, Ambrose, reflect. A golfer needs a wife, true. It is essential that he has a sympathetic listener always handy, to whom he can relate the details of the day's play. But what sort of a life companion would a tennis player be?"

He sighed ecstatically.

"Just let me get this tennis player as a life companion, and you won't find me beefing. I love her, I love her, I love her, I love her, I love her," said Ambrose Gussett, summing up.

A few days later I found him beside my chair once more. His clean-cut face was grave.

"Say, listen," he said. "You know that great love of mine?"

"Ah, yes. How is it coming along?"

"Not too well. Every time I call at her home, I find her festooned in tennis players."

"Her natural mates. Female tennis players always marry male tennis players, poor souls. Abandon this mad enterprise, Ambrose," I pleaded, "and seek for some sweet girl with a loving disposition and a low handicap."

"I won't. My stethoscope is still in the ring. I don't care if these germs are her natural mates. I defy them. Whatever the odds, however sticky the going, I shall continue to do my stuff. But, as I say, the course is heavily trapped and one will need to be at the top of one's form. Looking over the field, I think my most formidable rival is a pin-headed string bean of a fellow named Dwight Messmore. You know him?"

"By sight. She would naturally be attracted by him. I believe he is very expert at this outdoor ping-pong."

"In the running for a place in the Davis Cup team, they tell me."

"What is the Davis Cup team?"

"A team that plays for a sort of cup they have."

"They have cups, do they, in the world—or sub-world—of tennis? And what are you proposing to do to foil this Davis Cup addict?"

"Ah, there you have me. I keep asking her to let me give her a golf lesson. I feel that in the pure surroundings of the practice tee her true self would come to the surface, causing her to recoil with loathing from men like Dwight Messmore. But she scoffs at the suggestion. She says golf is a footling game and she can't understand how any except the half-witted can find pleasure in it."

"And that appalling speech did not quench your love?"

"Of course it didn't quench my love. A love like mine doesn't go around getting itself quenched. But I admit that the situation is sticky, and I shall have to survey it from every angle and take steps."

It was not until several weeks had elapsed, a period in which I had seen nothing of him, that I learned with a sickening qualm of horror how awful were the steps which he had decided to take.

He became a tennis player.

It was, of course, as I learned subsequently, not without prolonged and earnest wrestling with his conscience that a man like Ambrose Gussett, playing even then to a handicap of two and destined in the near future to be scratch, had been able to bring himself to jettison all the principles of a lifetime and plunge into the abyss. Later, when the madness had passed and he was once more hitting them sweetly off the tee, he told me that the struggle had been terrific. But in the end infatuation had proved too strong. If, he said to himself, it was necessary in order to win Evangeline Tewkesbury to become a tennis player, a tennis player he would be.

And, inquiries having informed him that the quickest way of accomplishing this degradation was to put himself in the hands of a professional, he turned up his coat collar, pulled down the brim of his hat, and snaked off to the lair where the man plied his dark trade. And presently he found himself facing a net with a racquet in his hand. Or rather, hands, for naturally he had assumed the orthodox interlocking grip.

This led the professional to make his first criticism.

"You hold the racquet in one hand only," he said.

Ambrose was astounded, but he was here to learn, so he followed out the instruction, and having done so peered about him, puzzled.

"Where," he asked, "is the flag?"

"Flag?" said the professional. "But it isn't the fourth of July."

"I can't shoot unless I see the flag."

The professional was now betraying open bewilderment. He came up to the net and peered at Ambrose over it like someone inspecting a new arrival at the Zoo.

"I don't get this about flags. We don't use flags in tennis. Have you never played tennis? Never? Most extraordinary. Are there other games?"

"I play golf."

"Golf? Golf? Ah, yes, of course. What they call cow-pasture pool."

Ambrose stiffened.

"What *who* call cow-pasture pool?"

"All right-thinking men. Well, well, well! Well, listen," said the professional. "It looks to me as if our best plan would be to start right at the beginning. This is a racquet. This is the net. That is what we call a ball . . ."

It was toward the end of the lesson that a string-bean-like young man sauntered on to the court, and the professional turned to him with the air of one seeking sympathy.

"Gentleman's never played tennis before, Mr. Messmore."

"Well, he certainly isn't playing it now," replied Dwight Messmore. "Ha, ha, ha, ha, ha, ha, ha," he added, with scarcely veiled derision.

Ambrose felt the hot blood coursing in his cheeks, but all he could find to say was "Is that so?" and the lesson proceeded to its end.

It was followed by others, every morning without respite, and at long last the professional declared him competent to appear in—if one may use the term—a serious game, at the same time counselling him not to begin too ambitiously. There was a cripple he knew, said the professional, a poor fellow who had lost both legs in a motor accident, who would be about Ambrose's form, always provided that the latter waited his opportunity and caught him on one of his off days.

But it was with no cripple that Ambrose Gussett made his first appearance. With incredible audacity he sought out Evangeline Tewkesbury and asked her for a game.

The fixture came off next day before an audience consisting of Dwight Messmore, who, though Ambrose gave him every opportunity of remembering another engagement elsewhere, remained on the side lines throughout, convulsed with merriment and uttering, in Ambrose's opinion, far more catcalls than were necessary. Having learned that morning that he had been selected to play in the Davis Cup team, whatever that may be, the man was thoroughly above himself. As early as the middle of the first set he was drawing audible comparisons between Ambrose and a cat on hot bricks, seeming to feel that the palm for gracefulness should be awarded to the latter.

When the game was over—6–0, 6–0—Ambrose inquired of Evangeline if she thought he would ever be a good tennis player. The girl gave him a curious look and asked if he had read any nice books lately. Ambrose mentioned a few, and she said that she had enjoyed them, too, and wondered how authors managed to think up these things. She was starting to touch on the new plays, when Ambrose, bluntly bringing up once more a subject which he had a feeling that she was evading, repeated his question.

Again the girl seemed to hesitate, and it was Dwight Messmore who took upon himself the onus of reply, sticking his oar in with insufferable heartiness.

"The problem which you have propounded, my dear fellow," he said, "is one which it is not easy to answer. A 'good' tennis player, you say. Well, I feel sure that you will always be a moral tennis player, a virtuous, upright tennis player, but if you wish to know whether I think you will ever be able to make a game of it with a child of six, I reply No. Abandon all hope of reaching such heights. Console yourself with the reflection that you have great entertainment value. You are what I should call an amusing tennis player, a tennis player who will always be good for a laugh from the most discriminating audience. I can vouch for this, for I have been filming you from time to time with my ciné-kodak, and whenever I have run the result off at parties it has been the success of the evening. My friends are hard critics, not easy to please, but you have won them. 'Show us Ambrose Gussett playing tennis,' is their cry, and when I do so they guffaw till their eyes bubble."

And scooping Evangeline up he led her off, leaving Ambrose, as you may well imagine, a prey to the most violent and disturbing emotions. If a patient had described to him the symptoms which he was experiencing, he would have ordered him cold compresses and a milk diet.

You will have no difficulty in guessing for yourself the trend his thoughts were taking. He was a doctor, and a doctor is peculiarly situated. He must be a dignified, venerable figure, to whom patients can show their tongues without secret misgivings as to his ability to read their message. And Ambrose, recalling some of his recent activities, could not but feel that a ciné-kodak record of these must lower, if not absolutely destroy, his prestige.

One moment in particular stood out in his memory, when in a fruitless effort to reach and return one of Evangeline's testing drives he had got his left foot entangled with his right elbow and had rolled over and over like a shot rabbit, eventually coming to rest with his head between his legs. Such a picture, exhibited to anything like a wide audience, might well ruin his practice irretrievably.

He woke from a troubled sleep next morning filled with a stern resolve. He had decided to confront Dwight Messmore and demand that film from him. So after a light breakfast he got in his car and drove to the other's residence. Alighting at the door with tight lip and a set face, he beat a sharp tattoo on it with the knocker. And simultaneously there came from within a loud cry, almost a scream, if not a shriek. The next moment the door opened and Dwight Messmore stood before him.

"Holy smoke!" said Dwight Messmore. "I thought it was an atom bomb."

It was plain to Ambrose's experienced eye that the man was not in his customary vigorous health. He was wearing about his forehead a towel which appeared to have ice in it, and his complexion was a curious greenish-yellow.

"Come in," said Dwight Messmore, speaking in a hollow, husky voice, like a spirit at a *séance*. "I was just going to send for you. Walk on tip-toe, do you mind, and speak very softly. I am on the point of expiring."

As he led the way into the living-room, shuffling along like a Volga boatman, a genial voice with a rather nasal intonation cried "Hello!" and Ambrose perceived a handsome parrot in a cage on the table.

"I didn't know you had a parrot," he said.

"I didn't know it myself till this morning," said Dwight Messmore. "It suddenly arrived out of the unknown. A man in a sweater came in a van and left it. He insisted that I had ordered it. Damn fool. Do I look like a man who orders parrots?"

"Ko-ko," observed the bird, which for some moments had taken no part in the conversation.

"Cocoa!" whispered Dwight Messmore with a powerful shudder. "At a moment like this!"

He lowered himself into a chair, and Ambrose gently placed a thermometer in his mouth.

"Can we think of anything that can have caused this little indisposition?" he asked.

"Charcoal poisoning," said Dwight Messmore promptly. "I gave a little party last night to a few fellows to celebrate my making the Davis Cup team——"

"Did we drink anything?"

"Not a thing. Well, just a bottle or two of champagne, and liqueurs . . . brandy, chartreuse, benedictine, curaçao, crème de menthe, kummel and so forth . . . and, of course, whisky. But nothing more. It was practically a teetotal evening. No, what did the trick was that charcoal. As you are probably aware, the stuff they sell you as caviare in this country isn't caviare. It's whitefish roe, and they colour it with powdered charcoal. Well, you can't sit up half the night eating powdered charcoal without paying the penalty."

"Quite," said Ambrose. "Well, I think our best plan will be to remain perfectly quiet with our eyes closed, and presently I will send us a little sedative."

"Have a nut," suggested the parrot.

"No nuts, of course," said Ambrose.

It was only after Ambrose had returned to his car and was driving off to the Tewkesbury home in the hope of seeing Evangeline that it occurred to him that he had forgotten all about that film. Feeling, however, that there would be plenty of time to collect that later, he fetched up at *chez* Tewkesbury and was informed by Miss Martha that Evangeline was out.

"She's upset to-day," said the adored object's aunt. "Not ill, just in a temper. She's gone for a walk. She said it might make her feel better. She is very angry because nobody has remembered her birthday."

Ambrose reeled. He had not remembered it himself. How he had come to allow so vital a date to slip his mind, he was at a loss to understand. He could only suppose that the strain of learning tennis had sapped his intellect.

"She is particularly annoyed," proceeded Miss Tewkesbury, "with Mr. Messmore. She is passionately fond of birds, and Mr. Messmore faithfully promised her a parrot for her birthday. Her birthday arrives, and what happens? No parrot."

She was going on to speak further, but Ambrose was no longer there. With a brief "Excuse me" he had shot from her presence as if Walter Hagen in his prime had driven him off the tee. His alert mind had seen the way.

Once again his knock on Dwight Messmore's door produced that loud cry that was almost a scream, if not a shriek. And once again the invalid presented himself, looking like a full-page illustration from a medical treatise on bubonic plague.

"Ye gods!" he moaned. "Must you? Rap, rap, rap. Tap, tap, tap. Are you a doctor or a woodpecker?"

"Listen," said Ambrose. He had no time for these unmanly complaints. "It just occurred to me. We need perfect relaxation and repose, and we cannot enjoy perfect relaxation and repose if we are consistently hampered by parrots. I will take the bird off our hands."

Although one would have said that such a thing was impossible, the look that came into Dwight Messmore's pea-green face made it seem almost beautiful.

"You will? You really will? Then heaven bless you, you Boy Scout of a physician! Take this bird, Gussett, and my blessing with it. Maybe in the days to come when acquaintance has ripened into friendship and it feels justified in becoming confidential, it will reveal to you what it is that it expects people to have seen by the dawn's early light. So far it has maintained a complete reserve on the point. It just says 'Oh, say have you seen by the dawn's early light?' and then stops and makes a noise like someone drawing a cork. After a brief interval for mental refreshment it then starts all over again at the beginning. Gosh!" said Dwight Messmore, having struggled with his emotion for a while. "It's lucky you came along, you United States marine! I was very near the breaking point, very near. And, by the way," he proceeded, "as a fitting expression of my gratitude I am going to destroy those films I took of you playing—I use the word loosely—tennis. I feel that it is the least I can do. 'Oh, say have you seen by the dawn's early light?' it says, and then the popping noise. Be prepared for this. Well, I will now take a short and, I anticipate, refreshing nap. Good-bye, Gussett. Don't forget your parrot."

It was with a light heart that Ambrose returned to his car, dangling the cage on a carefree finger. And it was with a still lighter heart that, as he rounded a corner, he

saw Evangeline coming along at a quick heel-and-toe. Her brow, he noticed, was
overcast and her lips tightly set, but these were symptoms which he hoped very
shortly to treat and correct.

Evangeline Tewkesbury was, indeed, in no sunny frame of mind. A queen
accustomed to the homage of her little court, she could have betted her Sunday cami-
knickers that her birthday would have found her snowed under with parcels and
flowers, the gift of adoring males of her entourage, and she had imagined that on this
important morning her telephone would never have stopped ringing. Instead of
which, no parcels, no flowers, and out of the telephone not a yip. She might have
been celebrating her birthday on some lonely atoll in the South Seas.

Could she have known that every male friend on her list was suffering, like
Dwight Messmore, from too lavish indulgence in whitefish roe powdered with charcoal, she might have understood and forgiven. But she did not know, and so missed
understanding and forgiveness by several parasangs. Her only feeling towards these
faithless wooers was a well-marked urge to skin them all with a blunt knife and
dance on the remains.

"Good morning, Miss Tewkesbury," cried Ambrose gaily. Good morning, good
morning, good morning. Many happy returns of the day. Happy birthday to you,
happy birthday to you, in short. I have a little present here which I hope you will
accept. Just a trivial parrot, but you may be able to fit it in somewhere."

And, encouraged by the sudden softening of her eyes, he parked the car, stood on
one leg and asked her to be his wife.

When he had finished, she stood silent for a space, and a close observer would
have seen that a struggle was proceeding in her mind. She was weighing the pros and
cons.

She had always liked Ambrose and admired his clean-cut good looks. And the fact
that he had remembered her birthday argued that he was kind, courteous and con-
siderate; of the stuff, in short, of which good husbands are made. For a while the
word "Yes" seemed to be trembling on her lips.

And then, chillingly, there came into her mind the picture of this man as he
had appeared on the tennis court. Could she, she asked herself, link her lot with that
of such a super-rabbit? There rose before her a vision of that awful moment when
Ambrose had got his left foot entangled with his right elbow.

"No, no, a thousand times no," she told herself. Then aloud, with a remorseful
sweetness which she hoped would rob the words of their sting: "I'm sorry . . . I'm
afraid . . . In fact . . . Well, you know what I mean."

Ambrose, disjointed through her utterance was, knew but too well what she
meant, and his eager face fell as if it, too, had got its left foot entangled with its
right elbow.

"I see," he said. "Yes, I get your drift."

"I'm sorry."

"Don't mention it."

"But you know how it is."

"Oh, quite."

There was a silence, broken only by the parrot, asking one or both of them—it was impossible to say to whom the question was addressed—if they had seen by the dawn's early light. Despite his efforts to keep a stiff upper lip, Ambrose Gussett was showing plainly how deeply this stymie had gashed his soul. His aspect caused the girl's tender heart to bleed for him. She yearned for some means of softening the blow which she had been compelled to deliver.

And then she saw how this might be done.

"You used to speak," she said, "of giving me a golf lesson."

Ambrose raised his bowed head.

"So I did."

"Would you like to give me one now?"

Ambrose's sombre face lit up.

"May I really?"

"Do. I'll go and fetch my racquet."

"You don't use a racquet."

"Then how do you get the ball over the net?"

"There isn't a net."

"No net. What a peculiar game."

She was still sniggering a little to herself, for she was a girl with a strong sense of the ridiculous, when they came on to the practice tee.

"Now," said Ambrose, having teed up the ball and placed the driver in her hands and adjusted her stance and enjoined upon her to come back slowly, "let's see you paste it into the next county."

Years of tennis playing (which, however bad for the soul, does, I admit, strengthen the thews and sinews) had given Evangeline Tewkesbury a fine physique, and Ambrose tells me that it was an inspiring sight to see her put every ounce of wrist and muscle into her shot. The only criticism which could have been made of her performance was that she missed the ball by about three inches.

It was her salvation. Evangeline Tewkesbury's was an arrogant mind, and I think there can be no question that had she succeeded at her first effort in accomplishing an outstanding drive, she would have abandoned the game on the plea that it was too easy. For this, Ambrose had shocked me by telling me, was one of the things she had said about golf when urged to take a lesson.

But she had failed, and now it was but a question of time before the golf bug ran up her leg and bit her to the bone. Suddenly Ambrose saw come into her face that strange yearning look, composite of eagerness and humility, which is the infallible first symptom.

"Let me show you," he said, seizing his opportunity with subtle skill. And taking the club from her he waggled briefly and sent a screamer down the fairway. "That—

roughly—is the idea," he said.

She was staring at him, in her gaze awe, admiration, respect, homage and devotion nicely blended.

"You must be terribly good at golf," she said.

"Oh, fairish."

"Could you teach me to play?"

"In a few lessons. Unfortunately I shall be leaving almost immediately for the Rocky Mountains, to shoot grizzly bears."

"Oh, must you?"

"Surely it is the usual procedure for a man in my position."

There was a silence. Her foot made arabesques on the turf.

"It seems rather tough on the grizzlies," she said at length.

"Into each life some rain must fall."

"Look," said Evangeline. "I think I see a way out."

"There is only one way out."

"That is the way I mean."

Ambrose quivered from the top of his head to the soles of his sure-grip shoes, as worn by all the leading professionals.

"You mean——?"

"Yes, that's what I mean."

"You really—?"

"Yes, really. I can't imagine what I was thinking of when I said No just now. One makes these foolish mistakes."

Ambrose dropped the club and folded her in a long, lingering embrace.

"My mate!" he cried. "Now," he added, picking up the driver and placing it in her hands. "Slow back, don't press, and keep your'ee on the ba'."

26

FEET OF CLAY

WITH THE coming of dusk the blizzard which had been blowing all the afternoon had gained in force, and the trees outside the club-house swayed beneath it. The falling snow rendered the visibility poor, but the Oldest Member, standing at the smoking-room window, was able to recognize the familiar gleam of Cyril Jukes's heather-mixture plus-fours as he crossed the icebound terrace from the direction of the caddie shed, and he gave a little nod of approval. No fair weather golfer himself when still a player, he liked to see the younger generation doing its round in the teeth of November gales.

On Cyril Jukes's normally cheerful face, as he entered the room some moments later, there was the sort of look which might have been worn by a survivor of the last days of Pompeii. What had been happening to Cyril Jukes in the recent past it was impossible to say, but the dullest eye could discern that it had been plenty, and the Oldest Member regarded him sympathetically.

"Something on your mind, my boy?"

"A slight tiff with the helpmeet."

"I am sorry. What caused it?"

"Well, you know her little brother, and you will agree with me, I think that his long game wants polishing up."

"Quite."

"This can be done only by means of unremitting practice."

"Very true."

"So I took him out for a couple of rounds after lunch. We've just got back. We found the little woman waiting for us. She seemed rather stirred. Directing my attention to the fact that the child was bright blue and that icicles had formed on him, she said that if he expired his blood would be on my head. She then took him off to thaw him out with hot-water bottles. Life can be very difficult."

"Very."

"I suppose there *was* a sort of nip in the air, though I hadn't noticed it myself, but I had meant so well. Do you think that when a man's wife calls him a fatheaded sadist, she implies that married happiness is dead and the home in the melting pot?"

The Sage patted him on the shoulder.

"Courage," he said. "She may be a little annoyed for the moment, but the mood will pass and she will understand and forgive. Your wife is a golfer and, when calmer, cannot fail to realize how lucky she is to have married a man with the true golfing spirit. For that is what matters in this life. That is what counts. I mean the spirit that animated Horace Bewstridge, causing him to spank his loved one's mother on the eighteenth green when she interfered with his putting; the inner fire that drove Rollo Podmarsh on to finish his round, though he thought he had been poisoned, because he had a chance of breaking a hundred for the first time; the spirit which saved Agnes Flack and Sidney McMurdo, bringing them at last to peace and happiness. I think I may have mentioned Agnes Flack and Sidney McMurdo to you before. They were engaged to be married."

"She was a large girl, wasn't she?"

"Very large. And Sidney was large, also. That was what made the thing so satisfactory to their friends and well-wishers. Too often in this world you find the six-foot-three man teaming up with the four-foot-ten girl and the five-foot-eleven girl linking her lot with something which she would seem to have dug out of Singer's troupe of midgets: but in the union of Agnes Flack and Sidney McMurdo there was none of this discrepancy. Sidney weighed two hundred pounds and was all muscle, and Agnes weighed a hundred and sixty pounds and was all muscle, too. And, more important still, both had been assiduous golfers since childhood. Theirs was a love based on mutual respect. Sidney's habit of always getting two hundred and fifty yards from the tee fascinated Agnes, and he in his turn was enthralled by her short game, which was exceptionally accurate."

It was in warmer weather than this (the Sage proceeded, having accepted his companion's offer of a hot toddy) that the story began which I am about to relate. The month was August, and from a cloudless sky the sun blazed down on the popular sea-shore resort of East Bampton, illuminating with its rays the beach, the pier, the boardwalk, the ice-cream stands, the hot doggeries and the shimmering ocean. In the last-named, about fifty yards from shore, Agnes Flack was taking her customary cooler after the day's golf and thinking how much she loved Sidney McMurdo.

Sidney himself was not present. He was still in the city, working for the insurance company which had bespoken his services, counting the days to his vacation and thinking how much he loved Agnes Flack.

When girls are floating in warm water, dreaming of the man they adore, it sometimes happens that there comes to them a sort of exaltation of the soul which demands physical expression. It came now to Agnes Flack. God, the way she looked at it, was in His heaven and all right with the world, and it seemed to her that something ought to be done about it. And as practically the only thing you can do in the way of physical expression in the water is to splash, she splashed. With arms and feet she churned up great fountains of foam, at the same time singing a wordless song of ecstasy.

The trouble about doing that sort of thing when swimming is that people are apt to be misled. Agnes Flack's was one of those penetrating voices which sound like the down express letting off steam at a level crossing, and in the number which she had selected for rendition there occurred a series of high notes which she held with determination and vigour. It is not surprising, therefore, that a passing stranger who was cleaving the waves in her vicinity should have got his facts twisted.

A moment later Agnes, in the middle of a high note, was surprised to find herself gripped firmly beneath the arms and towed rapidly shorewards.

Her annoyance was extreme, and it increased during the trip, most of which was made with her head under water. By the time she arrived at the beach, she had swallowed perhaps a pint and a half, and her initial impulse was to tell her assailant what she thought of his officiousness. But just as she was about to do so friendly hands, seizing her from behind, pulled her backwards and started rolling her over a barrel. And when she fought herself free the man had vanished.

Her mood was still ruffled and resentful when she stepped out of the elevator that night on her way down to dinner, for the feeling that she was full of salt water had not wholly disappeared. And it was as she was crossing the lounge with a moody frown on her brow that a voice at her side said "Oh, hullo, there you are, what?" and she turned to see a tall, slender, willowy man with keen blue eyes and a sun-tanned face.

"Feeling all right again?" asked the handsome stranger.

Agnes, who had been about to draw herself to her full height and say "Sir!" suddenly divined who this must be.

"Was it you——?" she began.

He raised a deprecating hand.

"Don't thank me, dear lady, don't thank me. I'm always saving people's lives, and they will try to thank me. It was nothing, nothing. Different, of course, if there had been sharks."

Agnes was staring like a child at a saucer of ice-cream. She had revised her intention of telling this man what she thought of him. His eyes, his clean-cut face, his perfect figure and his clothes had made a profound and instantaneous impression on her, giving her the sort of sensation which she had experienced on the occasion when she had done the short third at Squashy Hollow in one, a sort of dizzy feeling that life had nothing more to offer.

"Sharks get in the way and hamper a man. The time I saved the Princess della Raviogli in the Indian Ocean there were half a dozen of them, horsing about and behaving as if the place belonged to them. I had to teach one of two of them a sharp lesson with my Boy Scout pocket knife. The curse of the average shark is that if you give it the slightest encouragement it gets above itself and starts putting on airs."

Agnes felt that she must speak, but there seemed so little that she could say.

"You're English, aren't you?" she asked.

He raised a deprecating hand.

"Call me rather a cosmopolite, dear lady. I was born in the old country and have resided there from time to time and even served my sovereigns in various positions of trust such as Deputy Master of the Royal Buckhounds, but all my life I have been a rover. I flit. I move to and fro. They say of me: 'Last week he was in Pernambuco, but goodness knows where he is now. China, possibly, or Africa or the North Pole.' Until recently I was in Hollywood. They were doing a film of life in the jungle, where might is right and the strong man comes into his own, and they roped me in as adviser. By the way, introduce myself, what? Fosdyke is the name. Captain Jack Fosdyke."

Agnes's emotion was now such that she was unable for a moment to recall hers. Then it came back to her.

"Mine is Flack," she said, and the statement seemed to interest her companion.

"No, really? I've just been spending the week-end with an old boy named Flack, down at Sands Point."

"Josiah Flack?"

"That's right. Amazing place he has. Absolute palace. They tell me he's one of the richest men in America. Rather pathetic. This lonely old man, rolling in the stuff, but with no chick or child."

"He is my uncle. How was he?"

"Very frail. Very, very frail. Not long for this world, it seemed to me." A sharp tremor ran through Captain Jack Fosdyke. It was as if for the first time her words had penetrated to his consciousness. "Your *uncle*, did you say?"

"Yes."

"Are you his only niece?"

"Yes."

"God bless my soul!" cried Captain Jack Fosdyke with extraordinary animation. "Here, come and have a cocktail. Come and have some dinner. Well, well, well, well, well!"

At the dinner table the spell which her companion was casting on Agnes Flack deepened in intensity. There seemed no limits to the powers of this wonder man. He met the head waiter's eye and made him wilt. He spoke with polished knowledge of food and wine, comparing the hospitality of princes of his acquaintance with that of African chiefs he had known. Between the courses he danced like something dark and slithery from the Argentine. Little wonder that ere long he had Agnes Flack fanning herself with her napkin.

A girl who could, had she seen good reason to do so, have felled an ox with a single blow, in the presence of Captain Jack Fosdyke she felt timid and fluttering. He was turning on the charm as if through the nozzle of a hose-pipe, and it was going all over her and she liked it. She was conscious of a dreamlike sensation, as if she were floating on a pink cloud over an ocean of joy. For the first time in weeks the image of Sidney McMurdo had passed completely from her mind. There was still, presumably, a McMurdo, Sidney, in the telephone book, but in the thoughts of Agnes Flack, no.

The conversation turned to sports and athleticism.

"You swim wonderfully," she said, for that salt water had long since ceased to rankle.

"Yes, I've always been a pretty decent swimmer. I learned in the lake at Wapshott."

"Wapshott?"

"Wapshott Castle, Wapshott-on-the-Wap, Hants., the family seat. I don't go there often nowadays—too busy—but when I do I have a good time. Plenty of ridin', shootin', fishin' and all that."

"Are you fond of riding?"

"I like steeplechasin'. The spice of danger, don't you know, what? Ever seen the Grand National?"

"Not yet."

"I won it a couple of times. I remember on the second occasion Lady Astor saying to me that I ought to saw off a leg and give the other fellows a chance. Lord Beaverbrook, who overheard the remark, was much amused."

"You seem to be marvellous at everything."

"I am."

"Do you play golf?"

"Oh, rather. Scratch."

"We might have a game tomorrow."

"Not tomorrow. Lunching in Washington. A bore, but I can't get out of it. Harry insisted."

"Harry?"

"Truman. We'll have a game when I get back. I may be able to give you a pointer or two. Bobby Jones said to me once that he would never have won the British and American Amateur and Open, if he hadn't studied my swing."

Agnes gasped.

"You don't know Bobby Jones?"

"We're like brothers."

"I once got his autograph."

"Say the word, dear lady, and I'll get you a signed photograph."

Agnes clutched at the table. She had thought for a moment that she was going to faint. And so the long evening wore on.

Mark you, I do not altogether blame Agnes Flack. Hers had been a sheltered life, and nothing like Captain Jack Fosdyke had ever happened to her before. Here was a man who, while looking like something out of a full page coloured advertisement in a slick paper magazine, seemed to have been everywhere and to know everybody.

When he took her out in the moonlight and spoke nonchalantly of Lady Astor, Lord Beaverbrook, Borneo head hunters, Mervyn Leroy and the brothers Schubert one can appreciate her attitude and understand how inevitable it was that Sidney McMurdo should have gone right back in the betting. In accepting the addresses of

Sidney McMurdo, she realized that she had fallen into the error of making her selection before walking the length of the counter.

In short, to hurry on this painful part of my story, when Sidney McMurdo eventually arrived with his suitcase and bag of clubs and was about to clasp Agnes Flack to his forty-four-inch bosom, he was surprised and distressed to observe her step back and raise a deprecating hand. A moment later she was informing him that she had made a mistake and that the photograph on her dressing-table at even date was not his but that of Captain Jack Fosdyke, to whom she was now betrothed.

This, of course, was a nice bit of news for a devoted *fiancé* to get after a four-hour journey on a hot day in a train without a dining-car, and it is not too much to say that for an instant Sidney McMurdo tottered beneath it like a preliminary bout heavyweight who has been incautious enough to place his jaw *en rapport* with the fist of a fellow member of the Truck Drivers' Union. Dimly he heard Agnes Flack saying that she would be a sister to him, and this threat, for he was a man already loaded up with sisters almost beyond capacity, brought him out of what had promised to be a lasting coma.

His eyes flashed, his torso swelled, the muscles leaped about all over him under his pullover, and with a muttered "Is zat so?" he turned on his heel and left her, but not before he had asked for and obtained his supplanter's address. It was his intention to visit the latter and begin by picking him up by the scruff of the neck and shaking him like a rat. After that he would carry on as the inspiration of the moment dictated.

My efforts up to the present having been directed towards limning the personalities of Agnes Flack and Captain Jack Fosdyke, I have not as yet given you anything in the nature of a comprehensive character study of Sidney McMurdo. I should now reveal that he was as fiercely jealous a man as ever swung an aluminium putter. Othello might have had a slight edge on him in that respect, but it would have been a very near thing. Rob him of the girl he loved, and you roused the lion in Sidney McMurdo.

He was flexing his muscles and snorting ominously when he reached the cosy bungalow which Captain Jack Fosdyke had rented for the summer season. The Captain, who was humming one of the song hits from last year's war dance of the 'Mgubo-Mgompis and cleaning an elephant gun, looked up inquiringly as he entered, and Sidney glowered down at him, his muscles still doing the shimmy.

"Captain Fosdyke?"

"The same."

"Pleased to meet you."

"Naturally."

"Could I have a word with you?"

"A thousand."

"It is with reference to your sneaking my girl."

"Oh, that? Are you this McMurdo bird of whom I have heard Agnes speak?"

"I am."

"You were engaged, I understand, till I came along?"

"We were."

"Too bad. Well, that's how it goes. Will you be seeing her shortly?"

"I may decide to confront her again."

"Then you might tell her I've found that elephant gun I mentioned to her. She was anxious to see the notches on it."

Sidney, who had been about to call his companion a sneaking, slinking serpent and bid him rise and put his hands up, decided that later on would do. He did not at all like this talk of notches and elephant guns.

"Are there notches on your elephant gun?"

"There are notches on all my guns. I use them in rotation. This is the one I shot the chief of the 'Mgopo-Mgumpis with."

The chill which had begun to creep over Sidney McMurdo from the feet upwards became more marked. His clenched fists relaxed, and his muscles paused in their rhythmic dance.

"You shot him?"

"Quite."

"Er—do you often do that sort of thing?"

"Invariably, when chaps smirch the honour of the Fosdykes. If a bally bounder smirches the honour of the Fosdykes, I shoot him like a dog."

"Like a dog?"

"Like a dog."

"What sort of dog?"

"Any sort of dog."

"I see."

There was a pause.

"Would you consider that being plugged in the eye smirched the honour of the Fosdykes?"

"Unquestionably. I was once plugged in the eye by the chief of the 'Mgeebo-Mgoopies. And when they buried him the little port had seldom seen a costlier funeral."

"I see," said Sidney McMurdo thoughtfully. "I see. Well, goodbye. It's been nice meeting you."

"It always is," said Captain Jack Fosdyke. "Drop in again. I'll show you my tommy gun."

Sidney McMurdo had not much forehead, being one of those rugged men whose front hair finishes a scant inch or so above the eyebrows, but there was just room on it for a ruminative frown, and he was wearing this as he left the bungalow and set out for a walk along the shore. He was fully alive to the fact that in the recent interview he had cut a poorish figure, failing entirely to express himself and fulfil himself.

But how else, he asked himself, could he have acted? His was a simple nature, easily baffled by the unusual, and he frankly did not see how he could have coped with a rival who appeared to be a combination of mass murderer and United States Armoury. His customary routine of picking rivals up by the scruff of the neck and shaking them like rats plainly would not have answered here.

He walked on, brooding, and so distrait was he that anyone watching him would have given attractive odds that before long he would bump into something. This occurred after he had proceeded some hundred yards, the object into which he bumped being a slender, streamlined, serpentine female who looked like one of those intense young women who used to wreck good men's lives in the silent films but seem rather to have died out since the talkies came in. She was dark and subtle and exotic, and she appeared to be weeping.

Sidney, however, who was a close observer, saw that the trouble was that she had got a fly in her eye, and to whip out his pocket handkerchief and tilt her head back and apply first aid was with him the work of an instant. She thanked him brokenly, blinking as she did so. Then, for the first time seeming to see him steadily and see him whole, she gave a little gasp, and said:

"You!"

Her eyes, which were large and dark and lustrous, like those of some inscrutable priestess of a strange old religion, focused themselves on him as she spoke, and seemed to go through him in much the same way as a couple of red-hot bullets would go through a pound of butter. He rocked back on his heels, feeling as if someone had stirred up his interior organs with an egg beater.

"I have been waiting for you—oh, so long."

"I'm sorry," said Sidney. "Am I late?"

"My man!"

"I beg your pardon?"

"I love you," explained the beautiful unknown. "Kiss me."

If she had studied for weeks she could not have found a better approach to Sidney McMurdo and one more calculated to overcome any customer's sales resistance which might have been lurking in him. Something along these lines from a woman something along her lines was exactly what he had been feeling he could do with. A lover who has just got off a stuffy train to find himself discarded like a worn-out glove by the girl he has worshipped and trusted, is ripe for treatment of this kind.

His bruised spirit began to heal. He kissed her, as directed, and there started to burgeon within him the thought that Agnes Flack wasn't everybody and that it would do her no harm to have this demonstrated to her. A heartening picture flitted through his mind of himself ambling up to Agnes Flack with this spectacular number on his arm, saying to her: "If you don't want me, it would appear that there are others who do."

"Nice day," he said, to help the conversation along.

"Divine. Hark to the wavelets, plashing on the shore. How they seem to fill one with a sense of the inexpressibly ineffable."

"That's right. They do, don't they?"

"Are they singing us songs of old Greece, of Triton blowing on his wreathed horn and the sunlit loves of gods and goddesses?"

"I'm afraid I couldn't tell you," said Sidney McMurdo. "I'm a stranger in these parts myself."

She sighed.

"I, too. But it is my fate to be stranger everywhere. I live a life apart; alone, aloof, solitary, separate; wrapped up in my dreams and vision. 'Tis ever so with the artist."

"You're a painter?"

"In ink, not in oils. I depict the souls of men and women. I am Cora McGuffy Spottsworth."

The name was new to Sidney, who seldom got much beyond the golf weeklies and the house organ of the firm for which he worked, but he gathered that she must be a writer of sorts and made a mental note to wire Brentano's for her complete output and bone it up without delay.

They walked along in silence. At the next ice-cream stand he bought her a nut sundae, and she ate it with a sort of restrained emotion which suggested the presence of banked-up fires, one hand wielding the spoon, the other nestling in his like a white orchid.

Sidney McMurdo was now right under the ether. As he sipped his sarsaparilla, his soul seemed to heave and bubble like a Welsh rarebit coming to the boil. From regarding this woman merely as a sort of stooge, to be exhibited to Agnes Flack as evidence that McMurdo Preferred, even if she had seen fit to unload her holdings, was far from being a drug on the market, he had come to look upon her as a strong man's mate. So that when, having disposed of the last spoonful, she said she hoped he had not thought her abrupt just now in saying that she loved him, he replied "Not at all, not at all," adding that it was precisely the sort of thing he liked to hear. It amazed him that he could ever have considered a mere number-three-iron-swinging robot like Agnes Flack as a life partner.

"It needs but a glance, don't you think, to recognize one's mate?"

"Oh, sure."

"Especially if you have met and loved before. You remember those old days in Egypt?"

"Egypt?" Sidney was a little bewildered. The town she mentioned was, he knew, in Illinois, but he had never been there.

"In Egypt, Antony."

"The name is Sidney. McMurdo, Sidney George."

"In your present incarnation, possibly. But once, long ago, you were Mark Antony and I was Cleopatra."

"Of course, yes," said Sidney. "It all comes back to me."

"What times those were. That night on the Nile!"

"Some party."

"I drew Revell Carstairs in my *Furnace of Sin* from my memories of you in the old days. He was tall and broad and strong, but with the heart of a child. All these years I have been seeking for you, and now that I have found you, would you have had me hold back and mask my love from respect for outworn fetishes of convention?"

"You betcher. I mean, you betcher not."

"What have we to do with conventions? The world would say that I have known you for a mere half-hour——"

"Twenty-five minutes," said Sidney, who was rather a stickler for accuracy, consulting his wrist-watch.

"Or twenty-five minutes. In Egypt I was in your arms in forty seconds."

"Quick service."

"That was ever my way, direct and sudden and impulsive. I remember saying once to Mr. Spottsworth——"

Sidney McMurdo was conscious of a quick chill, similar to that which had affected him when Captain Jack Fosdyke had spoken of elephant guns and notches. His moral code, improving after a rocky start in his Mark Antony days, had become rigid and would never allow him to be a breaker-up of homes. Besides, there was his insurance company to be considered. A scandal might mean the loss of his second vice-presidency.

"Mr. Spottsworth?" he echoed, his jaw falling a little. "Is there a Mr. Spottsworth?"

"Not now. He has left me."

"The low hound."

"He had no option. Double pneumonia. By now, no doubt, he has been reincarnated, but probably only as a jellyfish. A jellyfish need not come between us."

"Certainly not," said Sidney McMurdo, speaking warmly, for he had once been stung by one, and they resumed their saunter.

Agnes Flack, meanwhile, though basking in the rays of Captain Jack Fosdyke, had by no means forgotten Sidney McMurdo. In the days that followed their painful interview, in the intervals of brushing up her fifty yards from the pin game in preparation for the Women's Singles contest which was shortly to take place, she found her thoughts dwelling on him quite a good deal. A girl who has loved, even if mistakenly, can never be indifferent to the fortunes of the man whom she once regarded as the lode star of her life. She kept wondering how he was making out, and hoped that his vacation was not being spoiled by a broken heart.

The first time she saw him, accordingly, she should have been relieved and pleased. He was escorting Cora McGuffy Spottsworth along the boardwalk, and it was abundantly obvious even from a casual glance that if his heart had ever been broken, there had been some adroit work done in the repair shop. Clark Gable could have improved his technique by watching the way he bent over Cora McGuffy Spottsworth and stroked her slender arm. He also, while bending and stroking, whispered into her shell-like ear, and you could see that what he was saying was good stuff. His whole attitude was that of a man who, recognizing that he was on a good thing, was determined to push it along.

But Agnes Flack was not relieved and pleased; she was disturbed and concerned. She was perhaps a hard judge, but Cora McGuffy Spottsworth looked to her like the sort of woman who goes about stealing the plans of forts—or, at the best, leaning back negligently on a settee and saying "Prince, my fan". The impression Agnes formed was of something that might be all right stepping out of a pie at a bachelor party, but not the type you could take home to meet mother.

Her first move, therefore, on encountering Sidney at the golf club one morning, was to institute a probe.

"Who," she demanded, not beating about the bush, "was that lady I saw you walking down the street with?"

Her tone, in which he seemed to detect the note of criticism, offended Sidney.

"That," he replied with a touch of hauteur, "was no lady, that was my *fiancée*."

Agnes reeled. She had noticed that he was wearing a new tie and that his hair had been treated with Sticko, the pomade that satisfies, but she had not dreamed that matters had proceeded as far as this.

"You are engaged?"

"And how!"

"Oh, Sidney!"

He stiffened.

"That will be all of that 'Oh, Sidney!' stuff," he retorted with spirit. "I don't see what you have to beef about. You were offered the opportunity of a merger, and when you failed to take up your option I was free, I presume, to open negotiations elsewhere. As might have been foreseen, I was snapped up the moment it got about that I was in the market."

Agnes Flack bridled.

"I'm not jealous."

"Then what's your kick?"

"It's just that I want to see you happy."

"I am."

"How can you be happy with a woman who looks like a snake with hips?"

"She has every right to look like a snake with hips. In a former incarnation she used to be Cleopatra. I," said Sidney McMurdo, straightening his tie, "was Antony."

"Who told you that?"

"She did. She has all the facts."

"She must be crazy."

"Not at all. I admit that for a while at our first meeting some such thought did cross my mind, but the matter is readily explained. She is a novelist. You may have heard of Cora McGuffy Spottsworth?"

Agnes uttered a cry.

"What? Oh, she can't be."

"She has documents to prove it."

"But Sidney, she's awful. At my school two girls were expelled because they were found with her books under their pillows. Her publisher's slogan is 'Spottsworth for Blushes'. You can't intend to marry a woman who notoriously has to write her love scenes on asbestos."

"Well, what price your intending to marry a prominent international plug-ugly who thinks nothing of shooting people with elephant guns?"

"Only African chiefs."

"African chiefs are also God's creatures."

"Not when under the influence of trade gin, Jack says. He says you have to shoot them with elephant guns then. It means nothing more, he says, than if you drew their attention to some ruling by Emily Post. Besides, he knows Bobby Jones."

"So does Bobby Jones's grocer. Does he play golf himself? That's the point."

"He plays beautifully."

"So does Cora. She expects to win the Women's Singles."

Agnes drew herself up haughtily. She was expecting to win the Women's Singles herself.

"She does, does she?"

"Yes, she does."

"Over my dead body."

"That would be a mashie niblick shot," said Sidney McMurdo thoughtfully. "She's wonderful with her mashie niblick."

With a powerful effort Agnes Flack choked down her choler.

"Well, I hope it will be all right," she said.

"Of course it will be all right. I'm about the luckiest man alive."

"In any case, it's fortunate that we found out our mistake in time."

"I'll say so. A nice thing it would have been, if all this had happened after we were married. We should have had one of those situations authors have to use a row of dots for."

"Yes. Even if we had been married, I should have flown to Jack."

"And I should have flown to Cora."

"He once killed a lion with a sardine opener."

"Cora once danced with the Duke of Windsor," said Sidney McMurdo, and with a proud tilt of the chin, went off to give his betrothed lunch.

As a close student of the game of golf in all its phases over a considerable number of years, I should say that Women's Singles at fashionable seashore resorts nearly always follow the same general lines. The participants with a reasonable hope of bringing home the bacon seldom number more than three or four, the rest being the mere dregs of the golfing world who enter for the hell of the thing or because they know they look well in sports clothes. The preliminary rounds, accordingly, are never worth watching or describing. The rabbits eliminate each other with merry laughs and pretty squeals, and the tigresses massacre the surviving rabbits, till by the time the semi-final is reached, only grim-faced experts are left in.

It was so with the tourney this year at East Bampton. Agnes had no difficulty in murdering the four long handicap fluffies with whom she was confronted in the early stages, and entered the semi-final with the feeling that the competition proper was now about to begin.

Watching, when opportunity offered, the play of the future Mrs. Sidney McMurdo, who also had won through to the penultimate round, she found herself feeling a little easier in her mind. Cora McGuffy Spottsworth still looked to her like one of those women who lure men's souls to the shoals of sin, but there was no question that, as far as knowing what to do with a number four iron when you put it into her hands was concerned, she would make a good wife. Her apprehensions regarding Sidney's future were to a certain extent relieved.

It might be that his bride at some future date would put arsenic in his coffee or elope with the leader of a band, but before she did so, she would in all essential respects be a worthy mate. He would never have to suffer that greatest of all spiritual agonies, the misery of the husband whose wife insists on his playing with her daily because the doctor thinks she ought to have fresh air and exercise. Cora McGuffy Spottsworth might, and probably would, recline on tiger skins in the nude and expect Sidney to drink champagne out of her shoe, but she would never wear high heels on the links or say Tee-hee when she missed a putt. On the previous day, while eliminating her most recent opponent, she had done the long hole in four, and Agnes, who had just taken a rather smelly six, was impressed.

The afternoon of the semi-final was one of those heavy, baking afternoons which cause people to crawl about saying that it is not the heat they mind, but the humidity. After weeks of sunshine the weather was about to break. Thunder was in the air, and once sprightly caddies seemed to droop beneath the weight of their bags. To Agnes, who was impervious to weather conditions, this testing warmth was welcome. It might, she felt, affect her adversary's game.

Cora McGuffy Spottsworth and her antagonist drove off first, and once again Agnes was impressed by the lissom fluidity of the other's swing. Sidney, who was hovering lovingly in the offing, watched her effort with obvious approval.

"You won't want that one back, old girl," he said, and a curious pang shot through Agnes, as if she had bitten into a bad oyster. How often had she heard him say the same thing to her! For an instant she was aware of a sorrowful sense of loss. Then her eye fell on Captain Jack Fosdyke, smoking a debonair cigarette, and the anguish abated. If Captain Jack Fosdyke was not a king among men, she told herself, she didn't know a king among men when she saw one.

When the couple ahead were out of distance, she drove off and achieved her usual faultless shot. Captain Jack Fosdyke said it reminded him of one he had made when playing a friendly round with Harry Hopkins, and they moved off.

From the moment when her adversary had driven off the first tee, Agnes Flack had realized that she had no easy task before her, but one that would test her skill to the utmost. The woman in question looked like a schoolmistress, and she hit her ball as if it had been a refractory pupil. And to increase the severity of Agnes's ordeal, she seldom failed to hit it straight.

Agnes, too, being at the top of her form, the result was that for ten holes the struggle proceeded with but slight advantage to either. At the sixth, Agnes, putting superbly, contrived to be one up, only to lose her lead on the seventh, where the schoolmistress holed out an iron shot for a birdie. They were all square at the turn, and still all square on the eleventh tee. It was as Agnes was addressing her ball here that there came a roll of thunder, and the rain which had been threatening all the afternoon began to descend in liberal streams.

It seemed to Agnes Flack that Providence was at last intervening on behalf of a good woman. She was always at her best in dirty weather. Give her a tropical deluge, accompanied by thunderbolts, and other Acts of God, and she took on a new vigour. And she just had begun to be filled with a stern joy, the joy of an earnest golfer who after a gruelling struggle feels that the thing is in the bag, when she was chagrined to observe that her adversary appeared to be of precisely the same mind. So far from being discouraged by the warring elements, the schoolmistress plainly welcomed the new conditions. Taking in the rain at every pore with obvious relish, she smote her ball as if it had been writing rude things about her on the blackboard, and it was as much as Agnes could do to halve the eleventh and twelfth.

All this while Captain Fosdyke had been striding round with them, chatting between the strokes of cannibals he had met and lions which had regretted meeting him, but during these last two holes a strange silence had fallen upon him. And it was as Agnes uncoiled herself on the thirteenth tee after another of her powerful drives that she was aware of him at her elbow, endeavouring to secure her attention. His coat collar was turned up, and he looked moist and unhappy.

"I say," he said, "what about this?"

"What?"

"This bally rain."

"Just a Scotch mist."

"Don't you think you had better chuck it?"

Agnes stared.

"Are you suggesting that I give up the match?"

"That's the idea."

Agnes stared again.

"Give up my chance of getting into the final just because of a drop of rain?"

"Well, we're getting dashed wet, what? And golf's only a game, I mean, if you know what I mean."

Agnes's eyes flashed like the lightning which had just struck a tree not far off. "I would not dream of forfeiting the match," she cried. "And if you leave me now, I'll never speak to you again."

"Oh, right ho," said Captain Jack Fosdyke. "Merely a suggestion."

He turned his collar up a little higher, and the game proceeded.

Agnes was rudely shaken. Those frightful words about golf being only a game kept ringing in her head. This thing had come upon her like one of the thunderbolts which she liked to have around her when playing an important match. In the brief period of time during which she had known him, Captain Jack Fosdyke's game had appealed to her depths. He had shown himself a skilful and meritorious performer, at times brilliant. But what is golfing skill, if the golfing spirit is absent?

Then a healing thought came to her. He had but jested. In the circles in which he moved, the gay world of African chiefs and English dukes in which he had so long had his being, lighthearted badinage of this kind was no doubt *de rigueur*. To hold his place in that world, a man had to be a merry kidder, a light josher and a mad wag. It was probably because he thought she needed cheering up that he had exercised his flashing wit.

Her doubts vanished. Her faith in him was once more firm. It was as if a heavy load had rolled off her heart. Playing her second, a brassie shot, she uncorked such a snorter that a few moments later she found herself one up again.

As for Captain Jack Fosdyke, he was fully occupied with trying to keep the rain from going down the back of his neck and reminding himself that Agnes was the only niece of Josiah Flack, a man who had a deep sense of family obligations, more money than you could shake a stick at and one foot in the grave.

Whether or not Agnes's opponent was actually a schoolmistress, I do not know. But if she was, the juvenile education of this country is in good hands. In a crisis where a weaker woman might have wilted—one down and five to play—she remained firm and undaunted. Her hat was a frightful object, but it was still in the ring. She fought Agnes, hole after hole, with indomitable tenacity. The fourteenth and fifteenth she halved, but at the sixteenth she produced another of those inspired iron shots and the match was squared. And, going from strength to strength, she won the seventeenth with a twenty-foot putt.

"Dormy one," she said, speaking for the first time.

It is always a mistake to chatter on the links. It disturbs the concentration. To this burst of speech I attribute the fact that the schoolmistress's tee shot at the eighteenth was so markedly inferior to its predecessors. The eighteenth was a short hole ending just outside the club-house and even rabbits seldom failed to make the green. But she fell short by some yards, and Agnes, judging the distance perfectly, was on and near the pin. The schoolmistress chipped so successfully with her second that it seemed for an instant that she was about to hole out. But the ball stopped a few inches from its destination, and Agnes, with a three-foot putt for a two, felt her heart leap up like that of the poet Wordsworth when he saw a rainbow. She had not missed more than one three-foot putt a year since her kindergarten days.

It was at this moment that there emerged from the club-house where it had been having a saucer of tea and a slice of cake, a Pekinese dog of hard-boiled aspect. It strolled on to the green, and approaching Agnes's ball subjected it to a pop-eyed scrutiny.

There is a vein of eccentricity in all Pekes. Here, one would have said, was a ball with little about it to arrest the attention of a thoughtful dog. It was just a regulation blue dot, slightly battered. Yet it was obvious immediately that it had touched a chord. The animal sniffed at it with every evidence of interest and pleasure. It patted it with its paw. It smelled it. Then, lying down, it took it in its mouth and began to chew meditatively.

To Agnes the mere spectacle of a dog on a green had been a thing of horror. Brought up from childhood to reverence the rules of Greens Committees, she had shuddered violently from head to foot. Recovering herself with a powerful effort, she advanced and said 'Shoo!' The Peke rolled its eyes sideways, inspected her, dismissed her as of no importance or entertainment value, and resumed its fletcherizing. Agnes advanced another step, and the schoolmistress for the second time broke her Trappist vows.

"You can't move that dog," she said. "It's a hazard."

"Nonsense."

"I beg your pardon, it is. If you get into casual water, you don't mop it up with a brush and pail, do you? Certainly you don't. You play out of it. Same thing when you get into a casual dog."

They train these schoolmistresses to reason clearly. Agnes halted, baffled. Then her eye fell on Captain Jack Fosdyke, and she saw the way out.

"There's nothing in the rules to prevent a spectator, meeting a dog on the course, from picking it up and fondling it."

It was the schoolmistress's turn to be baffled. She bit her lip in chagrined silence.

"Jack, dear," said Agnes, "pick up that dog and fondle it. And," she added, for she was a quick-thinking girl, "when doing so, hold its head over the hole."

It was a behest which one might have supposed that any knight, eager to win his lady's favour, would have leaped to fulfil. But Captain Jack Fosdyke did not leap. There was a dubious look on his handsome face, and he scratched his chin pensively.

"Just a moment," he said. "This is a thing you want to look at from every angle. Pekes are awfully nippy, you know. They make sudden darts at your ankles."

"Well, you like a spice of danger."

"Within reason, dear lady, within reason."

"You once killed a lion with a sardine opener."

"Ah, but I first quelled him with the power of the human eye. The trouble with Pekes is, they're so shortsighted, they can't see the human eye, so you can't quell them with it."

"You could if you put your face right down close."

"If," said Captain Jack Fosdyke thoughtfully.

Agnes gasped. Already this afternoon she had had occasion to stare at this man. She now stared again.

"Are you afraid of a dog?"

He gave a light laugh.

"Afraid of dogs? That would amuse the boys at Buckingham Palace, if they could hear it. They know what a dare-devil I was in the old days when I was Deputy Master of the Royal Buckhounds. I remember one morning coming down to the kennels with my whistle and my bag of dog biscuits and finding one of the personnel in rather an edgy mood. I spoke to it soothingly—'Fido, Fido, good boy, Fido!'— but it merely bared its teeth and snarled, and I saw that it was about to spring. There wasn't a moment to lose. By a bit of luck the Bluemantle Pursuivant at Arms had happened to leave his blue mantle hanging over the back of a chair. I snatched it up and flung it over the animal's head, after which it was a simple task to secure it with stout cords and put on its muzzle. There was a good deal of comment on my adroit-ness. Lord Slythe and Sayle, who was present, I remember, said to Lord Knubble of Knopp, who was also present, that he hadn't seen anything so resourceful since the day when the Chancellor of the Duchy of Lancaster rang in a bad half-crown on the First Gold Stick in Waiting."

It was the sort of story which in happier days had held Agnes Flack enthralled, but now it merely added to her depression and disillusionment. She made a last appeal to his better feelings.

"But, Jack, if you don't shift this beastly little object, I shall lose the match."

"Well, what does that matter, dear child? A mere tiddly seaside competition."

Agnes had heard enough. Her eyes were stony.

"You refuse? Then our engagement is at an end."

"Oh, don't say that."

"I do say that."

It was plain that a struggle was proceeding in Captain Jack Fosdyke's soul, or what one may loosely call his soul. He was thinking how rich Josiah Flack was, how fond of his niece, and how frail. On the other hand, the Peke, now suspecting a plot against its well-being, had bared a small but serviceable tooth at the corner of its mouth. The whole situation was very difficult.

As he stood there at a man's cross-roads, there came out of the club-house, smoking a cigarette in a sixteen-inch holder, an expensively upholstered girl with platinum hair and vermilion finger-nails. She bent and picked the Peke up.

"My little angel would appear to be interfering with your hockey-knocking," she said. "Why, hello, Captain Fosdyke. You here? Come along in and give me a cocktail."

She kissed the Peke lovingly on the top of its head and carried it into the club-house. The ball went with them.

"She's gone into the bar," said the schoolmistress. "You'll have to chip out from there. Difficult shot. I'd use a niblick."

Captain Jack Fosdyke was gazing after the girl, a puzzled wrinkle on his forehead. "I've met her before somewhere, but I can't place her. Who is she?"

"One of the idle rich," said the schoolmistress, sniffing. Her views were Socialistic.

Captain Jack Fosdyke started.

"Idle *rich*?"

"That's Lulabelle Sprockett, the Sprockett's Superfine Sardine heiress. She's worth a hundred million in her own right."

"In her own right? You mean she's actually got the stuff in the bank, where she can lay hands on it whenever she feels disposed? Good God!" cried Captain Jack Fosdyke. "Bless my soul! Well, well, well, well, well!" He turned to Agnes. "Did I hear you mention something about breaking our engagement? Right ho, dear lady, right ho. Just as you say. Nice to have known you. I shall watch your future career with considerable interest. Excuse me," said Captain Jack Fosdyke.

There was a whirring sound, and he disappeared into the club-house.

"I concede the match," said Agnes dully.

"Might just as well," said the schoolmistress.

Agnes Flack stood on the eighteenth green, contemplating the ruin of her life. It was not the loss of Captain Jack Fosdyke that was making her mourn, for the scales had fallen from her eyes. He had shown himself totally lacking in the golfing spirit, and infatuation was dead. What did jar her was that she had lost Sidney McMurdo. In this dark hour all the old love had come sweeping back into her soul like a tidal wave.

Had she been mad to sever their relations?

The answer to that was "Certainly".

Had she, like a child breaking up a Noah's Ark with a tack hammer, deliberately sabotaged her hopes and happiness?

The reply to that was "Quite".

Would she ever see him again?

In the space allotted to this question she could pencil in the word "Undoubtedly", for he was even now coming out of the locker-room entrance.

"Sidney!" she cried.

He seemed depressed. His colossal shoulders were drooping, and his eyes were those of a man who has drunk the wine of life to the lees.

"Oh, hello," he said.

There was a silence.

"How did Mrs. Spottsworth come out?" asked Agnes.

"Eh? Oh, she won."

Agnes's depression hit a new low. There was another silence.

"She has broken the engagement," said Sidney.

The rain was still sluicing down with undiminished intensity, but it seemed to Agnes Flack, as she heard these words, that a blaze of golden sunshine had suddenly lit up the East Bampton golf course.

"She wanted to quit because of the rain," went on Sidney, in a low, toneless voice. "I took her by the ear and led her round, standing over her with upraised hand as she made her shots, ready to let her have a juicy one if she faltered. On one or two occasions I was obliged to do so. By these means I steered her through to victory, but she didn't like it. Having holed out on the eighteenth for a nice three, which gave her the match, she told me that I had completely changed since those days on the Nile and that she never wished to see or speak to me again in this or any other incarnation."

Agnes was gulping like one of those peculiar fish you catch down in Florida.

"Then you are free?"

"And glad of it. What I ever saw in the woman beats me. But what good is that, when I have lost you?"

"But you haven't."

"Pardon me. What about your Fosdyke?"

"I've just broken my engagement, too. Oh, Sidney, let's go right off and get married under an arch of niblicks before we make any more of these unfortunate mistakes. Let me tell you how that Fosdyke false alarm behaved."

In molten words she began to relate her story, but she had not proceeded far when she was obliged to stop, for Sidney McMurdo's strong arms were about her and he was crushing her to his bosom. And when Sidney McMurdo crushed girls to his bosom, they had to save their breath for breathing purposes, inhaling and exhaling when and if they could.

27
EXCELSIOR

ALFRED JUKES and Wilberforce Bream had just holed out at the end of their match for the club championship, the latter sinking a long putt to win, and the young man sitting with the Oldest Member on the terrace overlooking the eighteenth green said that though this meant a loss to his privy purse of ten dollars, his confidence in Jukes remained unimpaired. He still considered him a better golfer than Bream.

The Sage nodded without much enthusiasm.

"You may be right," he agreed. "But I would not call either of them a good golfer."

"They're both scratch."

"True. But it is not mere technical skill that makes a man a good golfer, it is the golfing soul. These two have not the proper attitude of seriousness towards the game. Jukes once returned to the club-house in the middle of a round because there was a thunderstorm and his caddie got struck by lightning, and I have known Bream to concede a hole for the almost frivolous reason that he had sliced his ball into a hornet's nest and was reluctant to play it where it lay. This was not the Bewstridge spirit."

"The what spirit?"

"The spirit that animated Horace Bewstridge, the finest golfer I have ever known."

"Was he scratch?"

"Far from it. His handicap was twenty-four. But though his ball was seldom in the right place, his heart was. When I think what Horace Bewstridge went through that day he battled for the President's Cup, I am reminded of the poem, Excelsior, by the late Henry Wadsworth Longfellow, with which you are doubtless familiar."

"I used to recite it as a child."

"I am sorry I missed the treat," said the Oldest Member courteously. "Then you will recall how its hero, in his struggle to reach the heights, was laid stymie after stymie, and how in order to achieve his aim, he had to give up all idea of resting his head upon the maiden's breast, though cordially invited to do so. A tear, if you remember, stood in his bright blue eye, but with a brief 'Excelsior!' he intimated that no business could result. Virtually the same thing that happened to Horace Bewstridge."

"You know," said the young man, "I've always thought that Excelsior bird a bit of a fathead. I mean to say, what was there in it for him? As far as I can make out, just the walk."

"Suppose he had been trying to win his first cup?"

"I don't recollect anything being said about any cup. Do they give cups for climbing mountains 'mid snow and ice?"

"We are getting a little muddled," said the Oldest member. "You appear to be discussing the youth with the banner and the clarion voice, while I am talking about Horace Bewstridge. It may serve to clear the air and disperse the fog of misunderstanding if I tell you the latter's story. And in order that you shall miss none of the finer shades, I must begin by dwelling upon his great love for Vera Witherby."

It was only after the thing had been going on for some time (said the Oldest Member) that I learned of this secret romance in Horace's life. As a rule, the Romeos who live about here are not backward in confiding in me when they fall in love. Indeed, I sometimes feel that I shall have to begin keeping them off with a stick. But Bewstridge was reticent. It was purely by chance that I became aware of his passion.

One rather breezy morning, I was sitting almost exactly where we are sitting now, thinking of this and that, when I observed fluttering towards me across the terrace a sheet of paper. It stopped against my foot, and I picked it up and read its contents. They ran as follows: —

MEM

OLD B.	Ribs. But watch eyes.
MA B.	Bone up on pixies. Flowers. Insects.
I.	Symp. breeziness.
A.	Concil. If poss. p., but w.o. for s.d.a.

That was all, and I studied it with close attention and, I must confess, a certain amount of alarm. There had been a number of atom-bomb spy scares in the papers recently, and it occurred to me that this might be a secret code, possibly containing information about some local atoms.

It was then that I saw Horace Bewstridge hurrying towards me. He appeared agitated.

"Have you seen a piece of paper?" he asked.

"Would this be it?"

He took it, and seemed to hesitate for a moment.

"I suppose you're wondering what it's all about?"

I admitted to a certain curiosity, and he hesitated again. Then there crept into his eyes the look which I have seen so often in the eyes of young men. I saw that he was about to confide in me. And presently out it all came, like beer from a bottle. He was in love with Vera Witherby, the niece of one Ponsford Botts, a resident in the neighbourhood.

In putting it like that, I am giving you the thing in condensed form, confining myself to the gist. Horace Bewstridge was a little long-winded about it all, going rather deeply into his emotions and speaking at some length about her eyes, which he compared to twin stars. It was several minutes before I was able to enquire how he was making out.

"Have you told your love?" I asked.

"Not yet," said Horace Bewstridge. "I goggle a good deal, but for the present am content to leave it at that. You see, I'm working this thing on a system. All the nibs will tell you that everything is done by propaganda nowadays, and that your first move, if you want to get anywhere, must be to rope in a *bloc* of friendly neutrals. I start, accordingly, by making myself solid with the family. I give them the old salve, get them rooting for me, and thus ensure an impressive build-up. Only then do I take direct action and edge into what you might call the *blitzkrieg*. This paper contains notes for my guidance."

"With reference to administering the salve?"

"Exactly."

I took the document from him, and glanced at it again.

"What," I asked, "does 'Old B. Ribs. But watch eyes' signify?"

"Quite simple. Old Botts tells dialect stories about Irishmen named Pat and Mike, and you laugh when he prods you in the ribs. But sometimes he doesn't prod you in the ribs, merely stands there looking pop-eyed. One has to be careful about that."

"Under the heading 'Ma B.', I see you say: 'Bone up on pixies.' You add the words 'flowers' and 'insects'."

"Yes. All that is vitally important. Mrs. Botts, I am sorry to say, is a trifle on the whimsy side. Perhaps you have read her books? They are three in number—*My Chums the Pixies, How to Talk to the Flowers*, and *Many of My Best Friends are Mosquitoes*. The programme calls for a good working knowledge of them all."

"Who is 'I', against whose name you have written the phrase: 'Symp. breeziness'?"

"That is little Irwin Botts, the son of the house. He is in love with Dorothy Lamour, and not making much of a go of it. He talks to me about her, and I endeavour to be breezily sympathetic."

"And 'A'?"

"Their poodle, Alphonse. The note is to remind me to conciliate him. He is a dog of wide influence, and cannot be ignored."

"'I poss., p., but w.o. for s.d.a.'?"

"If possible, pat, but watch out for sudden dash at ankles. He is extraordinarily quick on his feet."

I handed back the paper.

"Well," I said, "it all seems a little elaborate, and I should have thought better results would have been obtained by having a direct pop at the girl, but I wish you luck."

In the days which followed, I kept a watchful eye on Horace, for his story had interested me strangely. Now and then, I would see him pacing the terrace with Ponsford Botts at his side and catch references to Pat and Mike, together with an occasional "Begorrah," and I noted how ringing was his guffaw as the other suddenly congealed with bulging eyes.

Once, as I strolled along the road, I heard a noise like machine-gun fire and turned the corner to find him slapping little Irwin's shoulder in a breezy, elder-brotherly manner. His pockets were generally bulging with biscuits for Alphonse, and from time to time he would come and tell me how he was getting along with Mrs. Botts's books. These, he confessed, called for all that he had of resolution and fortitude, but he told me that he was slowly mastering their contents and already knew a lot more about pixies than most people.

It would all have been easier, he said, if he had been in a position to be able to concentrate his whole attention upon them. But of course he had his living to earn and could not afford to neglect his office work. He held a subordinate post in the well-known firm of R. P. Crumbles Inc., purveyors of Silver Sardines (The Sardine with A Soul), and R. P. Crumbles was a hard taskmaster. And, in addition to this, he had entered for the annual handicap competition known as the President's Cup.

It was upon this latter topic, as the date of the tourney drew near, that he spoke almost as frequently and eloquently as upon the theme of his love. He had been playing golf, it appeared, for some seven years, and up till now had never come within even measurable distance of winning a trophy. Generally, he said, it was his putting that dished him. But recently, as the result of reading golf books, he had adopted a super-scientific system, and was now hoping for the best.

It was a stimulating experience to listen to his fine, frank enthusiasm. He spoke of the President's Cup as some young knight of King Arthur's Round Table might have spoken of the Holy Grail. And it was consequently with peculiar satisfaction that I noted his success in the early rounds. Step by step, he won his way into the semi-finals in his bracket, and was enabled to get triumphantly through that critical test owing to the fortunate circumstance of his opponent tripping over a passing cat on the eve of the match and spraining his ankle.

Many members of the club would, of course, have been fully competent to defeat Horace Bewstridge if they had sprained both ankles, or even broken both arms, but Mortimer Gooch, his antagonist, was not one of these. He scratched, and Horace walked over into the final.

His chances now, it seemed to me, were extremely good. According to how the semi-final in the other bracket went, he would be playing either Peter Willard, who would be as clay in his hands, or a certain Sir George Copstone, a visiting Englishman whom his employer, R. P. Crumbles, had put up for the club, and who by an odd coincidence was residing as a guest at the house of Ponsford Botts. I had watched this hand across the sea in action, and was convinced that Horace, provided he did not lose his nerve, could trim him nicely.

A meeting on the fifteenth green the afternoon before the match enabled me to convey these views to the young fellow. We were there to watch the finish of the opposition semi-final, and when Sir George Copstone had won this, I linked by arm in Horace's and told him that in my opinion the thing was in the bag.

"If Peter Willard, our most outstanding golfing cripple, can take this man to the fifteenth, your victory should be a certainty."

"Peter was receiving thirty-eight."

"You could give him fifty. What is this Copstone? A twenty-four like yourself, is he not?"

"Yes."

"Then you need feel no anxiety, my boy," I said, for when I give a pep talk I like it to be a pep talk. "If you are not too busy to-night reading about pixies, you might be looking around your living-room for a spot to put that cup."

He snorted devoutly, and I think he was about to burst into one of those ecstatic monologues of his, but at this moment we reached the terrace. And, as we did so, a harsh, metallic voice called his name, and I perceived, standing at some little distance, a beetle-browed man of formidable aspect, who looked like a cartoon of capital in a Labour paper. He was smoking a large cigar, with which he beckoned to Horace Bewstridge imperiously, and Horace, leaving my side, ambled up to him like a spaniel. From the fact that, as he ambled, he was bleating "Oh, good evening, Mr. Crumbles. Yes, Mr. Crumbles. I'm coming, Mr. Crumbles," I deduced that this was the eminent sardine fancier who provided him with his weekly envelope.

Their conversation was not an extended one. R. P. Crumbles spoke rapidly and authoritatively for some moments, emphasising his remarks with swift, captain-of-industry prods at Horace's breast-bone, and then he turned on his heel and strode off in a strong, economic royalist sort of way, and Horace came back to where I stood.

Now, I had noticed once or twice during the interview that the young fellow had seemed to totter on his axis, and as he drew nearer, his pallid face, with its staring eyes and drooping jaw, told me that all was not well.

"That was my boss," he said, in a low, faint voice.

"So I had guessed. Why did he call the conference?"

Horace Bewstridge beat his breast.

"It's about Sir George Copstone."

"What about him?"

Horace Bewstridge clutched his hair.

"Apparently this Copstone runs a vast system of chain stores throughout the British Isles, and old Crumbles has been fawning on him ever since his arrival in the hope of getting him to take on the Silver Sardine and propagate it over there. He says that this is a big opportunity for the dear old firm and that it behoves all of us to do our bit and push it along. So——"

"So——?"

Horace Bewstridge rent his pullover.

"So," he whispered hoarsely, "I've got to play Customer's Golf to-morrow and let the man win that cup."

"Horace!" I cried.

I would have seized his hand and pressed it, but it was not there. Horace Bewstridge had left me. All that my eye encountered was a swirl of dust and his flying form disappearing in the direction of the bar. I understood and sympathized. There are moments in the life of every man when human consolation cannot avail and only two or three quick ones will meet the case.

I did not see him again until we met next afternoon on the first tee for the start of the final.

You, being a newcomer here (said the Oldest Member) may possibly have formed an erroneous impression regarding this President's Cup of which I have been speaking. Its name, I admit, is misleading, suggesting as it does the guerdon of some terrific tourney battled for by the cream of the local golfing talent. One pictures perspiring scratch men straining every nerve and history being made by amateur champions.

As a matter of fact, it is open for competition only to those whose handicap is not lower than twenty-four, and excites little interest outside the ranks of the submerged tenth who play for it. As a sporting event on our fixture list, as I often have to explain, it may be classed somewhere between the Grandmothers' Umbrella and the All day Sucker competed for by children who have not passed their seventh year.

The final, accordingly, did not attract a large gate. In fact, I think I was the only spectator. I was thus enabled to obtain an excellent view of the contestants and to follow their play to the best advantage. And, as on the previous occasions when I had watched him perform, I found myself speculating with no little bewilderment as to how Horace's opponent had got that way.

Sir George Copstone was one of those tall, thin, bony Englishmen who seem to have been left over from the eighteen-sixties. He did not actually wear long side-whiskers of the type known as Piccadilly Weepers, nor did he really flaunt a fore-and-aft deer-stalker cap of the type affected by Sherlock Holmes, but you got the illusion that this was so, and it was partly the unnerving effect of his appearance on his opponents that had facilitated his making his way into the final. But what had been the basic factor in his success was his method of play.

A deliberate man, this Copstone. Before making a shot, he would inspect his enormous bag of clubs and take out one after another, slowly, as if he were playing spillikens. Having at length made his selection, he would stand motionless beside his ball, staring at it for what seemed an eternity. Only after one had begun to give up hope that life would ever again animate the rigid limbs, would he start his stroke. He was affectionately known on our links as The Frozen Horror.

Even in normal circumstances, a sensitive, highly-strung young man like Horace Bewstridge might well have found himself hard put to it to cope with such an antagonist. And when you take into consideration the fact that he had received those special instructions from the front office, it is not surprising that he should have failed in the opening stages of the encounter to give of his best. The fourth hole found him four down, and one had the feeling that he was lucky not to be five.

At this point, however, there occurred one of those remarkable changes of fortune which are so common in golf and which make it the undisputed king of games. Teeing up at the fifth, Sir George Copstone appeared suddenly to have become afflicted with some form of shaking palsy. Where before he had stood addressing his ball like Lot's wife just after she had been turned into a pillar of salt, he now wriggled like an Ouled Nail dancer in the throes of colic. Nor did his condition improve as the match progressed. His movements took on an ever freerer abandon. To cut a long story short, which I am told is a thing I seldom do, he lost four holes in a row, and they came to the ninth all square.

And it was here that I observed an almost equally surprising change in the demeanour of Horace Bewstridge.

Until this moment, Horace had been going through the motions with something of the weary moodiness of a Volga boatman, his face drawn, his manner listless. But now he had become a different man. As he advanced to the ninth tee, his eyes gleamed, his ears wiggled and his lips were set. He looked like a Volga boatman who has just learned that Stalin has purged his employer.

I could see what had happened. Intoxicated with this unexpected success, he was beginning to rebel against those instructions from up top. The almost religious fervour which comes upon a twenty-four handicap man when he sees a chance of winning his first cup had him in its grip. Who, he was asking himself, was R. P. Crumbles? The man who paid him his salary and could fire him out on his ear, yes, but was money everything? Suppose he won this cup and starved in the gutter, I could almost hear him murmuring, would not that be better than losing the cup and getting his three square a day?

And when on the ninth green, by pure accident, he sank a thirty-foot putt, I saw his lips move and I knew what he was saying to himself. It was the word "Excelsior."

It was as he stood gaping at the hole into which his ball had disappeared that Sir George Copstone spoke for the first time.

"Jolly good shot, what?" said Sir George, a gallant sportsman. "Right in the old crevasse, what, what? I say, look here," he went on, jerking his shoulders in a convulsive gesture, "do you mind if I go and shake out the underlinen? Got a beetle or something down my back."

"Certainly," said Horace.

"Won't keep you long. I'll just strip off the next-the-skins and spring upon it unawares."

He performed another complicated writhing movement, and was about to leave us, when along came R. P. Crumbles.

"How's it going?" asked R. P. Crumbles.

"Eh? What? Going? Oh, one down at the turn."

"He is?"

"No, I am," said Sir George. "He, in sharp contradistinction, is one up. Sank a dashed find putt on this green. Thirty feet, if an inch. Well, excuse me, I'll just buzz off and bash this beetle."

He hastened away, twitching in every limb, and R. P. Crumbles turned to Horace. His face was suffused.

"Do I get no co-operation, Bewstridge?" he demanded. "What the devil do you mean by being one up? And what's all this nonsense about thirty-foot putts? How dare you sink thirty-foot putts?"

I could have told him that Horace was in no way responsible for what had occurred and that the thing must be looked on as an Act of God, but I hesitated to wound the young man's feelings, and R. P. Crumbles continued.

"Thirty-foot putts, indeed! Have you forgotten what I told you?"

Horace Bewstridge met his accusing glare without a tremor. His face was like granite. His eyes shone with a strange light.

"I have not forgotten the inter-office memo. to which you refer," he said, in a firm, quiet voice. "But I am ignoring it. I intend to trim the pants off this stranger in our midst."

"You do, and see what happens."

"I don't care what happens."

"Bewstridge," said R. B. Crumbles, "nine more holes remain to be played. During these nine holes, think well. I shall be waiting on the eighteenth to see the finish. I shall hope to find," he added significantly, "that the match has ended before then."

He walked away, and I think I have never seen the back of any head look more sinister. Horace, however, merely waved his putter defiantly, as if it had been a banner with a strange device and the other an old man recommending him not to try a pass.

"Nuts to you, R. P. Crumbles!" he cried, with a strange dignity. "Fire me, if you will. This is the only chance I shall ever have of winning a cup, and I'm going to do it."

I stood for a moment motionless. This revelation of the nobility of this young man's soul had stunned me. Then I hurried to where he stood, and gripped his hand. I was still shaking it, when an arch contralto voice spoke behind us.

"Good afternoon, Mr. Bewstridge."

Mrs. Botts was in our midst. She was accompanied by her husband, Ponsford, her son Irwin, and her dog, Alphonse.

"How is the match going?" asked Mrs. Botts.

Horace explained the position of affairs.

"We shall all be on the eighteenth green, to see the finish," said Mrs. Botts. "But you really must not beat Sir George. That would be very naughty. Where is Sir George?"

As she spoke, Sir George Copstone appeared, looking quite his old self again.

"Bashed him!" he said. "Whopping big chap. Put up the dickens of a struggle. But I settled him in the end. He'll think twice before he tackles a Sussex Copstone again."

Mrs. Botts uttered a girlish scream.

"Somebody attacked you, Sir George?"

"I should say so. Whacking great brute of a beetle. But I fixed him."

"You killed a beetle?"

"Well, stunned him, at any rate. Technical knockout."

"But, Sir George, don't you remember what Coleridge said—He prayeth best who loveth best all things both great and small?"

"Not beetles?"

"Of course. Some of my closest chums are beetles."

The other seemed amazed.

"This friend of yours, this Coleridge, really says—he positively asserts that we ought to love beetles?"

"Of course."

"Even when they get under the vest and start doing buck and wing dances along the spine?"

"Of course."

"Sounds a bit of a silly ass to me. Not the sort of chap one would care to know. Well, come on, Bewstridge, let's be moving, what? I say," went on Sir George, as they passed out of earshot, "do you know that old geezer? Potty, what? Over in England, we'd have her in a padded cell before she could say 'Pip, pip'. Beetles, egad! Coleridge, forsooth! And do you know what she said to me this morning? Told me to be careful where I stepped on the front lawn, because it was full of pixies. Can't stand that husband of hers, either. Always talking rot about Irishmen. And what price the son and heir? There's a young blister for you. And as for that flea storage depot she calls a dog . . . Well, I'll tell you If I'd known what I was letting myself in for, staying at her house, I'd have gone to a hotel. Carry on, Bewstridge. It's your honour."

It was perhaps the exhilaration due to hearing these frank criticisms of a quartette whom he had never liked, though he had striven to love them for Vera Witherby's sake, that lent zip to Horace's drive from the tenth tee. Normally, he was a man who alternated between a weak slice and a robust hook, but on this occasion his ball looked neither to right nor left. He pasted it straight down the middle, and with such vehemence that he had no difficulty in winning the hole and putting himself two up.

But now the tide of fortune began to change again. His recent victory over the beetle had put Sir George Copstone right back into the old mid-season form. Once more he had become the formidable Frozen Horror whose deliberate methods of play had caused three stout men to succumb before his onslaught in the preliminary rounds. With infinite caution, like one suspecting a trap of some kind, he selected clubs from his bulging bag; with unremitting concentration he addressed and struck his ball. And for a while there took place as stern a struggle as I have ever witnessed on the links.

But gradually Sir George secured the upper hand. Little by little he recovered the ground he had lost. He kept turning in steady sevens, and came a time when Horace began to take nines. The strain had uncovered his weak spot. His putting touch had left him.

I could see what was wrong, of course. He was being much too scientific. He was remembering the illustrated plates in the golf books and trying to make the club head move from Spot A. through Line B. to ball C. and that is always a fatal thing for a high handicap man to do. I have talked to a great many of our most successful high handicap men, and they all assured me that the only way in which it was possible to obtain results was to shut the eyes, breathe a short prayer and loose off into the unknown.

Still, there it was, and there was nothing that could be done about it. Horace went on studying the line and taking the Bobby Jones stance and all the rest of it, and gradually, as I say, Sir George recovered the ground he had lost. One down on the thirteenth, he squared the match at the fifteenth, and it was only by holing out a fortunate brassie shot to win on the seventeenth that Horace was enabled to avoid defeat by two and one. As it was, they came to the eighteenth on level terms, and everything, therefore, depended on what Fate held in store for them there.

I had a melancholy feeling that the odds were all in favour of the older man. At the time of which I am speaking, the eighteenth was not the long hole which we are looking at as we sit here, but that short, tricky one which is now the ninth— the one where you stand at the foot of the hill and pop the ball up vertically with a mashie, trusting that you will not overdrive and run across the green into the deep chasm on the other side. At such a hole, a cautious, calculating player like Sir George Copstone inevitably has the advantage over a younger and more ardent antagonist, who is apt to put too much beef behind his tee shot.

My fear, however, that Horace would fall into this error was not fulfilled. His ball soared in a perfect arc, and one could see at a glance that it must have dropped very near the pin. Sir George's effort, though sound and scholarly, was not in the same class, and there could be no doubt that on reaching the summit we should find that he was away. And so it proved. The first thing I saw as I arrived, was a group consisting of Ponsford Botts, little Irwin Botts and the poodle, Alphonse; the second, Horace's ball lying some two feet from the flag; the third, that of his opponent at least six feet beyond it.

Sir George, a fighter to the last, putting to within a few inches of the hole, and I heard Horace draw a deep breath.

"This for it," he said. And, as he spoke, there was a rapid pattering of feet, and what looked like a bundle of black cotton-wool swooped past him, seized the ball in its slavering jaws and bore it away. At this crucial moment, with Horace Bewstridge's fortunes swaying in the balance, Alphonse had got the party spirit.

The shocked "Hoy!" that sprang from my lips must have sounded to the animal like the Voice of Conscience, for he started visibly and dropped the ball. I had at least prevented him from going to the last awful extreme of carrying it down into the abyss.

But the spot where he had dropped it was the very edge of the green, and Horace Bewstridge stood motionless, with ashen face. Once before, in the course of this match, he had sunk a putt of this length, but he was doubting if that sort of thing happened twice in a lifetime. He would have to concentrate, concentrate. With knitted brow, he knelt down to study the line. And, as he did so, Alphonse began to bark.

Horace rose. Almost as clearly as if he had given them verbal utterance, I could read the thoughts that were passing through his mind.

This dog, he was saying to himself, was the apple of Irwin Botts's eye. It was also the apple of Ponsford Botts's eye. To seek it out and kick it in the slats, therefore, would be to shoot that system of his to pieces beyond repair. Irwin Botts would look at him askance. Ponsford Botts would look at him askance. And if they looked at him askance, Vera Witherby would look at him askance, too, for they were presumably the apples of her eye, just as Alphonse was the apple of theirs.

On the other hand, he could not putt with a noise like that going on.

He made his decision. If he should lose Vera Witherby, it would be most unfortunate, but not so unfortunate as losing the President's Cup. Horace Bewstridge, as I have said, was a golfer.

The next moment, the barking had broken off in a sharp yelp, and Alphonse was descending into the chasm like a falling star. Horace was descending into the chasm like a falling star. Horace returned to his ball, and resumed his study of the line.

The Bottses, Irwin and Ponsford, had been stunned witnesses of the assault. They now gave tongue simultaneously.

"Hey!" cried Irwin Botts.

"Hi!" cried Ponsford Botts.

Horace frowned meditatively at the hole. Even apart from the length of it, it was a difficult shot. He would have to allow for the undulations of the green. There was a nasty little slope there to the right. That must be taken into consideration. There was also, further on, a nasty little slope to the left. The thing called for profound thought, and for some reason he found himself unable to give his whole mind to the problem.

Then he saw what the trouble was. Irwin Botts was standing beside him, shouting "Hey!" in his left ear, and Ponsford Botts was standing on the other side, shouting "Hi!" in his right ear. It was this that was affecting his concentration.

He gazed at them, momentarily at a loss. How, he asked himself, would Bobby Jones have handled a situation like this? The answer came in a flash. He would have taken Irwin Botts by the scruff of his neck, led him to the brink of the chasm and kicked him into it. He would then have come back for Ponsford Botts.

Horace did this, and resumed the scrutiny of the line. And at this moment, accompanied by a pretty, soulful-looking girl in whom I recognized Vera Witherby, R. P. Crumbles came on to the green. As his eye fell on Horace, his face darkened. He asked Sir George Copstone how the match stood.

"I should have thought," he said, chewing his cigar ominously, "that it would have been over long before this. I had supposed that you would have won on about the fifteenth or sixteenth."

"It is a point verging very decidedly on the moot," replied Sir George, "if I'm going to win on the eighteenth. He's got this for it, and I expect him to sink it, now that there's nothing to distract his mind. He was being a bit bothered a moment ago," he explained, "by Botts senior, Botts junior and the Botts dog. But he has just kicked them all into the chasm, and can now give his whole attention to the game. Capable young feller, that. Just holed out a two hundred yard brassie shot. Judged it to a nicety."

I heard Vera Witherby draw in her breath sharply. R. P. Crumbles, switching his cigar from one side of his mouth to the other, strode across to where Horace was bending over his ball, and spoke rapidly and forcefully.

It was a dangerous thing to do, and one against which his best friends would have advised him. There was no "Yes, Mr. Crumbles", "No, Mr. Crumbles" about Horace Bewstridge now. I saw him straighten up with a testy frown. The next moment, he had attached himself to the scruff of the other's neck and was adding him to the contents of the chasm.

This done, he returned, took another look at the hole with his head on one side, and seemed satisfied. He rose, and addressed his ball. He was drawing the club head back, when a sudden scream rent the air. Glancing over his shoulder, exasperated, he saw that their little group had been joined by Mrs. Botts. She was bending over the edge of the chasm, endeavouring to establish communication with its inmates. Muffled voices rose from the depths.

"Ponsford!"

"Wah, wah, wah."

"Mr. Crumbles!"

"Wah, wah, wah."

"Irwin!"

"Wah, wah, wah."

"Alphonse!"

"Woof, woof, woof."

Mrs. Botts bent still further forward, one hand resting on the turf, the other cupped to her ear.

"What? What did you say? I can't hear. What are you doing down there? What? I can't hear. What is Mr. Crumbles doing down there? Why has he got his foot in Irwin's eye? Irwin, take your eye away from Mr. Crumbles' foot immediately.

What? I can't hear. Tell whom he is fired, Mr. Crumbles? I can't hear. Why is Alphonse biting Mr. Crumbles in the leg? What? I can't hear. I wish you would speak plainly. Your mouth's full of what? Ham? Oh, sand? Why is your mouth full of sand? Why is Alphonse now biting Irwin? Skin whom, Mr. Crumbles? What? I can't hear. You've swallowed your cigar? Why? What? I can't hear."

It seemed to Horace Bewstridge, that this sort of thing, unless firmly checked at the source, might go on indefinitely. And to attempt to concentrate while it did, was hopeless. Clicking his tongue in annoyance at these incessant interruptions, he stepped across to where Mrs. Botts crouched. There was a sound like a pistol shot. Mrs. Botts joined the others. Horace came back, rubbing his hand, studied the line again and took his stance.

"Mr. Bewstridge!"

The words, spoken in his left ear just as he was shooting, were little more than a whisper, but they affected Horace as if an ammunition dump had exploded beneath him. Until this moment, he had evidently been unaware of the presence of the girl he loved, and this unexpected announcement of it caused him to putt rather strongly.

His club descended with a convulsive jerk, and the ball, as if feeling that now that all that scientific nonsense was over, it knew where it was, started off for the hole at forty miles an hour in a dead straight line. There were slopes to the right. There were slopes to the left. It ignored them. Sizzling over the turf, it struck the back of the cup, soared into the air like a rocket, came down, soared up again, fell once more bounced and rebounded and finally, after rattling round and round for perhaps a quarter of a minute, rested safe at journey's end. The struggle for the President's Cup was over.

"Nice work," said Sir George Copstone. "Your match, what?"

Horace was gazing at Vera Witherby.

"You spoke?" he said.

She blushed in pretty confusion.

"It was nothing. I only wanted to thank you."

"Thank me?"

"For what you did to Aunt Lavender."

"Me, too," said Sir George Copstone, who had joined them. "Precisely what the woman needed. Should be a turning point in her life. That'll take her mind off pixies for a bit. *And* beetles."

Horace stared at the girl. He had thought to see her shrink from him in loathing. Instead of which, she was looking at him with something in her eyes which, if he was not very much mistaken, was the love light.

"Vera . . . Do you mean . . . ?"

Her eyes must have given him his answer, for he sprang forward and clasped her to his bosom, using the interlocking grip. She nestled in his arms.

"I misjudged you, Horace," she whispered. "I thought you were a sap. I mistrusted anyone who could be as fond as you seemed to be of Aunt Lavender, Uncle

Ponsford, little Irwin and Alphonse. And I had always yearned for one of those engagements where my man, like Romeo, would run fearful risks to come near me, and I would have to communicate with him by means of notes in hollow trees."

"Romantic," explained Sir George. "Many girls are."

Into the ecstasy of Horace Bewstridge's mood there crept a chilling thought. He had won her love. He had won the President's Cup. But, unless he had quite misinterpreted the recent exchange of remarks between Mrs. Botts and R. P. Crumbles at the chasm side, he had lost his job and so far from being able to support a wife, would now presumably have to starve in the gutter.

He explained this, and Sir George Copstone pooh-poohed vehemently.

"Starve in the gutter? Never heard such bally rot. What do you want to go starving in gutters for? Join me, what? Come over to England, I mean to say, and accept a prominent position in my chain of dashed stores. Name your own salary, of course."

Horace reeled.

"You don't mean that?"

"Of course I mean it. What do you think I meant? What other possible construction could you have put on my words?"

"But you don't know what I can do."

Sir George stared.

"Not know what you can do? Why, I've seen you in action, dash it. If what you have just done isn't enough to give a discerning man an idea of your capabilities, I'd like to know what is. Ever since I went to stay at that house, I've wanted to find someone capable of kicking that dog, kicking that boy, kicking old Botts and giving Ma Botts a juicy one right on the good old spot. I'm not merely grateful to you, my dear chap, profoundly grateful, I'm overcome with admiration. Enormously impressed, I am. Never saw anything so adroit. What I need in my business is a man who thinks on his feet and does it now. Ginger up some of my branch managers a bit. Of course, you must join me, dear old thing, and don't forget about making the salary big. And now that's settled, how about trickling off to the bar and having a few? Yoicks!"

"Yoicks!" said Horace.

"Yoicks!" said Vera Witherby.

"Tallo-ho!" said Sir George.

"Tallo-ho!" said Horace.

"Tally-ho!" said Vera Witherby.

"Tally-bally-ho!" said Sir George, driving the thing home beyond any possibility of misunderstanding. "Come on, let's go."

28

RODNEY HAS A RELAPSE

THE OLDEST MEMBER, who had been in a reverie, came out of it abruptly and began to speak with the practised ease of a raconteur who does not require a cue to start him off on a story.

When William Bates came to me that afternoon with his tragic story (said the Oldest Member, as smoothly as if we had been discussing William Bates, whoever he might be, for hours), I felt no surprise that he should have selected me as a confidant. I have been sitting on the terrace of this golf club long enough to know that that is what I am there for. Everybody with a bit of bad news always brings it to me.

"I say," said William Bates.

This William was a substantial young man constructed rather on the lines of a lorry, and as a rule he shared that vehicle's placid and unruffled outlook on life. He lived mainly on chops and beer, and few things were able to disturb him. Yet, as he stood before me now, I could see that he was all of a twitter, as far as a fourteen-stone-six man full of beer and chops can be all of a twitter.

"I say," said William. "You know Rodney?"

"Your brother-in-law, Rodney Spelvin?"

"Yes. I believe he's gone cuckoo."

"What gives you that impression?"

"Well, look. Listen to this. We were playing our usual foursome this morning, Rodney and Anastatia and me and Jane, a bob a corner, nip and tuck all the way around, and at the eighteenth Jane and I were lying dead in four and Rodney had a simple chip to reach the green in three. You get the set-up?"

I said I got the set-up.

"Well, knowing my sister Anastatia's uncanny ability to hole out from anywhere within fifteen yards of the pin, I naturally thought the thing was in the bag for them. I said as much to Jane. 'Jane,' I said, 'be ready with the stiff upper lip. They've dished us.' And I had already started to feel in my pocket for my bob, when I suddenly saw that Rodney was picking up his ball."

"Picking up his ball?"

"And what do you think his explanation was? His explanation was that in order to make his shot he would have had to crush a daisy. 'I couldn't crush a daisy,' he said. 'The pixies would never forgive me.' What do you make of it?"

I knew what I made of it, but I had not the heart to tell him. I passed it off by saying that Rodney was one of those genial clowns who will do anything for a laugh and, William being a simple soul, my efforts to soothe him were successful. But his story had left me uneasy and apprehensive. It seemed to me only too certain that Rodney Spelvin was in for another attack of poetry.

I have generally found, as I have gone through the world, that people are tolerant and ready to forgive, and in our little community it was never held against Rodney Spelvin that he had once been a poet and a very virulent one, too; the sort of man who would produce a slim volume of verse bound in squashy mauve leather at the drop of the hat, mostly on the subject of sunsets and pixies. He sad said good-bye to all that directly he took up golf and announced his betrothal to William's sister Anastatia.

It was golf and the love of a good woman that saved Rodney Spelvin. The moment he had bought his bag of clubs and signed up Anastatia Bates as a partner for life's medal round, he was a different man. He now wrote mystery thrillers, and with such success that he and Anastatia and their child Timothy were enabled to live like fighting cocks. It was impossible not to be thrilled by Rodney Spelvin, and so skilful was the technique which he had developed that he was soon able to push out his couple of thousand words of wholesome blood-stained fiction each morning before breakfast, leaving the rest of the day for the normal fifty-four holes of golf.

At golf, too, he made steady progress. His wife, a scratch player who had once won the Ladies' Championship, guided him with loving care, and it was not long before he became a skilful twenty-one and was regarded in several knowledgeable quarters as a man to keep your eye on for the Rabbits Umbrella, a local competition open to those with a handicap of eighteen or over.

But smooth though the putting green of Anastatia Spelvin's happiness was to the casual glance, there lurked on it, I knew, a secret worm-cast. She could never forget that the man she loved was a man with a past. Deep down in her soul there was always the corroding fear lest at any moment a particularly fine sunset or the sight of a rose in bud might undo all the work she had done, sending Rodney hot-foot once more to this Thesaurus and rhyming dictionary. It was for this reason that she always hurried him indoors when the sun began to go down and refused to have rose trees in her garden. She was in the same position as a wife who has married a once heavy drinker and, though tolerably certain that he has reformed, nevertheless feels it prudent to tear out the whisky advertisements before giving him his *Tatler*.

And now, after seven years, the blow was about to fall. Or so I felt justified in supposing. And I could see that Anastatia thought the same. There was a drawn look on her face, and she was watching her husband closely. Once when I was dining at her house and a tactless guest spoke of the June moon, she changed the subject hurriedly, but not before I had seen Rodney Spelvin start and throw his head up like a war horse at the sound of the bugle. He recovered himself quickly, but for an instant he had looked like a man who has suddenly awakened to the fact that "June" rhymes with "moon" and feels that steps of some sort ought to be taken.

A week later suspicion became certainty. I had strolled over to William's cottage after dinner, as I often did, and I found him and Anastatia in the morning-room. At a glance I could see that something was wrong. William was practising distrait swings with a number three iron, a moody frown on his face, while Anastatia in what seemed to me a feverish way sat knitting a sweater for her little nephew, Braid Bates, the son of William and Jane, at the moment away from home undergoing intensive instruction from a leading professional in preparation for the forthcoming contest for the Children's Cup. Both William and Jane rightly felt that the child could not start getting the competition spirit too soon.

Anastatia was looking pale, and William would have been, too, no doubt, if it had been possible for him to look pale. Years of incessant golf in all weathers had converted his cheeks into a substance resembling red leather.

"Lovely evening," I said.

"Beautiful," replied Anastatia wildly.

"Good weather for the crops."

"Splendid," gasped Anastatia.

"And where is Rodney?"

Anastatia quivered all over and dropped a stitch.

"He's out, I think," she said in a strange, strangled voice.

William's frown deepened. A plain, blunt man, he dislikes evasions.

"He is not out," he said curtly. "He is at his home, writing poetry. Much better to tell him," he added to Anastasia, who had uttered a wordless sound of protest. "You can't keep the thing dark, and he will be able to handle it. He has white whiskers. A fellow with white whiskers is bound to be able to handle things better than a couple of birds like us who haven't white whiskers. Stands to reason."

I assured them that they could rely on my secrecy and discretion and that I would do anything that lay in the power of myself and my whiskers to assist them in their distress.

"So Rodney is writing poetry?" I said. "I feared that this might happen. Yes, I think I may say I saw it coming. About pixies, I suppose?"

Anastatia gave a quick sob and William a quick snort.

"About pixies, you suppose, do you?" he cried. "Well, you're wrong. If pixies were all the trouble, I wouldn't have a word to say. Let Rodney Spelvin come in at the door and tell me he has written a poem about pixies, and I will clasp him in my arms. Yes," said William, "to my bosom. The thing has gone far, far beyond the pixie stage. Do you know where Rodney is at this moment? Up in the nursery, bending over his son Timothy's cot, gathering material for a poem about the unfortunate little rat when asleep. Some bolony, no doubt, about how he hugs his teddy bear and dreams of angels. Yes, that is what he is doing, writing poetry about

Timothy. Horrible whimsical stuff that . . . Well, when I tell you that he refers to him throughout as 'Timothy Bobbin', you will appreciate what we are up against."

I am not a weak man, but I confess that I shuddered.

"Timothy Bobbin?"

"Timothy by golly Bobbin. No less."

I shuddered again. This was worse than I had feared. And yet, when you examined it, how inevitable it was. The poetry virus always seeks out the weak spot. Rodney Spelvin was a devoted father. It had long been his practice to converse with his offspring in baby talk, though hitherto always in prose. It was only to be expected that when he found verse welling up in him, the object on which he would decant it would be his unfortunate son.

"What it comes to," said William, "is that he is wantonly laying up a lifetime of shame and misery for the wretched little moppet. In the years to come, when he is playing in the National Amateur, the papers will print photographs of him with captions underneath explaining that he is the Timothy Bobbin of the well-known poems——"

"Rodney says he expects soon to have sufficient material for a slim volume," put in Anastatia in a low voice.

"——and he will be put clean off his stroke. Misery, desolation and despair," said William. "That is the programme, as I see it."

"Are these poems so very raw?"

"Read these and judge for yourself. I swiped them off his desk."

The documents which he thrust upon me appeared to be in the nature of experimental drafts, intended at a later stage to be developed more fully; what one might perhaps describe as practice swings.

The first ran:

> Timothy Bobbin has a puppy,
> A dear little puppy that goes Bow-wow. . . .

Beneath this were the words:

> Whoa! Wait a minute!

followed, as though the writer had realized in time that this "uppy" rhyming scheme was going to present difficulties, by some scattered notes:

> Safer to change to rabbit?
> (Habit . . . Grab it . . . Stab it . . . Babbitt)

> Rabbit looks tough, too. How about canary?
> (Airy, dairy, fairy, hairy Mary, contrary, vary)

Note: Canaries go tweet-tweet.
(Beat, seat, feet, heat, meet, neat, repeat, sheet, complete, discreet).
Yes, canary looks like goods.

Timothy Bobbin has a canary.

Gosh, this is pie.
Timothy Bobbin has a canary.
As regards its sex opinions vary.
If it just goes tweet-tweet,
We shall call it Pete,
But if it lays an egg, we shall switch to Mary.

(*Query: Sex motif too strongly stressed*)

That was all about canaries. The next was on a different theme:

Timothy Bobbin has ten little toes.
He takes them out walking wherever he goes.
And if Timothy gets a cold in the head,
His ten little toes stay with him in bed.

William saw me wince, and asked if that was the toes one. I said it was and hurried on to the third and last.
It ran:

Timothy
    Bobbin
        Goes
            Hoppity
             Hoppity
            Hoppity
            Hoppity
             Hop.

With this Rodney appeared to have been dissatisfied, for beneath it he had written the word

Reminiscent ?

as though he feared that he might have been forestalled by some other poet, and there was a suggestion in the margin that instead of going Hoppity-hoppity-hop his hero might go Boppity-Boppity-bop. The alternative seemed to me equally melancholy, and it was with a grave face that I handed the papers back to William.

"Bad," I said gravely.

"Bad is right."

"Has this been going on long?"

"For days the fountain pen has hardly been out of his hand."

I put the question which had been uppermost in my mind from the first.

"Has it affected his golf?"

"He says he is going to give up golf."

"What! But the Rabbits Umbrella?"

"He intends to scratch."

There seemed to be nothing more to be said. I left them. I wanted to be alone, to give this sad affair my undivided attention. As I made for the door, I saw that Anastatia had buried her face in her hands, while William, with brotherly solicitude, stood scratching the top of her head with the number three iron, no doubt in a well-meant effort to comfort and console.

For several days I brooded tensely on the problem, but it was all too soon borne in upon me that William had over-estimated the results-producing qualities of white whiskers. I think I may say with all modesty that mine are as white as the next man's, but they got me nowhere. If I had been a clean-shaven juvenile in the early twenties, I could not have made less progress towards a satisfactory settlement.

It was all very well, I felt rather bitterly at times, for William to tell me to "handle it", but what could I do? What can any man do when he is confronted by these great natural forces? For years, it was evident, poetry had been banking up inside Rodney Spelvin, accumulating like steam in a boiler on the safety valve of which someone is sitting. And now that the explosion had come, its violence was such as to defy all ordinary methods of treatment. Does one argue with an erupting crater? Does one reason with a waterspout? When William in his airy way told me to "handle it", it was as if someone had said to the young man who bore 'mid snow and ice the banner with the strange device Excelsior—"Block that avalanche."

I could see only one gleam of light in the whole murky affair. Rodney Spelvin had not given up golf. Yielding to his wife's prayers, he had entered for the competition for the Rabbits Umbrella, and had shown good form in the early rounds. Three of the local cripples had fallen victims to his prowess, leaving him a popular semi-finalist. It might be then, that golf would work a cure.

It was as I was taking an afternoon nap a few days later that I was aroused by a sharp prod in the ribs and saw William's wife Jane standing beside me.

"Well?" she was saying.

I blinked, and sat up.

"Ah, Jane," I said.

"Sleeping at a time like this," she exclaimed, and I saw that she was regarding me censoriously. If Jane Bates has a fault, it is that she does not readily make allowances. "But perhaps you are just taking a well-earned rest after doping out the scheme of a lifetime?"

I could not deceive her.

"I am sorry. No."

"No scheme?"

"None."

Jane Bates's face, like that of her husband, had been much worked upon by an open-air life, so she did not pale. But her nose twitched with sudden emotion, and she looked as if she had foozled a short putt for hole and match in an important contest. I saw her glance questioningly at my whiskers.

"Yes," I said, interpreting her look, "I know they are white, but I repeat: No scheme. I have no more ideas than a rabbit; indeed not so many."

"But William said you would handle the thing."

"It can't be handled."

"It must be. Anastatia is going into a decline. Have you seen Timothy lately?"

"I saw him yesterday in the woods with his father. He was plucking a bluebell."

"No, he wasn't."

"He certainly had the air of one who is plucking a bluebell."

"Well, he wasn't. He was talking into it. He said it was a fairy telephone and he was calling up the Fairy Queen to invite her to a party on his teddy bear's birthday. Rodney stood by, taking notes and that evening wrote a poem about it."

"Does Timothy often do that sort of thing?"

"All the time. The child has become a ham. He never ceases putting on an act. He can't eat his breakfast cereal without looking out of the corner of his eye to see how it's going with the audience. And when he says his prayers at night his eyes are ostensibly closed, but all the while he is peering through his fingers and counting the house. And that's not the worst of it. A wife and mother can put up with having an infant ham in the home, constantly popping out at her and being cute, provided that she is able to pay the household bills, but now Rodney says he is going to give up writing thrillers and devote himself entirely to poetry."

"But his contracts?"

"He says he doesn't give a darn for any contracts. He says he wants to get away from it all and give his soul a chance. The way he talks about his soul and the raw deal it has had all these years, you would think it had been doing a stretch in Wormwood Scrubs. He says he is fed up with bloodstains and that the mere thought of bodies in the library with daggers of Oriental design in their backs make him sick. He broke the news to his agent on the telephone last night, and I could hear the man's screams as plainly as if he had been in the next room."

"But is he going to stop eating?"

"Practically. So is Anastatia. He says they can get along quite nicely on wholesome and inexpensive vegetables. He thinks it will help his poetry. He says look at Rabindranath Tagore. Never wrapped himself around a T-bone steak in his life, and look where he fetched up. All done on rice, he said, with an occasional draft of cold water from the spring. I tell you my heart bleeds for Anastatia. A lunatic husband and a son who talks into bluebells, and she'll have to cope with them on Brussels sprouts. She certainly drew the short straw when she married that bard."

She paused in order to snort, and suddenly, without warning, as so often happens, the solution came to me.

"Jane!" I said, "I believe I see the way out."

"You do?"

There flashed into her face a look which I had only once seen there before, on the occasion when the opponent who had fought her all the way to the twentieth hole in the final of the Ladies' Championship of the club was stung by a wasp while making the crucial putt. She kissed me between the whiskers and was good enough to say that she had known all along that I had it in me.

"When do you expect your son Braid back?"

"Some time to-morrow afternoon."

"When he arrives, send him to me. I will outline the position of affairs to him, and I think we can be safe in assuming that he will immediately take over."

"I don't understand."

"You know what Braid is like. He has no reticences."

I spoke feelingly. Braid Bates was one of those frank, uninhibited children who are not afraid to speak their minds, and there had been certain passages between us in the not distant past in the course of which I had learned more about my personal appearance from two minutes of his conversation than I could have done from years of introspective study. At the time, I confess, I had been chagrined and had tried fruitlessly to get at him with a niblick, but now I found myself approving whole-heartedly of this trait in his character.

"Reflect. What will Braid's reaction be to the news that these poems are being written about Timothy? He will be revolted, and will say so, not mincing his words. Briefly, he will kid the pants off the young Spelvin, and it should not be long before the latter, instead of gloating obscenely, will be writhing in an agony of shame at the mention of Timothy Bobbin and begging Rodney to lay off. And surely even a poet cannot be deaf to the pleadings of the child he loves. Leave it to Braid. He will put everything right."

Jane had grasped it now, and her face was aglow with the light of mother love.

"Why, of course!" she cried, clasping her hands in a sort of ecstasy. "I ought to have thought of it myself. People may say what they like about my sweet Braid, but they can't deny that he is the rudest child this side of the Atlantic Ocean. I'll send him to you the moment he clocks in."

Braid Bates at that time was a young plug-ugly of some nine summers, in appearance a miniature edition of William and in soul and temperament a combination of Dead End Kid and army mule; a freckled hard-boiled character with a sardonic eye and a mouth which, when not occupied in eating, had a cynical twist to it. He spoke little as a general thing, but when he did speak seldom failed to find a chink in the armour. The impact of such a personality on little Timothy must, I felt, be tremendous, and I was confident that we could not have placed the child in better hands.

I lost no time in showing him the poem about the Fairy Queen and the bluebell. He read it in silence, and when he had finished drew a deep breath.

"Is Timothy Bobbin Timothy?"

"He is."

"This poem's all about Timothy?"

"Precisely."

"Will it be printed in a book?"

"In a slim volume, yes. Together with others of the same type."

I could see that he was deeply stirred, and felt that I had sown the good seed.

"You will probably have quite a good deal to say about this to Timothy at one time and another," I said. "Don't be afraid to speak out for fear of wounding his feelings. Remind yourself that it is all for his good. The expression 'cruel to be kind' occurs to one."

His manner, as I spoke, seemed absent, as if he were turning over in his mind a selection of good things to be said to his little cousin when they met, and shortly afterwards he left me, so moved that on my offering him a ginger ale and a slice of cake he appeared not to have heard me. I retired to rest that night with the gratifying feeling that I had done my day's good deed, and was on the verge of falling asleep when the telephone bell rang.

It was Jane Bates. Her voice was agitated.

"You and your schemes!" she said.

"I beg your pardon?"

"Do you know what has happened?"

"What?"

"William is writing poetry."

It seemed to me that I could not have heard her correctly.

"William?"

"William."

"You mean Rodney——"

"I don't mean Rodney. Let me tell you in a few simple words what has happened. Braid returned from your house like one in a dream."

"Yes, I thought he seemed impressed."

"Please do not interrupt. It makes it difficult for me to control myself, and I have already bitten a semi-circle out of the mouthpiece. Like one in a dream, I was saying. For the rest of the evening he sat apart, brooding and not answering when spoken to. At bedtime he came out of the silence. And how!"

"And what?"

"I said 'And how!' He announced that that poem of Rodney's about the Fairy

Queen was the snappiest thing he had ever read and he didn't see why, if Rodney could write poems about Timothy, William couldn't write poems about *him*. And when we told him not to talk nonsense, he delivered his ultimatum. He said that if William did not immediately come through, he would remove his name from the list of entrants for the Children's Cup. What did you say?"

"I mean nothing. I was gasping."

"You may well gasp. In fact, it will be all right with me if you choke. It was you who started all this. Of course, he had got us cold. It has been our dearest wish that he should win the Children's Cup, and we have spent money lavishly to have his short game polished up. Naturally, when he put it like that, we had no alternative. I kissed William, shook him by the hand, tied a wet towel around his head, gave him pencil and paper and locked him up in the morning-room with lots of hot coffee. When I asked him just now how he was making out, he said that he had had no inspiration so far but would keep on swinging. His voice sounded very hollow. I can picture the poor darling's agony. The only thing he has ever written before in his life was a stiff letter to the Greens Committee beefing about the new bunker on the fifth, and that took him four days and left him as limp as a rag."

She then turned the conversation to what she described as my mischief-making meddling, and I thought it advisable to hang up.

A thing I have noticed frequently in the course of a long life, and it is one that makes for optimism, is that tragedy, while of course rife in this world of ours, is seldom universal. To give an instance of what I mean, while the barometer of William and Jane Bates pointed to "Further Outlook Unsettled", with Anastatia Spelvin the weather conditions showed signs of improvement.

That William and his wife were in the depths there could be no question. I did not meet Jane, for after the trend of her telephone conversation I felt it more prudent not to, but I saw William a couple of times at luncheon at the club. He looked weary and haggard and was sticking cheese straws in his hair. I heard him ask the waiter if he knew any good rhymes, and when the waiter said "To what?" William replied "To anything". He refused a second chop, and sighed a good deal.

Anastatia, on the other hand, whom I overtook on my way to the links to watch the final of the Rabbits Umbrella a few days later, I found her old cheerful self again. Rodney was one of the competitors in the struggle which was about to begin, and she took a rosy view of his chances. His opponent was Joe Stocker, and it appeared that Joe was suffering from one of his bouts of hay fever.

"Surely," she said, "Rodney can trim a man with hay fever? Of course, Mr. Stocker is trying Sneezo, the sovereign remedy, but, after all, what is Sneezo?"

"A mere palliative."

"They say he broke a large vase yesterday during one of his paroxysms. It flew across the room and was dashed to pieces against the wall."

"That sounds promising."

"Do you know," said Anastatia, and I saw that her eyes were shining, "I can't help feeling that if all goes well Rodney may turn the corner."

"You mean that his better self will gain the upper hand, making him once again the Rodney we knew and loved?"

"Exactly. If he wins his final, I think he will be a changed man."

I saw what she meant. A man who has won his first trophy, be it only a scarlet umbrella, has no room in his mind for anything but the improving of his game so that he can as soon as possible win another trophy. A Rodney Spelvin with the Rabbits Umbrella under his belt would have little leisure or inclination for writing poetry. Golf had been his salvation once. It might prove to be so again.

"You didn't watch the preliminary rounds did, you?" Anastatia went on. "Well, at first Rodney was listless. The game plainly bored him. He had taken a note-book out with him, and he kept stopping to jot down ideas. And then suddenly, half-way through the semi-final, he seemed to change. His lips tightened. His face grew set. And on the tenth a particularly significant incident occurred. He was shaping for a brassie shot, when a wee little blue butterfly fluttered down and settled on his ball. And instead of faltering he clenched his teeth and swung at it with every ounce of weight and muscle. It had to make a quick jump to save its life. I have seldom seen a butterfly move more nippily. Don't you think that was promising?"

"Highly promising. And this brighter state of things continued?"

"All through the semi-final. The butterfly came back on the seventeenth and seemed about to settle on his ball again. But it took a look at his face and moved off. I feel so happy."

I patted her on the shoulder, and we made our way to the first tee, where Rodney was spinning a coin for Joe Stocker to call. And presently Joe, having won the honour, drove off.

A word about this Stocker. A famous amateur wrestler in his youth, and now in middle age completely muscle-bound, he made up for what he lacked in finesse by bringing to the links the rugged strength and directness of purpose which in other days had enabled him to pin one and all to the mat: and it had been well said of him as a golfer that you never knew what he was going to do next. It might be one thing, or it might be another. All you could say with certainty was that he would be in there, trying. I have seen him do the long fifteenth in two, and I have seen him do the shorter second in thirty-seven.

To-day he made history immediately by holing out his opening drive. It is true that he holed it out on the sixteenth green, which lies some three hundred yards away and a good deal to the left of the first tee, but he holed it out, and a gasp went up from the spectators who had assembled to watch the match. If this was what Joseph Stocker did on the first, they said to one another, the imagination reeled stunned at the prospect of the heights to which he might soar in the course of eighteen holes.

But golf is an uncertain game. Taking a line through that majestic opening drive, one would have supposed that Joe Stocker's tee shot at the second would have beaned a lady, too far off to be identified, who was working in her garden about a quarter of a mile to the south-west. I had, indeed, shouted a warning "Fore!"

So far from doing this, however, it took him in a classic curve straight for the pin, and he had no difficulty in shooting a pretty three. And as Rodney had the misfortune to sink a ball in the lake, they came to the third all square.

The third, fourth and fifth they halved. Rodney won the sixth, Stocker the seventh. At the eighth I fancied that Rodney was about to take the lead again, for his opponent's third had left his ball entangled in a bush of considerable size, from which it seemed that it could be removed only with a pair of tweezers.

But it was at moments like this that you caught Joseph Stocker at his best. In some of the more scientific aspects of the game he might be forced to yield the palm to more skilful performers, but when it came to a straight issue of muscle and the will to win he stood alone. Here was where he could use his niblick, and Joe Stocker, armed with his niblick, was like King Arthur wielding his sword Excalibur. The next instant the ball, the bush, a last year's bird's nest and a family of caterpillars which had taken out squatter's rights were hurtling toward the green, and shortly after that, Rodney was one down again.

And as they halved the ninth, it was in this unpleasant position that he came to the turn. Here Stocker, a chivalrous antagonist, courteously suggested a quick one at the bar before proceeding, and we repaired thither.

All through these nine gruelling holes, with their dramatic mutations of fortune, I had been watching Rodney carefully, and I had been well pleased with what I saw. There could be no doubt whatever that Anastatia had been right and that the game had gripped this backslider with all its old force. Here was no poet, pausing between shots to enter stray throughts in a note-book, but something that looked like a Scotch pro in the last round of the National Open. What he had said to his caddie on the occasion of the lad cracking a nut just as he was putting had been music to my ears. It was plain that the stern struggle had brought out all that was best in Rodney Spelvin.

It seemed to me, too, an excellent sign that he was all impatience to renew the contest. He asked Stocker with some brusqueness if he proposed to spend the rest of the day in the bar, and Stocker hastily drained his second ginger ale and Sneezo and we went out.

As we were making our way to the tenth tee, little Timothy suddenly appeared from nowhere, gambolling up in an arch way like a miniature chorus-boy, and I saw at once what Jane had meant when she had spoken of him putting on an act. There was a sort of ghastly sprightliness about the child. He exuded whimsicality at every pore.

"Daddee," he called, and Rodney looked round a little irritably, it seemed to me, like one interrupted while thinking of higher things.

"Daddee, I've made friends with such a nice beetle."

It was a remark which a few days earlier would have had Rodney reaching for his note-book with a gleaming eye, but now he was plainly distrait. There was an absent look on his face, and watching him swing his driver one was reminded of a tiger of the jungle lashing its tail.

"Quite," was all he said.

"It's green. I call it Mister Green Beetle."

This idiotic statement—good, one would have thought, for at least a couple of stanzas—seemed to arouse little or no enthusiasm in Rodney. He merely nodded curtly and said "Yes, yes, very sensible".

"Run away and have a long talk with it," he added.

"What about?"

"Why—er—other beetles."

"Do you think Mister Green Beetle has some dear little brothers and sisters, Daddee?"

"Extremely likely. Good-bye. No doubt we shall meet later."

"I wonder if the Fairy Queen uses beetles as horses, Daddee?"

"Very possibly, very possibly. Go and make inquiries. And you," said Rodney, addressing his cowering caddie, "if I hear one more hiccough out of you while I am shooting—just one—I shall give you two minutes to put your affairs in order and then I shall act. Come on, Stocker, come on, come on, come on. You have the honour."

He looked at his opponent sourly, like one with a grievance, and I knew what was in his mind. He was wondering where this hay fever of Stocker's was, of which he had heard so much.

I could not blame him. A finalist in a golf tournament, playing against an antagonist who has been widely publicized as a victim of hay fever, is entitled to expect that the latter will give at least occasional evidence of his infirmity, and so far Joseph Stocker had done nothing of the kind. From the start of the proceedings he had failed to foozle a single shot owing to a sudden sneeze, and what Rodney was feeling was that while this could not perhaps actually be described as sharp practice, it was sailing very near the wind.

The fact of the matter was that the inventor of Sneezo knew his stuff. A quick-working and harmless specific highly recommended by the medical fraternity and containing no deleterious drugs, it brought instant relief. Joe Stocker had been lowering it by the pailful since breakfast, and it was standing him in good stead. I have fairly keen ears, but up to now I had not heard him even sniffle. He played his shots dry-eyed and without convulsions, and whatever holes Rodney had won he had had to win by sheer unassisted merit.

There was no suggestion of the hay fever patient as he drove off now. He smote his ball firmly and truly, and it would unquestionably have travelled several hundred yards had it not chanced to strike the ladies' tee box and ricocheted into the rough. Encouraged by this, Rodney played a nice straight one down the middle and was able to square the match again.

A ding-dong struggle ensued, for both men were now on their mettle. First one would win a hole, then the other: and then, to increase the dramatic suspense, they would halve a couple. They arrived at the eighteenth all square.

The eighteenth was at that time one of those longish up-hill holes which present few difficulties if you can keep your drive straight, and it seemed after both men had driven that the issue would be settled on the green. But golf, as I said before, is an uncertain game. Rodney played a nice second to within fifty yards of the green, but Stocker, pressing, topped badly and with his next missed the globe altogether, tying himself in the process into a knot from which for an instant I thought it would be impossible to unravel him.

But he contrived to straighten himself out, and was collecting his faculties for another effort, when little Timothy came trotting up. He had a posy of wild flowers in his hand.

"Smell my pretty flowers, Mr. Stocker," he chirped. And with a arch gesture he thrust the blooms beneath Joseph Stocker's nose.

A hoarse cry sprang from the other's lips, and he recoiled as if the bouquet had contained a snake.

"Hey, look out for my hay fever!" he cried, and already I saw that he was beginning to heave and writhe. Under a direct frontal attack like this even Sneezo loses its power to protect.

"Don't bother the gentleman now dear," said Rodney mildly. A glance at his face told me that he was saying to himself that this was something like family teamwork. "Run along and wait for Daddy on the green."

Little Timothy skipped off, and once more Stocker addressed his ball. It was plain that it was going to be a close thing. A sneeze of vast proportions was evidently coming to a head within him like some great tidal wave, and if he meant to forestall it he would have to cut his customary deliberate waggle to something short and sharp like George Duncan's. And I could see that he appreciated this.

But quickly though he waggled, he did not waggle quickly enough. The explosion came just as the club head descended on the ball.

The result was one of the most magnificent shots I have ever witnessed. It was as if the whole soul and essence of Joseph Stocker, poured into that colossal sneeze, had gone to the making of it. Straight and true, as if fired out of a gun, the ball flew up the hill and disappeared over the edge of the green.

It was with a thoughtful air that Rodney Spelvin prepared to play his chip shot. He had obviously been badly shaken by the miracle which he had just observed. But Anastatia had trained him well, and he made no mistake. He, too, was on the green and, as far as one could judge, very near the pin. Even supposing that Stocker was lying dead, he would still be in the enviable position of playing four as against the other's five. And he was a very accurate putter.

Only when we arrived on the green were we able to appreciate the full drama of the situation. Stocker's ball was nowhere to be seen, and it seemed for a moment as it it must have been snatched up to heaven. Then a careful search discovered it nestling in the hole.

"Ah," said Joe Stocker, well satisfied. "Thought for a moment I had missed it."

There was good stuff in Rodney Spelvin. The best he could hope for now was to take his opponent on the nineteenth, but he did not quail. His ball was lying some four feet from the hole, never at any time an easy shot but at the crisis of a hard-fought match calculated to unman the stoutest, and he addressed it with a quiet fortitude which I like to see.

Slowly he drew his club back, and brought it down. And as he did so, a clear childish voice broke the silence.

"Daddee!"

And Rodney, starting as if a red-hot iron had been placed against the bent seat of his knickerbockers, sent the ball scudding yards past the hole. Joseph Stocker was the winner of that year's Rabbits Umbrella.

Rodney Spelvin straightened himself. His face was pale and drawn.

"Daddee, are daisies little bits of the stars that have been chipped off by the angels?"

A deep sigh shook Rodney Spelvin. I saw his eyes. They were alight with a hideous menace. Quickly and silently, like an African leopard stalking its prey, he advanced on the child. An instant later the stillness was disturbed by a series of reports like pistol shots.

I looked at Anastatia. There was distress on her face, but mingled with the distress a sort of ecstasy. She mourned as a mother, but rejoiced as a wife.

Rodney Spelvin was himself again.

That night little Braid Bates, addressing his father, said:

"How's that poem coming along?"

William cast a hunted look at his helpmeet, and Jane took things in hand in her firm, capable way.

"That," she said, "will be all of that. Daddy isn't going to write any poem and, we shall want you out on the practice tee at seven sharp to-morrow, my lad."

"But Uncle Rodney writes poems to Timothy."

"No he doesn't. Not now."

"But . . ."

Jane regarded him with quiet intentness.

"Does Mother's little chickabiddy want his nose pushed sideways?" she said. "Very well, then."

29

TANGLED HEARTS

A MARRIAGE was being solemnized in the church that stands about a full spoon shot from the club-house. The ceremony had nearly reached its conclusion. As the officiating clergyman, coming to the nub of the thing, addressed the young man in the cutaway coat and spongebag trousers, there reigned throughout the sacred edifice a tense silence, such as prevails upon a racecourse just before the shout goes up, "They're off!"

"Wilt thou," he said, "—hup—Smallwood, take this—hup—Celia to be thy wedded wife?"

A sudden gleam came into the other's horn-rimmed spectacled eyes.

"Say, listen," he began. "Lemme tell you what to——"

He stopped, a blush mantling his face.

"I will," he said.

A few moments later, the organ was pealing forth "The Voice That Breathed O'er Eden". The happy couple entered the vestry. The Oldest Member, who had been among those in the ringside pews, walked back to the club-house with the friend who was spending the week-end with him.

The friend seemed puzzled.

"Tell me," he said. "Am I wrong, or did the bridegroom at one point in the proceedings start to *ad lib* with some stuff that was not on the routine?"

"He did, indeed," replied the Oldest Member. "He was about to advise the minister what to do for his hiccoughs. I find the fact that he succeeded in checking himself very gratifying. It seems to show that his cure may be considered permanent."

"His cure?"

"Until very recently Smallwood Bessemer was a confirmed adviser."

"Bad, that."

"Yes. I always advise people never to give advice. Mind you, one can find excuses for the young fellow. For many years he had been a columnist on one of the morning papers, and to columnists, accustomed day after day to set the world right on every conceivable subject, the giving of advice becomes a habit. It is an occupational risk. But if I had known young Bessemer better, I would have warned him that he was in danger of alienating Celia Todd, his betrothed, who was a girl of proud and independent spirit.

"Unfortunately, he was not a member of our little community. He lived in the city, merely coming here for occasional week-ends. At the time when my story begins, I had met him only twice, when he arrived to spend his summer vacation. And it was not long before, as I had feared would be the case, I found that all was not well between him and Celia Todd."

The first intimation I had of this (the Sage proceeded) was when she called at my cottage accompanied by her Pekinese, Pirbright, to whom she was greatly attached, and unburdened her soul to me. Sinking listlessly into a chair, she sat silent for some moments. Then, as if waking from a reverie, she spoke abruptly.

"Do you think," she said, "that true love can exist between a woman and a man, if the woman feels more and more every day that she wants to hit the man over the head with a brick?"

I was disturbed. I like to see the young folks happy. And my hope that she might merely be stating a hypothetical case vanished as she continued.

"Take me and Smallwood, for instance. I have to clench my fists sometimes till the knuckles stand out white under the strain, in order to stop myself from beaning him. This habit of his of scattering advice on every side like a sower going forth sowing is getting me down. It has begun to sap my reason. Only this morning, to show you what I mean, we were walking along the road and we met that wolfhound of Agnes Flack's, and it said something to Pirbright about the situation in China that made him hot under the collar. The little angel was just rolling up his sleeves and starting in to mix it, when I snatched him away. And Smallwood said I shouldn't have done it. I should have let them fight it out, he said, so that they could get it out of their systems, after which a beautiful friendship would have resulted. I told him he was the sort of human fiend who ought to be eating peanuts in the front row at a bull fight, and we parted on rather distant terms."

"The clouds will clear away."

"I wonder," said Celia. "I have a feeling that one of these days he will go too far, and something will crack."

In the light of this conversation, what happened at the dance becomes intelligible. Every Saturday night we have a dance at the club-house, at which all the younger set assembles. Celia was there, escorted by Smallwood Bessemer, their differences having apparently been smoothed over, and for a while all seems to have gone well. Bessemer was an awkward and clumsy dancer, but the girl's love enabled her to endure the way in which he jumped on and off her feet. When the music stopped, she started straightening out her toes without the slightest doubt in her mind that he was a king among men.

And then suddenly he turned to her with a kindly smile.

"I'd like to give you a bit of advice," he said. "What's wrong with your dancing is that you give a sort of jump at the turn, like a trout leaping at a fly. Now, the way to cure this is very simple. Try to imagine that the ceiling is very low and made of very thin glass, and that your head just touches it and you mustn't break it. You've dropped your engagement ring," he said, as something small and hard struck him on the side of the face.

"No, I haven't," said Celia. "I threw it at you."

And she strode haughtily out on to the terrace. And Smallwood Bessemer, having watched her disappear, went to the bar to get a quick one.

There was only one man in the bar, and yet it looked well filled. This was because Sidney McMurdo, its occupant, is one of those vast, muscled individuals who bulge in every direction. He was sitting slumped in a chair, scowling beneath beetling brows, his whole aspect that of one whose soul has just got the sleeve across the windpipe.

Sidney was not in any sense an intimate of Smallwood Bessemer. They had met for the first time on the previous afternoon, when Bessemer had advised Sidney always to cool off slowly after playing golf, as otherwise he might contract pneumonia and cease to be with us, and Sidney, who is a second vice-president of a large insurance company, had taken advantage of this all-flesh-is-as-grass note which had been introduced into the conversation to try to sell Bessemer his firm's all-accident policy.

No business had resulted, but the episode had served to make them acquainted, and they now split a bottle. The influence of his share on Sidney McMurdo was mellowing enough to make him confidential.

"I've just had a hell of a row with my *fiancée*," he said.

"I've just had a hell of a row with *my fiancée*," said Smallwood Bessemer, struck by the coincidence.

"She told me I ought to putt off the right foot. I said I was darned well going to keep right along putting off the left foot, as I had been taught at my mother's knee. She then broke off the engagement."

Smallwood Bessemer was not a golfer, but manlike he sympathized with the male, and he was in a mood to be impatient of exhibitions of temperament in women.

"Women," he said, "are all alike. They need to be brought to heel. You have to teach them where they get off and show them that they can't go about the place casting away a good man's love as if it were a used tube of toothpaste. Let me give you a bit of advice. Don't sit brooding in bars. Do as I intend to do. Go out and start making vigorous passes at some other girl."

"To make her jealous?"

"Exactly."

"So that she will come legging it back, pleading to be forgiven?"

"Precisely."

Sidney brightened.

"That sounds pretty good to me. Because I mean to say there's always the chance that the other girl will let you kiss her, and then you're that much ahead of the game."

"Quite," said Smallwood Bessemer.

He returned to the dance room, glad to have been able to be of assistance to a fellow man in his hour of distress. Celia was nowhere to be seen, and he presumed that she was still cooling off on the terrace. He saw Sidney, who had stayed behind for a moment to finish the bottle, flash past in a purposeful way, and then he looked about him to decide who should be his assistant in the little psychological experiment which he proposed to undertake. His eyes fell on Agnes Flack, sitting in a corner, rapping her substantial foot on the floor.

Have you met Agnes Flack? You don't remember? Then you have not, for once seen she is not forgotten. She is our female club champion, a position which she owes not only to her skill at golf but to her remarkable physique. She is a fine, large, handsome girl, built rather on the lines of Pop-Eye the Sailor, and Smallwood Bessemer, who was on the slender side, had always admired her.

He caught her eye, and she smiled brightly. He went over to where she sat, and presently they were out on the floor. He saw Celia appear at the French windows and stand looking in, and intensified the silent passion of his dancing, trying to convey the idea of being something South American, which ought to be chained up and muzzled in the interests of pure womanhood. Celia sniffed with a violence that caused the lights to flicker, and an hour or so later Smallwood Bessemer went home, well pleased with the start he had made.

He was climbing into bed, feeling that all would soon be well once more, when the telephone rang and Sidney McMurdo's voice boomed over the wire.

"Hoy!" said Sidney.

"Yes?" said Bessemer.

"You know that advice you gave me?"

"You took it, I hope?"

"Yes," said Sidney. "And a rather unfortunate thing has occurred. How it happened, I can't say, but I've gone and got engaged."

"Too bad," said Bessemer sympathetically. "There was always that risk, of course. The danger on these occasions is that one may overdo the thing and become too fascinating. I ought to have warned you to hold yourself in. Who is the girl?"

"A frightful pie-faced little squirt named Celia Todd," said Sidney and hung up with a hollow groan.

To say that this information stunned Smallwood Bessemer would scarcely be to overstate the facts. For some moments after the line had gone dead, he sat motionless, his soul seething within him like a welsh rabbit at the height of its fever. He burned with rage and resentment, and all the manhood in him called to him to make a virile gesture and show Celia Todd who was who and what was what.

An idea struck him. He called up Agnes Flack.

"Miss Flack?"

"Hello?"

"Sorry to disturb you at this hour, but will you marry me?"

"Certainly. Who is that?"

"Smallwood Bessemer."

"I don't get the second name."

"Bessemer. B. for banana, e for erysipelas——"

"Oh, Bessemer? Yes, delighted. Good night, Mr. Bessemer."

"Good night, Miss Flack."

Sometimes it happens that after a restorative sleep a man finds that his views on what seemed in the small hours a pretty good idea have undergone a change. It was so with Bessemer. He woke next morning oppressed by a nebulous feeling that in some way, which for the moment eluded his memory, he had made rather a chump of himself overnight. And then, as he was brushing his teeth, he was able to put his finger on the seat of the trouble. Like a tidal wave, the events of the previous evening came flooding back into his mind, and he groaned in spirit.

Why in this dark hour he should have thought of me, I cannot say, for we were the merest acquaintances. But he must have felt that I was the sort of man who would lend a sympathetic ear, for he called me up on the telephone and explained the situation, begging me to step round and see Agnes and sound her regarding her views on the matter. An hour later, I was able to put him abreast.

"She says she loves you devotedly."

"But how can she? I scarcely know the girl."

"That is what she says. No doubt you are one of those men who give a woman a single glance and—bing!—all is over."

There was a silence at the other end of the wire. When he spoke again, there was an anxious tremor in his voice.

"What would you say chances were," he asked, "for explaining that it was all a little joke, at which I had expected that no one would laugh more heartily than herself?'

"Virtually nil. As a matter of fact, that point happened to come up, and she stated specifically that if there was any rannygazoo—if, in other words, it should prove that you had been pulling her leg and trying to make her the plaything of an idle moment —she would know what to do about it."

"Know what to do about it."

"That was the expression she employed."

"Know what to do about it," repeated Smallwood Bessemer thoughtfully. " 'M yes. I see what you mean. Know what to do about it. Yes. But why on earth does this ghastly girl love me? She must be cuckoo."

"For your intellect, she tells me. She says she finds you a refreshing change after her late *fiancé*, Sidney McMurdo."

"Was she engaged to Sidney McMurdo?"

"Yes."

"H'm!" said Bessemer.

He told me subsequently that his first action after he had hung up was to go to his cupboard and take from it a bottle of tonic port which he kept handy in case he required a restorative or stimulant. He had fallen into the habit of drinking a little of this whenever he felt low, and Reason told him that he was never going to feel lower than he did at that moment. To dash off a glass and fill another was with him the work of an instant.

Generally, the effect of this tonic port was to send the blood coursing through his veins like liquid fire and make him feel that he was walking on the tip of his toes with his hat on the side of his head. But now its magic seemed to have failed. Spiritually, he remained a total loss.

Nor, I think, can we be surprised at this. It is not every day that a young fellow loses the girl he worships and finds that he has accumulated another whom he not only does not love but knows that he can never love. Smallwood Bessemer respected Agnes Flack. He would always feel for her that impersonal admiration which is inspired by anything very large, like the Empire State Building or the Grand Canyon of Arizona. But the thought of being married to her frankly appalled him.

And in addition to this there was the Sidney McMurdo angle.

Smallwood Bessemer, as I say, did not know Sidney McMurdo well. But he knew him well enough to be aware that his reactions on finding that another man had become engaged to his temporarily ex-*fiancée* would be of a marked nature. And as the picture rose before his eyes of that vast frame of his and those almost varicose muscles that rippled like dangerous snakes beneath his pullover, his soul sickened and he had to have a third glass of tonic port.

It was while he was draining it that Sidney McMurdo came lumbering over the threshold, and so vivid was the impression he created of being eight foot high and broad in proportion that Smallwood Bessemer nearly swooned. Recovering himself, he greeted him with almost effusive cordiality.

"Come in, McMurdo, come in," he cried buoyantly. "Just the fellow I wanted to see. I wonder, McMurdo, if you remember what you were saying to me the other day about the advisability of my taking out an all-accident insurance with your firm? I have been thinking it over, and am strongly inclined to do so."

"It's the sensible thing," said Sidney McMurdo. "A man ought to look to the future."

"Precisely."

"You never know when you may not get badly smashed up."

"Never. Shall we go round to your place and get a form?"

"I have one with me."

"Then I will sign it at once," said Bessemer.

And he had just done so and had written out a cheque for the first year's premium, when the telephone bell rang.

"Yoo-hoo, darling," bellowed a voice genially, and he recognized it as Agnes Flack's. A quick glance out of the corner of his eye told him that his companion had recognized it, too. Sidney McMurdo had stiffened. His face was flushed. He sat clenching and unclenching his hands. When Agnes Flack spoke on the telephone, there was never any need for extensions to enable the bystander to follow her remarks.

Smallwood Bessemer swallowed once or twice.

"Oh, good morning, Miss Flack," he said formally.

"What do you mean—Miss Flack? Call me Aggie. Listen, I'm at the club-house. Come on out. I want to give you a golf lesson."

"Very well."

"You mean 'Very well, darling'."

"Er—yes. Er—very well, darling."

"Right," said Agnes Flack.

Smallwood Bessemer hung up the receiver, and turned to find his companion scrutinizing him narrowly. Sidney McMurdo had turned a rather pretty mauve, and his eyes had an incandescent appearance. It seemed to Bessemer that with a few minor changes he could have stepped straight into the Book of Revelations and no questions asked.

"That was Agnes Flack!" said McMurdo hoarsely.

"Er—yes," said Bessemer. "Yes, I believe it was."

"She called you 'darling'."

"Er—yes. Yes, I believe she did."

"You called her 'darling'."

"Ee—yes. That's right. She seemed to wish it."

"Why?" asked Sidney McMurdo, who was one of those simple, direct men who like to come straight to the point.

"I've been meaning to tell you about that," said Smallwood Bessemer. "We're engaged. It happened last night after the dance."

Sidney McMurdo gave a hitch to his shoulder muscles, which were leaping about under his pullover like adagio dancers. His scrutiny, already narrow, became narrower.

"So it was all a vile plot, was it?"

"No, no."

"Of course it was a vile plot," said Sidney McMurdo petulantly, breaking off a corner of the mantelpiece and shredding it through his fingers. "You gave me that advice about going out and making passes purely in order that you should be left free to steal Agnes from me. If that wasn't a vile plot, then I don't know a vile plot when I see one. Well, well, we must see what we can do about it."

It was the fact that Smallwood Bessemer at this moment sprang nimbly behind the table that temporarily eased the strain of the situation. For as Sidney McMurdo started to remove the obstacle, his eye fell on the insurance policy. He stopped as if spellbound, staring at it, his lower jaw sagging.

Bessemer, scanning him anxiously, could read what was passing through his mind. Sidney McMurdo was a lover, but he was also a second vice-president of the Jersey City and All Points West Mutual and Co-operative Life and Accident Insurance Company, an organization which had an almost morbid distaste for parting with its money. If as the result of any impulsive action on his part the Co. were compelled

to pay over a large sum to Smallwood Bessemer almost before they had trousered
his first cheque, there would be harsh words and raised eyebrows. He might even be
stripped of his second vice-president's desk in the middle of a hollow square. And
next to Agnes Flack and his steel-shafted driver, he loved his second vice-presidency
more than anything in the world.

For what seemed an eternity, Smallwood Bessemer gazed at a strong man
wrestling with himself. Then the crisis passed. Sidney McMurdo flung himself into
a chair, and sat moodily gnashing his teeth.

"Well," said Bessemer, feeling like Shadrach, Meshach and Abednego, "I suppose
I must be leaving you. I am having my first golf lesson."

Sidney McMurdo started.

"Your *first* golf lesson? Haven't you ever played?"

"Net yet."

A hollow groan escaped Sidney McMurdo.

"To think of my Agnes marrying a man who doesn't know the difference between
a brassie and a niblick!"

"Well, if it comes to that," retorted Bessemer, with some spirit, "what price my
Celia marrying a man who doesn't know the difference between Edna St. Vincent
Millay and Bugs Baer?"

Sidney McMurdo stared.

"Your Celia? You weren't engaged to that Todd pipsqueak?"

"She is not a pipsqueak."

"She is too, a pipsqueak, and I can prove it. She reads poetry."

"Naturally. I have made it my loving task to train her eager mind to appreciate
all that is best and most beautiful."

"She says I've got to do it, too."

"It will be the making of you. And now," said Smallwood Bessemer, "I really
must be going."

"Just a moment," said Sidney McMurdo. He reached out and took the insurance
policy, studying it intently for a while. But it was as he feared. It covered everything.
"All right," he said sombrely, "pop off."

I suppose there is nothing (proceeded the Oldest Member) more painful to the
man of sensibility that the spectacle of tangled hearts. Here were four hearts as
tangled as spaghetti, and I grieved for them. The female members of the quartette
did not confide in me, but I was in constant demand by both McMurdo and Bessemer,
and it is not too much to say that these men were passing through the furnace. Indeed,
I cannot say which moved me the more—Bessemer's analysis of his emotions when
jerked out of bed at daybreak by a telephone call from Agnes, summoning him to
the links before breakfast, or McMurdo's description of how it felt to read W. H.
Auden. Suffice it that each wrung my heart to the uttermost.

And so the matter stood at the opening of the contest for the Ladies' Vase.

This was one of our handicap events, embracing in its comprehensive scope almost the entire female personnel of the club, from the fire-breathing tigresses to the rabbits who had taken up golf because it gave them an opportunity of appearing in sports clothes. It was expected to be a gift once more for Agnes Flack, though she would be playing from scratch and several of the contestants were receiving as much as forty-eight. She had won the Vase the last two years, and if she scooped it in again, it would become her permanent possession. I mention this to show you what the competition meant to her.

For a while, all proceeded according to the form book. Playing in her usual bold, resolute style, she blasted her opponents off the links one by one, and came safely through into the final without disarranging her hair.

But as the tournament progressed, it became evident that a platinum blonde of the name of Julia Prebble, receiving twenty-seven, had been grossly under-handicapped. Whether through some natural skill at concealing the merits of her game, or because she was engaged to a member of the handicapping committee, one cannot tell, but she had, as I say, contrived to scrounge a twenty-seven when ten would have been more suitable. The result was that she passed into the final bracket with consummate ease, and the betting among the wilder spirits was that for the first time in three years Agnes Flack's mantelpiece would have to be looking about it for some other ornament than the handsome silver vase presented by the club for annual competition among its female members.

And when at the end of the first half of the thirty-six hole final Agnes was two down after a gruelling struggle, it seemed as though their prognostications were about to be fulfilled.

It was in the cool of a lovely summer evening that play was resumed. I had been asked to referee the match, and I was crossing the terrace on my way to the first tee when I encountered Smallwood Bessemer. And we were pausing to exchange a word or two, when Sidney McMurdo came along.

To my surprise, for I had supposed relations between the two men to be strained, Bessemer waved a cordial hand.

"Hyah, Sidney," he called.

"Hyah, Smallwood," replied the other.

"Did you get that tonic?"

"Yes. Good stuff, you think?"

"You can't beat it," said Bessemer, and Sidney McMurdo passed along towards the first tee.

I was astonished.

"You seem on excellent terms with McMurdo," I said.

"Oh, yes," said Bessemer. "He drops in at my place a good deal. We smoke a pipe and roast each other's girls. It draws us very close together. I was able to do him a good turn this morning. He was very anxious to watch the match, and Celia wanted him to go into town to fetch a specialist for her Peke, who is off colour to-day. I told him to give it a shot of that tonic port I drink. Put it right in no time. Well, I'll be seeing you."

"You are not coming round?"

"I may look in toward the finish. What do you think of Agnes's chances?"

"Well, she had been battling nobly against heavy odds, but—"

"The trouble with Agnes is that she believes all she reads in the golf books. If she would only listen to me . . . Ah, well," said Smallwood Bessemer, and moved off.

It did not take me long after I had reached the first tee to see that Agnes Flack was not blind to the possibility of being deprived of her Vase. Her lips were tight, and there was a furrow in her forehead. I endeavoured to ease her tension with a kindly word or two.

"Lovely evening," I said.

"It will be," she replied, directing a somewhat acid glance at her antagonist, who was straightening the tie of the member of the handicapping committee to whom she was betrothed "if I can trim that ginger-headed Delilah and foil the criminal skul-duggery of a bunch of yeggmen who ought to be blushing themselves purple. Twenty-seven, forsooth!"

Her warmth was not unjustified. After watching the morning's round, I, too, felt that that twenty-seven handicap of Julia Prebble's had been dictated by the voice of love rather than by a rigid sense of justice. I changed the subject.

"Bessemer is not watching the match, he tells me."

"I wouldn't let him. He makes me nervous."

"Indeed?"

"Yes. I started teaching him golf a little while ago, and now he's teaching *me*. He knows it all."

"He is a columnist," I reminded her.

"At lunch to-day he said he was going to skim through Alex Morrison's book again, because he had a feeling that Alex hadn't got the right angle on the game."

I shuddered strongly, and at this moment Julia Prebble detached herself from her loved one, and the contest began.

I confess that, as I watched the opening stages of the play, I found a change taking place in my attitude towards Agnes Flack. I had always respected her, as one must respect any woman capable of pasting a ball two hundred and forty yards, but it was only now that respect burgeoned into something like affection. The way she hitched up her sleeves and started to wipe off her opponent's lead invited sympathy and support.

At the outset, she was assisted by the fact that success had rendered Julia Prebble a little overconfident. She did not concentrate. The eye which should have been riveted on her ball had a tendency to smirk sideways at her affianced, causing her to top, with the result that only three holes had been played before the match was all square again.

However, as was inevitable, these reverses had the effect of tightening up Julia Prebble's game. Her mouth hardened, and she showed a disposition to bite at the man she loved, whom she appeared to consider responsible. On the fifth, she told him not to stand in front of her, on the sixth not to stand behind her, on the seventh she asked him not to move while she was putting. On the eighth she suggested that if he had really got St. Vitus Dance he ought to go and put himself in the hands of some good doctor. On the ninth she formally broke off the engagement.

Naturally, all this helped her a good deal, and at the tenth she recovered the lead she had lost. Agnes drew level at the eleventh, and after that things settled down to the grim struggle which one generally sees in finals. A casual observer would have said that it was anybody's game.

But the strain of battling against that handicap was telling on Agnes Flack. Once or twice, her iron resolution seemed to waver. And on the seventeenth Nature took its toll. She missed a short putt for the half, and they came to the eighteenth tee with Julia Prebble dormy one.

The eighteenth hole takes you over the water. A sort of small lake lies just beyond that tee, spanned by a rustic bridge. Across the bridge I now beheld Smallwood Bessemer approaching.

"How's it going?" he asked, as he came to where I stood.

I told him the state of the game, and he shook his head.

"Looks bad," he said. "I'm sorry. I don't like Agnes Flack, and never shall, but one has one's human feelings. It will cut her to the heart to lose that Vase. And when you reflect that if she had only let me come along, she would have been all right, it all seems such a pity, doesn't it? I could have given her a pointer from time to time, which would have made all the difference. But she doesn't seem to want my advice. Prefers to trust to Alex Morrison. Sad. Very sad. Ah," said Smallwood Bessemer, "She didn't relax."

He was alluding to Julia Prebble, who had just driven off. Her ball had cleared the water nicely, but it was plain to the seeing eye that it had a nasty slice on it. It came to rest in a patch of rough at the side of the fairway, and I saw her look sharply round, as if instinctively about to tell her betrothed that she wished he wouldn't shuffle his feet just as she was shooting. But he was not there. He had withdrawn to the club-house, where, I was informed later, he drank six Scotches in quick succession, subsequently crying on the barman's shoulder and telling him what was wrong with women.

In the demeanour of Agnes Flack, as she teed up, there was something that reminded me of Boadicea about to get in amongst a Roman legion. She looked dominant and conquering. I knew what she was thinking. Even if her opponent recovered from the moral shock of a drive like that, she could scarcely be down in less than six, and this was a hole which she, Agnes, always did in four. This meant that the match would go to the thirty-seventh, in which case she was confident that her stamina and the will to win would see her through.

She measured her distance. She waggled. Slowly and forcefully she swung back. And her club was just descending in a perfect arc, when Smallwood Bessemer spoke.

"Hey!" he said.

In the tense silence the word rang out like the crack of a gun. It affected Agnes Flack visibly. For the first time since she had been a slip of a child, she lifted her head in the middle of a stroke, and the ball, badly topped, trickled over the turf, gathered momentum as it reached the edge of the tee, bounded towards the water, hesitated on the brink for an instant like a timid diver on a cold morning and then plunged in.

"Too bad," said Julia Prebble.

Agnes Flack did not reply. She was breathing heavily through her nostrils. She turned to Smallwood Bessemer.

"You were saying something?" she asked.

"I was only going to remind you to relax," said Smallwood Bessemer. "Alex Morrison lays great stress on the importance of pointing the chin and rolling the feet. To my mind, however, the whole secret of golf consists in relaxing. At the top of the swing the muscles should be——"

"My niblick, please," said Agnes Flack to her caddie.

She took the club, poised it for an instant as if judging its heft, then began to move forward swiftly and stealthily, like a tigress of the jungle.

Until that moment, I had always looked on Smallwood Bessemer as purely the man of intellect, what you would describe as the thoughtful, reflective, type. But he now showed that he could, if the occasion demanded it, be the man of action. I do not think I have ever seen anything move quicker than the manner in which he dived head-foremost into the thick clump of bushes which borders the eighteenth tee. One moment, he was there; the next, he had vanished. Eels could have taken his correspondence course.

It was a move of the highest strategic quality. Strong woman though Agnes Flack was, she was afraid of spiders. For an instant, she stood looking wistfully at the bushes; then, hurling her niblick into them, she burst into tears and tottered into the arms of Sidney McMurdo, who came up at this juncture. He had been following the match at a cautious distance.

"Oh, Sidney!" she sobbed.

"There, there," said Sidney McMurdo.

He folded her in his embrace, and they walked off together. From her passionate gestures, I could gather that she was explaining what had occurred and was urging him to plunge into the undergrowth and break Smallwood Bessemer's neck, and the apologetic way in which he waved his hands told me that he was making clear his obligations to the Jersey City and All Points West Mutual and Co-operative Life and Accident Insurance Co.

Presently, they were lost in the gathering dusk, and I called to Bessemer and informed him that the All Clear had been blown.

"She's gone?" he said.

"She has been gone some moments."

"Are you sure?"

"Quite sure."

There was a silence.

"No," said Bessemer. "It may be a trap. I think I'll stick on here a while."

I shrugged my shoulder and left him.

The shades of night were falling fast before Smallwood Bessemer, weighing the pro's and con's, felt justified in emerging from his lair. As he started to cross the bridge that spans the water, it was almost dark. He leaned on the rail, giving himself up to thought.

The sweet was mingled with the bitter in his meditations. He could see that the future held much that must inevitably be distasteful to a man who liked a quiet life. As long as he remained in the neighbourhood, he would be compelled to exercise ceaseless vigilance and would have to hold himself in readiness, should the occasion arise, to pick up his feet and run like a rabbit.

This was not so good. On the other hand, it seemed reasonable to infer from Agnes Flack's manner during the recent episode that their engagement was at an end. A substantial bit of velvet.

Against this, however, must be set the fact that he had lost Celia Todd. There was no getting away from that, and it was this thought that caused him to moan softly as he gazed at the dark water beneath him. And he was still moaning, when there came to his ears the sound of a footstep. A woman's form loomed up in the dusk. She was crossing the bridge towards him. And then suddenly a cry rent the air.

Smallwood Bessemer was to discover shortly that he had placed an erroneous interpretation upon this cry, which had really been one of agitation and alarm. To his sensitive ear it had sounded like the animal yowl of an angry woman sighting her prey, and he had concluded that this must be Agnes Flack, returned to the chase. Acting upon this assumption, he stood not on the order of going but immediately soared over the rail and plunged into the water below. Rising quickly to the surface and clutching out for support, he found himself grasping something wet and furry.

For an instant, he was at a loss to decide what this could be. It had some of the properties of a sponge and some of a damp hearthrug. Then it bit him in the fleshy part of the thumb and he identified it as Celia Todd's Pekinese, Pirbright. In happier days he had been bitten from once to three times a week by this animal, and he recognized its technique.

The discovery removed a great weight from his mind. If Pirbright came, he reasoned, could Celia Todd be far behind. He saw that it must be she, and not Agnes Flack, who stood on the bridge. Greatly relieved, he sloshed to the shore, endeavouring as best he might to elude the creature's snapping jaws.

In this he was not wholly successful. Twice more he had to endure nips, and juicy ones. But the physical anguish soon passed away as he came to land and found himself gazing into Celia's eyes. They were large and round, and shone with an adoring light.

"Oh, Smallwood!" she cried. "Thank heaven you were there! If you had not acted so promptly, the poor little mite would have been drowned."

"It was nothing," protested Bessemer modestly.

"Nothing? To have the reckless courage to plunge in like that? It was the sort of thing people get expensive medals for."

"Just presence of mind," said Bessemer. "Some fellows have it, some haven't. How did it happen?"

She caught her breath.

"It was Sidney McMurdo's doing."

"Sidney McMurdo's?"

"Yes. Pirbright was not well to-day, and I told him to fetch the vet. And he talked me into trying some sort of tonic port, which he said was highly recommended. We gave Pirbright a saucer full, and he seemed to enjoy it. And then he suddenly uttered a piercing bark and ran up the side of the wall. Finally he dashed out of the house. When he returned, his manner was lethargic, and I thought a walk would do him good. And as he came on to the bridge, he staggered and fell. He must have had some form of vertigo."

Smallwood Bessemer scrutinized the animal. The visibility was not good, but he was able to discern in its bearing all the symptoms of an advanced hangover.

"Well, I broke off the engagement right away," proceeded Celia Todd. "I can respect a practical joker. I can admire a man who is cruel to animals. But I cannot pass as fit for human consumption a blend of the two. The mixture is too rich."

Bessemer started.

"You are not going to marry Sidney McMurdo?"

"I am not."

"What an extraordinary coincidence. I am not going to marry Agnes Flack."

"You aren't?"

"No. So it almost looks——"

"Yes, doesn't it?"

"I mean, both of us being at a loose end, as it were . . ."

"Exactly."

"Celia!"

"Smallwood!"

Hand in hand they made their way across the bridge. Celia uttered a sudden cry causing the dog Pirbright to wince as if somebody had driven a red hot spike into his head.

"I haven't told you the worst," she said. "He had the effrontery to assert that you had advised the tonic port."

"The low blister!"

"I knew it could not be true. Your advice is always so good. You remember telling me I ought to have let Pirbright fight Agnes Flack's wolfhound? Well, you were quite right. He met it when he dashed out of the house after drinking that tonic port, and cleaned it up in under a minute. They are now the best of friends. After this, I shall always take your advice and ask for more."

Smallwood Bessemer mused. Once again he was weighing the pro's and con's. It was his habit of giving advice that had freed him from Agnes Flack. On the other hand, if it had not been for his habit of giving advice, Agnes Flack would never, so to speak, have arisen.

"Do you know," he said, "I doubt if I shall be doing much advising from now on. I think I shall ask the paper to release me from my columnist contract. I have a feeling that I shall be happier doing something like the Society News or the Children's Corner."

30

SCRATCH MAN

A DEVOUT expression had come into the face of the young man in plus fours who sat with the Oldest Member on the terrace overlooking the ninth green. With something of the abruptness of a conjurer taking a rabbit out of a hat he drew a photograph from his left breast pocket and handed it to his companion. The Sage inspected it thoughtfully.

"This is the girl you were speaking of?"

"Yes."

"You love her?"

"Madly."

"And how do you find it affects your game?"

"I've started shanking a bit."

The Oldest Member nodded.

"I am sorry," he said, "but not surprised. Either that or missing short putts is what generally happens on these occasions. I doubt if golfers ought to fall in love. I have known it to cost men ten shots in a medal round. They think of the girl and forget to keep their eyes on the ball. On the other hand, there was the case of Harold Pickering."

"I don't think I've met him."

"He was before your time. He took a cottage here a few years ago. His handicap was fourteen. Yet within a month of his arrival love had brought him down to scratch."

"Quick service."

"Very. He went back eventually to a shaky ten, but the fact remains. But for his great love he would not have become even temporarily a scratch man."

I had seen Harold Pickering in and about the club-house (said the Oldest Member) for some time before I made his acquaintance, and there was something in his manner which suggested that sooner or later he would be seeking me out and telling me the story of his life. For some reason, possibly because I have white whiskers, I seem to act on men with stories of their lives to tell like catnip on cats. And sure enough, I was sitting on this terrace one evening, enjoying a quiet gin and ginger, when he sidled up, coughed once or twice like a sheep with bronchitis and gave me the works.

His was a curious and romantic tale. He was by profession a partner in a publishing house, and shortly before his arrival here he had gone to negotiate with John Rockett for the purchase of his Reminiscences.

The name John Rockett will, of course, be familiar to you. If you are a student of history, you will recall that he was twice British Amateur Champion and three times runner-up in the Open. He had long retired from competition golf and settled down to a life of leisured ease, and when Harold Pickering presented himself he found the great veteran celebrating his silver wedding. All the family were there—his grand-mother, now ageing a little but in her day a demon with the gutty ball; his wife, at one time British Ladies Champion; his three sons, Sandwich, Hoylake and St. Andrew; and his two daughters, Troon and Prestwick. He called his children after the courses on which he had won renown, and they did not disgrace the honoured names. They were all scratch.

In a gathering so august, you might have supposed that a sense of what was fitting would have kept a fourteen-handicap man from getting above himself. But passion knows no class distinctions. Ten minutes after his arrival, Harold Pickering had fallen in love with Troon Rockett, with a fervour which could not have been more whole-hearted if he had been playing to plus two. And a week later he put his fortune to the test, to win or lose it all.

"Of course, I was mad . . . mad," he said, moodily chewing the ham sandwich he had ordered, for he had only a light lunch. "How could I suppose that a girl who was scratch—the sister of scratch men—the daughter of an amateur champion—would stoop to a fellow like me? Even as I started to speak, I saw the horror and amazement on her face. Well, when I say speak, I didn't exactly speak, I sort of gargled. But it was enough. She rose quickly and left the room. And I came here ——"

"To forget her?"

"Talk sense," said Harold Pickering shortly. "I came to try to make myself worthy of her. I intended to get myself down to scratch, if it choked me. I heard that your pro here was the best instructor in the country, so I signed the lease for a cottage, seized my clubs and raced round to his shop . . . only to discover what?"

"That he has broken his leg?"

"Exactly. What a sensible, level-headed pro wants to break his leg for is more than I can imagine. But there it was. No chance of any lessons from him."

"It must have been a shock for you."

"I was stunned. It seemed to me that this was the end. But now things have brightened considerably. Do you know a Miss Flack?"

I did indeed. Agnes Flack was one of the recognized sights of the place. One pointed her out to visitors together with the Lover's Leap, the waterfall and the curious rock formation near the twelfth tee. Built rather on the lines of the village blacksmith, she had for many seasons been the undisputed female champion of the club. She had the shoulders of an all-in wrestler, the breezy self-confidence of a sergeant-major and a voice like a toastmaster's. I had often seen the Wrecking Crew, that quartette of spavined septuagenarians whose pride it was that they never let anyone through, scatter like leaves in an autumn gale at the sound of her stentorian "Fore!" A dynamic and interesting personality.

"She is going to coach me," said Harold Pickering. "I saw her practising chip shots my first morning here, and I was amazed at her virtuosity. She seemed just to give a flick of the wrists and the ball fell a foot from the pin and flopped there like a poached egg. It struck me immediately that here was someone whose methods I could study to my great advantage. The chip is my weak spot. For the last ten days or so, accordingly, I have been following her about the course, watching her every movement, and yesterday we happened to fall into conversation and I confided my ambition to her. With a hearty laugh, she told me that if I wanted to become scratch I had come to the right shop. She said that she could make a scratch player out of a cheese mite, provided it had not lost the use of its limbs, and gave as evidence of her tuitionary skill the fact that she had turned a man named Sidney McMurdo from a mere blot on the local scene into something which in a dim light might be mistaken for a golfer. I haven't met McMurdo."

"He is away at the moment. He has gone to attend the sickbed of an uncle. He will be back to play for the club championship."

"As hot as that, is he?"

"Yes, I suppose he would be about the best man we have."

"Scratch?"

"Plus one, I believe, actually."

"And what was he before Miss Flack took him in hand?"

"His handicap, if I remember rightly, was fifteen."

"You don't say?" said Harold Pickering, his face lighting up. "Was it, by Jove? Then this begins to look like something. If she could turn him into such a tiger, there's a chance for me. We start the lessons tomorrow."

I did not see Harold Pickering for some little time after this, an attack of lumbago confining me to my bed, but stories of his prowess filtered through to my sick-room, and from these it was abundantly evident that his confidence in Agnes Flack's skill as an instructress had not been misplaced. He won a minor competition with such ease that his handicap was instantly reduced to eight. Then he turned in a series of cards which brought him down to four. And the first thing I saw on entering the clubhouse on my restoration to health was his name on the list of entrants for the club championship. Against it was the word "scratch".

I can remember few things that have pleased me more. We are all sentimentalists at heart, and the boy's story had touched me deeply. I hastened to seek him out and congratulate him. I found him practising approach putts on the ninth green, but when I gripped his hand it was like squeezing a wet fish. His whole manner was that of one who has not quite shaken off the effects of being struck on the back of the head by a thunderbolt. It surprised me for a moment, but then I remembered that the achievement of a great ambition often causes a man to feel for a while somewhat filleted. The historian Gibbon, if you recall, had that experience on finishing his

Decline and Fall of the Roman Empire, and I saw the same thing once in a friend of mine who had just won a Littlewood's pool.

"Well," I said cheerily, "I suppose you will now be leaving us? You will want to hurry off to Miss Rockett with the great news."

He winced and topped a putt.

"No," he said, "I'm staying on here. My *fiancé* seems to wish it."

"Your *fiancé*?"

"I am engaged to Agnes Flack."

I was astounded. I had always understood that Agnes Flack was betrothed to Sidney McMurdo. I was also more than a little shocked. It was only a few weeks since he had poured out his soul to me on the subject of Troon Rockett, and this abrupt switching of his affections to another seemed to argue a sad lack of character and stability. When young fellows are enamoured of a member of the other sex, I like them to stay enamoured.

"Well, I hope you will be very happy," I said.

"You needn't try to be funny," he rejoined bitterly.

There was a sombre light in his eyes, and he foozled another putt.

"The whole thing," he said, "is due to one of those unfortunate misunderstandings. When they made me scratch, my first move was to thank Miss Flack warmly for all she had done for me."

"Naturally."

"I let myself go rather."

"You would, of course."

"Then, feeling that after all the trouble she had taken to raise me to the heights she was entitled to be let in on the inside story, I told her my reason for being so anxious to get down to scratch was that I loved a scratch girl and wanted to be worthy of her. Upon which, chuckling like a train going through a tunnel, she gave me a slap on the back which nearly drove my spine through the front of my pullover and said she had guessed it from the very start, from the moment when she first saw me dogging her footsteps with that look of dumb devotion in my eyes. You could have knocked me down with a putter."

"She then said she would marry you?"

"Yes. And what could I do? A girl," said Harold Pickering fretfully, "who can't distinguish between the way a man looks when he's admiring a chip shot thirty feet from the green and the way he looks when he's in love ought not to be allowed at large."

There seemed nothing to say. The idea of suggesting that he should break off the engagement presented itself to me, but I dismissed it. Women are divided broadly into two classes—those who, when jilted, merely drop a silent tear and those who take a niblick from their bag and chase the faithless swain across country with it. It was to this latter section that Agnes Flack belonged. Attila the Hun might have broken off his engagement to her, but nobody except Attila the Hun, and he only on one of his best mornings.

So I said nothing, and presently Harold Pickering resumed his moody putting and I left him.

The contest for the club championship opened unsensationally. There are never very many entrants for this of course non-handicap event, and this year there were only four. Harold Pickering won his match against Rupert Watchett comfortably, and Sidney McMurdo, who had returned on the previous night, had no difficulty in disposing of George Bunting. The final, Pickering versus McMurdo, was to be played in the afternoon.

Agnes Flack had walked round with Harold Pickering in the morning, and they lunched together after the game. But an appointment with her lawyer in the metropolis made it impossible for her to stay and watch the final, and she had to be content with giving him some parting words of advice.

"The great thing," she said, as he accompanied her to her car, "is not to lose your nerve. Forget that it's a final and play your ordinary game, and you can trim the pants off him. This statement carries my personal guarantee."

"You know his game pretty well?"

"Backwards. We used to do our three rounds a day together, when we were engaged."

"Engaged?"

"Yes. Didn't I tell you? We were heading straight for the altar, apparently with no bunkers in sight, when one afternoon he took a Number Three iron when I had told him to take a Number Four. I scratched the fixture immediately. 'No man,' I said to him, 'is going to walk up the aisle with me who takes a Number Three iron for a Number Four iron shot. Pop off, Sidney McMurdo,' I said, and he gnashed his teeth and popped. I shall get the laugh of a lifetime, seeing his face when I tell him I'm engaged to you. The big lummox."

Harold Pickering started.

"Did you say *big* lummox?"

"That was the expression I used."

"He is robust, then?"

"Oh, he's robust enough. He could fell an ox with a single blow, if he wasn't fond of oxen."

"And is he—er—at all inclined to be jealous?"

"Othello took his correspondence course."

"I see," said Harold Pickering. "I see."

He fell into a reverie, from which he was aroused a moment later by a deafening bellow from his companion.

"Hey, Sidney!"

The person she addressed was in Harold Pickering's rear. He turned, and perceived a vast man who gazed yearningly at Agnes Flack from beneath beetling eyebrows.

"Sidney," said Agnes Flack, "I want you to meet Mr. Pickering, who is playing you in the final this afternoon, Mr. McMurdo, Mr. Pickering, my *fiancé*. Well, goodbye, Harold darling, I've got to rush."

She folded him in a long lingering embrace, the car bowled off, and Harold Pickering found himself alone with this oversized plug-ugly in what seemed to his fevered fancy a great empty space, like one of those ones in the movies where two strong men stand face to face and Might is the only law.

Sidney McMurdo was staring at him with a peculiar intensity. There was a disturbing gleam in his eyes, and his hands, each the size of a largish ham, were clenching and unclenching as if flexing themselves for some grim work in the not too distant future.

"Did she," he asked in an odd, hoarse voice, "say—*fiancé*?"

"Why, yes," said Harold Pickering, with a nonchalance which it cost him a strong effort to assume. "Yes, that's right, I believe she did."

"You are going to marry Agnes Flack?"

"There is some idea of it, I understand."

"Ah!" said Sidney McMurdo, and the intensity of his stare was now more marked than ever.

Harold Pickering quailed beneath it. His heart, as he gazed at this patently steamed-up colossus, missed not one beat but several. Nor, I think, can we blame him. All publishers are sensitive, highly strung men. Gollancz is. So is Hamish Hamilton. So are Chapman and Hall, Heinemann and Herbert Jenkins, Ltd. And even when in sunny mood, Sidney McMurdo was always a rather intimidating spectacle. Tall, broad, deep-chested and superbly muscled, he looked like the worthy descendant of a long line of heavyweight gorillas, and nervous people and invalids were generally warned if there was any likelihood of their meeting him unexpectedly. Harold Pickering could not but feel that an uncle who would want anything like that at his sickbed must be eccentric to the last degree.

However, he did his best to keep the conversation on a note of easy cordiality.

"Nice weather," he said.

"Bah!" said Sidney McMurdo.

"How's your uncle?"

"Never mind my uncle. Are you busy at the moment, Mr. Pickering?"

"No."

"Good," said Sidney McMurdo. "Because I want to break your neck."

There was a pause. Harold Pickering backed a step. Sidney McMurdo advanced a step. Harold Pickering backed another step. Sidney McMurdo advanced again. Harold Pickering sprang sideways. Sidney McMurdo also sprang sideways. If it had not been for the fact that the latter was gnashing his teeth and filling the air with a sound similar to that produced by an inexperienced Spanish dancer learning to play the castanets, one might have supposed them to be practising the opening

SCRATCH MAN   **449**

movements of some graceful, old-world gavotte.

"Or, rather," said Sidney McMurdo, correcting his previous statement, "tear you limb from limb."

"Why?" asked Harold Pickering, who liked to go into things.

"You know why," said Sidney McMurdo, moving eastwards as his vis-à-vis moved westwards. "Because you steal girls' hearts behind people's backs, like a snake."

Harold Pickering, who happened to know something about snakes, might have challenged this description of their habits, but he was afforded no opportunity of doing so. His companion had suddenly reached out a clutching hand, and only by coyly drawing it back was he enabled to preserve his neck intact.

"Here, just a moment," he said.

I have mentioned that publishers are sensitive and highly strung. They are also quickwitted. They think on their feet. Harold Pickering had done so now. Hodder and Stoughton could not have reacted more nimbly.

"You are proposing to tear me limb from limb, are you?"

"And also to dance on the fragments."

It was not easy for Harold Pickering to sneer, for his lower jaw kept dropping, but he contrived to do so.

"I see," he said, just managing to curl his lip before the jaw got away from him again. "Thus ensuring that you shall be this year's club champion. Ingenious, McMurdo. It's one way of winning, of course. But I should not call it very sporting."

He had struck the right note. The blush of shame mantled Sidney McMurdo's cheek. His hands fell to his sides, and he stood chewing his lip, plainly disconcerted.

"I hadn't looked at it like that," he confessed.

"Posterity will,'" said Harold Pickering.

"Yes, I see what you mean. Postpone it, then, you think, eh?"

"Indefinitely."

"Oh, not indefinitely. We'll get together after the match. After all," said Sidney McMurdo, looking on the bright side, "it isn't long to wait."

It was at this point that I joined them. As generally happened in those days, I had been given the honour of refereeing the final. I asked if they were ready to start.

"Not only ready," said Sidney McMurdo. "Impatient."

Harold Pickering said nothing. He merely moistened the lips with the tip of the tongue.

My friends (proceeded the Oldest Member) have sometimes been kind enough to say that if there is one thing at which I excel, it is at describing in meticulous detail a desperately closely fought golf match—taking my audience stroke by stroke from tee one to hole eighteen and showing fortune fluctuating now to one side, now to the other, before finally placing the laurel wreath on the perspiring brow of the ultimate winner. And it is this treat that I should like to be able to give you now.

Unfortunately, the contest for that particular club championship final does not lend itself to such a description. From the very outset it was hopelessly one-sided.

Even as we walked to the first tee, it seemed to me that Harold Pickering was not looking his best and brightest. But I put this down to a nervous man's natural anxiety before an important match, and even when he lost the first two holes by the weakest type of play, I assumed that he would soon pull himself together and give of his best.

At that time, of course, I was not aware of the emotions surging in his bosom. It was only some years later that I ran into him and he told me his story and its sequel. That afternoon, what struck me most was the charming spirit of courtesy in which he played the match. He was losing every hole with monotonous regularity, and in such circumstances even the most amiable are apt to be gloomy and sullen, but he never lost his affability. He seemed to be straining every nerve to ingratiate himself with Sidney McMurdo and win the latter's affection.

Oddly, as it appeared to me then, it was McMurdo who was sullen and gloomy. On three occasions he declined the offer of a cigarette from his opponent, and was short in his manner—one might almost say surly—when Harold Pickering, nine down at the ninth, said that is was well worth anyone's while being beaten by Sidney McMurdo because, apart from the fresh air and exercise, it was such an artistic treat to watch his putting.

It was as he paid this graceful tribute that the crowd, which had been melting away pretty steadily for the last quarter of an hour, finally disappeared. By the time Sidney McMurdo had holed out at the tenth for a four that gave him the match, we were alone except for the caddies. These having been paid off, we started to walk back.

To lose a championship match by ten and eight is an experience calculated to induce in a man an introspective silence, and I had not expected Harold Pickering to contribute much to any feast of reason and flow of soul which might enliven the homeward journey. To my surprise, however, as we started to cross the bridge which spans the water at the eleventh, he burst into animated speech, complimenting his conqueror in a graceful way which I thought very sporting.

"I wonder if you will allow me to say, Mr. McMurdo," he began, "how greatly impressed I have been by your performance this afternoon. It has been a genuine revelation to me. It is so seldom that one meets a man who, while long off the tee, also plays an impeccable short game. I don't want to appear fulsome, but it seems to me that you have everything."

Words like these should have been music to Sidney McMurdo's ears, but he merely scowled darkly and uttered a short grunt like a bulldog choking on a piece of steak.

"In fact, I don't mind telling you, McMurdo," proceeded Harold Pickering, still in that genial and ingratiating manner, "that I shall watch your future career with considerable interest. It is a sad pity that this year's Walker Cup matches are over, for our team might have been greatly strengthened. Well, I venture to assert that next season the selection of at least one member will give the authorities little trouble."

Sidney McMurdo uttered another grunt, and I saw what seemed like a look of discouragement come into Harold Pickering's face. But after gulping a couple of times he continued brightly.

"Tell me, Sidney," he said, "have you ever thought of writing a golf book? You know the sort of thing, old man. Something light and chatty, describing your methods and giving advice to the novice. If so, I should be delighted to publish it, and we should not quarrel about the terms. If I were you, I'd go straight home and start on it now."

Sidney McMurdo spoke for the first time. His voice was deep and rumbling.

"I have something to do before I go home."

"Oh, yes?"

"I am going to pound the stuffing out of a snake."

"Ah, then in that case you will doubtless want to be alone, to concentrate. I will leave you."

"No, you won't. Let us step behind those bushes for a moment, Mr. Pickering," said Sidney McMurdo.

I have always been good at putting two and two together, and listening to these exchanges I now sensed how matters stood. In a word, I saw all, and my heart bled for Harold Pickering. Unnecessarily, as it turned out, for even as my heart started to bleed, Harold Pickering acted.

I have said that we were crossing the bridge over the water at the eleventh, and no doubt you have been picturing that bridge as it is today—a stout steel structure. At the time of which I am speaking it was a mere plank with a rickety wooden rail along it, a rail ill adapted to withstand the impact of a heavy body.

Sidney McMurdo's was about as heavy a body as there was in the neighbourhood, and when Harold Pickering, with a resource and ingenuity which it would be difficult to overpraise, suddenly butted him in the stomach with his head and sent him reeling against it, it gave way without a moment's hesitation. There was a splintering crash, followed by a splash and a scurry of feet, and the next thing I saw was Harold Pickering disappearing over the horizon while Sidney McMurdo, up to his waist in water, petulantly detaching an eel from his hair. It was a striking proof of the old saying that a publisher is never so dangerous as when apparently beaten. You may drive a publisher into a corner, but you do so at your own peril.

Presently, Sidney McMurdo waded ashore and started to slosh sullenly up the hillside towards the club-house. From the irritable manner in which he was striking himself between the shoulder blades I received the impression that he had got some sort of a water beetle down his back.

As I think I mentioned earlier, I did not see Harold Pickering again for some years, and it was only then that I was enabled to fill in the gaps, in what has always seemed to me a singularly poignant human drama.

At first, he told me, he was actuated by the desire, which one can understand and sympathize with, to put as great a distance as possible between Sidney McMurdo and himself in the shortest possible time. With this end in view, he hastened to his car, which he had left standing outside the club-house, and placing a firm foot on the accelerator drove about seventy miles in the general direction of Scotland. Only when he paused for a sandwich at a wayside tavern after completing this preliminary burst did he discover that all the money he had on his person was five shillings and a little bronze.

Now, a less agitated man would, of course, have seen that the policy to pursue was to take a room at a hotel, explain to the management that his luggage would be following shortly, and write to his bank to telegraph him such funds as he might require. But this obvious solution did not even occur to Harold Pickering. The only way out of the difficulty that suggested itself to him was to drive back to his cottage, secure the few pounds which he knew to be on the premises, throw into a suitcase some articles of clothing and his cheque book and then drive off again into the sunset.

As it happened, however, he would not have been able to drive into the sunset, for it was quite dark when he arrived at his destination. He alighted from his car, and was about to enter the house, when he suddenly observed that there was a light in the sitting-room. And creeping to the window and peering cautiously through a chink in the curtains, he saw that it was precisely as he had feared. There on a settee, scowling up at the ceiling, was Sidney McMurdo. He had the air of a man who was waiting for somebody.

And scarcely had Harold Pickering, appalled by this spectacle, withdrawn into a near-by bush to think the situation over in all of its aspects and try to find a formula, when heavy footsteps sounded on the gravel path and, dark though it was, he had no difficulty in identifying the newcomer as Agnes Flack. Only she could have clumped like that.

The next moment, she had delivered a resounding buffet on the front door, and Sidney McMurdo was opening it to her.

There was a silence as they gazed at one another. Except for that brief instant when she had introduced Harold Pickering to Sidney McMurdo outside the club-house, these sundered hearts had not met since the severance of their relations, and even a fifteen-stone man and an eleven-stone girl are not immune from embarrassment.

Agnes was the first to speak.

"Hullo," she said. "You here?"

"Yes," said Sidney McMurdo, "I'm here all right. I am waiting for the snake Pickering."

"I've come to see him myself."

"Oh? Well, nothing that you can do will save him from my wrath."

"Who wants to save him from your wrath?"

"Don't you?"

"Certainly not. All I looked in for was to break our engagement."

Sidney McMurdo staggered.

"Break your engagement?"

"That's right."

"But I thought you loved him."

"No more. The scales have fallen from my eyes. I don't marry men who are as hot as pistols in a friendly round with nothing depending on it, but blow up like geysers in competition golf. Why are you wrathful with him, Sidney?"

Sidney McMurdo gnashed his teeth.

"He stole you from me," he said hoarsely.

If Agnes Flack had been about a foot shorter and had weighed about thirty pounds less, the sound which proceeded from her might have been described as a giggle. She stretched out the toe of her substantial shoe and made a squiggle with it on the gravel.

"And did you mind that so much?" she said softly—or as softly as it was in her power to speak.

"Yes, I jolly well did," said Sidney McMurdo. "I love you, old girl, and I shall continue to love you till the cows come home. When I was demolishing the reptile Pickering this afternoon, your face seemed to float before me all the way round, even when I was putting. And I'll tell you something. I've been thinking it over, and I see now that I was all wrong that time and should unquestionably have used a Number Four iron. Too late, of course," said Sidney McMurdo moodily, thinking of what might have been.

Agnes Flack drew a second arabesque on the gravel, using the toe of the other shoe this time.

"How do you mean, too late?" she asked reasonably softly.

"Well, isn't it too late?"

"Certainly not."

"You can't mean you love me still?"

"Yes, I jolly well can mean I love you still."

"Well, I'll be blowed! And here was I, thinking that all was over and life empty and all that sort of thing. My mate!" cried Sidney McMurdo.

They fell into an embrace like a couple of mastodons clashing in a primaeval swamp, and the earth had scarcely ceased to shake when a voice spoke.

"Excuse me."

In his hiding-place in the bush Harold Pickering leaped as if somebody had touched off a land mine under his feet and came to rest quivering in every limb. He had recognized that voice.

"Excuse me," said Troon Rockett. "Does Mr. Pickering live here?"

"Yes," said Sidney McMurdo.

"If," added Agnes Flack, "you can call it living when a man enters for an important competition and gets beaten ten and eight. He's out at the moment. Better go in and stick around."

"Thank you," said the girl. "I will."

She vanished into the cottage. Sidney McMurdo took advantage of her departure to embrace Agnes Flack again.

"Old blighter," he said tenderly, "let's get married right away, before there can be any more misunderstandings and rifts and what not. How about Tuesday?"

"Can't Tuesday. Mixed foursomes."

"Wednesday?"

"Can't Wednesday. Bogey competition."

"And Thursday I'm playing in the invitation tournament at Squashy Heath," said Sidney McMurdo. "Oh, well, I daresay we shall manage to find a day when we're both free. Let's stroll along and talk it over."

They crashed off, and as the echoes of their clumping feet died away in the distance Harold Pickering left the form in which he had been crouching and walked dizzily to the cottage. And the first thing he saw as he entered the sitting-room was Troon Rockett kissing a cabinet photograph of himself which she had taken from place on the mantelpiece. The spectacle drew from him a sharp, staccato bark of amazement, and she turned, her eyes wide.

"Harold!" she cried, and flung herself into his arms.

To say that Harold Pickering was surprised, bewildered, startled and astounded would be merely to state the facts. He could not remember having been so genuinely taken aback since the evening when, sauntering in his garden in the dusk, he had trodden on the teeth of a rake and had the handle jump up and hit him on the nose.

But, as I have had occasion to observe before, he was a publisher, and I doubt if there is a publisher on the list who would not know what to do if a charming girl flung herself into his arms. I have told this story to one or two publishers of my acquaintance, and they all assured me that the correct procedure would come instinctively to them. Harold Pickering kissed Troon Rockett sixteen times in quick succession, and Macmillan and Faber and Faber say they would have done just the same.

At length, he paused. He was, as I have said, a man who liked to go into things.

"But I don't understand."

"What don't you understand?"

"Well, don't think for a moment that I'm complaining, but this flinging-into-arms sequence strikes me as odd."

"I can't imagine why. I love you."

"But when I asked you to be my wife, you rose and walked haughtily from the room."

"I didn't."

"You did. I was there."

"I mean, I didn't walk haughtily. I hurried out because I was alarmed and agitated. You sat there gasping and gurgling, and I thought you were having a fit of some kind. So I rushed off to phone the doctor, and when I got back you had gone. And then a day or two later another man proposed to me, and he, too, started gasping and gurgling, and I realized the truth. They told me at your office that you were living here, so I came along to let you know that I loved you."

"You really do?"

"Of course I do. I loved you the first moment I saw you. You remember? You were explaining to father that thirteen copies count as twelve, and I came in and our eyes met. In that instant I knew that you were the only man in the world for me."

For a moment Harold Pickering was conscious only of a wild exhilaration. He felt as if his firm had brought out *Gone With the Wind*. Then a dull, hopeless look came into his sensitive face.

"It can never be," he said.

"Why not?"

"You heard what that large girl was saying outside there, but probably you did not take it in. It was the truth. I was beaten this afternoon ten and eight."

"Everybody has an off day."

He shook his head.

"It was not an off day. That was my true form. I haven't the nerve to be a scratch man. When the acid test comes, I blow up. I suppose I'm about ten, really. You can't marry a ten-handicap man."

"Why not?"

"You! The daughter of John Rockett and his British Ladies Champion wife. The great-grand-daughter of old Ma Rockett. The sister of Prestwick, Sandwich, Hoylake and St. Andrew Rockett."

"But that's just why. It has always been my dream to marry a man with a handicap of about ten, so that we could go through life together side by side, twin souls. I should be ten, if the family didn't make me practise five hours a day all the year round. I'm not a natural scratch. I have made myself scratch by ceaseless, unremitting toil, and if there's one thing in the world I loathe it is ceaseless, unremitting toil. The relief of being able to let myself slip back to ten is indescribable. Oh, Harold, we shall be so happy. Just to think of taking three putts on a green! It will be heaven!"

Harold Pickering had been reeling a good deal during these remarks. He now ceased to do so. There is a time for reeling and a time for not reeling.

"You mean that?"

"I certainly do."

"You will really marry me?"

"How long does it take to get a licence?"

For an instant Harold Pickering sought for words, but found none. Then a rather

neat thing that Sidney McMurdo had said came back to him. Sidney McMurdo
was a man he could never really like, but his dialogue was excellent.

"My mate!" he said.

31

SLEEPY TIME

IN HIS office on the premises of Popgood and Grooly, publishers of the Book Beautiful, Madison Avenue, New York, Cyril Grooly, the firm's junior partner, was practising putts into a tooth glass and doing rather badly even for one with a twenty-four handicap, when Patricia Binstead, Mr. Popgood's secretary, entered, and dropping his putter he folded her in a close embrace. This was not because all American publishers are warmhearted impulsive men and she a very attractive girl, but because they had recently become betrothed. On his return from his summer vacation at Paradise Valley, due to begin this afternoon, they would step along to some convenient church and become man, if you can call someone with a twenty-four handicap a man, and wife.

"A social visit?" he asked, the embrace concluded. "Or business?"

"Business. Popgood had to go out to see a man about subsidiary rights, and Count Dracula has blown in. Well, when I say Count Dracula, I speak loosely. He just looks like him. His name is Professor Pepperidge Farmer, and he's come to sign his contract.

"He writes books?"

"He's written one. He calls it Hypnotism As A Device To Uncover The Unconscious Drives and Mechanism In An Effort To Analyse The Functions Involved Which Gives Rise To Emotional Conflicts In The Waking State, but the title's going to be changed to Sleepy Time. Popgood thinks it's snappier."

"Much snappier."

"Shall I send him in?"

"Do so, queen of my soul."

"And Popgood says Be sure not to go above two hundred dollars for the advance," said Patricia, and a few moments later the visitor made his appearance.

It was an appearance, as Patricia had hinted, of a nature to chill the spine. Sinister was the adjective that automatically sprang to the lips of those who met Professor Pepperidge Farmer for the first time. His face was gaunt and lined and grim, and as his burning eyes bored into Cyril's the young publisher was conscious of a feeling of relief that this encounter was not taking place down a dark alley or in some lonely spot in the country. But a man used to mingling with American authors, few of whom look like anything on earth, is not readily intimidated and he greeted him with his customary easy courtesy.

"Come right in," he said. "You've caught me just in time. I'm off to Paradise Valley this afternoon."

"A golfing holiday?" said the Professor, eyeing the putter.

"Yes, I'm looking forward to getting some golf."

"How is your game?"

"Horrible," Cyril was obliged to confess. "Mine is a sad and peculiar case. I have the theory of golf at my fingertips, but once out in the middle I do nothing but foozle."

"You should keep your head down."

"So Tommy Armour tells me, but up it comes."

"That's Life."

"Or shall we say hell?"

"If you prefer it."

"It seems the mot juste. But now to business. Miss Binstead tells me you have come to sign your contract. I have it here. It all appears to be in order except that the amount of the advance has not been decided on."

"And what are your views on that?"

"I was thinking of a hundred dollars. You see," said Cyril, falling smoothly into his stride, "a book like yours always involves a serious risk for the publisher owing to the absence of the Sex Motif, which renders it impossible for him to put a nude female of impressive vital statistics on the jacket and no hope of getting banned in Boston. Add the growing cost of paper and the ever-increasing demands of printers, compositors, binders and . . . why are you waving your hands like that?"

"I have French blood in me. On the mother's side."

"Well, I wish you wouldn't. You're making me sleepy."

"Oh, am I? How very interesting. Yes, I can see that your eyes are closing. You are becoming drowsy. You are falling asleep . . . you are falling asleep . . . asleep . . . asleep . . . asleep . . ."

It was getting on for lunch time when Cyril awoke. When he did so, he found that the recent gargoyle was no longer with him. Odd, he felt, that the fellow should have gone before they had settled the amount of his advance, but no doubt he had remembered some appointment elsewhere. Dismissing him from his mind, Cyril resumed his putting, and soon after lunch he left for Paradise Valley.

On the subject of Paradise Valley the public relations representative of the Paradise Hotel has expressed himself very frankly. It is, he says in his illustrated booklet, a dream world of breath-taking beauty, and its noble scenery, its wide open spaces, its soft mountain breezes and its sun-drenched pleasances impart to the jaded city worker a new vim and vigour and fill him so full of red corpuscles that before a day has elapsed in these delightful surroundings he is conscious of a *je ne sais quoi* and a *bien être* and goes about with his chin up and both feet on the ground, feeling as if he had just come back from the cleaner's. And, what is more, only a step from the hotel lies the Squashy Hollow golf course, of whose amenities residents can avail themselves on payment of a green fee.

What, however, the booklet omits to mention is that the Squashy Hollow course is one of the most difficult in the country. It was constructed by an exiled Scot who, probably from some deep-seated grudge against the human race, has modelled the eighteen holes on the nastiest and most repellent of his native land, so that after negotiating—say—the Alps at Prestwick the pleasure-seeker finds himself confronted by the Stationmaster's Garden at St. Andrew's, with the Eden and the Redan just around the corner.

The type of golfer it attracts, therefore, is the one with high ideals and an implicit confidence in his ability to overcome the toughest obstacles; the sort who plays in amateur championships and mutters to himself "Why this strange weakness?" if he shoots worse than a seventy-five, and one look at it gave Cyril that uncomfortable feeling known to scientists as the heeby-jeebies. He had entered for the medal contest which was to take place tomorrow, for he always entered for medal contests, never being able to forget that he had once shot a ninety-eight and that this, if repeated, would with his handicap give him a sporting chance of success. But the prospect of performing in front of all these hardened experts created in him the illusion that caterpillars to the number of about fifty-seven were parading up and down his spinal cord. He shrank from exposing himself to their bleak contemptuous stares. His emotions when he did would, he knew, be similar in almost every respect to those of a mongrel which has been rash enough to wander into some fashionable Kennel Show.

As, then, he sat on the porch of the Paradise Hotel on the morning before the contest, he was so far from being filled with *bien être* that he could not even achieve *je ne sais quoi,* and at this moment the seal was set on his despondency by the sight of Agnes Flack.

Agnes Flack was a large young woman who on the first day of his arrival had discovered that he was a partner in a publishing firm and had immediately begun to speak of a novel which she had written and would be glad to have his opinion of when he had a little time to spare. And experience had taught him that when large young women wrote novels they were either squashily sentimental or so Chatterleyesque that it would be necessary to print them on asbestos, and he had spent much of his leisure avoiding her. She seemed now to be coming in his direction, so rising hastily he made on winged feet for the bar. Entering it at a rapid gallop, he collided with a solid body, and this proved on inspection to be none other than Professor Pepperidge Farmer, looking more sinister than ever in Bermuda shorts, a shirt like a Turner sunset and a Panama hat with a pink ribbon round it.

He stood amazed. There was, of course, no reason why the other should not have been there, for the hotel was open to all whose purses were equal to the tariff, but somehow he seemed out of place, like a ghoul at a garden party or a vampire bat at a picnic.

"You!" he exclaimed. "What ever became of you that morning?"

"You allude to our previous meeting?" said the Professor. "I saw you had dozed off, so I tiptoed out without disturbing you. I thought it would be better to resume our acquaintance in these more agreeable surroundings. For if you are thinking that my presence here is due to one of those coincidences which are so strained and inartistic, you are wrong. I came in the hope that I might be able to do something to improve your golf game. I feel I owe you a great deal."

"You do? Why?"

"We can go into that some other time. Tell me, how is the golf going? Any improvement?"

If he had hoped to receive confidences, he could not have put the question at a better moment. Cyril did not habitually bare his soul to comparative strangers, but now he found himself unable to resist the urge. It was as though the Professor's query had drawn a cork and brought all his doubts and fears and inhibitions foaming out like ginger pop from a ginger pop bottle. As far as reticence was concerned, he might have been on a psychoanalyst's couch at twenty-five dollars the half hour. In burning words he spoke of the coming medal contest, stressing his qualms and the growing coldness of his feet, and the Professor listened attentively, clicking a sympathetic tongue from time to time. It was plain that though he looked like something Charles Addams might have thought up when in the throes of a hangover, if Mr. Addams does ever have hangovers, he had a feeling heart.

"I'm paired with a fellow called Sidney McMurdo, who they tell me is the club champion, and I fear his scorn. It's going to take me at least a hundred and fifteen shots for the round, and on each of those hundred and fifteen shots Sidney McMurdo will look at me as if I were something slimy and obscene that had crawled out from under a flat stone. I shall feel like a crippled leper, and so," said Cyril, concluding his remarks, "I have decided to take my name off the list of entrants. Call me weak if you will, but I can't face it."

The Professor patted him on the shoulder in a fatherly manner and was about to speak, but before he could do so Cyril heard his name paged and was told that he was wanted on the telephone. It was some little time before he returned, and when he did the dullest eye could see that something had occurred to ruffle him. He found Professor Farmer sipping a lemon squash, and when the Professor asked him if he would care for one of the same, he thundered out a violent No.

"Blast and damn all lemon squashes!" he cried vehemently. "Do you know who that was on the phone? It was Popgood, my senior partner. And do you know what he said? He wanted to know what had got into me to make me sign a contract giving you five thousand dollars advance on that book of yours. He said you must have hypnotized me."

A smile, probably intended to be gentle, but conveying the impression that he was suffering from some internal disorder, played over the Professor's face.

"Of course I did, my dear fellow. It was one of the ordinary business precautions an author has to take. The only way to get a decent advance from a publisher is to hypnotize him. That was what I was referring to when I said I owed you a great deal. But for you I should never have been able to afford a holiday at a place like Paradise Valley where even the simplest lemon squash sets you back a prince's ransom. Was Popgood annoyed?"

"He was."

"Too bad. He should have been rejoicing to think that his money had been instrumental in bringing a little sunshine into a fellow creature's life. But let us forget him and return to this matter of your golfing problems."

He had said the one thing capable of diverting Cyril's thoughts from his incandescent partner. No twenty-four handicap man is ever deaf to such an appeal.

"You told me you had all the theory of the game at your finger-tips. Is that so? Your reading has been wide?"

"I've read every golf book that has been written."

"You mentioned Tommy Armour. Have you studied his preachings?"

"I know them by heart."

"But lack of confidence prevents you putting them into practice?"

"I suppose that's it."

"Then the solution is simple. I must hypnotize you again. You should still be under the influence, but the effects may have worn off and it's best to be on the safe side. I will instil into you the conviction that you can knock spots off the proudest McMurdo. When you take club in hand, it will be with the certainty that your ball is going to travel from Point A to Point B by the shortest route and will meet with no misadventures on the way. Whose game would you prefer yours to resemble? Arnold Palmer's? Gary Player's? Jack Nicklaus's? Palmer's is the one I would recommend. Those spectacular finishes of his. You agree? Palmer it shall be, then. So away we go. Your eyes are closing. You are feeling drowsy. You are falling asleep . . . asleep . . . asleep . . ."

Paradise Valley was at its best next day, its scenery just as noble, its mountain breezes just as soft, its spaces fully as wide and open as the public relations man's booklet had claimed them to be, and Cyril, as he stood beside the first tee of the Squashy Hollow course awaiting Sidney McMurdo's arrival, was feeling, as he had confided to the caddie master when picking up his clubs, like a million dollars. He would indeed scarcely have been exaggerating if he had made it two million. His chin was up, both his feet were on the ground, and the red corpuscles of which the booklet had spoken coursed through his body like students rioting in Saigon, Moscow, Cairo, Panama and other centres. Professor Farmer, in assuring him that he would become as confident as Arnold Palmer, had understated it. He was as confident as Arnold Palmer, Gary Player, Ray Venturi, Jack Nicklaus and Tony Lema all rolled into one.

He had not been waiting long when he beheld a vast expanse of man approaching and presumed that this must be his partner for the round. He gave him a sunny smile.

"Mr. McMurdo? How do you do? Nice day. Very pleasant, those soft mountain breezes."

The newcomer's only response was a bronchial sound such as might have been produced by an elephant taking its foot out of a swamp in a teak forest. Sidney McMurdo was in dark and sullen mood. On the previous night Agnes Flack, his *fiancé*, had broken their engagement owing to a trifling disagreement they had had about the novel she had written. He had said it was a lot of prune juice and advised her to burn it without delay, and she had said it was not, too, a lot of prune juice, adding that she never wanted to see or speak to him again, and this had affected him adversely. It always annoyed him when Agnes Flack broke their engagement, because it made him overswing, particularly off the tee.

He did so now, having won the honour, and was pained to see that his ball, which he had intended to go due north, was travelling nor'-nor'-east. And as he stood scowling after it, Cyril spoke.

"I wonder if you noticed what you did wrong there, Mr. McMurdo," he said in the friendliest way. "Your backswing was too long. Length of backswing does not have as much effect on distance as many believe. You should swing back only just as far as you can without losing control of the club. Control is all-important. I always take my driver to about the horizontal position on the back swing. Watch me now."

And so saying Cyril with effortless grace drove two hundred and eighty yards straight down the fairway.

"See what I mean?" he said.

It was on the fourth green, after he had done an eagle, that he spoke again. Sidney McMurdo had had some difficulty in getting out of a sand trap and he hastened to give him the benefit of his advice. There was nothing in it for him except the glow that comes from doing an act of kindness, but it distressed him to see a quite promising player like McMurdo making mistakes of which a wiser head could so easily cure him.

"You did not allow for the texture of the sand," he said. "Your sand shot should differ with the texture of the sand. If it is wet, hard or shallow, your clubhead will not cut into it as deeply as it would into soft and shifting sand. If the sand is soft, try to dig into it about two inches behind the ball, but when it is hard penetrate it about one and a half inches behind the ball. And since firm sand will slow down your club considerably, be sure to give your swing a full follow-through."

The game proceeded. On the twelfth Cyril warned his partner to be careful to remember to bend the knees slightly for greater flexibility throughout the swing, though—on the sixteenth—he warned against bending them too much, as this often led to topping. When both had holed out at the eighteenth, he had a word of counsel to give on the subject of putting.

"Successful putting, Sidney," he said, for he felt that they might now consider themselves on first name terms. "Depends largely on the mental attitude. Confidence is everything. Never let anxiety make you tense. Never for an instant harbour the thought that your shot may miss. When I sank that last fifty-foot putt, I *knew* it was going in. My mind was filled with a picture of the ball following a proper line to the hole, and it is that sort of picture I should like to encourage in you. Well, it has been a most pleasant round. We must have another soon. I shot a sixty-two, did I not? I thought so. I was quite on my game today, quite on my game."

Sidney McMurdo's eyebrows, always beetling, were beetling still more darkly as he watched Cyril walking away with elastic tread. He turned to a friend who had just come up.

"Who is that fellow?" he asked hoarsely.

"His name's Grooly," said the friend. "One of the summer visitors."

"What's his handicap?"

"I can tell you that, for I was looking at the board this morning. It's twenty-four."

"Air!" cried Sidney McMurdo, clutching his throat. "Give me air!"

Cyril, meanwhile, had rounded the club-house and was approaching the practice green that lay behind it. Someone large and female was engaged there in polishing her chip shots, and as he paused to watch he stood astounded at her virtuosity. A chip shot, he was aware, having read his Johnny Farrell, is a crisp hit with the club-head stopping at the ball and not following through. "Open your stance," says the venerable Farrell, "Place your weight on the left foot and hit down at the ball," and this was precisely what this substantial female was doing. Each ball she struck dropped on the green like a poached egg, and as she advanced to pick them up he saw that she was Agnes Flack.

A loud gasp escaped Cyril. The dream world of breathtaking beauty pirouetted before his eyes as if Arthur Murray were teaching it dancing in a hurry. He was conscious of strange, tumultuous emotions stirring within him. Then the mists cleared, and gazing at Agnes Flack he knew that there before him stood his destined mate. A novelist she might be and no doubt as ghastly a novelist as ever set finger to typewriter key, but what of that? Quite possibly she would grow out of it in time, and in any case he felt that as a man who went about shooting sixty-twos in medal contests he owed it to himself to link his lot with a golfer of her calibre. Theirs would be the ideal union.

In a situation like this no publisher hesitates. A moment later, Cyril was on the green, his arms as far around Agnes Flack as they would go.

"Old girl," he said. "You're a grand bit of work!"

Two courses were open to Agnes Flack. She could draw herself to her full height, say "Sir!" and strike this clinging vine with her number seven iron, or, remembering that Cyril was a publisher and that she had a top copy and two carbons of a novel in her suitcase, she could co-operate and accept his addresses. She chose the latter alternative, and when Cyril suggested that they should spend the honeymoon in Scotland, playing all the famous courses there, she said that that would suit her perfectly. If, as she plighted her troth, a thought of Sidney McMurdo came into her mind, it was merely the renewed conviction that he was an oaf and a fathead temperamentally incapable of recognizing good literature when it was handed to him on a skewer.

These passionate scenes take it out of a man, and it is not surprising that Cyril's first move on leaving Agnes Flack should have been in the direction of the bar. Arriving there, he found Professor Farmer steeping himself, as was his custom, in lemon squashes. The warm weather engendered thirst, and since he had come to the Paradise Hotel the straw had seldom left his lips.

"Ah, Cyril, if you don't mind me calling you Cyril, though you will be the first to admit that it's a hell of a name," said the Professor. "How did everything come out?"

"Quite satisfactorily, Pepperidge. The returns are not all in, but I think I must have won the medal. I shot a sixty-two, which, subtracting my handicap, gives me a thirty-eight. I doubt if anyone will do better than thirty-eight."

"Most unlikely."

"Thirty-four under par takes a lot of beating."

"Quite a good deal. I congratulate you."

"And that's not all. I'm engaged to the most wonderful girl."

"Really? I congratulate you again. Who is she?"

"Her name is Agnes Flack."

The Professor started, dislodging a drop of lemon squash from his lower lip.

"Agnes Flack?"

"Yes."

"You couldn't be mistaken in the name?"

"No."

"H'm!"

"Why do you say H'm?"

"I was thinking of Sidney McMurdo."

"How does he get into the act?"

"He is—or was—betrothed to Agnes Flack, and I am told he has rather a short way with men who get engaged to his *fiancé*, even if technically ex. Do you know a publisher called Pickering?"

"Harold Pickering? I've met him."

"He got engaged to Agnes Flack, and it was only by butting Sidney McMurdo in the stomach with his head and disappearing over the horizon that he was able to avoid being torn by the latter into little pieces. But for his ready resource he would have become converted into, as one might say, a sort of publishing hash, though, of course, McMurdo might simply have jumped on him with spiked shoes."

It was Cyril's turn to say H'm, and he said it with a good deal of thoughtful fervour. He had parted so recently from Sidney McMurdo that he had not had time to erase from his mental retina what might be called the over-all picture of him. The massive bulk of Sidney McMurdo rose before his eyes, as did the other's rippling muscles. The discovery that in addition to possessing the physique of a gorilla he had also that animal's easily aroused temper was not one calculated to induce a restful peace of mind. Given the choice between annoying Sidney McMurdo and stirring up a nest of hornets with a fountain pen, he would unhesitatingly have cast his vote for the hornets.

And it was as he sat trying to think what was to be done for the best that the door flew open and the bar became full of McMurdo. He seemed to permeate its every nook and cranny. Nor had Professor Farmer erred in predicting that his mood would be edgy. His eyes blazed, his ears wiggled and a clicking sound like the manipulation of castanets by a Spanish dancer told that he was gnashing his teeth. Except that he was not beating his chest with both fists, he resembled in every respect the gorilla to which Cyril had mentally compared him.

"Ha!" he said, sighting Cyril.

"Oh, hullo, Sidney."

"Less of the Sidney!" snarled McMurdo. "I don't want a man of your kidney calling me Sidney," he went on, rather surprisingly dropping into poetry. "Agnes Flack tells me she is engaged to you."

Cyril replied nervously that there had been some informal conversation along those lines.

"She says you hugged her."

"Only a little."

"And kissed her."

"In the most respectful manner."

"In other words, you have sneaked behind my back like a slithery serpent and stolen from me the woman I love. Perhaps, if you have a moment to spare, you will step outside."

Cyril did not wish to step outside, but it seemed that there was no alternative. He preceded Sidney McMurdo through the door, and was surprised on reaching the wide open spaces to find that Professor Farmer had joined the party. The Professor was regarding Sidney with that penetrating gaze of his which made him look like Boris Karloff on one of his bad mornings.

"Might I ask you to look me in the eye for a moment, Mr. McMurdo," he said. "Thank you. Yes, as I thought. You are drowsy. Your eyes are closing. You are falling asleep."

"No, I'm not."

"Yes, you are."

"By Jove, I believe you're right," said Sidney McMurdo, sinking slowly into a conveniently placed deck chair. "Yes, I think I'll take a nap."

The Professor continued to weave arabesques in the air with his hands, and suddenly Sidney McMurdo sat up. His eye rested on Cyril, but it was no longer the flaming eye it had been. Almost affectionate it seemed, and when he spoke his voice was mild.

"Mr. Grooly."

"On the spot."

"I have been thinking it over, Mr. Grooly, and I have reached a decision which, though painful, I am sure is right. It is wrong to think only of self. There are times when a man must make the great sacrifice no matter what distress it causes him. You love Agnes Flack, Agnes loves you, and I must not come between you. Take her, Mr. Grooly. I yield her to you, yield her freely. It breaks my heart, but her happiness is all that matters. Take her, Grooly, and if a broken man's blessing is of any use to you, I give it without reserve. I think I'll go to the bar and have a gin and tonic," said Sidney McMurdo, and proceeded to do so.

"A very happy conclusion to your afternoon's activities," said Professor Farmer as the swing door closed behind him. "I often say that there is nothing like hypnotism for straightening out these little difficulties. I thought McMurdo's speech of renunciation was very well phrased, didn't you? In perfect taste. Well, as you will now no longer have need of my services, I suppose I had better de-hypnotize you. It will not be painful, just a momentary twinge," said the Professor, blowing a lemon-squash-charged breath in Cyril's face, and Cyril was aware of an odd feeling of having been hit by an atom bomb while making a descent in an express elevator. He found himself a little puzzled by his companion's choice of the expression 'momentary twinge', but he had not leisure to go into what was after all a side issue. With the removal of the hypnotic spell there had come to him the realization of the unfortunate position in which he had placed himself, and he uttered a sharp "Oh, golly!"

"I beg your pardon?" said the Professor.

"Listen," said Cyril, and his voice shook like a jelly in a high wind. "Does it count if you ask a girl to marry you when you're hypnotized?"

"You are speaking of Miss Flack?"

"Yes, I proposed to her on the practice green, carried away by the super-excellence of her chip shots, and I can't stand the sight of her. And, what's more, in about three weeks I'm supposed to be marrying someone else. You remember Patricia Binstead, the girl who showed you into my office?"

"Very vividly."

"She holds the copyright. What am I to do? You couldn't go and hypnotize Agnes Flack and instil her, as you call it, with the idea that I'm the world's leading louse, could you?"

"My dear fellow, nothing easier."

"Then do it without an instant's delay," said Cyril. "Tell her I'm scratch and pretended to have a twenty-four handicap in order to win the medal. Tell her I'm sober only at the rarest intervals. Tell her I'm a Communist spy and my name's really Groolinsky. Tell her I've two wives already. But you'll know what to say."

He waited breathlessly for the Professor's return.

"Well?" he cried.

"All washed up, my dear Cyril. I left her reunited to McMurdo. She says she wouldn't marry you if you were the last publisher on earth and wouldn't let you sponsor her novel if you begged her on bended knees. She says she is going to let Simon and Schuster have it, and she hopes that will be a lesson to you."

Cyril drew a deep breath.

"Pepperidge, you're wonderful!"

"One does one's best," said the Professor modestly. "Well, now that the happy ending has been achieved, how about returning to the bar? I'll buy you a lemon squash."

"Do you really like that stuff?"

"I love it."

It was on the tip of Cyril's tongue to say that one would have thought he was a man who would be more likely to share Count Dracula's preference for human blood when thirsty, but he refrained from putting the thought into words. It might, he felt, be lacking in tact, and after all, why criticize a man for looking like something out of a horror film if his heart was so patently of the purest gold. It is the heart that matters, not the features, however unshuffled.

"I'm with you," he said. "A lemon squash would be most refreshing."

"They serve a very good lemon squash here."

"Probably made from contented lemons."

"I shouldn't wonder," said the Professor.

He smiled a hideous smile. It had just occurred to him that if he hypnotized the waiter, he would be spared the necessity of disbursing money, always a consideration to a man of slender means.

ABOUT THE AUTHOR

P. G. Wodehouse (Sir Pelham Grenville Wodehouse), 1881–1975, has enter-
tained generations with his comic novels and stories set in a timeless
Edwardian England. His numerous works include the famous "Jeeves" novels,
which have been developed into a popular PBS series.